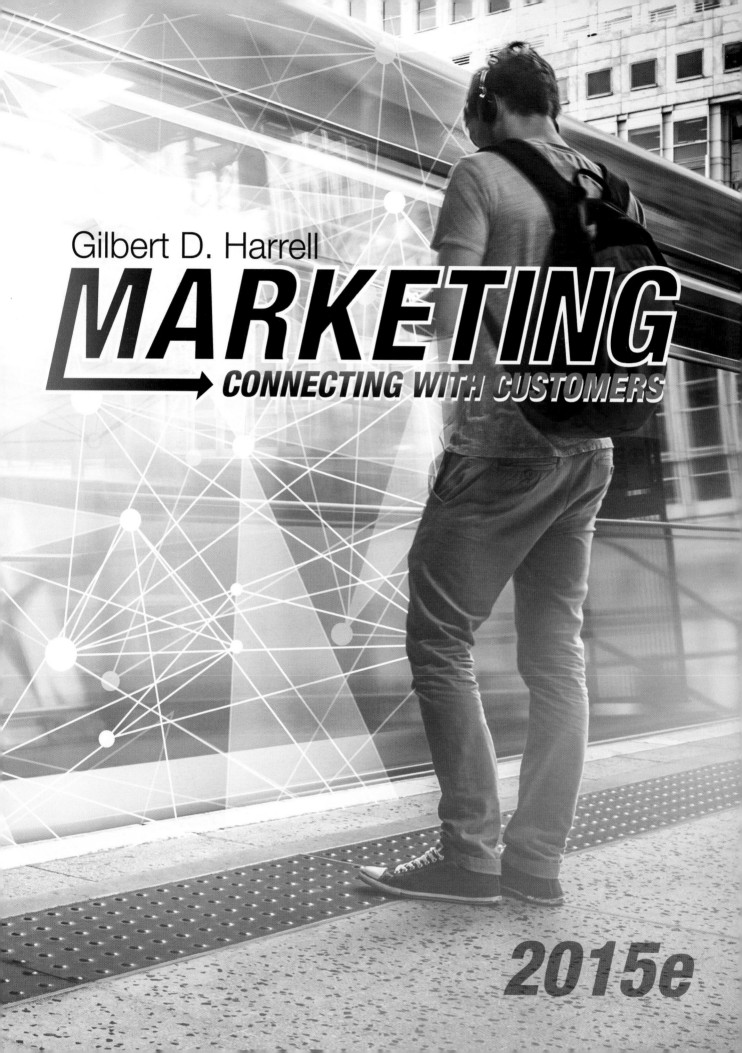

Gilbert D. Harrell

MARKETING
CONNECTING WITH CUSTOMERS

2015e

Printed in the United States of America

10 9 8 7 6 5 4 3 2

CASE BOUND: ISBN 13: 978-0-9905178-2-5

SOFT COVER: ISBN 13: 978-0-9905178-3-2

Executive Editor: Karen Sadler

Cover Design: Troy Miller

Cover Image: ©iStockphoto.com/Adam Petto

CHICAGO EDUCATION PRESS

Chicago Education Press, LLC
27 N. Wacker Drive, Suite 390
Chicago, IL 60606-2800
USA

www.chicagoeducationpress.com

To My Wife, Susanna, and Our Children

Contents

CHAPTER 5

UNDERSTANDING CONSUMER BEHAVIOR

CHAPTER 6

UNDERSTANDING BUSINESS MARKETING

CHAPTER 7

CREATING CUSTOMER SATISFACTION & LOYALTY

CHAPTER 8

SEGMENTATION, TARGETING & POSITIONING

CHAPTER 16

RETAILING, DIRECT MARKETING & WHOLESALING

CHAPTER 17

PRICING OBJECTIVES & INFLUENCES

CHAPTER 18

PRICING STRATEGIES

About the Author

GILBERT D. HARRELL, PH.D.

Gilbert D. Harrell, Ph.D., is Professor of Marketing in the Eli Broad College of Business and Graduate School of Management at Michigan State University. Professor Harrell has been featured by Business Week as one of the top American educators in leading business schools. He has received The John D. and Dortha J. Withrow Teacher-Scholar Award which is presented to members of the business school faculty who have achieved the highest level of distinction for service to Michigan State University through excellence in teaching and scholarship; the Phi Chi Theta Professor of the Year Award; and the Golden Key National Honor Society Teaching Excellence Award as the top teacher at Michigan State University. He has taught over 50,000 students in the undergraduate, MBA, Executive MBA and Ph.D. programs at MSU. Professor Harrell is a highly respected consultant with business clients from around the world.

Professor Harrell earned his Ph.D. at The Pennsylvania State University, where he was elected to the Phi Kappa Phi Honorary and the American Marketing Association Consortium. He earned his bachelor's and master's degrees at Michigan State University. He lives with his wife, Susanna, near the campus of Michigan State University. They are frequent travelers on Study Abroad missions and enjoy all aspects of college life.

Preface

INTRODUCTION

Marketing affects all of us -- all of the time. This text demonstrates current, relevant examples of exactly how pervasive marketing is in all of our lives as citizens and consumers. From a business perspective, excellent marketing separates corporate winners from losers, and it facilitates efficient functioning of our growing global consumer-based economy. Few companies can compete without excellent marketing – so it is a terrific career choice! Rising managers and executives from all disciplines must have a solid foundation in marketing concepts. This book is designed to present contemporary marketing principles in a way that is engaging and interesting for you, the reader.

The context in which marketing concepts are described is critical because, by their very nature, marketing actions are designed to alter the status quo. They are designed to prompt action. From sporting events to education to food, marketing surrounds us. We can't ignore it! Since the marketing landscape changes daily, a text on the subject must be more up-to-date with current examples than many other subjects. Our objective is to use examples from actual events that have occurred within the past year or two, with a significant number from 2014. They illustrate marketing programs and decisions made by executives and their teams in real organizations.

And, what about marketing theory – the marketing discipline? Does it also undergo rapid change? We are constantly learning more about how consumers behave and how companies interface with customers. Certainly social media and technology have made consumer to consumer and consumer to company interactions much more fluid. Big data, real time analysis and multidimensional communication enable marketing principles to be implemented more quickly than ever before. So, the marketing discipline is evolving as the world shifts. Many excellent theories developed by marketing scholars are core to the principles outlined in this text. Rigorous academic research supports most of what is written; the remaining aspects are from observations of outstanding executives, from consulting with a large number of companies in numerous industries for several decades and from various media sources.

ACKNOWLEDGEMENTS

Many people have made important contributions to this book, including the team at Chicago Education Press, university and business colleagues, reviewers from many universities and experiences with outstanding students.

I especially want to thank Troy Miller, Executive Director, Chicago Education Press, and Karen Sadler, Editor, for their important contributions to this edition. Troy, for his leadership with every aspect of the project from planning through execution! He has managed the production of this book with great imagination, spirit, and insight. Karen, for skillfully editing the entire manuscript! She made terrific contributions by bringing life to concepts, integrating new material and sculpting sentences to communicate what is intended. John Wilson, Business Director, Chicago Education Press, deserves special thanks regarding business planning and execution.

I want to thank Dale Wilson and Roger Calantone for their enthusiasm of this work at MSU and Dean Stephanie Lenway, Pat Dougherty and Cheri Speir-Pero for support during 2013 of the earlier Watson Edition including sponsorship of student presentations based on that edition's content. I also want to thank additional colleagues at Michigan State University for ideas, content, and for making MSU an overall, great place to be everyday, including: Forest Carter, Dave Closs, Bix Cooper, David Frayer, Rick Simonds, Chen Lin, Doug Hughes, Tomas Hult, Rich Spreng, Cornelia Droge, Ahmet Kirca, Glen Omura, Tom Page, Clay Voorhees, Brenda Sternquist, Hang Nguyen, Irina Kozlenkova Ayalia Ruvio, and Stephanie Mangus, to name a few. From the business world, Neil Ferranti, Bruce Leech, Pete Pendergast, Dan Wolf, Jake Lestan, Carolyn Calzavara, Pete Macking and other executives from many organizations have been very important – thank you. I also want to thank Gary Frazier for contributions to an earlier edition, although he was unable to participate in this edition due to prior commitments. Special gratitude is expressed to Peter Bennett (The Pennsylvania State University), my valued mentor, who contributed greatly to my enthusiasm for the subject.

Special thanks go to the following marketing faculty members from over 50 different schools who contributed in-depth reviews of this and/or other editions. Many have adopted the text for their students. Their excellent suggestions have been incorporated into the production of this book:

David Andrus	*Kansas State University*
Bob Balderstone	*Western Melbourne Institute of TAFE (Australia)*
Richard Brand	*Florida State University*
Jim Brock	*Susquehanna University*
Bruce Buskirk	*Pepperdine University*
William Carner	*University of Texas at Austin*
George Chrysschoidis	*University of Wales*
Howard Combs	*San Jose University*
John Cronin	*Western Connecticut State University*
Bernard Delagneau	*University of Wales*
Peter Doukas	*Westchester Community College*
Jim Dupree	*Grove City College*
John Durham	*San Francisco State University*
William Flatley	*Principia College*
James S. Gould	*Pace University*
Joyce Grahn	*University of Minnesota at Duluth*
Robert F. Guinner	*Arizona State University*
Pola Gupta	*University of Northern Iowa*
Lynn Harris	*Shippensburg University*
Benoit Heilbrunn	*Le Groupe ESC Lyon/Lyon Graduate School of Business (France)*
George Kelley	*Erie Community College*
Stephen Koernig	*California State University at Fullerton*
Rex Kovacevich	*University of Southern California*
Frank Krohn	*SUNY Fredonia*
Felicia G. Lassk	*Western Kentucky University*
Ken Lawrence	*New Jersey Institute of Technology*
Chong S. K. Lee	*California State University at Hayward*

Marilyn Liebrenz-Himes	*George Washington University*
Elizabeth Mariotz	*Philadelphia College of Textiles and Science*
Mike Mayo	*Kent State University*
Gary McCain	*Boise State University*
G. Stephen Miller	*St. Louis University*
Herbert Miller	*University of Texas at Austin*
Mark Mitchell	*University of South Carolina*
David Mothersbaugh	*University of Alabama*
Robert O'Keefe	*DePaul University*
Cliff Olson	*Southern State College of SDA*
Stan Paliwoda	*University of Calgary*
Eric Pratt	*New Mexico State University*
Abe Qastin	*Lakeland College*
Zahir Quaraeshi	*Western Michigan University*
Mohammed Rawwas	*University of Northern Iowa*
Deborah Reed Scarfino	*William Jewell College*
A.J. Taylor	*Austin Peay State University*
David Urban	*Virginia Commonwealth University*
Anthony Urbaniak	*Northern State University*
Simon Walls	*Western Washington University*
Mike Welker	*Franciscan University*
Ken Williamson	*James Madison University*
Mark Young	*Winona State University*
George Zinkham	*University of Houston*

Thank you all for your energy, creativity and dedication.

For me, working on a text that students will enjoy has been a lot of fun, particularly because of the people who have been involved in this and previous editions. I am truly lucky in this regard.

Most importantly, my great thanks go to my wife, Susanna, and to our family for their support and joy.

Gil Harrell
East Lansing, Michigan

Chapter 01

MARKETING:
CREATING & CAPTURING
VALUE

STARBUCKS®

Many of you, consciously or unconsciously, have been tempted by seeing a distinctive coffee cup in the hand of someone walking by. When a person chooses to drink Starbucks coffee, he or she is experiencing a rich blend of exceptional business and marketing practices. No matter where you travel in the world, you will find a powerful and consistent message conveyed — from its logo, to a rewarding experience in retail stores, and to the quality of the coffee in your cup. Even after your coffee is gone, you might find yourself on the Starbucks website to view your coffee reward status, find new stores or even connect with other coffee lovers through social media.

For Starbucks loyalists, coffee is not a trend — it's a lifestyle, one that Starbucks has promoted since its inception. The company has been elevating the overall coffee experience since 1971, when three men opened a gourmet coffee shop in Seattle. Today, Starbucks connects with millions of customers daily in 20,000 retail stores in over 64 countries. Starbucks' commitment is to put the customers' interest first by using the highest-quality ingredients while maintaining unrivaled global responsibility.

Recently, Starbucks bought 385 million pounds of coffee from farms around the world, 77 percent of which was known to be responsibly grown and ethically traded. The Starbucks Shared Planet program includes purchasing certified organic coffee, employing small-scale fair-trade farmers, and creating biodiversity in the world's coffee regions. To cement relations among the farmers it employs, Starbucks has opened several Farmer Support Centers. A center in Costa Rica has helped increase crop yield by 20 percent and reduced the use of pesticides by 80 percent. In the next year, Starbucks' goal is to make sure 100 percent of its coffee is grown using ethical trading and responsible growing practices.

Investing in the coffee communities worldwide is another way Starbucks enforces global sustainability. The Black Apron Exclusives is an initiative that set out to find some of the most unique, coveted kinds of coffee around the globe, particularly in remote regions of Africa and South America. Starbucks donated $15,000 to the community that produces the beans for this program, and to date there are 15 coffees available. Starbucks has used The Black Apron to help protect wildlife in these communities, teaming with the African Wildlife Foundation to produce coffee while maintaining an ecological balance. The program also includes tasting rooms so local farmers who have never tasted the final product can appreciate the complexity of coffee they produce.

Starbucks has done a great deal for sustainability in the outdoors, and plans to reinvent its own stores to maintain consistently high standards in all aspects of its business. Working with the LEED (Leadership in Energy and Environmental Design) building program, it has outlined a total reconstruction plan to be accomplished by 2015.

Two decades ago "latte," "cappuccino" and "espresso" were not part of America's everyday lexicon and "short" and "tall" were used to describe your height, not the size of your cup. You can largely thank Starbucks for changing our coffee vocabulary.[1]

<< Outside Starbucks in Austin, Texas

Courtesy of Starbucks

Learning Objectives

1. Understand the concept of marketing, including its definition, purpose and role in creating exchanges.
2. Contrast the periods of marketing evolution from its early history through the eras of production, sales, customer marketing, value marketing and social media.
3. Learn what is involved in the marketing strategy process in making marketing decisions, including examples of product, price, promotion and place decisions to create a marketing mix.
4. Understand the six key forces that are dramatically influencing how organizations create and capture value.
5. Realize how marketing affects you.

THE CONCEPT OF MARKETING

Starbucks has the uncanny ability to fit into your world at home or abroad: The company understands and accommodates diversity; it's ethically and socially responsible, focusing on sustainability; its executives work hard to understand what you want and form a lasting connection. Organizations like Starbucks know you have plenty of choices, so they practice marketing at its highest level to win your loyalty.

Ideally, organizations are created, grow and continue to grow. In reality, many decline, and some die. For one reason or another, declining organizations fall out of favor with customers, who replace them with more popular ones. Winning organizations set themselves above the rest by doing an exceptional job of creating and capturing value for customers. They are extraordinary marketers. They understand the marketing concept, use a full range of marketing tools and techniques, and help customers experience the satisfaction that occurs when products precisely match their needs and wants. Every time satisfaction occurs, value is created.

Today's business environment is global, diverse and ethically challenging. It is based on serving customers in ways unimaginable just a short time ago. Marketing is about much more than just selling a product; it is about providing value to customers in ways that are deeply rewarding for them. Marketing is also about serving the needs of society and accomplishing the goals of the organization. It includes researching potential customers' needs and wants; understanding competitors' strategies; developing appropriate goods and services; communicating with the market; creating, selecting and managing channels to reach customers; and pricing to deliver superior customer value. It is about satisfying customers so they will reward the business with the loyalty necessary to reach organizational objectives.

This chapter introduces marketing. As it presents ideas, it references chapters that discuss topics in more detail, providing a brief overview of the book. It begins by defining marketing and

discussing its purpose, including how marketing creates and facilitates economic exchanges, followed by a discussion of how marketing has evolved. Then a section on the marketing strategy process introduces the basic elements used to build a marketing plan. Next are descriptions of six factors that are huge influences on the practice of marketing. Finally, the chapter ends with a note about how marketing affects you on a daily basis.

www.starbucks.com

Visit Starbuck's website to learn about the company's sustainability initiatives.

MARKETING IS...

How do you view marketing? Is your impression positive or negative? Most people have been exposed to advertising, point-of-purchase displays and personal selling, so marketing is often seen strictly as the promotion and sale of existing products. However, excellent marketing is much more extensive, beginning long before a product exists. This allows all marketing decisions — including promotion — to be made with customer needs and wants in mind. Marketing extends far beyond a purchase to ensure customer satisfaction and loyalty. You can gain a good idea about the extent of marketing by understanding each element in its definition.

Marketing is the activity, set of institutions and processes for creating, communicating, delivering and exchanging offerings that have value. This value is intended for customers, clients, partners and society at large.

The American Marketing Association (AMA), an organization of professionals interested in furthering the marketing discipline, developed the following definition. **Marketing** is the activity, set of institutions and processes for creating, communicating, delivering and exchanging offerings that have value. This value is intended for customers, clients, partners and society at large.[2] As an introduction to the subject, the first part of this chapter discusses the definition in depth.

AMERICAN MARKETING ASSOCIATION

Marketing

The activity, set of institutions, and processes for creating, communicating, delivering, and exchanging offerings that have value for customers, clients, partners, and society at large.

THE ACTIVITY

Marketing activity focuses on understanding the needs and wants of customers and engaging in competitive behavior to satisfy those needs and wants. Organizations that do this well tend to grow and prosper. The quest to understand and satisfy customers provides the basis for a competitive system that dramatically benefits society. Because needs and wants are numerous, diverse and dynamic, there are unlimited opportunities for marketing.

Understand the Needs and Wants of Customers
Understanding customer needs and wants is central to marketing activities. It is impossible to implement appropriate marketing without this understanding. Marketers use **customer orientation**, an organizational philosophy that focuses on satisfying customer needs and wants.

Needs and wants are not the same. A **need** is a fundamental requirement — meeting it is the ultimate goal of behavior. Of course, there are many needs,

Customer Orientation

An organizational philosophy that focuses on satisfying consumer needs and wants.

Need

A fundamental requirement, the meeting of which is the ultimate goal of behavior.

from those that allow survival to those that produce personal enrichment. A need becomes apparent when there is a gap between a desired state and an actual state. For example, you need proper nutrition on a regular basis to have a healthy and energetic body. When nutrition drops below the desired state, your body signals the deprivation — you feel hungry. When the need is satisfied, the hunger goes away. Needs represent what people and organizations must have to survive and thrive. The degree to which needs are satisfied determines the quality of life for all people and organizations.

A **want** is the specific form of consumption desired to satisfy a need. Therefore, a want is simply one of many desires a person may have to help fulfill a particular need. For instance, hunger can be satisfied with a candy bar, an orange or a chicken sandwich. Taken a step farther, a consumer may want a Snickers® bar or a Sunkist® orange or a McChicken® sandwich.

Want

A specific form of consumption desired to satisfy a need.

Like people, organizations have objectives that must be met. For-profit companies must make a sizable return on the owners' investment or they will go out of business. Nonprofit companies have other needs: The Red Cross, for example, must help increasing numbers of disaster victims if it is to meet its organizational objectives. Every organization needs customers or clients — the people they serve. There are many ways to obtain them, as well as specific types of suppliers, employee characteristics and profit objectives. The aerospace company, Boeing, addresses the need of United Airlines for aircraft by designing planes the airline will want with attributes that satisfy United's *needs*. Figure 1.1 shows the relationship between needs and wants.

NEEDS	→	WANTS
Fundamental Requirements	←	Form of Consumption Desired to Satisfy a Need

Figure 1.1   Needs and Wants

Potential customers try to satisfy wants in ways that produce the greatest amount of need satisfaction. This makes wants dynamic. Marketing leaders facilitate and adjust to change rapidly by learning how to serve customers in new and creative ways. Marketers that learn how to best serve customers can gain tremendous competitive advantages.

Competitive Behavior

Strong marketers compete, and they measure success by the way their customers judge them, especially relative to competitors. Competition is the key to our economic system. You see aggressive global competition occurring every day: Coke vs. Pepsi, McDonald's vs. Burger King, and American Airlines vs. British Airways.

Unilever's Dove recently released a commercial for its Men+Care Clean Comfort to directly compete with market leader Old Spice High Endurance Pure Sport. The commercial depicts a Dove representative interviewing Jay Wright, Villanova Head Basketball Coach, depicted as a good decision maker. Asked if he would choose the competitor Old Spice soap that "cleans," or the Dove soap that "cleans and protects against dryness," Wright, without hesitation, chooses Dove. [3]

Even nonprofit groups compete. Mail-order catalogs from the Art Institute of Chicago, the Metropolitan Museum of Art, the Smithsonian Institution and Boston's Museum of Fine Arts all compete for your purchases. The United Way competes for your discretionary income, and political parties compete for your donations. With fierce competition for donations, nonprofit marketing is more important than ever. Marketers outperform competitors by being more effective, efficient and agile. According to the Interactive Investment Benchmark Study from Char-

Dove directly competes with Old Spice by identifying the advantages of choosing its Clean Comfort soap.

ity Dynamics, nonprofits are increasing investment in interactive solutions to gain a competitive advantage. Donation and e-commerce solutions, social media, websites, and email marketing are among the top categories for nonprofit digital spending. Charity Dynamics CEO and Founder, Donna Wilkins, said: "As we all spend more time online, be it shopping or socializing, we start to expect a higher level of online engagement. These results show nonprofits understand that and are responding by investing in solutions to improve the online experience for their supporters."[4]

Effectiveness occurs when the organization's activities produce results that matter to consumers. **Efficiency** means operating with minimal waste of time and money. Baxter International, a hospital products company with more than $15 billion in annual sales, is successful on both counts.[5] First, it recognized that its customers — hospitals — were spending too much money storing and distributing supplies. Baxter developed an electronic ordering system to indicate which supplies a hospital requires on a daily basis and where in the hospital the supplies should go. This system is effective because it meets the wants of Baxter's customers better than the competition. It is efficient because it saves both the hospitals and Baxter substantial amounts of money and time. In many cases, hospitals choose Baxter as their only supplier, which leads to higher sales and profits for Baxter.

Agility is the anticipation of market dynamics and speed of response to changing customer desires and competitors' actions. Organizations that possess agility continually sense and explore marketplace opportunities. For example, organizations that consider the environmental impact of decisions are more agile than competitors that lag in this area. McDonald's prides itself on its ability to evolve; one of the company's core values states, "We are a learning organization that aims to anticipate and respond to changing customer, employee, and system needs through constant evolution and innovation."[6]

SET OF INSTITUTIONS

The most basic set of marketing institutions is comprised of the market and buyers and sellers who want to exchange value. A **market** consists of all the organizations and individuals with potential desire and ability to acquire value — that is, to own a particular idea, good or service. Generally, we talk about marketing products, which are usually goods that are manufactured or services that are performed. Marketing can also be applied to any idea that can be used in an exchange of value. These include, for example, marketing events, causes, people, and places. Ideas, goods and services are exchanged in consumer markets, business-to-business markets, nonprofit markets and internal markets.

Nearly every type of organization, large or small, public or private, has the need for marketing. That is why marketing professionals find a vast array of career opportunities. Peter Drucker, renowned educator and author, has said the two critical functions of an organization are innovation and marketing. All other functions, such as finance, accounting and personnel management, support these two key functions. To him, innovation involves rearranging what currently exists or creating something entirely new. These innovations provide the "raw materials" that can be used by organizations to advance the standard of living for people. From a societal point of view, marketing is the function that creates exchanges, which allow those innovations to be delivered and consumed by society. Looking at marketing from a societal point of view is often called **macro-marketing.**

From an organizational point of view, marketing is so important that it is often seen as a function of the entire business or the responsibility of one or more depart-

> **Nearly every type of organization, large or small, public or private, has a need for marketing.**

Effectiveness

An organizational philosophy that focuses on satisfying consumer needs and wants.

Efficiency

The ability of an organization to execute activities with minimal waste of time and money.

Agility

The flexibility and speed with which organizations can identify or create new wants and take action to satisfy them.

Market

All the individuals and organizations with potential desire and ability to acquire a particular good or service.

Macro-marketing

Viewing marketing from a societal point of view, marketing is the function that creates exchanges that facilitates the delivery of the standard of living to society.

Micro-marketing

Marketing from the point of view of the firm or organization – (the definition of marketing described in detail in this book)

Consumer (B2C) Marketing

When organizations sell to individuals or households that buy, consume, and dispose of products.

Business-to-business (B2B) Marketing

When a business purchases goods or services to produce other goods, to support daily operations, or to resell at a profit.

ments. When marketing is viewed in this way, from the perspective of a single organization, it is called **micro-marketing.** Professionals in these marketing roles often have titles such as chief marketing officer, marketing manager, director of marketing research, and so forth. Most leading organizations have marketing departments that report directly to the leader of the organization or to the head of major sections of the organization. In a great number of cases, top executives of the organization have a strong background in marketing.

Many top executives have a very strong background and experience in marketing.

Consumer (B2C) Marketing
Literally millions of products are marketed, targeting diverse consumers. **Consumer (B2C) marketing** occurs when organizations sell to individuals or households that buy, consume and dispose of products. Leading consumer marketers include such companies as Procter & Gamble, Johnson & Johnson, General Mills, Hewlett-Packard, and Nike.

You know the products of these companies very well. You have probably already purchased or used many of them and will continue to do so over the years. Because you buy, consume and dispose of products such as these daily, you are an important part of consumer marketing. Consumer marketing is often referred to as B2C, business-to-consumer, because businesses like Nike market to consumers like you. We will learn more about consumer marketing throughout this book.

Business-to-Business (B2B) Marketing
Business-to-business (B2B) marketing occurs when a business purchases goods or services to produce other goods, to support daily operations, or to resell at a profit. Although there are many more consumers than companies, business-to-business purchases far outweigh the consumer market in dollar amount.

Organizations belong either to the public or private sector. The public sector consists of federal, state and local government organizations. The private sector includes industrial firms, professionals, retailers and service organizations. Utility companies, which provide water, electricity, gas and waste disposal, fall between the public and private sectors because they are regulated by the government but may be privately owned. Most of these organizations rely on business-to-business marketing to sell and purchase goods or services. For example, Dell uses LinkedIn groups to give its B2B marketing campaign an advantage over competitors. Using this social media platform with more than 300 million members, Dell has successfully linked over 8000 professionals in the fields of IT, Engineering and Consulting. Seventy percent of the LinkedIn group members are top management, c-level and business owners. This gives Dell direct access to the key decision makers of its target market, and will likely influence purchasing decisions of group member companies. Additionally, Dell gains a network of professionals related to its core business that can improve its operations and buying decisions.[7] In Chapter 6, we will explore many of the topics involved in business-to-business marketing.

Courtesy of LinkedIn

in

300

MILLION MEMBERS

We now have 300 million LinkedIn members, more than half of whom live outside of the U.S. That's enough to make LinkedIn the fourth largest country in the world. In celebration, we took a look back to see how much our membership has grown and diversified over the past five years. It's a helpful reminder of not only where we've been, but also where we're headed as we work to create economic opportunity for every professional in the world.

Nonprofit Marketing **Nonprofit marketing** occurs when an organization does not try to make a profit but instead attempts to influence others to support its cause by using its service or by making a contribution. It is generally used to benefit a particular segment of society. Marketing has many applications in the not-for-profit sector. Churches, museums, hospitals, universities, symphonies and municipalities regularly create marketing plans in an effort to be more consumer-oriented. The organization *charity: water* is a non-profit bringing clean and safe drinking water to people in developing nations. One-hundred percent of all public donations directly fund water projects in 20 countries. Since 2007, *charity: water* has successfully funded over 8,000 water projects, providing clean drinking water for more than 3 million people.[8]

Like businesses that seek profit, many of these organizations want to please their constituents, and they have competition. Although they may not be motivated by profit, many are interested in obtaining revenues that equal or exceed expenses, requiring a full range of marketing knowledge. We will learn in Chapter 9 that, in making marketing decisions, many not-for-profit groups seek the same quality of talent as for-profit companies.

Nonprofit marketing

When an organization does not try to make a profit but instead attempts to influence others to support its cause by using its service or by making a contribution.

Internal Marketing **Internal marketing** occurs when managers of one functional unit market their capabilities to other units within their own organization. This type of marketing addresses the needs and wants of internal customers, the employees of the firm, so these people can ultimately contribute to the external customers, who are the end users of a company's products or services. For example, Dr. Lew Dotterer, Director of Learning and Organizational Development at Sparrow Health System in Lansing, Michigan, is responsible for maintaining the knowledge and skills of employees in all units of the system. Applying marketing techniques, he first identified the key customers: doctors, nurses, administrators and so forth. Next, he researched each group to determine its learning needs. He then created educational programs to address the learning needs of each group and promoted these programs throughout the organization. Through internal marketing, one functional unit was able to help employees in other units to better serve Sparrow's external customers (patients).

Internal marketing

When managers of one functional unit market their capabilities to other units within their own organization.

PROCESSES

Marketing is composed of many ongoing processes, which are used to manage complex, changing phenomena. New competitors enter the market, customers change, and the economic climate shifts. What works today may be totally wrong tomorrow. Consequently, those who practice marketing must take a long-distance view of events. They must not focus on a single transaction but on the enduring, systematic management of change. Marketers look for patterns, trends and surprises that signal what is likely to happen in the future while being responsive to current circumstances. In fact, marketing has its greatest value when it helps guide organizations in highly dynamic environments.

Marketers look for patterns, trends and surprises that signal what is likely to happen in the future.

Marketing is concerned with the process of planning and providing the guidance system for companies. Planning sets direction before action takes place. It addresses what is to be accomplished and how to accomplish it. Competitors force each other to make strategic marketing plans, to develop ways to better satisfy customer needs and wants. Later we will see that plans are created for a whole organization as well as for select products. No matter what is being planned, marketing involves a broad range of people in order for plans to be effective. Consequently, marketing usually means working in groups rather than working alone. Many internal marketing processes help groups of people work together to build strategies and plans.

Marketing is also responsible for processes involved in executing or carrying out the plan. Marketing manages people and events in line with the plan, which serves as a guide. To carry out plans, marketing must acquire and develop many of the organization's human resources. Effective marketers are energetic, creative managers who make use of processes to guide their actions.

For companies to stay on the leading edge, they must focus on market-oriented product development processes and innovation. Consider the dynamic computing field, in which the marketing plan is crucial. In 1978, the world's fastest computer processed at a speed of 160 MHz and cost about $20 million. It occupied the space of a small room and required special cooling to function properly. Today, most personal computers cost less than $1,000 and use inexpensive and rapid-processing microchips. In the next 20 years, speed compression and cost reduction for computing power will be even more pronounced, and the number of new products and services will be staggering.

In 2001, Apple released an industry-breaking portable MP3 music player called the iPod; it could hold 1,000 songs, weighed just 6.5 ounces, and cost $400. The iPod revolutionized the music industry by combining both form and function to produce a consumer-friendly MP3 player and the world's largest music download store, containing millions of songs, podcasts, movies, and TV shows. Since the release of the original iPod, the company has continued to evolve through innovation. Today, iPods are available in many different models, ranging from $59 to $399, and can hold up to 40,000 songs, 25,000 photos or 200 hours of video.[9]

Apple's first generation iPod was an innovative design that quickly became the interface of choice by consumers around the world.

No company today can enter a major market expecting that a single product and strategy will sustain it for long. Rather, it is agility - the ability to change in response to market demand - that separates great marketers from others.

Apple used a marketing process for the introduction of the iPhone which integrated media, global positioning, satellite and communication technologies to bring consumers one of the most advanced personal communication devices to date. The latest iPhone 5S model uses a A7 chip for faster graphics and improved browsing and gaming experiences, a Touch ID fingerprint identity sensor, ultrafast LTE wireless, an iSight camera with a larger 8MP sensor.[10]

When Apple released its highly anticipated tablet device, the iPad, it featured a 9.7-inch, capacitive multi-touch display, weighed 1.5 pounds and measured 0.5 inches thick. The device is positioned to bridge the gap between the iPhone and laptop computers in an interactive, innovative way. While some didn't believe there was a market for such a device, Apple sold 3 million iPads in the first weekend of the release of the second generation iPad 2. Numbers continue to pile on, with more than 210 million iPads sold to date.[11]

Because of Apple's quick success in the new market, competitors quickly responded with their own tablet devices. Apple's early success in the tablet market has actually been blamed for a recent slump in global tablet sales. It is conceivable that the majority of prospective buyers already have an iPad and love it enough to have no interest in buying a different or new device. CEO Tim Cook had a slightly different perspective, explaining Apple's drop in sales are because of differences in channel inventory. He later reiterated that the iPad has been the fasting growing product in the company's history.

"We've sold over 210 million [iPads], which is more than we or anyone thought was possible," he said. "It's interesting to note that that's over twice as many iPhones as we had sold in a comparable period of time and over seven times as many iPods as we had sold in the period of time." Cook is still awfully confident on the iPad's future and said that things look "very, very good" over the long haul, even if Apple occasionally can't put up sales numbers "every 90 days that everyone's thrilled with."[12]

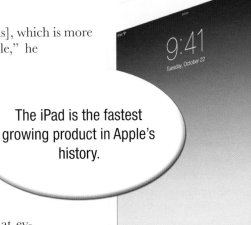

The iPad is the fastest growing product in Apple's history.

Courtesy of Apple

CREATING, COMMUNICATING & DELIVERING

Professor James Culliton once described the business executive as a "decider" and "artist" — a "mixer of ingredients" who sometimes follows a recipe as he or she goes along, sometimes adapts a recipe to the ingredients immediately available, and sometimes experiments with or invents ingredients no one else has tried. This description gave Neil Borden, another noted professor, the idea that there is a list of elements the marketer mixes together. He called these elements the **marketing mix.**[13] Today they are known as the four Ps: product, price, promotion and place. Several other elements can be classified under one of these points. For example, product development, branding, packaging and service are included in the product area. Leasing and credit terms are part of pricing. Advertising, personal selling and sales promotion are included in promotion. Distribution, logistics, retailing and direct marketing are part of place. A dramatic shift in the mix produces a huge winner, and minor shifts create day-to-day competition. It is through the mixing process that organizations arrive at unique ways of addressing customers. Marketing creativity and imagination play a key role.

Marketing mix

The four controllable variables - product, price, promotion, and place (distribution) - that are combined to appeal to the company's target markets.

EXCHANGING OFFERINGS THAT HAVE VALUE

Value occurs for customers and for the organization only when an exchange is created. An **exchange** is a process in which two or more parties provide something of value to one another. At the most basic level, an exchange generally involves a seller who provides a good or service to a buyer for money or some other item. Most exchanges are much more complex than that, involving several parties in a social system exchanging all kinds of items.[14]

Relationship marketing is the development and maintenance of successful relational exchanges. It involves interactive, ongoing, two-way connections among customers, organizations, suppliers and other parties for mutual benefit. For example, Unilever Group's Dove soap's market researchers found that too many ads focused on young, thin models. The group spoke to women of all ages in its markets and found an overwhelming response that the way beauty was being portrayed was unrealistic. Realizing that aging baby boomers were especially active and had tremendous spending power, Dove found a way to connect with the aging market. The company began using ordinary women in ads featuring slogans such as, "Why aren't women glad to be gray?" Dove sales rose 3.4 percent within a year of the campaign's launch.[15]

Exchange

The process in which two or more parties provide something of value to one another.

Relationship Marketing

The development and maintenance of successful relational exchanges through interactive, ongoing, two-way connections among customers, organizations, suppliers, and other parties for mutual benefit.

Emotion is a key ingredient in relationships, so in addition to providing logical reasons for buyers to prefer particular brands, marketers involve customers by being trustworthy, supportive and a part of their lives. Coca-Cola Worldwide President of Marketing Mary Minnick captured this idea: "Historically, we thought 'enjoyment' was great taste. But it's a very complex 'need' state. ... We don't just want to entertain customers, we want Coke (brands) to be more relevant, an integral part of consumers' everyday lives. We want to build a relationship with consumers, not hold a mirror up to them."[16] Relationship marketing builds customer loyalty, a critical goal that dramatically improves business performance.

Marketers need to be sensitive to the fact that not all customers are looking for strong relationships in all exchanges. However, there is a clear trend showing that, in recent years, marketing has evolved from transaction-based exchanges toward relationship-based exchanges. The change goes far beyond the interaction between an organization and its customers; suppliers and other parties also have roles to play. The relationships range from informal to contractual or even ownership. On the informal level, incentives make it difficult or inconvenient for customers to switch to a new organization. For example, Land Rover has a club for customers that publishes a newsletter and sends invitations to off-road rallies. Service managers call customers to see how their Land Rover Discovery is performing.[17]

Marketing brings the many parties together and facilitates exchanges. This provides utility, which in turn creates value. Utility is a term economists use to describe the want-satisfying potential of a good or service. There are four fundamental types of utility: form, place, time and ownership.

Form, Place, Time, and Ownership Utility

Form Utility

A want-satisfying value that is created when knowledge and materials are converted into finished goods and services.

Form utility occurs when knowledge and materials are converted into finished goods and services. Marketing provides form utility when it guides decisions about what products to create. When McDonald's created grilled chicken salads with low-fat salad dressing as alternatives for health-conscious consumers, the company provided form utility. Beech-Nut, the nation's third-largest baby-food manufacturer, has just launched 40 new products that have no additives or preservatives. Its independent research revealed that 70 percent of parents make isome of their baby food at home because they believe the supermarket products are overprocessed, contain too many additives, or are unhealthy for their baby.[18] Generally, the marketing function is responsible for specifying what form utility the final product should possess, and it works closely with research and development (R&D), engineering, manufacturing and other units.

this is not baby food

This is real food for babies™.
Welcome to a new kind of Beech-Nut®.
Homemade is our inspiration.

hear our story

new!

Just real, whole fruits and vegetables are inside our new jars. And nothing else.

Place Utility

A want-satisfying value that is created by making goods and services conveniently available.

Place utility makes goods and services conveniently available. Fresh bananas on a remote tree are not nearly as want-satisfying as those at a local supermarket, convenience store or restaurant. Their accessibility makes them worth many times more at those locations than where they are grown. Marketing brings products to customers for the sake of convenience. When FedEx, operator of a premiere global delivery network, delivers more than

10 million shipments a day to more than 220 countries and territories, it is providing place utility.[19]

Time utility makes goods and services available when they are wanted. You can watch DVDs at your convenience, which is one reason for their tremendous popularity. UPS, Federal Express, DHL and other overnight carriers offer outstanding time utility. L. L. Bean now receives an order one day and has the item at your home the next, 15 times faster than the Sears, Roebuck & Co. mail orders that dominated the 1970s and earlier. Netflix allows subscribers to watch thousands of movies instantly on their computer, Xbox 360, AppleTV, TiVo or other compatible instant devices.[20]

Courtesy of Netflix

Netflix provides time utility by allowing subscribers to watch movies and television shows anytime, anywhere.

Ownership utility makes it possible to transfer the title of goods and services from one party to another. The most obvious way is through cash transactions, but credit card purchases and leasing are other means. Later we will learn how this functions on an international scale. Even airplane travel is a form of ownership utility. By leasing a seat (buying a ticket), you can possess the vast resources of the air transportation system during the time required to reach nearly any destination on the planet. Marketing has progressed by finding better ways to produce increasing amounts of utility.

CUSTOMERS, CLIENTS, PARTNERS & SOCIETY

For Customers and Clients **Customer value** refers to what consumers perceive they gain from owning or using a product when weighed against the cost of acquiring it—a topic we will consider in more detail in Chapter 6. **Satisfaction** refers to the consumer's overall rating of his or her experience with a company and its products. **Loyalty** is a measure of how often, when selecting from a product class, a customer purchases a particular brand. In combination, satisfaction and customer value help create customer loyalty. Loyal customers provide a continuous revenue stream through repeated purchases of a product. They also provide word-of-mouth of their satisfaction, which is one of the most effective and inexpensive forms of promotion. To increase customer satisfaction, Xerox's Total Satisfaction Guarantee allows unsatisfied customers to return any equipment and Xerox will replace it without charge.[21] Hampton Hotels led the industry when it became the first national hotel brand to offer guests an unconditional 100-percent satisfaction guarantee. "It's a philosophy we continue to live by today. Our guarantee ... Friendly service, clean rooms, comfortable surroundings every time. If you're not satisfied, we don't expect you to pay. That's our commitment and your guarantee. That's 100% Hampton."[22]

Sears allows customers to request a repair online. These organizations are responding to a request from customers to make their lives easier, thereby adding customer value. A level of satisfaction strong enough to create product loyalty requires an organizational commitment to customer value in every aspect of the business.

Time Utility

A want-satisfying value that is created when goods and services are made available when they are wanted.

Ownership Utility

A want-satisfying value that is created by making it possible to transfer the title of goods and services from one party to another.

Customer value

What consumers perceive they gain from owning or using a product over and above the cost of acquiring it.

Satisfaction

The consumer's overall rating of his or her experience with a company and its products.

Loyalty

A measure of how often, when selecting from a product class, a customer purchases a particular brand.

Partners (Organization and its Stakeholders)
All organizations have objectives. Many focus on financial measures such as profit margins and return on investment to evaluate performance. In order to stay in business, companies must make money when they fulfill consumer needs. Profit provides the financial fuel that allows companies to innovate and grow. Nonprofit organizations, in contrast, use measures such as donation levels, membership and services provided to evaluate performance. Although nonprofit organizations must be effective and efficient, by definition they do not seek profit as a primary goal. Still, even nonprofit organizations strive to satisfy their constituents in a cost-effective way. For example, the national organizations for Boy Scouts and Girl Scouts have rigorous financial goals. They often strive for growth in sales and in number of members as well as certain levels of customer satisfaction relative to competitors.

An organization increases its own value by creating value for customers and society. Organizations that do the best job of competing require profits to grow and prosper. These profits are used to further create and deliver innovations to waiting customers. In

> **An organization increases its own value by creating value for customers and society.**

turn, society, employees and owners benefit. The organization grows and the process continues.

Both private and public companies strive to increase the value of the organization to its stakeholders. Stakeholders of an organization include employees, customers, suppliers, and stockholders. The single most important role of the marketing effort is to increase stakeholder value by establishing and implementing an effective marketing strategy. This can be accomplished in many ways. For example, it can involve focusing on a new set of customers, expanding the organization's base, or focusing on the types of customers that the company has targeted in the past, relying on loyalty and its established reputation.

Increasing the value of the organization can also be achieved by introducing an entirely new product. For example, Smith Klein Beecham created a vaccine for Lyme disease in an attempt to limit new cases of the disease. The organization was able to increase the value to all stakeholders: its employees, its customers, its suppliers and its stockholders. Creating value for the organization and its stakeholders is an important part of marketing.

Sustainability

The steps and processes organizations undertake to manage growth without detrimentally affecting the resources or biological systems of the earth.

Society
Marketing offers great value to society. It stimulates demand, promotes innovation, and improves life by providing an array of goods and services that benefit every citizen. The marketing industry has also provided a significant percentage of the population with employment. When marketing decisions contribute to the profit of firms, they fuel economic growth. Today, leading edge companies also accomplish their objectives through the concept of sustainability.

Sustainability consists of the steps and processes that organizations undertake to manage growth without detrimentally affecting the earth's resources or biological systems. It is the fundamental concept of meeting the needs of today without compromising the ability of future generations to meet their needs.[23] As consumer awareness of environmental sustainability increases, organizations have focused on marketing their sustainable initiatives. Some organizations are doing this by offering green products to consumers. Green products provide energy-saving options or inflict minimal damage on the surrounding environment. Other organizations may focus on reducing waste and emissions.

An example of involvement in environmental causes is Aveda, a skin- and hair-care company committed to protection of the environment, animals and humans. Using organic ingredients, plant-based alternatives to chemicals and responsible packaging, Aveda reflects commitment to its environmental sustainability policy.[24]

In another example, S.C. Johnson & Sons, the maker of popular household cleaning products such as Windex, implemented a sustainability process titled Greenlist. Through Greenlist, the company searches for the most environmentally friendly inputs and raw materials. By reformulating Windex brand glass cleaner, S.C. Johnson & Sons cut 1.8 million pounds of volatile organic compounds (VOCs) from the product while giving it 30 percent more cleaning power.[25]

THE EVOLUTION OF MARKETING

Marketing activities, in the broadest sense, can be traced to the trading and bartering that occurred thousands of years ago. The ancient Egyptians had vending machines as early as 200 B.C.! But it wasn't until the 1500s in England and the 1600s in Germany and North America that modern marketing began. Most people lived in rural areas and produced all necessary goods themselves. Nevertheless, enterprising business people — early marketers — discovered they could make money by providing luxury items to the upper class and more practical goods to others in the population.

Although large trading companies had existed for centuries, many merchants and craftsmen built their businesses by satisfying individual customers. People often bought their shoes from a cobbler who knew the exact dimensions of their feet, their preferred shoe style, and their ability to pay. During the late 1700s and early 1800s, major improvements in production and transportation, along with growing urbanization, fostered the development of mass marketing. **Mass marketing** is the mass production, mass distribution and mass promotion of a product to all buyers. A free-enterprise system based on competition began to develop. Starting in the late 1800s, advertising, marketing research, improved physical distribution methods and retailing were used to help find and develop markets for mass production. Unlike the days when the consumer came into direct contact with the producer, more goods began to be purchased through an intermediary. The producer had no contact with the end user. During the 20th and 21st centuries, the economy moved through five basic eras in terms of the focus of business: the production era, the sales era, the customer era, the value era and the social media era, depicted in Figure 1.2.

> **Marketing activities, in the broadest sense, can be traced to the trading and barter that occurred thousands of years ago.**

Mass Marketing

The mass production, mass distribution, and mass promotion of a product to all buyers.

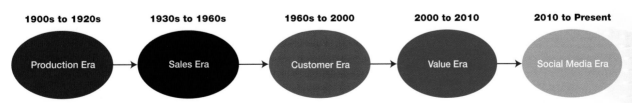

1900s to 1920s	1930s to 1960s	1960s to 2000	2000 to 2010	2010 to Present
Production Era	Sales Era	Customer Era	Value Era	Social Media Era

Figure 1.2   Needs and Wants

THE PRODUCTION ERA

Production Orientation

Historical marketing period that emphasized new products and the efficiency of production.

During the production era, which lasted until about 1925, companies focused on ways to make products in mass quantities. They achieved production economies that often led to lower prices. This **production orientation** emphasized new products and creating them with efficiency. Businesses were primarily concerned with ways to speed physical production. Manufacturers did not address the consumer until after the goods had been made. They assumed a good product would sell itself. Salespeople were more interested in helping the manufacturer take orders than in helping the customer. Demand for these new lower-priced products was often greater than supply, which led to the growth of large manufacturing organizations.

Henry Ford's approach is a prime example of production orientation. Until Ford came along, automobiles were made one at a time in small factories. Often each car was unique; perhaps a few of each type were made. Ford standardized the design of the Model T and mass-produced it on an assembly line. This dramatically reduced costs and made cars affordable to more people. Visualizing a ready demand for this cheap form of transportation, he remarked that people "can have any color they want, as long as it's black."

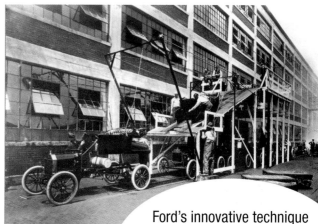

Ford's innovative technique of using assembly lines transformed the automobile industry and dramatically reduced costs.

THE SALES ERA

Sales Orientation

Historical marketing period that emphasized that consumers must be convinced to buy.

Seller's Market

The marketing environment in which scarcity of products lets the seller control the market.

Buyer's Market

The marketing environment in which an abundance of product lets the buyer control the market.

As production methods improved and more firms entered markets, competition increased. Eventually, the supply of many products outpaced demand. Since businesses had more goods than their regular customers could buy, the need for personal selling and advertising arose. The sales era focused on ways to sell more effectively. This period was spurred on by the Great Depression of the 1930s, when spending power was drastically reduced. Consumers resisted purchasing nonessential goods and services, so organizations developed sales forces and sales tactics to overcome customer resistance.

The **sales orientation** emphasized that consumers must be convinced to buy. Consumer tastes, preferences and needs did not receive much consideration. Rather, companies tried to shape consumers' ideals to fit the attributes of the products offered.

After World War II, a vastly different economic environment emerged in the United States. The country was moving from the **seller's market**, in which scarcity of products lets the seller control the market, to a **buyer's market**, in which abundance of products lets the buyer control the market. With the emergence of the buyer's market came rewards to organizations that gave customers a prominent place in their business thinking.

THE CUSTOMER MARKETING ERA

A company with a sales philosophy focuses internally. Emphasis is placed on making the product, then on selling it. The sales force has to push existing products to the consumer through increased promotion and personal selling. In contrast, the customer marketing concept emphasizes customer satisfaction, value and loyalty. After an organization determines consumer needs, it coordinates its activities so that the product will satisfy customer needs and wants.

During the past 50 years, marketing has evolved into a tremendously important business function. Before the 1960s, the prevailing economic philosophy in the United States was caveat emptor — "Let the buyer beware." In other words, consumers had to be cautious when purchasing a product. Once they did, they were stuck with it — and any injuries or inconveniences that might result. It didn't matter if the product was defective.

Led by the efforts of President John F. Kennedy, legislators began to be more responsive to consumer rights. Throughout the 1960s and '70s, government agencies and private consumer protection groups advanced this cause. Successful companies realized they could gain a competitive edge by treating customers fairly. They also became keenly aware that a loyal repeat buyer is more profitable than a one-time buyer (which you will learn more about in Chapter 7). Businesses began to realize that customer satisfaction was paramount.

In the early 1980s, executives turned their attention to competitors. For the first time in U.S. history, foreign rivals seriously threatened the dominance enjoyed for years by U.S.-based global companies. Competition, beyond mere price and promotion, was developed and refined in many ways. During the '80s, strategic planning became widely accepted. The role of marketing was elevated from understanding consumer behavior to assessing customer expectations, learning about competitors' practices, and determining how to make the organization an industry leader in a continuously changing world.

In the early 1990s, business executives began building teams designed to focus all of a given organization's resources on customer satisfaction. Achieving customer satisfaction depends on how well the various branches of the organization work together. A business is like any other team; success is determined not only by individual talents but also by the ability to do well as a unit. The organization that can form fast, flexible, powerful teams is most capable of competing in global markets. An organization must be designed to maximize both the speed of its responsiveness to customers and its ability to work as a team.

Value-driven Organizations

An organization that implements the marketing concept by ensuring that all parts of the organization make the maximum contribution toward creating value for the customer.

THE VALUE MARKETING ERA

Today, **value-driven organizations** are implementing the marketing concept by ensuring that all parts of the organization make the maximum possible contribution toward creating value for the customer. They make sure that every part of the organization has a clear focus on its customers, researching their satisfaction and loyalty to the company. Value-driven organizations also make sure that all the costs they incur over the long run provide at least as much value in customer-want satisfaction. For example, Microsoft is value-driven. By listening to its users' reviews on past systems, Microsoft brings software to market that creates want satisfaction with its latest operating system, Windows 8.1. It is the first operating system to unify the experience for touchscreen devices and desktop systems. Microsoft willingly supports millions of users, one at a time, with cus-

tomer service and 800 numbers to ensure that its products can be used as intended.[26] Customers have rewarded Microsoft with loyalty that yields enormous profits. These, in turn, fuel further innovation in Microsoft, making it one of the most competitive companies in the world. Companies such as Microsoft are using their value-driven approaches to produce great benefit for customers.

> **Today, organizations want lasting relationships so customers become assets of the organization, not just one-time buyers**

Today, organizations want lasting relationships so that customers become long-term assets of the organization, not just one-time buyers. How do marketers develop such relationships to create value for customers? They go through the steps of target marketing, positioning and development of the marketing mix. Then with value-driven marketing practices, they respond to customer needs and wants. When all parts of an organization strive for maximum customer value, stakeholders benefit and the company thrives.

CREATING & CAPTURING VALUE THROUGH *Sustainability*

Aveda - Makes the Earth a More Beautiful Place

Has "green" hair become a major trend? Aveda has been able to create green products that make its customers feel beautiful without sacrificing the earth's natural resources. The company is known globally for its ecologically friendly hair products, cosmetics and skin-care line. The company, founded in 1978 and purchased by Estee Lauder in 1997, has a mission to create beauty as part of a larger web of authentic care for the environment.

Every April, the company sponsors an Earth Month campaign to raise money and awareness for different environmental issues. Since Earth Month began in 1999, it has raised more than $22 million to combat global warming, assist clean water projects and protect endangered species, among other causes. Aveda takes its care for the environment a step beyond philanthropy by including sustainable ingredients in its products and using green packaging techniques. Many of the ingredients are derived from sustainable plant sources. The company utilizes eco-friendly product containers made from cornstarch or post-consumer recycled materials. It has recently initiated a bottle-cap collecting campaign to minimize pollution from bottle trash. The collected soda and shampoo caps are ground down to make plastic for their product containers.

Aveda is also merging with communities around the world to inspire economic growth. It has partnered with 21 communities in Nepal to help strengthen families through business opportunities. Families were provided access to manage local forests and assist in the paper-making process for Aveda gift-set packaging. Since the program's arrival in Nepal, household income among participants has increased 318 percent, and 4,800 children have been able to stop working and go to school with the help of child-rights advocates. In the future, Aveda's goal is to partner with non-profit organizations to strengthen unstable communities worldwide.

www.aveda.com, website visited February 22, 2014.

THE SOCIAL MEDIA ERA

Social media marketing is a recent and exciting addition to many organizations' marketing plans. Rapidly growing online social networking has impacted the way organizations communicate. The networks allow people to build social and business connections, share information, and collaborate in ways never possible before. Social media marketing usually focuses on efforts to draw attention to featured content and encourages users to share it with their social networks. If the content is successful, the message can spread from user to user at incredible rates. Typically the message resonates well with users because it is coming from a trusted source, instead of the company or brand itself.

Social media has become a platform that can increase communication for organizations, create brand awareness, elevate customer service, and move customers through the buying cycle. A study conducted by E-tailing Group shows that Facebook posts influence 31 percent of respondents' buying behaviors, while Twitter has an impact on 17 percent of customers. The report indicates that consumers use social media to get reviews about products and services.

CAREER TIP!

Want to get your feet wet in another city this summer while doing more than pushing paper? Marketing internships with Ford Motor Company require candidates to be willing to relocate and enable them to work on a variety of projects such as product placement and pricing evaluation, export and growth initiatives, and chief marketing office strategy. To explore your opportunities with Ford Motor Company, visit www.mycareer.ford.com.

Social media serves as a relatively inexpensive platform for organizations to implement marketing campaigns. With emergence of services like Facebook, YouTube, Twitter, and Pinterest, the barrier to entry in social media is greatly reduced. Some companies are striving to change the social media landscape with innovative ideas. For example, coupon sites like Groupon and LivingSocial offer businesses the opportunity to post discount offers on the sites. Revenue from the purchases are good, but exposing a large group of customers to your product or service is even more valuable.

At the 2014 Olympic Games in Sochi, social media changed many aspects of how the games were perceived globally. Many fans and athletes posted photos and comments about the living conditions in Sochi, and activists used the opportunity to spread the word of the anti-gay laws in Russia. In this case, social media avenues generated enough negative chatter to create a looming cloud over the image of Sochi and the winter games. Suddenly, fans and athletes have become inside reporters giving millions of people access to information that may have otherwise never been reported. Activists now have a way to spread their point of view from their couch, instead of picketing in Russia. Marketers must consider both the positive and the negative aspects of social media and respond with agility. For example, McDonald's launched a twitter feed with the hashtag #CheersSochi intended to send positive messages to athletes. It was later forced to remove it all together after it was flooded with activists challenging McDonald's sponsorship role in the games.[27]

THE MARKETING STRATEGY PROCESS

The marketing concept is implemented through the marketing strategy process, the series of steps the organization takes to interface with the rest of the world. Chapter

2 defines the elements of that process in depth. Figure 1.3 illustrates the steps of the marketing strategy process.

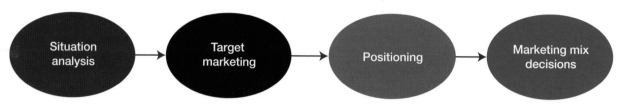

Figure 1.3   Marketing Strategy Process

Situation Analysis Situation analysis includes all the marketing activities required to understand the global marketing environment, the customer's needs and wants, and the competition. It provides the context around which plans are created, altered, and adjusted. It includes analysis of the marketing environment (covered in Chapter 3), an assessment of customer needs and behaviors (covered in Chapters 5, 6, and 7), and the competition. Understanding the situation requires a thorough knowledge of consumer behavior or, in business-to-business marketing, of organizational buying behavior. Understanding consumer behavior gives marketers insight into why buyers respond to goods and services as they do. As we will see in Chapter 6, consumer behavior involves more than just purchasing patterns. It also includes the ways in which consumers perceive and use information and how they arrive at feelings of satisfaction and dissatisfaction. Organizational buying behavior is more complex in terms of the functions and personnel involved in the buying decision, and marketer relationships with these buyers are often more direct. Chapter 6 covers organizational buying in the context of business-to-business marketing. An important function of the situation analysis is to provide the information needed to select certain customers for emphasis — targeting.

Target Marketing Most markets have a wide range of customers so attempting to satisfy all of their needs and wants isn't feasible. Consequently, leading organizations divide customers into groups with similar characteristics. Then they select one or more of these groups, called target markets, to try to address better than their competitors. Leading companies identify potential market segments by making effective use of research methods covered in Chapter 4. Nike has used target marketing to focus attention on college sport teams. Many leading college basketball teams wear the Nike swoosh in clear view on their uniforms. Seeing the brand prominently displayed on their favorite teams and players, fans are more likely to purchase Nike gear for themselves. At store.nike.com, fans can easily purchase athletic gear to look just like their favorite player. Chapter 8 explores target marketing in depth.

Positioning Consumers often perceive well-known brands as having a certain image or reputation. While this perception exists in consumers' minds, marketing organizations undergo a deliberate process, called positioning, to influence it. Nike says, "Just do it," reinforcing the image of an aggressive, action-oriented company. It's no accident that both amateur and professional athletes perceive Nike as producing high-quality shoes that help athletes perform to their maximum potential. Everything Nike does is designed to create this impression, including the use of outstanding athletes such as Kobe Bryant and Lebron James to promote the brand. Chapter 9 examines positioning strategies in more detail.

Marketing Mix Decisions
Once the target market is selected, marketing mix decisions have to be made. How do you go about blending the elements into an appealing mix? Clearly, there needs to be a focus and a purpose. That's where the target market enters the picture. Since it is composed of similar customers, it is possible to address them with one marketing mix. Adjustments to individual customers then can be made within this framework. Figure 1.4 illustrates elements of the marketing mix and target marketing. The marketing mix is based on product, place, promotion and pricing decisions.

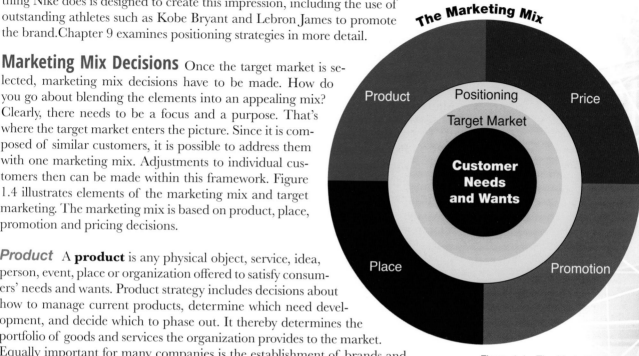

Figure 1.4 The Marketing Mix

Product
Any physical object, service, idea, person, event, place, or organization offered to satisfy consumers' needs and wants.

Place
Providing products where and when they are needed, in the proper quantities, with the greatest appeal, and at the lowest possible cost.

Distribution Channel
A set of independent organizations that make a good or service available for purchase by consumers or businesses.

Physical Distribution
The movement of products through the channels to consumers.

Retailing & Direct Marketing
Selling products directly to end users.

Product A **product** is any physical object, service, idea, person, event, place or organization offered to satisfy consumers' needs and wants. Product strategy includes decisions about how to manage current products, determine which need development, and decide which to phase out. It thereby determines the portfolio of goods and services the organization provides to the market. Equally important for many companies is the establishment of brands and the creation of brand equity (the value associated with a brand). Marketers carefully establish brand names to effectively communicate their products' unique attributes and protect their reputation. For example, Pepsi introduced Pepsi MAX, a soft drink with zero calories, while preserving the original Pepsi flavor. Propel, a Pepsi company product, is offering many different flavored waters. While the consumer shift toward healthier alternatives may account for the new beverages, these products keep Pepsi current in the changing environment. Both products are a part of the company's product strategy. Techniques for making product decisions will be discussed in Chapter 11, "Product Innovation and Management."

Place **Place** strategy is developed to serve customers by providing products where and when they are needed, in the proper quantities, with the greatest appeal, and at the lowest possible cost. The first task is to determine which distribution channels to use. A **distribution channel** is a set of independent organizations that make a good or service available for purchase. Some companies sell directly, such as your local dry cleaner, whereas others use longer channels with more members. For example, a company may sell to wholesalers, who sell to retailers, who sell to you. This becomes increasingly complex in global markets, where numerous channel members are required to move products to customers around the world. **Physical distribution** is the movement of products through the channels to consumers. Companies need order entry systems, transportation, and shipping and inventory storage capacity. Sophisticated information systems are creating some extremely innovative ways of serving customers better.

Retailing and direct marketing provide direct contact with customers. Retailing involves selling products directly to end users, often in retail outlets such as McDonald's or Walmart. Chapter 15, "Supply Chain Management and Channels," and Chapter 16, "Retailing, Direct Marketing, and Wholesaling," address the place strategy.

Promotion

Setting objectives to be attained, creating messages and forms they will take.

Price

Setting prices to reflect the value received by customers and to achieve volume and profit required by the organization.

Promotion **Promotion** involves communicating with customers in a variety of ways. The promotion strategy includes determining the objectives to be attained, as well as creating messages and the forms they will take. In addition, the communication mechanism or media must be selected. Will two-way communication be used, such as personal selling, the phone or Internet, or will one-way radio, television or other media carry the message? Since many messages are carried by numerous media, these decisions can be complex and tremendously interesting. Marketers have a vast number of options when developing promotions, such as training and managing a sales force or creating advertising. Because these mechanisms work together, coordination is vital. The promotion strategy is addressed in Chapter 12, "Integrated Marketing Communications;" Chapter 13, "Mass Communications: Advertising, Sales Promotions, and Personal Selling;" and Chapter 14, "Personal Selling."

Price **Price** strategy affects nearly every part of a business. The objective is to set prices to reflect the value received by customers and to achieve the volume and profit required by the organization. When prices are too high, customers are dissatisfied and refuse to buy, or will switch to a competitor. When prices are too low, companies don't have money to cover costs, invest in new development, and provide a fair return to owners. Pricing must focus on determining value, which is based on what customers expect and desire and what competitors charge, as well as the unique qualities of the products. Marketers must also determine how their prices will influence the volume sold relative to the competition, and what competitors are likely to do with their prices. Prices not only need to be set but also must be communicated and administered. Will warranty charges be extra? What is charged for the base product or add-on? What financing is available? These questions must be answered and factored in. Pricing strategy is covered in Chapter 17, "Pricing Objectives & Influences," and Chapter 18, "Pricing Strategies."

FORCES IMPORTANT TO CREATE & CAPTURE VALUE

The future will center around better ways of creating value for customers. How marketers create and capture value for customers is embodied in the six supporting themes of this book. They are:

- Technology and e-commerce
- Relationships
- Global forces
- Diversity
- Ethics
- Sustainability

These supporting themes were carefully selected to describe how marketers build lasting connections. These six key forces, depicted in Figure 1.5, will reappear throughout the book.

CREATING AND CAPTURING VALUE THROUGH TECHNOLOGY AND E-COMMERCE

New technology is all around us, but two types are particularly noteworthy: (1) product technology that spawns new goods and services; (2) the Internet, which facilitates two-way global connectivity with customers. Additionally, we will discuss the concept of a marketspace, which is bringing many of these technological forces into a single focus.

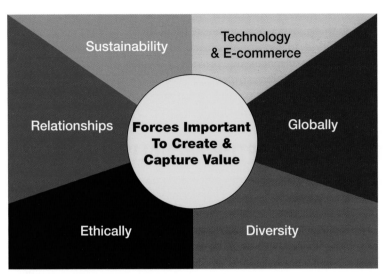

Figure 1.5   Six Forces Important to Create & Capture Value

Product Technology

Product technology is technology that spawns the development of new goods and services. Product technology provides the raw material that fuels improvements in our standard of living. Examples of innovative technology that has produced radically new goods and services are everywhere. Nanotex, a Crypton Company, applies nanotechnology to fabrics, which changes the molecular structures of fibers to create improved performance and comfort in 5 textile technology segments -- repellency/stain resistance, moisture management, odor control, static elimination and wrinkle free. The technology also has applications in other industries, such as energy, high-tech, building and construction, medical, and paints.[28] Cellular systems support telephone calls, fax and data transmissions, as well as global positioning from moving vehicles everywhere. Digital television and flat-screen technology support in-home theater systems that rival movie theaters. And although there are many practical and ethical issues, we can clone the "best" sheep, tomatoes and viruses.

E-commerce and the Internet

We tend to think of marketing as activities that occur in a physical **marketplace**. With new developments in technology, it is now also possible to market goods and services in marketspace, an electronic space where business occurs.

Marketspace transactions take place via the Internet, interactive television, ATMs, online services, shopping channels, 800 numbers and others. You can visit your local music store and buy music or movies — or visit iTunes online and purchase digital music, television shows and movies. Some new artists or the organizations behind them use marketspaces to expand their audience, encouraging them to sample music free of charge.

Numerous Internet marketspaces allow users to search for nearly every good or service — for example, obscure recordings not easily found in a store. You can even experience music from around the world, including Russian, Pakistani or Chinese selections. Other Internet marketspaces provide information about nearly every other type of purchase. Pandora, a free personalized online music player, is present on consumer electronic devices from smartphones to TVs to Blu-ray players. It is able to stream visual, audio and interactive advertising to users along with music. Even Facebook allows users to market their goods for just a few dollars per day.

Some predict that the growth of marketspace will eventually result in the eradication of marketplaces. Indeed, U.S. online retail sales are expected to reach $370 billion by 2017.[29] Although this is a significant growth, the eradication of marketplaces altogether is unlikely; technology does not offer the social dimension of shop-

Product Technology

Technology that spawns the development of new goods and services.

Marketplace

A physical arena where marketing exchanges take place.

Marketspace

An electronic space where business occurs

ping in a marketplace, where consumers can interact with store personnel and other shoppers. In addition, in a store, consumers can physically touch, test, compare and try on products. Marketspaces can provide a similar experience with media, but with products such as clothes or tools, there is no suitable substitute. Shopping in a marketplace also gives some consumers greater reassurance that their credit card transactions will remain confidential.

CREATING AND CAPTURING VALUE THROUGH RELATIONSHIPS

Before the production era, marketers embraced customer orientation. They created products on demand for specific customers. Manufacturers and customers did business directly, building relationships on a personal level. As mass production took root and more levels of distribution channels were added — including retailers and wholesalers, the consumer's voice was heard less and less. In an effort to become more connected to their markets, organizations today are enthusiastically embracing relationship marketing. Figure 1.6 describes a continuum of marketing exchanges from pure transactions to repeated transactions to relationships.[30]

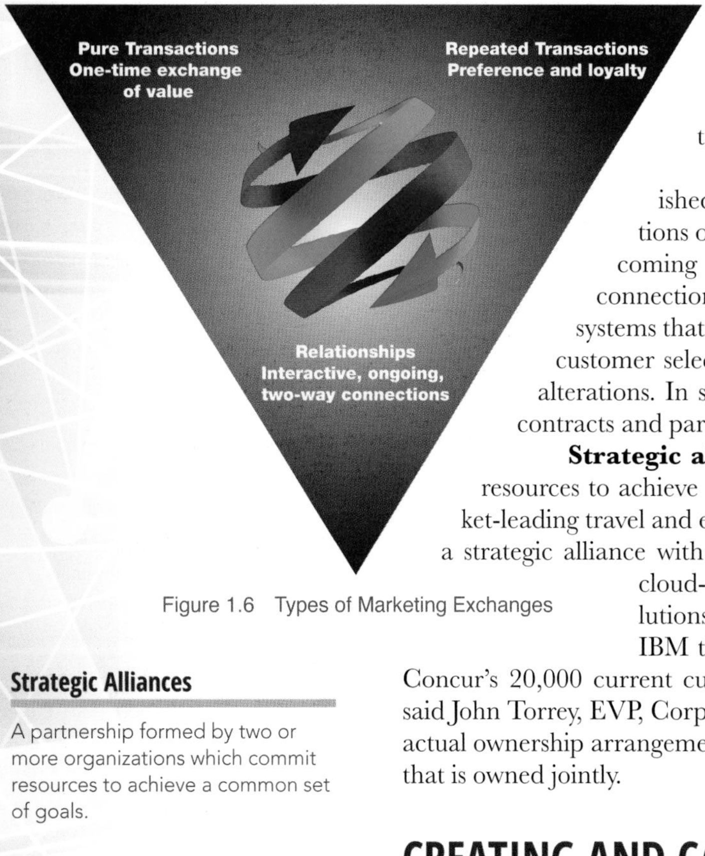

A pure transaction occurs only once. When it is finished, both parties go their separate ways. Repeated transactions occur when customers have strong preferences, often becoming loyal customers. Relationships create an even stronger connection. In business markets, suppliers develop computerized systems that are tied to a customer's manufacturing processes. If the customer selects a new supplier, the computer system will also need alterations. In some cases, these relationships are based on long-term contracts and partnerships.

Strategic alliances occur between firms in which each commits resources to achieve a common set of objectives. Concur, owner of a market-leading travel and expense management platform, has recently announced a strategic alliance with IBM. Together, the companies will market Concur's cloud-based solutions to IBM Global Expense Reporting Solutions clients. "We are thrilled to enter into this alliance with IBM to help their customers experience the same benefits as Concur's 20,000 current customers and the 25 million travelers they represent," said John Torrey, EVP, Corporate Strategy of Concur.[31] Some alliances may involve actual ownership arrangements. In these cases, several parties form an organization that is owned jointly.

Figure 1.6   Types of Marketing Exchanges

Pure Transactions
One-time exchange of value

Repeated Transactions
Preference and loyalty

Relationships
Interactive, ongoing, two-way connections

Strategic Alliances

A partnership formed by two or more organizations which commit resources to achieve a common set of goals.

CREATING AND CAPTURING VALUE GLOBALLY

Marketers are connecting globally like never before. The global marketplace is tremendously important for U.S. companies, as the United States reigns as the world's third leading exporter, shipping approximately $1.6 trillion in goods and services per year. China, the world's leader, exports approximately $2.2 trillion annually.[32] Marketers should not ignore or lose sight of the importance of a global organization. Compared to domestic firms, global companies have an increased customer reach and a better understanding of diversity and competition. They can also offset economic downturns with the implementation of appropriate strategies.

The global marketplace can be very complex. Marketers evaluate many considerations and implement well-planned strategies to ensure their success. The Internet has had a tremendous impact on global marketing. Experts predict that the number of brands around the globe will actually decrease, as companies use the same brand name to market a product regardless of its location. Procter & Gamble, for example, has chosen to decrease the number of its brands from 600 to 400, to focus more on global marketing, especially via the Internet.[33] Throughout this book, you will learn that organizations need to research and accommodate differences at many levels. These include language, culture, currency, infrastructure, laws and regulations, consumer preferences, and negotiating style. Marketers also need to understand the different preferences and needs of global customers.

CREATING AND CAPTURING VALUE THROUGH DIVERSITY

Professor Warren Plunkett teaches what he calls the "new golden rule." The traditional golden rule states that you should do unto others as you would have them do unto you, but that assumes all people are the same. In an increasingly diverse society, you must be able to see others' point of view. People from different cultures or backgrounds don't necessarily have the same perceptions, needs and wants. Plunkett's new rule is: Do unto others as they would have you do unto them. In other words, as a marketer, you must remember to satisfy your customer on the basis of your customer's desires and social norms—not your own.[34]

As marketers move to a more personalized, one-on-one connection with customers, it is imperative to understand and respect diversity among customers, because no two are alike. As you will learn in Chapter 5, some commonalities exist within various subcultures and social classes. But marketers today are much more sensitive to the needs of a diverse population.

It is important to understand that cultural diversity refers to far more than just ethnic groups. U.S. West Airlines, which recognizes diversity as part of its corporate culture, distinguishes among the following categories: race/color, gender, age, sexual orientation, religion, cultural heritage, veteran status, marital status, liberal/conservative, and national origin. The companies you will work for may have even more distinguishing factors. According to Marsha Farnsworth Riche, director of the U.S. Bureau of the Census, "We're all minorities now. If you count men and women as separate groups, all Americans are now members of at least one minority group."[35]

When marketing to ethnic groups, it is important to distinguish between ethnic background and ethnicity. A person's **ethnic background** is usually determined by birth and related to one or more of four elements: country of origin, native language, race, and religion. Hispanics are an ethnic group, but members have diverse interests and beliefs depending on country of origin, length of time in the United States, geographic placement, and other factors. **Ethnicity** is an individual identifying with a particular ethnic group. According to Lafayette Jones, president and CEO of Segmented Marketing Services, Inc., marketers should "look at the market not in terms of black and white, but in terms of true ethnicity. We use terms like 'African American' because these terms really describe what we're talking about, without the social and political implications of race. … Every culture has its own food, music and religious practices. They're diverse in competition, flavorings, attitudes and expressions."[36] In Chapter 5, we'll look more specifically at various ethnic markets. Applying what you learn can help you as a marketer cultivate and satisfy customers from varied ethnic backgrounds.

Marketers recognize that there is tremendous diversity in marketing. They also recognize the immense spending power of diverse groups. African Americans, Hispanic Americans, and Asian Americans will spend in excess of $2.1 trillion by 2015, more than quadruple their level of $454 billion in 1990.[37] Mature customers (age

> As marketers move to a more personalized, on-on-one connection with customers, it is imperative to understand and respect diversity among customers.

Ethnic Background

Subculture membership usually determined by birth and related to one or more of four elements: country of origin, native language, race, and religion.

Ethnicity

The amount of identification an individual feels with a particular ethnic group.

Companies like Allstate recognize the importance of marketing to Hispanic Americans and other diverse groups.

Courtesy of Lapiz and Allstate

50 and older) control half the U.S. buying power. Young adults spend $200 billion annually, whereas women reportedly buy 85 percent of all consumer goods.[38] These are just a few of the diverse customers you will be learning about in this book. It is both profitable and rewarding for marketers to connect and build relationships with every type of customer. By acknowledging, understanding, and accommodating the needs of diverse groups, marketers can create a loyal base of customers for future business.

CREATING AND CAPTURING VALUE ETHICALLY

Today, most marketers understand the importance of social responsibility and ethical behavior. In fact, ethical initiatives by businesses have more than doubled in the past five years. Responsible marketers make decisions with a clear code of ethics in mind and consider the standards of conduct for an organization. A worldwide poll conducted by Environics International asked 25,000 people in 23 countries to name the factors that most affected their impressions of individual companies. A majority mentioned factors related to social responsibility (e.g., labor practices and business ethics) and felt that companies should go beyond the traditional goals of "making a profit, paying taxes, and providing employment."[39] Ethics and social responsibility are two directly related forces, but they are not the same.

Ethics **Ethics** are the values or standards that govern professional conduct. **Marketing ethics** deal specifically with the application of moral standards to marketing decisions, behaviors and institutions.[40] Nearly every area of marketing has significant ethical dimensions that raise difficult questions. Throughout this book, we will evaluate many ethical situations, including issues of fairness, equity, conflict of interest, privacy, confidentiality and product safety. You will also find that every area of marketing can present an ethical dilemma, including product development, promotion, distribution and pricing.

In order to promote ethical behavior in each area of marketing, both large and small businesses implement a code of conduct, sometimes referred to as value statements or management integrity statements. These may provide a wide range of guidelines, depending on the beliefs and values of a particular organization. For example, Johnson & Johnson established one of the first codes in 1947. It embodies a commitment to ethical business practices as well as a responsibility to consumers, employees, the community and shareholders. You will learn more about Johnson & Johnson in Chapter 2.

Responsible organizations don't simply implement a code of ethics; they make it clear that ethics are a priority by communicating standards to employees. An ethical organization requires the support of top management, and many companies aim to manage beyond compliance by exceeding the standards defined by federal, state,

Ethics

Values or standards that govern professional conduct.

Marketing Ethics

The ethics that deal specifically with how moral standards are applied to marketing decisions, behaviors, and institutions.

and local regulations.

Because the marketing function within an organization relies heavily on interaction with customers, it is often subject to public scrutiny. This emphasizes the power of ethics as a force in making business decisions. Over the long run, organizations with a strong ethical culture and code of conduct likely will be better equipped to handle ethical dilemmas.

Social Responsibility Many people believe that a socially responsible business must satisfy the needs of customers in ways that provide profits to the owners or meet other requirements outlined by the owners. Some argue that profits represent the response of consumers to businesses that best serve their needs. As mentioned previously, social responsibility and ethics are closely related. The **societal marketing concept** seeks to balance customer satisfaction against corporate profits and the well-being of the larger society. It extends the marketing concept to include satisfying the citizen as well as the customer. Social responsibility reflects "the consequences of a person or firm's acts as they might affect the interest of others."[41]

Method, one of the fastest-growing privately owned companies proves the successful products can also be responsible. Makers of safe and effective home cleaning products, Method eliminates hazardous chemicals and replaces them with natural ingredients like coconut, soy and palm oils. The company's humanifesto uses clever statements like "role models in bottles," and "good always prevails over stinky" to help describe its socially responsible pursuit. [42]

Many companies are well known for their commitment to social causes and for acting in the best interest of the citizen as well as the consumer. Consider Ben & Jerry's, which contributes about $2 million each year to charitable causes. Ben & Jerry's is well known for its environmental initiatives, including innovative recycling, energy saving and waste reduction. The company incorporated its dedication to societal marketing into this part of its mission statement: "to operate the Company in a way that actively recognizes the central role that business plays in society by initiating innovative ways to improve the quality of life locally, nationally, and internationally."[43]

Societal Marketing Concept

The marketing concept extended to include satisfying the citizen as well as the consumer.

CREATING AND CAPTURING VALUE THROUGH SUSTAINABILITY

It's a common misconception that sustainability pertains strictly to environmental issues. However, the Brundtland Commission outlined in its classic report "Our Common Future" that sustainable development is a complex process involving three components: the environment, economy and society. It is important to understand that these elements are closely linked. The environment is where we live, while economic and social development are the actions we take to improve our conditions within the environment.[44] How does this relate to creating and capturing value? Increased environmental concerns among consumers lead them to assess an organization's value not only by its products but how its products and processes affect the environment.

The result of consumer environmental consciousness has been the creation of green marketing campaigns — the marketing of eco-friendly products or processes, or marketing using eco-friendly methods — by many organizations. For example, S.C. Johnson and Sons markets how its manufacturing facilities use waste methane gas, a byproduct of decomposition in landfills, for energy.[45] Marketers must weigh the importance of sustainability to its customers and implement a strategy accordingly. Throughout this book, you will learn of different companies undertaking environmental initiatives in order to create and capture value for customers.

MARKETING: YOUR INVOLVEMENT

By now it should be clear that marketing affects you in many ways. Your exploration of marketing begins from many angles — the prospective marketer, member of a target market, customer, and citizen. Each of these roles gives you a slightly different point of view, which can lead to the development of valuable marketing skills. One in three of you will be in a job that directly involves marketing. Throughout this text, we will highlight opportunities in the Career Tip feature. Your career may involve strategic marketing planning, personal selling, promotion or advertising, retailing, product development, social media marketing, getting products to market (distribution), or establishing pricing criteria. No matter what career you choose — working for a political campaign, a not-for-profit organization, a religious organization, or a Fortune 500 company — your job will require an understanding of marketing.

In a sense, you are already a marketer through your everyday actions. You market yourself when you apply to schools or pursue a scholarship. You are a marketer when you seek election to an organization or attempt to influence its members. You are a marketer when you interview for an internship or job. In all likelihood, you will be applying marketing in a professional sense in the future. Since marketing is so important, this is true no matter what your college major happens to be.

You also belong to a target market, which makes you tremendously important to other marketers. You are part of a target market when political candidates appear on popular TV shows to ask for your votes, when a TV network produces a show designed to appeal to you, and when sports teams, theme parks and movies compete for your entertainment dollars.

Marketing affects you through your role as a customer. You are a customer every time you purchase. You are a loyal customer when you have a strong preference that results in your repeated purchase of a company's goods or services. You are part of a marketing relationship when a company that knows you by name wants to customize its actions to fit your desires.

Finally, marketing pertains to you as a citizen. You are affected by marketing when McDonald's selects paper over Styrofoam packaging to reduce pollution. You are affected when Mothers Against Drunk Driving (MADD) reduces your chance of injury from a traffic accident. You are affected when General Motors designs a Cadillac that is completely recyclable.

Marketing is a relevant, fun subject. It is filled with examples that you see every day. It touches your life directly in countless ways — something as simple as sending a Tweet makes you one of millions of consumers and marketers participating in emerging trends in social media marketing.

CHAPTER SUMMARY

Objective 1: Understand the concept of marketing, including its definition, purpose and role in creating exchanges.
Marketing is an organizational function and a set of processes for creating, communicating, and delivering value to customers and for managing customer relationships in ways that benefit the organization and its stakeholders. The purpose of marketing is to identify the needs and wants of customers within markets and to create customer value in ways that will ensure the long-run success of the organization by making connections between companies and customers. Many people refer to the purpose as the marketing concept. Marketing works by creating

valuable exchanges that provide utility. Utility is produced when products are created or adjusted, when goods and services are placed so consumers can discover and acquire them, when products are delivered at the right time, and when the transfer of ownership is facilitated.

Objective 2: Contrast the periods of marketing evolution from its early history through the eras of production, sales, customer marketing, value marketing and social media.
Marketing has progressed through five eras — the production era, the sales era, the customer marketing era, the value marketing era and the

social media era. As the names suggest, the production era focused on ways to efficiently mass-produce new products, while the sales era focused on getting people to buy products. The customer marketing era moved management's attention toward satisfying customer needs and wants. The value driven era required every part of an organization to create maximum value for its customers. And today, the social media era has significantly improved the efficiency and effectiveness of how organizations communicate.

Objective 3: Learn what is involved in making marketing decisions, including examples of product, price, promotion and place decisions to create a marketing mix.

The marketing strategy process has four steps — situation analysis, targeting, positioning and marketing mix decisions. Situation analysis provides information about the marketing environment and specific company elements. It is based on insights gained from the use of marketing information systems and marketing research. Targeting occurs when groups of customers with identifiable characteristics are selected for attention. Targeting helps focus resources. The best marketing strategies do an excellent job of addressing the needs and wants of customers within these targets. Positioning is used to determine what image or impression the marketer wants customers within a target segment to possess regarding the organization or its products. By blending the marketing mix — product, price, promotion and place — marketing decisions are made to support the positioning strategy. These decisions can be blended into a vast array of combinations, each producing different results.

Objective 4: Understand the six key forces that are dramatically influencing how organizations will connect with customers in the future.

Marketing is influenced by relationships, technology, ethics, diversity, globalization and sustainability. Today, more organizations are implementing the marketing concept by forging relationships with valued customers. These are creating loyalty and repeat business that help the organization to achieve its objectives. Product technology develops radically new goods and services, and process technology makes it possible to be more responsive to customers by altering how marketing occurs. The Internet is a particularly noteworthy technological advance because it brings us new distribution, communication, scanning and research capabilities. The global economy has an impact on all customers and competitors. Consequently, global factors must be considered when making marketing decisions. Ethics and social responsibility are also important forces, because they help guide many marketing decisions. Ethics involve making decisions based on what is right and wrong. Social responsibility involves decisions that affect citizens, customers, and the environment. Finally, supporting sustainability enables a company to work toward protecting the environment, our economy and society.

Objective 5: Determine how marketing pertains to you.

You are intimately involved in marketing — as a marketer, as a member of a target market, as a customer, and as a citizen. Marketing pertains to you personally, and you begin your study of the subject having already experienced many of its facets. Professionally, marketing is important no matter which major or career you choose. In a sense, you are often a marketer when you attempt to advance yourself or your views. Along with other people similar to yourself, you are part of a target market toward which certain marketers direct their attention. As a customer, you experience the actions of marketers. As a citizen, you are impacted positively and negatively by many organizations whether or not you purchase their products.

REVIEW YOUR UNDERSTANDING

1. What is marketing? What are the key elements in its definition?
2. What are the four basic areas (types of markets) in which marketing is typically applied?
3. What is utility? What are the four types of utility involved in marketing exchanges?
4. What is the difference between a need and a want? Give examples of each.
5. What is the marketing concept? What are its three key aspects?
6. What are the stages in marketing evolution? Describe each of the five marketing eras.
7. What is a marketing strategy? Describe each of its four steps.
8. How do product, place, promotion and price decisions form the marketing mix? Give examples of each decision.
9. What are the five key forces shaping marketing as we enter the 21st century? Describe each.
10. How does marketing relate to you? List four ways.

DISCUSSION OF CONCEPTS

1. Describe marketing, highlighting examples from your daily life that illustrate each of its four aspects.
2. Identify one company with which you are familiar and describe four ways in which it provides utility.
3. Discuss the activities involved in implementing the marketing concept. How do they pertain to customers, competitors and the marketing organization?
4. Describe the steps in developing a marketing strategy. Why is it important to target prior to positioning? Why is positioning important prior to marketing mix decisions?
5. Compare and contrast the various eras of marketing, assessing the role each era played in reaching the current social media era.
6. Discuss the five forces shaping marketing by showing how they help implement the marketing concept.

KEY TERMS & DEFINITIONS

1. **Agility:** The flexibility and speed with which organizations can identify or create new wants and take action to satisfy them.
2. **Business-To-Business marketing:** When a business purchases goods or services to produce other goods, to support daily operations or to resell at a profit.
3. **Buyer's market:** The marketing environment that exists when an abundance of product lets the buyer control the market.
4. **Consumer marketing:** When organizations sell to individuals or households that buy, consume, and dispose of products.
5. **Consumer orientation:** An organizational philosophy that focuses on satisfying consumer needs and wants.
6. **Customer value:** What consumers perceive they gain from owning or using a product over and above the cost of acquiring it.
7. **Distribution channel:** A set of independent organizations that make up a good or service available for purchase by consumers or business.
8. **Effectiveness:** The degree to which an organization's activities produce results that matter to consumers.
9. **Efficiency:** The degree to which activities are carried out without waste of time or money.
10. **Ethics:** Standards or values that govern professional conduct.
11. **Ethnic background:** Subculture membership usually determined by birth and related to one or more of four elements: country of origin, native language, race, and religion.
12. **Ethnicity:** The amount of identification an individual feels with a particular ethnic group.
13. **Exchange:** A process in which two or more parties provide something of value to one another.
14. **Form utility:** A want-satisfying value that is created when knowledge and materials are converted into finished goods and services.
15. **Internal marketing:** When managers of one functional unit market their capabilities to other units within their own organization.
16. **Loyalty:** A measure of how often, when selecting from a product class, a customer purchases a particular brand.
17. **Macro-marketing:** Viewing marketing from a societal point of view, marketing is the function that creates exchanges that facilitates the delivery of the standard of living to society.
18. **Market:** All the individuals and organizations with potential desire and ability to acquire a particular good or service.
19. **Marketing:** The process of planning and executing the conception, pricing, promotion, and distribution of ideas, goods, and services to create exchanges that satisfy individual and organizational objectives.
20. **Marketing ethics:** The ethics that deal specifically with how moral standards are applied to marketing decisions, behaviors, and institutions.
21. **Marketing mix:** The four controllable variables—product, price, promotion, and place (distribution)—that are combined to appeal to the company's target markets.
22. **Marketplace:** A physical arena where marketing exchanges take place.
23. **Marketspace:** An electronic space where business occurs.
24. **Mass marketing:** The mass production, mass distribution, and mass promotion of a product to all buyers.
25. **Micro-marketing:** Marketing from the point of view of the firm or organization
26. **Need:** Fundamental requirements the meeting of which is the ultimate goal of behavior.
27. **Nonprofit marketing:** When an organization does not try to make a profit but instead attempts to influence others to support its cause by using its service or by making a contribution.
28. **Ownership utility:** A want-satisfying value that is created by making it possible to transfer the title of goods and services from one party to another.
29. **Physical distribution:** The movement of products through the channels to consumers.
30. **Place:** Providing products where and when they are needed, in the proper quantities, with the greatest appeal, and at the lowest possible cost.
31. **Place utility:** A want-satisfying value that is created by making goods and services conveniently available.
32. **Positioning:** The process of creating an image, reputation, or perception of the company or its goods and services in the consumer's mind.
33. **Price:** Setting prices to reflect the value received by customers and to achieve volume and profit required by the organization.
34. **Product:** Any physical object, service, idea, person, event, place, or organization offered to satisfy consumers' needs and wants.
35. **Product technology:** Technology that spawns the development of new goods and services.
36. **Production orientation:** Historical marketing period that emphasized new products and the efficiency of production.
37. **Promotion:** Setting objectives to be attained, creating messages and forms they will take.
38. **Relationship marketing:** The development and maintenance of successful relational exchanges; it involves interactive, ongoing, two-way connections among customers, organizations, suppliers, and other parties for mutual benefit.
39. **Retailing & direct marketing:** Selling products directly to end users.
40. **Sales orientation:** Historical marketing period that emphasized that consumers must be convinced to buy.
41. **Satisfaction:** The customer's overall rating of his or her experience with a company's products.
42. **Seller's market:** The marketing environment that exists when scarcity of products lets the seller control the market.
43. **Societal marketing concept:** The marketing concept extended to include satisfying the citizen as well as the consumer.
44. **Strategic alliances:** A partnership formed by two or more organizations for a new venture.
45. **Sustainability:** The steps and processes organizations undertake to manage growth without detrimentally affecting the resources or biological systems of the earth.

46. **Time utility:** A want-satisfying value that is created when goods and services are made available when they are wanted.
47. **Value-Driven organization:** An organization that implements the marketing concept by ensuring that all parts of the organization make the maximum contribution toward creating value for the customer.
48. **Want:** A specific form of consumption desired to satisfy need.

REFERENCES

1. www.starbucks.com, website visited July 22, 2014
2. www.ama.org, website visited February 20, 2014.
3. Jay Wright Soap Commercial, www.youtube.com, website visited May 8, 2014.
4. Rebecca Horsley, "Study finds nonprofit digital spending on the rise," Charity Digital News, May 12, 2014.
5. Form 10-K for BAXTER INTERNATIONAL INC, Annual Report, February 21, 2014.
6. McDonald's Values, www.aboutmcdonalds.com, website visited June 9, 2014.
7. "Case Study: Dell Builds Brand Equity with Business Solutions Exchange LinkedIn Group," www.linkedselling.com, February 6, 2014.
8. www.charitywater.org, website visited February 6, 2014.
9. www.apple.com, website visited February 23, 2014.
10. Ibid.
11. James Kendrick, "Dropping tablet sales: Blame Apple," Mobile News, May 5, 2014; Chris Velazco , "Apple's iPhone sales soar while the iPad slumps slightly," Engadget.com, April 23, 2014.
12. Ibid.
13. Culliton, James W., The Management of Marketing Costs, cited in Borden, Neil H., "The Concept of the Marketing Mix," Journal of Advertising Research, June 1964, pp. 2-7.
14. Bagozzi, Richard P., "Marketing as Exchange," Journal of Marketing, October 1975, pp. 32-39.
15. "Love Those Boomers," Business Week, October 25, 2005. www.dove.us, website visited March 23, 2014.
16. "Coke Unveils Global Strategy," Adweek, www.adweek.com, website visited July 27, 2014.
17. www.roversclub.org, website visited February 20, 2014.
18. Stacy Finz, "Homemade baby food biting into sales," San Francisco Chronicle, May 13, 2014.
19. www.fedex.com website visited March 22, 2014.
20. www.netflix.com, website visited March 22, 2014.
21. www.xerox.com, website visited February 28, 2014.
22. www.facebook.com/Hampton, website visited February 28, 2014.
23. The President's Council on Sustainable Development.
24. www.aveda.com, website visited January 29, 2014.
25. www.scjohnson.com, website visited January 29, 2014.
26. www.microsoft.com, website visited February 14, 2014.
27. Avi Dan, "For Coke And McDonald's, Ignoring The Power Of Social Media To Disrupt Means No Medals In Sochi," CMO Network, February 05, 2014.
28. Constance Gustke, "Nanotechnology Now an Unseen Success," CNBC.com, May 29, 2012; www.nano-tex.com, website visited May 14, 2014.
29. US Online Retail Sales To Reach $370 Billion By 2017, Forrester, March 13, 2013
30. Webster, Frederick, E., "The Changing Role of Marketing in the Corporation," Journal of Marketing, October 1992, pp.1-17.
31. Concur Announces Strategic Alliance with IBM, PRNewswire, May 6, 2014.
32. CIA World Factbook, www.cia.gov, website visited May 15, 2014.
33. Schmidt, Kathleen, "Outlook 2000: Globalization," Marketing News, January 17, 2000. pp. 9-12.
34. Plunkett, Warren, Instructor's Manual for Supervision, 7th ed. (Boston: Allyn & Bacon, 1993), pp. 6-7.
35. Mogelonsky, Marcia, Everybody Eats: Supermarket Consumers in the 1990s (Ithaca, NY: American Demographic Books, 1995), pg. 185.
36. Ibid., p. 163.
37. "Despite recession, Hispanic and Asian buying power expected to surge in U.S., according to annual UGA Selig Center Multicultural Economy study," www.terry.uga.edu, website visited July 28, 2012.
38. "Young, with tons of purchasing power," www.marketwatch.com, website visited June 10, 2014.
39. "Great Expectations," Across the Board, January 1, 2000.
40. Laczniak, Gene R., Murphy, Patrick E., Ethical Marketing Decisions: The Higher Road (Boston: Allyn & Bacon, 1993), pg. 3.
41. Bennet, Peter D., Dictionary of Marketing Terms (Chicago: American Marketing Association, 1995), pg. 267.
42. www.methodhome.com, website visited May 5, 2014.
43. "Activism," Benjerry.com website visited August 9, 2014.
44. Mandese, Joe, "Talk Show Stalwart P&G Cans 'Trash,'" Advertising Age, November 20, 1995, pg. 1.
45. Our Common Future: Report of World Commission on Environment and Development, United Nations, 1987.
46. www.scjohnson.com, website visited March 16, 2014.

Chapter 02

THE MARKETING & STRATEGY
PLANNING PROCESS

Coca-Cola, the world's leading manufacturer, marketer and distributor of nonalcoholic beverages, has an unprecedented ability to fit into people's lives. Its global footprint is staggering, with nearly 500 brands and 3,000 products served 1.8 billion times daily in more than 200 countries. Its broad beverage portfolio includes sparkling drinks, bottled water, sports drinks, energy drinks, juices, teas and coffees. It is one of the most powerful brands in the world.

With a history of strong and consistent messages, including slogans such as "Enjoy," "The Coke Side of Life," and "Open Happiness," the Coke brand has found prominence in markets around the world. Over the company's long history, Coke has built an image embraced by generation after generation and continues to be the drink preferred by most consumers. From its use of polar bears in advertising to its signature contoured bottles, Coca-Cola's innovative marketing campaigns have provided impressive strategic advantages.

The power of the Coke brand has transcended national borders and cultural barriers. Because of regional taste differences, Coke has tapped into foreign markets by renaming or adding flavors to existing products, even creating entirely new brands. For example, in Europe, Diet Coke is called Coke Light; in Peru, you may enjoy an Inca Kola, the national beverage of the country.

With great success comes great responsibility, and Coca-Cola rises to the challenge. Faced with the growing social movement of sustainability and a world "going green," Coca-Cola quickly implemented global sustainability goals and targets to reduce energy consumption, increase global climate protection, implement sustainable packaging and improve water efficiency. Coca-Cola is a member of the Plant PET Technology Collaborative (PTC), which also includes Ford Motor Company, H.J. Heinz Company, Nike and Procter & Gamble. The group is working to develop 100% plant-based PET materials for its products. This technology will dramatically reduce the use of petroleum-based plastics.

As a proud sponsor of the Olympic Games since 1928, Coca-Cola also sponsors other world events like the 2014 FIFA World Cup. The brand launched a special FIFA World Cup Trophy Tour, a flight to various cities around the world, to promote the event. During the tour, Coca-Cola rolled out its "Get Happiness Rolling" program to spread happiness and encourage healthy, active lifestiles around the world.

Coke's quick adoption of the environmentally responsible social movement goes beyond helping to save the planet. With a redefined green-company persona, Coke markets itself and its vast array of products to a rapidly growing green consumer base. Coke believes that "investing in the economic, environmental and social development of communities will help our business grow."

Coke's rapid product innovations are also part of a winning formula. Recently, it developed a fountain that dispenses more than 100 beverages with the press of a button. Consumers now have the freedom to choose any type of beverage in any flavor that the company produces. Introducing a new brand to the dispenser is as easy as switching a cartridge, so Coke can introduce consumers to new brands with ease. The consumer decision may no longer come down to Coke vs. competitor, but to which Coca-Cola product to choose.[1]

<< Official 2014 FIFA World Cup Trophy Tour Plane

Courtesy of Coca-Cola

Learning Objectives

1. Understand how the strategic marketing planning hierarchy fits together to provide a complete planning system.
2. Describe the four elements of an organization's vision that provide guidance for all actions.
3. Integrate components of the strategic marketing plan with the vision.
4. Understand why elements of the marketing mix must be integrated and outline the steps of the marketing control process.
5. Identify the four major ways that organizations enter and cultivate global markets.

THE CONCEPT OF THE STRATEGIC MARKETING PLANNING PROCESS

Connecting with customers to create and capture value requires both long- and short-term efforts.

Marketing can be described as philosophy, as strategy and as tactics. Leading-edge businesses such as Coca-Cola, Eli Lilly and Johnson & Johnson develop marketing plans that address each of these aspects to help them connect with customers. Figure 2.1 outlines the type of planning that corresponds with each aspect of marketing, including the people who usually implement it.

Marketing as philosophy is embodied within the organization's statement of **vision**. It is usually developed by top executives, and it articulates the codes of conduct guiding organizational behavior, what customer value will be delivered, specific strategic objectives, and the resources that will be developed and deployed. The vision describes the fundamental contributions the business intends to make to society, its position relative to competitors, and the attributes that make the organization unique. Those developing the statement may seek input from all organizational levels.

Marketing as strategy is formalized in the **strategic marketing plan,** a document describing the company's objectives and how to achieve them in light of competitive activities. Essentially, this plan outlines the decisions executives have made about how to accomplish their vision. The strategic marketing plan generally requires input and guidelines from marketing executives and a planning team of top- and middle-level personnel.

Marketing as tactics refers to precisely how each part of the marketing mix (product, price, promotion and place) will be managed to meet requirements of the strategic marketing plan. Marketing mix plans are developed by specialists in each component, such as product managers, advertising executives and sales personnel.

In a small company, the owner may perform all of these planning roles, whereas a larger company could employ several hundred people in this area. You will find that

Vision

Statement of an organization's operating philosophy including core values, business definition, strategic direction and strategic infrastructure.

Strategic Marketing Plan

The document describing the company's objectives and how to achieve them in light of competitive activities.

Marketing Aspect	Type of Planning	Responsibility
Marketing as philosophy	Vision	Top executive and top management team
Marketing as strategy	Strategic marketing plan	Marketing executive and other members of the strategic marketing team
Marketing as tactics	Marketing mix plans	Managers responsible for product, price, promotion, and place programs

Figure 2.1   Strategic Marketing Planning Hierarchy

Figure 2.2   Marketing Planning as Philosophy, Planning, Tactics

companies tend to blend philosophy, strategy and tactics into a range of planning, but traces of all three will be present in varying degrees, depending on what is most appropriate for a given organization. The hierarchy in Figure 2.2 describes what takes place as companies develop plans that address the three marketing aspects. Each of the major components of the vision, strategic marketing plan, and marketing mix plans depicted here is examined in detail in the following sections. The final section of the chapter focuses on the strategies companies use to enter and build strength in foreign markets.

THE ORGANIZATION VISION

Outstanding performers have a vision that focuses marketing efforts purposefully. The vision helps maintain consistent direction despite volatile market environments. When President John F. Kennedy said, "...I believe this nation should commit itself to achieving the goal, before this decade is out, of landing a man on the Moon and returning him safely to the Earth," he created an effective vision. He provided a picture that inspired the U.S. space program, largely because the vision was simple, clear and easy to remember. If Kennedy had described the enormity of the challenge in detail (how many people were needed, what talents they must possess, what type of equipment would be required), it's doubtful the venture would have succeeded. Instead, Kennedy's vision was fulfilled in 1969, when Neil Arm-

President John F. Kennedy in his historic vision to a joint session of the Congress, on May 25, 1961.

strong took "one small step for man, one giant leap for mankind," and walked on the moon.

If you visualize your life now and in five years, 15 years, and beyond, you are forming a personal vision. To make that vision a reality, what values will guide your behaviors? What will you contribute to people around you? What is your idea of excellence? What skills and attributes do you possess or will you develop? Organizations have to answer the same questions. This is the visioning process. Discovering the vision is critical for companies (or people) that wish to deliver superior value.

The corporate vision provides a common understanding of what the organization is trying to accomplish in the broadest sense. Most company visions are composed of four parts: a set of core values, a business definition, the strategic direction of the company, and the strategic infrastructure.

CORE VALUES: THE ETHICAL FOUNDATION

Core Values

A set of statements describing the type of behavior expected of the company and its employees.

Core values describe the type of behavior expected from a company's employees. They are the articulation of ethics and social responsibility, which were discussed in Chapter 1. Whole Foods Market considers its values the underpinning of its company culture and says, "We're not just about selling groceries; we believe we have a responsibility toward all people involved in our business." The company commits to selling the highest-quality natural and organic products available, satisfying and delighting customers, supporting team member excellence and happiness, creating wealth through profits and growth, caring about communities and the environment, creating ongoing win-win partnerships with suppliers and promoting the health of stakeholders through healthy eating education. By sustaining these core values, Whole Foods believes it will preserve what has made it special since its beginning, regardless of how large the company becomes.[2] Employees believe that if they do this, business will be grounded on a firm foundation. Core values often express the company's philosophy about societal well-being, good corporate citizenship and treatment of employees. Employees believe that if they do this, business will be grounded on a firm foundation. Core values often express the company's philosophy about societal well-being, good corporate citizenship and treatment of employees.

For example, a team of top executives and managers at Sparrow Health System in Lansing, Michigan, gathered to articulate the core values of its organization, as shown in Figure 2.3. Sparrow considers "ICARE" — innovation, compassion, accountability, respect and excellence — as values fundamental in defining its behaviors.[3] By embracing these values, Sparrow can better serve its customers and the community, providing "quality, compassionate care to everyone, every time."

Sparrow Health System Core Values:

Innovation
finding new ways to improve the quality of health services
Compassion
providing 'radical loving care' for everyone
Accountability
accepting responsibility for our actions and attitudes
Respect
valuing diversity, inclusion and working well together
Excellence
achieving the best results in all we do

Figure 2.3   Sparrow Health System Core Values

Johnson and Johnson (JNJ) puts people first. Founded more than 120 years ago, JNJ has grown to 250 companies in 57 countries. Today, it excels at connecting with its customers while contributing to a greener world. For three years running, it has been awarded the prestigious Environmental Protection Agency Green Power Partnership Award.[4]

Core values provide an ethical guide that may be particularly useful in a crisis. It is possible Johnson & Johnson would not be around today if it had not adhered to its core values when Tylenol capsules laced with cyanide were linked to several deaths in the early 1980s. The company's values are described in a credo, outlined in the early 1940s, which today reads in part: "We believe our first responsibility is to the doctors, nurses, and patients, to mothers and all others who use our products and services. In meeting their needs, everything we do must be of high quality."[5] That credo represents the organization's main purpose: to supply products responsibly with consumer safety in mind.

The Tylenol tragedy was one that few companies could withstand. By following the guidelines set forth in its credo, however, Johnson & Johnson did not just survive, but emerged stronger. This ethics issue, one of the most heavily covered of its type by the Wall Street Journal, provides a fascinating example of core values.[6] Johnson & Johnson owns McNeil Consumer Products Company, the maker of Tylenol, which in 1982 generated $500 million in annual sales and contributed eight percent of Johnson & Johnson's annual revenues. It was outselling Bayer aspirin, Bufferin, Excedrin and Anacin combined.

On September 30, 1982, when Extra-Strength Tylenol capsules laced with cyanide were reportedly linked with five deaths and one serious illness, McNeil immediately and voluntarily withdrew the lot that had contained the two bottles from the market — removing 93,000 units in total. That same day, 500 sales agents were sent to remove the product from store shelves. By mid-afternoon, the company had sent half a million messages to physicians, hospitals and distributors notifying them of the deaths and indicating the lot number.

Tougher times were ahead. Another death occurred in April that was linked

©istockphoto.com/skhoward

to poisoned Tylenol. The company removed all 22 million bottles of Tylenol capsules from the market, valued at $79 million. To offset the loss in consumer goodwill, the marketing focus shifted to selling Tylenol tablets and voluntarily exchanging these for bottles of capsules. Nevertheless, by October 25, 1982, sales of all Tylenol products had slipped more than 25 percent. A letter was sent to approximately 61,000 doctors nationwide in which McNeil's Dr. Thomas N. Gates outlined the steps taken in response to the product tampering. In addition, two million pieces of literature were sent to doctors, dentists, nurses and pharmacists emphasizing that the company was not the source of the poison. A special promotion offered coupons for Tylenol, and customers who had thrown away their bottles following the scare could have them replaced for free by calling an 800 number. Investor confidence improved, and Johnson & Johnson stock, which had fallen 17 percent after the first deaths were reported, bounced back. Johnson & Johnson had all stores restocked with tamper-proof capsules by New Year's Day.

It's unlikely that the Tylenol brand could have withstood this if not for Johnson & Johnson's early decision to stand by its credo. The credo concludes: "We are responsible to the communities in which we live and work and to the world community as well. ... We must experiment with new ideas. Research must be carried on, innovative programs developed, and mistakes paid for."

BUSINESS DEFINITION (MISSION)

Business Definition

Describes the contributions the business makes to customers and society; also called the company mission.

Marketing Myopia

A focus on company products rather than on how the products benefit consumers.

The **business definition**, also referred to as the company mission, describes the fundamental contributions the organization provides to customers. The mission of clothing company Patagonia is "to build the best product, cause no unnecessary harm, and use business to inspire and implement solutions to the environmental crisis."[7] Patagonia continually demonstrates environmental consciousness, including the use of eco-friendly dyes and materials, energy-efficient computer configurations, and power conservation in product development and manufacturing. In a different industry, Sparrow Health System's mission, "to improve the health of the people in our communities by providing quality, compassionate care to everyone, every time," has remained consistent for more than 110 years.

Noted scholar Ted Levitt has had a tremendous influence on how companies develop their business definition. In a classic Harvard Business Review article, "Marketing Myopia," he explains why customer orientation is absolutely critical to a company's business definition. **Marketing myopia** occurs when executives focus on their company's current products and services rather than on benefits to consumers. Levitt uses U.S. railroads as an example. They didn't stop growing when the need for passenger and freight transportation declined but continued to expand. They got into trouble because they saw themselves as being in the railroad business supplying a product rather than in the transportation business offering a service. Trucking and airline companies took customers away from railroads because they better met their needs. In addition, the railroads' failure to focus on customers meant they also failed to make themselves more competitive. If the railroads had defined their business as transportation, they would have likely retained a strong influence in the market even with the introduction of alternative methods. Levitt adds that "the entire corporation must be viewed as a customer-creating and customer-satisfying organization. Management must think of itself not as producing products but as providing customer-creating value satisfactions."

eBay's community philosophy has provided customer-creating value satisfaction across the world to the 100 million members who buy and sell on its marketplace. Its online culture uses five principal values to create a foundation for its users.

Customer-creating values for the eBay community:

- We believe people are basically good.

- We believe everyone has something to contribute.

- We believe an honest, open environment can bring out the best in people.

- We recognize and respect everyone as a unique individual.

- We encourage you to treat others the way you want to be treated.[8]

The organization's business definition should be stated in basic, benefit-rich terms and should focus on consumer benefits, not product features. It should always answer this question: "What business are we really in?" For example, Johnson & Johnson sees itself in the business of bettering lives. It innovates with this in mind and participates in multiple environmental partnerships, such as the World Research Institute, a research organization dedicated to finding ways to protect the earth.

The organization's business definition should be stated in basic, benefit-rich terms and should focus on consumer benefits, not product features.

STRATEGIC DIRECTION (INTENT)

Strategic direction is the desired leadership position of an organization and the measures used to chart progress toward this position. Strategic intent is another term for strategic direction: "Strategic intent captures the essence of winning."[9] Strategic direction addresses the competitiveness of the organization and often sets specific growth, profit, share or scope goals relative to the competition and market opportunities.

Strategic direction may identify competitors by name or by type. Facebook's strategic direction is aimed at overtaking Microsoft in advertising revenue. Volkswagen's "Strategy 2018" is geared to be the most successful automaker in the world.[10] Strategic direction may guide organizations toward becoming one of the largest in an industry. General Electric wants to be either a leader or close follower in each venture it pursues. Google, Mozilla and Microsoft's strategic directions each involve a battle for dominance of the web. Microsoft's Internet Explorer web browser dropped the top spot in market share after a steady decline to Mozilla Firefox and Google Chrome.[11] In 2008 Internet Explorer controlled nearly 70 percent of the market. Today, it continues to lose users and only holds approximately 21 percent of the market. Firefox holds about 19 percent of the market and Chrome has captured about 45 percent.[12]

The Volkswagen XL1, with 261 mpg, is the most fuel-efficient car in the world.

> **Strategic Direction**
>
> The desired leadership position of an organization as well as the measures used to chart progress toward reaching that position.

STRATEGIC INFRASTRUCTURE

Executives must develop and organize the company's **strategic infrastructure**, the corporate configuration that produces the company's distinctive or core competencies and provides the resources necessary to satisfy customer wants. This often means dividing the business into functional units and determining which core competencies to develop. The idea is to focus energy on specific goods, services and talents necessary to create customer value in specific market segments.

Strategic Business Units (SBUs)
Most medium-sized and large companies have several strategic departments or units. A **strategic business unit (SBU)** is a part of the firm that can be managed separately for marketing purposes; it may be a division within the company, a separate product or product line, a distinct group of customers, or a unique technology. Johnson & Johnson has three SBUs: consumer and medical devices, pharmaceutical, and diagnostic. The consumer and medical SBU concentrates its efforts on marketing consumer products such as Band-Aids, No More Tears shampoo, and Tylenol. The pharmaceutical SBU mainly markets prescription drugs to the health-care industry. The diagnostic SBU produces sutures, surgical equipment, and medical supplies for physicians, dentists and others. Coca-Cola has many SBUs, including Coffees, Energy Drinks, Juices and Juice Drinks, Soft Drinks, Sports Drinks, Teas and Waters.[13]

Consider the corporation illustrated in Figure 2.4. It has two divisions: ground transportation and air transportation. The ground transportation division can be divided into SBUs according to products (motorcycles, trucks and cars), types of markets (business, consumer and military) and technology (electric and gas). The air transportation division can be divided similarly (products are passenger planes, fighter planes and training planes; markets are military, airlines and consumers; and

> **Strategic Infrastructure**
>
> The corporate configuration that produces the company's distinctive or core competencies and provides the resources necessary to satisfy customer wants.
>
> **Strategic Business Unit (SBU)**
>
> A part of the firm that can be managed separately for marketing purposes; it may be a division, a product or product line, a distinct group of customers, or a unique technology.

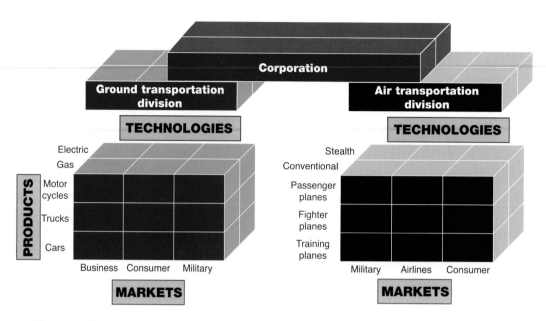

Figure 2.4   Strategic Business Units

technologies are conventional and stealth).

The total SBUs possible for this company is 36, but not all combinations would make sense (such as an SBU that produces stealth passenger planes for civilian consumers). There are several ways to structure the SBUs in this company. Grouped by technology, there would be four (electric, gas, conventional and stealth); based on products, there would be six (motorcycles, trucks, cars, passenger planes, fighter planes and training planes); and according to type of market, there would be four (airlines, other businesses, consumers and the military). Many companies, lacking a customer focus, form SBUs by product line. In market-oriented companies, SBUs often address specific segments. That's why UPS Logistics Group is organized by the industries it serves: automotive, healthcare, industrial manufacturing, retailing, and so forth.[14]

Typically, an SBU is managed by a team from several different functional areas, such as marketing, accounting and engineering. The corporate executives are responsible for managing the collection of SBUs — often called a portfolio — that makes up the organization. The general health of the company depends on how well the SBU portfolio performs. **Portfolio-planning tools** measure the contribution each SBU makes to the overall performance of the company. We will discuss two tools that are widely used: the growth-share matrix developed by the Boston Consulting Group (BCG) and the attractiveness-strength matrix developed by General Electric.

Portfolio-Planning Tools

Tools that measure the contribution that each SBU makes to the overall performance of the company.

Assessing SBUs: The Growth-Share Matrix

Marketers need to understand market opportunities and the strength of their organization's resources relative to competitors. The growth-share matrix, shown in Figure 2.5, uses market growth as a measure of opportunity and the company's market share as the measure of resource strength. SBUs are placed in a matrix according to their scores on these two dimensions. Different actions are recommended, depending on the category in which the SBU falls.

In the low-share/high-growth category are SBUs called Problem Children or question marks. Although they are in a market that is growing quickly, most have not yet achieved competitive advantage or begun generating substantial revenues. An airborne transportation

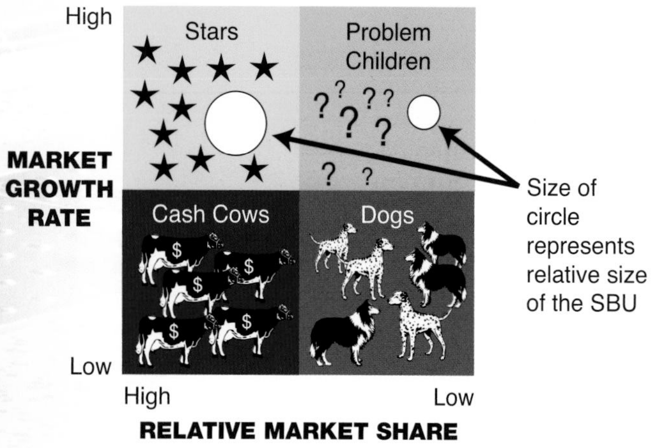

Figure 2.5 Boston Consulting Group Growth-share Matrix

vehicle, dubbed "SkyCat," was introduced by Britain's Advanced Technologies Group. Combining the better qualities of airplanes and hovercraft, the SkyCat can land or fly virtually anywhere. Though SkyCat might have potential to revolutionize global air transport, it has not received wide adoption. Because many believe the SkyCat is risky, marketers have to take careful consideration before choosing how much time and resources should be invested in it. If time is not pressing, gathering more information about the market is an advisable option.

Stars (high-share/high-growth SBUs) are a lot like movie personalities—give them lots of attention and expect a lot of success. Because they're growing, stars require a high investment, but it can result in a high return. Products such as the Microsoft Xbox One and the Apple iPad are examples.

Cash cows (high-share/low-growth SBUs) require a relatively small investment but should yield fairly substantial returns. Although the market is growing at a very low rate, the SBU has enough share to generate substantial cash flow. Companies want at least one product in this category and often have more, since revenues from these products can support the development of others. Two huge cash cows are Microsoft Office and Procter & Gamble's Ivory soap.

Procter & Gamble's Ivory soap is a classic example of a cash cow.

Attribution: Adam Cuerden

Dogs (low-share/low-growth SBUs) typically provide less than desirable returns. They're often considered competitively disadvantaged and unlikely to generate profits. They may actually consume resources, becoming cash drains that create negative value for the company. An example is Playboy magazine. It loses significant money, but it is still valuable as the cornerstone of Playboy Enterprises. The astoundingly profitable Playmate videos (an SBU star) and other Playboy businesses are possible largely because of the magazine.

Assessing SBUs: The Attractiveness-Strength Matrix

The growth-share matrix is useful, but it fails to address competitive behavior or the dynamic characteristics of the market. To obtain a larger picture, most marketing strategists use the attractiveness-strength matrix. As illustrated in Figure 2.6, the marketer first examines such factors as market size, market growth, competitive pressure, price levels and government regulation to develop a composite industry attractiveness score. Next, the marketer assesses the business

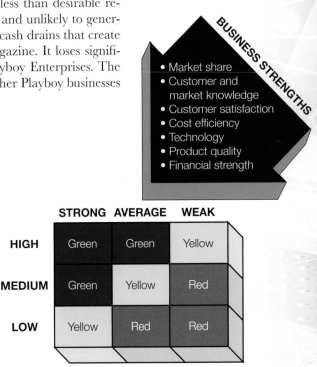

Figure 2.6   The General Electric Attractiveness-Strength Matrix

strengths of each SBU based on estimates of the company's market share, customer and market knowledge, customer satisfaction with the company, cost efficiency, level of technology, product quality, and financial strength. Each SBU is then graphed in the matrix based on these several measures.

The attractiveness-strength matrix uses colors to signal whether executives should stop (red), be cautious (yellow) or go ahead (green) with the SBU. Unfortunately, during the 1960s and '70s, "red" SBUs were sometimes categorically denied the resources required to compete, dooming them to failure. At the same time, "green" SBUs were allowed to charge ahead, regardless of the vision of the company. All that was important was the amount of investment required and the SBU's potential return.

Today, portfolio-planning tools are considered useful indicators, not predictors. Even SBUs that fall in the same category may require vastly different management strategies. Portfolio techniques are helpful in identifying the current business situation, but they are inappropriate for making resource allocations. These, as we shall see later, should be made only after the strategic marketing plan has been developed. Because portfolio techniques say little about strategy, they should be used only as a first step in strategic marketing.

Core Competencies

As shown previously in Figure 2.2, core competency is the other important aspect of strategic infrastructures. **Core competencies** are the unique resources a company employs as its specialty to create superior customer value. They are the fundamental building blocks of competitive advantage.

McDonald's core competencies in food distribution and preparation give it the ability to reproduce precisely the same taste, texture and service millions of times a day, anywhere in the world. Recently, McDonald's has added competencies in coffee-based drinks in order to compete with Starbucks. FedEx has developed a core competency in computerized information and tracking system technology so it can determine the location of any package worldwide within seconds.

Core competencies form the foundation of the success of any one SBU and also span several SBUs or corporate divisions. Marketing's role is to interpret market forces so that the proper core competencies can be developed to provide maximum benefit to consumers in the marketplace. When they succeed, companies are rewarded with the profit necessary to support continued improvement and growth.

An understanding of core competencies is necessary to comprehend how technology is shaping marketing practices. Through the rapid growth of technologies, companies build millions of products and services that produce superior customer value. The many types of core competencies can be grouped into five categories: (1) base technologies, (2) process technologies, (3) product technologies, (4) people systems and (5) information systems.

Base Technologies Base technologies refer to a broad innovation that a given organization is especially effective at harnessing, or even one it pioneered. The best base technologies are adaptable and can be applied to several different products. For example, one of Canon's core competencies, vision optics, can be used to deliver outstanding cameras, copiers and other inventive products. DuPont, known for basic chemistry, has developed multitudes of industrial and consumer products. General Dynamics is skilled in the wave technology necessary for radar and other types of vision systems. General Electric has spent billions of dollars developing its extensive knowledge of physics. Base technologies can be applied simultaneously to a number of diverse industries and product areas.

Process Technologies Process technologies allow the firm to produce quality

Core Competencies

The unique resources a company develops and employs to create superior customer value; the fundamental building blocks of competitive advantage.

products in the most effective and flexible manner possible. Marketing's job is to make sure that the development of processes is consistent with market trends and is in the customer's best interest. In an effort to decrease time customers spend waiting for their orders, fast food companies use a wireless device for inputting orders during peak hours. The device can significantly reduce the amount of time customers wait in drive-thru lines.[15] This improvement requires extensive changes in employee training, as well as the technologies used to process food.

ARAMARK is another food-service example. Over 40 years, ARAMARK has been selected 15 times to provide meals at the Olympic Games. ARAMARK served a record-breaking 3.5 million meals in 60 days using its superior process technologies during the Summer Olympics held in Beijing.[16]

ARAMARK's Work Apparel and Uniforms division designs thousands of new products each year for the custom clothing market. An order for a shirt with a company logo or Little League team name can be received over the phone and shipped within 24 hours. In fact, ARAMARK maintains a tracking system on its website for checking the status and location of a customer's order 24 hours a day.[17] Its production is tied so closely to the customer order process that no time is spent without contributing value to the customer.

Product Technologies A company's ability to create new goods and services is supported by product technologies. Many organizations have worked hard to develop competency in moving quickly from the idea stage through a series of well-defined steps to commercialization. Others follow the leader, copying competitors' products, sometimes improving upon them slightly. Followers benefit from the innovation of leaders without having to invest substantially in developing their own product technology.

The cellphone industry, for instance, has been dramatically affected by changes in technology. Motorola, formerly the market leader in the industry, lost significant share to competitors as rivals introduced smartphones with advanced technologies. Apple took an early lead in the market leaving competitors like Samsung and LG scrambling to gain market share. In the U.S., Apple continues to lead with 40.6 percent of total smartphone owners. Samsung, with arguably the best technologies available today, holds 26.7 percent of the market and Motorola has only been able to capture 6.4 percent.[18] While Samsung continues to gain on Apple, the race will largely be determined by product technologies.

Courtesy of Samsung

Samsung's Galaxy series smartphones continue to push product technologies in the cellphone industry.

People Systems The procedures that provide the human connection between companies and consumers are called people systems. Johnson and Johnson's website offers a specific section titled "our stories," which recounts customers' stories of how Johnson and Johnson products have made a difference in their lives. Johnson and Johnson employees also share stories of successes and failures they have faced in bringing new products, ideas and services to their customers.[19]

The Walt Disney Company has always placed high value on its team of employees. Walt once said: "The whole thing here is the organization. Whatever we accomplish belongs to our entire group, a tribute to our combined effort. I feel that there is no door with which the kind of talent we have cannot be opened." Today Disney has updated those sentiments: "The Disney name — and the image it con-

Coolcaesar / GFDL

veys — is one of our greatest assets, second only to the people who have contributed their talents and dreams toward the achievement of the goals we have set for ourselves."[20] The importance of Disney's employees is reflected in the organization's retail operation. To foster a spirit of teamwork, employees are called cast members; they refer to the customers as their guests. On the retail floor, they are onstage; in the storeroom, they are backstage. Such role-playing helps employees keep the desired goal in mind: Exceed guests' expectations.[21]

Information Systems An information system that is robust enough to give an organization a competitive advantage is a core competency. Historically, companies were located close to their customers, so organizations could feasibly research their markets firsthand. Even executives talked directly with customers. Today, the situation is very different because of the increasing diversity of products, customers, competitors and geographical distances. Information-processing technologies are especially important in global marketing because they provide vast amounts of data almost instantly. Companies that don't possess this core competency are at a dramatic competitive disadvantage.

UPS's information systems infrastructure is made up of the largest privately owned wireless network and database on earth. Its Supply Chain Solutions division uses information systems to oversee the entire supply chain of customers, anticipating delays, bottlenecks and other problems, and allowing issues to be quickly resolved. These systems also allow better, faster communication with third parties, speeding international shipping and the time necessary to clear customs.[22]

Basing a marketing strategy on core competency gives companies the long-term flexibility required for sustained leadership. SBUs should be treated as relatively temporary reservoirs of competencies that may be phased in, phased out or adjusted radically according to strategic marketing conditions. According to Prahalad and Hamel, noted educators, "The real sources of advantage are to be found in management's ability to consolidate corporate-wide technologies and production skills into competencies that empower the individual business to adapt quickly to changing opportunities."[23]

THE STRATEGIC MARKETING PLAN

In an organization, many people, not just the marketing department, have at least some responsibility toward developing and executing strategic marketing plans. As noted scholar and business consultant Frederick Webster Jr. says: "Everyone in the firm must be charged with responsibility for understanding customers and contributing to developing and delivering value to them."[24] Marketing is so pervasive in customer-focused, competition-driven companies that teams from diverse areas of the firm (such as accounting, engineering and manufacturing) often work together with marketers to implement it.

THE PLANNING TEAM

Cross-Functional Planning Team

Employees from several areas responsible for developing the company's strategic marketing plan.

In the past, the planning process included only marketing personnel. Today, strong marketers generally assemble a **cross-functional planning team**. This team works together with a total understanding of the market and the organization's ca-

TITLE	RESPONSIBILITY
Marketing	Development of strategic plan and team leader
Engineering	Technological product development
Manufacturing	Efficient manufacturing
Finance	Financial modeling of strategies
Marketing Intelligence	Estimate competitor strengths, vulnerabilities
Marketing Research	Customer and consumer requirements
Sales	Potential sales strategies
Promotion and Advertising	Support program development
Procurement	Available supply partners and costs
Human Resources	Union and employee relations
Logistics	Distribution systems approaches
Accounting	Analysis of cost data

Figure 2.7   A Cross-Functional Strategic Planning Team

pabilities.[25] Just as relationships with stakeholders outside the company are important, so are internal relationships. Since each member of the planning team has a unique perspective, these people must bring all parts of the picture together. Figure 2.7 gives each person's functional area and a short description of his or her main responsibility.

WHAT IS STRATEGY?

Before we talk about strategic marketing plans, we need to discuss one of the most overused and misused terms in business. The military defines strategy as "the art of meeting the enemy in battle under advantageous conditions." Although there are several "correct" definitions of strategy, we will use the following: A **strategy** is the development and/or deployment of resources with the intent of accomplishing goals and objectives in competitive arenas. Executives, for instance, must determine how best to use companies with limited resources to accomplish organizational goals. Note that "competitive arena" implies the presence of competitors. They all have their own goals to achieve, and some of them overlap and affect each others' ability to succeed. Japanese companies tend to be acutely aware of competitors. Consider Honda's public statement, "Yamaha No Tsubusu" "We will crush, squash and slaughter Yamaha." But beating competitors with the intent of hurting them is not really what strategy is all about. The idea is to win outright by serving customers better through relationships and technology, with attention to diversity, global dimensions, sustainability and ethics.

> Strategy is not just about meeting competitors face to face. It also involves seizing the moment to create change in a timely manner. Observe any group of planners and you're sure to hear someone refer to the **strategic window**. Derek Abell, noted business strategist, coined the term to describe the moment when requirements of the market and competencies of the firm fit together to create a significant opportunity.[26] Now, more than ever, the strategic window is important. Products and technologies change so rapidly that organizations must be prepared to respond quickly when opportunities arise to gain sales and market share. Companies slow to respond often find their product(s) sitting in inventory after spending millions of dollars on product development.

> For example, after Apple introduced its iPad tablet, a host of competitors quickly followed: the HP Touchpad, the Dell Streak, the 16GB BlackBerry Play-

Strategy

The development and/or deployment of resources with the intent of accomplishing goals and objectives in a competitive arena.

Strategic Window

The time during which market needs and the competencies of the firm fit together to create a significant opportunity.

Book, all of which have since been shelved.[27] Savvy marketers know that the strategic window is open for a relatively short period as consumers consider new technology. During this short time, organizations can and should create sustainable strategies.

Low-Cost Strategy

Low-Cost Strategy

Strategy whose objective is to be the low-cost leader, thereby allowing the company to have higher margins than competitors and pass some savings on to customers through lower prices; works through efficiency.

A **low-cost strategy** focuses on winning through efficiency. The objective is to be the low-cost leader, which allows the company to have higher margins than competitors and to pass some savings on to customers through lower prices. There are many ways to gain a favorable cost position:

- *Process technology.* Invent a low-cost way to create and deliver a product.

- *Product design.* Create a product that provides the same level of functionality with lower cost than predecessors or competitors, often through new materials or miniaturization.

- *Consolidation of the value chain.* Combine several steps in the value chain into one.

- *Low-cost suppliers.* Reduce costs by purchasing materials and other inputs at lower prices.

- *Location.* Put facilities in low-wage areas or nearby markets to lower distribution costs.

- *Economies of scale and scope.* Produce more and market in a larger area so costs are spread over more units and customers.[28]

Differentiation Strategy

Differentiation Strategy

Strategy based on delivering customer value in a way that clearly distinguishes the product from competitors; works through effectiveness.

A **differentiation strategy** involves delivering customer value in a way that clearly distinguishes the product from its competitors. Differentiation works through effectiveness by giving superior benefits or reducing customer cost rather than price. There are several ways to achieve differentiation.

- *New functional capabilities.* Create products that do new things.

- *Improved performance.* Make products that work better

- *Product tailoring.* Make products that more closely suit the needs of select groups.

- *Lower Costs.* Make products that are more energy efficient, require less maintenance, or are less expensive to operate.

Customer Intimacy Strategy

Customer Intimacy Strategy

Strategy based on delivering value through superior empathy for customers and solutions tailored to specific customer needs.

A **customer intimacy strategy** is based on delivering value through superior empathy for customers and solutions tailored to specific customer needs. Intimacy requires developing close relationships with the customer. There are several ways to achieve this:

- Take on additional responsibilities, including those normally assumed by customers. Automatically update and support products at the customer's site.

- Mass customization. Use a process that creates products precisely to the specifications of individual customers.

- Information. Collect and maintain databases regarding customers' product usage.

- Product bundling. Develop product configurations specifically suited for individual customers.

Sustainable Competitive Advantage

Sustainable Competitive Advantage

The strategy that competitors cannot easily duplicate or surpass.

Sustainable competitive advan-

tage refers to a strategy that competitors cannot easily duplicate or surpass. These various strategies are meant to create sustainable competitive advantages for the company. Once such a strategy is attained, competitors generally try to copy it or develop their own advantages. Organizations that create sustainable advantages have less volatility and better long-run performance.

COMPONENTS OF THE STRATEGIC MARKETING PLAN

Guided by the corporate vision, the strategic marketing plan essentially describes how to accomplish that vision. Keep in mind that many organizations are complex and may have more than one strategic marketing plan. General Electric has a strategic marketing plan for the company itself and additional ones for selected parts of the organization, such as aircraft engines and lighting. It even developed a separate plan for its participation in the 2014 Olympic Games in Sochi.

The planning team has to address several areas: objectives, situation analysis, target markets, positioning, and integration of the marketing mix. The first step is to state the objectives the business will pursue and the specific goals it expects to obtain. The second step is a situation analysis, which describes the current business environment and how well the company will be able to compete in it. The third step is to determine target markets to identify which customers the organization will serve. The fourth step is to decide positioning relative to competitors — the image the organization wants customers to have about it and its products. The fifth step is to develop plans for each aspect of the marketing mix and integrate these into the overall strategic plan.

We will discuss each step in detail following this logical order, but as actual plans are developed, the various steps usually interact with one another. For example, objectives are stated first but may later be changed to reflect information uncovered during the situation analysis. Finally, like a baseball pitch, a good strategic marketing plan needs follow-through or control measures that provide feedback on how well the plan is working.

OBJECTIVES

The strategic marketing plan must support the business definition laid out in the organization's vision. Since the objectives are an outgrowth of the vision, they tend to be stated up-front. But they must take into account all of the remaining parts of the plan as well, so objectives might be recast as strategies emerge during subsequent steps in the planning process. Companies usually set objectives in terms of desired profit, market share or total sales. Profit is the most common choice and may be stated in various ways, such as return on investment, cash flow (amount of cash returned to the business), or profit margins. Market share refers to a proportion relative to competitors that the company captures: the percentage of customers within a given market, the percentage of dollars spent on similar products, or the percentage of all similar product units that are sold (unit sales). Finally, businesses determine a total sales objective,

A good strategic marketing plan needs follow-through like a baseball pitch.

defined as either a dollar amount or a quantity of products sold. Most organizations state objectives in these ways, but many may add others: number of loyal customers, customer-retention rates, and customer-satisfaction scores.

Often, it's appropriate to state very specific objectives such as "Forty-four percent market share by 2020." Notice that objectives always provide a time frame and must be verifiable (meaning it will be clear whether or not the objective has been met). You will see why this is important when we talk later about the marketing control process.

SITUATION ANALYSIS

All marketing activities required to understand the marketing environment, customer needs and wants, and the competition are examined in the situation analysis. This analysis predicts market conditions for the period that the strategic marketing plan is in effect. If the plan extends through 2020, for example, then predictions should be made up to that time. Developing possible scenarios generally requires bringing

CREATING & CAPTURING VALUE THROUGH *Technology*

Skittles Creates Buzz on Twitter

Since hitting the scene in 2006, Twitter has become a technological force that is changing the way individuals connect with others, discover breaking news and communicate ideas. Businesses are realizing the power of Twitter — which has more than 255 million monthly active users— and searching for effective ways reach their target customers.

The popular candy brand Skittles launched one of the first major marketing campaigns centered on social media. Instead of taking the traditional route, where the company creates the message and delivers it via TV and radio ads, Skittles boldly let customers have a say.

The company transformed its homepage into a streaming feed of its Twitter, Facebook, Flickr and YouTube content, where any customer could upload a message, picture or video. This means that every Tweet or Facebook post containing the word "Skittles" appeared on the Skittles' homepage. When the campaign launched, Twitter and Facebook were buzzing about Skittles. Fans of the fruity candy were thrilled to participate, and soon Skittles became a trending topic on Twitter.

Social media marketing is a new avenue for companies using innovative ways to reach customers, and it is not without hurdles — as Skittles learned. A number of Internet pranksters took advantage of the live feed by writing inappropriate messages, and the company had to quickly react to the negative publicity. Yet even with the mishap, critics agreed the campaign was a success in reaching new markets, trying an innovative approach and increasing profits.

The constant evolution of technology affects all businesses. The companies that maximize the potential of technology will capture a valuable market, increase customer loyalty and see huge financial gains in the coming decade.

https://about.twitter.com/company

together data and expertise from different parts of the company to provide an accurate picture.

The situation analysis can be very elaborate or fairly simple, depending on the circumstances. At a minimum, it should give the planning team a general idea about the future, including potential size of the market, types of customers, competitors, technology, channels of distribution, economic conditions, governmental regulations, and the resources the company will have at its disposal, both globally and in individual countries.

As a final step in the situation analysis, the planning team must determine how well the company's skills and resources match the predicted market opportunities. This is typically called a **SWOT analysis**, which is an acronym for strengths, weaknesses, opportunities and threats. An example is shown in Figure 2.8.

Strengths and weaknesses are defined by such measures as market share, number of loyal customers, level of customer satisfaction and rate of success with new products. Strengths describe the unique resources or circumstances that can be used to take advantage of opportunities. Weaknesses suggest aspects of the organization or product that need improvement or, if that is not possible, ways to minimize any negative effects. Opportunities indicate advancements that can be made in new or existing markets. They identify areas in which the organization can gain competitive advantages. The threats section describes how the competition, new technology, the business environment or government may possibly impede the company's development.

Companies are constrained by their weaknesses and are vulnerable to threats. When the government eliminated the use of certain environmentally hazardous resins in

SWOT Analysis

An analysis of strengths, weaknesses, opportunities, and threats to determine how well the company's skills and resources match the predicted market opportunities.

Strengths

Assess good use of competencies and results in the market:
 Share increase
 High loyalty and satisfaction ratings
 Excellent sales force
 Unique products, services

Opportunities

Assess areas where advantage may be gained:
 Add a new product
 Promote to new segment
 Sell more to existing customers
 Use a new form of distribution to reach new markets

Weaknesses (Constraints)

Assess poor use of competencies and results in the market:
 Share decrease
 Disloyal customers
 Not enough salespeople
 Product launch delays

Threats (Vulnerability)

Assess external forces that may prevent the company from accomplishing its objectives:
 Competitor with a new technology
 New government regulations
 Changing customer preferences

Figure 2.8   An Example of SWOT Analysis

the manufacture of recreational boats, irate customers complained that colors faded in the sun. White didn't fade, but the lack of color reduced much of the excitement of new models and designs, convincing many customers to stop purchasing designer-style boats for that reason. Today, technological breakthroughs in environmentally friendly but stable colors have eliminated this threat.

TARGET MARKETING

Once the situation analysis is complete, the planning team determines the characteristics of viable customer groups. Businesses cannot be "all things to all people;" given their competencies, they must choose which segments have the greatest potential.

Target marketing is the process of selecting which market segments the firm will emphasize in attempts to satisfy customers better than its competitors. Many consumer businesses target the Generation Y customers (born in the 1980s and 1990s). As marketers are well aware, Gen Y is 72 million strong and spends about $200 billion a year. Gen Y-ers are also considerably more tech- and design-savvy than their predecessors. "With this generation, everything has to be visual and contextual. … They will form impressions about a product based on how it looks and what it does, not what advertisers say about it," says Kit Yarrow, Professor of

Target Marketing

The process of selecting which market segments the organization will emphasize in attempts to satisfy customers better than its competitors.

Psychology and Marketing at Golden Gate University and author of the book *Gen BuY.*[29]

This market is also getting a lot of attention from companies such as Toyota, Honda, Ford, Volkswagen and Saturn. Ford was one of the first automobile companies in the U.S. to target Gen Y, using the Ford Focus. Ford specifically aimed at winning Generation Y customers by providing a vehicle with a Sync sound system, affordable pricing, and fashionable design. Other companies followed suit with powerful factory stereo systems, faster designs, and sporty interiors. Ford has also been actively pursuing Generation Y as the core market for its subcompact Fiesta. Market research indicates this demographic consists of around 70 million licensed drivers — the largest segment of any generation, according to Ford, constituting 28 percent of the car-buying public, many of whom have no specific brand loyalty yet. Ford is using the web as a main source to reach out to Generation Y through sites such as Facebook, Flickr, Twitter and YouTube.[30]

POSITIONING

Positioning

Creating an image or perception in the minds of consumers about the organization or its products relative to the competition.

Planning teams often decide to pursue different positioning strategies with different target market segments. **Positioning**, as you recall, refers to creating a perception in the minds of consumers about the company and/or its products relative to competitors. A more common word for positioning is image, often evoked by the brand name. For example, Tiffany & Co. wants to convey an image of high quality and status. If consumers see the company that way, then the marketing team has been successful in its positioning efforts.

Value Proposition

The compelling reason customers should select your brand.

Positioning is closely related to the **value proposition**, which is the compelling reason customers should select your brand. For example, the value proposition for Advanced Micro Devices Inc. (AMD) is simple: AMD offers superior products at competitive costs and industry-standard products at lower costs.

"Everyone is after everyone's business. The mind of your customer or prospect is the battleground and that's where you win or lose," says Jack Trout, author of numerous marketing books and president of Trout & Partners, Ltd. According to him, "just as each product needs to be positioned in the mind (of consumers) against competitors, so does a company need to be positioned. Customers want to know where you're going. So do your employees."

INTEGRATED MARKETING MIX PLANS

Once the desired positioning is established, the marketing mix — product, place, promotion, and price — must be integrated to make the strategy happen. An effective strategy incorporates all elements of the mix in order to produce a unified effect.

Numerous companies have managed to integrate all elements of the marketing mix to form successful strategies. As previously mentioned, Disney offers multiple products — amusement parks, MGM Studios, Epcot Center, Blizzard Beach, Discovery Island and others. Each provides a high-quality experience, whether for vacations, weddings or business meetings. Disney is constantly adding new products in order to remain relevant to current consumer lifestyles. Disney carefully chooses theme park locations that are easily accessible to consumers. It also makes information about its products readily available through websites and thousands of travel agents around the world. The variety of pricing options — deluxe, moderate, or economy — makes it easy for customers from all walks of life to purchase. And Disney takes care to promote its products to a variety of customers. Some are aimed directly at children, others at young singles, and still others at married couples whose children have left home. This communicates to consumers that Disney parks are for everyone. Their integrated strategy is clearly paying off: Disney's annual sales are more than $45 billion and rising.[31]

A company needs a plan for each part of the marketing mix: product, place, promotion and price. The plan for each element often is developed within specific functional areas of marketing, such as the product development department. In some cases, all of these plans are combined into one. Each mix element will be covered in depth in future chapters, but a brief discussion of the issues is provided here. Figure 2.9 illustrates some of the questions marketers consider when developing plans for each aspect of the marketing mix. This list is far from comprehensive; other issues will be covered in later chapters.

Each plan for an element of the marketing mix deals with both strategies and tactics. For example, the decision to enter a new product area or distribution channel is strategic. Changes to an existing product or the addition of a new retailer in distribution are tactical. Tactics are used to achieve strategies. Strategies are long-term and broad in scope; **tactics** are short-term, well-defined actions suited to specific market conditions. Strategies describe how a company will compete to serve customers, whereas tactics specifically describe who will do what and when.

Companies usually employ several tactics to accomplish a given strategy. McDonald's strategy is to provide high-quality, moderately priced food and friendly, fast service to families. One tactic is to have a mini-playground at some of its restaurants. Another is colorful packaging of children's meals and personal appearances by Ronald McDonald. McDonald's strategy involves the use of major cartoon stars, such as The Penguins of Madagascar, and well-known toy brands like the Littlest Pet Shop.[32] Subway, which targets a more adult audience, pursues a strategy of preparing customized

Tactics

Short-term actions and reactions to specific market conditions through which companies pursue their strategy.

Marketing Mix Element	Types of Decisions
Product/Service	What new products/services should we introduce? Which ones should we drop? What are our objectives with each product or service? Are any new technologies available to improve our product/service?
Place	Where do our customers shop? Should our product/service be available at all these places or just a few? Should we sell directly to our customers or through middlemen, such as retailers, wholesalers, or dealers? How should we ship the product—by rail, truck, air, ship, or others?
Promotion	What are our promotion objectives? Are we trying to create awareness, encourage purchases, or others? What medium should we use: television or radio advertising, coupons, free trials, personal selling, public relations campaign, or a combination of these?
Price	What type of message do we want to send out? What is our overall pricing philosophy? Do we want to exceed, meet, or underprice our competitors? Is our price consistent with the amount of value we deliver to our customers?

Figure 2.9 The Marketing Control Process: Assessing the Strategic Marketing Plan

sandwiches quickly. Its assembly-line tactic allows patrons to build their own sandwiches. Another aspect of the Subway strategy focuses on providing healthy alternatives to other fast-food restaurants. Its efforts paid off when the five-dollar foot-long deal became a huge hit, leading to an explosion of business for Subway.[33] The business's specific tactic to preassemble the meat element of the sandwich, leaving only the toppings to be added, speeds the process up while maintaining patron selection. Both of these franchises employ strategies that make use of their core competencies. It would be tactically inconsistent for McDonald's to add gourmet items to its menu or for Subway to offer complicated full-course meals.

Product Plans A company may sell physical goods (such as automobiles or textbooks) or intangible services (a college education, legal counsel or health care). Many companies sell both. In the business world, "product" has come to mean services as well as physical goods. Unless specified otherwise, we shall use product to mean either goods or services. Product decisions are critical for most companies, and they are among the most difficult to make. Marketers must help determine which products or product lines to develop and which ones to drop. Because products go through a life cycle, product strategy decisions are ongoing. Most organizations use systematic processes to develop and manage products over their life cycles, including decisions regarding product attributes, warranties, package design, and customer service features.

A **product line** consists of several closely related products marketed by an organization. For example, Nabisco offers many different types of snack foods, including Oreos, Fig Newtons, Chips Ahoy!, and Ritz crackers; each of these is a separate product line. Items are constantly being added, such as seasonal Oreos with different colored fillings.

Marketers must take consumers into account when making product decisions. Each year, Coach, the maker of handbags and fine accessories, interviews more than 60,000 customers through Internet questionnaires, phone surveys and face-to-face encounters. The information has helped executives spot trends and extend the Coach brand beyond the traditional leather bags. After hearing customers complain that they couldn't find decent carry-on luggage for weekend getaways, Coach launched its successful Signature Stripe travel bags.[34]

Product plans challenge marketers to continuously monitor, assess and make decisions based on the ever-changing environment. Technological products go through a rapid life cycle, requiring marketers to make frequent and sometimes difficult product decisions. In the console game industry, leaders have changed often, from Atari and Coleco to Sega and Nintendo to Sony and Microsoft. In addition to increasing graphics and sound technology, companies have brought further innovations to gaming. The Nintendo Wii introduced motion controls, bringing new interest and technology to the industry. Microsoft launched Kinect 1.0, a motion sensor that was touted to change the gaming industry forever. However, Nintendo quickly refocused to duel screen controllers and Sony decided virtual reality would be the next "game-changer." Sony could be right; Facebook recently acquired the virtual reality technology Oculus and Samsung is rumored to beat both Sony and Oculus to the virtual reality market. Microsoft's recent announcement to deliver the new Xbox One without Kinect 2.0 could indicate that traditional motion sensing will become obsolete. This rapid shift in technologies will likely keep the console game industry, and its marketers, working to position their companies for the next major change.[35]

Product Line

Closely related products marketed by the organization.

CAREER TIP!

Ranked as the No. 1 Best Company to Work For in 2014 by Fortune magazine, Google provides its employees innovative benefits, flexibility and the opportunity to pursue ideas that challenge the status quo. Google recognizes that every employee has something important to say and is integral to the company's success. Nooglers (new Googlers) are welcomed into an invigorating, positive environment, committed to creating search perfection while having a great time doing it. Internships and full-time positions are available ranging from science to business, from Mountain View, California, to Cairo, Egypt. To explore the life of a Noogler, visit www.google.com/jobs.

Distribution Channels

A set of independent organizations involved in making the product available for purchase.

Place Plans   **Distribution channels** are the set of independent organizations involved in making the product available for purchase. A channel describes the route a product follows as it moves from manufacturer to consumers. First, marketers must determine where target customers shop: malls, shopping centers, downtown areas, discount outlets, drive-throughs or at home via mail or telephone. People also shop in many different types of stores: supermarkets, merchandise marts, hyperstores, specialty shops and outdoor markets. In each area of the world, consumer shopping patterns are unique. Parisians buy bread baked daily at small shops located throughout the city. The Japanese prefer to purchase fresh fish, caught within hours of eating, from small neighborhood retailers. Suburban Americans often shop once a week and freeze many items for use days or even weeks later. They like one-stop supermarkets within driving distance. Obviously, it's important for marketers to know where consumers prefer to shop for the types of products or services that their company makes.

Physical distribution (or logistics) involves getting the right product, in the right condition, to the right customer, at the right time, for the minimum cost. This is one of the fastest-growing and most important areas of business. Annual spending on supply-chain logistics services has reached $3 trillion globally. Apple alone spent $10.5 billion on additional supply-chain robots and machinery in 2013.[36]

Physical distribution decisions can greatly affect the profitability of the company. For example, excess inventory in the channel increases storage costs. The marketing team is responsible for ensuring inventory keeps flowing through the channel. Recent data from financial information company Sageworks Inc. shows that later customer payments and slow-moving inventory are tying up private companies' cash for 16 percent longer than just three years ago. "Their cash is tied up in inventory as well as receivables, and that has a significant effect on cash flow and consequently, a significant effect on how much they can use for capital expenditures or new jobs," said Michael W. McNeilly, Sageworks' Director of Advisory Services.[37]

Promotion Plans
The third element of the marketing mix, promotion, provides information about a company's product or service in an effort to encourage purchase. Marketers develop integrated marketing communications by coordinating advertising, sales promotion, personal selling, and public relations to get consistent messages to all types of customers. These messages provide information necessary for the decision process. Promotion also increases demand for products, describes unique product characteristics, and helps build customer loyalty by creating expectations and reinforcing buying decisions.

Even formerly narrow marketers have expanded their audience through promotions. Broadway shows were once only promoted in theater directories. Today, ads appear on water towers and subways. The musical "Book of Mormon," from the directors of South Park, is marketing itself to younger audiences. Its splashy website has links to ticket sales, social media sites for the show and even a store where fans can buy "The Book of Mormon," a coffee table book containing the comical story and lyrics.[38]

Pricing Plans
Prices send strong signals to buyers. When Reebok aerobic shoes were first introduced into the women's market segment, demand was disappointing. The product was priced incorrectly — in this case, too low. When Reebok raised its prices, demand increased. Consumers often equate low prices with poor quality, whereas higher prices signal high quality, and perhaps something unique or difficult to obtain. Porsche raised prices in the American market. Ralph Lauren found it worked with men's and women's clothing. The perfume industry has used this technique since its inception.

In other cases, price increases can be devastating to sales volume. Think about the airline industry, with many different providers offering service between the same cities. What do you think would happen to ticket sales at United Airlines if it raised its prices above those of Northwest? Unless United offered a unique benefit to its flights, demand would start dropping. That's why a

Physical Distribution

The movement of finished products through channels of distribution to customers.

price shift in one airline triggers shifts in most others.

THE MARKETING CONTROL PROCESS

Control Process

Procedures designed to provide feedback on how well the marketing strategy is working.

Control Review Meeting

Meeting of members of the planning team to see whether objectives are being met.

Once a strategic marketing plan is implemented, results seldom occur precisely as expected. The **control process** provides feedback on how well the strategy is working. In a typical **control review meeting**, members of the planning team assemble to determine whether they are reaching objectives. As described in Figure 2.10, the team reviews the original objectives, including sales volume projections, order quantities, customer loyalty and satisfaction rates, and market share projections. These

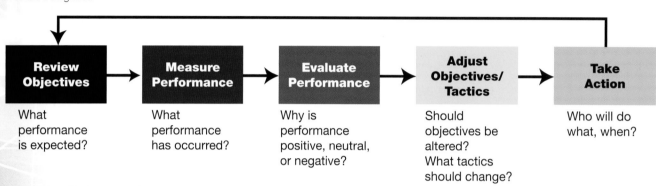

Figure 2.10   The Marketing Control Process: Assessing the Strategic Marketing Plan

projections are compared to the actual results for each target market segment and the total. This procedure is often called metrics, or metering (measuring) what actually happened.

By comparing actual results to the stated objectives, the team can assess the organization's performance. During these reviews, the planning team can spot trends. For example, sales and market share may be higher than expected because competitors were late in launching a new product, or sales may be low because the company's price was too high compared to competitors' prices. An unclear cause for results points to a need for more intensive marketing research.

Next, the team may decide to adjust objectives or plans. If results are strong, then objectives may be elevated. If not, objectives can be lowered, but the team usually resists this step, because it can be viewed as a sign of weakness.[39] Adjustments to the plans usually are tactical rather than strategic, done through changes in the marketing mix elements. A change in overall strategy requires a more involved and lengthy process. Sometimes teams go back to ground zero and start fresh. In either case, time is critical. One executive says that adjusting plans and taking action can be "like changing a flat tire on a moving automobile." It happens rapidly in companies that are flexible, efficient and competitive.

CONNECTING GLOBALLY: ENTERING WORLD MARKETS TO CAPTURE VALUE

Once the domain of a few corporate giants, global marketing is fast becoming a requirement for most companies. Why? First, world markets offer tremendous opportunities. Many foreign market segments are larger and growing more rapidly than segments in the United States. Second, for better or worse, U.S. business is no longer safe from global competitors. Most U.S. companies are in some form of competition with foreign ones, even in local markets. The United States' relatively few restrictions on foreign entry provide opportunities for that competition. Third, a company intent on becoming an industry leader must operate globally or be placed at a severe competitive disadvantage.

GEOGRAPHIC SCOPE

World trade has skyrocketed in recent years: U.S. exports exceed $2.2 trillion annually. The United States also imports a large amount of foreign goods and services — approximately $2.7 trillion each year.[40] From a planning standpoint, marketers must identify the **geographic scope** of the strategy, which is the extent of a company's international activities. Generally, geographic scope is divided into four categories, as outlined in Figure 2.11.

Geographic Scope

The extent of a company's international activities.

International Scope

When a company conducts business in one or a very few foreign countries, it has an international scope. Generally, international companies treat foreign business as a supplement to their domestic operations rather than as a strategic necessity. Yet expansion in even one country can provide useful experience for further global activity at a

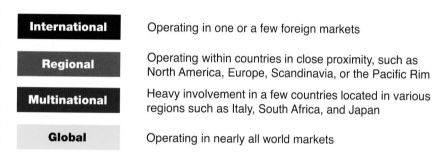

International	Operating in one or a few foreign markets
Regional	Operating within countries in close proximity, such as North America, Europe, Scandinavia, or the Pacific Rim
Multinational	Heavy involvement in a few countries located in various regions such as Italy, South Africa, and Japan
Global	Operating in nearly all world markets

Figure 2.11   Geographic Scope

later date. Topps, a trading card company in the U.S., recently launched a brand-new marketing campaign to market cricket sports collectables in India. While the U.S. trading card industry is suffering, the decision to build a trading card market in India could prove to be successful for the business.[41]

Regional Scope
A company with operations in several adjacent countries has regional scope. In essence, regional companies are competing within one large market that crosses national borders, generally only in one area of the world. Regional operations tend to be efficient because the markets are close together. The benefits of large market size, combined with localized production and distribution provide a viable strategy. This was the approach of Starbucks Corporation, the specialty coffee chain, as it expanded outside the United States. The company opened its first Pacific Rim outlet in Tokyo and from there expanded into other nations in the Asian-Pacific region, including Singapore, Hong Kong, Taiwan and Indonesia.

Multinational Scope
When companies operate in several countries around the world, unrestricted by region, their scope is multinational. For example, Westinghouse Process Control sells services to electric utilities in the United States and several selected countries in many regions of the world. However, Westinghouse has decided to avoid marketing to certain countries in several areas. Multinational companies carefully choose their target areas and use an appropriate method of operation (if any) for each area of the world.

Global Scope
Operations in nearly all countries around the world constitute a global scope. Kenichi Ohmae, previous global consultant for McKinsey & Company, describes global scope with the mental image of hovering like a satellite over the

earth.[42] Global businesses develop totally integrated strategies that maximize competitiveness worldwide over the long term. The Quaker Oats Company has committed to this type of integrated global strategy. Its Quaker International Branding Program is designed to ensure that the Quaker name means "healthy," no matter where you live. The company has a basic advertising, packaging and promotion plan that is tailored to meet local conditions. This helps keep the Quaker image consistent around the globe.

A global market reaches nearly all countries. Differences among market areas are recognized, but so are similarities, so that similar segments of buyers within the various regions can be targeted with a universal image.[43]

Global marketing is based on the notion that consumers around the world are growing more alike and that modern technology has created a degree of commonality. Travel and communication have exposed more and more people to the same types of goods and services. Global companies appreciate the differences in consumer preferences, shopping behavior, cultural institutions, and promotional media, but they believe that these preferences and practices can and will become more similar.[44]

STRATEGIES FOR FOREIGN MARKET ENTRY

There are several different approaches for entering and developing markets. Small companies may use only one or two methods, due to resource limitations or a focused target market, whereas larger companies may use several simultaneously. Figure 2.12 outlines the most important approaches.

Exporting and Importing

Exporting and importing are the least risky and most common forms of international marketing. Exporting sends domestically manufactured products into foreign countries for resale. Importing brings products from foreign countries for resale within the home market, usually as part of another product. Exporting and importing are relatively easy ways to enter foreign trade, because the investment is lower than most other methods. In addition, most governments offer support and expertise to help domestic companies with these activities.

Because foreign trade can involve many complicated details, most firms use **export and import intermediaries**, which are firms with specialized expertise in exporting or importing. Intermediaries come in two types, indirect and direct. **Indirect export intermediaries** are located in the domestic market and help send products abroad. They specialize in knowledge about foreign customs, regulations affecting businesses and products, laws, and market conditions. **Direct export intermediaries** are located in the foreign market. Since they are very familiar with the local business environment, they can help clients in special ways, such as offering unique government contacts. Intermediaries can be very beneficial because they assume many of the risks involved with distribution. At the same time, the exporting company must give up a significant amount of control over how its product is distributed.

Export and Import Intermediaries

Domestic or foreign firm that assists with exporting or importing activity.

Indirect Export Intermediaries

Firm located in a domestic market which specializes in knowledge about foreign customs, regulations affecting businesses and products, laws, and market conditions.

Export—Import	Send products abroad for resale (exporting) or purchase products from foreign companies for resale, usually as part of another product, within the home market (import)
Foreign Licensing and Franchising	Agreements that permit foreign companies to produce and distribute merchandise, often using trademarks and/or selected merchandising and customer delivery approaches
Overseas Marketing and Manufacturing	A marketing infrastructure and/or manufacturing facilities abroad
Joint Ventures and Strategic Alliances	The shared ownership of operations by two or more local and foreign companies (joint venture) or the pooling of resources by two or more companies for the purpose of competing as one entity (strategic alliance)

Figure 2.12   Approaches for Entering and Building Foreign Markets

Direct Export Intermediaries

Firm located in a foreign market which specializes in knowledge about foreign customs, regulations affecting businesses and products, laws, and market conditions.

Trading companies are large intermediaries that facilitate the movement of goods in and out of countries. For example, Koch is an international trading company that aids in the sale of goods to and from a variety of regions, such as crude oil, petroleum products, and other commodities. In order to provide customers a diverse array of products and commodities, Koch companies have access to major international trading regions in the United States, Europe, Asia, and the Middle East.[45]

Foreign Licensing and Franchising
Foreign licensing assigns the rights to a patent, trademark or manufacturing process to a foreign company for a fee, often called a royalty. Licensing allows companies to gain entry into a foreign market at almost no cost or risk, but control of the marketing strategy is turned over to the licensee. **Franchising** is a special type of licensing arrangement whereby the marketer provides not only the product, technology, process and/or trademark but also most of the marketing program. In nearly any major city around the world, you are likely to find McDonald's, Burger King and Taco Bell, or Holiday Inn, Hilton and Marriott. They are there because local entrepreneurs have bought the franchise. Franchising allows companies to maintain marketing control while passing along many of the costs, risks, and responsibilities to the foreign licensees. These often function quite autonomously from the parent company but benefit from being part of a large corporation.

Overseas Marketing and Production
Also called subsidiaries, overseas marketing and production operations, whether a small sales office or something more elaborate, are owned by a parent company in foreign countries. A subsidiary operation may simply assemble finished goods or may function as an independent business, responsible for product development, manufacturing, marketing and so on. For example, General Motors operates assembly plants for automotive components in Mexico, while its German and British subsidiaries produce entire automobiles. Subsidiaries can be very costly to establish and very risky to operate, since the owner is liable for any mishaps. Foreign operations also are subject to a host of circumstances beyond the company's control. For example, several oil companies lost billions of dollars when their Iranian subsidiaries were closed after the invasion of Kuwait. The major advantage of a subsidiary is that the parent company retains control and can carry out its own strategy while benefiting from a presence in foreign markets.

Foreign Strategic Alliances
Strategic alliances involve partnership. Sony, for instance, develops many of its innovative computer and communications products through strategic alliances and joint ventures with companies in the United States. A **joint venture** occurs when two companies combine resources for a new venture. They are formed to provide products and services more competitively than a single organization could do independently. Typically, a foreign joint venture has one company in each of two countries, but more partners or countries are possible. National laws often require any business to have a certain percentage of domestic ownership. When the Soviet bloc dissolved, joint ventures were formed rapidly as foreign firms attempted to gain access to these markets. Often, the first strategy was to buy ownership, as Volkswagen did in the Czech Republic. The Germans beat out other contenders, such as Renault of France, and acquired a significant percent of the Czech auto leader Skoda.

Global strategic alliances are joint ventures that involve actions taken internationally by two or more companies contributing an agreed amount of resources. The arrangement often resembles a well-funded startup operation. This approach may be preferred when competition is tough or technology and capital requirements are relatively large for one partner. General Motors has global alliances with Suzuki, Isuzu and Fiat. Ford has allied with Volkswagen and Nissan, Daimler-Chrysler with Mitsubishi and Honda. General Mills created an alliance with Nestlé in Europe, called Cereal Partners Worldwide (CPW), to compete against Kellogg's grow-

---

Trading Companies

Large intermediaries that facilitate the movement of goods in and out of countries.

Foreign Licensing

Assigning the rights to a patent, trademark, or manufacturing process to a foreign company for a fee, often called a royalty.

Franchising

A special type of licensing arrangement whereby the marketer provides not only the product, technology, process, and/or trademark but also the entire marketing program.

Joint Venture

An alliance of two companies that combine resources to provide products and services more competitively than either could do independently.

ing global share. They agreed to pool part of their product lines and distribution system. Etisalat, one of the largest telecommunications companies in the world, and GE Healthcare recently signed a Memorandum of Understanding (MoU) to mark its strategic alliance. The joint initiative aims to improve synergies between health care and telecom, setting the highest standards for health care in the United Arab Emirates (UAE).

Some companies are competitors in certain regions of the world, but not in others, and they may choose to form a global strategic alliance in those areas. Toshiba, for example, has allied with a number of firms in the United States (United Technologies, Apple, Sun Microsystems, Motorola, and National Semiconductor) as well as a number of firms in Europe (Olivetti, Seimens, Rhore-Poulenc Ericcson, and SGS Thomson). Notice that many of these are rivals in various markets, but each works with Toshiba.

Whether its scope of operations is global or local, a company needs in-depth knowledge of its targeted markets in order to shape the strategic plan and meet its goals. In the next chapter, we will look at the importance of e-commerce and its role in the global marketing environment.

CHAPTER SUMMARY

Objective 1: Understand how the strategic marketing planning hierarchy fits together to provide a complete planning system.

Strategic marketing proceeds from a company's vision, to the strategic marketing plan, to the marketing mix plans. The vision describes what the organization is trying to accomplish in the broadest sense. It includes the organization's marketing philosophy. The strategic marketing plan is developed in line with the vision by a cross-functional team representing several business areas, such as manufacturing, accounting, finance and engineering. The plan describes the company's goals and states how the company will achieve them. Specialists in each component of the marketing mix prepare a plan for that area.

Objective 2: Describe the four elements of an organization's vision that provide guidance for all actions.

The vision statement expresses the company's core values, business definition, strategic direction and strategic infrastructure. Core values reflect the company's beliefs about the types of behavior acceptable from employees and the company as a whole, as well as its relationship to employees, customers and society in general. A business definition describes the contributions a company seeks to make to customers and society. It is important to avoid marketing myopia when developing a mission statement. Marketing myopia occurs when executives focus on the company's goods and services rather than on the benefits these goods and services provide to consumers. Strategic direction is the desired leadership position of an organization as well as the measures used to chart progress toward reaching that goal. It captures the "essence of winning" and addresses the competitiveness of the organization. A company's strategic infrastructure consists of both strategic business units and core competencies. SBUs can be managed using portfolio planning tools, such as the growth-share matrix or the attractiveness-strength matrix. Core competencies are the unique resources a company develops and employs to create superior customer value.

They are the fundamental building blocks of competitive advantage and can be developed in one or more of the following areas: base technologies, process technologies, product technologies, people systems or information systems.

Objective 3: Integrate components of the strategic marketing plan with the vision.

The strategic marketing plan describes how to accomplish the vision for a particular part of the business. It has five components: objectives, situation analysis, target marketing, positioning and integration of the marketing mix. Objectives are developed in line with the vision and the situation analysis. They state aims regarding profit, market share and total sales as well as customer satisfaction and loyalty. The situation analysis describes the marketing environment for the period in which the plan is in effect. It gives all the information required to estimate possible business scenarios, including market size, customer characteristics, competitors and technology. A key part of the situation analysis is to examine strengths, weaknesses, opportunities and threats (SWOT). The target marketing phase of strategic marketing planning focuses the organization on select groups of customers. In the positioning phase, the image of the organization relative to the competition is developed. The final step is to integrate the marketing mix plans to accomplish the overall strategy. It is important to look at the total effect of the marketing mix, rather than a single element, on the market.

Objective 4: Understand why elements of the marketing mix must be integrated and outline the steps of the marketing control process.

Plans for each part of the marketing mix are usually developed by specialists in the respective areas. Often a separate plan is created for product, place, promotion and price, but sometimes these plans are combined. Plans for any of these elements are both strategic and tactical. Strategies are long term and broad in scope, whereas tactics are short-term actions suited to specific market conditions. Several tactics may be used to carry out a single strategy. To determine whether the strategic marketing plan is accomplishing the intended objectives, a marketing control process is needed. It has five steps. First, the original performance objectives are reviewed. Second, measures indicate what performance has occurred. Third, performance is evaluated by interpreting the results obtained and looking for any trends. Fourth, it is decided whether actions or objectives should be altered. Fifth, the strategy proceeds as planned or another course is developed and implemented.

Objective 5: Identify the four major ways that organizations enter and cultivate global markets.

Organizations enter and cultivate global markets through exporting and importing, foreign licensing and franchising, overseas marketing and manufacturing, and joint ventures and strategic alliances. Exporting involves sending domestically manufactured products into foreign markets. It is usually the low-risk and low-cost way to enter markets. There are many forms of help for companies just getting started in exporting or importing. Foreign licensing and franchising simply assign the rights to a patent, trademark or process to a foreign company. Overseas marketing and manufacturing involve setting up operations in a foreign country. This requires the commitment of direct investment in a foreign country. Strategic alliances and joint ventures involve sharing resources with a partner to enter markets. Often the partner has strong contacts in the country or region where the venture takes place. Joint ventures can simply involve contracts between companies or shared ownership of new organizations. In some cases, these joint ventures require huge investments and substantial risks.

REVIEW YOUR UNDERSTANDING

1. What are the elements of the marketing planning hierarchy?
2. What are the components of a vision?
3. What is marketing myopia? How is the company's mission related to myopia?
4. In what ways can strategic business units be structured?
5. What are portfolio planning tools and how are they used?
6. What are core competencies? Give examples of five types.
7. Which people in an organization create the strategic marketing plan?
8. What is the difference between a strategy and a tactic? How do they work together?
9. What are the components of the strategic marketing plan? Describe each.
10. What are the elements of a SWOT analysis?
11. How are marketing mix plans strategic and tactical?
12. What is the marketing control process, and what are its steps?
13. In what four ways can an organization enter foreign markets? Describe each.

DISCUSSION OF CONCEPTS

1. Define strategy. Define tactics. How is strategy related to tactics? What strategy do you think Coca-Cola is following? What tactics is it using to support this strategy?
2. How are a company's core values, business definition, strategic infrastructure and strategic direction interrelated? Do you think it is important for a company to develop an explicit statement about each of these?
3. Imagine that the following companies describe their business as shown: (a) Black & Decker: drills and sanders; (b) Sherwin-Williams: paint; (c) Schwinn: bicycles; (d) U.S. Post Office: mail delivery. Do you think these companies are suffering from marketing myopia? How may they better define their business?
4. Why is it important for a company to have a well-defined strategic direction? In your opinion, what may happen to a company that lacks strategic direction?
5. How would you assess the contribution made by each strategic business unit? Do you think it is important for technology to be shared among SBUs? Why or why not?
6. Who should be involved in the development of a strategic marketing plan? Why?
7. What is the purpose of a situation analysis? What type of information should be included?
8. Why do most companies engage in some type of target marketing? What market do you think Nintendo is targeting with its handheld DS product line?

KEY TERMS & DEFINITIONS

1. **Business definition:** Describes the contributions the business makes to customers and society; also called the company mission.
2. **Control process:** Procedures designed to provide feedback on how well the marketing strategy is working.
3. **Control review meeting:** Meeting of members of the planning team to see whether objectives are being met.
4. **Core competencies:** The unique resources a company develops and employs to create superior customer value; the fundamental building blocks of competitive advantage.
5. **Core values:** A set of statements describing the type of behavior expected of the company and its employees.
6. **Cross-functional planning team:** Employees from several areas responsible for developing the company's strategic marketing plan.
7. **Customer intimacy strategy:** Strategy based on delivering value through superior empathy for customers and solutions tailored to specific customer needs.
8. **Differentiation strategy:** Strategy based on delivering customer value in a way that clearly distinguishes the product from competitors; works through effectiveness.
9. **Direct export intermediary:** A firm located in a foreign market that specializes in knowledge about foreign customs, regulations affecting businesses and products, laws, and market conditions.
10. **Distribution channel:** A set of independent organizations involved in making the product available for purchase.
11. **Export & import intermediary:** Domestic or foreign firm that assists with exporting or importing activity.
12. **Foreign licensing:** Assigning the rights to a patent, trademark or manufacturing process to a foreign company for a fee, often called a royalty.
13. **Franchising:** A special type of licensing arrangement whereby the marketer provides not only the product, technology, process, and/or trademark but also the entire marketing program.
14. **Geographic scope:** The extent of a company's international activities.
15. **Indirect export intermediary:** Firm located in a domestic market that specializes in knowledge about foreign customs, regulations affecting businesses and products, laws, and market conditions.
16. **Joint venture:** An alliance of two companies that combine resources to provide products and services more competitively than either could do independently.
17. **Low-cost strategy:** Strategy whose objective is to be the low-cost leader, thereby allowing the company to have higher margins than competitors and pass some savings on to customers through lower prices; works through efficiency.
18. **Marketing myopia:** A focus on company products rather than on how these products benefit consumers.
19. **Physical distribution:** The movement of finished products through channels of distribution to customers.
20. **Portfolio planning tools:** Tools that measure the contribution each SBU makes to the overall performance of the company.
21. **Positioning:** Creating an image or perception in the minds of consumers about the organization or its products relative to the competition.
22. **Product line:** Closely related products marketed by the organization.
23. **Strategic business unit (SBU):** A part of the firm that can be managed separately for marketing purposes; it may be a division, a product or product line, a distinct group of customers, or a unique technology.
24. **Strategic direction:** The desired leadership position of an organization as well as the measures used to chart progress toward reaching that position.
25. **Strategic infrastructure:** The corporate configuration that produces the company's distinctive or core competencies and provides the resources necessary to satisfy customer wants.
26. **Strategic marketing plan:** The document describing the company's objectives and how to achieve them in light of competitive activities.
27. **Strategic window:** The time during which market needs and the competencies of the firm fit together to create a significant opportunity.
28. **Strategy:** The development and/or deployment of resources with the intent of accomplishing goals and objectives in a competitive arena.
29. **Sustainable competitive advantage:** The strategy that competitors cannot easily duplicate or surpass.
30. **SWOT analysis:** An analysis of strengths, weaknesses, opportunities and threats to determine how well the company's skills and resources match the predicted market opportunities.
31. **Tactics:** Short-term actions and reactions to specific market conditions through which companies pursue their strategy.
32. **Target marketing:** The process of selecting which market segments the organization will emphasize in attempts to satisfy customers better than its competitors.
33. **Trading companies:** Large intermediaries that facilitate the movement of goods in and out of countries.
34. **Value proposition:** The compelling reason customers should select your brand.
35. **Vision:** Statement of an organization's operating philosophy including core values, business definition, strategic direction and strategic infrastructure.

REFERENCES

1. www.coca-cola.com, website visited July 6, 2014.

2. Whole Foods Market, Mission & Values, www.wholefoodsmarket.com, website visited May 13, 2014.

3. Sparrow Health System, http://ourfuture.sparrow.org, website visited May 13, 2014.

4. www.jnj.com, website visited April 3, 2014.

5. www.jnj.com/our_company/our_credo/, website visited March 21, 2014.

6. Waldholz, Michael, Kneale, Dennis, "Tylenol's Maker Tries to Regain Good Image in Wake of Tragedy," Wall Street Journal, October 8, 1982.

7. "Patagonia Company Information: Our Reason for Being," www.patagonia.com, website visited February 20, 2014.

8. "Our Community," eBay, www.ebay.com, website visited March 2, 2014.

9. "Strategic Intent," Harvard Business Review, May-June 1989, pg. 64.

10. www.volkswagenag.com, website visited March 2, 2014.

11. StatCounter Global Stats, http://gs.statcounter.com, website visited June 1, 2014.

12. Ibid.

13. www.coca-cola.com, website visited February 22, 2014.

14. www.upslogistics.com, website visited February 23, 2014.

15. www.infologixsys.com, website visited February 22, 2014.

16. www.aramark.com, website visited March 18, 2014.

17. www.aramark-uniform.com, website visited March 18, 2014.

18. "comScore Reports January 2014 U.S. Smartphone Subscriber Market Share," comScore.com, March 7, 2014.

19. www.jnj.com, website visited February 2, 2014.

20. Recruiting brochure for the Disney Store.

21. Ibid.

22. www.pressroom.ups.com/about/info, website visited June 3, 2014.

23. "The Core Competence of the Corporation," Harvard Business Review, May/June 1990, pg. 81.

24. "The Changing Role of Marketing in the Corporation, Journal of Marketing, October 1992, pg. 14.

25. Schmidt, Jeffery B., Montoya-Weiss, Mitzi M., Massay, Anne P., "New Product Development Decision Making Effectiveness: Comparing Face-to-Face Teams and Virtual Teams," Decision Sciences, Fall 2001.

26. Abell, Derek F., "Strategic Windows," Journal of Marketing, July 1978, pg. 21.

27. "iPad Competitors From Samsung, Sony, And RIM Leak; Retina Display Galaxy Tab Coming?", The Huffington Post, www.huffingtonpost.com, August 1, 2012.

28. Porter, Michael, Competitive Advantage: Creating and Sustaining Superior Performance (New York: The Free Press, 1985.)

29. "Gen Y: The Next Generation of Spenders," Destination CRM, http://www.destinationcrm.com, website visited August 13, 2014.

30. "Ford Engages Generation-Y with a Special 2011 Fiesta Contest," Autotropolis, www.autotropolis.com, site visited March 2, 2014.

31. www.hoovers.com, website visited March 2, 2014.

32. "Toys," Happy Meal, www.happymeal.com, website visited March 2, 2014.

33. "The diabolical geniuses behind Subway's 'five-dollar foot-long' song," Slate, www.slate.com, site visited March 2, 2014.

34. "The 50 best stocks of the S&P 500," BusinessWeek, April 30, 2007.

35. Alex Carlson, "A Kinect-less Xbox One Signals the Death of Motion Gaming," http://www.hardcoregamer.com, May 19, 2014; Hayley Tsukayam, "Samsung rumored to race Oculus and Sony to the virtual reality market," http://www.washingtonpost.com, May 23, 2014.

36. Neil Hughes, "Apple investing record $10.5 billion in supply chain robots & machinery," http://appleinsider.com, November 13, 2013.

37. "Companies' cash tied up in inventory, slow payers," Forbes, www.forbes.com, May 25, 2012.

38. http://www.bookofmormonbroadwaystore.com, website visited May 13, 2014.

39. Schmidt, Jeffery, Ph.D. dissertation, Michigan State University, 1996.

40. CIA World Factbook, www.cia.gov/library, website visited May 21, 2014.

41. "Topps going global: will produce IPL cricket products," Sports Business Digest, www.sportsbusinessdigest.com, website visited May 24, 2014.

42. Ohmae, Kinichi, The Borderless World (New York: Harper Business, 1990), pp. 17-31.

43. Calantore, Roger J., Kim, Daekwan, Schmidt, Jeffery B., Clavusgil, S.T., "The Influence of Internal and External Firm Factors on International Product Adoption Strategy and Export Performance," Journal of Business Research, April 19, 2004.

44. Erickson, David A., "Standardized Approach Works Well in Establishing Global Presence," Marketing News, October 7, 1996, pg. 9.

45. www.kochoil.com, website visited March 3, 2012.

Chapter 03

THE GLOBAL MARKETING ENVIRONMENT INCLUDING MARKETING E-COMMERCE

MARS

In 1950, Mars Corporation printed the first "m" on the plain candy-coated chocolates called M&M's. The company wanted to ensure consumers would get the "real thing" and coined the slogan, "Look for the M on every piece." Since then, the delicious candies that "melt in your mouth, not in your hand" are recognized around the globe as one of the world's favorite candy snacks.

Mars is the world's leading confectionery company, producing seven of the world's 20 best-selling chocolate snacks. It is a $30 billion business and employs approximately 70,000 associates at 230 sites in 73 countries. Despite sizable growth, Mars has remained a family-owned company guided by its Five Principles: quality, responsibility, mutuality, efficiency and freedom. These principles have provided a foundation for success in the global marketing environment and in e-commerce.

Through successful global marketing strategies, Mars has been able to connect with millions of consumers each day. Recently, Mars took top honors at the Promotion Marketing Association's Reggie Awards for its Global Color Vote, which gave consumers worldwide a chance to vote for the newest M&M's color. More than 10 million votes from 78 countries were cast, with the color purple winning the most votes. More importantly for Mars, the global brand grew 21 percent during the promotion.

A big success for Mars M&M's was the introduction of its "spokescandies" Red and Yellow (with Blue, Green, and Orange arriving later). These life-sized M&M's characters with lovable and unique personalities grace much of the M&M packaging, advertisements and memorabilia, from T-shirts to lunchboxes to candy dispensers. Now, Mars is using the Internet to leverage the popularity of the iconic characters to the next level. Users can visit the "Become an M&M" site and create personalized spokescandies that look just like them. To coincide with the launch of the website, Mars constructed a 50-foot Lady Liberty statue in the New York City Harbor. The smiling statue kicked off the campaign, encouraging consumers to create their M&M's characters at www.mms.com.

Through scanning the environment, Mars launched an e-commerce website, www.mymms.com. Its emergence in the e-commerce market surprised many, but My M&M is a clever example of how to use the value of the Internet to reach a new market. The site lets customers create and order personalized M&M's with custom colors, messages and images (even faces). This interactive platform makes it possible to have customized M&M's perfect for any occasion: pink "It's a Girl!" candies at baby showers, logos of NFL teams for a Super Bowl party, or a picture of a happy couple for a wedding reception. Recently, Mars released limited edition Kiss M&M's to be sold in Walmart stores during the promotion of the album Sonic Boom. The My M&M Kiss Blend features four customized packages that include images of the iconic faces of band members Gene Simmons, Paul Stanley, Tommy Thayer and Eric Singer.

By following its Five Principles, engaging the global market and harnessing the power of the Internet, Mars Corporation will continue producing over 400 million M&M's each day — good news for chocolate lovers around the world!

<< Mars in China

Courtesy of Mars

Learning Objectives

1. Describe the marketing environment and environmental scanning.
2. Understand how the roles that stakeholders play influence the accomplishment of marketing objectives. Know why marketing must address stakeholder desires when making decisions.
3. Be able to integrate an understanding of industry competition into environmental analysis.
4. Synthesize aspects of the global macroenvironment, including technological, economic, demographic, cultural and legal/regulatory elements in order to be in step with long-term trends.
5. Recognize the importance of ethics and guides to ethical behavior.
6. Understand the impact that e-commerce is making on the global business environment and understand the structure of Internet marketing.

THE GLOBAL MARKETING ENVIRONMENT INCLUDING MARKETING E-COMMERCE

Change abounds. It can be your friend or enemy, depending on how it is handled. Some organizations are reactive — they do not adjust strategies until the environmental changes have occurred. That can be dangerous, since it may be too late to construct a successful new strategy. Other organizations are proactive — they anticipate environmental changes in order to adjust ahead of time.

THE GLOBAL MARKETING ENVIRONMENT

Marketing Environment

The sum of all factors that affect a business.

Environmental Scanning

Collecting and analyzing information about the marketing environment in order to detect important changes or trends that can affect a company's strategy.

The **marketing environment** is the sum of all factors that affect a business. Figure 3.1 depicts the marketing environment surrounding our theme: creating and capturing value. First is the microenvironment, then the all-encompassing global macroenvironment. You will learn about both in the following sections.

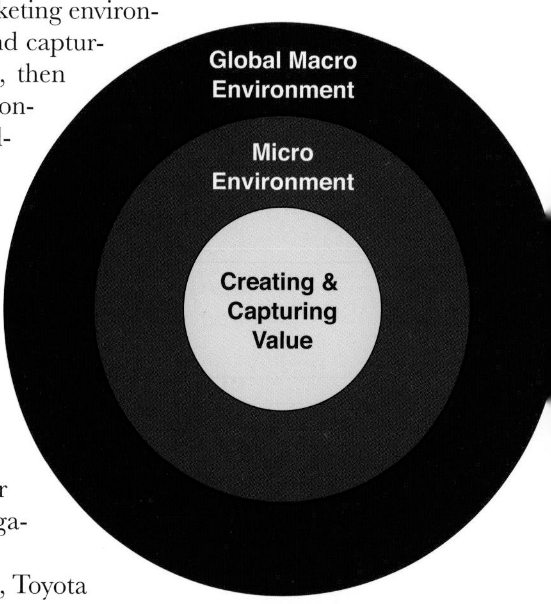

An organization has to be sensitive to its surroundings; many factors can dramatically influence it. These create opportunities, but they can also limit the company from pursuing its desired strategy. **Environmental scanning** collects and analyzes information in order to detect any trends that can affect a company's strategy. It can be performed by the company itself, by a professional or industry association, or by a consulting organization that specializes in forecasting.

Through scanning the environment, Toyota monitors the technological needs and wants of its

Global Macro Environment

Micro Environment

Creating & Capturing Value

Figure 3.1   The Marketing Environment

market in order to deploy state-of-the-art advances in its vehicles. One new feature is Entune, a collection of mobile applications and data services accessible from the car. It includes satellite radio; smart-phone, iPod and USB storage connectivity; navigation; and services such as search engine Bing, reservation-finder OpenTable and streaming music player Pandora. One recent study by Deloitte and Michigan State University assistant professor Clay Voorhees found that Generation Y consumers are highly focused on in-dash technology, with 59 percent calling it the most important part of a vehicle's interior to them.[2] The Internet is an extraordinary environmental scanning tool. It enables marketers to investigate press releases, news stories, online magazines, journals, newspapers and company websites highlighting product offerings, as well as technical and financial data. A skilled marketing analyst can even glean company strategies from this information.

Getting information about the market is much faster and easier on the Internet than through other methods. The U.S. Bureau of the Census website (www.census.gov) provides demographic information, and online magazines such as American Demographics (www.demographics.com) identify cultural trends. When scanning for legal/regulatory information, marketers can check government sites. For example, data on pending designs can be found at the U.S. Patent Office website (www.uspto.gov). The most authoritative sources for economic and demographic information about foreign countries are globalEDGE™ (www.globaledge.msu.edu), the CIA (www.cia.gov) and Economist Intelligence Unit (www.eiu.com) websites. The Internet also offers research opportunities, surveys and other means for studying web user behavior and surfing habits. All this is used extensively to collect marketing information, which we will discuss in Chapter 4.

Scanning resources and assistance are readily available. Companies that specialize in competitive intelligence even offer subscriptions to access data they have assembled. GE Information Services (Global Exchange) and Factiva (a Dow Jones & Reuters Company) are two leading providers of these services.[3]

THE MICROENVIRONMENT

The **microenvironment** is made up of the forces close to the company that influence how it connects with customers. As you'll notice in Figure 3.2, stakeholders and industry competition are part of the microenvironment. Stakeholders, as the name suggests, have a stake in an organization. Marketers need to understand stakeholders, recognizing that marketing decisions affect them and are affected by their influence. Since companies deal with stakeholders on a daily basis, marketers need to have their needs in mind. Competition is another force that impacts an organization daily. Competitors challenge your organization—some-

Microenvironment

The forces close to a company that influence how it connects with customers.

MICROENVIRONMENT

RELATIONSHIPS WITH STAKEHOLDERS
- Owners
- Employees
- Suppliers
- Intermediaries
- Action groups
- Others

COMPETITIVE INDUSTRY
- Competitors
- Competitive groups

Figure 3.2　The Microenvironment

times you win, and sometimes they win. In either case, healthy competition is beneficial because it stimulates innovation and change. An organization must consider its competitors and stakeholders in nearly every major marketing decision.

RELATIONSHIPS WITH STAKEHOLDERS

Stakeholder

A group who can influence or be influenced by the firm's actions.

Any group or individual, other than competitors, that can influence or be influenced by an organization's actions is a **stakeholder**, including customers, owners shareholders), employees, suppliers, intermediaries, action groups, and many others. In the previous chapter we stressed the importance of building relationships with customers. In this chapter we stress building relationships with other stakeholders. Marketers form interactive, ongoing, two-way connections with stakeholders so they will be a positive influence on the organization. Stakeholders can help serve customer needs and wants as well as help accomplish other

> **Marketers form interactive, ongoing, two-way connections with stakeholders so they will be a positive influence on the organization.**

objectives of the organization. Consequently, marketers try to act in the best long-term interest of all the firm's stakeholders. Because one organization can have a diverse array of stakeholders with conflicting objectives, this can be difficult. Balanced score cards are used to set objectives that address the needs of all stakeholders. Let's examine some of these stakeholders.

Owners and Employees
Whether public or private, an organization operates to benefit its owners, or shareholders. For companies, these benefits usually stress increasing the value of the business — making substantial profit. In nonprofit organizations, the benefits usually relate to helping constituents. For example, members of the Sierra Club are concerned about a safe and healthy community, smart energy solutions to combat global warming, and protecting America's wild places. The club urges members to contact political leaders about environmental issues and endorses candidates who support its goals.[4]

Shareholders have purchased, been given or inherited a share of the business. Typically, owners either represent themselves or are represented by a board of directors, which is charged with the responsibility to speak for all the owners. Marketers need to understand the goals, risks and reward levels acceptable to owners, who only invest in a company that continues to reach its objectives.[5] For example, Panera Bread Company had a 100 percent increase in stock price in a single year. It took an aggressive and somewhat risky market approach by introducing several new menu items and announcing plans to open 500 new

stores. Panera continues to grow at an impressive rate and now operates 1,800 bakery-cafes in 45 U.S. states and Ontario, Canada.[6] These actions produced results in line with shareholders' expectations, so they were willing to pay more for the stock.

Employees are also key stakeholders. Their livelihood depends on the company. Since every employee helps create and deliver value to the end consumer, each employee has a very important influence on the organization. Content employees are likely to be pleasant and helpful in their interactions with customers. W. L. Gore & Associates Inc., a top 100 company to work for, encourages hands-on innovation by involving those closest to a project in decision-making. The founder, Bill Gore, created an organization with no chains of command or pre-determined channels of communication. Employees are called "associates," communicate directly with each other and are accountable to fellow members of multi-disciplined teams. Instead of bosses, "sponsors" guide associates to reach team objectives in an environment that combines freedom with cooperation and autonomy with synergy. "We work hard at maximizing individual potential, maintaining an emphasis on product integrity and cultivating an environment where creativity can flourish," says Terri Kelly, the company's new president and CEO. "A fundamental belief in our people and their abilities continues to be the key to our success, even as we expand globally."[7]

Suppliers and Intermediaries
Suppliers are stakeholders who provide a company with necessary services, raw materials and components. Very few organizations can exist without suppliers, who also can be a major factor in creating customer satisfaction. For example, Ford relies on more than 1,300 production suppliers to provide many of the parts that are assembled into Ford vehicles. Another 11,000 suppliers provide a wide range of goods and services, from production equipment to computers to advertising.[8] If you like the dashboard, seats or electronics on the new Ford F-150, chances are a supplier worked with Ford to design it. Suppliers manufacture many of the components that go into vehicles — no matter what brand.

Suppliers

Organizations that provide a company with necessary services, raw materials, or components.

Courtesy of Ford

The new Ford F-150 contains a 360-degree birds-eye camera view.

Since they are specialized in their product, suppliers are an excellent source of new technology and are likely to speed the introduction of the latest designs and techniques. They give companies access to technology and expertise that an organization could not obtain with its own resources. For example, until 1987, DuPont sold only adhesives to Reebok. Then DuPont technicians suggested that Reebok use a plastic tube technology, originally designed for the automobile industry. The tubes made Reebok shoes "bouncier" and the new feel was a hit with consumers. Chances are that Reebok never would have developed this technology on its own at the time. This single idea dramatically influenced the entire industry.

Companies rely on suppliers, so when suppliers have their own problems, it can mean trouble. Failure to develop and maintain good working relationships with suppliers can have consequences. In May 2014, Wolverine Packing Co. issued a recall for 1.8 million pounds of ground beef after people were sickened during a fifteen-state E. coli outbreak. If the food makers had better visibility with their suppliers, the recall may have been avoided.[9]

Intermediaries are independently owned organizations that act as links to

Intermediaries

Stakeholders who move products from the manufacturer to the final user.

move products between producers and end users. They have an important influence on organizations because they dramatically extend the ability of marketers to reach customers at home and abroad. Book wholesalers and campus bookstores help publishers sell textbooks to students. Beverage manufacturers such as Gatorade, Dole and Ocean Spray use intermediaries to deliver their goods to outlets that sell them to the final consumer. Kawasaki, Sea-Doo and Honda market their personal watercrafts through dealerships.

Some intermediaries specialize in international markets, using their unique skills and capabilities to give a company global reach. For example, an intermediary with special expertise in an emerging market may provide access to channels necessary to reach select customers. Companies that want to expand into untapped markets find intermediaries invaluable in delivering their product to the consumer. It is very beneficial for companies to establish solid working relationships with their intermediaries.

Action Group

A number of people who support some cause in the interest of consumers or environmental safety.

Action Groups **Action groups** are stakeholders that support some cause in the interest of consumers or environmental safety. The hundreds of action groups act as "watchdogs," making sure that companies keep the interests of people and the environment in balance with those of profit.

A vocal and well-known environmental advocate, former Vice President Al Gore, is fighting to stop global warming and is calling for action through his web-

site, AlGore.com. Users can sign a virtual postcard, which will help take his message to Congress. Gore's book, Our Choice, describes his take on the real solutions to global warming through his experiences. The Our Choice app allows you to interact with graphics, animations and video.[10] He is also the Chairman of the Board for the Alliance For Climate Protection, which is committed to finding and implementing comprehensive solutions for the climate crisis.[11] Many movie and television personalities lend their names and celebrity status to consumer or environmental causes. StopGlobalWarming. org has an impressive list of celebrity supporters including Jon Bon Jovi, Kobe Bryant, Reggie Bush, Sheryl Crow, Leonardo DiCaprio, Tony Hawk, Gretchen Bleiler and Shaun White.[12] Al Gore introduced "Live Earth: The Concerts for a Climate in Crisis," and is supported by many of the greatest entertainers around the globe.

Marketers are very aware of consumer groups that frequently criticize the pursuits of business. A marketer may have to make difficult decisions when there is a conflict between the desires of action groups and other stakeholders. For instance, the Washington D.C. Center for Gay, Lesbian, Bisexual and Transgender People is a member of Walmart's affiliate program. When the American Family Association learned of this, it initiated a national boycott, claiming that the deal suggests Walmart executives believe "the homosexual agenda is worthy of their support." Nevertheless, Walmart did not give in to protesters, stating that it forges business partnerships with many minority organizations to help it attract a diverse array of suppliers. While stressing its support for diversity and nondiscrimination, Walmart said in its statement that it "will not make corporate contributions to support or oppose highly controversial issues unless they directly relate to our ability to serve our customers." In response to Walmart's comments, The American Family Association later abandoned the boycott.[13]

Action groups can also help marketers gain positive publicity and may help businesses make a greater contribution to society. In recent years, NFL players have worn and used pink equipment, such as cleats, wristbands and gloves, during October — Breast Cancer Awareness Month — to help draw attention to the issue. Merchandise and footballs used during the game are later autographed and auctioned off to benefit the American Cancer Society.[14]

INDUSTRY COMPETITION

The word *competition* brings to mind an image of two giant companies vying against each other; however, competition also involves companies of differing types and sizes. Well-established and new companies, along with suppliers and customers, form an industry structure that dictates the intensity of competition. Competitors may be individual companies or the industry as a whole.

The competitive environment can be marked by intense change, making it difficult to successfully launch a new product.[15] It is important for companies to assess the risks and ask the following questions: Who are our existing rivals? What new competitors may emerge? What is the relative strength of suppliers and buyers within the industry? Finally, what substitutes are likely to appear? The answers give a complete picture of the overall nature of competition within an industry. Figure 3.3 depicts the forces that shape the competitive environment.

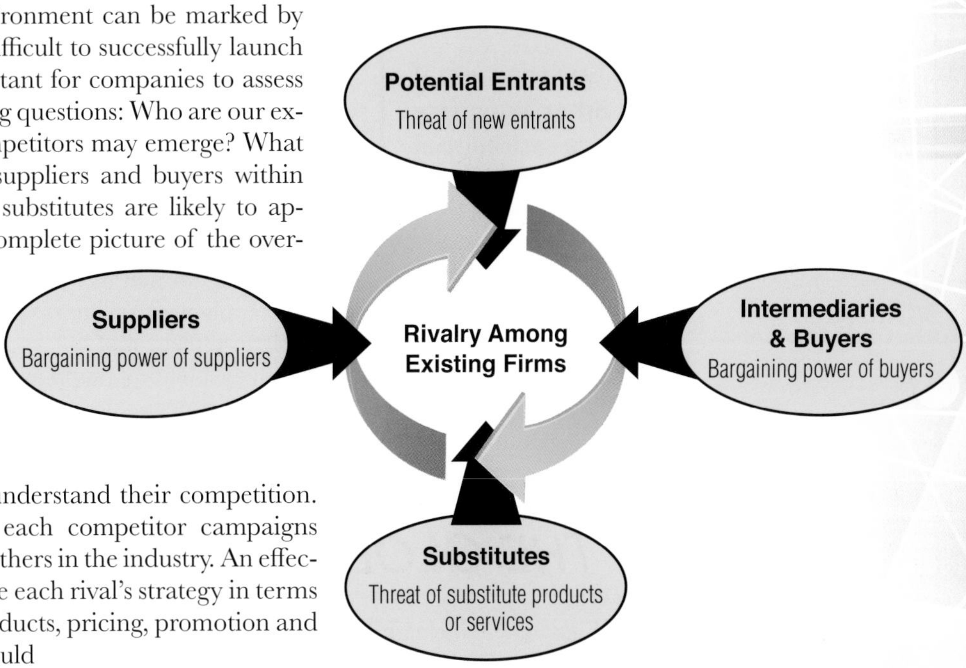

Figure 3.3   Forces Driving Industry Competition
Source: The Free Press, a division of Simon & Schuster, from Competitive Strategy: Techniques for Analyzing Industries and Competitors, by Michael Porter. Copyright 1980

Existing Firms
Marketers need to thoroughly understand their competition. They need to know how each competitor campaigns against their company and others in the industry. An effective marketer would examine each rival's strategy in terms of current and potential products, pricing, promotion and distribution. They also should identify key customers and suppliers, the types of technologies used, current performance, and strengths and weaknesses. From all this information, the marketing manager attempts to determine the plans of every competitor and how every competitor will react to the marketer's actions.

Potential Competitors
At any time a company may enter an industry with similar products. Recently, 3,231 new snack, cookie and cracker products, including 382 types of potato chips, were introduced in a single year.[16] This is not a welcome statistic to established competitors such as Lays and Pringles, but one advantage is that aggressive marketing by several companies will often draw attention to the overall product category and cause industry-wide sales to increase. New competitors are not always upstart companies, but are sometimes established ones branching into a

new market. Taco Bell's entry into the breakfast market with innovative products like the waffle taco, required new strategies by the leader, McDonald's, which responded with a promotion to offer a free cup of coffee with a breakfast purchase. McDonald's move appears to have worked in the short term, as its breakfast sales rose 1.2 percent just one month after Taco Bell's entry.[17]

Substitutes A **substitute product** is any good or service that performs the same function or provides the same benefit as an existing one. For example, who competes with Federal Express for overnight delivery of letters? If you said United Parcel Service (UPS), the U.S. Postal Service, Airborne Express or other overnight delivery companies, then you are correct, but you probably left out two important ones: fax and email.

Marketers should not limit their analysis to the same industry. Companies in other industries that make or develop substitutes may be an even greater competitive threat. For example, JPMorgan Chase, a successful marketer of financial services, faces such industry rivals as Merrill Lynch and Paine Webber but also experiences tough competition from insurance companies, banks, brokers and others. Often information about substitutes can be found on the Internet.

The Bargaining Power of Buyers and Suppliers

Marketers must also ask which group—buyers or suppliers—has the most power in an industry. The answer affects both company strategy and competition. Generally, when there are many suppliers, buyers are the most powerful, because one buyer may have several suppliers competing for business. For example, Walmart is powerful because there are fewer retailers than in the past and many, many small suppliers. Walmart spends more than $200 billion annually on merchandise through its 61,000 vendors.[18] If a vendor does not go comply with Walmart's policies, there are many others available to replace it.of

When buyers are extremely plentiful, suppliers tend to be more powerful. Since demand is great, suppliers can negotiate contracts on their terms and generally command higher prices. A supplier has the most power when it offers a unique and superior good or service that buyers are clamoring to purchase.

THE GLOBAL MACROENVIRONMENT

Like stakeholders and industry forces in the microenvironment, the global macroenvironment also influences the company, but it does so indirectly. The **global macroenvironment** consists of large external influences considered vital to long-term decisions but not directly affected by the company itself. It is critical for marketers to identify, anticipate, and plan for the effects of those factors. Larger forces — each of which constitutes an environment in itself — tend to shift slowly, so they have long-term implications for the organization, but they do have an effect on day-to-day operations as well. Figure 3.4 lists the most important forces or environments — technological, economic, demographic, cultural, legal/regulatory, and ethical — that make up the global macroenvironment.

Constituents of the Global Macroenvironment
- Technological environment
- Economic environment
- Demographic environment
- Cultural environment
- Legal/regulatory environment
- Ethical environment

Figure 3.4   The Global Macroenvironment

Substitute Product

Any good or service that performs the same function or provides the same benefit as an existing one.

UPS was awarded the Environmental Protection Agency's SmartWay Excellence Award. Explore additional awards it has received for "working green and working smart."

www.ups.com

Global Macroenvironment

The large external influences considered vital to long-term decisions but not directly affected by the company itself.

TECHNOLOGICAL ENVIRONMENT

As you know, technology is one of the six key elements in connecting with customers. The **technological environment** refers to the collective knowledge available for use in developing, manufacturing and marketing products. Companies spend huge sums each year to increase this body of knowledge. Merck Pharmaceutical Company, an industry leader, annually invests about $8 billion in research and development (R&D) activities.[19] The government contributes to this body of knowledge as well. When the U.S. government announced a war against AIDS, it included federally sponsored studies on the disease. Several pharmaceutical companies used this research as the fundamental knowledge required to make patentable products. On their own, many companies would not have the time or resources to make the uncertain and risky investment in AIDS R&D. Sustained research is too costly, with no guarantee of resulting revenue, so the government contributing its studies was necessary to progress in the field.

> **Technological Environment**
>
> The total body of knowledge available for development, manufacturing, and marketing of products and services.

A huge technological effect has resulted from microprocessor R&D. Leading computer companies spend several billion dollars each year. Intel Corporation, for instance, spends more than $10 billion on R&D annually.[20] R&D has accelerated the rate of technological change; what was innovative a short time ago is now obsolete. The personal computer (PC) is an example. First introduced on a broad scale by Steve Jobs and Steve Wozniak in 1976, the PC is still evolving rapidly. Many of the first models used the same cassette technology for memory that was once used to record music. This quickly gave way to floppy discs, then compact discs, DVDs and flash drives. The world's first gigabyte disk drive, built in 1980, was the size of a refrigerator and cost $40,000. Today, Apple easily packs two gigabytes into a MP3 player the size of a matchbook and sells it for less than $50. Processing capability is also growing phenomenally: At the end of the 1980s, Intel's 20 MHz chip offered state-of-the-art speed. Intel is now producing speeds up to 4GHz with the its Intel Core i7-4960X.[21] Obviously, changes such as these create great opportunities and challenges for companies.

Ed Uthman / CC-BY-SA-2.0

Apple's first computer (Apple-1) had a 1MHz processor and 4KB of memory.

"With new processes and technologies, you want to replace [your own product] instead of letting someone else do it," says Gary Tooker, former CEO of Motorola, adding that "success comes from a constant focus on renewal."[22] The rapid rate of change requires businesses to invest in R&D and creative innovation. If a computer company cannot build a machine that processes information quickly and can support future additions, it will soon be as obsolete as its products. However, top spending does not necessarily equal innovation; according to a report by Booz & Company. It found that "many companies — notably, Apple — consistently underspend their peers on R&D investments while outperforming them on a broad range of corporate success measures, such as revenue growth, profit growth, margins, and total shareholder return" and that company culture was the most important factor in innovativeness.[23]

ECONOMIC ENVIRONMENT

Economic Environment

Financial and natural resources that are available to consumers, businesses and countries.

Disposable Income

The income consumers have left after paying taxes.

Discretionary Income

The amount of money consumers have left after paying taxes and purchasing necessities.

Spending Power

The ability of the population to purchase goods and services.

Gross Domestic Product

The total market value of all goods and services produced by a country in a single year.

The **economic environment** refers to financial and natural resources that are available to consumers, businesses and countries. An understanding of consumer economic factors such as income, spending behavior, spending power and wealth dispersion is essential in assessing opportunities that may emerge. Global marketers also must be familiar with the economic features of the world's major trading blocs.

Income and Spending Behavior
Benjamin Franklin said that only two things are certain in life: death and taxes. **Disposable income** is the money consumers have left after paying taxes, and many marketers prefer to use this as the measure of consumer wealth. People spend some of their disposable income on necessities, such as food, clothing and shelter; anything left over is called **discretionary income**. Marketers of nonessentials, such as vacation packages, jewelry and stereos, target consumers' discretionary income.

No less important than the amount of income is the willingness, or propensity, to spend. The typical middle-income American family is spending more on luxury goods. According to the U.S. Bureau of the Census, the average income of the top fifth of households rose 38 percent in the past 10 years. Marketers have seized this opportunity to focus on promoting nonessential items, especially over the Internet.

Spending Power and Wealth Dispersion
Marketers must realize that a large population does not always provide a large marketing opportunity. They should consider the residents' **spending power**, or the ability of people to purchase goods and services. A common measure of spending power is the gross domestic product of a country. **Gross domestic product (GDP)** is the total market value of all final goods and services produced for consumption during a given period by a particular country. The European Union has the highest GDP, at approximately $15.65 trillion, followed closely by the United States at $15.29 trillion. The next closest GDP is China ($11.44 trillion), followed by India ($4.51 trillion) and Japan ($4.49 trillion).[24]

When the GDP of every nation is added together, the gross world product (GWP) today is about $70.16 trillion. That figure is not spread equally among countries, however. The United States accounts for about 21 percent of the GWP. Considering that the United States has less than 5 percent of the world's population, this is a high figure. In comparison, with 36 percent of the world's population, China and India contribute about 22 percent to GWP (China at 16 percent and India at 6 percent).[25]

Many marketers do not look solely at GDP, because it does not indicate how much each person in the country has to spend. For example, Mexico and Sweden have approximately the same GDP, but we know that the standard of living is lower in Mexico than in Sweden. Because Mexico has a larger population, a smaller portion of GDP is allocated to each inhabitant. Consequently, many marketers use GDP per capita ("per person") to assess the standard of living. This way, they can estimate the living conditions of a country's individuals.

Even GDP per capita has limitations, because it ignores the dispersion of wealth within a country. Often there are a few rich people and many, many poor

CAREER TIP!

eBay "has jobs as unique as you!" The company has a summer internship program for college students looking for experience. The summer internship is a 12-week structured program where students are able to get a glimpse of the real world with guidance from eBay mentors and participation in hands-on projects. For more information about the internship program and job opportunities, check out eBay's website at www.ebaycareers.com/university.html

ones. In Brazil, for example, the richest 10 percent of the population controls 46 percent of the wealth. In the United States, that figure is 29 percent.[26] In Japan and Spain, the dispersion of wealth is much more even.[27]

Trading Blocs

The world's three major trading blocs — North America, Europe and the Pacific Rim — are shown in Figure 3.5. Often called the world's economic superpowers, they are expected to compete for the mastery of international markets well into the 21st century. Combined, these three regions are responsible for about 80 percent of the world's economic activity. Customers in the superpower triad buy, for instance, a great majority of all computers and consumer electronics. The triad contains over a half-billion consumers with converging preferences. Among others, IBM, Motorola and Gucci are found nearly everywhere in the triad. Today, each of these blocs is basically equal in terms of economic activity, but current trends point toward shifts. The Pacific Rim is growing the fastest, Europe next, then North America.

Despite their collective power, the triad's constituent economies are not without difficulties. Many of these countries have a mature economy, rising social welfare costs, an aging population, and escalating research and development costs.[28] Let's look at each of the trading blocs in more detail.

North America When the United States, Canada and Mexico entered into the North American Free Trade Agreement (NAFTA), they created the largest single market in the world. The objective was to make all three nations more competitive globally by combining their strengths. The United States and Canada have capital, skills, technology and natural resources; Mexico has low-cost labor. Proponents of NAFTA believe efficient North American companies will be able to offer lower-priced products to consumers. Overall, the open market means removal of tariffs and other trade barriers, increased investment opportunities, stronger protection of intellectual property, and more environmentally sound business practices. Today, the NAFTA market boasts a total gross domestic product of more than $18 trillion.[29]

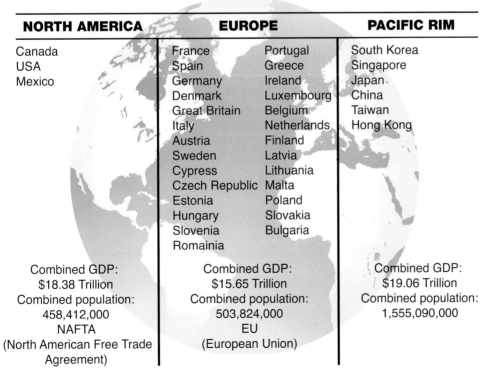

NORTH AMERICA	EUROPE		PACIFIC RIM
Canada	France	Portugal	South Korea
USA	Spain	Greece	Singapore
Mexico	Germany	Ireland	Japan
	Denmark	Luxembourg	China
	Great Britain	Belgium	Taiwan
	Italy	Netherlands	Hong Kong
	Austria	Finland	
	Sweden	Latvia	
	Cypress	Lithuania	
	Czech Republic	Malta	
	Estonia	Poland	
	Hungary	Slovakia	
	Slovenia	Bulgaria	
	Romainia		
Combined GDP: $18.38 Trillion	Combined GDP: $15.65 Trillion		Combined GDP: $19.06 Trillion
Combined population: 458,412,000	Combined population: 503,824,000		Combined population: 1,555,090,000
NAFTA (North American Free Trade Agreement)	EU (European Union)		

Figure 3.5   The Three Superpower Trading Blocks

NAFTA is not without critics. Companies are becoming more mobile, and some will go where labor is cheapest. If U.S. technology does not create enough high-paying jobs at home, U.S. workers will ultimately be fighting for low-paying jobs with fewer benefits.

Europe The European Union (EU) has tremendous economic relevance in Europe and around the world. It has the goal of eliminating barriers that restrict the flow of people, goods, services and money within the union. The objective is to restructure Europe economically so that it can better compete against the United States, Japan and other developed nations. The EU members include Austria, Belgium, Bulgaria, Cyprus, the Czech Republic, Denmark, Estonia, Finland, France, Germany, Greece, Hungary, Ireland, Italy, Latvia, Lithuania, Luxembourg, Malta, the Netherlands, Poland, Portugal, Romania, Slovakia, Slovenia, Spain, Sweden and the United Kingdom.[30]

The **Maastricht Treaty** consists of 282 directives that eliminate border controls and customs duties, strengthen external borders, establish a single European currency, coordinate defense and foreign policy, unify product standards and working conditions, protect intellectual property, and deregulate many industries, including telecommunications, airlines, banking, and insurance. This will make it much easier to move products from one region to another. Eventually, a company will be able to create a more unified marketing strategy for the EU as a whole; today its different market environments still have to be addressed.

Pacific Rim The Pacific Rim (PAC Rim), which comprises much of East Asia, is named for the ocean it borders. It is made up of Japan and the four "dragons" — South Korea, Singapore, Taiwan and China (including Hong Kong), and it is known for its enormous manufacturing potential. Depending on the outcome of attempts at economic reform, Thailand, Malaysia and Indonesia could join soon. Economic integration in the PAC Rim is based primarily on market forces, not a formal agreement such as NAFTA. Much of the growth in East Asia has been spurred by Japanese investors, such as Matsushita Electric, which has established 10 major operations in Southeast Asia since 1961.

Asia-Pacific Economic Cooperation, or APEC, is a forum for 21 Pacific Rim countries to cooperate on regional trade and investment in the Asia Pacific region. APEC's 21 members, referred to as "Member Economies," include Australia, Brunei, Canada, Chile, China, Hong Kong, Indonesia, Japan, South Korea, Malaysia, Mexico, New Zealand, Papua New Guinea, Peru, the Philippines, Russia, Singapore, Taiwan, Thailand, the United States and Vietnam. These members account for approximately 40 percent of the world's population, 54 percent of world GDP and about 44 percent of world trade.[31]

East Asia has recently undergone explosive economic growth. China has experienced at least an 8 percent annual growth rate since 2000, making it the fastest-growing area in the region.[32] These Asian nations are feeding their home markets with the net gain in money received from other economies, which is possible when a country exports more than it imports. The domestic markets are increasing in size as companies and workers earn more money. With cash reserves of several hundred billion dollars and personal wealth, they can buy large amounts of goods from other countries. In Japan, for instance, annual household savings amount to a hefty $6.6 trillion.[33]

General Agreement on Tariffs and Trade and the World Trade Organization In 1947, the General Agreement on Tariffs and Trade (GATT) was founded under the United Nations. GATT is responsible for many of the current trade agreements among its 155 members. This organization has successfully negotiated significant reductions in trade restrictions and import duties that countries would otherwise impose in their own interests. GATT has successfully reduced import duties and tariffs from more than 40 percent in 1947 to less than 5 percent today.

Maastricht Treaty

Consists of 282 directives that eliminate border controls and customs duties among members of the European Union.

In 1995, GATT was absorbed by the World Trade Organization (WTO), which will carry out the traditional role of GATT. The WTO deals with a broad range of issues, including pollution, tariffs, trade agreements and trade disputes.

Natural Resources The availability of natural sources of wealth (which can be minerals, vegetation, wildlife, water and others) within a given region or nation is an important economic factor. For example, the U.S. Pacific Northwest provides a rich source of timber for the paper and construction industries, while countries in the Middle East control approximately 65 percent of the world's crude oil. In both cases, natural resources provide income to the area's inhabitants. Resource availability affects a marketer's pricing strategy. If a company operates a large plant in an area where energy or raw materials are expensive, production costs will be high, and its price must be set accordingly.

When seeking natural resources, marketers must balance their company's efforts against preservation of the environment. For instance, environmentalists and locals in some areas claim that "fracking," or injecting a combination of water, sand and chemicals into shale in order to extract natural gas, is responsible for groundwater contamination as well as releasing methane into the atmosphere.[34]

Marketers have to consider environmental regulations, since they may threaten current business practices or create new opportunities. For example, the Strategic Environment Initiative (SEI) recommends that the government provide tax breaks to companies using environmentally friendly technologies and levy high taxes on those using older, unsafe methods. This has encouraged companies to come up with innovations in order to cut down on emissions. In the product area, for example, companies can retrofit antipollution devices or engineer more environmentally friendly designs. The environment has become an increasingly prominent factor for marketers to consider. When it became known that the chlorofluorocarbons (CFCs) released from aerosol cans were thinning the ozone layer, many companies switched to pump spray bottles. Starbucks recently unveiled a new beverage sleeve, made with 34 percent less raw fiber material and 25 percent more post-consumer content. The company says the "EarthSleeve" will save 100,000 trees.[35]

Some experts believe "fracking" is extremely harmful to our environment. You can learn more at dangersoffracking.com

DEMOGRAPHIC ENVIRONMENT

The **demographic environment** consists of the data that describe a population in terms of age, education, health and so forth. Marketers examine such information to gain an understanding of current opportunities and discover trends that may indicate future opportunities. Some frequently studied demographics include population size and density, urbanization and age structure.

Demographic Environment

The statistical data used to describe a population.

Population There are approximately 7 billion people in the world, and there are expected to be over 9 billion by 2050.[36] If marketing opportunities were defined solely by population size, then the prospects would be bright indeed. Marketers need to look at trends within populations to get a more accurate picture.

Population growth depends on the number of live births plus the number of immigrants entering a country. The birthrate, which is measured as the number of live births per 1,000 people, is increasing throughout the world, but the rate of increase has begun to slow. Still, there are about 252 worldwide births per minute, or 4.2 births every second.[37] At the same time, advances in medicine and technology mean that people are healthier, and the number of deaths per 1,000 people is decreasing. Longer life spans combined with births result in an even larger world population.

Movement from one country to another redistributes the world's population, and the United States is gaining considerable numbers this way. Although U.S. immigration laws have become more restrictive, immigration is still expected to contribute as much to U.S. population growth as natural births. The multicultural population is over 30 percent today and is expected to climb to 54 percent of the total U.S. population by 2050.[38]

The U.S. population is expected to grow to 349 million in 2025 and to 403 million in 2050.[39] As with the world population, the average annual growth rate is expected to decrease by nearly half from 1.1 percent in the 1990s to around .54 percent by 2045. This predicted decline, which would be the lowest growth rate in U.S. history, is attributed to numerous factors, including the general aging of the population, increased age at first marriage, delayed childbearing, a growing proportion of childless couples, and the greater participation of women in the labor force.[40]

Population Density

The concentration of people within some unit of measure, such as per square mile or per square kilometer.

Density

Density A country with a large population may seem to offer a large marketing opportunity, but it is important to know where those people live. **Population density** refers to the number of people within a standard measurement unit, such as a square mile. Canada has more than 34 million people and 8.9 people, on average, per square mile. Yet, because three-quarters of Canadians live in a few large cities, such as Quebec and Toronto, large areas of the country are quite sparsely populated. Singapore's population of about 5.3 million is highly concentrated, with an average of over 20,000 people per square mile.[41] When people are concentrated, it's easier and more cost-effective to reach them with advertising campaigns and products. When they are spread out, marketing can be difficult, time-consuming and expensive. Consider the Pacific Rim countries, where many more people live in the coastal regions than inland, or Australia with its sparsely populated Outback. Delivering products to consumers in the thinly populated areas takes far more effort than delivering to consumers in a city. Even promoting products can be more difficult: billboards won't be seen by as many people, and magazine subscribers are spread out. Organizations are likely to focus marketing efforts on densely populated areas.

Urbanization

The shift of population from rural to urban areas.

Urbanization

Urbanization **Urbanization** refers to the population shift from rural areas to cities. About half of the world's population lives in an urban area, including the vast majority of some countries' populations. In Germany, for example, 74 percent of the population lives in urban areas; in Singapore, 100 percent.[42] In the United States, four out of five people live in or near a

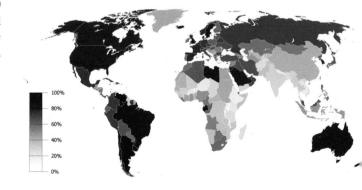

Global representation of the percent of population urbanized.

city. Over a quarter of the U.S. population is concentrated in the 10 largest metropolitan areas, with New York City (19 million), Los Angeles (12.9 million), and Chicago (9.5 million) at the top.[43] Urbanization is significant to marketers for three important reasons. First, as noted earlier, it is easier to reach a concentrated population. Second, as a group, people in cities tend to have enough income to purchase luxuries and support the arts, such as opera or theater. Third, people in urban areas tend to demand a wider variety of products than do rural inhabitants.

When the city population spills into the suburbs, neighboring cities may eventually join together. The U.S. Bureau of the Census uses the following to categorize urban concentrations. A **metropolitan statistical area (MSA)** is a stand-alone population center, not linked to other cities, with more than 50,000 people. Examples are San Antonio, Texas; Montgomery, Alabama; and Spokane, Washington.

A **consolidated metropolitan statistical area (CMSA)** is two or more overlapping urban communities with a combined population of at least 1 million. An example is the area that includes New York City, northern New Jersey, and southwestern Connecticut.

Age Structure

Because generations differ in their tastes, age-related marketing research has become popular. An **age cohort** is a group of people close in age who have been shaped by their generation's experience with the media, peers, events and the larger society. Often these cohorts are divided into four groups. "Matures" were born between 1909 and 1945, "baby boomers" between 1946 and 1964, "Generation X" between 1965 and 1976, "Generation Y" between 1977 and 1994, and "Generation Z" thereafter. Research reveals substantial differences among them in values, tastes and needs.

Globally, the average age is less than 25 years and getting younger. Many countries, such as Mexico, have rapidly growing populations that contribute to this statistic. In some industrialized nations, however, the picture is different. Children constitute a declining proportion of the German population, which is aging slowly but is older than the U.S. population, with a median age of 44.9.[44] Today the median age in the United States is 37.2; by 2030,

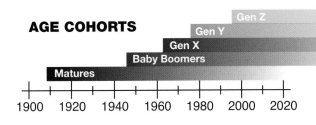

AGE COHORTS

Gen Z
Gen Y
Gen X
Baby Boomers
Matures

1900 1920 1940 1960 1980 2000 2020

almost 20 percent of the population will be age 65 or older. This is partly due to the baby boom after World War II, which will affect U.S. demographics for many years. In addition to varying by history, the U.S. age distribution also varies according to race. About 80 percent of Americans are Caucasian, but that percentage increases with age. Among the 12.9 percent of all Americans who are African American, nearly 15 percent are younger than 10. Sixteen percent of Americans are Hispanic, and 20 percent of them are 10 or younger.[45]

Now that U.S. baby boomers are migrating into senior-life status, when spending power is substantial, marketers are focusing on older consumers; this age group currently makes up 44 percent of the population but controls 70 percent of its disposable income. There's even been a surge in gray-haired models as companies try to appeal to the boomer demographic, who want to see versions of themselves — not twentysomethings — in ads. Even youth-oriented clothing retailer American Apparel has hired "seasoned" model Jacky, who sports long gray hair and laugh lines.[46] In the years ahead, marketers will face the growing task of serving an aging market and addressing its unique concerns. You will learn more about age structure, and how to use it for segmentation, in Chapter 8.

Metropolitan Statistical Area (MSA)

A stand-alone population center, unlinked to other cities, that has more than 50,000 people.

Consolidated Metropolitan Statistical Area (CMSA)

Two or more overlapping urban communities with a combined population of at least 1 million.

Age Cohort

A group of people close in age who have been shaped by their generation's experience with the media, peers, events, and society at large.

CULTURAL ENVIRONMENT

Cultural Environment

The learned values, beliefs, language, symbols, and patterns of behavior shared by people in a society and passed on from generation to generation.

The **cultural environment** consists of the learned values, beliefs, language, symbols and behaviors shared by people in a society and passed on from one generation to the next. Culture includes morals, values, religion, art, customs, traditions, folkways, technology, myths and norms. These and other characteristics distinguish different societies, define the way we think about ourselves and the world, what we want, and how we behave. Marketers must be in touch with the cultural environment because it helps them to make stronger connections with diverse customers. This connection has even been made between culture and environmental practices. According to a study about Chinese consumers' green purchase behavior, the tra-

CREATING & CAPTURING VALUE *Globally*

Global Player: McDonald's

Nothing is more American than those golden arches, golden fries, and delicious Big Macs. Imagine this scenario: After a long day of work or play, the familiar craving draws your car to the nearest McDonald's, which is probably right around the corner. Whether you choose the convenience of the drive thru or settle into a booth to enjoy your Big Mac or McNuggets, you can always count on the same distinct taste. It's a typical scene that we have all experienced, but now you can replay it in 123 countries worldwide. The hamburger is no longer just an American delight.

Making the Mickey D's hamburger a global icon has put a cultural twist on the traditionally American burger and fries. McDonald's has created menus that reflect the tastes of the local cuisine while keeping in mind everything from religious values to the availability of resources. To accommodate Hinduism in India, where beef is not consumed, the Maharaja Burger, with mutton or chicken patties, replaces the traditional Big Mac. In many Middle Eastern countries, food is prepared within Muslim guidelines, and in China customers can enjoy localized tastes such as Szechuan-style spicy chicken wings and seafood soup. In Germany you can even throw back a cold beer with your meal. These modifications have led McDonald's to rack up approximately $70 billion in global

revenue annually. To accompany their custom menus, the company wanted to revamp their look to blend in with conventional, local architecture.

When one sits down to enjoy their "McWhatever," there is something nostalgic and comforting about the traditional McDonald's atmosphere. But what was typical for American McDonald's restaurants now varies regionally. In the fashion forward city of Paris, upscale café styling is used to convince people that McDonald's too can be chic. One wouldn't notice the golden arches as they blend in with the airy, whitewashed buildings in metropolitan areas of Iraq. Even here in the United States, where the fast food chain originated, architects have used inspiration from the happy meal box in designing some of their children-oriented restaurants. Some restaurants even include plush couches and fireplaces.

This emphasis on customer value and customization has provided McDonald's with a competitive advantage and a way to make a hamburger not just a hamburger, but an institution. Their overwhelming global campaign will keep people saying "I'm loving it" for many years to come.

www.mcdonalds.com, website visited June 12, 2014.

ditional collectivist and nature-oriented Chinese culture has a positive impact on Chinese consumers' attitude toward green purchases.

Most people are socialized to be part of the culture in which they grow up. The socialization process is so strong that even marketers may be influenced by their own learned values when trying to understand another culture. This is called the **self-reference criterion**, and it is not always acceptable to rely on it. For example, most people in the United States would not think twice about eating a candy bar as they walk down the street, but in Japan this is considered impolite. In China, when people approach a bus, the first person is expected to buy tickets for the group. It is easy to embarrass yourself and others in a foreign culture unless you take the time to understand it.

Because of people's tendency to use the self-reference criterion, it's often difficult to assess opportunities in other countries, but global success requires precisely that. McDonald's targets the same audience around the world — young families with children — but the basic concept must be "translated" into local conditions: In Singapore, you could try a burger served on toasted rice cakes instead of a bun, or visit Mexico to try Mc-Molletes — refried beans, cheese and pico de gallo on an English muffin.[47] Understanding different cultures has helped McDonald's establish itself in the new global market.

In a memorable article, Edward Hall notes that perceptions of time, space, property, friendships, agreements, and negotiations cause the greatest misunderstanding between people of different cultures.[48] In order to succeed as a global marketer, you need to acknowledge and understand these differences.

Self-Reference Criterion

The unconscious reliance on values gained from one's own socialization when trying to understand another culture.

In Mexico, McMolletes are a breakfast staple at McDonald's.

Perceptions of Time

It's extremely important to consider a culture's perception of time, which communicates several subtle points. For example, in some cultures the most significant decisions are given the greatest amount of time. In contrast, Americans tend to operate within deadlines, and time is a scarce resource to be used efficiently. In the United States, if visitors are kept waiting, then they infer that they are unimportant. In a Latin culture, schedules are not rigid, and it is acceptable to use time more flexibly. More recently, many Latin American countries have redefined time for business. In some cultures, a very long time may pass between customer awareness of a product and the actual purchase, something marketers need to plan for in these regions. In cultures in which decisions are made quickly, this time frame is usually much shorter.

Size and Space

In the United States, size is equated with importance; the larger and taller a building, the greater the degree of status represented. The dean of a college of business is likely to be located in a spacious office on the top floor; the university president is likely to have a larger office in a taller building. In contrast, the French try to place important executives close to the scene of action, where their influence can be most strongly felt. The distance between people during conversations also can be culturally related. In many Latin cultures, people show friendship by talking closely, sometimes within two or three inches of each other. In the U.S., a distance of three to five feet is usually considered respectful. Marketers must be sensitive to space when promoting products in different regions. In commercials or promotional materials, the wrong interpersonal distance among the actors or models could deliver the wrong message.

Negotiations and Agreements Business agreements may have different meanings in various parts of the world. In highly legalistic cultures, they must be written and signed prior to acceptance. In other cultures, legal documents are viewed as inconveniences; more important is a meeting of the minds, sealed with a handshake. When Americans consult a lawyer, visit a doctor or take a taxi, they assume the charge will be at the going rate, something that cannot be taken for granted in other cultures. For example, in the Middle East, it's best to settle the charge in advance or the person providing the service is likely to set an arbitrary price. It is important to know a culture's stance on payment and agreements when developing a pricing strategy for your products. Whereas a predetermined price is expected in the United States, bartering is part of the social process elsewhere, and a preset price upsets or offends consumers.

LEGAL/REGULATORY ENVIRONMENT

Legal / Regulatory Environment

International, federal, state, and local regulations and laws, the agencies that interpret and administer them, and the court system.

The **legal/regulatory environment** is comprised of international, federal, state and local regulations and laws, the agencies that interpret and administer them, and the court system. It also includes the ethical standards and theories that guide marketing decisions. This environment reflects long-standing political and economic philosophies and varies dramatically from one country or region to another. It indicates the general outlook of government toward business practices and ethical issues. It also includes the effect that legal/regulatory decisions can have on an organization, individuals, and society as a whole. Marketers need to be aware of this environment so they can estimate how tolerant or cooperative the government will be with their company's operations.

In the United States, several agencies are charged with the responsibility of regulating businesses to comply with the intentions of major laws, the most important of which are listed in Figure 3.6. These agencies must interpret laws and develop policies and procedures to gain compliance. In some cases, the agency only sets guidelines so businesses can self-regulate within them. Businesses that step out of line may be taken to court by the agency. In other

Consumer Products Safety Commission (CPSC)
• Enforces regulations to protect consumers from being harmed by products.

Environmental Protection Agency (EPA)
• Regulates business actions to prevent damage to the environment.

Federal Communication Commission (FCC)
• Regulates communications on telephone, radio, television, and other aspects including allocations of frequencies.

Federal Trade Commission (FTC)
• Enforces laws to prevent unfair or deceptive marketing practices.

Food and Drug Administration (FDA)
• Enforces laws to maintain safety in food and drug products.

Figure 3.6   Federal Agencies Regulating Marketing

cases, a company's product needs to obtain approval from an agency. For example, the Food and Drug Administration (FDA) must approve all drugs prior to their release in the United States.

Although the U.S. legal and regulatory sphere covers hundreds of specific practices, for our purposes these can be divided into four basic types: laws promoting competition, laws restricting big business, laws protecting consumers, and laws protecting the environment.

U.S. Laws Promoting Competition

During the 1800s and early 1900s, a few U.S. enterprises grew to the point of monopoly. Companies such as Standard Oil and Pennsylvania Railroad could exercise economic control over smaller firms, in many cases forcing them into bankruptcy by temporarily lowering prices. In 1890, due to a strong political movement led by Midwestern farmers, Congress passed the Sherman Antitrust Act, which prohibits business practices designed to create monopolies or restrict trade across state lines or internationally. The Sherman Antitrust Act laid the foundation for many related laws. The premise behind them is that fair competition allows more companies to serve the market, which in turn keeps prices down and provides more choices to consumers. As you can see from Figure 3.7, many laws since 1890 are designed to ensure fair competition.

Sherman Antitrust Act (1890)
Outlaws monopolies and any business practice that restricts interstate or international commerce.

Federal Trade Commission Act (1914)
Declares as unlawful "unfair methods of competition in or affecting commerce, and unfair or deceptive acts or practices in or affecting commerce."

Clayton Act (1914)
Prohibits mergers and acquisitions that may "substantially lessen competition or tend to create a monopoly"; outlaws tie-in and exclusive dealing arrangements; allows violators to be held criminally liable.

Robinson-Patman Act (1936)
Developed primarily to protect small retailers. Amends the Clayton Act. Makes it illegal to sell "commodities of like grade and quality" to competing buyers at different prices if it will restrict competition. Also makes it illegal knowingly to receive an illegal price break.

Miller-Tydings Act (1937)
Protects interstate fair-trade (price fixing) agreements from antitrust prosecution.

Wheeler-Lea Act (1938)
Outlaws the pursuit of unfair or deceptive practices or actions.

Antimerger Act (1950)
Prevents corporate acquisitions or mergers that may substantially reduce competition.

Figure 3.7 U.S. Laws Promoting Competition

U.S. Laws Restricting Big Business

The U.S. approach to competition has tended to restrict company size and power. The Federal Trade Commission (FTC) has explored numerous accusations of monopolistic control. For example, Johnson & Johnson proposed a $16.6 billion acquisition of Pfizer's health-care division. The proposal underwent extensive review by the FTC for a possible violation of the Federal Trade Commission Act and monopolistic activity. The FTC ruled that the acquisition would be allowed.[49]

Some countries have laws that favor monopolies and cartels, which are outlawed in the United States. A **cartel** is a group of businesses or nations working together to control the price and output of a particular product. The U.S. government has recognized that laws intended to provide a fair environment for domestic competition can be restrictive and sometimes put American companies at competitive disadvantages in the global market. In the late 1970s, the Department of Justice began to lighten its enforcement of traditional antitrust laws.

Cartel

A group of businesses or nations that work together to control the price and production of a particular product.

U.S. Laws Protecting Consumers

Recall that the early economic philosophy in the United States was typically caveat emptor: "Let the buyer beware." Essentially, consumers were responsible for protecting themselves against the unscrupulous acts of sellers. The Pure Food and Drug Act and the Meat Inspection Act, both introduced in 1906, were the first attempts to protect consumers. For four decades, regulations concentrated on making the food supply safe. Then they extended to regulating products such as automobiles and toys, and eventually protecting consumers from misleading and deceptive advertising. By 1960, the consumer movement was so powerful that President Kennedy issued the Consumer Bill of Rights. This enforced the idea that it was not up to the consumer alone to assess the quality and safety of a product. The Consumer Bill of Rights guaranteed consumers:

Pure Food and Drug Act (1906)
Regulates the manufacture and labeling of food and drugs.

Meat Inspection Act (1906)
Permits federal inspection of companies selling meat across state line and allows for enforcement of sanitary standards.

Lanham Trademark Act (1946)
Outlaws misrepresentation of goods and services sold across state lines; forces trademarks to be distinctive.

Automobile Information Disclosure Act (1958)
Forces auto manufacturers to disclose the suggested retail price of their new cars, which keeps car dealers from inflating prices.

National Traffic and Safety Act (1958)
Provides a set of automobile and tire safety standards.

Fair Packaging and Labeling Act (1966)
Permits the FTC and FDA to create standards for packaging and labeling content.

Child Protection Act (1966)
Makes illegal the sale of dangerous toys and children's articles as well as products creating a thermal, mechanical, or electrical danger.

Federal Cigarette Labeling and Advertising Act (1967)
Requires cigarette manufacturers to label cigarettes as dangerous. Outlaws use of television media for cigarette advertisements.

Truth-in-Lending Act (1968)
Also called the Consumer Credit Protection Act. Forces lenders to disclose in writing, before the credit transaction: (1) the actual cash price, (2) the required down payment, (3) how much cash is being financed, (4) how much the loan will actually cost, (5) estimated annual interest rate, and (6) penalty for late payments or loan default.

Fair Credit Reporting Act (1970)
Allows consumers to see free of charge a copy of their credit report. Forces credit reporting agencies to remove any false information. Protects the confidentiality of the consumer.

Consumer Product Safety Act (1972)
Created the Consumer Product Safety Commission. It collects and disperses information on all consumer goods except automobiles, food, and a few others. It also has the authority to develop and enforce product standards, when deemed necessary.

Consumer Goods Pricing Act (1975)
Prevents retailers and manufacturers from entering into certain types of price maintenance agreements.

Magnuson-Moss Warranty/FTC Improvement Act (1975)
Requires the company or individual who offers a warranty to explain fully what the warranty covers and what its limitations are. This information allows consumers to file a lawsuit if the warranty is breached.

Equal Credit Opportunity Act (1975)
Forces creditors to disclose the reason for any credit denial. Credit connot be denied on the basis of sex, marital status, race, national origin, region, age, or receipt of public assistance.

Fair Debt Collection Practice Act (1978)
Prohibits debt collectors from using harassment, abuse, or deceit when collecting a debt.

Toy Safety Act (1984)
Allows the government immediately to remove dangerous toys from the market.

Figure 3.8 Consumer Protection Laws

1. The right to choose freely from a variety of goods and services.

2. The right to be informed about specific products and services so that responsible purchase decisions can be made.

3. The right to be heard when voicing opinions about products and services offered.

4. The right to be safe from defective or harmful products and services when used properly.

In 1959, the FTC held a landmark conference at which consumer action groups and businesses discussed harmful practices. This activity led to the FTC assuming responsibility for the enforcement of truth-in-packaging and truth-in-lending laws. The FTC tackled tobacco advertising, forcing manufacturers to include a strong warning about the dangers of cigarette smoking in ads and on packages. Shortly thereafter, the Supreme Court ruled it illegal to create advertising gimmicks that would mislead the public or exaggerate product benefits.

Today the FTC and the FDA aggressively focus on the tobacco industry. In the late 1990s, the FTC investigated the R. J. Reynolds Tobacco Company for unfair advertising with its Joe Camel campaign, allegedly aimed at minors. The campaign was part of the industry's $4.8 billion annual expenditure on ads and promotions.[50] R. J. Reynolds agreed to drop the Joe Camel cartoon figure from such items as hats, lighters, bags and T-shirts, and it agreed not to use the character in billboard advertising or in the sponsorship of entertainment events. Recently two other tobacco companies, Phillip Morris and Brown & Williamson, agreed to reduce cigarette advertising in magazines read by teens. All told, the companies pulled ads from 42 magazines with more than 2 million readers under 18 years of age.[51] The FTC also examines the Internet for tobacco- and alcohol-related websites that may violate advertising guidelines.

There are numerous consumer protection laws (see a partial list in Figure 3.8), and marketers need to know which ones affect their company. Consumer safety legislation has a direct effect on important marketing decisions, such as product design, label information and design, and advertising claims. Interest in consumer safety has provided opportunities to marketing as well: It resulted in the development of seat belts, air bags, shatterproof windshields, antilock brakes, and other features. But marketers need to manage these carefully. Consider the effect of air bags on marketing in the auto industry: Although air bags have saved approximately 17,000 lives since 1990, they have caused at least 256 deaths, 135 of whom were children.[52] As a result, Ford Motor Company was the first to introduce less forceful air bags in 1998. Since the 2006 model year, all passenger cars and light-duty trucks are equipped with sensors that identify children and very small adults and don't deploy the airbag, or do so less forcefully. The Buick Lucerne uses airbag technology that identifies both size and position of the occupant and adjusts the airbag's size and force accordingly.[53]

U.S. Laws Protecting the Environment By the early 1960s, people were consuming the world's natural resources at an alarming rate. The most basic resources—air and water—were often so polluted that they were unfit to sustain life. Although little was done internationally, the U.S. Congress enacted the National Environmental Policy Act in 1969 to direct environmental protection activities. The following year, the Environmental Protection Agency (EPA) was formed so that one agency would be responsible for enforcing all federal environmental regulation.

U.S. companies are required to adequately disclose potential environmental threats from their operations. The EPA maintains that those responsible for environmental contamination must pay for the cleanup and subsequently protect citizens' health. The EPA's Water Alliances for Volunteer Efficiency (WAVE) seeks to encourage commercial businesses and institutions to reduce water consumption while simultaneously increasing efficiency, profitability and competitiveness. WAVE is a part of EPA's long-standing effort to prevent pollution and reduce demand on America's water and energy infrastructure.[54]

Environmental groups such as the Audubon Society, Greenpeace and the Sierra Club have drawn attention to numerous environmental disasters and are actively seeking remedies and legislation to repair or avert damage.

ETHICAL ENVIRONMENT

Questions of ethics are not always straightforward. In many countries bribery is regarded as highly unethical, but in others it is considered standard business practice. There is an important difference between what is legal and what is ethical. To determine legality, you must examine the relevant law. If the meaning is unclear, then a court may have to interpret it. Without a precedent, you may have to assess whether the action would be deemed legal or illegal.

Ethical issues are not so easily defined. Is it ethical for a pharmaceutical company to charge a price for a new drug that is much higher than the cost to produce it? After all, the company has poured millions into R&D and is trying to recoup its investment. Yet the high price makes the drug unaffordable to many people who desperately need it to survive. Is the drug company acting unethically?

The matrix in Figure 3.9 shows that marketing decisions may fall into one of four categories: legal and ethical, illegal and ethical, legal and unethical, or illegal and unethical.

	Legal	**Illegal**
Ethical	Market FDA-approved cold medicine	Market a safe AIDS vaccine not yet approved by the FDA
Unethical	Market a harmful drug banned by the FDA in a country with no drug review agencies	Market contraband drugs

Figure 3.9   Ethics Situations

The appropriate behavior is easy to assess when the proposed action is clearly legal and ethical (acceptable) or clearly illegal and unethical (unacceptable). However, legality and ethics are open to different interpretations, so marketers must be sensitive to issues in both categories.

Perhaps the most difficult circumstances occur when legal and ethical standards conflict. Some people place more weight on the ethical side ("Should we do it?"), others emphasize the legal ("Can we do it?"), while still others believe it is best to altogether avoid any actions that are either illegal or unethical. Most laws that affect business are interpreted in the courts, which set precedents to be followed. Every legislative session can create new laws that lead to new regulations, which often require new court decisions to set new precedents. As with every other environment, the legal field is constantly changing and marketers need to keep in step with it.

Many companies have developed written guidelines for employees. This helps ensure that everyone in the company is following the same set of ethical standards. For instance, eBay took action against the unethical slaughter of endangered elephants by banning all ivory from its website. Senior regulatory counsel Jack Christin from eBay's blog "eBay Ink" explained, "Due to the unique nature of eBay's global online marketplace and the growing complexity of the rules and regulations surrounding the sale of legal ivory, we will be moving from a ban on cross-border sales to rolling out a complete ban of the sale of ivory on eBay."[55]

The American Marketing Association also has a code of ethics. The code goes beyond stating simply "Follow the law." It impresses upon marketers the importance of being honest and acting with integrity. It covers basic responsibilities, what a customer should be able to expect from an exchange, and ethics surrounding the marketing mix areas of product, promotion, place, and price—as well as in marketing research and relationships with others.

Members of the American Marketing Association (AMA) are committed to ethical professional conduct. They have joined together in subscribing to the following Code of Ethics.

To protect the endangered and protected species, eBay banned the sale of ivory.

ETHICAL NORMS

As marketers, we must:

- Do no harm. This means consciously avoiding harmful actions or omissions by embodying high ethical standards and adhering to all applicable laws and regulations in the choices we make.

- Foster trust in the marketing system. This means striving for good faith and fair dealing so as to contribute toward the efficacy of the exchange process as well as avoiding deception in product design, pricing, communication and delivery of distribution.

- Embrace ethical values. This means building relationships and enhancing consumer confidence in the integrity of marketing by affirming these core values: honesty, responsibility, fairness, respect, transparency and citizenship.

ETHICAL VALUES

Honesty — to be forthright in dealings with customers and stakeholders. To this end, we will:

- Strive to be truthful in all situations and at all times.

- Offer products of value that do what we claim in our communications.

- Stand behind our products if they fail to deliver their claimed benefits.

- Honor our explicit and implicit commitments and promises.

Responsibility — to accept the consequences of our marketing decisions and strategies. To this end, we will:

- Strive to serve the needs of customers.

- Avoid using coercion with all stakeholders.

- Acknowledge the social obligations to stakeholders that come with increased marketing and economic power.

- Recognize our special commitments to vulnerable market segments such as children, seniors, the economically impoverished, market illiterates and others who may be substantially disadvantaged.

- Consider environmental stewardship in our decision-making.

Fairness — to balance justly the needs of the buyer with the interests of the seller. To this end, we will:

- Represent products in a clear way in selling, advertising and other forms of communication; this includes the avoidance of false, misleading and deceptive promotion.

- Reject manipulations and sales tactics that harm customer trust.

- Refuse to engage in price fixing, predatory pricing, price gouging or "bait-and-switch" tactics.

- Avoid knowing participation in conflicts of interest.

- Seek to protect the private information of customers, employees and partners.

Respect — to acknowledge the basic human dignity of all stakeholders. To this end, we will:

- Value individual differences and avoid stereotyping customers or depicting demographic groups (e.g., gender, race, sexual orientation) in a negative or dehumanizing way.

- Listen to the needs of customers and make all reasonable efforts to monitor and improve their satisfaction on an ongoing basis.

- Make every effort to understand and respectfully treat buyers, suppliers, intermediaries and distributors from all cultures.

- Acknowledge the contributions of others, such as consultants, employees and co-workers, to marketing endeavors.

- Treat everyone, including our competitors, as we would wish to be treated.

Transparency — to create a spirit of openness in marketing operations. To this end, we will:

- Strive to communicate clearly with all constituencies.

- Accept constructive criticism from customers and other stakeholders.

- Explain and take appropriate action regarding significant product or service risks, component substitutions or other foreseeable eventualities that could affect customers or their perception of the purchase decision.

- Disclose list prices and terms of financing as well as available price deals and adjustments.

Citizenship — to fulfill the economic, legal, philanthropic and societal responsibilities that serve stakeholders. To this end, we will:

- Strive to protect the ecological environment in the execution of marketing campaigns.

- Give back to the community through volunteerism and charitable donations.

- Contribute to the overall betterment of marketing and its reputation.

- Urge supply chain members to ensure that trade is fair for all participants, including producers in developing countries.

"Statement of Ethics," AMA Publishing, www.ama.org, website visited June 12, 2014.

MARKETING E-COMMERCE

Business-To-Business (B2B) E-Commerce

Trade involving Internet sales in which businesses sell to other businesses, including governments and organizations.

Business-To-Consumer (B2C) E-Commerce

Trade involving businesses selling to consumers over the Internet.

Internet marketing can be divided into two sectors. **Business-to-consumer (B2C) e-commerce** is trade involving businesses selling to consumers over the Internet. **Business-to-business (B2B) e-commerce** is trade involving Internet sales in which businesses sell to other businesses, including governments and organizations.

The U.S. consumer retail e-commerce sales (e-sales) is increasing by approximately 14 percent annually, much higher than the total retail sales of 4 percent. The mobile e-commerce market is quickly making a statement too. Recent forecasts predict global e-commerce sales made on mobile devices will top $638 billion in 2018. To put that in perspective, that was roughly the entire size of the world's e-commerce market in 2013. Tablet devices, not smartphones, are predicted to contribute the majority of those sales.[56]

The dramatic online consumer spending increase also has an direct impact on the B2B sector. The typical B2B buyer is also a consumer buyer in his or her personal life. They are aware of Amazon, Zappos, eBay, and other e-commerce giants. With those positive and common online experiences in their personal life, they begin to expect the same experiences at the workplace. When the office runs low on toner, would you rather call vendors for pricing, search dusty catalogs and phone in orders, or jump on Amazon to have it at your office door the next day? B2B sellers must be very aware of these shifts, and adapt as quickly and effectlively as the B2C sellers or they could miss out on huge opportunies.[57] There is no doubt that both the B2B and B2C e-commerce markets demand serious attention.

Cloud computing has quickly impacted B2B and B2C e-commerce. Cloud computing is a general term used to incorporate a variety of information services and applications remotely operated by users across the web. It allows companies to access scalable computing power and intelligent networks, while reducing labor needs, physical space and energy consumption.[58] Salesforce.com sells its customer relationship management (CRM) system over the cloud, eliminating the requirement for businesses to download bulky software and create in-house databases. Other companies have created cloud computing products, including Amazon Web Services, Google AppEngine and Microsoft Azure, Zoho, and Rackspace, offering both B2B and B2C solutions.[59]

Internet Marketing Economy

All organizations that are set up to conduct commercial transactions with business partners and buyers over the Internet.

THE STRUCTURE OF INTERNET MARKETING

Most organizations benefit from the Internet by having a web presence and nearly every winning organization can be reached via the web in one form or another. Organizations that are set up to conduct commercial transactions over the Internet are part of e-commerce, which we term the **Internet marketing economy**.[60] As shown in Figure 3.10, the Internet marketing economy has three components, each with a different role: web portals, web market makers, and web product-service providers.[61] Together they provide a market space that is globally expansive and personalized.

Type of Player	Role	Business-to-Consumer	Business-to-Business
Web Portals	Bring together information for consumers or businesses and direct them to the Web sites of product-service providers and intermediaries	Google Yahoo! MSN	ZDNet Marketsite
Web Market Makers	Facilitate transactions between buyers and sellers by providing information about each party and by helping to ensure secure, low-cost exchanges	Ebay Priceline Travelocity	Bloomberg ChemConnect NetBuy
Web Product-Service Providers	Deal directly with consumers in an Internet transaction and customize processes to accommodate online customers	Amazon Barnes&Noble Toys-R-Us	Cisco Dell Compaq

Figure 3.10 The Structure of E-Commerce
Source: Based on California Management Review, Vols. 1 & 2, No. 4.

Web Portals

The purpose of **web portals** is to direct consumers or businesses to websites of product providers or intermediaries. They offer information and web linkages that enable consumers and businesses to connect with the right commercial sites for their needs. Good portals are valuable because they remain up-to-date with the constantly changing web and assist users with the sorting and matching process.

Web Portals

Organizations that direct consumers or businesses to the websites of product-service providers and intermediaries.

Portals allow users to sort information so that companies, products and messages can be accessed in useful ways. Marketers can make the most of this resource by classifying their website with appropriate key words, descriptors and categories. That begins by selecting a domain name that labels an organization's Internet presence, much like branding is used to identify products. Each domain has a numerical address, and a company may use the same address for several domain names or split them up. For example, Coke can be reached at www.cocacola.com, www.coca-cola.com, www.coke.com or by specifying the numerical IP address (216.64.210.28) directly.

Portals can be powerful search engines, such as Google, that help users reach the sites they want. These sites are usually owned by web market makers or by web product-service providers. Google has expanded its brand to include a suite of online applications tailored to businesses, non-profit organizations, educational institutions and the government. More than 5 million businesses use the cloud-based Google Apps, creating a substantial B2B sector for Google. These applications, such as Google Docs, Google Calendar and Google Drive, utilize the cloud by allowing users to interact and collaborate in real time over the Internet. This has tremendous business implications, because it enables a team of employees from all over the world to complete projects in real time without physically being in the same place. Many universities have adopted Google Apps to comply with students' demanding schedules and lack of time to meet outside of the classroom.[62]

Web Market Makers

Web Market Makers

Organizations that help buyers and sellers by providing information about each party and by facilitating secure, low-cost exchanges.

Web Market Makers The purpose of **web market makers** is to help buyers and sellers obtain information about each other and to facilitate secure, low-cost exchanges. Market makers have a great deal of knowledge about domains and are usually specialized in certain product types. They also add an element of security and trust to the business transaction. When eBay acquired PayPal nearly a decade ago, it quickly became the preferred payment processor for eBay transactions. PayPal provides a safe, efficient and trusted way to transfer money online.[63]

In the business-to-business arena, market makers include organizations like Chendex (chemicals), HoustonStreet.com (electricity), FastParts (electronic components) and BigBuyer.com (small business products). They can organize auctions, set up exchanges and integrate product and service catalogs from several suppliers.[64] In addition, they can offer **virtual trade shows**, that is, online sites that display new products and technologies from several suppliers to current or potential customers. Industry associations, trade associations or companies sponsor these trade shows. This versatility has experts predicting business-to-business market makers will experience tremendous growth.

Virtual Trade Shows

Online sites that display new products and technologies from several suppliers to current and potential customers.

Web Product-Service Providers

Companies that customize processes to accommodate online customers.

Web Product-Service Providers

Web Product-Service Providers Because they deal directly with customers, **web product-service providers** customize processes to accommodate online transactions. They go to great lengths to make online buying a major aspect of their business. This doesn't include companies that make minor changes like adding a "buy online" option to their website; rather, these companies adjust their entire infrastructure so that web-based business can become an integral part of their marketing strategy. These providers connect directly with customers, and the Internet becomes a business channel. Popular organizations in this category are Amazon for consumers and Dell for both businesses and consumers. Amazon, originally a marketplace for printed books, has transformed the way literature is read. Instead of letting books pile up on shelves, Amazon's Kindle e-reader allows readers to download entire books wirelessly from around the globe and read them on a screen. Some Kindle models weigh less than 6 ounces and can store around 1,500 books at a time.[65]

How the Structure Interacts

Figure 3.11 shows how consumers and businesses interact with the three major parts of the Internet marketing economy. Market makers and product-service providers gain the attention of customers by working with portals as well as through traditional efforts, such as advertising, personal selling and word of mouth. The revenue stream of a portal depends on how well it supports the web market makers and product-service providers. At the same time, market makers depend on product-service providers for items to sell, and product-service providers depend on market makers for many of their customers. All parties are roughly interdependent.

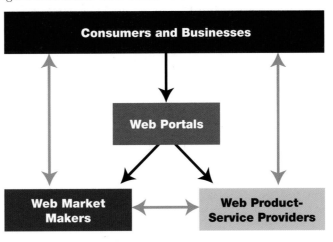

Figure 3.11   Participation in E-Commerce

Many new marketing companies have used the benefits of the Internet to establish themselves, but the online market is not without risks. Thousands of dot-com companies that boomed in the late '90s flopped soon after the turn of the century. Some companies like Google, Yahoo!, and Amazon emerged victoriously, but many simply failed.[66] Yet, Michael Krauss, a regular columnist for Marketing News, notes that traditional brick-and-mortar firms are becoming increasingly aware of the Internet marketing economy. "The dinosaurs are starting to dance," he says, mentioning such alliances as Walmart and America Online, Kmart and Yahoo!, and Best Buy and Microsoft.[67]

VALUE OF THE INTERNET TO BUYERS AND SELLERS

E-commerce is gaining ground because, as Figure 3.12 indicates, both buyers and sellers receive great value from it. Compared to traditional channels, buyers get better information, greater convenience, wider and more customized selection, and better prices. Marketers have access to more customers, reduced supply-chain costs, efficient two-way communication with customers, and the ability to personalize messages and products.

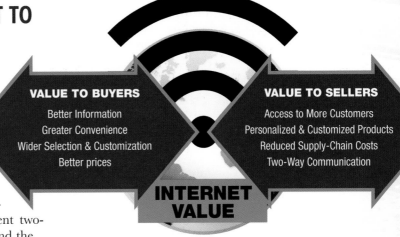

VALUE TO BUYERS
Better Information
Greater Convenience
Wider Selection & Customization
Better prices

VALUE TO SELLERS
Access to More Customers
Personalized & Customized Products
Reduced Supply-Chain Costs
Two-Way Communication

INTERNET VALUE

Figure 3.12   Internet Marketing Benefits

Value to Buyers *Better Information* The Internet enables buyers to obtain a

great deal of information about products, including availability, costs, attributes and use instructions, as well as information about manufacturers and sellers of particular brands. Some Internet services perform the difficult task of comparison shopping, helping users find the right product configuration at the lowest price. In many cases, before selecting an item, potential buyers can even see other customers' reactions to products. At Amazon.com, readers can browse customer reviews based on a five-star system prior to making a buying decision.

Greater Convenience Shopping at home or in the office via computer reduces the amount of travel and time associated with in-store purchases. Buyers in rural or remote communities benefit by saving a lengthy trip to a store. In urban and suburban settings, buyers can avoid traffic congestion, and long checkout lines. In addition, savings in gasoline and other vehicle costs can be substantial, not to mention the social benefits of less auto pollution and congestion.

Wider Selection and Customization Online buyers can choose from a wide selection of products, and if that's not enough, they can customize their own. Retail

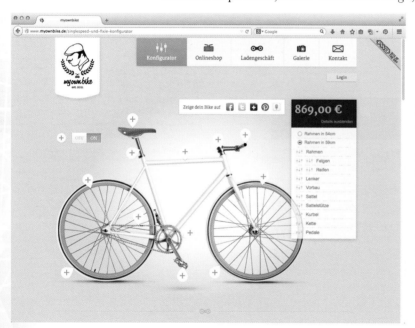

outlets may carry only certain brands and sizes, but online sources offer all possible configurations for buyers to compare. Even scarce products, such as an obscure book, can be found very quickly. If the book's in print, you'll likely find it on Amazon. At the same time, more customization is possible, because buyers can interface with a seller's manufacturing facilities, which in turn are networked with suppliers, so sellers can build or manufacture on demand. UberPrints.com will print customer designed t-shirts, hats, and more at increadibly low prices and no minimum order. Many custom bicycle shops allow users to build their own bike online and deliver the finished product to their door in weeks or even days.

Better Prices Due to the efficiency and competitive nature of the Internet marketing economy, shoppers may benefit from lower prices. One company asks: "Would you like to buy this camera [a popular brand is shown] at $169 or $149 or at $129? Shop at MySimon.com." Internet retailers tend to be driven by price because many buyers go online specifically to save. The pioneers of e-commerce used a low-price strategy to attract business in a then-unfamiliar market, and this strategy has continued, because online shoppers have become accustomed to the competitive prices.

Values to Sellers *Access to More Customers* On the seller side of the

market, Internet businesses have access to a world of customers. A firm in Chicago can communicate with a potential customer in India as easily as with one next door. E-commerce has grown by leaps and bounds, which means that more businesses and customers are being brought together in more uniquely personal ways than could be imagined a decade ago. With the advent of smartphones, staying connected is easier than ever. The computing that people used to do at their desks can increasingly be done from anywhere with the help of mobile applications. The Apple App

Store has more than 1.2 million applications available, from simple games to time-management helpers to guitar tuners. It made $10 billion in 2013 alone, and there are expectations for even larger profits in the coming years.[68]

There are more than 2.9 billion people around the world with Internet access, penetrating 40 percent of the world population. That's a major increase from the mere one percent penetration when many of you were born 18-19 years ago.[69] Obviously, not all users make web purchases. In fact, only 15 percent of holiday sales in 2013 were made online.[70] Many shoppers go online to do research, but still prefer to go to shops in order to make purchases. In the reverse scenario, some shoppers will go to stores to try on clothing or shoes, or check out high-end items, then buy them for less online, in a practice known as "showrooming." Showrooming is particularly common for items $100 or more, and has hit appliance and electronics stores particularly hard.[71]

Personalized and Customized Products E-commerce makes it easier for sellers to cater to customer needs. This can be done through product representation and product configuration.[72] Product representation refers to how the product is presented to customers. With the web it is possible to use the customer's name in a communication or arrange information about the product to reflect more closely the potential buyer's preferences. A more complex customization occurs with product configuration, which promotes selected products or brands directly to a consumer or adjusts attributes to user specifications. In addition, buyers themselves can make adjustments online. For example, eBay has partnered with the U.S. Postal Service to provide purchasers with a new packaging option for priority mail. This new priority packaging, free to eBay customers through its website, uses an environmentally intelligent design.[73]

Reduced Supply Chain Costs E-commerce reduces not only the **supply chain costs** associated with procuring goods and services from suppliers but also the costs of distributing products to consumers. Savings occur throughout the supply chain, including lower inventory costs due to better demand forecasting, streamlined manufacturing, warehousing, and transportation. Better communication among all members of the value chain reduces errors. Dell has been successful in the computer server market by integrating its supply chain through the Internet. For example, Dell allows purchasers to specify precisely which computer configuration they want by providing the option to "Build Your Own" computer.[74] All members of Dell's supply chain are connected online and are given intensive information linked to customer demand. This allows each supplier to operate efficiently while knowing the context of the customer's requests and supplying precisely what Dell customers want.

The web itself is not a supply chain, but a marketing channel used to enhance companies' supply chains. What makes this channel unique is that so many customers are within a few keystrokes of a shopping experience. Because many e-commerce companies take advantage of the latest technologies, their supply chains tend to be very efficient.

Two-Way Communication A significant benefit of the Internet for marketers is how efficiently it allows two-way communication and customization to take place. It costs less than telephone or mail contact and is significantly less expensive and more convenient than face-to-face communication. This technology is as revolutionary for communication today as the telephone, radio and television were when they were introduced. The web wasn't initially designed with that purpose; it began as a way to present and send information, such as online newspapers or reports. Then it allowed access on demand to all sorts of data, helping users find information among the most widely ranging sources imaginable. In the most significant communication advance to date, however, the web can personalize contact (between two people or millions). This two-way, multiple-person communication enables marketers to create dialogues among consumers quickly and inexpensively, so marketers can learn con-

Supply Chain Costs

Costs associated with procuring goods and services from suppliers and with distributing products from businesses to consumers.

sumers' views on products and issues in real time.

Web communication also facilitates personalization and customization of both products and messages. Marketers can easily collect opinions and test reactions to marketing activities. They can also collect data on a buyer's previous purchases, which reveals the buyer's preferences and buying patterns.

Customers can order, customize and pay for items online. Perhaps even more importantly, there are opportunities for two-way dialogue about product attributes, ordering and customer service. The amount and type of communication, including product options and pricing, is extremely malleable. This kind of contact helps marketers develop and maintain customer loyalty.

CHAPTER SUMMARY

Objective 1: Describe the marketing environment and the use of environmental scanning.

The marketing environment comprises all factors that affect a business. The factors are divided into two groups — the microenvironment and the global macroenvironment. The microenvironment includes factors that marketers interact with regularly. Consequently, the microenvironment influences and is influenced by marketing. The global macroenvironment includes factors that marketers must take into account when making decisions. However, marketers seldom influence these factors. Together, the environments can facilitate or inhibit organizations from reaching their objectives. Proactive organizations anticipate changes in the marketing environment and plan accordingly. Organizations use environmental scanning in order to keep up with environmental changes. The web is a great technological tool to help maintain currency in knowledge of the environment.

Objective 2: Understand how the roles that stakeholders play influence the accomplishment of marketing objectives. Know why marketing must address stakeholder desires when making decisions.

Stakeholders are important parts of the microenvironment and directly participate in accomplishing the organization's goals. They include owners, employees, suppliers, intermediaries and action groups. Stakeholders participate with the organization in order to accomplish their own goals; consequently, marketers must take their desires into consideration when making decisions. Because owners are entitled to a fair return on their investment, companies need to make a substantial profit, and nonprofit organizations must accomplish the goals their owners (sponsors) intend. Employees are also important; happy employees produce happy customers. Suppliers provide necessary services, raw materials and components. They also provide technology in specialized areas. Suppliers have a dramatic influence on your customers. Intermediaries help move products between you and your customers. They often contact customers directly. Since they represent your organization, you must carefully interface with them. Action groups are "watchdogs" that keep the interests of the environment and people

in balance with profit seeking. They can help marketers interface better with society. Marketers must address stakeholders' desires, because stakeholders support marketers in order to attain their goals. In turn, marketers depend on stakeholders to accomplish their organization's objectives.

Objective 3: Be able to integrate an understanding of industry competition into environmental analysis.

An understanding of industry competition provides an integrated picture about the major forces that determine competitive intensity. Competition involves single competitors and groups of company types that compete. We look at the rivalry among existing firms to understand one-on-one competition. Potential competitors are also viewed, because firms enter and exit industries. At the same time, substitute products can play a role, especially when new technologies bring new ways to perform old functions. The bargaining power of buyers and suppliers determines how a company competes. Suppliers have more power when there are few suppliers and many buyers. All of these aspects of industry competition need to be understood in order to build appropriate marketing strategies.

Objective 4: Synthesize aspects of the global macroenvironment, including technological, economic, demographic, cultural and legal/regulatory elements, in order to be in step with long-term trends.

The global macroenvironment is being influenced by many forces. The technological environment provides knowledge and tools that companies can acquire to produce better products. By phasing in new technology, progressive companies stay abreast of the best ways to create customer value. Economic factors are also important. Changes in income and spending power and other factors help determine which countries have the ability to purchase. The world has three major trading areas. The regions offer large markets, but they also compete against one another. The natural resources environment also comes into play. It provides raw materials and must be protected. Global demographics are changing. Shifts in population density and dispersion are important, as are age shifts. It is important to grasp the cultural environment and to view things from other perspectives. The values, beliefs and behaviors f others may differ from your own. Finally, the legal/regulatory environment is complex. Laws must be interpreted and followed. They help promote competition, influence business size, protect customers and protect the environment.

Objective 5: Recognize the importance of ethics and guides to ethical behavior.

Marketers often face ethical dilemmas, particularly when legal and ethical standards conflict. Many companies have developed codes of ethics for their employees to help ensure that everyone in the company is following the same standards. The American Marketing Association has a code of ethics that covers the basic responsibilities of marketers in each of the areas in which they are likely to be active. It stresses the importance of fairness and integrity.

Objective 6: Understand the impact that e-commerce is making on the global business environment and understand the structure of Internet marketing.

Both business-to-consumer and business-to-business organizations are using the Internet increasingly. However, the business-to-business sector is growing faster. The Internet marketing economy is composed of three structural elements. Web portals direct consumers or businesses to websites of product providers or intermediaries. Web market makers help buyers and sellers enter into transactions on the web by providing information and making arrangements for selling and buying between parties. Web product-service providers deal directly with customers utilizing special technologies developed to facilitate sales over the Internet. These three entities interact to provide a viable infrastructure to conduct marketing over the Internet in several types of marketspaces, including virtual shopping malls and virtual trade shows. The Internet marketing economy is growing because it offers great value for buyers as well as marketers.

REVIEW YOUR UNDERSTANDING

1. What is environmental scanning and what technology is being used for it today?
2. What is the microenvironment and what are its elements?
3. What is the global macroenvironment and what are its elements?
4. Who are stakeholders and why are they important? List five different types of stakeholders.
5. What are the elements of industry competition? Describe each.
6. Why is the technological environment important?
7. What are the elements of the economic environment? List three aspects that are influencing global marketing.
8. What are the three major trading blocs in the world economy?
9. What demographic trends are influencing marketing?
10. What is the self-reference criterion? What are some cultural differences to be aware of?
11. What are the types of laws that affect marketing?
12. What is the difference between unethical and illegal behavior?

DISCUSSION OF CONCEPTS

1. Suppose that IBM and Microsoft announced plans to merge into one company. Would U.S. laws allow this to happen? Why? Do you think that other countries around the world would have the same reaction?
2. What is culture, and how does it affect marketing? Can you think of any products that are successful in the United States but would fail in Japan because of cultural differences?
3. In the 1980s, McDonald's discontinued the use of Styrofoam containers for its sandwiches. What other changes have occurred recently in the natural resources environment? What types of legislation do you expect in the future? How would that legislation affect marketing?
4. Do you think that General Motors should invest a significant amount of money in research and development projects? Why or why not?
5. In recent years, discount stores such as Walmart and Kmart have become extremely large and powerful. How does this affect industry structure and competitive intensity?
6. As the director of marketing for Dow Chemical Company, you are required to interact regularly with a number of different publics. List these publics, the concerns that each might have, and how you would address each of those concerns.
7. What effect do you expect the new Euro have on trade among the three superblocs? Which trading relationships will be most affected? In what ways?
8. Which do you feel is more important — ethics or the law? Why?

KEY TERMS & DEFINITIONS

1. **Action Group:** A number of people who support some cause in the interest of consumers or environmental safety.
2. **Age cohort:** A group of people close in age who have been shaped by their generation's experience with the media, peers, events and society at large.
3. **Business-to-business (B2B) e-commerce:** Trade involving Internet sales in which businesses sell to other businesses, including governments and organizations.
4. **Business-to-consumer (B2C) e-commerce:** Trade involving businesses selling to consumers over the Internet.
5. **Cartel:** A group of businesses or nations that work together to control the price and production of a particular product.
6. **Consolidated metropolitan statistical area (CMSA):** Two or more overlapping urban communities with a combined population of at least 1 million.
7. **Cultural environment:** The learned values, beliefs, language, symbols and patterns of behavior shared by people in a society and passed on from generation to generation.
8. **Demographic environment:** The statistical data used to describe a population.
9. **Discretionary income:** The amount of money consumers have left after paying taxes and purchasing necessities.
10. **Disposable income:** The income consumers have left after paying taxes.
11. **Economic environment:** The financial and natural resources available to consumers, businesses and countries.
12. **Environmental scanning:** Collecting and analyzing information about the marketing environment in order to detect important changes or trends that can affect a company's strategy.
13. **Global macroenvironment:** The large external influences considered vital to long-term decisions but not directly affected by the company itself.
14. **Gross domestic product (GDP):** The total market value of all goods and services produced by a country in a single year.
15. **Intermediaries:** Stakeholders who move products from the manufacturer to the final user.
16. **Internet marketing economy:** All organizations that are set up to conduct commercial transactions with business partners and buyers over the Internet.
17. **Legal/regulatory environment:** International, federal, state, and local regulations and laws, the agencies that interpret and administer them, and the court system.
18. **Maastricht Treaty:** Consists of 282 directives that eliminate border controls and custom duties among members of the European Union.
19. **Marketing environment:** The sum of all the factors that affect a business.
20. **Metropolitan statistical area (MSA):** A stand-alone population center, unlinked to other cities, that has more than 50,000 people.
21. **Microenvironment:** The forces close to a company that influence how it connects with customers.
22. **Population density:** The concentration of people within some unit of measure, such as per square mile or per square kilometer.
23. **Self-reference criterion:** The unconscious reliance on values gained from one's own socialization when trying to understand another culture.
24. **Spending power:** The ability of the population to purchase goods and services.
25. **Stakeholder:** A group that can influence or be influenced by the firm's actions.
26. **Substitute product:** Any good or service that performs the same function or provides the same benefit as an existing one.
27. **Suppliers:** Organizations that provide a company with necessary services, raw materials or components.
28. **Supply chain costs:** Costs associated with procuring goods and services from suppliers and with distributing products from businesses to consumers.
29. **Technological environment:** The total body of knowledge available for development, manufacturing and marketing of products and services.
30. **Urbanization:** The shift of population from rural to urban areas.
31. **Virtual trade shows:** Online sites that display new products and technologies from several suppliers to current and potential customers.
32. **Web market makers:** Organizations that help buyers and sellers by providing information about each party and by facilitating secure, low-cost exchanges.
33. **Web portals:** Organizations that direct consumers or businesses to the websites of product-service providers and intermediaries.
34. **Web product-service providers:** Companies that customize processes to accommodate online customers.

REFERENCES

1. www.mars.com; www.mms.com, websites visited February 8, 2014.
2. "Gen Y's embrace of hybrids may be auto market's tipping point," http://news.msu.edu, January 18, 2012; www.toyota.com/entune, website visited August 13, 2014.
3. www.factiva.com and www.gegxs.com, websites visited February 22, 2014.
4. Sierra Club, www.sierraclub.org, website visited March 13, 2014.
5. Laczniak, Gene R., Murphy, Patrick E., Ethical Marketing Decisions: The Higher Road (Boston: Allyn & Bacon, 1993), pp. 14-15.
6. www.panerabread.com, website visited March 13, 2014.
7. Kiger, Patrick J., "Small Groups, Big Ideas," Workforce Management, February 27, 2006, pg. 1, 22-27.
8. Ford Sustainability Report, 2012-13, www.ford.com, website visited May 14, 2014.
9. Jonel Aleccia, "College Student Sickened in Big Beef Recall: Lawsuit," NBC News, May 27, 2014.
10. "'Our Choice': Al Gore's New Book Follows On 'Inconvenient Truth'," Huffington Post, www.huffingtonpost.com, website visited March 9, 2014.

11. www.allianceforclimateprotection.org, website visited March 9, 2014; www.algore.com, website visited March 9, 2014.

12. www.stopglobalwarming.com, website visited March 9, 2014.

13. Geewax, Marilyn, "Gay link prompts call for Walmart boycott," The Austin American-Statesman, November 11, 2006. Crary, David, "Conscrvatives abandon planned boycott of Walmart over outreach to gay groups," Associated Press, November 22, 2006.

14. "NFL Supports Breast Cancer Awareness Month with Third-Annual "A Crucial Catch" Campaign Benefitting American Cancer Society," www.nfl.com, September 28, 2011, website visited August 2014.

15. Anthony, C., Bendetto, D., Calantone, Roger, Schmidt, Jeffrey, "New Product Activities and Performance: The Moderating Role of Environmental Hostility," J Product Innovation Management, 1997.

16. "SWEETS and SNACKS 2012 Trends: Sharing Sweets, Mango Mania, Healthy Snacking," Business Journals, www.bizjournals.com, May 8, 2012.

17. John Kell, "McDonald's so far unfazed by latest entrant in breakfast war," Fortune, May 8, 2014.

18. "Corporate Fact Sheet," www.walmartfacts.com, website visisted February 22, 2014.

19. Merck Annual Report, www.merck.com, website visited February 22, 2014.

20. "Top 10 Semiconductor R&D Leaders Ranked for 2013," http://www.icinsights.com, February 25, 2014.

21. www.intel.com, website visited May 29, 2014.

22. Deal, Terrence E., Kennedy, Allan A., Corporate Cultures: The Ethics and Rituals of Corporate Life (Massachusetts: Addison-Wesley Publishing, 1982), pg. 8.

23. "Why Culture Is Key," Booz & Company, www.booz.com, Winter 2011, website visited August 13, 2012.

24. www.cia.gov, website visited May 29, 2014.

25. Ibid.

26. "What Latin America Can Teach Us," New York Times, www.nytimes.com, website visited May 29, 2014.

27. "Wealth distribution: Which nations are the best?," Rediff, www.rediff.com, website visited May 29, 2014.

28. "Becoming a Triad Power: The New Global Corporation," International Marketing Review, Autumn 1986.

29. www.cia.gov, website visited May 29, 2014.

30. www.europa.eu, website visited May 29, 2014.

31. www.apec.org, website visited May 29, 2014.

32. www.chinability.com/GDP.htm, website visited May 29, 2014.

33. "Japan's household savings deposits fall for 1st time since 1964," AFXNEWS.com, January 5, 2007.

34. "Fracking causes the most harm to Earth," Poughkeepsie Journal, www.poughkeepsiejournal.com, August 11, 2012.

35. "Starbucks' new environmentally friendly coffee-cup sleeve validated by Western Michigan University paper program," MLive, www.mlive.com, July 12, 2012.

36. www.prb.org, website visited May 29, 2014.

37. www.cia.gov, website visited May 29, 2014.

38. Chang-Hoan Cho, Ph.D., John Holcombe & Daniel Murphy, "Multicultural Marketing in Contemporary U.S. Markets," www.greenbook.org/marketing-research.cfm/multicultural-marketing, website visted May 29, 2014.

39. http://esa.un.org/unpd/wpp/, website visited June 2, 2014.

40. Bennett, Claudette, "Current Population Reports (Washington, DC: Bureau of the Census, U.S. Department of Commerce," January 1995, pg. 2.

41. CIA World Factbook, www.cia.gov, website visited June 2, 2014.

42. Ibid.

43. www.census.gov, website visited June 2, 2014.

44. CIA World Factbook, www.cia.gov, website visited June 2, 2014.

45. www.census.gov, website visited June 2, 2014.

46. "Are Baby Boomers an Invisible Goldmine for Marketers?", Forbes, www.forbes.com, August 10, 2012; "Gray-haired models growing in popularity as baby boomers age," Boston.com, www.boston.com, July 24, 2012.

47. "McDonald's food you can't get here," Chicago Tribune, www.chicagotribune.com, website visited June 2, 2014.

48. Hall, Edward T., "The Silent Language in Overseas Business," Harvard Business Review, May-June 1960, pg. 87.

49. "0610220 Johnson & Johnson and Pfizer Inc," Federal Trade Commission, www.ftc.gov, website visited June 2, 2014.

50. "FTC and FDA Team UP Against Tobacco," Wall Street Journal Interactive Edition, May 1, 1997.

51. Melillo, Wendy, "PM Claims Withdrawal of Ads Was voluntary," AdWeek East, June 12, 2000.

52. www.ihs.org/safety_facts, website visited June 2, 2014.

53. www.buick.com, website visited June 2, 2014.

54. www.epa.gov/nscep/, website visited June 2, 2014.

55. "eBay Bans Ivory Trading to Protect Endangered Elephants," Environmental News Service, October 22, 2008, www.ens-newswire.com, website visited June 2, 2014.

56. Cooper Smith, "US E-Commerce Growth Is Now Far Outpacing Overall Retail Sales," http://www.businessinsider.com, April 2, 2014.

57. Brian Walker, "Why E-Commerce Still Isn't Clicking with B2B Executives," Forbes, May 6, 2014.

58. Service Management and Cloud Computing, www-01.ibm.com, website visited February 11, 2010.

59. Armbrust, M., Fox, A., Griffith, R., et.al. "Above the Clouds: A Berkeley View of Cloud Computing," UC Berkely Reliable Adaptive Distributed Systems Laboratory, http://radlab.cs.berkeley.edu/, website visited June 14, 2014.

60. Mahadevan, B., "Business Models for Internet-based E-Commerce," California Management Review, 42 Summer 2000, pg. 56.

61. Ibid.

62. www.google.com/apps, website visited June 14, 2014.

63. "Buying & Paying," www.ebay.com, website visited June 14, 2014.

64. Mahadevan, B., "Business Models," pg. 57.

65. www.amazon.com/Kindle, website visited June 14, 2014.

66. Friedman, Thomas L., "The World Is Flat, Further Updated and Expanded: Release 3.0" New York: Farrar, Straus and Giroux, 2007.

67. Ibid.

68. "App Store Sales Top $10 Billion in 2013," Apple Press Info, January 7, 2014.

69. http://www.internetlivestats.com, website visited June 19, 2014.

70. "Online holiday sales climb 15 percent to $30.9B," MSNBC, http://www.msnbc.msn.com, website visited June 19, 2014.

71. "Showrooming Challenges Brick-and-Mortar Retailers," Practical eCommerce, www.practicalecommerce.com, July 25, 2012.

72. Hansen, Ward, Principles of Internet Marketing (Cincinnati: South-Western College Pub, 1999) pg. 197.

73. "eBay Inc. Global Citizenship: Environmental Activities," eBay, pages.ebay.com, website visited June 19, 2014.

74. www.dell.com, website visited June 19, 2014.

Chapter 04

MARKETING
INFORMATION
& RESEARCH

What began as a small, family-operated business in the 1830s has grown into the largest consumer-products corporation in the world. Procter & Gamble brands serve about 4.4 billion of the nearly 7 billion people in the world today. The company makes many brands you probably use every day: Tide, Bounty, Folgers, Pringles and Pampers. Its commitment to product innovation and the environment lands Procter & Gamble a spot among Fortune's 10 Most Admired Corporations year after year, as well as an induction into the Global 100 list of the World's Most Sustainable Corporations.

With hundreds of scientists and engineers responsible for assuring the environmental safety of products and operations, P&G is truly dedicated to the protection of the environment. Rather than developing a separate line of green products, compromising the reputation of non-green ones, Procter & Gamble holds all of its products to high environmental standards. For example, Ariel Excel Gel laundry detergent makes it possible to wash clothes in cold water, reducing energy consumption by up to 50 percent.

Procter & Gamble is one of the few companies with a division dedicated solely to consumer and marketing knowledge, a self-proclaimed "secret weapon." When considering product innovation, P&G combines consumer understanding and science to deliver sustainable new products that don't compromise performance or value. Employees explore what consumers think and want, influencing company decisions and direction. P&G develops strategies for brands entering new markets and analyzes market trends to predict future customer behavior.

The division acquires robust lists of email and mailing addresses. It uses this information to inform consumers of new products, offer free samples and conduct surveys. When surveys are completed, customers are offered vouchers for gift certificates or other incentives. The Consumer and Market Knowledge (CMK) division uses the survey information to analyze trends, target customers, adjust advertising campaigns and generate ideas for new products. CMK studies consumer and shopper decision processes, market and retailer dynamics, external influences, and key drivers of business growth. This helps P&G identify opportunities and make robust predictions of business outcomes.

With customers in 180 countries, Procter & Gamble is truly a global company. To gain insight on customers, particularly in foreign markets, P&G uses a method called immersion research. Instead of using focus groups, marketers visit customers in their homes or other local settings to help understand the roles its products play in their lives. This research method provides valuable information in markets where consumers use its products differently than American consumers. P&G has invested more than $400 million annually in market research and consumer understanding, more than any other company in the world.[1]

<< A Small Collection of P&G Products

Courtesy of Procter & Gamble

Learning Objectives

1. Understand the roles that marketing information systems (MIS) and research play in marketing decision making.
2. Recognize how data are transformed into information to be used in a variety of marketing decisions.
3. Understand the types of research and the steps of a typical marketing research process.
4. Describe widely used marketing research techniques.
5. Explore how marketing information is being influenced by technology and is obtained globally.
6. Understand the ethical issues that surround the use and dissemination of research.

THE CONCEPT OF MARKETING INFORMATION & RESEARCH

Connecting with customers requires vast amounts of information. You can't connect if you can't locate, understand and respond to customers. That's where marketing information and research enter the picture. Technology has completely changed the process of marketing information, making it possible to gather data at incredible speeds for anyone with a tablet and an Internet connection. The director of strategic planning at a large Midwestern hospital commented recently, "We have access to more information than we can possibly use. The trick is to determine which information will be useful to us in making decisions that positively affect our future."[2]

In fact, a major problem for executives today is data overload — access to so much that their minds simply can't process all of it. To help decision makers, most companies carefully structure the way data are collected, stored and made available through marketing information systems and marketing research.

Marketing information systems (MIS) are computerized systems that collect and organize marketing data on a timely basis to provide information for decision making. The results become part of the MIS so that executives have constant feedback. Note that the abbreviation MIS can be confusing because many organizations have a **management information system**, also called an MIS. Many times the marketing information system is considered part of that larger system. Management information systems usually contain additional data, such as employee records and various internal documents.

Marketing research is the formal assembly and analysis of data about specific issues surrounding a marketing strategy. When there's little or no information available about a particular marketing situation, organizations often conduct research on the problem. For example, Tantau Software Inc., a developer of computer programs for wireless Internet, hired IntelliQuest Research to provide marketing data on the attitudes of current and potential wireless users. IntelliQuest discovered that finance-based transactions

Marketing Information Systems (MIS)

A computerized system used to collect and analyze the data needed for management decision making. The marketing information system is often considered a part of this system.

Management Information System

A computerized system used to collect and analyze the data needed for management decision making. The marketing information system is often considered a part of this system.

Marketing Research

The formal assembly and analysis of information about specific issues surrounding the marketing of goods and services.

showed the most promise for a wireless Internet market. However, it also found that many customers were concerned with the security of their transactions and were hesitant to use the medium. As a result, Tantau was able to use IntelliQuest's research to better focus on e-commerce wireless security software, something that consumers obviously needed. Tantau Software was later acquired by 724 Solutions Inc., a provider of Internet infrastructure software for online banking transactions and m-commerce (mobile commerce).[3]

Marketing research addresses a specific issue with a clearly identified objective regarding marketing strategy. Once the research is completed, it's typically saved as part of the MIS. Figure 4.1 depicts the relationships of the MIS and marketing research to marketing decision making.

Figure 4.1   Marketing information and Decision Making

This chapter starts with an examination of marketing information systems and their role in marketing decisions. This is followed by a discussion of the marketing research process, which is also key in decision making. The chapter concludes with sections on the all-important technological, global, and ethical dimensions of information generation and usage.

MARKETING INFORMATION SYSTEMS & DATA

Marketing information systems often include a **marketing decision support system (MDSS)**, which allows decision makers to access raw data from the MIS and manipulate it into a useful form. A typical MDSS consists of a computer database, data retrieval and modeling software, and a user-friendly graphical interface. Let's say that a marketing manager wants to know how the price of the company's downhill skis compares to that of a competitor. The information is probably in the MIS on a store-by-store basis, which would be difficult for the manager to sort through and use for insightful results. Instead, the manager may sit down at a computer and access the company's MDSS. A user-friendly display appears and, through interactive directions, helps the user determine how to manipulate the raw data. The marketing manager may want to compare average prices across the entire country or for one region or state. Once that is decided, the MDSS software retrieves and models the relevant data. Now the manager can interpret the data and make an informed decision.

A **transaction-based information system (TBIS)** is a specialized type of MIS that serves as an electronic link between a firm and its customers, distributors and suppliers. Originally designed for ordering, billing, shipping and inventory control, these systems are now designed to provide data on customer preferences, loyalty, sales trends and an array of marketing issues. As part of an initiative to streamline communications, Walmart requires all of its suppliers to adopt Applicability Statement 2 (AS2), a company-created connectivity standard designed to standardize trading and facilitate data interchange over the Internet.[4]

To develop an excellent MIS and design a useful MDSS, the organization needs to assess its marketing information needs. This assessment begins by identifying the types of executive decisions, what information will help make them, and the best formats and timetables for presenting it. Figure 4.2 describes the types of questions used to assess marketing information needs.

Marketing Decision Support System (MDSS)

A two-way communication bridge between the people who collect and analyze information and the executives who use it.

Transaction-Based Information System (TBIS)

A computerized link between a firm and its customers, distributors, and suppliers.

1. What decisions are made, with what frequency?
2. What information helps make those decisions?
3. What information is currently supplied?
4. What additional information is required?
5. What information do you get now that is unnecessary?
6. How would you like the information displayed?
7. What sources of information would you like to receive on a regular basis?

Figure 4.2   How to Determine Marketing Information Needs

TURNING DATA INTO INFORMATION

In order to comprehend marketing information systems and marketing research, it is important to understand how data becomes information useful for decision making. Keep in mind that data and information are not the same. Data are raw facts and statistics. **Information** is composed of data that have been analyzed and put in useful form, as depicted in Figure 4.3. It is difficult to draw marketing conclusions from data in simple tabular form. In other words, market analysts and researchers need to interpret data — turn them into information — to assist upper-level managers and executives in making quick, informed decisions.

Information

Data that has been analyzed and put into useful form.

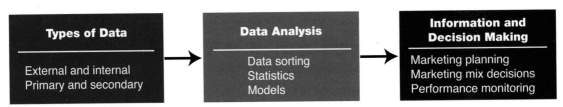

Figure 4.3   How Data Becomes Information

Types of Data   Data provides the starting point from which marketing information is derived. **Data** can be any set of facts or statistics obtained from outside (external) or inside (internal) the company. Usually the data are stored in a **database**, which is a collection of material that can be retrieved by a computer.

External data comes from outside the company. Popular external databases include LEXIS®-NEXIS®, Dow Jones Interactive, Hoover's Online and Dialog. They provide raw data as well as articles, newsletters, breaking news stories, financial reports and nearly any other type of data imaginable. For specific needs, there are sources such as Forrester Research Group's Technographic Data, which provides continuous surveys of 260,000 households in North America and Europe. Technographic Data gives valuable survey information on how consumers think about, buy and use technology in the categories of devices and media, health care, financial services, retail, and travel — survey information that many companies need.[5]

To track competitors, one approach is the source in the Nexis® service, which analyzes specific industries and companies. For research of business customers, Dun & Bradstreet can provide information on almost 130 million businesses in 190 countries.[6] It can give in-depth financial and operational reports on most of the companies in its database. These databases are rarely free; companies charge either for time online or for each piece of data, such as a name or news release.

Internal data include a company's own sales and accounting records and sales force call reports. They are likely to reside in several different departments. For example, the accounting department often has detailed records of sales costs and how much revenue is generated by each product. In some cases, these figures are available for each market segment. The manufacturing and shipping departments

Data

Facts or statistics obtained from inside or outside the company.

Database

A collection of data that can be retrieved by a computer.

External Data

Data obtained outside the company

Internal Data

Data obtained within the company.

track production schedules, amount of capacity utilized, shipping dates, and inventory levels. In many companies, the supply-chain management department provides detailed records of the flow of goods into the company and out to each customer, including the frequency of orders, stock levels and purchase rates. The marketing department will usually have such data as type and frequency of sales calls, orders received from each location, and advertising schedules.

Primary data are those gathered for the first time for a particular issue being addressed. **Secondary data** are obtained from sources that have already gathered the data. Since primary data can be costly and time-consuming to gather, secondary data are far more common. While obtaining secondary data is much easier and considerably cheaper than primary data, it can still be expensive, costing thousands of dollars for access to studies by primary researchers.

Primary Data

Information collected for the first time.

Secondary Data

Information that already has been collected.

Data Analysis Data analysis transforms material into a usable form, so analysts can develop insights. It usually involves data sorting, statistics and models. Data sorting uses several tools for grouping data. For example, Burger King may want to know sales by time of day to determine whether certain items are more popular at certain times.

> **Data analysis transforms material into a usable form, so analysts can develop insights.**

Statistics help describe data in more detail or tell us how representative certain occurrences are relative to overall patterns. Most information systems have readily available statistical packages that can easily be applied to the data. In some cases they simply count frequencies of occurrence or describe using cross-tabulations or averages. Gannett Co., a leading international news and information company, hired The Advanced Marketing & Media Group to provide it with an advertising performance measurement system. The AMM Group is a marketing technology business that uses technological innovation to help companies capitalize on marketing performance. The system it created for Gannett Co. will be designed to "offer its advertisers an opportunity to measure marketing return on investment across Gannett media assets, including newspapers, television stations, websites and mobile devices." This information system will add value to the company by unifying statistical marketing data.[7]

Models are simplified, miniaturized representations of marketing phenomena. Marketers need models for the same reasons that architects need blueprints. With a blueprint, the architect can visualize various parts of the building without actually being there. Marketing models describe what variables are important for specific marketing situations.

INFORMATION IS FOR DECISION MAKING

Using information is not easy; however, it's absolutely critical to have good information if you expect to develop a good marketing strategy. In the past, marketers often relied on their experience and intuition. Instinct and prior knowledge remain useful tools today, but the world is more complex, requiring an organization to possess outside information about the market. Good information helps executives make key marketing decisions. Marketing information plays a key role in marketing planning, marketing mix decisions and performance monitoring.

Marketing Planning Marketing planning requires input about customers, competitors, market trends, technology, channels of distribution and economic conditions. Marketing information helps marketers make better decisions about which segments to target and how to position the organization in response to competitors.

Marketing planning should always place priority on complete, fact-based data, not opinion or conjecture. Most planning teams have a marketing information specialist who collects relevant information and shares it with the team.

Marketing Mix Decisions Marketing information is necessary for making decisions based on any component of the marketing mix. In fact, decision methods have developed for each of the individual components (product, place, promotion and price). Radius Global Market Research is a research and consulting firm headquartered in New York. The company provides in-depth research and analysis that enable clients to make informed decisions on product ventures.[8]

Product Decisions Marketing information on new products is essential. Marketing information monitors test markets, helps monitor customer satisfaction with goods and services, forecasts technology trends, and indicates when to introduce new products or phase out old ones. JCPenney conducted in-depth research in order to determine the needs of "the missing middle," defined as middle-income married women between ages 35 and 54. The company did a telephone survey of 900 women asking them about casual clothes. It also conducted video interviews with 30 women for up to six hours, recording their feelings about fashion and shopping preferences. The research shows the target women have a more casual lifestyle, want to look trendy without sacrificing quality, and crave something suitable for relaxed occasions. As a result, JCPenney launched two lines of moderately priced casual clothes, one by designer Nicole Miller.[9]

Place Decisions Marketing information helps with place decisions such as determining the appropriate distribution channel, either directly to consumers or through intermediaries, such as wholesalers and retailers. It can be used to identify specific distributors or the inventory requirements for selected channels. One form of marketing information tracks every item sold in every store.

Courtesy of Amazon

At Amazon.com, users can shop online yet still receive personal attention. Visitors are encouraged to log in with each visit so the company can access the user's previous purchases to create a recommended product list to cross sell items. Attention to customization and personalization has elevated Amazon.com to a dominant position in the market because customers are satisfied and respond with return visits. At the same time, Amazon executives are able to track the sales of all items to the minutest detail. Once executives gain a good understanding of market phenomena, they are able to make quality decisions regarding the distribution of products and services.

Promotion Decisions In order for a promotion campaign to accomplish desired objectives, it needs to deliver the proper combination of advertising, personal selling, and other approaches, which require a great deal of information. For advertising, decision makers need to determine the most effective numbers of Internet, print, television and radio ads to reach targeted consumers. Internet advertising is continuously growing while an explosion of companies race to compete. Google now holds an impressive 44 percent of the online advertising market.[10] Information is available regarding the number of target audience members that can be reached by each media, including variations by type of television programming, time of day and region of the country. The Nielsen Company provides data to help decide whether to advertise during particular programs and time slots for several groups of targeted customers. There is even available data that determines the cost for each airing of a promotion.[11] Information about promotion variations, such as the use of in-store coupons, is also available and helpful.

Pricing Decisions Because prices send strong signals to the market about the value of a product, information on pricing is critical for almost every marketing decision. Walmart and Toys "R" Us advertise that they will meet or beat (local) competitors' prices. They monitor local competition and collect competitors' ads, feeding the information into a centralized MIS. Automobile companies look not only at the prices of major competitors but also at finance and leasing terms. Information is collected about the effectiveness of cash discounts and rebates as well as the likelihood of buyers switching from one brand to another at various price points. The airline industry, whose profits are highly sensitive to volume, continually monitors how price affects demand in local, national and international markets. Internet ticket sellers such as Expedia.com and Travelocity.com are especially helpful in this regard, as commercial websites are an excellent source of consumer information.

Performance Monitoring

The third area supported by marketing information is performance monitoring. This helps managers make sure that plans and programs are progressing as scheduled. Information is required to track progress, identify unexpected obstacles, and make corrections to accomplish objectives. For British Columbia-based Robeez Footwear, a manufacturer of children's soft-soled leather footwear, customer input is not an occasional goal, it's a way of life. "We have a very loyal group of customers who love to give us feedback," explains Tricia Burton, Robeez's Internet marketing manager. Robeez launched a post-purchase online survey to gauge the effectiveness of a recent website redesign. The survey, which appears as a popup, includes eight questions on the quality of the content, ease of navigation, and the ordering process. So far, the survey has both validated the site redesign and given Robeez a strong direction for the future.[12]

Marketing information also provides valuable feedback. "Without indicators like increased sales or market share gain, we really have no way of knowing how effective our plan for a brand really is," says Dana Anderson, media buyer for United Airlines at Leo Burnett Company Inc., a major advertising agency. Marketing information also tells how well an advertising plan meets specific marketing objectives, like an increase in brand awareness or an improved image of a brand relative to competitors. Today, nearly every organization monitors customer service levels. Marketing information provides data on customer expectations and how well the company meets them.

Outside rating services can provide unbiased information on how consumers evaluate performance. You're probably familiar with the Nielsen ratings, which usually appear weekly in publications such as USA Today. Nielsen Media Research, the leading international television information services company, monitors thousands of homes. A Nielsen People Meter is installed to monitor tuning records for every channel: the time of day, duration of tuning, and which household members are watching. The result is television show rankings, weekly ratings, and season-to-date rankings. Nielsen also provides reports on consumer trends including social media, smartphones and video games.[13]

According to Nielson, NBC's America's Got Talent opened its ninth season with 12 million viewers.

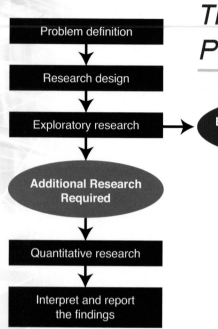

Figure 4.4   The Marketing Research Process

THE MARKETING RESEARCH PROCESS

Marketing research is a key aspect of the organization's ability to make good marketing decisions. It starts with a clear understanding of the problem to be addressed and ends with an interpretation of findings that will aid in decision making. Each step is shown in Figure 4.4.

DEFINING THE PROBLEM

A highly respected marketing research executive for Pfizer Corporation said, "Never begin a research process with a search for market information. Always start by understanding the decisions to be made and the managerial circumstances surrounding those decisions." This isn't as easy as it sounds, but it's a critical step in the research process. As Albert Einstein said, "The formulation of a problem is often more essential than its solution."[14]

The marketing researcher and key decision makers should work together to specify the problem. The researcher usually must ask probing questions to determine exactly how pressing the problem is and the time and resources available to address it.

A researcher must carefully isolate the symptoms from the actual problem. For instance, if Pepsi's sales were to experience a sudden decline, that would be a symptom, not the source. The real problem may be a new promotional campaign by Coca-Cola that Pepsi has failed to address, or a shift in their marketing toward a new product offering. Just as a fever is a sign of the flu, declining sales usually indicate a deeper problem. Once it is isolated, the variables or factors causing it can be identified. Defining the problem is necessary before any marketing research begins.

RESEARCH DESIGN

A **research design** is an outline of what data will be gathered, what sources will be used, and how the data will be collected and analyzed. The research design is, in effect, a master plan for the research project as shown in Figure 4.4.

Most designs call for two types of research: exploratory and quantitative. **Exploratory research** clarifies the problem and searches for ways to address it. **Quantitative research** provides the information needed to select the best course of action and forecast probable results. Research generally starts with an exploratory study, may include a pilot phase, and ends with quantitative research. A **pilot study** is a small-scale project that allows the researcher to refine and test the approaches that ultimately will be used.

EXPLORATORY RESEARCH

Exploratory research enables investigators to obtain a better understanding of the issues. Specifically, it helps to:

- Determine the exact nature of the problem or opportunity

- Search for causes or explanations for the problem

- Define the magnitude of the problem

Research Design

An outline of what data will be gathered, what sources will be used, and how the data will be collected and analyzed.

Exploratory Research

Research designed to clarify the problem and suggest ways to address

Quantitative Research

Research designed to provide the information needed to select the best course of action and estimate the probable results.

Pilot Study

A small-scale project that allows the researcher to refine and test the approaches that eventually will be used.

- Create hypotheses about underlying causes

- Describe why or how the causes may affect the situation

- Understand competitors' actions and reactions

- Estimate how courses of action may affect the market.

Exploratory research seeks information that will enlighten marketers in the decision-making process. It generally begins by finding and reviewing secondary data. This information has already been collected, so it's usually the quickest and most cost-effective way to get started. Primary data are usually required at some point, but sometimes information from secondary sources is enough. A simple Google search for sports sites reveals 621 million results for baseball, 700 million for basketball, and 1.66 billion for football.[15] By starting with exploratory research, companies can learn a lot about sports, such as how fans follow the game, how leagues, teams, and players market themselves, and what products and services sports fans buy.

Although exploratory research seldom reveals the best solution, it helps define the problem and suggests options. Exploratory research is conducted with focus groups, interviews, projective techniques, observation, and case analysis. Each is discussed next.

Focus Groups

A **focus (focused) group** usually involves eight to 12 people whose opinions provide qualitative insights into a problem. This approach is particularly useful in clarifying problems with a company's products, services, advertising, distribution channels and the like. It's possible to gather a wide range of information about customers' feelings on these subjects and discover the reasons for their attitudes or purchase behaviors. Researchers ask questions and encourage participants to interact with one another to discover unexpected attitudes, behaviors and ideas that may suggest innovative marketing strategies. In a sense, the group interviews itself. The social interaction often yields insights that could not be obtained through one-on-one interviews.

Focus groups have been used for a variety of purposes. Although most focus groups are conducted in person with a facilitator, other formats can be used, such as videoconferencing through monitors, remote control cameras, and digital transmission. The Internet is an excellent — and cost-effective — tool for focus group research. The Atlanta-based ActiveGroup has emerged as one of the leading providers of Internet-based focus group technology. This technology is allowing marketing specialists to conduct focus groups from their homes, hotels and boardrooms. Lately, ActiveGroup has focused on website and computer-usability testing by using cam-to-cam technology, so researchers can view consumer facial expressions of satisfaction, confusion, like or dislike.[16]

When selecting participants for a focus group, it's generally best to choose them all from similar demographics, since common experiences provide the basis for

Focus Group

A group, usually composed of eight to twelve people, whose opinions are elicited by an interviewer to provide exploratory insights into a problem.

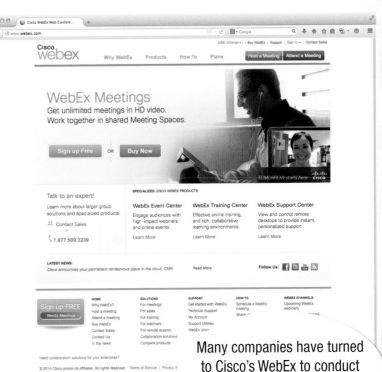

Many companies have turned to Cisco's WebEx to conduct focus groups without expensive videoconferencing equipment.

more in-depth discussion. Researchers can cover other groups in future focus groups, since just one is rarely enough to obtain an accurate sampling. The researcher should use several groups to ensure that the findings are somewhat representative. Even though many individuals may be involved, the unit of analysis is the group and not the individual. Six groups with eight people each, in effect, yields six interviews, not 48.

Depth Interviews

Depth Interviews **Depth interviews** are relatively unstructured conversations that allow researchers to probe into a consumer's thought processes. Often they are used to investigate the mechanisms of purchase decisions. Although the discussion may appear casual to the participant, the skilled researcher exerts a great deal of control, subtly discovering the participant's attitudes, opinions or motivations. The marketer uses these results both as individual case studies and as comparative data to examine commonalities among respondents.

Depth Interviews

A relatively unstructured conversation that allows the researcher to probe deeply into a consumer's thoughts.

Projective Techniques

Projective Techniques **Projective techniques** enable respondents to project their thoughts onto a third party, or through some type of contrived situation. This is often done using word associations, sentence completion and role playing. Because projective approaches do not require respondents to provide answers in a structured format, people are more likely to interpret the situation creatively and in the context of their own experiences and emotions. When asked directly why they purchase a particular item, they may describe a far more rational process than the one that actually occurs. For example, if a recent college graduate is asked why she would purchase an Audi or a Ford Mustang, she may cite performance, gas mileage and overall value of the product. But if asked to project the feelings of a person who purchases this kind of automobile, she may focus on status, self-esteem and the need to be noticed.

Projective Techniques

A technique that enables respondents to project their thoughts onto a third party or object or through some type of contrived situation.

Observation

Observation **Observation** is a technique whereby the participants are simply watched. In one classic study, researchers stationed themselves in both crowded and uncrowded supermarkets to see if buying behavior differed. In less crowded stores, shoppers tended to use the information on labels and shelves, whereas in crowded conditions they tended to make decisions more hastily. This exploratory observation was followed by a more formal survey that enabled the researchers to draw conclusions about buyer behavior in crowded situations.[17]

Observation

A research technique whereby researchers simply watch the participants they are studying.

> **In less crowded stores, shoppers tended to use the information on labels and shelves, whereas in crowded conditions they tended to make decisions more hastily.**

Structured observation is made through mechanical means. Tachistoscopes measure visual stimuli, while galvanometers record electrical resistance in the skin, associated with sweating and other responses. Special cameras often are used to study eye movement as a subject reads advertising copy. By observing pupil dilation, blinking and eye tracking, it is possible to judge what receives attention in ads, on packaging or on the Internet.

Case Analysis

Case Analysis **Case analysis** takes a few select examples and studies them in-depth. This technique is particularly appropriate for complex buying and competitive situations. For example, how industrial companies make decisions for particular components or capital goods is often studied this way. A single researcher may spend several days interviewing a firm's employees who purchase and use the product in question. In addition, buying policies, documents and actual purchase history are investigated. When researchers give this treatment to enough companies (perhaps 10), they start to get a larger picture of how suppliers are selected. The information

Case Analysis

The in-depth study of a few examples.

can help suppliers determine the appropriateness of various marketing approaches.

Case analysis can also be used to study the competition. Researchers may select two or three activities of key competitors and examine them in depth. By knowing all aspects of the strategies used to introduce a couple of products, researchers can assess competitors' strengths and weaknesses and also predict how they might behave in the future with other products. Researchers can also use competitors' sales and expense figures to set benchmarks for their own organization.

QUANTITATIVE RESEARCH

Quantitative research provides information that helps decision makers select the best course of action and estimate the probable results. Rigorous statistical procedures allow researchers to estimate how confident they can be about their conclusions. Since quantitative research uses widely accepted methods, duplicating the study should arrive at approximately the same results. Certain techniques also indicate how closely the findings represent the views or attitudes of the whole population at large, not just the sample studied.

CAREER TIP!

Amazon.com offers unique opportunities for marketing interns. You can work with full-time employees to help manage projects in strategy development, market research, positioning and other related areas. At Amazon, you will partner with some of the most innovative minds in business, marketing and e-commerce. If Amazon sounds like the place for you, visit their Careers page at Amazon.com.

Quantitative research played an enormous role in the successful positioning and launch of Kimberly-Clark's Expressions facial tissue line. In the face of increasing competition from a new product line of super soft tissues by Procter & Gamble, the company began looking for an innovative way to increase market share for its Kleenex brand. Through quantitative research, it found that the second most important feature to consumers behind softness was the box design. Nearly 37 percent of buyers said they disliked the look of tissue boxes and often hid them in closets or bathrooms. Product testing in eight U.S. cities revealed consumer preferences for six styles: traditional, country, Southwestern, contemporary, Asian and Victorian. The new designs were a great success, partly because marketers took the time to learn the opinions of consumers.[18] Recently, Kimberly-Clark has taken box design a step further by giving consumers the ability to create and print their own custom box design through their website.

Quantitative research usually follows the **scientific method** to prevent faulty conclusions. The scientific method is a systematic way to gather, analyze and interpret data in order to confirm or refute a prior conception. First, researchers develop a **hypothesis** about an issue based on a limited amount of information. A hypothesis is a tentative assumption about a particular event or issue. Second, rigorous tests are conducted to determine whether the hypothesis is supported by the information.

Let us say we have an idea that more men and women shop in malls on the weekend because they're not working, so we hypothesize that malls will obtain greater sales volumes on Saturday and Sunday than on weekdays. We then gather information to test the hypothesis. The key is for researchers to state beforehand what they believe the results may be and why. This enables appropriate data to be gathered and analyzed to assess whether the hypothesis is true.

Data-Collection Methods
Two of the most common methods for collecting quantitative data are experiments and surveys. **Experiments** usually take place either where the marketing problem occurs or in a laboratory setting that is contrived

Scientific Method

A systematic way to gather, analyze, and interpret data in order to confirm or disconfirm a prior conception.

Hypothesis

A tentative assumption about a particular event or issue.

Experiments

A test conducted under controlled conditions in order to prove or disprove a marketing hypothesis.

Causal Research

Research that attempts to show a cause-and-effect relationship between two phenomena.

Likert Scales

A scale that measures the respondent's intensity of agreement with a particular statement.

to match research needs. To test new packaging for a pain reliever, for example, the manufacturer may invite consumers to "shop" in a simulated supermarket. In that way shopping patterns can be observed to see whether the packaging is eye-catching. Experiments are often used for **causal research**, which attempts to show a cause-and-effect relationship between two events. One of the most important forms of causal research is test marketing. A test market provides a limited trial of a product strategy under realistic conditions.

Surveys are the most popular way to collect data. When researchers want to ensure that each subject is asked for the same information, they prepare a written survey questionnaire. It is a measurement device, much like a thermometer or a ruler. Two common units of measure for questionnaire items are the points along Likert scales and bipolar adjective scales.

Likert scales allow the intensity of feelings to be expressed and tend to provide information about a person's attitude toward something. Subjects are asked to indicate the extent to which they agree or disagree with each statement in the survey. The Likert scale shown in Figure 4.5 has five points (units of measure). A seven-point scale often is used, adding "somewhat disagree" and "somewhat agree" on either side of the middle point.

Bipolar adjective scales allow respondents to choose along a range between two extremes. Figure 4.6 shows a typical bipolar adjective scale. In general, there are three, five, or seven points in the scale. This scale is used frequently in marketing research, likely because it can cover a wide range of opinions with relatively few questions.

The wording of an item can make quite a difference. A classic example occurred in the 1980s during the battles between Burger King and McDonald's. Burger King asked respondents: "Do you prefer your hamburgers flame-broiled or fried?" When Burger King's method

---

INSTRUCTIONS: Please put an X in the space that indicates how strongly you agree or disagree with the following statements about The Daily Show with John Stewart.

	Strongly Disagree	Disagree	Neither Agree Nor Disagree	Agree	Strongly Agree
Watching The Daily Show is enjoyable	——	——	——	——	——
The Daily Show is more educational than most evening programming	——	——	——	——	——
The Daily Show appeals more to those with higher income	——	——	——	——	——

Figure 4.5   A Typical Likert Scale

INSTRUCTIONS: Please put an X in the space that most appropriately indicates your feelings about shopping at Gap.

	Very	Moderately	Slightly	Neither One nor the Other	Slightly	Moderately	Very	
Inexpensive	——	——	——	——	——	——	——	Expensive
Helpful Salespeople	——	——	——	——	——	——	——	Unhelpful Salespeople
High-quality Products	——	——	——	——	——	——	——	Low-quality Products

Figure 4.6   A Typical Bipolar Adjective Scale

of flame-broiling was preferred three to one, the chain aggressively publicized this in an ad campaign. The results were completely different when McDonald's researchers asked: "Do you prefer a hamburger that is grilled on a hot stainless-steel grill or cooked by passing the warmed meat through an open-gas flame?" McDonald's frying method received a clear majority. When the question was modified to include the fact that the gas-flame burgers were warmed in a microwave oven prior to serving, McDonald's won seven to one.[20]

Administering Surveys
A survey can be administered through personal interviews, mall intercepts, telephone, mail or the Internet. Each technique has benefits and disadvantages, as shown in Figure 4.7. The researcher needs to select the method most appropriate for the current project.

	Personal Interviews	Mall Intercepts	Telephone	Mail	Internet
Speed of Completion	Slowest	Fast	Fast	Moderate	Fastest
Response Rate	High	Moderate	Moderate	Low	Moderate
Quality of Response	Excellent	Good	Good	Limited	Good
Interviewer Bias	High	Moderate	Moderate	Low	Low
Geographic Reach	Limited	Limited	Excellent	Excellent	Excellent
Cost	Very expensive	Moderate	Moderate	Inexpensive	Inexpensive

Figure 4.7　Comparative Advantages of Interviews, Mall Intercepts, Telephone Surveys, Mail Questionnaires and Internet Surveys

Personal Interviews Personal interviews require face-to-face, two-way communication between the interviewer and the respondent. This method is particularly useful in probing complex answers or observing the respondent's behavior. The setting usually is comfortable, and the respondent is given undivided attention. Gen-X Press is a leading full-service consulting group that helps companies to better market to Generations X and Y, usually collecting data through face-to-face interviews with members of these generations. Their interviewers ask questions about motivation, the relationship between pay and happiness, and empowerment in the workplace. Marketers believe that the opinions of individuals can be used to predict future actions among mainstream members of Generations X and Y.[20]

One benefit of personal interviews is the high participation rate. It's unlikely that any questions will go unanswered, and props or visual aids can be used. But there are several disadvantages. Subjects may be influenced by the interviewer, and they give up anonymity when meeting face-to-face, so they may withhold information or answer in unnatural ways. Interviewing is expensive, since professionals must be trained and then transported to the various locations. The cost can range from $25 per average consumer to thousands of dollars per top executive, surgeon, legislator or others.

Mall Intercepts Mall intercepts, as the name implies, occur at a shopping mall, and the interviewer chooses respondents on some objective basis, such as every fifth person encountered. Mall intercepts are simple to conduct, and data can be collected quickly and cost-effectively. They can ask questions about actual purchases during some specified period, which helps determine actual behaviors as well as opinions and attitudes. One variation of this method is a shopping basket study, or simply looking at what a consumer purchases during a particular trip to the store. Grocery stores often want this kind of information in order to identify which products are purchased together, the total amount of spending, and the shopping patterns of individuals while in the store.

Telephone Surveys Telephone surveys offer speed and relatively low cost. Using banks of telephones, marketers can contact a large number of people at approximately the same time. This method is particularly effective with professionals, who tend to be articulate and willing to discuss matters over the telephone. By prearranging the call, it's possible to gain considerable cooperation from respondents. Now that fax machines and the Internet are so prevalent, a common procedure is to call ahead, fax the information or ask respondents to get it from a website, and obtain reactions over the telephone. This enables interviewers not only to probe for thoughts and ideas but also to elicit responses to printed materials. Another advantage of the telephone is that a follow-up call can be arranged easily if the individual cannot respond at that moment. Today, computer-assisted technology allows respondents to register their answers using the touch-tone pad, which works particularly well with a large panel of subjects. Also, computerized systems that are voice-activated save on telephone charges and make online data analysis possible.

The major drawback of telephone interviews is the large number of unlisted numbers, which makes it very difficult to obtain a valid sample. In some cities more than half the population has an unlisted number. Many consumers have done away with landlines, using (typically unlisted) cell phones as their primary phone lines. One way to overcome this is through random-digit dialing by a computer, although many consumers are adding Caller ID service to screen out unwanted surveys. In addition, phone surveys have an obvious limitation if respondents are required to see something, as in evaluating ads or product renderings.

Mail Surveys In mail surveys, a questionnaire is sent directly to the respondent's home or place of business. An advantage is that people can answer at their own pace and at a convenient time. Mailed questionnaires can be extremely useful for surveying professionals, who have a high response rate and tend to give thoughtful answers. Publishers regularly survey professors by mail concerning textbooks they have adopted, teaching methods, and their ideas about innovative materials that can be created. Associations often obtain good response quality and return rates from membership surveys by mail.

Many techniques are used to encourage people to answer mail questionnaires. Including an explanatory cover letter or small incentive can increase return rates. Research also reveals that the rate can be boosted considerably by multiple prior notifications, while sending only one has no influence. Mailing a second survey has a significant effect on response rates as well.[21]

According to a study reported in *Industrial Marketing Management*, surveys get better receptions when sponsored by a legitimate organization, such as a professional association. The mean response rates for the questionnaires from a university and an honor society sponsor were significantly higher than for those sponsored by a marketing research firm and an unidentified source.[22] The greatest problem with mail questionnaires is that many people simply refuse to answer them. This causes significant problems for researchers, since those who do respond may differ from the rest of the population. For example, people may be motivated to answer because they intensely like or dislike a product.

Internet Surveys Many researchers use the Internet to gain individuals' participation in surveys. The main advantage of using the Internet instead of traditional methods is that the information is available very quickly. Additionally, researchers can survey a greater number of people with a lower cost compared to written and mailed surveys, and data can be analyzed as they are collected.

There are four main types of online surveys:

1. **Pop-up surveys:** When a user leaves a website, another window, containing a questionnaire, pops up on the screen. Internet users have the option of either completing the survey or closing the browser window. The response rate for this type of survey ranges from 15 to 45 percent.

2. **Email or web surveys:** Via e-mail, a company can invite someone to participate in an online questionnaire. The response rates for these surveys range from 25 to 50 percent and are usually completed by the user in two to three days.

3. **Online groups:** A research company can organize what is essentially a focus group discussion on Internet chat rooms.

4. **Consumer-generated media:** Researchers can carry on long discussions with individuals by communicating through blogs, forums, podcasts and email portals like Yahoo!.[23]

Marketers also observe discussions among web users to gather information about current and prospective customers. Many companies encourage customers to fill out a website registration form. The participant is usually asked to volunteer some personal information in exchange for a free gift, coupon, or some other incentive. For example, Best Buy targets its consumers online to provide store feedback. A customer is given the chance to win a $5,000 Best Buy shopping spree by going online to fill out its Best Buy Cares Survey. By providing an incentive, the company in return gets extremely useful comments about the store's atmosphere and the overall shopping experience.[24]

Best Buy Cares Survey allows customers a chance to win a $5,000 shopping spree for completing the survey.

SAMPLING

Surveys are conducted to gain insights about the groups of consumers or companies being studied. The **population (universe)** is composed of all the individuals or organizations relevant to the marketing research project. For example, if the a company wants to know the average number of jobs a U.S. resident holds during the first 10 years out of high school, the relevant population is all U.S. residents age 28 or older — millions of people. The company could attempt to interview all of them, but that would be impractical, if not impossible, and far too costly. Researchers have developed methods for surveying a subset of people from whom they draw inferences about the larger population.

The first step is to obtain a **sampling frame**, which is a list of people in the

Population (Universe)

All the individuals or organizations relevant to the marketing research project

Sampling Frame

A list of people in the universe who potentially could be contacted.

Sample

The group participating in a research project that represents the entire population of potential respondents.

Probability Sample

A sample in which the chance of selecting a given individual from the sampling frame or population can be calculated.

Simple Random Sampling

A sampling technique in which each member of the study population has an equal and known chance of being chosen.

Stratified Random Sampling

A sampling technique in which each member of a selected sub-group of the population has an equal chance of selection.

Nonprobability Sample

A sample in which the likelihood of selecting a particular respondent from the sampling frame cannot be calculated.

Judgment Sample

A sample selected by the research-ers or interviewers based on their belief that those chosen represent a majority of the study population.

Convenience Sample

A sample composed of people who happen to come along, such as shoppers in a store at a given time, whoever answers the doorbell, or travelers passing through an airport.

universe who potentially could be contacted. From this, researchers select the **sample:** the group of people who are asked to participate in the research.

There are two categories of samples: probability and nonprobability. In a **probability sample**, the chance of selecting a given individual can be calculated. One popular method is **simple random sampling**, whereby each individual has an equal chance of being chosen (say, every third name is selected). Another is **stratified random sampling**, whereby each individual within a selected subgroup of the sample has a known chance of selection (say, every third household with income of $50,000 or more). This method is often used in marketing, since much research focuses on market segments. If some form of random sampling is adopted, then statistics can be used to determine the likelihood that responses from the sample will be similar to the responses of the larger population.

When using **nonprobability samples**, the researcher does not know the likelihood of selecting a particular respondent. The two most common types are judgment and convenience samples. **Judgment samples** are chosen by the re-searcher based on the belief that these people represent a majority of the study population.

Convenience samples are people who happen to come along, such as shoppers in a given store at a certain time or travelers passing through an airport. Convenience samples are relatively inexpensive, and the selection can be purposely unrepresentative, such as interviewing only females. In general, this method does not provide data reliable enough for quantitative research. Even probability samples can become like convenience samples if care is not taken regarding the smallest details, such as when interviews are conducted. Tom Brokaw, renowned broadcast anchor, once remarked that election polls could not be taken on Friday night. It seems the results would be skewed because so many people go out that evening.

INTERPRETING AND REPORTING SURVEY FINDINGS

Once the research is completed, results are reported to the appropriate decision makers. No matter how sophisticated or reliable, marketing research is of little use unless it can be easily understood by the decision makers who act upon it. Most managers and executives have little experience with research techniques and little interest in learning about them. Thus, presentation of understandable research results is an important skill for marketing researchers. Good research moves succinctly from data to information to insight. Unfortunately, to demonstrate the hard work that has gone into a project, many researchers give too much extraneous information. A report that describes each table in detail instead of using the information to reach conclusions is not likely to meet the needs of executives.

Experience pays off in interpreting research. When the Museum of Fine Arts (MFA) in Boston held focus groups on an upcoming exhibition of Winslow Homer's works, the researchers found that the public did not know much about the artist and might not attend. A museum executive used her experience, including the MFA shop's sales records of items linked to Homer, to indicate that while the public may not know his name, it knows his pictures and would turn out for the show. Because the museum relied on the executive's experience to help interpret the focus group, it was able to create a blockbuster event. On the other hand, sometimes research is right when the experts are wrong. Ford didn't listen to marketing research in the mid-1950s. The Edsel was built with features that consumers said they wanted, but the car itself did poorly in several rounds of consumer testing. Ford went ahead anyway, believing it could push the car with a strong sales force. The mistake cost about $350 million (in 1950s dollars)!

There is some debate about whether marketing researchers should recommend action. Whether marketing researchers make recommendations must depend on the total data available, the inclinations of the researcher and the desires of decision makers. In keeping with team spirit, most executives would like knowledgeable people to provide as many insights as possible. If recommendations are made, then the circumstances they are based on should be made clear.

WHO DOES MARKETING RESEARCH?

The first commercial research department was founded in 1911 at the Saturday Evening Post, when Charles C. Parlin completed his now-famous study of Campbell's soup users. He undertook the research because Campbell's executives refused to purchase advertising in the Post, believing that its working-class readership did not represent a significant market for the company. The soup sold at 10 cents a can, a cost they believed only wealthy consumers could afford. By counting cans in the garbage from different neighborhoods, Parlin proved they were wrong. He showed that canned soup was bought mainly by the time-constrained working class, whereas the wealthy enjoyed homemade soup prepared by servants. Campbell's became a big advertiser in the magazine and one of the top brand names in the United States.

In-Company Research An American Marketing Association (AMA) survey indicates that three out of four large companies have a formal in-company marketing research department. In fact, nearly all consumer products manufacturers, retailers, wholesalers, advertising agencies and publishers have such a department. Most were created within the last decade.

Most in-company marketing research departments are headed by experienced personnel who report to top executives. The research staff usually includes project directors, analysts and specialists. The project director is responsible for designing projects, which may be conducted within the department or by outside agencies. The position of analyst is an entry-level job with the function of interpreting specific types of data for select decisions. Analysts are usually part of a marketing team from several units or divisions, although they report directly to the head of their department. Marketing research specialists have expertise in one aspect of a project, such as survey design, data collection, statistics, modeling or marketing science.

Marketing research has developed to a point where few organizations have employees that cover the full range of skills required to conduct state-of-the-art research. Consequently, research is conducted by both in-house personnel and outside agencies, which may or may not work together. Data collection is a particularly broad field, and many companies are in the business of offering that service to others. Even if external agencies are used, however, most companies still need internal staff to help identify the research problem and interface with the outside agency.

External Research Companies often hire out marketing research. As you can see from Figure 4.8, conducting research can be a very lucrative business.

Outside agencies include consulting companies, full-service research firms, specialty research firms and syndicated data companies. Such consulting companies often conduct all phases of marketing research for clients

Rank	Organization	Headquarters	Total Research Revenue (Millions)
1	The Nielsen Co.	New York, NY	$2,651.0
2	Kantar	Fairfield, CT	$ 929.4
3	Ipsos	New York, NY	$ 590.0
4	Westat Inc.	Rockville, MD	$ 491.1
5	Information Resources, Inc.	Chicago, IL	$ 478.7
6	Arbitron Inc.	Columbia, MD	$ 444.1
7	GfK USA	Nuremberg, Germany	$ 330.9
8	IMS Health Inc.	Norwalk, CT	$ 271.3
9	The NPD Group Inc.	Port Washington, NY	$ 191.8
10	ICF International Inc.	Fairfax, VA	$ 191.2

Figure 4.8 Top 10 U.S. Research Organizations
Source: "Top 50 U.S. Market Research Organizations," Marketing News, June, 2013, p35

with whom they have an ongoing relationship, as well as with new clients who have unique information needs. Full-service firms focus on all aspects of data collection and analysis, and their personnel can handle the entire project. Specialty research firms concentrate on certain aspects of a project. There are more than 180 research firms in the United States, and U.S. companies spend more than $7 billion annually on external research.[25] Some only conduct surveys, relying on others to supply questionnaires and even others to perform data analysis. Certain specialty research firms help marketers better understand diversity or particular segments. Companies such as VNU Inc., IMS Health Inc. and Westat earn hundreds of millions of dollars

CREATING & CAPTURING VALUE THROUGH *Technology*

Nielsen: Forecasting Consumer Trends

Walking into a newsroom each morning is either tense or energizing, depending on how the previous day's shows performed in the Nielsen ratings. For media conglomerates, knowing their viewers' or listeners' next move drives the entire scope of their company's success. The Nielsen rating system is a marketing research company that calculates consumer behavior ratings and trends. A news organization, for example, would track how many viewers tuned in to watch the 11 o'clock newscast to see how it fared among other shows in that timeslot. The Nielsen ratings allow companies to not only know the quantity of their followers but also the quality of them. They are actively used in 100 countries and have proven to be one of the most respected marketing research firms on the planet. In addition to providing hard numbers for media outlets, Nielsen studies how people react to in-store environments and how they spend their time on the Internet. Companies can contract Nielsen to compile research information to create extensive profiles based on consumer trends. The company prides itself on its ability to forecast trends with a margin of error of 9 percent, 95 percent of the time, while maintaining high ethical standards. Currently, consumer activity with online media is at the forefront of Nielsen's marketing research.

But how is Nielsen able to obtain all of this information about online users without violating people's right to privacy? One way the company makes observations is simply by reading what people write in blogs, chat rooms, forum threads and comment boards. The company scours these sources to get feedback on products, media and general website attributes. This may seem simplistic, but Nielsen has developed a systematic way of combining this kind of information to create effective consumer trend information. Companies utilizing websites for advertising have chosen Nielsen to create the most suitable campaigns for their products.

Recently, Nielsen joined forces with DataLogix to help companies utilize online advertising more effectively. The program named PRIZM splits households within a database into 66 segments based on lifestyle, shopping behavior and media choices. This allows advertisers to market their campaigns at a household level using a sophisticated web of information. Gathering information about offline consumer behavior helps create a total lifestyle profile that is more comprehensive than ever before. This program will ultimately allow advertisers to target specific individuals as opposed to an entire demographic.

Within the global marketplace, there is tenacious competition among online media outlets. Online media will continue to be the focus of Nielsen's attention as long as millions of websites flourish yearly. The company's goal is to better understand online consumer behavior so it can help other companies successfully compete for advertising dollars.

www.nielsen.com, website visited April 20, 2014.

in research revenue each year.[26] Syndicated data companies also research one type of information or a single industry. For example, the Bureau of the Census and the Bureau of Labor Statistics are experts on census data and use the data to model various scenarios for clients. Neurocommunication Research Laboratory specializes in customized information about how broadcast and print advertisements trigger the maximum responses in viewers.

Because marketing research is critical for good decision making but expensive to conduct, most companies build a long-term association with one or more outside sources. This enables the agency to become familiar with the typical problems faced by the organization and to establish a good working relationship with in-company marketing research staff.

TECHNOLOGY'S EFFECT ON MARKETING RESEARCH

Technology has brought many changes to marketing research. Today's marketers can acquire and analyze information faster than ever before. Technology has also made it easier for them to connect with an increasing number of customers and information sources. In the past, marketing research was a relatively static process in the face of constantly changing markets. Now marketers can track the marketplace in real time, quickly collecting data and converting it into information just as quickly.

In addition to making the research process faster, technology has made it more convenient and more accurate. Computers can create a virtual model of a store to quiz consumers about. Consumers can make product selections as they scroll through the computer image, effortlessly changing brands or features. The virtual store gives marketers a no-risk way to exercise their imagination early in the product development process.[27] For an example, virtual tours of the hotel room became an important feature of online travel sites such as Travelocity, Expedia and Orbitz.[28] Technology helps reduce the cost as well as the risk of marketing innovations.

INTERNET SEARCHES

The web can be an excellent source of marketing data. In fact, it is sometimes referred to as the world's largest resource library. It contains information on literally millions of topics and is updated instantly. The trick is to sift through all of it to find what you need. Marketers do this through the use of a search engine such as Google, Yahoo! or Bing. Google is expanding its search capabilities to include offline library content in online search results. All 12 universities of the Big Ten consortium joined Google's efforts, adding more than 10 million volumes of material to Google's current collection of over 15 million. Books are scanned and digitized, and when a user searches a key word, the Google results will show information about the book and a few sentences that display that search term within the book. Google estimates there are approximately 130 million unique books in the world, and it plans to scan all of them by the end of the decade.[29]

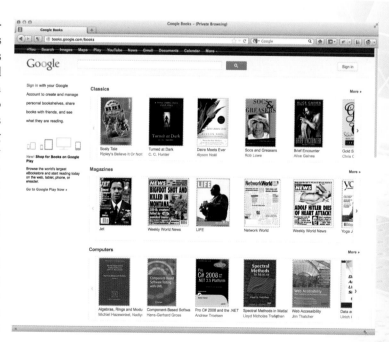

GLOBAL MARKETING RESEARCH

Global marketing research involves the same process as any other kind — from research design to the interpretation and presentation of results. And usually the same techniques are employed — interviews, focus groups and surveys. However, the level of difficulty increases exponentially when conducting global marketing research.

It is not easy to locate secondary data in foreign countries. Some national governments simply don't gather certain information. For example, Ethiopia and Chad don't gather population statistics.[30] Many developing countries lack mechanisms for collecting data about retail and wholesale activities. Even if secondary data are available, they may be incomplete or inaccurate. The data may be manipulated by the government for political reasons — for instance, some countries report an artificially low inflation rate. In developing countries, data are likely to be based on estimates or outdated processes.[31] Industrialized nations usually have sophisticated collection procedures, at least for basic statistics on population and economic activity. One resource that marketers can utilize is globalEDGE™. It was developed by MSU-CIBER at Michigan State University as the ultimate international marketing research tool. GlobalEDGE™ has up-to-date information on 200 countries including maps, governmental information, key statistics and history, as well as economic, stock market and country-specific marketing resources and news.

Because secondary data are difficult to find, global research often requires the collection of primary data.

Because secondary data are difficult to find, global research often requires the collection of primary data. This comes with challenges of its own, not the least of which is the language barrier. It's very difficult to ensure an exact translation, especially when slang is used. Many researchers use a technique called back translation: The research question is translated into the foreign language by one person, and then it is put back in the original language by a second person. This helps catch any errors. It certainly helped an Australian soft-drink company hoping to market its product in Hong Kong. Its slogan, "Baby, it's cold in here," translated into Chinese as: "Small mosquito, on the inside it is very cold."[32]

Once the survey instrument is translated, the equally difficult task of finding participants begins. In Mexico, there are only 17 (unreliable) phones lines per 100 citizens.[33] In Brazil, nearly 30 percent of all mail is never delivered, a situation that is not unique. Even if the mail gets through, literacy can be another barrier. Sometimes even individual interviews present challenges. In many cultures, it's considered embarrassing to discuss personal hygiene, such as which shampoo or soap you use. The Germans tend to avoid conversations about personal finances, and the Dutch would rather talk about sex than money. Nevertheless, companies that avoid global marketing research find themselves in trouble. When Gerber started selling baby food in Africa, they used the same packages they did in the U.S., featuring the classic image of a baby on the front. What they did not realize was that because the primary language was not English in every African country, companies routinely put pictures on the label to represent what's inside. In Taiwan, the Pepsi slogan "Come alive with the Pepsi Generation" was translated as "Pepsi will bring your ancestors back from the dead."[34] Proper marketing research would have caught these mistakes.

Global marketing research is becoming more and more prevalent as companies expand their scope of operations. The time it takes to conduct worldwide research has been reduced by online interviews, the global expansion of telephones and fax machines, and express delivery services. For example, one software company conducted a worldwide survey of more than 80 clients in only three weeks. This amazing feat, which would have been virtually impossible without use of the Internet, involved modeling tasks, computer programming, list development, respondent recruiting, and data retrieval, analysis and reporting. As a result of the research, the company was able to improve its pricing strategy.

ETHICS IN MARKETING RESEARCH AND INFORMATION USE

J. D. Power is paid by automakers to provide research on customer satisfaction, the results of which are used in publication to promote autos. Some magazine editors receive "consulting fees" from auto companies and write reviews of car performance. These are certainly legal practices, but are they ethical? With the information explosion comes the potential for deceptive research that can be used to alter consumers' opinions. Historically, studies were sponsored by scientists, the federal government and academic institutions. Today, with government and universities on tight budgets, private companies fill the void with so-called objective research for hire. Corporations, litigants, political candidates, trade associations, lobbyists and special-interest groups can buy research to use as they like.[35]

A study by the Boston Center for Strategy Research revealed that some marketing managers believe market research is likely to reflect biases rather than present objective information. They also believe much of it is conducted to confirm a preconceived conclusion or validate a client's position. In other words, it arrives at the desired outcome, no matter what the facts may indicate. Research of this nature is confirmatory, not exploratory.[36]

The scientific method is supposed to prevent this type of bias, because anyone else duplicating a study or experiment should come up with the same results. More and more of the information available to consumers is created to sell a product or advance a cause, though; buying and selling information to advance a private agenda demonstrates how the modern sense of truth may be warped.[37] Companies obviously want their products portrayed in a positive light, and privately sponsored studies often downplay negative information.[38] This becomes an ethical or legal problem if information that indicates potential harm to customers is suppressed.

Although consumers are increasingly suspicious about "facts," they often have little basis for questioning them. The average consumer does not have enough personal knowledge to dispute the research that almost daily shapes our beliefs about social, political, economic and environmental issues. That is why many groups exist to assist and protect consumers. Interested in truth, objectivity and accuracy, these groups consist of representatives from industry, individual companies, academia and the government. They have taken action to regulate the content of information and to defend the average consumer from distorted messages. Some industries have collectively formulated policies in order to reduce litigation, prevent mandatory regulation and increase consumer trust. Still, questionable information finds its way to consumers.

Consider a study sponsored by Procter & Gamble, the leading maker of disposable diapers. For several years, the company had been fighting a public relations battle against environmentalists and the cloth diaper industry. Environmentalists pushed cloth diapers, and their sales skyrocketed; more than a dozen state legislatures were considering various regulations for disposable diapers. Under pressure, Procter & Gamble decided to finance a public policy study. The researchers found that disposable and cloth diapers were environmentally equivalent, when factors such as energy and water use were taken into account. P&G's public relations improved, as did their diaper sales. Gerber Products, the largest supplier of cloth diapers at the time, closed three plants and laid off 900 workers. Gerber's CEO said: "There was a dramatic change in the cloth diaper market caused by reduced environmental concern about disposable diapers."[39] Procter & Gamble won back lost market share and gained, at least temporarily, acceptance of disposables. Today, new companies have emerged to make cloth diapering a popular option again. bumGenius cloth diapers are designed to make cloth diapering easy for every-day people while being wallet and planet friendly. It claims buying cloth diapers instead of disposables will save up to $1,200 and prevent up to 1 ton of landfill waste.[40]

bumGenius cloth diapers have been a huge success. The company now produces a variety of colors, styles, and even its own laundry detergent.

Although a marketer may occasionally benefit from biased information, those who connect ethically are more likely to create a profitable long-term relationship based on trust and loyalty. Often, as companies seek to build such relationships, the first question they must answer is: What customers are we trying to reach and how do we go about it? One concern for parents is the ethical use of information about children under the age of 18. The Children's Online Privacy Act of 1998 covers targeting children. In response, Kibu.com has promised to keep all information regarding its 13- to 18-year-old target market private.[41]

Another dimension of the ethical use of marketing research information lies in information obtained about the Internet and its users. Privacy is an important issue for most Internet users. The Online Privacy and Disclosure Act of 2003, passed in California, requires all commercial entities that collect personal information online to clearly post a privacy policy and makes it unlawful for an online entity to violate it.[42]

CHAPTER SUMMARY

Objective 1: Understand the roles that marketing information systems (MIS) and research play in marketing decision making.

You can't connect with customers if you can't locate, understand and respond to them. An MIS is critical in making informed decisions about nearly every aspect of marketing. It is used to systematically collect and analyze data to support decision making. An MIS often includes a marketing decision support system (MDSS), which puts information in convenient forms for executives to use. An MIS is ongoing and encompass all information. Marketing research is conducted to address a particular opportunity, problem or issue. Marketing information is used in planning, marketing mix decisions and performance monitoring.

Objective 2: Recognize how data are transformed into information to be used in a variety of marketing decisions.

Data and information are not the same. Data must be translated into information before they are useful for decision making. External data come from outside the firm, and internal data originate inside the firm. Both types are stored in databases so they can be retrieved through a computer. Primary data are collected for the first time to address a specific issue. Secondary data already exist and can be accessed immediately by a broad range of users. Once data are assembled, they must

be analyzed through data sorting, the use of statistics and models. A of this is done with particular issues and decision areas in mind.

Objective 3: Understand the types of research and the steps of a typical marketing research process.

The marketing research process starts with the problem definition which focuses on the needs of decision makers to ensure that the re search will be useful. The research design is then based on what deci sions need what information, what data and data sources will provid that information, and how the data will be collected and analyzed Next, exploratory research helps investigators better understand issue by defining problems, searching for possible explanations, and creating hypotheses. Quantitative research yields information to help decision makers select the best course of action. Because it is quantitative, esti mates usually can be made of the likely results of actions. This require appropriate measurement and sampling. The last steps are to interpre and report findings. Experience and insight are useful at this stage be cause the same information can be interpreted in various ways.

Objective 4: Describe widely used marketing research techniques.

Exploratory research techniques include focus groups, depth inter views, projective techniques, observation, and case analysis. A focu

oup usually has eight to twelve people. Several sessions must be used
ace the group, not individuals, provide the data. Depth interviews
e one-on-one conversations. Researchers spend a lot of time probing
few respondents about their opinions and actions. With projective
chniques, subjects are asked to analyze contrived situations or to give
pinions about how they believe others may respond. Observation pro-
des insights by watching consumers in a range of situations. Finally,
ase analysis is the study of a few situations in depth. It is particularly
seful for benchmarking. Quantitative research often involves using the
ientific method. Surveys and test markets are common in this type
research. Survey data are usually collected from a sample of the
opulation. Questionnaire design is important. Likert scales or bipolar
djective scales frequently are used in questionnaires.

Objective 5: Explore how marketing information is being influenced by technology and is obtained globally.

Both internal and external marketing research is being dramatically influenced by technology. It facilitates the faster collection and analysis of greater quantities of information than was possible in the past. The Internet is a revolutionary way of interacting with customers. Research in global markets is complicated because secondary data may be scarce. Surveys must be carefully translated, and data collection is often diffi-cult. Still, global research is becoming more and more important.

Objective 6: Understand the ethical issues that surround the use and dissemination of research.

There are many ethical issues surrounding marketing research. One problem is that it sometimes can reflect the biases of marketers. When research is conducted to confirm a preconceived conclusion or vali-date a position, the results are not likely to be objective. The scientific method can eliminate this type of bias. A number of groups exist to prevent the manipulation of marketing research. They are interested in accuracy and want to protect consumers.

REVIEW YOUR UNDERSTANDING

1. What is a marketing information system (MIS)? What is a market-ing decision support system (MDSS)? What is a transaction-based information system (TBIS)?
2. What is marketing research? How is it different from an MIS?
3. How are data transformed into information? What are the three steps?
4. What are the differences between primary and secondary data?
5. What are the three major uses of marketing information? Explain.
6. What are the steps in a typical marketing research project?
7. What is exploratory research? List five exploratory research meth-ods.
8. What is quantitative research? Name two quantitative methods.
9. Give two challenges associated with global marketing research.
10. What are the pros and cons of each type of survey data collection?

DISCUSSION OF CONCEPTS

1. How is an MIS used? What are the two components of a typical MIS? Describe them.
2. What is the difference between data and information? Why is it important for marketers to provide executives with information rather than data?
3. Explain the objective of the marketing decision support system.
4. List and describe the four types of information an MIS provides. What is the importance of each type for decision making?
5. Describe each step of the marketing research process. Why is it critical to lay out each step in detail prior to beginning any research project?
6. Select a marketing problem and design a suitable marketing re-search approach to address it.
7. After completing an exploratory research study, how would you decide whether quantitative research is in order?
8. What would be the major considerations in developing a market-ing research capability for a small company?
9. Under what circumstances would you consider it to be ethical to withhold marketing research from interested consumers? When would it be unethical?

KEY TERMS & DEFINITIONS

1. **Case analysis:**   The in-depth study of a few examples.
2. **Causal research:**   Research that attempts to prove a cause-and-effect relationship between two phenomena.
3. **Convenience sample:**   A sample composed of people who happen to come along, such as shoppers in a store at a given time, whoever answers the doorbell, or travelers passing through an airport.
4. **Data:**   Facts or statistics obtained from outside or inside the company.
5. **Database:**   A collection of data that can be retrieved by a computer.
6. **Depth interview:**   A relatively unstructured conversation that allows the researcher to probe deeply into a consumer's thoughts.
7. **Experiment:**   A test conducted under controlled conditions in order to prove or disprove a marketing hypothesis.
8. **Exploratory research:**   Research designed to clarify the problem and suggest ways to address it.
9. **External data:**   Data obtained outside the company.
10. **Focus group:**   A group, usually composed of eight to twelve people, whose opinions are elicited by an interviewer to provide exploratory insights into a problem.
11. **Hypothesis:**   A tentative assumption about a particular event or issue.
12. **Information:**   Data that has been analyzed and put in useful form.
13. **Internal data:**   Data obtained within the company.
14. **Judgment sample:**   A sample selected by the researchers or interviewers based on their belief that those chosen represent a majority of the study population.
15. **Likert scale:**   A scale that measures the respondent's intensity of agreement with a particular statement.
16. **Management information system (MIS):**   A computerized system used to collect and analyze the data needed for management decision making. The marketing information system is often considered a part of this system.
17. **Marketing decision support system (MDSS):**   A two-way communication bridge between the people who collect and analyze information and the executives who use it.
18. **Marketing information system (MIS):**   A computerized system used to collect and analyze marketing data.
19. **Marketing research:**   The formal assembly and analysis of information about specific issues surrounding the marketing of goods and services.
20. **Nonprobability sample:**   A sample in which the likelihood of selecting a particular respondent from the sampling frame cannot be calculated.
21. **Observation:**   A research technique whereby researchers simply watch the participants they are studying.
22. **Pilot study:**   A small-scale project that allows the researcher to refine and test the approaches that eventually will be used.
23. **Population (universe):**   All the individuals or organizations relevant to the marketing research project.
24. **Primary data:**   Information collected for the first time.
25. **Probability sample:**   A sample in which the chance of selecting a given individual from the sampling frame or population can be calculated.
26. **Projective technique:**   A technique that enables respondents to project their thoughts onto a third party or object or through some type of contrived situation.
27. **Quantitative research:**   Research designed to provide the information needed to select the best course of action and estimate the probable results.
28. **Research design:**   An outline of what data will be gathered, what sources will be used, and how the data will be collected and analyzed.
29. **Sample:**   The group participating in a research project that represents the entire population of potential respondents.
30. **Sampling frame:**   A list of people in the universe who potentially could be contacted.
31. **Scientific method:**   A systematic way to gather, analyze, and interpret data in order to confirm or disconfirm a prior conception.
32. **Secondary data:**   Information that already has been collected.
33. **Simple random sampling:**   A sampling technique in which each member of the study population has an equal and known chance of being chosen.
34. **Stratified random sampling:**   A sampling technique in which each member of a selected subgroup of the population has an equal chance of selection.
35. **Transaction-based information system (TBIS):**   A computerized link between a firm and its customers, distributors, and suppliers.

REFERENCES

1. P&G 2013 Sustainability Overview; P&G 2013 Annual Report.
2. Dazzo, Olga, personal interview, Sparrow Health System, Lansing, MI.
3. "IntelliQuest Research Identifies Key Concerns About Mobile eCommerce," Canadian Corporate Newswire, August 14, 2000.
4. Fusaro, Dave, "Meeting Wal-Mart's Mandates," www.foodprocessing.com, website visited April 16, 2010.
5. www.forrester.com, website visited June 28, 2014.
6. www.dnb.com, website visited June 28, 2014.
7. "Gannett Selects the AMM Group to Provide Advertising Performance Measurement System," Reuters. www.reuters.com, website visited March 3, 2014.
8. Radius Global Market Research. www.radius-global.com, website visited March 3, 2014.
9. Byron, Ellen, "New Penney: Chain Goes for 'Missing Middle,'" The Wall Street Journal, February 14, 2005, pg. B1.
10. Miranda Miller, "Google Now Owns 44% of Global Advertising Market," www.searchenginewatch.com, website visited June 13, 2014.
11. www.acnielsen.com, website visited April 16, 2014.
12. Gill, Tracy A., "Online Survey Facilitates Customer Feedback," Target Marketing, (Philadelphia: July 2005), Vol. 28, Iss. 7, pg. 13.
13. www.nielsen.com, website visited June 18, 2014.
14. Einstein, A.; Infeld, L., The Evolution of Physics (New York: Simon & Schuster, 1942), pg. 95.
15. www.google.com, website visited June 31, 2014.
16. www.activegroup.com, website visited June 18, 2014.
17. Harrell, Gilbert D.; Hutt, Michael D.; Anderson, James C., "Path Analysis of Buyer Behavior Under Conditions of Crowding," Journal of Marketing Research, February 1980, pg. 47.
18. ADD, www.meridianai.com/success_product_kimberly-clark.html, website visited June 15, 2014.
19. Marshall, Christy, "Have It Your Way with Research," Advertising Age, April 4, 1983.
20. "Fusing the Generational Gap," Business Wire, April 4, 2000.
21. Schmidt, Jeffery B.; Calantone, Roger J.; Griffin, Abbie; Montoyaweiss, Mitzi M., "Do Certified Mail Third-Wave Follow-Ups Really Boost Response Rates and Quality?" Marketing letters 16:2, 2005, pp. 129-141.
22. Girard, Peter, "Alloy's Online/Offline Dividends," Catalog Age, May 2000, pg. 12.
23. Cross, Richard, "Real-Time and Online Research Is Paying Off," Direct Marketing, May 2000, pg. 61.
24. "Best Buy Customer Voice Survey," Best Buy, www.bestbuycares.com, site visited June 15, 2014.
25. Honomichl, Jack, "Strong Progress, U.S. research firms see healthy growth in '04," Marketing News, June 15, 2005, pg. 3.
26. "Top 50 U.S. Research Organizations," Marketing news, June 15, 2005, pg. 4.
27. "Tru Dynamics Launches E-Commerce Virtual Mall," Business Wire, June 20, 2000.
28. Lewis, Len, "Paddle Surfing," Stores Vol. 88, November 2006, pg. 136.
29. Joab Jackson, "Google: 129 Million Different Books Have Been Published," www.pcworld.com, website visited May 27, 2014.
30. Henessey, Jeannet, Global Marketing Strategies, 3rd ed. (Boston: Houghton Mifflin, 1995), pg. 202.
31. "The Good Statistics Guide," Economist, September 11, 1993, pg. 34.
32. Onkvisit, Sak; Shaw, John J., International Marketing, 2nd ed. (Upper Saddle River, New Jersey: Prentice Hall, 1993), pg. 398.
33. www.cia.gov, website visited July 31, 2014.
34. Bush, Ian; Damminger, Rachelle; Daniels, Lisa Marie; Laoye, Elizabeth, "Communication Strategies: Marketing to the 'Majority Minority,'" Villanova University Publications, 2005.
35. Crossens, Cynthia, Tainted Truth: The Manipulation of Fact in America (New York: Simon & Schuster, 1994, pg. 19.
36. "Respondents Assail Quality of Research," Marketing news, May 8, 1995, pg. 14.
37. Crossens, Tainted Truth, pg. 14.
38. Ibid., pg. 19.
39. Kluger, Jeffrey, "Poll Vaulting," Discover, May 1995.
40. www.bumgenius.com, website visited June 5, 2014.
41. "They Know What Girls Want," Marketing News, March 27, 2000, pg. 3.
42. Swartz, Nikki, "California Passes Online Privacy Bill," Information Management Journal, Lemexa: September/October 2004, Vol. 38, Iss. 5, pg. 11.

Chapter 05

UNDERSTANDING CONSUMER BEHAVIOR

The do-it-yourself home improvement industry was revolutionized when Bernie Marcus and Arthur Blank opened the first Home Depot in 1978. As one of the largest retailers in the world, The Home Depot has captured the spirit of customers looking to improve their homes. Through trained associates, The Home Depot provides the tools and knowledge on how to lay tile, install faucets and use power tools to the ordinary homeowner. Customers will find up to 40,000 top-of-the-line products, including building materials, home improvement supplies, and lawn and garden products. Each store is tailored to the local market, offering products based on climate needs.

Understanding the needs of its different customers has made The Home Depot the success it is today. The company acknowledges that for many people, their home is the biggest financial investment they make and improvements can be costly and stressful. The company strives to make home improvements as easy as possible for all of its customers. As a result, the company divides its customers into three categories. The first category is the do-it-yourself customers. For these customers, the company provides free "how-to" clinics every Saturday and Sunday for common household projects. The second category is the do-it-for-me customers who purchase the materials themselves but hire a third party for installations. The Home Depot readily provides installation for a variety of projects through independent contractors. Lastly, The Home Depot provides for the needs of professional customers through will-call services, expanded credit programs, and merchandise selection.

Today, the company is transforming the home improvement industry through the aggressive introduction of the Eco-Option brand. Recognizing increased customer awareness of the environment, the company has labeled every product that benefits sustainable forestry, energy efficiency, healthy homes, clean air and water conservation. Fluorescent light bulbs, natural insect killers and bamboo flooring are just a few of the 3,000 environmentally friendly products the company is offering in its stores. To further its commitment to the Eco-Options line, Home Depot sponsored a Christmas light trade at all of its retail locations. Customers could trade in old strands of lights (both working and non-working) to be properly recycled. Customers then received a $3 coupon toward the purchase of new energy-efficient LED string lights. The new LED lights are said to last up to 10 percent longer and use 80 percent less energy.

While The Home Depot is influencing its customers to buy green products, it is encouraging its suppliers to do the same. As the world's largest buyer of building materials, The Home Depot has promoted suppliers who earn the Eco-Option label through prominent shelf space and marketing in weekly advertisements. The company's dedication to making positive environmental product-purchasing decisions is realized through policies such as wood purchasing. The Home Depot researched every wood-containing product it sells, from building lumber to broom handles, to understand where it was harvested. The company then pledged preference to wood that has come from managed forests that meet strict sustainable guidelines. "From our wood-purchasing policy to having our first store certified as green by the U.S. Green Building Council, we are committed to helping improve the environment and lessening our impact on it," said Home Depot Chairman Frank Blake. "And Eco-Options is the next step in expanding that commitment."[1]

<< The Home Depot Interior

Learning Objectives

1. Appreciate the importance of involvement in the decisions consumers make.
2. Evaluate the effect on consumer behavior of such psychological factors as motivation, perception, learning, attitudes and information processing.
3. Explain how social factors such as culture, subculture, social class, reference groups and family help explain consumer behavior.

THE CONCEPT OF CONSUMER BEHAVIOR

More than ever, consumers and markets are diversifying. The challenge for cutting-edge organizations is to enhance the life experiences of consumers with products that live up to their expectations. Every action must contribute in some way to consumer well-being, which requires a thorough knowledge of consumer decision making and the forces that influence it. To understand customers, we must comprehend the societal and psychological factors that determine their decisions. Leading organizations are bundling their knowledge of all these factors into systematic ways of influencing customer satisfaction, loyalty and relationships. Discovering and delivering value requires a thorough understanding of consumer behavior.

Consumer behavior involves the actions and decision processes of individuals and households in discovering, evaluating, acquiring, consuming, and disposing of products. Consider the key parts of that definition. First, it looks at both actions — what people do — and decision processes — how they think and feel. Marketers want to know how often the shopping occurs and for what reasons. Second, the definition refers to individuals and households. Usually an individual makes the purchase, but those decisions are often related to household considerations. When a mother shops, she may buy Pepsi for one person, Coke for another, bottled water for a third, and so forth. Third, evaluating, acquiring and consuming products are important parts of the process, but we need to remember that consumer behavior starts with discovery and proceeds through disposal.

Figure 5.1 provides an overview of the main topics covered in this chapter. We begin with the relationship between consumer involvement and decision making. Then we incorporate five psychological factors that influence consumer behavior and the social influences that affect the decisions of individual consumers. In the last sections, we look at ways in which technology is used to track consumer behavior, as well as ethical issues related to attempts to persuade consumers.

Consumer Behavior

Involves the actions and decision processes of individuals and households in discovering, evaluating, acquiring, consuming and disposing of products.

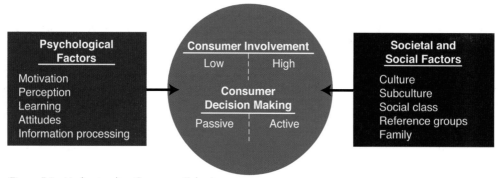

Figure 5.1   Understanding Consumer Behavior

CONSUMER INVOLVEMENT AND DECISION MAKING

Decision making and involvement are closely related processes. Involvement is a function of how important, complex and/or time-consuming a purchase may be. Decision making varies with the degree of involvement. For high-involvement purchases, the consumer is likely to devote time and attention to each of the five steps in the decision process. Understanding both concepts and how they relate provides insight into how and why consumers behave as they do.

CONSUMER INVOLVEMENT

Think about the difference between buying a box of breakfast cereal and a new home. Which purchase would you spend more time researching and generally care more about? Some purchases are more important to the consumer than others. **Low-involvement purchases** require only simple decision making; cereal, soap, soft drinks and similar items don't require much thought. Many people purchase the same brand every time they shop, which underscores the importance of brand awareness. **High-involvement purchases** demand more extensive and complex decision making. Buying a car, a computer or even a television requires a good deal of thought. The product is expensive and you will likely own it for a long time. Nontraditional products often fall in this category. An extreme example of high-involvement purchases involves Curtco Robb Media LLC, which publishes magazines such as The Robb Report and Showboats International. These magazines advertise such nontraditional products as Yves Saint Laurent's Waterproof Loafers; private jet-rental providers; vacation homes overlooking the Old Course in St. Andrews, Scotland; and luxury yachts. These magazines tout themselves as a one-stop resource for the luxury lifestyle. However, many high-involvement products are more frequently purchased items like jeans, jewelry and automobiles. What requires high involvement for one person might be a low-involvement purchase for another.[2]

Figure 5.2 shows how involvement influences decision making. The level of involvement with any product depends on its perceived importance to the consumer's self-image. High-involvement products tend to be tied to self-image, whereas low-involvement products are not. A middle-aged consumer who feels (and wants to look) youthful may invest a great deal of time in her decision to buy a sport-utility vehicle instead of a sedan. However, when purchasing an ordinary light bulb, she may buy without thinking, because the purchase has nothing to do with self-image. On the other hand, if she sees herself as a "green" consumer, her desire for energy conservation might get her to think a lot about which type of light bulb to buy. Generally, the more visible, risky or costly the product, the higher the level of involvement.

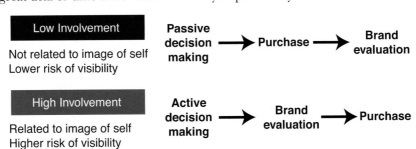

Figure 5.2   Low/High Involvement and Passive/Active Decision Making

Involvement also influences the relationship between product evaluation and purchasing behaviors. With low-involvement products, consumers generally purchase and try them first and then form an evaluation. With high-involvement

Low-involvement Purchase

A routine buying decision.

High-involvement Purchase

A complex buying decision made after extensive thought.

products, they first form an evaluation (expectation), and then purchase. Consumers do not actively research low-involvement products, instead they form an opinion of them through commercial advertisements or conversations with friends. This is called **passive learning,** which characterizes the passive decision-making process. Only when they acquire and use the product do they learn more about it. In contrast, consumers investigate high-involvement products through **active learning**—part of an active decision-making process—in order to form an opinion about which product to purchase.

Figure 5.3 shows that products fall on a continuum between low and high involvement. Moving toward the high end, decisions are made about more expensive, permanent and complex products that also are more related to self-concept. Consumers give these purchases more thought.

Figure 5.3   Examples of Products on an Involvement Continuum

CONSUMER DECISION MAKING

For a better understanding of consumer buying behavior, marketers have broken the decision process into the five steps shown in Figure 5.4 (along with examples). Consumers making low-involvement purchases may skip the first three steps altogether. As involvement increases, each step takes on greater importance, and more active learning occurs.

Problem recognition occurs when a consumer becomes aware of an unfulfilled desire. In a low-involvement situation, such as the purchase of a song, you might immediately go to a place such as iTunes and casually select recordings by two or three of your favorite artists. Or, if you're thirsty, you may simply run out and buy a soft drink. In a high-involvement purchase, the recognition of a need may arise long before it is acted upon. In the case of a house, the cost may prevent you from acting on your need for several years.

The **information search** consists of thinking through the situation, calling up experiences stored in memory (internal search), and probably seeking information from friends, salespeople, advertisements, online services and other sources (external search). Each source has its benefits and drawbacks: Experience is an effective learning device, but you may not have enough firsthand information. An external search is beneficial, but friends may have preferences different from yours, salespeople

Passive Learning

Learning in which little energy is devoted to thinking about or elaborating on information.

Active Learning

Learning in which substantial energy is devoted to thinking about and elaborating on information.

Problem Recognition

Becoming aware of an unfulfilled need or desire.

Information Search

Thinking through a situation by recalling information stored in memory or obtaining it from external sources.

STEPS IN DECISION MAKING

Figure 5.4   The Consumer Decision Making Process

EXAMPLES IN ERIN'S PURCHASE

Erin's old Ford Explorer is giving her trouble, so she starts thinking about a new vehicle.

Erin decides what she likes or dislikes about her old Explorer. She talks with family and friends and searches Internet sources on vehicles.

Erin establishes some decision rules (price, features, styling), test drives several vehicles, and evaluates her options.

Erin decides on a Ford Escape Hybrid and determines that leasing will work best for her.

Friends and family like the car, which reinforces Erin's decision. Interaction with the Ford dealer after the sale is positive.

may push the product that earns them the highest commission, and ads are often incomplete.

Alternatives evaluation is based on decision rules about which product or service is most likely to satisfy goals. These rules are personal; that is, they vary according to what the individual consumer considers important. At this point, complex thinking is likely to occur. Using the results of the information search, the consumer weighs the pros and cons of each choice.

The **purchase decision** emerges from the evaluation of alternatives. A consumer may decide to save the money instead or spend it on a different item altogether. He or she may play it safe by deciding to purchase a small amount for trial purposes, or by deciding to lease rather than to buy. The decision to buy often occurs some time before the actual **purchase** — the actual financial commitment and transaction made to acquire the product. It may take time to secure a mortgage or car loan, or the dealer may be temporarily out of stock.

The **purchase evaluation** stage results in satisfaction or dissatisfaction. Buyers often seek assurance from others that their choice was correct. Positive feedback reinforces the consumer's decision and affirms expectations, making it more likely that he or she will make a similar purchase in the future.

PSYCHOLOGICAL FACTORS THAT INFLUENCE CONSUMER DECISIONS

Although the decision-making process appears straightforward, it is influenced by many psychological factors. The most important are: (1) motivation, (2) perception, (3) learning, (4) attitudes and (5) information processing.

MOTIVATION

Marketers first conducted "motivation research" during the 1950s and early 1960s in an attempt to identify buyers' subconscious reasons for purchasing various products. This work has since been discredited, because it was based on a very limited theory and poor research techniques. The pioneering psychoanalyst Sigmund Freud suggested that most human behavior is determined not by conscious thought but by unconscious urges, passions, repressed feelings and underlying desires. Based on these beliefs, motivation researchers proposed ideas such as men purchasing a convertible as a substitute for a mistress, and women making cakes as a symbol of giving birth. About the best that can be said for this early work is that it inspired marketers to develop new methods of researching motivation. Today, motivation theories are much sounder, and they provide several basic insights for marketers.

Motivation is an internal force that directs behavior toward the fulfillment of needs. It involves the needs (or goals) a person has and the energy that is triggered to drive the person to action. The needs that underlie motivation can be classified as either biological or psychological. Biological needs have been called primary or innate needs, because they seem to exist in all people, regardless of environment. Needs in this category include food, water, shelter, fresh air and at least some degree of comfort. Products such as Evian spring water, Kellogg's Special K, and Fruit of the Loom T-shirts were developed in direct response to

Alternatives Evaluation

Use of decision rules that attempt to determine which product would be most likely to satisfy goals.

Purchase Decision

The decision of whether or not to buy and which competing product to buy, which is made after carefully weighing the alternatives.

Purchase

The financial commitment to acquire a product.

Purchase Evaluation

The process of determining satisfaction or dissatisfaction with a buying choice.

Motivation

An internal force that directs behavior toward the fulfillment of needs.

The 1942 Westinghouse poster was produced to boost morale in factories where women were working during World War II.

this type of need. **Psychological needs** are often called secondary or learned needs, because they result from socialization. Needs in this category include friendship, a sense of self-worth and achievement or self-fulfillment. The U.S. Army slogan "Be all that you can be" appeals directly to psychological needs. The 1942 Westinghouse poster depicting a female factory worker (Rosie the Riveter) rolling up her sleeve was produced to keep production up by boosting morale during World War II.

Maslow's Hierarchy of Needs

Abraham Maslow's famous classification is often used by marketers to help categorize consumer desires. According to Maslow, five basic needs underlie most human goals. He ranked them in a hierarchy to indicate that higher-level needs tend to emerge only after lower-level needs are satisfied. Figure 5.5 illustrates Maslow's hierarchy in the form of a pyramid.

At the base of the pyramid are physiological needs essential to survival, such as food, clean air and water, warmth, and sleep. Businesses tend to market products that fulfill physiological needs only if they meet higher level needs as well, such as Evian water. Water is the basic, physiological need, but the name "Evian" draws on one's need for esteem.

On the next level is the need for safety, which includes basic security and freedom from physical abuse. These needs are both biological and psychological. Insurance companies appeal to them with such slogans as "Nationwide is on your side."

The third level of the pyramid is the need for companionship, love and belonging. Family and friends are instrumental in satisfying this need. Advertisements for Kay Jewelers and 1-800-FLOWERS play on our need for human interaction, love and belonging.

The fourth level is the need for esteem, which comes from prestige, status and self-respect. Many consumers maintain and exhibit their social status through high-visibility products. Designer labels or symbols on clothing and recognizable automobile designs are two ways marketers have attempted to fulfill this need.

The final level of Maslow's hierarchy is the need for self-actualization. As people begin to feel physically satisfied, safe and secure, accepted, and esteemed by others, they may need a higher level of personal satisfaction, spurring them to develop themselves and their abilities. Education is directed toward this need by helping people attain knowledge and experiences that improve self-worth, sharpen talents, and promote personal growth. Self-actualization also may come from coaching youth soccer or playing in a basketball league. Backpacking, writing, skiing, painting and composing are other examples. The

Psychological Needs

A need that arises in the socialization process.

Self-Actualization	Self-fulfillment and personal enrichment
Esteem	Prestige and status
Love and Belonging	Friendship and acceptance
Safety	Security and protection
Physiological	Nutrition and air

Figure 5.5   Maslow's Hierarchy of Needs
Source: Adapted from Abraham H. Maslow, Motivation and Personality, 2nd ed. Copyright 1970 by Abraham H. Maslow. Reprinted by permission of Harper & Row Publishers, Inc.

Marine Corps has a new ad titled "The Sound of Chaos" and depicts troops heading into battle, then challenges the viewer, "Which way would you run?"

Motivational Conflict

People are motivated to attain some ends and avoid others. In marketing terms, consumers approach activities that help them attain desired outcomes but avoid activities that have negative consequences. Yet, because

Type	Description	Sample Situation	Possible Marketing Response
Approach-Approach	Two objectives are desired, but the consumer cannot have both	Toothpaste ↙ ↘ Health with fluoride / Sex appeal with breath freshener	**Provide both benefits:** Toothpaste with fluoride and a breath freshener.
Avoidance-Avoidance	The consumer must choose between two undesirable alternatives	Muffler repair ↙ ↘ Depleted savings / Bothersome exhaust noise	**Stress unpleasantness of one alternative to get desired action:** Muffler ads that emphasize how embarrassing a defective muffler can be or that offer financing or delayed payments.
Approach-Avoidance	The consumer's goal has both positive and negative aspects	College education ↙ ↘ Hard work and expense / Greater earnings opportunities	**Emphasize positive benefits of desired action:** A college ad campaign that illustrates how long-term earnings compare for a college graduate and a nongraduate.

Figure 5.6   Types of Motivational Conflict

human needs and wants are so varied, consumers may be faced with outcomes that combine both desirable and undesirable features. Three types of such motivational conflict have been identified: approach-approach, avoidance-avoidance, and approach-avoidance. These are summarized in Figure 5.6.

Approach-approach conflict occurs when a consumer desires two objectives but cannot have both. Suppose Anthony wants fuel-efficiency but SUV carrying capacity in a new car. Anthony has two desirable options, but unless he can afford to buy a both a Dart and a Durango, he will have to buy one or the other. Dodge attempts to circumvent the conflict with its midsize crossover Journey. It gets 26 mpg on the highway and still has room for life. It is targeted at consumers who want to combine good gas mileage with storage capacity in one vehicle.[3]

Avoidance-avoidance conflict results when a choice must be made between two undesirable alternatives. Elaine's car has a bad muffler, but the repairs will deplete Elaine's savings account. She wants to avoid spending money; however, she also wants to avoid driving around with a bad muffler. Elaine will have to resolve this conflict by selecting the least adverse choice. Midas Muffler offers a Midas Lifetime Guarantee option for mufflers for as long as a vehicle is owned. The appeal is to consumers who don't want engine problems yet also don't want to spend extra money on maintenance.

Approach-avoidance conflict occurs when a consumer desires an alternative that has positive and negative qualities. If Andrew lifts weights at the gym, his body will be stronger, but at the cost of time-consuming strenuous exercise and an expensive gym membership. Many types of purchases cause approach-avoidance

Approach-approach Conflict

Motivational conflict that occurs when a consumer desires two objectives but cannot have both.

Avoidance-avoidance Conflict

Motivational conflict that occurs when consumers must choose between two undesirable alternatives.

Approach-avoidance Conflict

Motivational conflict that occurs when a consumer desires an alternative that has positive and negative qualities.

conflict because they have drawbacks, side effects or other undesirable features. In a way, all purchases can be considered a mixed blessing, since the buyer must forfeit some money eventually. Consider the Army National Guard, which may offer tuition assistance and enlistment bonuses, but requires training obligations and a period of service.[4] The approach-avoidance conflict for people who join involves positive rewards in exchange for hard work and sacrificed time.

By understanding motivational conflicts, marketers can respond with new products as well as advertising, pricing and distribution plans that help minimize buyers' concerns.

PERCEPTION

Perception

The process of recognizing, selecting, organizing, and interpreting stimuli in order to make sense of the world around us.

Human beings use their sensory organs to see, hear, smell, taste, and touch an almost infinite variety of sensations. The sensations are caused by stimuli—the sound of a jackhammer, the fragrance of a flower, the texture of a fabric, and so on. **Perception** is the process of recognizing, selecting, organizing and interpreting these stimuli in order to make sense of the world around us.

We are constantly receiving stimuli, and can only process a limited number of them. Consumers must select — either consciously or subconsciously — which

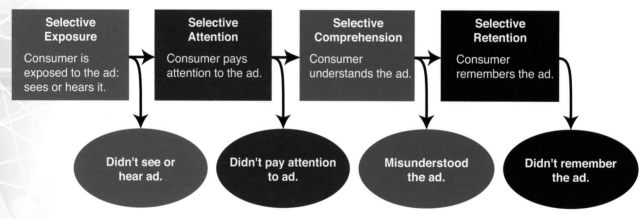

Figure 5.7   Process of Perception

stimuli to focus on. Typically, this selection occurs in four stages: selective exposure, selective attention, selective comprehension and selective retention. At each stage, one may lose messages, due to conscious or subconscious screening. Figure 5.7 illustrates the perception process.

Selective Exposure U.S. companies spend more than a billion dollars every day in hopes of communicating messages to consumers. However, a large portion of these messages are screened out in the first stage, when consumers choose whether to ignore or receive the message. How often do you reach for the remote and channel surf whenever an ad appears on television? Marketers call the consumer's ability to seek out or avoid information **selective exposure**. For example, Gatorade advertises on television with very unique commercials portraying athletes competing. Non-athletes exposed to this information might choose to tune out mentally or change the channel. This happens to all of us hundreds of times a day with other media — billboards, radio, newspaper, websites, etc.

Selective Exposure

The tendency to seek out or avoid information sources

Selective Attention Consumers pay attention to only a small percentage of messages. Noticing every one of them would lead to mental exhaustion from information overload, so consumers are extremely skilled at screening out irrelevant messages.

Through **selective attention,** people have a strong tendency to heed information that supports their current views. Democrats listen more often to Democratic than Republican politicians, and vice versa. Similarly, consumers pay attention to advertising for products they have already purchased or intend to purchase. They screen out much of the information that conflicts with their experience or goals because it is irrelevant and distracting. One of the most important challenges faced by any marketer is gaining the consumer's attention. Without it their message, no matter how well crafted, will have no effect on the intended target.

A good example is the ineffectiveness of smoking prevention campaigns. Forty-four million American adults continue to smoke, despite millions of dollars spent in anti-smoking campaigns trying to dissuade them. Even with warnings from the U.S. Surgeon General and proof that each year 480,000 Americans die prematurely from a tobacco-related illness, tobacco use remains the leading preventable cause of death in the United States.[5] Smokers may tune into advertisements about their brand but ignore prevention ads. This selective attention reinforces the likelihood that they will continue to smoke, since they choose not to hear the health warnings.

To help gain attention, a marketer initiates the message in a way relevant to the consumer — by using a known sports figure, a common activity, an attractive person or humor, while allowing the consumer to relate the brand to this central figure by association. Next, it is important to maintain attention by keeping the ad meaningful or interesting to the consumer. CoverGirl's choice to use talk-show sensation Ellen DeGeneres as a spokesmodel was a good one; Ellen's daily talk show appeals to middle-aged women, which makes her a recognizable and relatable face for the company's SimplyAgeless line of products.

Selective Comprehension

Marketers must take care to ensure that consumers understand their products and messages in the way intended. **Selective comprehension** refers to consumers' tendency to interpret messages with their biases. If a message runs counter to a consumer's strong beliefs, then the consumer is less likely to even attempt to hear the complete message. Consumers are likely to reject any information that contradicts their current beliefs or past behaviors. That is why marketers usually keep ads simple and avoid controversial images. A notable exception is political ads, since selective comprehension can work in the marketer's favor.

Selective Retention

Selective retention means that consumers remember some messages and forget others. The way information is understood determines how well it is remembered. People tend to recall what agrees with their own beliefs, desires or behaviors.

Once information is retained, it is held until replaced or altered. Old information may be forgotten when new, conflicting messages are received, or it may be reshaped if the new information is more consistent with the person's beliefs or goals. For instance, Joan wants a Samsung tablet but has heard it will be very expensive. After reading an ad comparing the cost of tablets, she sees that Samsung is not the highest priced. As a result, she discards the idea that Samsung tablets are expensive and retains the information that some other brands cost more.

Subliminal Perception

Since our conscious perceptions selectively and routinely filter messages, is it possible to bypass that level and market to the consumer's subconscious? The belief in subliminal persuasion began in 1957 in a New Jersey movie theater. Market researcher Jim Vicary coined the term "subliminal advertising" after claiming to flash messages such as "Drink Coca-Cola" and "Eat Popcorn" on the screen too fast to be recognized by the naked eye. According to him, the messages still registered in the brain, resulting in sales increases of 18 percent for Coke and almost 60 percent for popcorn. Researchers were never able to replicate his study, and there is no evidence to support his claim.[6]

Selective Attention

The tendency to heed information that supports current views and behaviors.

Selective Comprehension

The tendency to interpret products and messages according to current beliefs.

Selective Retention

The tendency to remember some and forget other information.

There is now evidence that subliminal messages may not work. A psychology study set out to determine whether self-improvement audio samples really help people lose weight, improve memory, raise self-esteem or quit smoking. Researcher Anthony Greenwald found that roughly half the people who listened to the audio claimed improvement in the area specified on the label. But the labels had been deliberately switched, so any effect has to be attributed to the power of suggestion, not the audio itself.[7] Even after this study, there is debate over the effectiveness of subliminal messages. Still, advertising agencies continue to push the envelope and attempt to submit messages that are considered taboo and subliminal to the general public.

LEARNING

The process in which people learn to acquire and use products starts at an early age and develops throughout life. It is through learning that consumers select the patterns of behavior that determine when, where, and how they purchase, consume, and discard goods. **Learning** is any change in consumers' behavioral tendencies caused by experience. There are two basic types of learning: cognitive and behavioral. Cognitive learning, often used in high-involvement purchases, emphasizes perception, reason and problem solving. The five decision steps outlined in Figure 5.4 deal with this type of learning. Behavioral learning occurs through either classical or operant (sometimes called instrumental) conditioning when consumers react to external events. Behavioral learning primarily concerns what consumers do, not what they are thinking.

Learning

Any change in consumer behavior caused by experience.

Classical Conditioning

After two stimuli are presented together repeatedly, people learn to respond to one in the same way as the other.

Classical Conditioning Classical conditioning gets its name from an early (and, therefore, classical) experiment by the Russian physiologist Ivan Pavlov in the 1920s. He presented meat paste to a dog, and the dog salivated. He then presented the paste while ringing a tuning fork, getting the same result. Pavlov repeated this several times. After repeating this several times, Pavlov found that the dog would salivate at the ring of the tuning fork, even with no meat paste present.[8] The basic idea behind **classical conditioning** is that people can learn to respond to one stimulus in the same way they respond to another if the two stimuli are presented together.

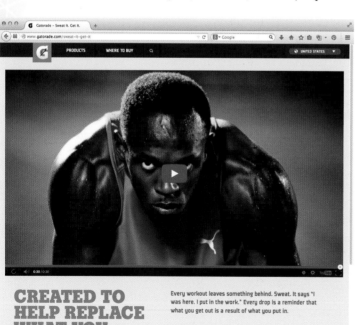

CREATED TO HELP REPLACE WHAT YOU SWEAT OUT

Every workout leaves something behind. Sweat. It says "I was here. I put in the work." Every drop is a reminder that what you get out is a result of what you put in.

Classical conditioning is used extensively in marketing. Think for a minute about a commercial that features an athlete, such as Gatorade's recent ad depicting athletes training while covered in sweat. It says, "Gatorade: created to help replace what you sweat out." Marketers want viewers to connect Gatorade with athletic prowess in much the same way that Pavlov's dogs associated the tuning fork with meat paste. The marketers' desired result is that consumers will drink Gatorade at the stimulus of an intense workout or game.

Oftentimes, it is aspects of advertising (stimuli) that influence a consumer's evaluation of a product, more so than the product itself. Marketers say that music helps define the emotional appeal of a certain brand. Classical music, for example, is often used to convey comfort, luxury and distinctive taste.[9] It is often played in spas and luxury hotel lobbies. The Gap also pays close attention to its audio identity. In one San Francisco location, shoppers can even use Rockbot's mobile apps to help customize the music they hear while shopping at the store. Rockbot lets customers pick the music playing at a restaurant, bar or business, right from their smartphones. Because of its early success, Google Ventures has invested in the company with hopes it will be successful enough to fully acquire into Google proper.[10]

Marketers need to understand that consumers may generalize stimuli or discriminate among them. **Generalization** occurs when people make the same response to different stimuli. **Discrimination** occurs when consumers make different responses to different stimuli. For instance, when oat bran cereals were first found to reduce cholesterol levels, the oat bran image was generalized to other bran cereals, such as Raisin Bran. With experience, however, consumers began to discriminate, aided by advertisers. The Quaker Oats Company distinguishes its oat bran from other bran products, saying "Oats contain soluble fiber that binds with and helps remove some of the cholesterol which can clog your arteries and lead to heart disease."[11]

To take advantage of a strong brand name, marketers establish visual consistency across categories. The various products in ConAgra's Healthy Choice line, including pasta sauces, cereals, breakfast bars, frozen dinners and ice cream, are branded under the distinctive green Healthy Choice label. Consumers can readily identify the brand and many are likely to generalize the health benefits its image conveys, attributing them to a wide range of ConAgra's products.

Marketers also try to take advantage of a buyer's ability to discriminate among brands. For example, McDonald's names its products "Mc," as in the case of the Egg McMuffin and the McFlurry, to ensure that its food is associated only with McDonald's.

Generalization

Making the same response to different stimuli.

Discrimination

Making different responses to different stimuli.

CAREER TIP!

Looking for the best internships available? Check out Forbes' annual list of the best internship programs, according to data such as pay and the percentage of interns who get full-time jobs, as well as feedback from career services directors across the U.S. Programs that ranked in the top 10 for 2014 include Google, Microsoft and Qualcomm.

Operant Conditioning
Even before Pavlov gained fame, Edward Thorndike, a noted psychologist, published work showing how rewards encourage certain responses and punishment discourages others. Behavior that is intermittently rewarded (positive or negative reinforcement) will be repeated in the expectation of eliciting the reward. Behavior that is punished will be avoided and diminish in frequency. Psychologist B. F. Skinner later termed this type of conditioning "operant" because the learning occurs as the subject responds to or "operates on" the environment. Thus, **operant conditioning** is the use of reinforcement or punishment to shape behavior. Today, marketers know that consumers associate positive and/or negative consequences with the items they consume.

Positive reinforcement can take place in different ways, the first being a product satisfying a need or want. If you drink Sierra Mist and your thirst disappears, then your action was reinforced, increasing the likelihood you'll reach for Sierra Mist the next time you're thirsty. Knowledge is the second source of reinforcement, and many organizations publish magazines to feed consumers information that supports their business: American Airlines has *American Way Magazine*, the National Hockey League publishes the online magazine *Impact,* and the Humane Society of the United States has *All Animals.*[12] These offer information that will reinforce purchases and stimulate new interests while maintaining brand loyalty. A third way consumer behavior can be reinforced is by seeing results. For example, Weight Watchers members are encouraged to attend weekly meetings to support other members in their area. Each member has a "weigh-in" to track his or her progress, and the group leader provides tips on subjects such as reducing emotional eating. Eating right and

Operant Conditioning

The use of reinforcement or punishment to shape behavior.

living a healthy lifestyle actually becomes reinforcement because consumers know they are making progress toward getting in shape.[13] Yet another way companies reward purchasers and encourage repeat purchases is the frequent-customer card promotion. Biggby Coffee offers its customers a frequent buyer card that rewards them with one free beverage for every 12 purchased. A consumer can feel punished (and subsequently become less receptive or outright reject the company) by a product that fails to perform as advertised, a service agent who acts in a curt, unfriendly manner, or even news stories that cast a corporation in a bad light and undermine the consumer's pride in owning its products.

ATTITUDES

An **attitude** is a state of readiness with cognitive, emotional and behavioral components, which reflects the beliefs of the consumer with regard to messages, brands, products, product characteristics, or other aspects of life. Attitudes are often described as consumer preferences — a like or dislike for products or their characteristics. Marketers usually think of attitudes as being the sum of three dimensions: cognitive, affective and behavioral. The **cognitive** aspect refers to knowledge about product attributes that is not influenced by emotion; the **affective** component relates to the emotional feelings of like or dislike; the **behavioral** element reflects the tendency to act positively or negatively.

Figure 5.8 shows how attitude can affect the purchase of a mountain bike. Attitudes are important because they help us understand why consumers take a particular action. Note that attitudes are not the same as beliefs: A **belief** is a descriptive thought or conviction that expresses an opinion about the characteristics of something. For example, a consumer may believe that a rapid-fire shifter is a feature of a Specialized brand bicycle. Beliefs may help shape attitudes but don't necessarily imply like or dislike. Attitudes also influence beliefs: If rapid-fire shifters increase the price, then a consumer who dislikes high cost may believe they are not a very useful feature.

Consumers frequently form attitudes to help evaluate whether products and brands fit into their lifestyle. These attitudes are drawn from a broad range of ideas, not just the characteristics of a product.

Generally, marketers use their knowledge of consumer attitudes to make sure that strategies are consistent with consumer tastes and preferences. From time to time, marketers attempt to change consumer attitudes, usually by influencing one of the three components. A common approach is to use promotion to influence the cognitive component. This may involve claims of product superiority such as the Calloway Golf Club claim "a better game by design."

Marketers also try to influence the affective component of consumer attitudes. For example, as the health and fitness craze swept the United States, many people developed a dislike for beef, believing it to be high in fat and cholesterol. The industry launched a campaign showing that beef is nutritious and easy to prepare, hoping to make consumers feel good about eating it. "Beef. It's what's for dinner" became a recognizable slogan for millions of Americans in the 1990s. Despite the efforts, sales have continued to decline since 1976, when beef consumption peaked at 94.4

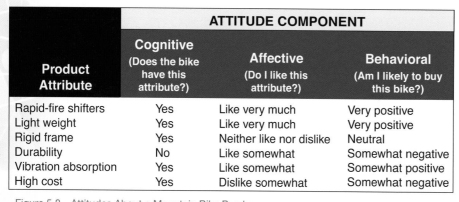

Figure 5.8   Attitudes About a Mountain Bike Purchase

Attitude
A state of readiness with cognitive, emotional, and behavioral components, which reflects the beliefs of the consumer with regard to messages, brands, products, product characteristics, or other

Cognitive
Knowledge about a product's attributes not influenced by emotion.

Affective
Emotional feeling of like or dislike.

Behavioral
Tendency to act positively or negatively.

Belief
A conviction that something is true or that descriptive statements are factual.

pounds per person. Today, healthier eating and higher beef prices have dropped the consumption to 57.5 pounds, a 39 percent decline.[14]

To change the behavioral aspect of consumer attitudes, companies will sometimes offer a coupon or free sample. This may involve claims of product superiority like claiming that your brand or product is clearly better than the nearest competitor.

INFORMATION PROCESSING

Information processing refers to ways in which consumers acquire, store and evaluate the data they use to make decisions. The human mind has a remarkable ability to process (understand and apply) the information it takes in. Perception, motivation, behavioral learning and attitudes are integrated into the human thought system, which processes data to arrive at goal-directed behaviors. The key to information processing is the encoding of information and its use in memory.

Encoding

Encoding is the process of converting information to knowledge. The brain is sometimes described as having two relatively distinct ways of encoding information.[15] These enable it to handle pictorial, geometric and nonverbal information as well as verbal, symbolic and analytical thinking. The mind combines all of this information and produces integrated perceptions.

The mental images encoded as thoughts are held in "picture" form called episodes. This is how human memory represents concepts such as aesthetics, tastes and symbolic meaning — in the form of a mental image that one can "feel." Ads and other phenomena are also likely to be retained as episodes.[16] Nike traditionally creates highly visual ads, targeting consumer emotions or values (often with dynamic imagery associated with competitive spirit). Nike appeals to consumers by focusing on professional athletes or athletic activities, and then ties their products and brand to those values. The "Swoosh" symbol actually represents the wing of the Greek goddess of victory, Nike.[17] The logo is a highly recognized trademark that elicits these desired effects because it is an episode encoded in the consumer's brain.

Verbal encoding occurs when words or symbols are stored in semantic memory. General knowledge, facts and principles gleaned from experience are held there. Many believe that the brain stores information such as package size, the meaning of brand names, and prices in this way. For example, advertisements for Johnson & Johnson's baby products use facts to appeal to concerned mothers. One ad states that Johnson's Baby Wash is the number one choice of hospitals.[18] Many mothers may form an impression in their semantic memory based on this information and call upon it later to make a purchase decision.

Marketers must remember that consumers in all markets encode both verbal and pictorial information.[19] In the early stage of information processing, the pictorial tends to dominate, giving way to verification and more analytical thoughts as the process continues. Striking images, memorable music and general creative advertisement will catch a consumer's attention. Then they're likely to consider the facts and details of product messages.

Memory

Memory is the brain function that stores and recalls encoded information (knowledge). There are three types of memory: sensory, short term and long term. Each operates differently and can be considered a separate step in the process of memory formation.

The first and most basic stage is sensory memory, which takes in an almost unlimited amount of encoded information. These sensory impressions are forgotten within a fraction of a second. But when attention is focused on a few stimuli, sensory information about them is transferred to short-term memory, where it can be coded and interpreted.

Short-term memory interprets what is sent from sensory memory. It usually

Information Processing

The process whereby consumers acquire, store, and evaluate the data they use in making decisions.

Encoding

The process of converting information to knowledge.

Memory

The brain function that stores and recalls encoded information; includes sensory, short-term, and long-term capacities.

can hold information for only a short time, and its capacity is much smaller than that of sensory memory—about four to seven chunks of information at once.[20] A chunk is a unit of organized information that can be recalled to solve specific problems of short duration. Different people focusing on the same object may form very different chunks. A first-time buyer of a used car is likely to have a more difficult time than a person who has purchased several. For example, the experienced buyer probably will ask for past service receipts to learn about repair history, whereas the novice may not think of it.

In long-term memory, a vast amount of information may be held for years or even indefinitely. It remains there until replaced by contradictory information through a process called interference. For example, you go to your favorite restaurant and receive a poor meal or poor service. This interferes with your positive memory of the place, and you then reclassify it to a lower status. Once a brand is stored in long-term memory, consumers can add relevant information to help with future choices.

SOCIAL FACTORS THAT INFLUENCE CONSUMER DECISIONS

Social factors have a great influence on how individual consumers and households behave. Consider something as simple as a pair of earrings. In some societies, children's ears are pierced at birth; other societies frown on ear piercing altogether. Some social groups regard earrings as a symbol of wealth and refinement; others consider them showy and in poor taste. They can be worn long-term or changed daily, and indicate status, membership or taste. Different social influences affect people's purchase decisions, but marketers focus on culture, subculture, social class, reference groups and family.

> **Different social influences affect people's purchase decisions, but marketers focus on culture, subculture, social class, reference groups and family.**

CULTURE

Culture

The learned values, beliefs, language, symbols, and patterns of behavior shared by people in a society that are passed on from generation to generation.

Perhaps the most pervasive influence on human beings is culture. **Culture** is the learned values, beliefs, language, symbols and patterns of behavior shared by people in a society and passed on from generation to generation. It produces manners and actions that are often taken for granted as the "appropriate" way.

Culture changes very slowly unless outside forces intervene. Historically, such forces have included political and religious wars and natural disasters. Today, global economics and technology are having enormous effects, as the swift exchange of ideas is making global culture more uniform. For example, the hugely popular NBC comedy *The Office* is an adaptation of a BBC show first broadcast in the UK that ran for two seasons. The original stories have already been sold in 80 countries worldwide, making it the most successful BBC comedy export of all time.[21] However, globalization extends beyond just entertainment. Banks, investment firms and credit card companies exchange capital and important knowledge-based information 24 hours a day, taking advantage of this emergent world culture.

Values

The shared norms about what is right to think and do; what culture considers to be worthy and desirable.

By taking cultural values into account, companies adjust to the particular customs of people in different societies. **Values** are the shared norms about what is considered appropriate to think and do. Marketers need to understand values so their actions don't oppose what consumers in a given market consider acceptable.

For a company like Whirlpool, a global provider of kitchen appliances and related products, it would be important to know how different societies view and utilize their kitchens. In Sweden, for example, the cooking facilities are more prized areas of the house, as indicated by the fact that utensils are often given as gifts and subsequently shown proudly to guests. On the other hand, in India, the kitchen is not usually shown to guests but serves as a strictly functional space. Thus, Swedes might be interested in more upscale kitchenware and appliances, while people in India might prefer space-saving, practical items.[22]

SUBCULTURE

Understanding a culture provides marketers with an overall picture, but they also need more specific information. A **subculture** is a group of people with shared values within a culture. In the United States, these groups may be defined by ethnicity, age, religion, geographic location, and national origin. In this section we will focus on ethnicity and look at three groups: Hispanic, Asian and African-American consumers.

Subculture

A subset of people with shared values within a culture.

An ethnic subculture can be a very broad category. For example, the U.S. Hispanic community includes Cubans, Puerto Ricans, Mexican Americans, Tejanos and Chicanos, among others. Within such groups are further distinctions—low or high ethnicity, length of time in the United States, place of birth, and place of residence, to name a few. A marketer can narrow this down to a very specific target, such as Cubans with high ethnicity living in New York City.

Marketers know that ethnic subgroups are much more likely to buy branded products and spend more for what they perceive as quality. Immigrants are often perplexed by the wide variety of choices, so they tend to stick with the major brands they knew at home.

Groups with strong ethnicity form some of the most important subcultures. You will learn that marketers are interested in identifying segments of the population with common needs, wants, and buying behaviors, since they can develop a single strategy to appeal to that entire segment. This encourages marketers to seek out segments with high ethnicity: Since they identify strongly with particular values and traditions, they are likely to have similar behavior in many aspects. Figure 5.9 illustrates the spending power, income and population percentages of several ethnic groups in the United States.

With the increase in ethnic populations, companies that produce, sell and market ethnic products may see a considerable growth. Use your knowledge of diversity to your advantage in interviews and by writing targeted cover letters. Remember that

	All Groups	White	African American	Hispanic	Asian
Percentage of U.S. Population	100%	67.6%	12%	12%	4%
Average Household Income	$46,326	$50,784	$30,858	$35,967	$61,094
Annual Spending Power	$9,710 billion	$7,811 billion	$760 billion	$736 billion	$396 billion

Figure 5.9   Subculture Spending Power in the United States
Source: Census Race and Hispanic Data, www.census.gov, U.S. Census Bureau.

companies in growing areas may offer you better opportunities for advancement.

Hispanic Consumers Hispanics are a booming subculture. Their number is growing rapidly due to births and immigration. There are more than 53 million Hispanics in the U.S. in 2014, and the Hispanic buying power will reach $1.5 trillion in 2015.[23] These numbers make the Hispanic community a very important target for marketers since they are the nation's largest ethnic minority.

Because Latinos share Spanish as a common language (except for Brazilians, who speak Portuguese), radio or television stations that broadcast in Spanish are obvious media choices for promotional messages. Although many Hispanics are fluent in English, most marketers believe that it is better to sell in Spanish. According to a pilot study by Skunkworks of New York, advertisers can gain a 20 percent increase in sales among Hispanics simply by advertising on Spanish-language network television.

Although many Hispanics are fluent in English, most marketers believe that it is better to sell in Spanish. According to a New York Times article, English-language television is struggling to attract the nation's more than 50 million Latinos. They do, however, continue to watch Spanish-language networks in huge number; in fact, during a recent season finale of the hit show "Modern Family," far more Hispanic viewers were watching the telenovela "La Que No Podía Amar" on Univision.[24] Some grocery stores are trying to create friendlier, more familiar atmospheres for Hispanic shoppers; for example, H.E. Butt Grocery's stores in Houston and Austin, Texas, added more bilingual employees, a masa factory, a tortilleria and a carniceria (Latino-style butcher shop). In Miami, one Winn-Dixie location added bilingual decor and a café serving Cuban-style espresso and pastries.[25]

Asian-American Consumers Imagine a market segment that's highly educated, affluent and geographically concentrated. That describes the 17.3 million Asian Americans, whose numbers are growing at a rapid rate. The Census Bureau estimates that the Asian-American population will grow to 40.6 million, or 9 percent of the total population, by 2050.[26] Moreover, segment generally spends more than other ethnic groups, particularly in categories such as computers and insurance.

However, just as with other ethnic groups, marketers must pay careful attention to cultural and language differences. For example, when an airline briefly used the number 1-800-FLY-4444, it failed to recognize that it was offending many in the Asian-American community to whom the number "four" implied death. The potential embarrassment in situations like this is causing some companies to avoid these markets altogether, rather than address them. Asian Americans make up only 5.6 percent of America's population, and that small proportion contains a wide variety of markets.[27] Because the Asian-American market segment is relatively small, and because companies may be unfamiliar with cultural and language differences, some marketers decide not to invest time or resources in this segment.

Some companies, however, are focusing their attention on Asian Americans during important cultural holidays such as the Asian Lunar New Year, and discovering the benefits of acknowledging other cultures. Hallmark Cards, for example, has developed a line of Lunar New Year greeting cards. According to Kim Newton, marketing manager for Hallmark's Ethnic Business Center, "We wanted to make sure we chose cards that are appropriate for the domestic market but still tie ethnic consumers to who they are. Our goal is to help them keep cultural traditions alive during the holidays that are important to them." Whereas Hallmark's advertising is a large-scale effort, Honest Tea is also realizing the value of the Asian-American market and increases promotion of its products during the Lunar New Year.[28]

Through future studies, marketers hope to learn more about the desires of Asian Americans, making advertising to them a more feasible task. Organizations like the Association of Asian-American Advertising Agencies seek to increase the information available to advertisers about this relatively unstudied group.

African-American Consumers African Americans represent about 13 percent of the total U.S. population and are expected to have an annual buying power of $1.3 trillion by 2017.[29] According to the Buying Power of Black America, a study conducted by Target Market News, African Americans are increasing their expenditures in various areas, from books to automobiles, making them an even more important market. In addition, they are a fast-growing group on the Internet and active on social media; a recent Pew Internet study found that 22 percent of African-American Internet users use Twitter at a high level, compared with 16 percent of white users.[30] In fact, Black Twitter (#blacktwitter) has emerged as a powerful subculture of the social media giant. Meredith Clark, a doctoral candidate at the University of North Carolina at Chapel Hill who is writing her dissertation on Black Twitter, compared it to the "Freedom's Journal," the first African-American newspaper in the United States. Armed with a social or political agenda, the group of devoted Twitter followers can be quite influential.[31] The group is credited for killing a book deal for a juror in the trial of George Zimmerman, who was acquitted in the shooting death of unarmed black teenager Trayvon Martin. Black Twitter is also the reason for the demise of Zimmerman's attempt to appear in a celebrity boxing match.[32]

Some companies are seeking to market goods directly to African Americans by focusing on African-American culture, much like Hallmark has done through its cards and e-cards celebrating Kwanzaa. However, some consumers are concerned about the lack of major advertising to African Americans outside of January and February, when Martin Luther King Jr.'s birthday and Black History Month are celebrated.

Many believe that marketers should be cognizant and sensitive toward cultural issues and tradition. The African-American community is distinct and "marketers should develop advertising and promotions specifically targeted to the African-American community, rather than assuming general-market advertising is enough because this ethnic group speaks English."[33]

SOCIAL CLASS

The third major social influence on consumer behavior is social class. A **social class** is a relatively homogeneous grouping of people based on similarities in income and occupation. Members tend to share values, interests and behaviors. How would you rank the following occupations by status: salesperson, high school teacher and accountant? What about a physician, a professor or a lawyer? Your views agree with research findings if, in both groups, you ranked them from highest to lowest in the order presented. Feelings about the relative prestige of these occupations reflect the tendency in most cultures to make social class distinctions. Figure 5.10 describes various social classes and gives examples of purchases for each.

Social Class

A relatively stable division of society based on education, income, and occupation.

Social Class	Percentage of U.S. Population	Examples of Purchases
Upper Upper	Less than 1%	Jewelry, fine wine, luxury cruises, yachts
Lower Upper	About 2%	Highly visible products such as cars
Upper Middle	12%	Condominiums, skiing, travel, outdoor furniture
Middle	32%	Brand-name clothing, family vacations
Working Class	38%	Used trucks and motorcycles
Upper Lower	9%	Fundamental necessities: food, rental housing, medical care
Lower Lower	7%	Food, used clothing, minimum necessities

Figure 5.10 A Breakdown of Social Classes

Global Social Class Dimensions Marketers increasingly look at social class from a global perspective. In some societies — such as India, South Africa and Brazil — class distinctions are clear, and status differences are prominent. In others — such as Australia, Denmark and Canada — differences are less extreme. In countries with strong class differences, where people live, the cars they drive, the restaurants they frequent, the sports in which they participate, the type of clothing they wear, how much they travel, and where (or whether) they go to college are largely determined by social class.

Class associations also have a great impact on commercial activity, particularly in business-to-business relations. For example, the president of a French company expects to deal only with the top executives of another firm. More than once, U.S. companies have failed at marketing in France because they did not know or ignored this, sometimes offending French executives by sending low-level managers to important meetings, other times losing stature by sending high-level executives to communicate with mid-level French managers. In a country with a more homogeneous class

CREATING & CAPTURING VALUE THROUGH *Relationships*

Walgreens: Consumer-centric Retailing

Without customers, businesses would just be four walls. But the customer is often overlooked in many companies, as not every employee has direct contact with customers every single day. However, Walgreens Pharmacy has revolutionized the way it interacts with its customers.

Walgreens has replaced its longtime strategy of reaching markets through sheer quantity of stores with redesigning those that already exist to be more customer-friendly. In what Walgreens calls "Customer-Centric Retailing," the company carefully examines what a customer wants and needs from a retail location, and delivers on these expectations. For example, the shelving in the aisles was lowered to 68 inches from 72 inches to alleviate the cramped and overcrowded feeling of the aisles. Reducing the shelf size also allowed Walgreens to eliminate about 4,000 products, decreasing the clutter on the shelves and allowing for more accurate inventorying.

Each store location is looked at carefully so it can be designed to serve the customers who frequent it the most. In locations where a supermarket is farther than 1.5 miles from a Walgreens, the grocery aisles are stocked with more inventory to capture some of the market that would otherwise go to the supermarket. Additionally, Walgreens continues to emphasize staple products to customers, especially Its private label products. The private label products are less expensive than the brand-name counterparts but carry a higher profit margin to the company.

Walgreens acquired Take Care Health Systems, and in doing so has brought convenient wellness care to its customers. Take Care clinics are staffed with board-certified nurse practitioners and physician assistants who are there to help customers with anything from basic ailments like the flu or an ear infection to health screening, vaccines and physicals. These walk-in clinics improve access to quality treatment or a prescription with minimal wait time.

http://files.shareholder.com/downloads/WAG, website visited June 3, 2014.

http://online.wsj.com/article/SB124566751732336741.html, website visited June 3, 2014.

www.takecarehealth.com/about/press-releases/press_051607_01.aspx, website visited June 3, 2014.

structure, such as Sweden or Denmark, it is not uncommon for executives from all levels to work as a team, so Americans of various ranks are accepted as well.

Marketers study global social class dimensions in order to understand consumer profiles, habits, interests, and purchasing behavior. For example, three national surveys costing more than $30 million were mailed to more than 24 million British homes by ICD Marketing Services. The research was designed to give insight into consumer preferences for cars, finance, travel, and other purchases.[34]

REFERENCE GROUPS

Another major influence on consumer behavior is reference groups. We all live with, depend on and are nurtured by other people. We influence and are influenced by those with whom we have frequent contact—friends, coworkers, and family members. We also are influenced by people we know only indirectly through the mass media. Research shows that groups have an immense effect on the purchasing behavior of their members, including their search for and use of information, their response to advertisements, and their brand choices.[35]

Reference groups are people whose norms and values influence a consumer's behavior. Consumers depend on them for product information, purchase comparisons, and rules about correct or incorrect buying behavior. In a college fraternity, for instance, each member is unique, but the group has certain norms and standards.

Marketers distinguish between two types of reference groups. **Associative reference groups** are considered desirable to belong to, even by those who are not part of one. In contrast, **dissociative reference groups** are those to which people do not want to belong. The same reference group can be associative to some people and dissociative to others. For example, The Gap chose its name because many younger people wanted to actively dissociate from parents and other older people not deemed "cool." Teens may choose these bands as associative or dissociative reference groups. On the other hand, famous faces can also be a positive reference group. For example, country and pop superstar Taylor Swift recently donated $4 million to the Country Music Hall of Fame to help establish the Taylor Swift Education Center, which will teach children about country music.[36]

Advertisers capitalize on the human tendency to rely on groups. In one form or another, groups are a part of almost all mass media advertisements and are used in many personal selling presentations. One Revlon campaign used a diverse collection of celebrities to create an atmosphere of intrigue playing to the characteristics of each celebrity. Recent Revlon spokespeople have included Halle Berry, Olivia Wilde and Emma Stone to target a number of different reference groups.[37]

Promotions that appeal to associative tendencies, such as consumers' dreams and hopes for the future, command a good deal of attention. Consider the number of advertisers that use famous spokespersons to tout their messages about products, particularly targeted toward a youth audience. Professional athletes are often seen as being members of associative reference groups. LeBron James has become a highly marketable athlete due to the exposure of the NBA and his ability to connect with a youthful audience. "King James" appeared as number 16 on Forbes' 2013 Celebrity 100 because of influential endorsements with large companies like Nike, McDonald's, Coca-Cola and State Farm.[38]

Reference Groups

A set of people whose norms and values influence a consumer's behavior.

Associative Reference Groups

A group with which people want to identify.

Dissociative Reference Groups

A group with which people do not want to identify.

Mtaylor848 / CC BY-SA 3.0

The Gap store name came about because many younger people wanted to dissociate from parents and other "uncool" people.

THE FAMILY

How much has your family influenced the way you behave, speak, or dress? Often, the family in which you grow up — known as your family of orientation — teaches you certain purchase habits that continue throughout your life. Many consumers buy the same brand of soap, toothpaste, mayonnaise, laundry detergent or gasoline that their mother or father did. Those consumers later start their own families, called the family of procreation, which also influences purchase habits.

The family is especially important to marketers because it forms a **household**, which is the standard purchase and consumption unit. If you do not already have a household, you are likely to purchase or rent a home, buy appliances and durable goods, and require banking and insurance services. In other words, your household will be a consumption unit.

Not all households consist of a mother, a father, and children. Many have only one person, or several nonrelatives, or a single parent with children. This section, however, focuses on the traditional nuclear family. Marketers generally look at three important aspects:

- How do families make decisions as a group?

- What roles can various members play in a purchase decision?

- How does family purchase behavior change over time?

Family Decision Making

Family decision making is "one of the most under-researched and difficult areas to study within all of consumer behavior."[39] How does your family make buying decisions? Most purchases are probably conceived and carried out by one member with little influence from the others. These are called autonomous decisions. In other cases, several family members may be involved. These are called joint decisions.

Marketers must remember that gender roles affect how family decisions are made. Decisions are termed "syncratic" when both spouses are jointly and equally involved; "autonomous" when either one of them makes the decision independently; and "husband- or wife-dominant" depending on which one has the influence. Research has found that gender especially affects financial decisions and that men and women approach finances differently. In general, men perceive themselves as advisers, active in business and in influencing their friends' financial decisions. Men are more likely to take independent financial risks, and they often place value on ego-gratifying opportunities. Women are less likely to take risks and are more open to advice from friends and others. Directing marketing activities to the wrong person in the household could be as wasteful as directing them to the wrong market segment altogether.[40] For this reason, it's important for marketers to understand the decision-making roles within a family.

Family Purchasing Roles

When children ask a parent to buy a certain type of cereal, they are influencing the purchase, but the parent still makes the final decision. In contrast, when teenagers go to the mall to buy clothing, while they certainly may be influenced by their parents, they usually make the final decision. Family members play certain roles in certain purchases and play different roles for different products. There are five key roles:

- Initiator: First suggests that a particular product be purchased.

- Influencer: Provides valuable input to the decision-making process.

- Decision maker: Makes the final buying decision.

Household

Family members (and occasionally others) who share the same housing unit; for marketers, the standard purchase and consumption unit.

- Purchaser: Physically goes out and makes the purchase.

- User: Uses the product.

The role a consumer plays is not always obvious. For example, women no longer rely on a husband or boyfriend to take care of home repairs and construction. Retailers such as Home Depot are now actively targeting this segment that spends $50 billion a year on hand tools, power tools and other equipment.[41] Children have a significant effect on family decisions. In fact, for certain products, the marketer may decide to focus on them rather than parents. Johnson & Johnson is among the many companies that market toward children. The company offers kid-friendly "easy-grip" bars of soap, body wash in scents such as "tropical blast" and detangling spray that smells like strawberries.[42] Cereal manufacturers also recognize the important role young children play. Eye-catching boxes and cartoon characters are designed to appeal directly to children. For instance, Kellogg's cereals targeted towards kids, such as Apple Jacks, frequently feature fun games on the box.[43] Children continue to influence their parents' purchasing decisions as they grow, but their interest may shift to other products — clothes, video or computer games, and such services as family vacations or video rentals.

Family Life Cycle As families age, they progress through a series of predictable stages, each presenting unique problems and situations to address. An understanding of each stage gives marketers powerful insight into the needs and expectations of families.

Only a few decades ago, everyone was expected to move in orderly progression from youth, to marriage, to childrearing, to retirement. Today, the picture is more complex because of widespread divorce and single parenting, as shown in Figure 5.11. As you can imagine, a family's needs and purchase decisions vary at each stage.

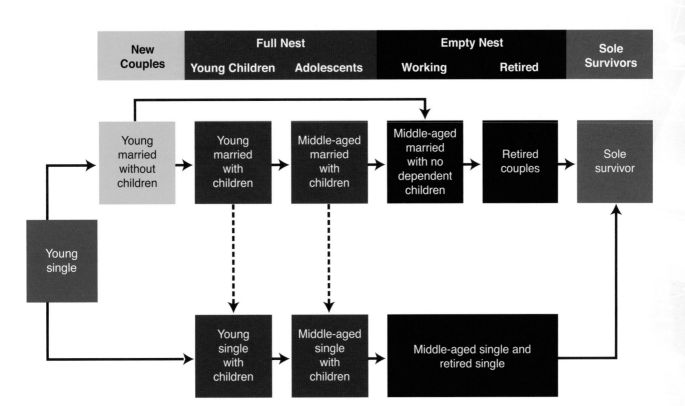

Figure 5.11   The Family Life Cycle

Young Singles Young singles are in the process of setting up their first household. Items they buy tend to be easily transportable from one location to another as living arrangements change or they find a new job. During this stage, courtship activities make social events, recreation and entertainment important. They may also look into purchasing advanced education or training to equip themselves for a career. This market category, when combined with middle-aged singles and sole survivors, has shown high growth.

New Couples Young married people without children generally try to build an economic foundation for later responsibilities. By combining resources, a new couple may have enough discretionary income to enjoy recreational activities while still saving for the future. This group spends more than other households on furnishings, new vehicles, and alcohol.

Full Nesters Caring for children consumes a great deal of time and resources, whether the guardian is single, married or divorced. Household budgets for full nesters increase for nearly every category of purchase, and new expenses emerge — diapers, day care, toys, lessons and so forth. As children reach adolescence, their sports activities may cost from several hundred to several thousand dollars per year. Many families prepare for the cost of college, which can consume a large amount of annual household income. The government has recently taken notice of the increase in student loan debt, which has now surpassed credit card debt for the first time ever. The current administration is trying to make college more accessible by doubling investments in Pell Grants, expanding education tax credits, and maintaining lower student loan interest rates.[44] Of course, purchase behavior will differ according to family structure — traditional family, divorced or widowed parent, or single parent. The latter group often has very limited spending power. A divorced or widowed parent may have some child support or death benefits to ease the burden a little, but often he or she must often work long hours to make ends meet and has very little free time. In traditional families, both parents usually work to provide for their children.

Working Empty Nesters This category consists of three types of consumers: middle-aged singles, married couples with no children, and married couples with grown children who have left home. These households are in their prime wage-earning years: According to the U.S. Census Bureau, the median income of people aged 45 to 54 is $67,992, the highest income bracket of any one group. Some 75 percent of Americans in their fifties still work, whereas the baby boomers who were born between 1946 and 1964 make up the largest segment of the U.S. population with nearly 80 million people.[45] Without children around, empty nesters are free to travel, pursue hobbies, and explore new lifestyle options. As baby boomers turn 50, this market will grow even more. For details on how to capture it, see the diversity feature, "Boomers Don't Act Like Seniors."

Retired Empty Nesters Americans aged 65 and older have considerably more purchasing power than the average American and over the next 20 years, this market is expected to grow by 30 percent. This wealthier group has changed the image of the retired couple over the last decade. Retirees are now viewed as financial investors willing to assume some risk, mobile and daring, physically active and health conscious, and willing to pamper themselves. It was once thought that advertising dollars were wasted on this segment, but this idea has reversed: It's a powerful niche that is targeted in television programming and advertising campaigns. The wealthy elderly are the focus of luxury cruise lines, automobile manufacturers and land developers.

Sole Survivors Sole survivors are men and women whose spouse has died, as well as older singles who never married. Their net worth and buying power have increased over the past two decades. A number of sole survivors are senior citizens, who today are targeted heavily by marketers, with products such as home health care and websites like CareScout.com.[46] Companies that produce television fitness programs and diet supplements also target the elderly.

USING TECHNOLOGY TO TRACK CONSUMER BEHAVIOR

Technology not only helps marketers better understand consumers, it also directly influences how companies build relationships. As computer usage rises in the classroom and at home, younger generations have increasing exposure to the Internet. Likewise, many seniors have begun using the Internet as a way to shop and stay in touch with others.

What implications does this have for marketing? Dozens of Internet survey groups such as CyberAtlas, Nua and Jupiter Communications maintain up-to-date databases and news sites with information on Internet demographics, advertising rates and industry-wide web spending and usage. These groups allow marketers to effectively track consumer behavior. For instance, these databases were capable of discovering that American web surfers visit an average of 87 unique domains and spend an average of nearly 32 hours online each month. Users are spending monthly averages of 1.5 hours on Google, 2 hours on Yahoo!, and over 7 hours on Facebook.[47] Currently the NPD Group maintains an "Online Panel" of consumers, demographically selected, who participate in continuous surveys of the web. For a fee, companies can access Online Panel reports, including attitude and usage studies, longitudinal tracking, as well as product and concept reviews. Together with names, addresses, and other data requested when a website is accessed, such research provides a reservoir of information about consumers.[48]

Marketers also make use of web-tracking software that allows them to track every website a surfer visits and to compile information such as purchases made. The resulting silhouette, or profile, provides the kind of precision targeting that marketers so eagerly desire. Google Analytics is an excellent example of web-tracking technology. This free tool is an enterprise-class web analytics solution that gives site owners rich insights into traffic and marketing effectiveness. The easy-to-use features allow users to see and analyze traffic data in an entirely new way. The main statistics Google Analytics provides include the length of time visitors stay at the specific site, where they live, and what pages of the website are most popular.[49]

Ultimately, the growing use of new technologies will provide marketers with greater insight into consumer

Google Analytics is the world's leading analytical data and tracking system.

behavior. Categorizing user behavior as well as providing consumers with easy web access enables marketers to reach many of their targeted audiences. This will benefit both consumers seeking information and the companies supplying it.

THE ETHICS OF INFLUENCING CONSUMER BEHAVIOR

For a long time, marketers have used sexual themes to heighten brand awareness and influence consumers. Today, ethical questions are being raised about some of these promotions, which many people find offensive. Procter & Gamble set up a "sex task force" to examine its policy toward sexually suggestive magazine articles and cover headlines. With nearly $500 million in magazine advertising per year, Procter & Gamble was concerned that it was overly connected with risqué content in magazines such as Cosmopolitan and Glamour.[50]

Controversial promotion risks losing consumers in the selective comprehension phase of perception. Some people screen out ads altogether that conflict with their values. At the same time, controversy generates free publicity, which can result in positive or negative impacts to a company. Ben & Jerry's liberal political view was controversial enough for three angry conservatives to launch their own brand of ice cream, Star Spangled Ice Cream, to target conservative consumers. Their flavors include Iraqi Road, I Hate the French Vanilla and Smaller GovernMINT.[51] Italian shoe company Geox S.p.A. donated several pairs of its anti-foot sweat system shoe to the Pope, hoping that they might be able to capitalize on a photograph of the Pope wearing the company's shoes. Although the Pope does not receive money for endorsing products, his use has created marketing opportunities. The Pope also owns Bushnell sunglasses and a specially engraved Apple iPod. These kinds of endorsement pursuits are seen as being unethical by some consumers and may result in backlash from the Pope's followers.[52]

Although consumers are free to seek out or avoid information, people often feel that children should not be exposed to objectionable images. When these are plastered on billboards or the side of a bus, it is hard to avoid them. Marketers face a challenge when deciding whether to promote a product with a sexual theme or shock tactics. They must weigh the risk of losing customers and crossing ethical boundaries against the advantages of gaining attention and strongly influencing purchase behavior.

Many of the factors that influence consumer decision making also play a role in the buying decisions of businesses because businesspeople are, after all, individuals with psychological motivations, perceptions and attitudes. Overall, however, the buying behavior of businesses is quite different from consumer buying behavior. Business-to-business transactions follow formalized procedures, involve many persons and functions, and require more personalized communication with the selling firm.

CHAPTER SUMMARY

Objective 1: Appreciate the importance of involvement in the decisions consumers make.

Marketers know that an understanding of consumer behavior lies at the heart of nearly every successful strategy for connecting with cus-

tomers. Consumer behavior is the actions and decision processes of individuals and organizations in discovering, evaluating, acquiring, consuming, and disposing of products. Consumers behave differently in low- and high-involvement purchasing situations. When involvement is high, they use an elaborate five-step decision process, and their atti tudes are learned actively. When involvement is low, they make choices without much effort, and learning is passive.

Objective 2: Evaluate the effect on consumer behavior of such psychological factors as motivation, perception, learning, attitudes and information processing.

The five important psychological factors influencing consumer behavior are motivation, perception, learning, attitudes and information processing. Motivation is an internal force that directs behavior toward the fulfillment of needs. Marketers often use Maslow's hierarchy to categorize needs. Consumers may experience one of three forms of motivational conflict: approach-approach, avoidance-avoidance, or approach-avoidance. Perception is the process of recognizing, selecting, organizing and interpreting stimuli in order to make sense of the world around us. It occurs in four stages: selective exposure, selective attention, selective comprehension and selective retention. Learning is any change in behavioral tendencies due to previous experience. The two basic types of learning are cognitive learning and behavioral learning. Behaviors can be learned (conditioned) by classical conditioning and operant conditioning. Attitudes have cognitive, affective, and behavioral components. Information processing involves encoding and memory processes. The human brain encodes information differently depending on the type of data. It processes nonverbal, emotional and visual concepts in one way, while it handles general knowledge, facts and justifications in another. Memory consists of sensory, short-term and long-term memory.

Objective 3: Explain how social factors such as culture, subculture, social class, reference groups, and family help explain consumer behavior.

Subcultures are groups that display homogeneous values and behaviors that diverge from the surrounding culture. Social class is a relatively stable division into groups based on such factors as education, income and occupation. Reference groups provide norms and values that become the perspectives that influence a consumer's behavior. Associative groups are ones with which people want to be associated, whereas dissociative groups are ones with which people do not want to identify. Families have a profound influence on consumer behavior.

REVIEW YOUR UNDERSTANDING

1. What is involvement? How does it influence passive and active learning?
2. Describe the five steps in decision making.
3. What is motivation? Describe Maslow's hierarchy of needs.
4. Describe the four elements of the perception process.
5. What is learning? Describe cognitive learning and two types of behavioral learning.
6. What are attitudes? What are their three components? How does knowledge of the components help in creating attitude change strategies?
7. What is information processing and how does it work?
8. What social influences are most important to marketers? List and define each.
9. How is social class measured?

DISCUSSION OF CONCEPTS

1. Name several subcultures in the United States. Which companies have target-marketed to them?
2. Why must marketers distinguish between a person's ethnic background and ethnicity?
3. How does social class affect consumer behavior? Which social classes exist in the United States?
4. What are the different ways families make purchase decisions? How do these affect marketing?
5. Imagine that you are the marketing manager for the Audi TT sports car. What product features would you include to meet each of the five types of needs described by Maslow's hierarchy? (For example, air bags might fulfill the safety need.)
6. What types of motivational conflict might be associated with the purchase of this Audi TT? How would you try to resolve the conflict?
7. You are in charge of marketing for a major league baseball team. How might you apply the principles of cognitive learning to your job? Could you also apply the principles of classical conditioning or reinforcement learning? How?

KEY TERMS & DEFINITIONS

1. **Active learning:** Learning in which substantial energy is devoted to thinking about and elaborating on information.
2. **Affective (component of attitude):** Emotional feeling of like or dislike.
3. **Alternatives evaluation:** Use of decision rules that attempt to determine which product would be most likely to satisfy goals.
4. **Approach-approach conflict:** Motivational conflict that occurs when a consumer desires two objectives but cannot have both.
5. **Approach-avoidance conflict:** Motivational conflict that

occurs when a consumer desires an alternative that has positive and negative qualities.

6. **Associative reference groups:** A group with which people want to identify.

7. **Attitude:** A state of readiness with cognitive, emotional, and behavioral components, which reflects the beliefs of the consumer with regard to messages, brands, products, product characteristics, and so forth.

8. **Avoidance-avoidance conflict:** Motivational conflict that occurs when consumers must choose between two undesirable alternatives.

9. **Behavioral (component of attitude):** Tendency to act positively or negatively.

10. **Belief:** A conviction that something is true or that descriptive statements are factual.

11. **Classical conditioning:** After two stimuli are presented together repeatedly, people learn to respond to one in the same way as the other.

12. **Cognitive (component of attitude):** Knowledge about a product's attributes not influenced by emotion.

13. **Consumer behavior:** The actions and decision processes of individuals and households in discovering, evaluating, acquiring, consuming, and disposing of products.

14. **Culture:** The learned values, beliefs, language, symbols, and patterns of behavior shared by people in a society that are passed on from generation to generation.

15. **Dissociative reference groups:** A group with which people do not want to identify.

16. **Discrimination:** Making different responses to different stimuli.

17. **Encoding:** The process of converting information to knowledge.

18. **Generalization:** Making the same response to different stimuli.

19. **High-involvement purchase:** A complex buying decision made after extensive thought.

20. **Household:** Family members (and occasionally others) who share the same housing unit; for marketers, the standard purchase and consumption unit.

21. **Information processing:** The process whereby consumers acquire, store, and evaluate the data they use in making decisions.

22. **Information search:** Thinking through a situation by recall-ing information from stored memory or obtaining it from extern sources.

23. **Learning:** Any change in consumer behavior caused experience.

24. **Low-involvement purchase:** A routine buying decision.

25. **Memory:** The brain function that stores and recalls e coded information; includes sensory, short-term, and long-ter capacities.

26. **Motivation:** An internal force that directs behavior toward t fulfillment of needs.

27. **Operant conditioning:** The use of reinforcement or punis ment to shape behavior.

28. **Passive learning:** Learning in which little energy is devot to thinking about or elaborating on information.

29. **Perception:** The process of recognizing, selecting, organizin and interpreting stimuli in order to make sense of the world.

30. **Problem recognition:** Becoming aware of an unfulfill need or desire.

31. **Psychological needs:** A need that arises in the socializatic process.

32. **Purchase:** A financial commitment to acquire a product.

33. **Purchase decision:** The decision of whether or not to bu and which competing product to buy, which is made after carefu weighing the alternatives.

34. **Purchase evaluation:** The process of determining satisfa tion or dissatisfaction with a buying choice.

35. **Reference groups:** A set of people whose norms and valu influence a consumer's behavior.

36. **Selective attention:** The tendency to heed information th supports current views and behaviors.

37. **Selective comprehension:** The tendency to interpret prod ucts and messages according to current beliefs.

38. **Selective exposure:** The tendency to seek out or avoid info mation sources.

39. **Selective retention:** The tendency to remember some an forget other information.

40. **Social class:** A relatively stable division of society based c education, income, and occupation.

41. **Subculture:** A subset of people with shared values within culture.

42. **Values:** The shared norms about what is right to think and d what a culture considers to be worthy and desirable.

REFERENCES

1. http://ir.homedepot.com/phoenix.zhtml?c=63646&p=irol-newsArticle&id=1345670; http://www6.homedepot.com/ecooptions/index.html?, websites visited April 11, 2014.

2. www.robbreport.com, website visited June 14, 2014.

3. www.dodge.com, website visited May 13, 2014.

4. The Army National Guard Recruiting Homepage, www.1800goguard.com, website visited May 13, 2014.

5. U.S. Department of Health and Human Services, "The Health Consequences of Smoking—50 Years of Progress," A Report of the Surgeon General. Atlanta: U.S. Department of Health and Human Services, Centers for Disease Control and Prevention, National Center for Chronic Disease Prevention and Health Promotion, Office on Smoking and Health, 2014.

6. Vivian, John, The Media of Mass Communication (Boston: Allyn & Bacon, 1993), pg. 296.

7. Spangenberg, Eric R.; Greenwald, Anthony G., "A Field Test of Subliminal Self-Help Audiotapes: The Power of Expectancies," Journal of Public Policy & Marketing, Fall 1992, Vol. 11, Issue 2, pp. 26-36.

8. Pavlov, Ivan, Conditioned Reflexes: An Investigation of the Physiological Activity of the Cerebral Cortex, trans. G.V. Anrep (London: Oxford University Press, 1927.

9. "Stand By Your Fans," Advertising Age, April 29, 1996, pg. M1.

10. "Google Ventures continues to precede acquisition with Divide," Slash Gear, May 19, 2014.

11. www.quakeroatmeal.com, website visited April 8, 2014.

12. http://www.americanwaymag.com, www.nhl.com/intheslot/read/impact, www.humanesociety.org, websites visited April 8, 2014.

13. "What Happens at a Meeting?" Weight Watchers. www.weightwatchers.com, website visited April 8, 2014.

14. Sarah Schoenborn, "Per capita meat consumption predicted lower for 2013; Prices moderately higher," www.agriview.com, February 21, 2013.

15. Hansen, Flemming, "Hemispherical Lateralization: Implications for Understanding Consumer Behavior," Journal of Consumer Research 8, June 1981, pp. 23-36.

16. Holbrash, Morris B.; Moore, William L., "Feature Interactions in Consumer Judgments of Verbal Versus Pictorial Presentations," Journal of Consumer Research 8, June 1981), pg. 103.

17. "Nike Logo," Logo Blog, www.logoblog.org, site visited March 29, 2014.

18. www.johnsonsbaby.com, website visited April 11, 2014.

19. Piave, Allan, "A Dual Coding Approach to Perception and Cognition," Modes of Perceiving and Processing Information (Hillsdale, New Jersey: Laurence Erlbaum, 1978), pg. 16.

20. Simon, Herbert A., "How Big Is a Chunk?" Science, February 8, 1974, pg. 183.

21. "The Office remade for French TV," news.bbc.co.uk., website visited April 11, 2014.

22. Fielding, Michael, "In One's Element," Marketing News, February 2006, Vol. 40, Issue 2, pg. 15.

23. Alan Gomez, "Voices: Fast-growing Hispanic market tough to tap," USA Today, February 28, 2014.

24. " The New York Times Highlights Univision's Continued Success in Drawing in Viewers," Univision, http://corporate.univision.com, August 8, 2012.

25. "CPG Growth Hinges on Success With Hispanics," Supermarket News, supermarketnews.com, May 22, 2012.

26. www.census.gov, website visited April 11, 2014.

27. Ibid.

28. Gates, Kelly, "Marketers Tie into Asian Lunar New Year," Brandmarketing, May 2000.

29. www.census.gov, website visited April 12, 2014; "Britni Danielle, "African Americans Have $1.1 Trillion in Buying Power, Are We Putting Our Money to Good Use?," Clutch Magazine, February 11, 2014.

30. Pew Internet, www.pewinternet.org, website visited June 14, 2014.

31. Jesse J. Holland, "Black Twitter Emerging As Major Force In A Technological Civil Rights Age," Associated Press, March 11, 2014.

32. Janelle Griffith, "DMX, George Zimmerman 'celebrity boxing match' canceled," The Star-Ledger, February 9, 2014.

33. Brumback, Nancy, "Ethnic Markets Are Growing Up," Brandmarketing, July 2000.

34. "Giant Lifestyle Survey to Hit U.K.," December 4, 1996, www.adage.com.

35. Peter, J.P.; Olson, Jerry C., Consumer Behavior and Marketing Strategy, 3rd ed, (Homewood, Illinois: Richard D. Irwin, 1993.

36. "Taylor Swift donates 4 million to charity. Wow," Sugarscape, www.sugarscape.com, May 18, 2012.

37. www.revlon.com, website visited April 14, 2014.

38. www.forbes.com, website visited April 14, 2014.

39. Wilkie, William L.; Moore-Shay, Elizabeth S.; Assar, Amardeep, Family Decision Making for Household Durable Goods (Cambridge, Massachusetts: Marketing Science Institute, 1992), pg. 1.

40. Plank, Richard E.; Greene, Robert C. Jr.; Greene, Joel M., "Understanding Which Spouse Makes Financial Decisions," Journal of Retail Banking, Spring 1994, Vol. 16, Issue 1, pp. 21-36.

41. Kwiatkowski, Jane, Women take on home improvement projects, big and small, McClatchy Tribune Business News, Washington, March 8, 2008.

42. www.drugstore.com, website visited April 14, 2014.

43. Kellogg's, hwww.kelloggs.com, website visited April 14, 2014.

44. www.whitehouse.gov, website visited April 14, 2014.

45. DeNavas-Walt, Carmen; Proctor, Smith, "Income, Poverty and Health Insurance Coverage in the United States: 2008.

46. www.carescout.com, website visited April 11, 2014.

47. The Nielsen Company, http://blog.nielsen.com/nielsenwire/online_mobile, website visited June 10, 2014.

48. www.internetnews.com, website visited May 12, 2014.

49. www.google.com/analytics, website visited May 12, 2014.

50. Kerwin, Anne M.; Neff, Jack, "Too Sexy? P&G 'Task Force' Stirs Magazine Debate," Advertising Age, April 10, 2000, www.adage.com.

51. "Companies in the Crossfire," BusinessWeek, April 17, 2006, Issue 3980, pg. 30.

52. Meichtry, Stacy, "Does the Pope Wear Prada," Wall Street Journal, April 25, 2006, pg. B1.

Chapter 06

UNDERSTANDING BUSINESS MARKETING

Before Intel, few computer users knew or cared about the microprocessor powering their PC or Mac. In 1992, the company began one of the most revolutionary corporate branding campaigns in history with "Intel Inside." Never before had an electrical component company tried to create brand identity with the end user, especially in a commodity market such as computer chips. Intel's share of the microprocessor market quickly climbed to about 80 percent.

The approach that Intel took to gain the end users' trust relied heavily on building a co-operative marketing strategy and advertising budgets with PC makers like Dell and Hewlett-Packard. Part of the deal that Intel struck with manufacturers was that if the Intel logo was included on a marketing piece then it would share the cost of advertising; Intel pays up to five percent in ad costs. The result? Now the Intel logo is as recognizable as Windows. The move shook up the entire microprocessor industry, transforming it into both a consumer and business-oriented company.

While PC companies were quick to adopt the branding strategy of Intel, Apple declined to participate. Steve Jobs, former CEO of Apple, noted that customers already know that Macs come equipped with Intel microprocessors and that including the badges on their machines would be redundant.

Recently, Intel launched 27 new products in its core line of micro processing units. The majority of these chips will be embedded in laptop computers and PCs, but they are also versatile enough to be used in banking machines as well as mobile technology with facial recognition software. Intel's approach in this most recent release was targeted at higher-volume but lower-priced segments in the market as the industry demands more energy-efficient and quicker processing units.

In 2012, Intel announced retail solutions developed in collaboration with HSN, Kraft Foods and Macy's. Using Intel-based technologies, retailers are able to provide the advantages of online shopping in brick-and-mortar stores. The solutions allow retailers to display visually appealing experiences to interact with customers, provide customized content and help shoppers make better-informed purchases.

"Today's consumers are increasingly mobile, connected and inundated with information," says Michelle Tinsley, general manager of Intel's Personal Solutions Division. "As a result, retailers are searching for new ways to deliver more personalized brand interactions that effectively reach their target audience. Intel is working with these industry leaders to drive the transformation of shopping through high-tech retail solutions that will change how brands engage and connect with shoppers."

These new technologies, powered by Intel, are making digital signage an exciting new method for marketers to deliver more relevant content for consumers. Intel understands how to execute effective business marketing. Its name resonates with end users and it's a powerhouse in the B2B market. As a corporation, Intel has been responsive to all of its stakeholders. Most notably, the company has rewarded shareholders with a 2643% return on investment since 1992.[1]

<< Intel booth at Mobile World Congress 2014

Courtesy of Intel

Learning Objectives

1. Describe the types of organizations and products involved in business-to-business marketing and understand the importance of this market.
2. Understand the link between consumer demand and business-to-business marketing.
3. Describe the organizational buying process.
4. Know how buyer-seller relationships work, including informal and contractual partnerships.
5. Learn what functions and roles within organizations influence the purchase of a broad range of products.

THE CONCEPT OF BUSINESS-TO-BUSINESS MARKETING

Intel, Dow Chemical Company and General Electric, like thousands of other companies, market directly to other companies. They connect with customers, one customer at a time, and each customer buys huge amounts of their products. Market Data Retrieval (MDR) has been selling data-rich marketing information and communication tools to colleges and universities for over 40 years. MDR doesn't normally sell directly to students or other consumers, but directly to schools and other businesses in need of such services.[2] This chapter describes the challenges of business-to-business marketing and its importance to the global economy. Business-to-business (B2B) marketing is the marketing of goods and services to other businesses, governments and institutions.

Total B2B sales are about five times greater than total business-to-consumer (B2C) sales. On the surface, this seems paradoxical, because most goods and services ultimately benefit the consumers who pay for them. However, consumer products result from a variety of components and processes, going through several different organizations before reaching the final consumer. Think about a product like an Apple iPad. Dow Chemical, for example, purchases petroleum to create a special plastic used for the case. A plastics manufacturer purchases the raw material from Dow to use in its manufacture of the case. The computer chips and communication components are manufactured by other suppliers like Intel. Corning supplies a tough, scratch-resistant glass called Gorilla Glass to protect the device from wear and tear. Each manufacturer adds some value to the process, and eventually Apple has a finished product to sell to consumers in the B2C arena. At each B2B step, increasing amounts of money, time and effort are spent on marketing. What the first party in the chain contributes is charged to the next party, which is included in the price to the next party as it moves along the chain.

In other cases of B2B marketing, a finished product is simply sold and re-sold along the line until it reaches the end consumer. For example, a deck of playing cards is purchased by a wholesaler, who resells it to a retailer such as Kmart, who then sells it to the final consumer, with each step requiring time, money and effort. In still other cases, one company sells products directly to another for its own internal use — whether copy machines, laptop computers or paper tablets.

Many types of organizations buy business products. For example, General Motors and Ford (B2C companies) have several thousand suppliers that support their auto divisions. Other for-profit and nonprofit organizations — from the Fortune 500 to small private firms — do the same and add to this total volume. Finally, the government market makes purchases nearly as large as all private organizations combined, ranging from country road repairs to army boots to toothbrushes. The

Business-to-Business Markets

Consumer Household Markets

Commercial

Extractor   Transportation

Telecommunication

Federal Government

State & Local

Military

Trade

THE SUPPLY CHAIN

Organizational Buying

Relationships between buyer and seller

Functions involved in business purchases

Organization's buying process

Figure 6.1   Connecting with Customers Through B2B Marketing

business market offers tremendous opportunities, and upon graduation, most business students enter the B2B arena.

Key aspects of the business-to-business market are depicted in Figure 6.1. The first half of this chapter discusses the nature of B2B markets, while the second half deals with business-buyer behavior.

This section begins by describing how B2B markets are formed from derived demand. Next we will look at the industries that comprise the overall market. Then we will see how supply links connect companies, following a supply chain that reaches from raw materials extractors to neighborhood retailers. Finally, we will discuss the globalization of business markets.

DERIVED BUSINESS MARKET DEMAND

Derived demand means that the amount of sales for business-to-business products ultimately depends on (is derived from) consumer demand. For example, when Xbox sales increase, so does the need for materials, components and subassemblies. The first (original) demand occurs among consumers and is reflected in the business-to-business market. This ripple effect is felt throughout the supply chain, and it drives economic growth.

Inelastic Demand
Certain products are so essential that they are less responsive than others to changes in the economy. **Inelastic demand** refers to products so necessary that a change in price has relatively little effect on the quantity demanded. If the price of sugar or another cola ingredient rises, it's doubtful that Coke or Pepsi will use less of it in making their product. The cost has little to do with their decision about what to buy, although it may affect the price charged to consumers.

Fluctuating Demand: The Accelerator Principle
Some business products are highly sensitive to changes in consumer demand. We see the **accelerator principle** operating when a small fluctuation (increase or decrease) in consumer demand has a larger effect on business demand. Suppose that the economy is sluggish. In an effort to save money, consumers are closely watching their energy consumption — turning off lights when not in use, running the air conditioner as little as possible, and so forth. A few dollars saved by each customer in the area will have a noticeable effect on the local power plant's revenue. Even a small drop in consumer demand may be enough to force the plant to postpone the purchase of multimillion-dollar equipment. Of course, if consumer demand exceeds expectations by only a little, the result may be blackouts, power outages or the need to buy energy from outside the system.

Derived Demand

A demand, such as the demand for business-to-business products, which depends ultimately on the demand of end customers.

Inelastic Demand

Demand that is influenced little by price changes.

Accelerator Principle

A small increase or decrease in consumer demand has a larger effect on business demand.

TYPES OF MARKETS

The business market is divided into the seven categories shown in Figure 6.2 and further described below. Each category is composed of organizations with similar business circumstances and general purchasing requirements.

Commercial Market

Commercial Market The **commercial market** category consists of organizations that acquire goods and services that are then used to produce other goods and services, eventually creating finished products used by consumers. For example, Pulte, the nation's largest home builder, has hundreds of suppliers of construction products used to build houses. These, in turn, have other suppliers. All the marketing activities leading up to and including the sale of goods and services to Pulte are part of the commercial market.

Extractor Industries

Extractor Industries The **extractor industries** category includes organizations that obtain and process raw materials, as in forestry or mining. Extractor companies are separated from the commercial segment because they acquire much of their supply from the earth, which requires expensive equipment such as drilling rigs and instrumentation. These industries consume a wide variety of products in vast quantities. Many of the companies in this category have global operations, such as Exxon-Mobil and BP.

The public is often especially demanding of extractor organizations to be environmentally sensitive, but this also provides these organizations unique opportunities to market ecological products. EnviroGroup is a firm that provides both consulting and testing services. Its expertise in vapor intrusion evaluation and mitigation helps clients deal with the technical, regulatory and risk communication challenges presented by vapor intrusion — an emerging focus of environmental agencies. With its expertise and advanced equipment, EnviroGroup manages environmental issues for clients worldwide.[3]

Trade Industries

Trade Industries The **trade industries** category is made up of organizations that acquire or distribute finished products to businesses or to consumers. It includes retailers, wholesalers and other intermediaries. These companies play an important role in the "place" component of the marketing mix. The importance of a reseller, a company that purchases a product and sells it in the same form for profit, has been gaining more and more recognition recently. The computer industry, for example, is now emphasizing the role of resellers in distribution and increasingly relies on them to install and service products, granting consumers the freedom to get computer maintenance at a location of their choice. Apple realizes the benefits of reselling and expanded its offerings to resellers by extending its build-to-order (BTO) capabilities to them, now allowing customers to order custom-built computers from their preferred reseller.[4]

In many cases, resellers repackage products to suit the needs of particular market segments. Humm Foods, the creator of LARABAR, uses Fair Trade Certified coffee and cocoa in its products. The certification ensures that the practice that goes into farming both coffee and cocoa "enables sustainable development and community empowerment by cultivating a more equitable global trade model that benefits farmers, workers, consumers, industry and the earth."[5]

Institutions

Institutions The **institutions** category covers public and private organizations that provide health, education and welfare services to consumers. It includes universities, hospitals, churches, nursing homes and museums. Institutional buyers purchase a broad range of products with funds of their own or from third parties, such as donors, insurance companies and government grants.

Institutions that rely largely or entirely on third-party funding must be especially prudent with their purchases, so potential suppliers need to take this into ac-

Category	Examples of Organizations	Purchase Examples
Commercial	Fabricators Component manufacturers Processors Original equipment manufacturers Designers	Raw materials Component parts Processing equipment Transportation Consulting services
Extractor	Agriculture Forestry Mining Drilling Water	Fertilizer and pesticides, seeds Heavy- and light-duty equipment Pipe Aircraft and transportation Real estate, mining rights Products for resale Loading equipment
Trade	Retailers Wholesalers Dealerships	Computer systems Buildings/real estate Advertising Transportation Warehousing Pharmaceuticals Equipment
Institutions	Hospitals Schools Day care centers Banks and finance organizations Insurance Churches Charities	Food Consulting Health care Suppliers Computer systems
Utilities	Electric utilities Gas utilities Water and waste disposal plants	Nuclear fuel Power generation equipment Electric components Motors Computers Chemicals Testing equipment
Transportation and Telecommunications	Airlines Trucking Rail companies Telephones Cellular	Fuel Equipment Computers Real estate
Government *Federal*	Senate and House Judicial Agencies Military	Consulting Offices Forms Computers Energy Aircraft Radar communications
State and Local	Highway commissions Health and social services Schools and universities Prisons Police Libraries Parks and recreation Museums	Health care items Food Logistics Equipment Energy Books Sports equipment Restoration

Figure 6.2   Types of B2B Markets

count when marketing to them. Solvay Chemical, for example, is a company that provides numerous chemical products for a number of industries including the pharmaceutical industry. In this industry, they provide products to hospitals and other businesses, requiring them to pay careful attention to the money they use so that they can charge accurate prices to their market.

Utilities

Utilities The **utilities** category is composed of companies that distribute gas, electricity and water. Once highly regulated by the government, utilities now have the opportunity to operate more like private organizations. Public service commissions continue to provide oversight, however, because even private utilities are considered to be part of the public sector to some degree. Consolidated Edison and Florida Power & Light are huge buyers of business products. General Electric sells billions of dollars in nuclear fuel, power generation equipment and design services to public and privately owned utilities like Consolidated Edison and Florida Power & Light.

Transportation and Telecommunications

Transportation and telecommunications make up another business market category. The transportation portion is composed of companies that provide passenger and freight service such as Union Pacific Railroad and United Airlines. Telecommunications companies supply local and long-distance telephone service as well as cable and broadcasting: CBS, AOL Time Warner and AT&T are some examples. Like utilities, this category was once subject to extensive government regulation that has been relaxed in recent years.

Although there are relatively few companies in this category, their purchases are huge. The cable and broadcast companies purchase satellite capacity, equipment and a huge range of services necessary to develop state-of-the-art telecasting.

Government Markets

In the United States, the subdivisions in the **government market** category are (1) the federal government, (2) the 50 different state governments and (3) 8,700 local units. Honeywell, a diverse company with many different services, markets to these government sectors by providing "government experts" to assist their customers with the challenges that come from navigating the demands of government while getting what they need.[6]

LARGE PURCHASES IN B2B MARKETS

Unlike B2C marketers, who sell a relatively small amount to a large number of buyers, business marketers choose to sell a large amount to a few customers. Often the price of a single item is high, like the cost of a corporate jet or a new information technology system for a company. In other cases, the buyer purchases a huge number of a lower priced item. For example, if EDS wins an order to replace computer work stations for a client, each work station might cost a little more than $1,000, but the total price tag could easily be several hundred million dollars. In some cases, these sales amounts are great enough to affect the companies' stock price. For example, when FedEx bought $3.5 billion of Boeing aircrafts, it had to back out of a deal with Boeing's competitor Airbus. Boeing's stock price increased by five percent in a single day, a huge win for Boeing's marketing team.[7]

Utilities
Companies that distribute gas, electricity and water.

Transportation & Telecommunications
Companies that provide passenger and freight service and/or local and long-distance telephone service.

Government Market
Market category including federal, state, and local government units.

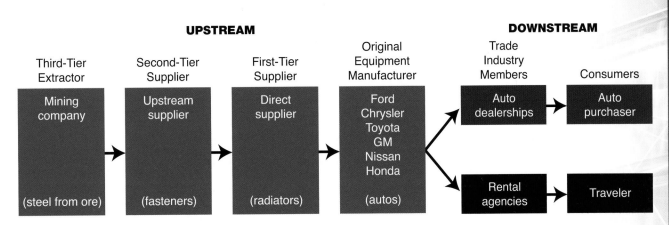

Figure 6.3   An Example of the Supply Chain in the Automotive Industry

BUSINESS MARKET LINKAGES: THE SUPPLY CHAIN

The **supply chain** links organizations involved in the creation and delivery of a product. Figure 6.3 is a simplified diagram of the supply chain for automobiles. The original equipment manufacturer (OEM), such as Toyota, is in the middle of the chain, with supply activities occurring on both sides. In B2B marketing, the word "**tier**" refers to the degree of contact between suppliers and the OEM. For example, there are third-tier suppliers (extractors who process steel from ore), second-tier suppliers (manufacturers of components such as wiring), and first-tier suppliers (makers of computer chips). The first tier is a direct supplier to the OEM such as LEAR Corporation which sells sophisticated electronic systems to auto manufactures like Ford.

Supply chain management involves establishing or improving linkages to maximize efficiency and effectiveness. Marketers view the supply chain in terms of activities that need to be coordinated to provide the greatest value to the consumer, who is at the end of the chain. For example, UPS is more than a $50 billion company with an extremely successful supply chain that delivers goods to more than 200 countries worldwide. It developed a unified organization called UPS Supply Chain Solutions. This system offers logistics, global freight, financial, and mail services to improve customers' profitability.[8]

Supply Chain

The linkage of organizations involved in the creation and delivery of a product.

Tier

The degree of contact between the supplier and the OEM.

GLOBALIZATION OF BUSINESS MARKETS

Because strong business-to-business marketers realize their success is tied to their clients', there is a lot of potential for overseas marketing. Companies such as International Data Group (IDG), the world's leading technology media, events and research company, is capable of providing multi-country coverage. IDG Communications, a division of the company, has globally branded product lines that extend to over 280 million consumers in 97 countries. IDG marketing services connect tech buyers and sellers around the world.[9] Global brand identity is as important in B2B marketing as in consumer marketing. JP Morgan, a highly recognized financial services firm in the United States, launched a global branding campaign to expand its customer base to include younger, high-tech and web-based firms.[10]

ORGANIZATIONAL BUYING

BUYING DECISIONS

Businesses decide whether to buy from suppliers or make the product in-house. When businesses decide to use a supplier, they then determine the best choice among competitors. Business consumers have to make many decisions about their own plan and potential suppliers before selecting one.

The Make or Buy Decision

Make or Buy Decision

The decision whether to supply products in-house, or to purchase them from other businesses.

The **make or buy decision** occurs when an organization determines whether to supply products or services in-house (the make decision) or to buy them from other businesses (the buy decision). The buy decision results in outsourcing from a supplier, which allows the buying company to focus on investments and its core business. An organization must evaluate its need for direct control over production or quality, and the costs associated with supplying internally versus externally. Other issues include supplier reliability, design secrecy and workforce stability.

The Outsourcing Decision

Outsourcing

Purchasing products and services from other companies.

Outsourcing, the purchasing of products and services from other companies has become widely popular. In fact, Dun & Bradstreet estimates that outsourcing is now a $4 trillion a year business globally.[11] Of the 300 largest global companies, about three-quarters use it as a strategy. The Global Outsourcing 100 listed in Fortune magazine are judged on four key characteristics: size and growth, customer references, organizational competencies, and management capabilities. Headquartered in Denmark, ISS is currently ranked as the best outsourcing service provider in the world.[12] It offers a wide range of services including facility management, cleaning, support, property management and maintenance, catering, and security. To do this on a global scale, ISS will outsource to organizations that can do a job better, faster, cheaper, or all three. It also looks to outsourcing partners to become a source for innovation and to help create new ways of improving business.[13] Outsourcing reduces need for in-house expertise and cuts costs, allowing companies to focus resources on primary business activities. Essentially, this allows B2B buyers to extend their enterprise by using the specialized talents and resources of suppliers.

Straight Rebuy

A routine purchase with which the organization has considerable experience.

Outsourcing may involve the purchase of a product on a routine basis, after evaluating a current product or supplier, or when purchasing a product for the first time. These three kinds of situations — straight rebuy, modified rebuy, and new task situations — are summarized in Figure 6.4. A **straight rebuy** is a purchase that the organization is very experienced at making, to the point of routine. For example, an exclusive furniture manufacturer may purchase leather for its sofas from only one supplier, which has a reputation for the highest quality. The two organizations have done business for years, and the manufacturer has made hundreds of purchases. In this case, a buying decision may take less than a week and involve only one or two people from each organization. In fact, it's normal for a purchasing agent to handle the entire transaction.

Modified Rebuy

Purchase of a familiar product from an unfamiliar supplier or a new or different product from a familiar supplier.

Suppose that the furniture manufacturer is dissatisfied with the leather supplier or doesn't want to depend on only one. A **modified rebuy** situation involves purchasing a familiar product from an unfamiliar supplier or a new product from a familiar supplier. A modified rebuy usually requires more personnel, time and energy.

TYPE	DESCRIPTION	PEOPLE INVOLVED
Straight rebuy	Reorder from current supplier	One purchasing agent
Modified rebuy	Evaluate alternative suppliers of a product purchased before or a new or different product from a current supplier	Purchasing agent plus one or a few others
New task	First-time purchase of a product	many people from several areas of the organization

Figure 6.4   Organizational Buying Situations

New Task Situation

Purchase of an unfamiliar product from an unfamiliar supplier.

Finally, let's say the furniture manufacturer decides to add a line of fabric sofas. This **new task situation** involves purchasing an unfamiliar product from an unfamiliar supplier. Because there is a great deal at risk, many people will likely provide input to the decision process, which may take several weeks, months or even years.

Competitive Bidding Some organizations use competitive bidding, especially for larger purchases. They want to obtain the lowest price rather than establish long-term relationships with suppliers. Most government purchases are required by law to use competitive bidding. Many companies, such as General Motors, have purchasing rules that require a minimum number of bids — usually three — for certain types of purchases. Even these companies will often make exceptions, as long as all parties agree and the justification is documented. In straight rebuy situations in the private sector, competitive bids are seldom required. Since both modified rebuys and new task situations often involve unfamiliar suppliers, bidding is likely to take place with either. In any of these cases, if the amount is very large, then the bidding procedure will probably be used.

Competitive bids may be sealed or negotiated. For the sealed bids, each seller is given a request for quotation (RFQ), which describes all of the product and purchase specifications. The responses are due on a given date, when envelopes are opened, and the lowest bidder is awarded the order. Negotiated bids are much more flexible, often allowing suppliers to be present and to comment on the results.

Web Auctions For competitive bidding, the auctions need to have enough bidders in the same place at the same time. The Internet has solved this problem, as there is no need for bidders to meet together physically; they simply need to be online while the auction is in process. Web auctions are conducted online and match buyers and sellers around the world. They are powerful and efficient to both buyers and sellers on two levels. First, they provide in-depth information that enhances bidders' understanding of the products. Buyers are more comfortable and feel that they can properly assess the products when they have adequate time to research. The fact that sellers, on average, obtain higher winning bids from web auctions than other formats is telling of the buyers' comfort levels. The second is that the web can increase the numbers of bidders. This helps the seller, leading to a higher winning bid. It also helps prevent an auction failure; when bids do not meet a designated price, the seller can later agree to accept a lower bid.[14] eBay has more than 145 million buyers and sellers on its online marketplace — the world's largest — which keeps competition healthy. In 2013, the company enabled $212 billion of commerce worldwide. Many of these buyers and sellers are B2B companies.[15]

STEPS IN THE ORGANIZATIONAL BUYING PROCESS

An organization may go through eight different stages when making a buying decision, but every purchase does not require all of them. New task situations may involve all eight, modified rebuys fewer, and straight rebuys the fewest. The eight possible steps in the organizational buying process are shown in Figure 6.5.

Problem recognition occurs when the buying organization realizes that a situation can be improved by acquiring a good or service. Potential problems include unsatisfactory materials, mechanical failure, or development of a new product that requires new equipment. The organization identifies the charac-

Figure 6.5 Steps in the Buying Process

teristics needed from the new product such as reliability, price, range and durability. Next, the organization prepares product specifications, which are usually technical and very detailed: precise dimensions, tolerances, quantity or the objectives of a consultant's study are included.

Unless it has been decided to make the product in-house, the search for suppliers now begins. Some may have been involved in the previous stages, but the organization usually looks for more to be certain no options are missed and to encourage price competition. New products and straight rebuys are both sought as necessary. During the proposal solicitation and supplier selection stage, the buying organization invites bids and assesses these according to the criteria set forth in the specifications. The lowest price usually wins, especially in the government sector, but such considerations as a reputation for quality and reliability may enter as well.

When a supplier has been selected, the buying organization negotiates the final terms of the agreement, called order routine specifications. At this point, fine-tuning of the agreement is not unheard of. During the purchase and use of product stage, the buyer signs the contract, takes the delivery and begins to evaluate whether the product does the job as anticipated. At this point, follow-through by the seller is critical to resolve any problems that may arise. The final step is performance review and feedback. After making a formal analysis, the buyer lets the supplier know how well the product meets the needs of the organization.

As the buying organization moves through this process repeatedly, creeping commitment may occur. If there is consistent satisfaction with a seller's products, the two parties may begin to build a lasting relationship. In that case, the buying process becomes simpler for both organizations, as modified or straight rebuys are more likely.

RELATIONSHIPS BETWEEN BUYERS AND SELLERS

Relationships grow in phases as the buying and selling organizations learn to work together. A marketer that understands the buyer's strategies, problems, and opportunities can help the company become more competitive. "With knowledgeable professional buyers, multiple decision makers, and fewer overall customers to choose from, B2B marketers have a more complex task than many realize," commented Nick Kaczmarek of Dow Chemical. Marketers that do a good job of understanding buying organizations are seen as valued members of their customers' supply chain.

Business relationships are not established overnight. It may take weeks, months or even years for the companies to understand and trust each other. There is a typical process involved (as illustrated in Figure 6.6) that consists of three phases: the courtship phase, the relationship-building phase, and the partnership phase. For example, a first-time customer of UPS will purchase only a few of their warehousing or shipping services. As the business comes to realize that UPS services are core aspects of the buyer's ability to satisfy its own customers, it purchases more services. Over time it is not unusual for UPS to supply all of a buyer's warehousing and transportation needs. UPS's high-technology information systems are not the only reason; UPS works to understand each customer's business thoroughly. This means that strategies and plans must be shared freely, and the client must trust UPS to keep them confidential. In many cases, UPS even helps customers develop the strategies and plans.

The Courtship Phase   During courtship, purchasers express their desires to sellers. This phase often begins when a seller is placed on the buyer's approved supplier list, which means it meets at least minimum standards. The criteria usually include financial health, size, licensing qualification, and delivery capabilities.

Unlike many people, businesses tend to look before they leap. Each company is trying to understand the other's requirements, so there are many discussions about product specifications, product design and order routines. After what can be a great

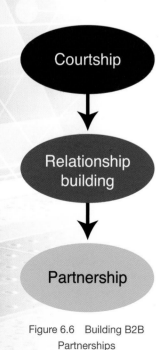

Figure 6.6   Building B2B
Partnerships

deal of time, the social distance begins to narrow. Often the buyer will grant the supplier a small order to test the waters, including the response to any problems that occur. In addition, the effectiveness of a solution depends on a customer's willingness to adapt to a supplier's offerings, and share relevant internal operations and political considerations with a supplier.[16]

The Relationship-Building Phase

The buyers and sellers work together for the first time in the relationship-building phase, which strengthens the bond between them. Unlike consumer marketing, business-to-business marketing tends to involve customizing the product, its delivery and its terms and conditions to each individual buyer. Buyers often grow to rely on suppliers for additional expertise, especially regarding new technologies. That is why trust, loyalty and compromise become so important in organizational buying activities. Due to the complexity and technical nature of most organizational purchasing, buyers and sellers must learn to work together, sometimes even adjusting their own internal practices to better satisfy the other's needs. Understanding the customer — and its customers — is critical.

CAREER TIP!

John A. Edwardson, retired chairman and CEO of Computer Discount Warehouse (CDW), says the culture of the company is more than great perks and benefits, and it is built on mutual respect. According to Edwardson, "Happy co-workers lead to happy customers, and that is fundamental in what shapes our business and help us continue to grow." Therefore, the company is willing to listen to its workers and give them the tools they need to succeed and celebrate in their success. As one of the "100 Best Companies to Work for in America," CDW states that it is a great place to work, and people do business with people they like.

During the relationship-building phase, the purchasing organization does not always have the upper hand. In fact, the relationship is sometimes said to be symmetrical — that is, the buyer and the seller may have equal power.[17] Both frequently feel a very strong need to interact in order to explore all options before signing a contract, especially if they are considering a formal partnership. Sellers generally offer information to help buyers formulate ideas about the purchase decision, while buyers provide information that helps the sellers do a better job of matching products to needs.

The Partnership Phase

After numerous purchases have been completed satisfactorily and long-term agreements are reached, the partnership phase begins. Because the buyer and seller have extensive experience with each other, they spend less time on the relationship itself and more time on ways to improve the productive aspects of the exchange, until it becomes routine. The seller may become an exclusive supplier or blanket orders may guarantee that the buyer will purchase a certain amount within a certain period.

The seller can commit resources to the buyer because it is assured that the business relationship will continue. Chrysler, for example, gets 70 percent of the value of its vehicles from its regular suppliers. Jeffrey Trimmer, Director of Operations and Strategy, says that the company's challenge is how to continue with its suppliers while using the Internet to facilitate that relationship and to identify and foster technology developments.[18] In many cases, computerized order entry systems are developed to link the buyer with the seller's manufacturing facilities. Nearly all big box retailers like Walmart give suppliers such a link. Vender-managed inventory, or VMI, is an order entry system that allows suppliers to monitor inventory and replenish stock without prior approval from the retailer. Through this close relationship with its suppliers, Walmart and other big box retailers can keep costs down and speed product distribution to avoid lost sales.[19]

Partnerships can be informal or contractual. Informally, each party may work without any guarantee of long-term business. An advertising agency and its client, for instance, both invest a lot of time and energy and share important information, so it's costly for either party to end the relationship.

A contractual partnership is formed when the buyer signs an agreement with a supplier for a specified period, usually three to five years. The trend in purchasing today is toward fewer suppliers, the use of programs that certify the qualifications of suppliers, and long-term contracts. Close relationships with a select few suppliers help ensure quality. Many buying organizations find that contractual partnerships have considerable advantages. The long-term relationship with suppliers allows the buying organization to concentrate energy on its customers. The buyer and supplier work as a team, each contributing its own expertise to provide products that better meet consumer needs. The longer the relationship, the better the results in terms of cooperation, efficiency, quality control and profits. In 2004, the National Broadcasting Company (NBC) and Vivendi Universal Entertainment combined to create NBC Universal. While this was the start of their official partnership, the two companies had worked together for decades, starting with the 1950 television premiere of "Stars Over Hollywood." Since then, the two companies have collaborated to produce hit television series such as "Miami Vice," "30 Rock" and "The Office." The company also owns and operates numerous cable channels, motion picture companies, and branded theme parks. The newest theme park, "The Wizarding World of Harry Potter," brings the magic of the screen to real life with a full-scale Diagon alley, complete with store fronts, Gringotts Bank, and other familiar haunts from the mind of J.K. Rowling. This long-lasting relationship has helped enhance NBC Universal's platform as one of the leading media and entertainment companies worldwide.[20]

Hogwarts Castle at NBC Universal's "Wizarding World of Harry Potter."

Many suppliers find contractual partnerships advantageous, but there are risks. The organizations often share highly confidential market and technological information as well as sensitive strategic marketing plans. An unethical buyer might reveal these secrets to competing suppliers in the hope of receiving price reductions. Contracts are usually designed to prevent this, and experienced suppliers will avoid dealing with buyers who have questionable histories. Another risk is the greater dependence that comes with strong relationships. If one partner experiences downsizing, strikes or financial failure, then the other party feels the consequences.

When each organization in a partnership has something of value to offer the other, it often results in strategic alliances, including joint R&D, licensing agreements, joint ventures and others. Suppose a Frito-Lay supplier has an idea for making chips stay fresh longer but lacks the money to conduct the necessary research. A joint R&D project might benefit both organizations.

Ethics and Business Relationships Unethical decisions can have a destructive effect on business relationships. Purchasing agents are often very familiar with the trade secrets, production plans and technologies of sellers. Misuse of this information has both ethical and legal implications. Employees may have trade secrets that need to be protected even if the employee takes a job with a new company. A former Intel employee, for example, was recently given a sentence of up to 20 years in prison for fraud due to taking trade secrets with him as he moved to Advanced

Micro Devices, Intel's main competitor. While in the process of transferring from Intel to AMD, Biswamohan Pani accessed data from Intel about one of its microprocessors. The value of the material he was found guilty of illegally accessing was between $200 and $400 million.[21]

Turning over trade secrets to a competitor is a serious breach of ethics with numerous repercussions. It tarnishes reputations, requires time and money in legal disputes, and creates friction between the buyer and supplier. An individual who steals and betrays company information may face serious criminal charges. Consider former employees of Coca-Cola that conspired to sell trade secrets to rival Pepsi for $1.5 million. They were discovered and exposed in an undercover sting by the FBI and ultimately had to pay fines in excess of $40,000.[22] The unethical Coca-Cola employees were also sentenced to serve eight- and five-year federal prison sentences for conspiring to steal and sell trade secrets.[23]

FUNCTIONS INVOLVED IN BUSINESS PURCHASES

Many employees are important to the purchasing process. Because of their different functions, they do not have the same motives for purchasing and do not use the same criteria. This section highlights functions most often involved in organizational buying: purchasing agents, functional managers, and the buying center.

Laterally, people at about the same level of management but from different functional areas (such as purchasing, engineering, production, sales and marketing) may take part in a purchasing decision. Although their status is roughly similar, each has a particular area of expertise and influence. Imagine that several vice presidents meet to select a strategic marketing consultant. Comments by the vice presidents of manufacturing and purchasing are certainly valuable, but the vice president of marketing probably will have the most influence on the final decision.

Vertically, people at different management levels within one functional area may participate in a buying decision. For example, the need for a new piece of equipment may be pointed out by a production floor worker to the foreman, who relays this to the production manager. The production manager seeks approval from the plant manager. If the purchase is costly, then the vice president of manufacturing or even the company president might be involved. If not, then the production engineer may have authority to approve the purchase.

Purchasing Agents Purchasing agents help buy a broad range of products most effectively. They establish and enforce purchase procedures, negotiate, and interact with suppliers. Through training programs, purchasing agents can learn how to obtain the best delivery schedules, prices and financing, while still meeting product specifications.

Purchasing agents are extremely important executives in some major corporations. In others, they simply process procurement requests. This function has received more attention in recent years, partly because of restricted supply in some industries and a greater general recognition of the cost savings from effective purchasing. College programs emphasizing the buying function have been developed, and graduates with this specialized education are finding increasing opportunities in global purchasing.

Functional Managers Functional managers have a position in a specific operational area of the buying organization. At one time or another in their career, most will be involved in negotiations to buy equipment or supplies. Typically, they come from the following areas:

- **Administration (including accounting and finance):** Help evaluate the cost effectiveness of projects.

- **Design engineering:** Buy equipment and material for products the company is marketing.

- **Research and development:** Look at basic materials and supplies rather than specific applications.

- **Manufacturing:** Often responsible for production equipment and processing approaches.

- **Technical specialists:** Advise others regarding the best brands and suppliers for a particular product type.

Buying Center

The group of people from the buying organization who make a purchase decision.

Gatekeeper

A person within the buying center who controls the flow of commercial (outside) information into the buying organization by screening all potential sellers and allowing only the most qualified to have access to decision makers.

The Buying Center

A group of people in the organization who make a purchase decision form the **buying center**. These people may play one of six important roles: gatekeeper, information seeker, advocate, linking pin, decision maker or user. It's important to note that buying center membership changes, depending on the type of purchase being considered. Often the selling organization that wins the order is the one that has made contact with each of the buying influencers. Figure 6.7 depicts the buying center roles.

Gatekeepers A **gatekeeper** controls the flow of commercial (outside) information into the buying organization. Purchasing agents have been referred to as gatekeepers because they are often the first people that sales representatives contact. They are responsible for screening all potential sellers and allowing only the most qualified to gain access to key decision makers. When dealing with unique or complicated products, a specialist can serve as the gatekeeper. For example, the head of engineering may recommend that only suppliers with which the company has a working relationship should be contacted for engineering consulting services.

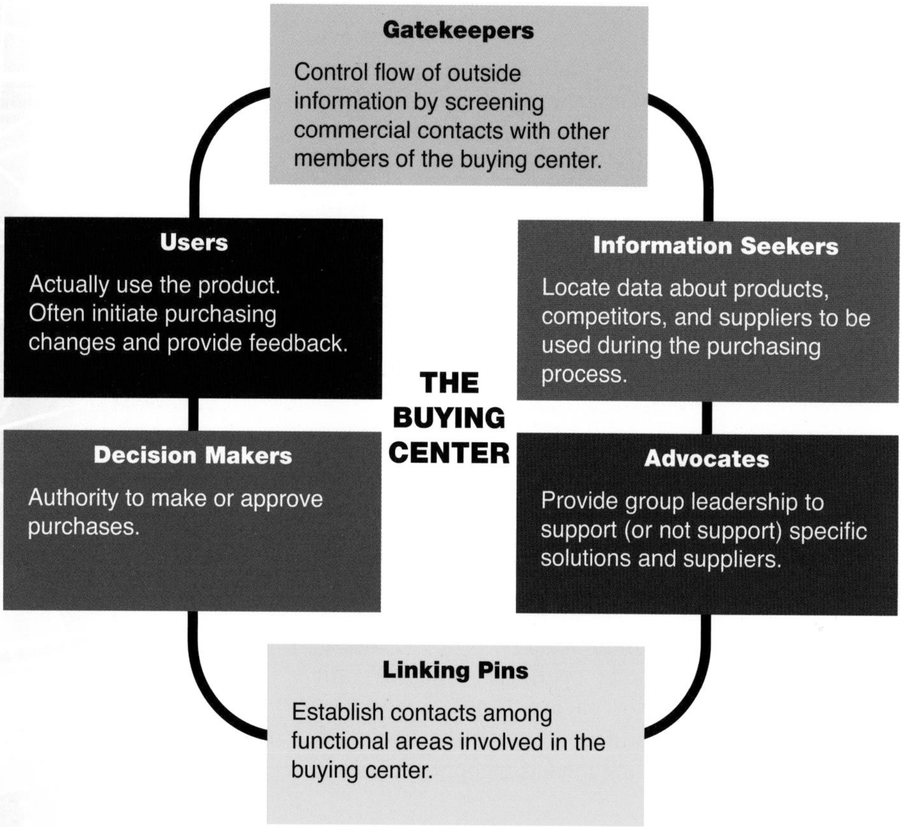

Experienced salespeople and gatekeepers will make efforts to understand each other and their organizations, and they will take action in the best interests of both. If the relationship is cooperative, a gatekeeper can efficiently direct a salesperson to the appropriate decision maker.

Gatekeepers
Control flow of outside information by screening commercial contacts with other members of the buying center.

Users
Actually use the product. Often initiate purchasing changes and provide feedback.

Information Seekers
Locate data about products, competitors, and suppliers to be used during the purchasing process.

THE BUYING CENTER

Decision Makers
Authority to make or approve purchases.

Advocates
Provide group leadership to support (or not support) specific solutions and suppliers.

Linking Pins
Establish contacts among functional areas involved in the buying center.

Figure 6.7   The Buying Center

Information Seekers

A person within the buying center who locates data that can be used during the purchasing process.

Information Seekers A great deal of information about products, competitors and suppliers is required for major purchases. **Information seekers** locate data that they or others can use during the purchasing process. Often the purchasing department is responsible for obtaining lists of firms or alternative types of products, but this task can also be performed by others. Think about the fundamental changes technology has brought to business-to-business marketing. Virtually every company in the world maintains a website to provide information about itself. The web can satisfy some of an information seeker's needs in only seconds.

The role of an information seeker differs from that of a gatekeeper. The former looks for sources of information, whereas the latter tends to reject sources of information and limits the number of people and companies allowed access to the buying firm. Naturally, marketers can make the job of the information seeker easier by clearly presenting relevant product data in an accessible way.

Advocates The **advocate** exercises a powerful influence over buying center decisions. Advocates are the most active participants in group discussions, have high status and play a leadership role. They often obtain their power from the amount of interaction they have with outside organizations and from their expertise on particular topics. Advocates sometimes use their position to inhibit the communications (or recommendations) of less powerful people in the organization. Thus, they may support one seller's offering while restricting the influence of competitors' presentations. Consequently, sellers often seek high-status, knowledgeable and articulate people within the buying organization to help promote their products. If salespeople are to succeed, then one or more advocates must take their side during purchase deliberations.

Linking Pins Contact among the functional areas involved in a buying center is provided by **linking pins**. They are particularly important to marketers of products that affect several parts of the buying company, such as electronic data-processing and telecommunications equipment. Linking pins communicate with one another both formally and informally. In many cases, information from the seller to one linking pin is then spread throughout the buying organization. A cooperative linking pin makes the seller's job easier.

Users Users purchase and operate the product in question. In manufacturing firms, for example, they are the employees who operate or service production equipment. When components are purchased, the **users** assemble the parts. In hospitals and other health care facilities, users may be nurses, physicians or the technicians who operate medical equipment. In other professional organizations, they may be programmers or technical support staff who interface with computers. There are almost as many types of users as there are job descriptions, and their influence on the purchasing process varies.

Users with a high degree of expertise may help develop product specifications. They are especially important in the last phase of the buying process, follow-through. The sophisticated salesperson values user feedback, in turn providing them with information to make the product function as smoothly as possible.

Decision Makers Sometimes it is difficult for the seller to identify **decision makers**, the people with authority to make or at least approve the purchase decision. It is also hard to determine when the decision is actually made. Often the selling organization wins enough support from the buyer to obtain the order by building the relationship over time, which is called creeping commitment. In competitive bidding situations, the decision to purchase occurs when the envelopes are opened. In these cases, however, much depends on how the specifications are drawn up in the first place. Some salespeople work closely with the buying organization at that stage to tilt the specs and ultimate decision in their favor.

Often the salesperson can identify exactly who will make the buying decision. In some organizations the decision maker is the purchasing agent. In most cases, however, the choice is made by a buying committee or by someone who has budgetary authority and long-term experience with the product. Salespeople are invited to make a presentation or to supply information so that the committee or a committee member can decide.

Advocate

A person within the buying center who exercises a powerful influence over group decisions.

Linking Pins

A person within the buying center who establishes contact among functional areas formed within the buying organization.

Users

A person within the buying center who actually uses the product.

Decision Makers

A person within the buying center who has the authority to make or approve a purchase decision.

INFLUENCES ON ORGANIZATIONAL BUYING BEHAVIOR

The buying process is seldom the same from one firm to the next, or even from one purchase to the next within a given firm. In each case, the decision-making process of the buying organization is affected by a number of factors.[24]

Background of Buying Center Members The background of the buying center members affects the buying process. Purchasing agents, engineers, users

CREATING & CAPTURING VALUE THROUGH *Technology*

IBM Wins With Watson

IBM Watson, named after IBM founder Thomas J. Watson, was built to accomplish a grand challenge – a computing system that could rival a human's ability to answer questions posed in natural language with speed, accuracy and confidence. In February 2011, Watson appeared on Jeopardy! competing "face-to-face" in a historic match against two of the most celebrated players ever to appear on the show. Watson won!

Jeopardy! was the ultimate test of a computing system's capabilities because it relied on many human cognitive functions such as ability to discern double meanings of words, puns, rhymes, and inferred hints – aspects beyond the realm of conventional computer systems. It also demanded extremely rapid responses and the ability to process vast amounts of information to make connections typically requiring a lifetime of immersion in pop culture and participation in the general human experience.

What began as a research project at IBM in 2006 is at the heart of IBM's strategic marketing today. Watson is being used by some of IBM's largest and most sophisticated business customers, with an initial emphasis on healthcare. For example, IBM Watson is used at Memorial Sloan Kettering Cancer Center in New York and M.D. Anderson Cancer Treatment Center in Houston. Watson quickly merges a patient's records with medical literature to suggest treatment options for cancer patients. IBM is also marketing Watson to commercial, government and educational markets.

IBM has a long history of B2B success. Its marketing teams know how to work with experts in most all types of organizations, including how to effectively communicate with key decision making groups in potential client businesses. IBM marketing leverages large amounts of research and expertise, and forms partnerships with leading organizations in Watson related industries, such as Memorial Sloan Kettering, M.D. Anderson, and WellPoint. In addition, Watson marketing works closely with analysts and industry experts in order to evaluate future potential industry applications for Watson.

Watson follows in the IBM tradition of value driven through innovation by working to transform how organizations think, act, and operate as it learns through interaction and co-evolves with its users. With the incredible volume of information available in the world today, Watson's evidence-based responses are improving business outcomes and changing people's expectations for technology's role in life.

http://www.washingtonpost.com/business/on-it/how-ibm-is-trying-to-commercialize-watson/2014/05/09/4f552506-d23c-11e3-937f-d3026234b51c_story.html, website visited June 19, 2014.

and others in the organization have expectations that are formed largely by their experiences. These expectations, in turn, influence the criteria used for decision making. Specialization has a great deal to do with the way people look at problems. Engineers, for instance, are highly trained in technical areas and are likely to judge a product accordingly, while financial managers are inclined to evaluate products on the basis of profitability.

Role orientation, which refers to the way people see themselves, is also a factor. Position or rank within the organization obviously can have an effect—one vice president among several lower-level managers has a stronger say in buying center decisions.

Finally, personal characteristics play a role. The lifestyles, interests, activities and general opinions of buying center members affect the buying process.

Information Sources

Organizational buying is influenced by the sources of information: salespeople, exhibitions and trade shows, direct mail, press releases, journal advertising, professional and technical conferences, trade news, word of mouth and others. Like direct selling, exhibitions provide one-on-one contact with a company's target audience. Although sales calls generally reach only a small number of potential customers per day, exhibitions can reach dozens more per hour.

The Internet is playing an increasing role in business-to-business marketing. Websites enable organizations to promote brand values, reduce printing costs, attract and qualify prospects and leads, and foster customer loyalty. Sites also can expand the customer database, provide customer service, showcase and sell products.

www.ibm.com

At IBM's website, read about how the company is protecting the environment by encouraging its business suppliers from around the world to operate more sustainably.

Product Factors: Time and Risk

Product and company factors tend to influence the organizational buying process. **Product factors** include time pressure and perceived risk. Time pressure relates to the speed with which a purchase must be made. When several members of the buying organization are involved in the decision, more time is required to make it. Perceived risk refers to what can be lost rather than gained when making the purchase.

Five types of uncertainty or risk aversion have been identified among buying organizations:

1. **Acceptance uncertainty:** Buyers are not sure of their need for a product.
2. **Need uncertainty:** The buying organization has not yet established product specifications.
3. **Technical uncertainty:** Buyers are unsure about the performance of a product in their own particular environment.
4. **Market uncertainty:** Buyers are unsure of the possible offerings from which they can select.
5. **Transaction uncertainty:** Buyers are unsure about the terms of the sale and product delivery.

When uncertainty is high, buyers strive to reduce perceived risk by either purchasing less or learning more. Decreasing the amount at stake means smaller orders or a reluctance to pay top prices. When much is at stake, the risk of the purchase decision may affect others in the organization.

Company Factors

Three company factors have particular influence on the purchasing process: the organization's orientation, its size and its degree of centraliza-

Product Factors

A factor such as time or perceived risk that influences the organizational buying process.

tion. An organization's orientation, or dominating function, is very important. Some companies are production oriented, others marketing oriented, while still others let finance or accounting control the decisions. When marketing dominates, sales factors tend to be very important in making purchase decisions. In production-oriented organizations, production factors are most important. In finance-oriented organizations, decisions are likely to be made on the basis of cost and other financial concerns. The seller must understand the organization's orientation in order to determine the basis for purchasing decisions and which members of the buying center are most influential.

The size of the organization is also likely to influence the number of people involved in purchasing. In very small companies, the purchasing process is typically informal, with the final decision made by a single high-ranking executive. Very large organizations use a formal purchasing process, and decisions are often made by members lower in the managerial structure.

Finally, highly decentralized organizations are likely to give various departments or divisions the autonomy to make their own purchases. Even these companies, requiring accountability, have formal buying procedures that can involve red tape.

Joint Decisions and Conflict Resolution

Whenever several people are involved in decision making, there is a potential for conflict. Purchase decisions are no exception and can be affected by how conflict is handled. When it occurs, members of the buying organization negotiate with one another to arrive at a solution. These negotiations can be shaped by task or non-task motives. Task motivation refers to solving the organization's problem, whereas non-task motivation refers to the personal needs of the buying group members. Organizations usually attempt to use problem solving and persuasion to make the best decision for the company. Non-task-oriented approaches to conflict involve bargaining and politicking. Each party is attempting to "get its own way" without considering the organization's goals or engaging in open communication. Sellers who are sensitive to the prevailing negotiating mode can plan their approach accordingly.

Problem solving in the buying context occurs when all decision makers agree on the goals of the particular purchase. Sellers address those goals and show how their product can help meet them. The fact that all parties agree to this method usually indicates the process will be straightforward.

Persuasion occurs when buying center members do not agree on purchase goals, and each tries to convince the others that his or her own goals should take precedence. In the case of buying a computer, for example, the purchasing agent may consider cost most important, whereas a user may put software compatibility first. When the two discuss the merits of the various trade-offs, they are engaging in persuasion. The seller needs to understand both parties and address both sets of goals.

Bargaining occurs when people in the buying center cannot arrive at a solution. Through dialogue, one person may try to obtain his or her preferred product by agreeing that someone else can choose the supplier for a different product. The supplier needs to make sure to address all individuals who might ultimately be in a good bargaining position.

Politicking occurs when buying center members of the organization have strong ego needs. In their search for power or self-esteem, they place their own goals before those of the organization as a whole. Such people are looking for support rather than the most functional purchase choice. What usually results is a "pecking order" within the buying firm, in which an employee's influence on the purchase is proportional to his or her status in the company. The superiority of a product is irrelevant if a buyer's ego is more important to him or her. Sellers must be very sensitive to personalities if they wish to conduct business under this circumstance.

Problem Solving

A task-oriented method of conflict resolution whereby all parties agree to put the organization's goals first.

Persuasion

A task-oriented mode of handling conflict in which persons with different goals attempt to convince the others that their goal should take precedence.

Bargaining

A non task-oriented mode of handling conflict in which one person obtains his or her goal by agreeing to allow the other's goal to prevail at another time.

Politicking

A non task-oriented mode of handling conflict in which personal ego needs take precedence over problem solving.

CHAPTER SUMMARY

Objective 1: Describe the types of organizations and products involved in business-to-business marketing and understand the importance of this market.

A large number of companies sell most of their products to other companies, which is known as business-to-business marketing. In total volume, business-to-business marketing is much larger than consumer marketing. Types of business markets include the commercial market, extractor industries, trade industries, institutions, utilities, transportation and telecommunications, and government markets. These markets can be segmented according to company demographics, geographic scope, buying approach and product/technology. Multiple steps bring the final product to consumers as businesses sell materials and processes to each other along the supply chain.

Objective 2: Understand the link between consumer demand and business-to-business marketing.

Business markets rely on derived demand to create opportunities for their products. When consumers purchase more, businesses buy more in order to produce more. The demand for business goods and services tends to be inelastic, which means that a price change does not greatly affect the types of products purchased. The accelerator principle recognizes that some business goods and services are highly sensitive to changes in consumer demand.

Objective 3: Describe the organizational buying process.

Organizations make purchases to support their production requirements and business needs. Buying decisions often start with the make or buy decision. Decisional situations in outsourcing include straight rebuy, modified rebuy and new task situations. The buying process can involve as many as eight steps: problem recognition, need description,

product specification, supplier search, proposal solicitation and supplier selection, order routine specification, purchase and use, and performance review and feedback. Good buyer-seller relationships are key to facilitating the process.

Objective 4: Know how buyer–seller relationships work, including informal and contractual partnerships.

The buyer-seller relationship between businesses develops over time, usually in three sequential phases: courtship, relationship building, and partnership. During courtship, buyers express their desires to sellers, who, in turn, propose products to satisfy the buyer's needs. In relationship building, the two parties work together for the first time, customizing the product, its delivery and conditions. In the partnership phase, long-term agreements are reached either informally or contractually, and close cooperation develops lasting relationships.

Objective 5: Learn what functions and roles within organizations influence the purchase of a broad range of products.

Different functional areas may be involved in business purchases, ranging from operational units to a purchasing department. The group of people who make a purchase decision forms the buying center. Having different backgrounds and functions in the company, they have different buying motives and use different criteria in evaluating products. Purchase decisions may be made laterally, through the interaction of people from different functional areas, or vertically, at one or more levels in the corporate hierarchy. Various buying center members play different roles: gatekeeper, information seeker, advocate, linking pin, decision maker and user. It is important that the salesperson identifies exactly who will make the purchase decision, whether it is the purchasing agent, a buying committee or someone with budgetary authority.

REVIEW YOUR UNDERSTANDING

1. What is business-to-business marketing? How does it differ from consumer marketing?
2. List the types of business-to-business markets.
3. What is the supply chain? Give an example.
4. What is derived demand? Inelastic demand? How do they apply to business markets?
5. What are two ways that globalization affects business marketing?
6. What is a make or buy decision?
7. What are three types of decisional situations in outsourcing?
8. What are the steps in the organizational buying process?
9. List the phases in buyer-seller relationships.
10. List six functions performed in the buying center.
11. What are purchasing agents? Functional managers?
12. List and explain five types of purchase uncertainty.

DISCUSSION OF CONCEPTS

1. Why is business-to-business marketing larger than consumer marketing? Explain the process of business-to-business marketing.
2. The private sector is composed of several classes of organizations. List examples of these classes, along with companies in each, and explain their importance within business-to-business marketing.
3. Explain the accelerator principle and how it is used in to business-to-business marketing. Give an example.
4. When making a purchase, an organization generally goes through a number of steps. Describe these and explain why some purchases require more steps than others.
5. Describe an informal partnership and a contractual partnership. What are the advantages and disadvantages to both buyer and seller of each type? How does price-only purchasing come into play?
6. Why are many employees within a buying organization essential to the purchasing process? Explain the different levels of involvement in business purchases. What roles do purchasing agents and functional managers play?
7. Several roles that people play within the buying center are essential to the purchasing process. Define these and explain why they are necessary. Is one more important than the other? Which has the most influence on the purchase decision?
8. Numerous factors influence the buying process. Explain the relevance of each in purchase decisions.

KEY TERMS & DEFINITIONS

1. **Accelerator Principle:** A small increase or decrease in consumer demand has a larger effect on business demand.
2. **Advocate:** A person within the buying center who exercises a powerful influence over group decisions.
3. **Bargaining:** A non task-oriented mode of handling conflict in which one person obtains his or her goal by agreeing to allow the other's goal to prevail at another time.
4. **Buying center:** The group of people from the buying organization who make a purchase decision.
5. **Commercial market:** Organizations and individuals that acquire goods and services to produce other goods and services sold to an end consumer for profit.
6. **Decision maker:** A person within the buying center who has the authority to make or approve a purchase decision.
7. **Derived demand:** A demand, such as the demand for business-to-business products, which depends ultimately on the demand of end consumers.
8. **Extractor industries:** Industries that obtain and process raw materials.
9. **Gatekeeper:** A person within the buying center who controls the flow of commercial (outside) information into the buying organization by screening all potential sellers and allowing only the most qualified to have access to decision makers.
10. **Government markets:** The federal, state, and local governments in their role as purchasers of goods and services.
11. **Inelastic demand:** Demand that is influenced little by price changes.
12. **Information seeker:** A person within the buying center who locates data that can be used during the purchasing process.
13. **Institutions:** Public and private organizations that provide services to consumers.
14. **Linking pin:** A person within the buying center who establishes contact among functional areas formed within the buying organization.
15. **Make or buy decision:** The decision to supply products in-house or to purchase them from other businesses.
16. **Modified rebuy:** Purchase of a familiar product from an unfamiliar supplier or a new or different product from a familiar supplier.
17. **New task situation:** Purchase of an unfamiliar product from an unfamiliar supplier.
18. **Outsourcing:** Purchasing products and services from other companies.
19. **Persuasion:** A task-oriented mode of handling conflicts in which persons with different goals attempt to convince the others that their goals should take precedence.
20. **Politicking:** A non task-oriented mode of handling conflict in which personal ego needs take precedence over problem solving.
21. **Problem solving:** A task-oriented method of conflict resolution whereby all parties agree to put the organization's goals first.
22. **Product factor:** A factor such as time or perceived risk that influences the organizational buying process.
23. **Straight rebuy:** A routine purchase with which the organization has considerable experience.
24. **Supply chain:** The linkage of organizations involved in the creation and delivery of a product.
25. **Tier:** The degree of contact between the supplier and the OEM.
26. **Trade industries:** Industries comprised of organizations that acquire finished products and distribute them to others.
27. **Transportation & Telecommunications:** Companies that provide passenger and freight service and/or local and long-distance telephone service.
28. **User:** A person within the buying center who actually uses the product.
29. **Utilities:** Companies that distribute gas, electricity, or water.

REFERENCES

1. www.informationweek.com/blog/main/archives, website visited March 14, 2014; Mitch Wagner, "Why No 'Intel Inside' Stickers on Macs?" Information Week, August 13, 2007; Jerry A. Dicolo, "Intel Unveils New PC Chips," The Wall Street Journal, January 7, 2010; Don Clark and Nick Wingfield, Intel, "Microsoft Offer Smart-Sign Technology," The Wall Street Journal, January 12, 2010; www.intel.com, website visited March 14, 2014; Total Return Calculator using June 15, 1992 as beginning invest date and June 15, 2014 as end, www.intel.com, website visited June 15, 2014.

2. www.schooldata.com, website visited April 12, 2014.

3. www.envirogroup.com, website visited April 12, 2014.

4. www.apple.com, website visited April 12, 2014.

5. www.larabar.com, website visited June 14, 2014.

6. www.honeywell.com, website visited June 14, 2014.

7. Frost, Laurence/Associated Press, "National-World Business," The Albuquerque Tribune, November 8, 2006.

8. "Global Commerce and Transportation," UPS. www.ups.com, website visited March 13, 2010.

9. "Corporate Profile," IDG, www.idg.com, site visited March 13, 2012.

10. www.jpmorgan.com, website visited June 13, 2014.

11. "Outsourcing History," www.issworld.com, website visited June 13, 2014.

12. www.iaop.org, website visited June 13, 2014.

13. "Introduction to ISS," www.issworld.com, website visited June 13, 2014.

14. Hanson, Ward; Kalyanam, Kirthi, "Internet Marketing & e-Commerce," 2007, pg. 410; Milgrom, Paul, "Auction and Bidding: A primer," Journal of Economic Perspectives 3, Summer 1989, pg. 3.

15. "Our Community," eBay, www.ebay.com, website visited June 13, 2014.

16. Tuli, Kapil R.; Kohil, Ajay; Bharadway, Sundar G., "Rethinking Customer Solutions: From Product Bundles to Relational Processes," Journal of Marketing, Vol. 71, No. 3, July 2007.

17. Hakanson, Hakan; Wootz, Bjorn, "A Framework of Industrial Buying and Selling," International Marketing Management 8, 1979, pp. 39-49.

18. Kachadourian, Gail, "DCX Relies on Supplier Innovations," Automotive News, June 19, 2000, pg. 28.

19. www.vendormanagedinventory.com, website visited June 23, 2014.

20. www.nbcuni.com, website visited June 13, 2014.

21. Gareth Halfacree, "Ex-Intel engineer pleads guilty to IP theft," bit-tech, April 10, 2012.

22. Day, Kathleen, "Three Accused in Theft of Coke Secrets," Washington Post, July 6, 2006.

23. "Two Sentenced in Coke Trade Secret Case," CNN Money, May 23, 2007.

24. Sheth, Jagdish N., "A Model of Industrial Buyer Behavior," Journal of Marketing 37, October 1973, pp. 50-58.

Chapter 07

CREATING CUSTOMER
SATISFACTION
& LOYALTY

THE RITZ-CARLTON®

Imagine you are traveling on a routine overnight business trip. You like your suit pressed by 6 a.m. sharp, and you take your coffee with one cream and two sugars. If you regularly stay at a Ritz-Carlton hotel, both your coffee and suit will be delivered at 6 a.m. — without a single call to the front desk. The company employs a sophisticated information technology system that tracks customers' previous requests and preferences.

That means if you stay at a Ritz-Carlton in Seoul, South Korea, and request to have green tea in your room, then when you visit a Ritz-Carlton anywhere else in the world, there will be green tea waiting in your room upon arrival. What's more, everyone from the bellhop to the front desk clerk will address you by name. These small touches form a cornerstone of the Ritz-Carlton strategy.

This dedication to extraordinary customer service distinguishes the brand and continues to earn it accolades. The Ritz-Carlton has won the Mal- colm Baldrige National Quality Award multiple times — only one other company has received this award more than once, and no other hotel has ever won it. How has the Ritz-Carlton accomplished this success? It starts at the top, with a team of senior executives who meet every week to review quality issues. This includes the company's products, services, customer satisfaction, loyalty, growth, profits, and evaluation of the competition.

In fact, Ritz executives spend 25 percent of their time working on quality-related issues. However, the ultimate responsibility for delivering customer value depends on 32,000 employees who complete 120 hours of on-the-job training in their first year. Every employee is given a "preference pad" to record the personal preferences of Ritz customers. Employees record the obvious guest requests like type of room preferred, but they also catch smaller details like requests for extra towels and whether the guest took apples or bananas from the fruit basket. This information is used to provide more personalized service to customers during future stays.

If you spill something on your shirt at breakfast and didn't pack an extra, don't fret. A Ritz employee will gladly go out and buy you a new shirt in time for your important meeting — free of charge. All employees, regardless of title, are given prior approval to do "whatever it takes" to make a customer happy. They are encouraged to anticipate potential issues and resolve them before they ever occur so guests can enjoy a flawless experience.

The Ritz-Carlton Hotel Company's impeccable standards make it an industry leader of customer satisfaction and loyalty. The 121 quality-related awards earned in one year alone speak volumes for the company. With a customer satisfaction rate of up to 97 percent, its reputation continues to attract high customer loyalty and repeat business.[1]

<< The Ritz-Carlton, Toronto
Courtesy of Ritz-Carlton

Learning Objectives

1. Understand why customer satisfaction and loyalty are the focus of marketing in winning organizations.
2. Learn how consumer expectations influence satisfaction.
3. See why connecting with customers through relationships achieves outstanding satisfaction and loyalty.
4. Understand the ideas that help organizations market quality goods and services.
5. Define quality and describe how it is obtained.

THE CONCEPTS OF CUSTOMER SATISFACTION, LOYALTY, AND QUALITY

People have millions of choices about where to spend their money. Ultimately, the decision depends on how much value they perceive they're getting for what they pay. Companies that consistently produce high value are likely to have satisfied customers who reward them with loyalty and repeat purchases. Winning organizations go to extremes to create customer satisfaction because they know that satisfaction leads to loyalty, which is the single most important factor in extraordinary business performance. Marketers who want to create and capture value must deliver goods and services worthy of their support. In this chapter, we will learn that satisfaction and loyalty usually go hand in hand.

Leading companies focus a good deal of effort on satisfaction and loyalty, but how do they achieve these two goals? There is no question that the ability to produce quality goods and services is required. Quality products that perform as promised make up the necessary starting point of a company attempting to create superior value. That requires the application of management principles to assure that processes throughout the company support the creation and delivery of products that produce satisfaction. Figure 7.1 describes the relationships among all these factors.

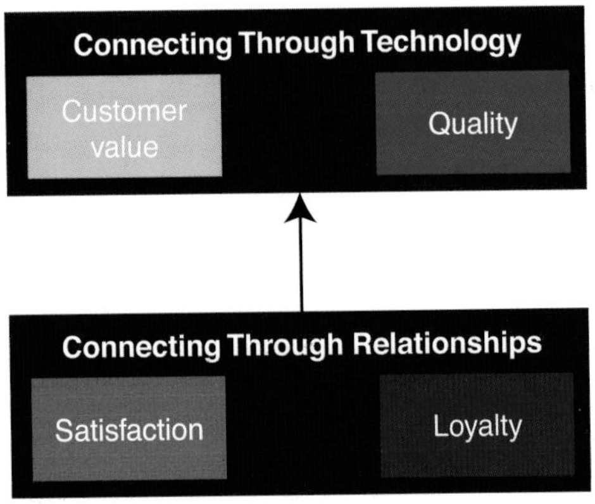

What are customer satisfaction and loyalty? What are value and quality? How do relationships and technology play into these factors? As a marketer, you need a strong foundation in these concepts. In this chapter, we'll consider each idea in detail.

Connecting Through Technology
Customer value | Quality

Connecting Through Relationships
Satisfaction | Loyalty

Figure 7.1 Customer Satisfaction, Customer Loyalty and Quality: Connecting Through Relationships Formed by Organizational Systems and Actions

CUSTOMER SATISFACTION AND CUSTOMER LOYALTY

A significant amount of marketing research is dedicated to measuring customer satisfaction and loyalty but customer-satisfaction ratings are an especially useful indicator of an organization's competitiveness. Today, the race to beat competitors in customer satisfaction is a powerful business objective, because satisfaction is an overall indicator of how well customers rate a company's performance. This section begins by exploring the importance of satisfaction and loyalty. Next, we look at how customer expectations affect satisfaction. We then tie all of these elements together by describing how relationships promote satisfaction and loyalty. We also examine how diversity and global competition affect efforts to build satisfaction and loyalty.

KEY ASPECTS OF SATISFACTION AND LOYALTY

Customer satisfaction is a customer's positive, neutral or negative feeling about the value received from an organization's product in specific use situations. In the past, product innovation was the major way to gain a competitive edge. Now, new products are copied by rivals, often within a few weeks or months, and the life span of new products is declining rapidly. Thus, organizations need to look beyond the immediate sale and focus on achieving the highest level of customer satisfaction if they want loyal customers and repeat business. Favorable satisfaction ratings not only boost sales but can also have a dramatic effect on overall company performance.[2]

In order to stay competitive in the cell phone service market, Sprint needed a quick solution to the steady decline in its customer satisfaction rankings. To combat customer churn, the company created an aggressive program to revamp its customer service and call center operations. The resulting metrics and strategies quickly improved Sprint's customer services and increased satisfaction. The remarkable turnaround resulted in the American Customer Satisfaction Index rating Sprint number one among all national carriers in customer satisfaction and most improved, across all 47 industries, since 2009.[3]

Customer loyalty refers to how often, when selecting from a product class, a customer purchases a particular brand. Customer satisfaction is a critical ingredient in building loyalty, and loyalty is essential to the long-term survival of a typical organization. It is estimated that companies lose 10 to 30 percent of their customers annually, and even more in the online world.[4] At this rate, few firms can achieve acceptable volume or profit without a strong base of loyal buyers. On average, 80 to 90 percent of a company's profits are generated by 10 to 20 percent of its customers.[5] A large number of satisfied, loyal customers helps a company's performance because these customers provide sales to increase revenues, are less concerned about price and help reduce the organization's costs. One study found that a one percent improvement in customer retention will improve firm value by five percent.[6] Sprint recently launched an initiative to improve loyalty by instituting "Thank You Thursdays" in which all Sprint employees are asked to write at least five handwritten notes to valued customers. Sprint customers who bring the note to a Sprint retail store will receive a 25 percent discount on any accessory.[7]

Customer Satisfaction

A customer's positive, neutral, or negative feeling about the value received from an organization's product in specific use situations.

Customer Loyalty

A measure of how often, when selecting from a product class, a customer purchases a particular brand.

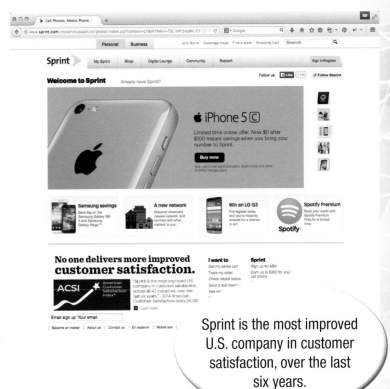

Sprint is the most improved U.S. company in customer satisfaction, over the last six years.

Sales to Increase Revenues   The revenue stream from one lifetime customer

can be tremendous. A loyal buyer of Starbucks may spend thousands of dollars, and a corporate buyer of Boeing aircraft equipment may invest billions of dollars. When you view the amount a customer buys over the lifetime of a relationship, you can see why customer retention is vital to an organization's prolonged success. In fact, many organizations develop compensation systems that offer pay incentives to executives and employees who contribute to customer satisfaction and loyalty.

The importance of satisfied customers for revenue generation is magnified by their influence on other buyers. If a typical customer purchases a new car once every four years and influences one new buyer each year, the loyal, satisfied customer can be worth nearly $1 million in revenues and more than $100,000 in profit. Some companies calculate the **customer lifetime value (CLV),** which is the amount

Customer Lifetime Value (CLV)

The amount of profit a company expects to obtain over the course of the relationship.

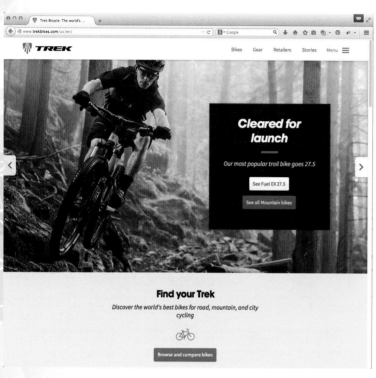

of profit an organization expects to obtain over the course of a customer relationship. For example, assume you are a marketing manager for a large bicycle equipment manufacturer. One of your customers, Trek, purchases about $80,000 in equipment each month. If Trek becomes dissatisfied and selects another supplier, how much will it cost your company? At $80,000 per month for 12 months, Trek purchases $960,000 annually. Assuming you earn a profit of 15 percent, that equals $144,000 per year. Over two decades, your company would forfeit more than $2.8 million in pure profit and $19.2 million in revenue. If the same problem that dissatisfied Trek results in the defection of other key customers, you face huge losses.

Less Concern About Price

Customer satisfaction has become a key to making sales at appropriate prices. Jeff Bezos, founder of Amazon.com, commented on the role of price: "We're known for competitive prices. ... That's very important online. But we're also known for great customer experience and great customer service. If your brand is based exclusively on price, you're in a fragile position, but if your brand is about great prices and great service and great selection, that is a much better position."[8] Essentially, creating satisfied customers through service and experience is often more important and successful than trying to create satisfied customers through price. In general, customers are willing to pay more because they are certain that the higher price is due to extra value or benefits. Also, satisfied customers will better tolerate price increases, showing little tendency to shop around. Overall, these factors lead to higher margins and profits.

Reduce the Organization's Costs

The percentage of loyal, satisfied customers is a very important determinant of an organization's costs and revenues. In addition to generating sales, loyal customers affect the **cost structure**, which is the amount of resources required to produce a specific amount of sales. The cost of acquiring a new customer is usually six to 10 times more expensive than keeping an existing one. In fact, loyal customers are often responsible for a company's seemingly disproportionate amount of profit. Loyal customers don't require high costs to retain, and they are likely to either demonstrate or tell others about their satisfaction with the company, prompting them to give the company a try. Some of these first-time purchasers may become loyal customers and, in turn tell others.

Cost Structure

The amount of resources required to produce a specific amount of sales.

CUSTOMER EXPECTATIONS

Customer expectations play an important role in determining satisfaction. **Customer expectations** are consumer beliefs about the performance of a product based on prior experience and communications. A consumer will be dissatisfied with a company that falls short of expectations, but delighted with one that exceeds them. In both cases, customers are emotionally charged by their experience — the delighted are more likely to be loyal, and the dissatisfied are more inclined to switch.

Customer expectations are based on personal experience, observation of others, company actions, advertising and promotion. Customers also expect companies to offer services to support their purchase decision. For example, because it is difficult for people to assess the quality of products in a catalog, companies such as Williams Sonoma and Crate & Barrel make it easy for people to return products that do not meet their expectations.

Higher and more varied expectations result when competition is intense. One Starbucks customer found the company pulling out all stops when a licensed store, not corporate owned, refused to honor a 10 percent corporate discount. Angered, he called Starbucks customer service and explained his frustration to the corporate representative. The representative told the customer he wanted to "make me whole, and give me an experience nothing short of fantastic." Expecting a free drink coupon, the customer was floored when he was mailed a $50 Starbucks card.[9]

A company benefits from exceeding customer expectations, but it also raises those expectations for the future. Similarly, each change in product, price, promotion or distribution can affect expectations. Companies have both competitors' efforts and consumer expectations to exceed, and it is a challenge to continually win over consumers without raising their expectations to unrealistic levels.

Customer Expectations

Consumer beliefs about the performance of a product based on prior experience and communications.

CUSTOMER DEFECTIONS AND COMPLAINING BEHAVIOR

Organizations look at **customer defections,** the percentage of customers who switch to another brand or supplier. Customer satisfaction and loyalty go hand-in-hand often, but loyal customers are not always highly satisfied, and satisfied customers are not always loyal. In some cases, customers continue to purchase a brand that doesn't fully meet expectations because defecting would be difficult or an alternative would be no better. In other cases, satisfied customers defect because they simply want to try something new. Consumers have degrees of satisfaction; they may be pleased by some aspects of a product, but not others. One study showed that 40 percent of all customers, though satisfied, would be willing to switch to a competitor, whereas highly satisfied customers are much less willing to do so.[10] The point is that just focusing on satisfaction isn't enough. You must build a bond of loyalty that is based on a relationship.

Figure 7.2 illustrates that, in a classic study completed in Sweden, 65 percent of customers defect primarily because they are dissatisfied with the way they are treated and 15 percent defect because of dissatisfaction with the product itself.[11] The remaining defect because they prefer a different product or for unrelated reasons. As this study indicates, treating people with respect is especially important when attempting to win their loyalty. The positive consequences of loyal customers can be

Customer Defections

The percentage of customers who switch to another brand or supplier

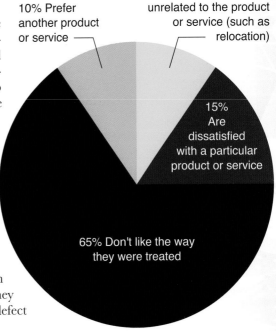

10% Prefer another product or service

10% Leave for reasons unrelated to the product or service (such as relocation)

15% Are dissatisfied with a particular product or service

65% Don't like the way they were treated

Figure 7.2   Why Customers Leave
Source: Eugene W. Anderson, Claes Fornell and Donald R. Lehmann, "Customer Satisfaction, Market Share and Profitability: Findings from Sweden," Journal of Marketing 58 (1994): 53.

seen everywhere and range by industry. A study by Temkin Group revealed that TV and Internet Service Providers have very few loyal customers in comparison to retailers and hotels. Companies such as DirectTV or Comcast would likely experience fewer defections if more emphasis was put on building a valuable relationship with its customers.[12]

Companies committed to customer satisfaction will deal with any complaints they receive in a way that still leads to overall satisfaction. On average, nine of every 10 customer problems that are discovered and resolved immediately will result in satisfaction and loyalty, with seven of those 10 customers willing to do repeat business with a company that makes a clear effort to resolve a problem. In fact, the average customer will tell five people about an effectively resolved problem, but may inform nine to 20 people about a negative experience or poor services.[13] This suggests that customers who complain and receive satisfactory attention are often more satisfied than those who don't complain at all.

Companies that respond to customer feedback and complaints are rewarded with customer loyalty and repeat business. They create a relationship through customer service. Companies that don't often do more harm than simply losing a customer. Perhaps you remember Dave Carroll, a young musician, who created the now-iconic "United Breaks Guitars" YouTube video after United Airlines damaged his Taylor guitar and would not address his claim and numerous complaints. The video quickly spread to over 5 million views in 2009 and has topped 14 million today. After the video went viral, United Airlines realized its mistake. It tried everything in its power to get Dave to remove the video, even offering him payment. The company's reaction was too late for Dave, though. He proceeded to post two additional YouTube videos that would further tarnish the airline's reputation and stock price. In retrospect, the entire situation could have been avoided if United Airlines had simply responded to his initial complaint. Instead, United lost a customer for life, and its image was tarnished with each YouTube hit. Taylor Guitars, on the other hand, seized the marketing opportunity to increase its sales by cleverly using the video to promote its brand through social media. It also rewarded Dave with a brand new Taylor guitar. To see the video, go to YouTube and search for "United Breaks Guitars."[14]

SATISFACTION RATINGS AND MEASUREMENT

Satisfaction Ratings

Ratings provided by testing agencies that compare purchase satisfaction with specified brands or with how well products perform.

Because satisfaction contributes so much to the success of an organization, it is no surprise that marketers are very interested in measuring satisfaction. **Satisfaction ratings** provide a way for consumers to compare brands, enable testing agencies to determine how well products perform, and allow companies to monitor how satisfied consumers are with their goods and services.

You may have used a rating system to help choose a cell phone, an insurance policy or even a college. Consumers have been sensitized to the importance of satisfaction by such publications as Consumer Reports, which routinely rates many products, and Motor Trend, which rates autos. Advertisers for autos and other products, as well as the press, place great emphasis on satisfaction ratings. For example, J.D. Power and Associates' annual U.S. Wireless Smartphone Satisfaction Study is based on responses from approximately 10,000 smartphone customers. In 2014 Apple won the tenth straight award for outscoring all others in the smartphone category. Key factors include performance, physical design, features, and ease of operation.[15]

The American Consumer Satisfaction Index (ACSI) is a quarterly rating that measures customer satisfaction in seven sectors of the economy broken down into 10 economic sections.[16] Even the U.S. government has entered the scene by sponsoring the Malcolm Baldrige National Quality Award, which is given to outstanding U.S. firms based partially on customer satisfaction.[17] We will discuss this award in more detail later in the chapter.

Competitive advantage comes to companies that can learn and adjust most quickly to market forces. One critical source of information is feedback from customers about how they behave and why they feel as they do. A **customer satisfaction measurement program** is an ongoing survey of customers (and competitors' customers) for the purpose of obtaining continuous estimates of satisfaction. Simply looking at sales data can tell us whether more or fewer products are purchased, but it does not reveal much about underlying reasons for behavior. Consequently, in addition to sales data, companies should measure customer satisfaction and loyalty rates. Marketers must not only measure their own company's performance but also that of their competitors. A company can work hard to build relationships critical to consumer satisfaction, yet the level of satisfaction may decline if a competitor has significantly improved its customer relationships more quickly.

The best consumer satisfaction program in the world is worth very little unless it feeds into the strategic and operational planning of the company. This information is then provided to all employees so the company can make adjustments to improve performance in its respective areas. Each functional area at all levels of the organization must be willing to undertake activities that lead to satisfied customers. One of the most important parts of the marketing executive's job is to get the entire organization to focus decisions on actions that directly affect customer satisfaction. So, much of a marketer's time is spent creating strategies that influence satisfaction.

RELATIONSHIPS BUILD SATISFACTION AND LOYALTY

Just a few years ago, marketers were content to sell to new customers with the goal of increasing sales faster than competitors. When one company's sales rise faster than all others, that organization's market share increases. Today, most companies realize that customer loyalty may be far more important than just market share.

You may try a new item once out of curiosity, but if you really like it, you will buy it again or tell others about it. The product becomes a more permanent fixture in your life and has more meaning. Very few organizations can survive without this loyalty and repeat business from customers. If an organization is forced to rely on single transactions, its costs escalate, and in many cases the company fails. Even companies that market products bought once in a lifetime depend on loyalty. The hospital that markets its heart surgery capabilities relies on positive word-of-mouth from loyal customers. Likewise, a Harley-Davidson dealer that sells a customer that one and only "dream machine" still builds the relationship after the sale. The customer tells friends and other prospective buyers of the experience, and they develop a positive perception of Harley David-son's customer relations.

In 1983, Harley established the Harley Owners Group (H.O.G.) for Harley riders across the nation to share their passion and pride for their Harleys. Today, there are over a million H.O.G. members worldwide.[18] How many companies have relationships so strong that consumers are willing to tattoo the brand or logo on their bodies, the way thousands of devoted Harley customers have? While few companies have connected with their customers to the extent of Harley-Davidson, it is clear that an effective connection creates a personal bond.

Customer Satisfaction Measurement Program

An ongoing survey of customers (and competitors' customers) for the purpose of obtaining continuous estimates of satisfaction.

There are over a million H.O.G members worldwide.

www.harley-davidson.com

At the Harley-Davidson website, learn how the company considers environmental impact when designing its motorcycles. You can also design your own bike or sign up for a tour of the factory.

That's what Harley-Davidson wants. When you buy a Harley, your new motorcycle is cleaned and polished to perfection. Your salesperson makes sure to take time, without interruptions, to discuss all of the features of your new purchase and answer any questions. Typically, a personal phone call from your salesperson, followed by a letter, provides the initial follow-through to begin furthering the relationship.

For a different demographic, BabyCenter.com, a one-stop shopping and information website for expectant and current mothers, allows users to set up personalized profiles with their children's names and birthdays. This allows the company to track demographic information and email relevant information regarding products, child development and safety to the parent, all based on the child's birth date. Therefore, just before a child's first birthday, BabyCenter.com can automatically email the mother about an appropriate and exciting birthday gift or important developmental milestones, increasing the probability that the mother will remain a customer. Similarly, Barnes and Noble has a membership program which customers can join on an annual basis to receive discounts on anything the company sells, including books, movies, music... even coffee. In return, the company receives information about each customer, including an email address and demographics, as well as enhanced loyalty.

CREATING A PERSONAL RELATIONSHIP

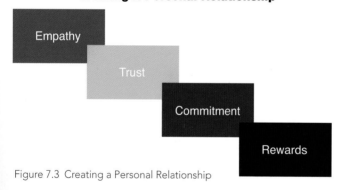

Creating A Personal Relationship

Figure 7.3 Creating a Personal Relationship

By its very nature, a relationship reflects the personal connection between two or more parties. While the core concept of marketing is to address customer needs and wants, marketers should seek to go beyond a minimalist effort and produce customer satisfaction and loyalty. Although not every customer seeks a relationship with every purchase, establishing one is typically the best way to address needs and wants. Involvement with customers is key in relationship marketing. More and more companies are embracing social media as a primary means to build relationships with customers. Proper social media management will enhance trust, increase communication and feedback, and develop a personal relationship that provides an emotional connection. Figure 7.3 lists empathy, trust, commitment and rewards as important aspects of creating personal relationships, which is true whether we are looking at consumer, B2B or other markets.

Empathy Empathy is the ability to put yourself in someone else's shoes, or from a marketing position, to understand the perspective of a consumer or another organization. Companies that build effective relationships and create inviting cultures often dedicate extensive marketing research to understanding consumers. But empathy works best when customers know that they are understood — that the organization has accurate knowledge of their circumstances. Marketers communicate this empathy in nearly everything they do. For example, when you call a pharmacy to renew a prescription and get courteous help, even if you don't have the prescription number handy, the company has communicated empathy. When a company goes out of its way to make things work just for you, you experience its empathy.

In addition to showing empathy through customer service, companies can also do so by being compassionate about the environment. A company's efforts to reduce its harmful impact on the environment show consumers its concern for the well-being of the community. Apple strives to preserve the earth by limiting environmentally harmful compounds, such as elemental forms of bromine and chlorine, in its materials and manufacturing processes. Even the aluminum enclosures on the popular MacBook Pro and other products are toxin-free and highly recyclable. Apple's packaging designs use post-consumer pulp fiber and vegetable-based inks. Even iTunes gift cards are made from 100 percent recycled paper. The steps Apple is taking to provide a greener environment for its customers helps it form a long-lasting personal relationship with consumers.[19]

Trust Trust is being able to rely on another party to perform as promised in the way you expect. The communications of marketers are filled with promises. For example, Coach's website states, "Our responsibility to our internal and external customers calls for impeccable service to ensure that their needs are always met. By treating customers like guests in our own home, we seek to establish long-term relationships based on trust and satisfaction."[20] Like people, companies that keep promises earn trust. This is a tremendously important element in building lasting connections with customers.

Coach understands that customer trust is an important aspect to creating a personal relationship.

Commitment Commitment occurs when companies go out of their way and deliver beyond what they promised in order to ensure customer satisfaction. When things go wrong, they work hard to fix them. This is particularly critical to relationships over time. For example, The Home Depot pledges to help its neighbors in troubled times with its "Team Depot." The company partnered with the American Red Cross to provide assistance in nearby communities to prevent disasters. The three-year joint venture is a $6.6 million program to teach one million people about emergency preparedness. The companies also work together if a disaster occurs. After one recent tornado outbreak in Northern Texas, The Home Depot sent 180 employees to board up broken windows, clear debris and fix fences while the American Red Cross handed out bottles of water and provided food to the hard-working employees. The Home Depot is deeply committed to its customers, thus forming a trusting relationship.[21]

Rewarding Loyalty Relationship marketing creates connections that make it unnecessary or difficult for customers to switch to competitors. In order for relationship marketing to work, companies must understand customers so well that competitors have little chance of new or unique offers that would entice a trial. This means that companies must be willing to provide superior value for their best customers. Louise O'Brien and Charles Jones, vice presidents with the successful consulting firm of Bain & Company, say that if companies want to realize the benefits of loyalty, they must admit that "all customers are not equal ... a company must give its best value to its best customers. That is, customers who generate superior profits for a company should enjoy the benefits of that value creation. As a result, they will then become even more loyal and profitable."[22]

In an effort to reward loyal customers, American Express teamed up with Starwood Hotels and Resorts to offer a credit card that earns points with each dollar spent, which can be redeemed for free hotel stays of Starwood Preferred Guests. When used to purchase a stay at any Starwood hotel, the cardholder earns three times the usual points. By becoming American Express cardholders and Starwood Preferred Guests, customers are rewarded for using American Express and staying at Starwood hotels.[23]

Starbucks Coffee Company is attempting a slight variant on this approach with its customer loyalty program, "My Starbucks Rewards." You earn one Star every time you pay with your Starbucks Card, and as you collect Stars, you move up to bigger benefits. A few Stars can earn you free refills on brewed coffee and tea or free flavored syrups. With more Stars, you can receive a Personalized Gold Card and special offers via email.[24]

It is important to remember that, often, competitors counter loyalty programs of rivals. For example, throughout the 1990s, an explosion of mileage-based incentive programs from airline companies allowed customers to get free travel after building up a certain number of paid travel miles. Because these programs were easy to copy, most airlines began offering some variation of their own. The result was competitive bidding wars with virtually no enhanced customer experience. Most programs failed.

DIVERSITY, GLOBAL COMPETITION AND SATISFACTION

The diversity of tastes and preferences presents opportunities for customer-centered marketers. Diversity helps explain why companies with the highest overall sales sometimes have lower satisfaction ratings than smaller companies. The latter can design products and services for very narrowly defined segments and can focus all of their attention on those customers. These companies may have lower market share but score high satisfaction points with a select few customers. As companies gain share by selling to more people, their products and services must appeal to more diversified customers with a broader range of expectations, something that requires a great deal of flexibility. Achieving satisfaction in the face of growth requires using the broadest range of marketing tools and techniques. If an organization expects impressive satisfaction scores, then it must understand all forms of diversity better than even its smallest competitors.

The success of a product or service in one market segment will not automatically transfer to consumers in another segment. The diverse nature of consumers makes universal buying preferences and behaviors very unlikely. Companies such as Coca-Cola, McDonald's, Apple and J.Crew address the individual wants and needs of people by acknowledging their unique differences. Attention to the diversity of consumers is often reflected in better market share and product sales. When McDonald's expanded to the Philippines about 25 years ago, few expected the local, 11-store Jollibee fast-food chain to survive. However, Jollibee reacted by first copying McDonald's business model and then tailoring its menu to better serve the preferences of the local market. It introduced a

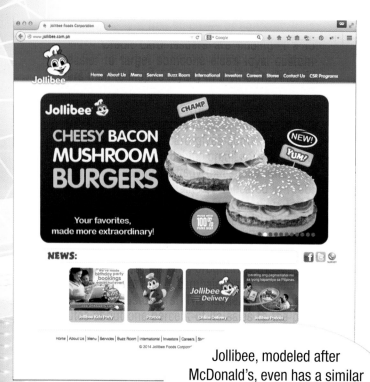

Jollibee, modeled after McDonald's, even has a similar look to its website. You can compare it to McDonald's on page 184.

slightly sweeter hamburger, a Philippine-style chicken product, and a kids-oriented spaghetti plate. Today, Jollibee is the widest store network in the Philippines with over 750 locations, and it has even opened 26 stores to compete with McDonald's in the United States. Its success in the U.S. has largely been contributed to strategic placement of stores across California and other areas with a high concentration of Filipinos.[26]

Groups based on ethnicity have such tremendous buying power that marketers have begun to recognize the advantages of addressing each group individually, to the point where many organizations have departments and positions for this very purpose. At Kraft, for example, there is a director of ethnic marketing. Today, most of the largest firms in the United States have created diversity management positions in an effort to modify corporate culture to reflect the growth of minority segments.

CAREER TIP!

If the title of crew member or captain suits you, then so might a job with Trader Joe's neighborhood grocery store. Trader Joe's makes creating an outstanding customer experience a priority. "We feel really close to our customers," says Audrey Dumper, vice president of marketing for Trader Joe's East. "When we want to know what's on their minds, we don't need to put them in a sterile room with a swinging bulb." Trader Joe's was recently highlighted in FastCompany Magazine as a "Leading Listener" in the industry.

The success of global companies is highly dependent on customer satisfaction. Throughout the 1960s and '70s, domestic firms dominated the U.S. market. By the early '80s, U.S. businesses were under the false impression that they could sustain success without making any major adjustments, which led to the neglect of changing customer needs and satisfaction. Many foreign companies spotted this weakness and entered U.S. markets quickly, putting great stock in customer satisfaction. Some of the strongest U.S. companies saw their market shares plummet because foreign rivals gained strong customer satisfaction ratings. Honda and BMW are examples. These foreign competitors raised consumer expectations for quality and speed of service to new levels and often at substantially lower overall prices. Essentially, foreign competitors created new levels of customer satisfaction in the U.S. market.

ORGANIZATIONAL SYSTEMS AND ACTIONS THAT DELIVER QUALITY

Technology has played an indispensable role in the creation of customer value. Overall, the functionality of products is increasing while costs are staying the same or decreasing. Most leading companies have systems that also deliver quality goods and services. It is this emphasis on quality largely made possible through technology and people that brings more satisfaction to customers. Products work as expected, last longer, and are user friendly. This section describes some of the aspects of quality that leading-edge organizations employ to help accomplish customer satisfaction and loyalty.

QUALITY & SATISFACTION

Quality describes the degree of excellence of a company's goods and services. Both organizations that sell physical products and those that sell services should emphasize quality. **Service quality** is the expected and perceived quality of all the services an organization offers. A quality good or service performs precisely to specifications that will satisfy customers. Consequently, quality is essential to achieving customer satisfaction. Some companies, such as Packard Electric, believe their product pos-

Quality

The degree of excellence of a company's products or services.

Service Quality

The expected and perceived quality of all the services an organization offers.

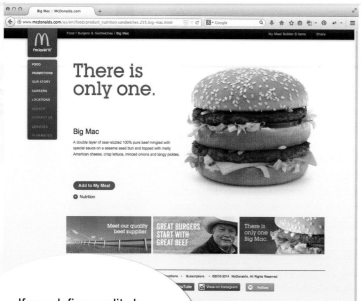

If you define quality by consistency, McDonald's Big Mac® might be a gold standard.

sesses quality to the degree that it meets or exceeds customer expectations. Elmer Reece, a former top executive at the company, introduced the "excellence concept" in a quest to deliver total quality. According to Reece, "being excellent means meeting or exceeding customer expectations in everything." Striving for excellence became a critical part of every employee's job at Packard, and Reece's philosophy turned the company into a real winner. In order to make the concept work, Reece elevated marketing from its traditional sales role to the leading force in every major decision. Reece often said that the customer, not the company, should be the judge of quality, and problems arise when quality is defined by the latter.

No two customers are precisely alike. We all want quality goods and services — but we each may view quality as being slightly different. For example, if you get an urge for a Big Mac® and can even taste its flavor in your mouth, then you might define quality by consistency (which McDonald's has perfected). But if you get an urge for a gourmet meal at a five-star restaurant, you might define quality as uniqueness and variety. Legendary restaurants such as Spago and Lutece take very different paths from McDonald's to achieve their standard of quality.

Similarly, customers are finding new ways of sharing their experiences, both positive and negative, with others. Outlets such as blogs, Facebook and Twitter are rising in popularity as a means for communicating quality and satisfaction to the world. Companies thus have to ensure that their presence in the social media sectors is being closely monitored. For example, Comcast operates a Twitter feed, @ComcastCares, where it responds to customer concerns much faster and more personally than over the phone. Presence in social media is allowing customers and companies to connect more frequently and ultimately facilitating a fuller customer experience.[27]

In many markets, quality is so important that if products do not meet a certain standard, they simply won't have a chance of success in the market. As more companies build quality into their products, quality alone ceases to provide a differential advantage. Quality has become a more complex concept. For some time, many consumers bought Japanese cars because they were perceived to be of much higher quality than U.S. brands. Today, most experts believe that U.S. vehicles are equal in quality to Japanese cars and that U.S. manufacturers are even beginning to take the lead in new areas of quality, such as design and performance. Quality in any of these areas can be evaluated subjectively by consumers or objectively by technical assessments. Toyota's recent product recall crisis of more than 5.3 million cars because of unintended acceleration caused by electrical problems resulted in a U.S. sales decline of 16 percent in a single month, and the company's stock value declined $21 billion in a single week. The crisis did cause Toyota to reflect and react to make dramatic changes to improve its responsiveness to customer concerns, and the automaker is positioned to emerge even stronger than before.[28]

Subjective Assessment of Quality

The degree to which a product does what consumers want it to do.

Assessments of Quality **Subjective assessment of quality** indicates to what degree the product does what consumers want it to do. For example, the hamburger tastes good. After an extensive review of a number of studies, one expert defined quality as "the consumer's judgment about a product's overall excellence or superiority."[29] From this perspective, different groups may evaluate quality altogether differently. When asked, adults may say Wendy's is higher in quality than

McDonald's, whereas children may have the opposite response. Health-conscious people might rate both items as low in quality.

Objective assessment of quality indicates to what degree the product does consistently what it's supposed to do. McDonald's and Burger King make what many consider to be high-quality hamburgers because each time one is served it consistently meets company standards. With hamburgers and other physical objects, it's possible to develop objective assessments of quality in the form of standards, such as fat and salt content or nutritional value.

Even objective assessments are open to interpretation, particularly in a global setting. For example, German and Japanese products are manufactured to precise specifications and will not perform in excess of their rating. If a product is rated to lift 1,000 kg, it will do precisely that and no more. In contrast, a similar U.S. product in some cases has a safety factor of 1.5, so the product will lift 1,500 kg. The extra capacity is a sign of quality in the United States but not in many other markets. Consequently, even measures of so-called objective quality are created in response to the subjective desires of various groups.[30]

Static and Dynamic Quality There are two other ways to categorize quality. **Static quality** results when an accepted practice is perfected. Many companies have processes designed to produce items to given quality standards that approach perfection. **Dynamic quality** results when a major change makes the existing standard obsolete. For example, Kodak once dominated the photography and film business by continually improving its extremely high-quality 35mm film. As consumers shifted to digital cameras and film became obsolete, Kodak's efforts to achieve static quality became irrelevant. A revolution had taken place as digital camera companies created value through change, a dynamic quality shift. Time will tell if hand-held digital cameras will face a similar shift with the increased camera technology and popularity of smartphones.

Focusing activities on static quality can divert resources from new ventures, and there seems little point in perfecting technology that is about to become obsolete. At the same time, dynamic quality shifts cannot be forced; the technology needs to be perfected and the market prepared. The task falls to marketers to discover what will be new and relevant, and what customers consider to be high quality. Marketers develop estimates of what attributes customers use to define quality, what quality standards must be met, and what various segments are willing to pay for quality.

TOTAL QUALITY MANAGEMENT

Total quality management (TQM) is an organizational philosophy that helps companies produce goods and services that deliver value to satisfy customers. TQM involves, first, assessing consumer needs and second, developing products or services that meet those needs. The approach seeks continuous improvement, reduced cycle time, and analysis of process problems. It also includes quality function deployment, which attempts to ensure that customer desires are built into the final product offering. When implemented correctly, TQM involves many company activities that affect customer satisfaction and ends with customer service and feedback. It deals with both deliverables (the goods and services provided) and interactions (how customers experience dealing with the provider).

Continuous Improvement **Continuous improvement** occurs as the organization strives to find better ways of satisfying customers. FedEx uses Service Quality Indications (SQI) in its efforts to achieve continuous improvement. The index measures a number of key service factors from the customer's perspective and then weighs them as to how seriously the customer will view a failure in any of those areas. Based on SQI, FedEx has set the goal of scoring better year after year. The

Objective Assessment of Quality

An evaluation of the degree to which a product does what it is supposed to do.

Static Quality

Quality that results when individuals or organizations perfect an accepted practice.

Dynamic Quality

Quality that results from a change that makes an existing standard obsolete.

Total Quality Management (TQM)

An organizational philosophy that helps companies produce goods and services that deliver value to satisfy customers.

Continuous Improvement

The enhancement process used by an organization to find the best ways of satisfying its customers.

University of Michigan's American Customer Satisfaction Index (ACSI) currently ranks FedEx tied with UPS as No. 1 in customer satisfaction out of 130 companies in the Express Delivery industry. Previously, FedEx had been the leader in customer satisfaction but tumbled four points during the 2013 holiday season. "The waning customer satisfaction is largely a result of delays caused by weather and overloaded systems during the winter. The holiday season was also shorter than usual this year, which resulted in a surge of packages that flooded delivery networks in the final days leading up to Christmas. The largest national shipping companies, FedEx and UPS, both struggled to sustain customer satisfaction over the holiday peak. In order to meet delivery commitments, FedEx used 25,000 temporary employees, while UPS added 55,000 extra workers and apparently chartered supplementary aircraft. FedEx declines 4% and UPS is down 2% to tie at an ACSI score of 82."[31]

Milliken & Company, another organization known for superior quality, pays particular attention to constant improvement. It calls its "Pursuit of Excellence" program an evolving process that continuously yields new ideas for enhancing quality, increasing customer satisfaction and improving business performance. Milliken's Policy Committee and Quality Council has created an environment conducive to constant innovation and improvement, calling employees "associates," and giving each one the training and responsibility to contribute to quality improvements. Managers must respond within one day to any suggestion by an associate to enhance customer satisfaction.

Reduced Cycle Time

Reduced cycle time is a TQM activity intended to help the company move more quickly from product inception to product delivery in the marketplace. The approach pays huge dividends by reducing costs while making possible very quick shipment of products matched specifically to customer requirements. This not only allows customers more flexibility in ordering but also results in lower inventories for business customers and quicker availability of products for consumers.

A Houston-based industrial distributor of pipes, valves, and fittings has used TQM principles to achieve reduced cycle time and has seen striking results. The company assigned a team of external salespeople and internal salespeople (customer service and sales representatives in the home office), and assigns receivable personnel to every customer account, allowing employees and customers to gain a great deal of familiarity with one another. Inventory turnover improved by 175 percent in five years, sales for newly introduced value-added products increased 75 percent in three years, and profits doubled.

Analysis of Process Problems

Analysis of process problems refers to the activities that find and fix problems in the production and delivery of products and services. For manufactured items, this includes procurement of raw materials and components that go into finished goods, the manufacture of the finished products themselves, and packaging and shipping to ensure that appropriate products get to their final destination. The International Standards Organization (ISO) has established an inclusive set of standards, called **ISO 9001**, to determine whether organizations are meeting quality requirements. These standards are being introduced into laws in the European community to ensure that firms have quality-management systems in place that meet specified criteria. ISO 9001 doesn't investigate individual products; it certifies organizations as a whole, providing they pass the certification process. In other words, this certification does not mean that the goods and services are certified, but that the organizational processes used to build and deliver the products are certified. Organizations such as Chrysler and Motorola require that all their suppliers be ISO 9001 certified.

An important outcome of the analysis is to establish rigid quality control, such as the Motorola Six-Sigma standard, which sets goals so that virtually all Motorola products perform as expected. Elaborate efforts are made in product and process

---

Reduced Cycle Time

A TQM activity that helps a company move more rapidly from product inception to final delivery of the product to the marketplace.

Analysis of Process Problems

Methods designed to find and fix problems that could reduce quality.

ISO 9001

An inclusive set of standards established by the International Standards Organization (ISO) to ensure that quality requirements are met.

design to ensure that the actual manufacturing activities efficiently produce quality items. In turn, the processes are monitored to make certain that the output is produced according to specifications. Six-Sigma is a total quality-management effort focused on eliminating defects to improve processes. It equates to only 3.4 defects per million opportunities. Caterpillar Inc. trains its employees in Six-Sigma methodologies, and they can earn green or black belts for their efforts. Caterpillar currently has more than 36,000 employees contributing to Six-Sigma projects worldwide, from divisions including safety, product quality and product availability.[32]

Although quality has been the focus of manufacturing for more than a decade, the same principles are now being applied to customer service. For example, FedEx Express Canada uses the Contact Center Employer of Choice ("CCEOC") program to help identify areas of improvement in its call centers. The program helps build exceptional work environments that attract and retain high-performing employees. By using recommendations outlined in the CCEOC Summary Reporting, customer service centers have increased employee and customer satisfaction. Jeff Doran, president of CCEOC Inc., says, "FedEx Express Canada has achieved the Platinum ranking for the fifth year in a row. They are the highest-ranking contact centre and have been certified for 10 consecutive years. This is an incredible feat!"[33]

Quality Function Deployment
Quality function deployment (QFD) is used during the product or service design process to make sure that features to fulfill customer desires are built into the final offering. The three most common concerns of QFD are to make the product or service faster, better and cheaper. Figure 7.4 shows what consumers desire in their dealings with the company and how those desires are translated into what the company delivers.

Quality Function Deployment (QFD)

A process that builds customer wants and desires into the final product offering.

	Faster	Better	Cheaper
COMPANY DELIVERS	Availability	Performance Features	Price
	Convenience	Reliability Conformance Serviceability Aesthetics Perceived Quality	
CUSTOMER DESIRES	Responsiveness	Reliability Security	Affordability
	Access	Competence Credibility Empathy Communications Style	

Figure 7.4   Faster-Better-Cheaper: What the Company Delivers and What the Customer Desires

Benchmarking
Benchmarking is the systematic evaluation of the practices of excellent organizations to learn new and better ways of serving customers. Benchmarking of **best practices**, those selected competencies for which leaders are known, has become so important that companies regularly send personnel to study and observe other organizations. Sparrow Health Systems, a leading provider in central Michigan, recently sent executives to Disney World to learn how to improve customer service. They also visited Saturn Corporation to obtain ideas for involving employees in the improvement process. Although Disney and Saturn are not in the same business as Sparrow or each other, Sparrow was able to learn several new ways of ultimately improving health-care delivery. By comparing its methods with those of known experts in other fields, Sparrow conducted benchmarking.

Benchmarking

The systematic evaluation of practices of excellent organizations to learn new and better ways to serve customers.

Best Practices

The competencies of industry leaders that other organizations use as benchmarks.

QUALITY AWARDS

To encourage companies to improve their quality and competitiveness, various governments have established awards for companies with the most outstanding quality initiatives. Two very distinguished annual awards are the Deming Prize in Japan and the Malcolm Baldrige National Quality Award in the United States.

The Deming Prize Everyone has heard of quality inspectors — people who examine finished products as they roll off the assembly line and remove defective goods before they are sold to customers. In the early 1900s, most companies used inspectors as their main source of quality control. Little or no effort was devoted to correcting the manufacturing problems that caused product defects.

Statistical Quality Control

The use of statistics to isolate and quantify production line problems that may cause product defects.

In the 1950s, Dr. Edward Deming took a new approach to the issue. He applied the idea of **statistical quality control**, a concept he learned while a statistician at AT&T's Bell Laboratories, to manufacturing. Statistical quality control involves using statistics to isolate and quantify production line problems that may cause defects, improving the overall process, not just the final product. The Japanese openly embraced Deming's philosophy, and this is viewed by many as one of the reasons for Japan's tremendous economic success during the 1970s and '80s. Deming's work transformed Japan from the maker of inferior products to one of the most powerful economies in the world. To honor Deming's contributions, the Japanese created the Deming Award as their highest recognition of quality.

To help business managers implement quality initiatives within their organization, Deming outlined 14 key issues, listed in Figure 7.5. Deming insisted, moreover, that top management be involved and supportive. If quality initiatives receive only lip service, without action, they will not be successful.

1. Create constancy of purpose toward improvement of product and service, with the aim to become competitive and stay in business, and to provide jobs.
2. Adopt this philosophy: We are in a new economic age created by Japan. Transformation of Western management style is necessary to halt the continued decline of industry.
3. Cease depending on inspection to achieve quality. Eliminate the need for inspection on a mass basis by building quality into the product in the first place.
4. End the practice of awarding business on the basis of price tag. Purchasing must be combined with design of product, manufacturing, and sales to work with the chosen suppliers; the aim is to minimize total cost, not merely initial cost.
5. Improve constantly and forever every activity in the company in order to improve quality and productivity and thus constantly decrease costs.
6. Institute training and education on the job for everyone, including management.
7. Institute supervision. The aim of supervision should be to help people and machines do a better job.
8. Drive out fear so that everyone may work effectively for the company.
9. Break down barriers between departments. People in Research, Design, Sales, and Production must work as a team to tackle usage and production problems that may be encountered with the product or service.
10. Eliminate slogans, exhortations, and targets for the work force that ask for zero defects and new levels of productivity. Such exhortations only create adversarial relationships; the bulk of the causes of low quality and low productivity belongs to the system and thus lies beyond the power of the work force.
11. Eliminate work standards that prescribe numerical quotas for the day. Substitute aids and helpful supervision.
12a. Remove the barriers that rob hourly workers of the right to pride of workmanship. The responsibility of supervisors must be changed from sheer numbers to quality.
12b. Remove the barriers that rob people in management and in engineering of their right to pride of workmanship. This means, among other things, abolition of the annual or merit rating and of management by objective.
13. Institute a vigorous program of education and retraining. New skills are required for changes in techniques, material, and service.
14. Put everybody in the company to work in teams to accomplish the transformation.

Figure 7.5   Edward Deming's 14 Points of Quality
Source: Reprinted from The New Economics for Industry, Government, Education by W. Edward Deming, by permission of MIT and The W. Edward Deming Institute. Published by MIT, Center for Advanced Educational Services, Cambridge, MA 02139. Copyright 1993 by the W. Edward Deming Institute.

The Malcolm Baldrige National Quality Award U.S. businesses have been late to emphasize quality. During the same period that the Japanese excelled in implementing quality initiatives, U.S. firms slipped dramatically in quality. Congress finally moved to establish a quality award for U.S. firms, named after the late Malcolm Baldrige, an advocate for quality and a former secretary of commerce. While considering the passage of the Malcolm Baldrige National Quality Improvement Act, the U.S. Senate Committee on Commerce, Science and Technology observed: "Strategic planning for quality improvement programs is becoming more and more essential to the well-being of our nation's companies and our ability to compete effectively in the global marketplace. Such an award would parallel the prize awarded annually in Japan."[34]

The 1987 legislation was enacted by Congress to encourage U.S. businesses and other organizations to practice effective quality control in the production of goods and services. At the time of its passage, the Senate and House produced a declaration reiterating the need for an incentive program for U.S. businesses and affirming that these businesses had been considerably challenged by foreign competitors. Slow growth in productivity and in product and process quality had, in some industries, resulted in annual losses of as much as 20 percent of sales revenues. It was evident that U.S. businesses needed to learn more about the importance of quality.

The **Malcolm Baldrige National Quality Award** is widely acknowledged as having raised quality awareness and practice among U.S. companies. Some consider the Baldrige an important catalyst for transforming U.S. business because it promotes quality excellence, recognizes achievements by companies that effectively improve quality, and supplies a guideline that business, industry, government and others can use to evaluate their quality improvement efforts.

A key criterion that winners must meet is "customer-driven excellence." "Performance and quality are judged by the organization's customer. Thus, the organization must take into account all product and service features and characteristics and all modes of customer access that contribute value to customers. Such behavior leads to customer acquisition, satisfaction, preference, referrals, retention, and loyalty and to business expansion. Customer-driven excellence means much more than reducing defects and errors, merely meeting specifications, or reducing complaints. In addition, the organization's success in recovering from defects, service errors, and mistakes is crucial for retaining customers and building customer relationships."[35] Awards are given each year in several categories: manufacturing companies or subsidiaries, service companies or subsidiaries, small businesses, education, and health care. Figure 7.6 lists companies that have most recently received the Malcolm Baldrige National Quality Award.

The Ritz-Carlton Hotel Company was an award winner in 1992 and 1999, making it the only two-time winner in its service category.[36] The Ritz-Carlton's qual-

Malcome Baldrige National Quality Award

A program designed to raise quality awareness and practice among U.S. businesses.

2007	PRO-TEC Coating Co.	**2010**	MEDRAD, Warrendale
	Mercy Health Systems		Nestlé Purina PetCare Co.
	Sharp HealthCare		Freese and Nichols Inc.
	City of Coral Springs, FL		K&N Management, Austin
	U.S. Army Armament Research,		Studer Group, Gulf Breeze
	Development and Engineering		Advocate Good Samaritan Hospital
	Center (ARDEC)		Montgomery County Public Schools
2008	Poudre Valley Health System	**2011**	Concordia Publishing House
	Cargill Corn Milling North America		Henry Ford Health System
	Iredell-Statesville Schools		Schneck Medical Center
2009	Honeywell Federal Manufacturing		Southcentral Foundation
	& Technologies	**2012**	Lockheed Martin Missiles and Fire Control
	MidwayUSA		MESA Products Inc.
	AtlantiCare		North Mississippi Health Services
	Heartland Health		City of Irving, Irving, TX
	VA Cooperative Studies Program	**2013**	Pewaukee School District
	Clinical Research Pharmacy		Sutter Davis Hospital
	Coordinating Center		

Figure 7.6   Winners of the Malcolm Baldrige National Quality Award

ity success comes from its dedicated focus on the customer. Its outspoken goal is to "Understand Customers in Detail" by relying on extensive data gathering and the dissection of key points where customer satisfaction problems generally occur. The Ritz-Carlton maintains a database of almost a million customer files, which enables hotel staff to anticipate needs of returning guests and to make sure in advance that requests are honored.[37]

DELIVERING VALUE TO IMPROVE SATISFACTION

Customer-centered marketing requires the development of unique competencies to satisfy customers within selected target market segments and to build their loyalty.

CREATING & CAPTURING VALUE THROUGH *Relationships*

The Customer Loyalty Card Game

More and more people are discovering that there is a free lunch — or coffee, haircut, video or even airline ticket — if you patronize certain shops and get your frequent-customer card punched. Retailers realize that building relationships with customers they already have is more profitable than luring first-timers with splashy ad campaigns or costly discounts. And for their loyalty, customers desire rewards more than anything else — from special rates in retail to frequent flyer miles in credit card companies.

Each time someone applies for a loyalty card, personal information and data can be collected about shopping habits. Advertised specials and new products can be marketed directly to the customers and data collected from shoppers about products they purchase can be analyzed to offer coupons on specific items the customers buy. However, many people are concerned about the use of personal information. Nearly a decade ago, Senate Bill 926, also known as the Supermarket Club Card Disclosure Act, became effective in California. The act allows companies to track purchases and analyze broad demographic trends but prohibits issuers of the cards from requiring applicants to provide identification such as a driver's license or Social Security card.

Even outside the privacy issue, some customers are disgruntled with carrying so many cards in their wallets. And research has found that multiple loyalty card memberships of geographically close retailers will reduce consumer lifetime duration on visiting a certain retailer.

Moreover, some experts believe that loyalty cards are simply a crutch for businesses struggling to find a way to differentiate from competitors. Consider the grocery store industry. A few superior chains like Whole Foods and Trader Joe's attract customers through better quality and unique products. ALDI Foods provides low-cost goods and no-frill's shopping. Not one of them uses a loyalty card, and they are all excelling in the industry because they provide shoppers with a compelling reason to return. Other grocery chains are clawing to collect customer-specific data, but often fail to use it correctly. Many times, paying more attention to the shopper's experience and what is driving satisfaction will far outweigh the volumes of data you can collect from a card.

Brian Palmer, "Ditch Your Loyalty Cards," www.slate.com, website visited June 18, 2014.

Many parties are involved in contributing to the delivery of products that benefit consumers. The value chain is used to describe the chain of activities involved in bringing products to consumers. Additionally, to improve customer satisfaction and loyalty, leading-edge companies operate ethically to fulfill commitments and involve employees and customers in performance-improving efforts.

INTEGRATED SUPPLY CHAIN

The **supply chain** is composed of all the activities that organizations undertake to deliver value to the customer, such as working with suppliers, and distribution through convenient channels. A simple supply chain starts by identifying customer needs. Most people seek products that perform as desired, portray the image they want, are easy to purchase and are priced fairly. Companies then identify the process required to deliver this value and ensure that each step of the process is carried out in quality fashion.

Supply Chain

All the activities that organizations undertake to deliver value to the customer, such as working with suppliers and distribution through convenient channels.

Many activities make a major difference in the amount of customer satisfaction. These include the procurement of raw materials as well as the manufacture and delivery of products to retailers and others in the channel of distribution. All functional areas — purchasing, operations, manufacturing, marketing, sales, and so on — are involved in delivering customer value and must clearly understand the customers of the final product. Many separate organizations may be involved in the process as well, and the respective organizations need to empathize with each other and the final customer.

Although customers have very little knowledge of these activities, they shape the quality of goods and services as well as the price that will be charged in the marketplace. For example, Gap's customers want a quality product at a good price, so Gap takes that into account when considering the costs of manufacturing locations. In the same manner, the cost of Gap's raw materials, its ability to deliver products efficiently to retail outlets, the effectiveness of its research and development, and many other activities affect the overall quality of the goods and services the company can provide to its customers. Even the quality of the commercials and print ads are important, since they largely shape the image of the product for users. Gap's competitiveness depends to a great degree on its abil-

Gap's 2014 "Lived-In" global marketing campaign celebrates an authentic attitude and features emerging young artists and musicians.

ity, and the ability of its suppliers and distributors, to perform well on all the factors that influence the amount of value delivered to the marketplace. All organizations in the chain must behave with the intent of creating satisfaction for others in the chain in order that consumers can ultimately benefit to the greatest degree possible.

ETHICAL BEHAVIOR IN FULFILLING COMMITMENTS

Many organizations that promise satisfaction and quality think it is not only good business but ethically correct to compensate customers when quality does not meet their expectations. Although "satisfaction guaranteed or your money back" usually applies to such purchases as clothes or pizza, today some colleges believe that a promise of a quality education should be backed by a guarantee as well.

Henry Ford Community College in Dearborn, Michigan, became the first school to offer a guarantee for its graduates. It provides up to 16 semester hours of further training if an employer feels a graduate lacks the expected job skills. Of course, many businesses offer satisfaction guarantees. Some make it very difficult for the customer to collect on such a guarantee, but others pay off with little hassle, like Meijer, a regional supermarket chain with an outstanding reputation for customer service. Despite the satisfaction that results when a customer problem is handled well, a number of companies have tightened their rules and changed generous exchange policies. Best Buy, for example, has quit taking back goods without a sales receipt, charging customers without one a restocking fee. Walmart has changed its open-ended return policy to one with a 90-day limit.

Customers are partly responsible for these changes. Imagine people returning goods actually purchased at a garage sale or bringing back clothes worn for an entire season. Or what about customers who pull items off store shelves and bring them to the counter for a refund? Nintendo has received returned game boxes containing underwear, soap and even a lizard. Although these are extreme examples, stores have tightened return policies to help prevent fraud. According to a recent study, U.S. merchants are incurring $191 billion in fraud losses each year, so the stricter policies may seem reasonable.[38] The important consideration, however, is the consumer response. If the ease of returning a defective or unwanted good is eliminated, then consumers feel negatively about the company or business. Since many aspects of satisfaction are based on how the organization and its products affect customers, it is important to make all employees aware of the importance of the customer to the overall health of the organization. That requires their involvement in knowing why products were returned and nearly every other aspect of customer evaluations.

EMPLOYEE AND CUSTOMER INVOLVEMENT

It's difficult to imagine making customers satisfied without having employees who are highly involved in the process. In turn, satisfied employees are much more likely to produce satisfied customers than are disgruntled employees, so the organization itself needs to ensure that employees feel appreciated. Strong companies involve the entire organization and its customers in efforts to improve performance in ways that will promote customer satisfaction. IBM integrates customers into its improvement planning process by inviting consumers from around the world to give direct input to top-level strategic planners. Executives at Procter & Gamble take time to interview consumers at grocery stores and answer customer service calls, while Hewlett-Packard recruits them to assist in developing products that will replace current offerings. All of these companies demonstrate how interaction between consumers and an organization's employees help ensure that the customer is a primary focus.[39]

The job of satisfying consumers cannot be left to the marketing or sales manager alone. Achieving customer satisfaction is nearly impossible without a well-defined process for focusing the entire organization on the customer. As with the most important marketing functions, everyone must participate, from top management to the workers on the factory floor. In fact, most companies that are serious about improving satisfaction consider it critical to involve their top managers. They sit in on meetings about customer satisfaction and demand that everyone "walk the walk" — not just discuss issues, but develop plans to address them. Compared to other organizations, managers in these companies spend more time talking with customers, and compensation structures often are based more on satisfying customers than on meeting short-term financial goals. Furthermore, all functional areas are involved in customer satisfaction, including marketing, sales, engineering, accounting and purchasing. Other channel members, such as manufacturers' representatives, wholesalers and distributors, are often part of the effort. The result is a customer-centered organization working to create satisfied purchasers.

Leading companies don't just build relationships with their own personnel and affiliates; customers are involved from the start. Customer Review, an Internet company that establishes online communities based around sports, electronics, and the home, works to develop relationships with customers of products. An online "facilitator" directs discussion about particular products among the company's 1.2 million website visitors. Establishing relationships with its customers is important to the success of Customer Review, but it also maintains quality relationships with the manufacturers of the products it reviews.[40] The quality of relationships and the accuracy of expectations that manufacturers of products establish with Customer Review's customers are reflected in the product reviews posted on its website.

The biggest mistake most companies make is to assume they know what their customers want without asking them. Unfortunately, most companies that guess do so incorrectly. For a true understanding of what consumers want, a company must establish a dialogue with not only current customers and those who have defected, but those of competitors and other potential purchasers. One way to achieve involvement is through formal marketing research, such as interviews or surveys. Industry leaders astutely include customers on their product planning teams.

CHAPTER SUMMARY

Objective 1: Understand why customer satisfaction and loyalty are the focus of marketing in winning organizations.

Satisfied, loyal customers generate profits because they are responsible for a large percentage of sales and are less costly to develop than new customers. Loyal, satisfied customers also influence others to buy products. Similar to product innovation, customer satisfaction has become a key to competitive advantage. In addition, satisfaction ratings help consumers compare products. Finally, loyal, satisfied customers will pay more and are less concerned about price and price increases.

Objective 2: Learn how consumer expectations influence satisfaction.

Customers form impressions about how well companies perform in relation to expectations. If performance falls short, then customers become dissatisfied. Often they defect when they don't like the way they are treated. When customers are delighted, their expectations are likely to increase. Loyal customers are not always satisfied, and they are likely to complain. If their complaint is handled quickly, then their loyalty may be even greater.

Objective 3: See why connecting with customers through relationships achieves outstanding satisfaction and loyalty.

The personal connection produces loyalty. Relationships are built, first, on empathy — the ability to understand another party and communicate that understanding. Second, trust is important, that is, behaving in line with promises you make and expectations you create. Third, commitment is also important. Commitment means making sure that the customer is better off because of the relationship.

Objective 4: Understand the ideas that help organizations market quality goods and services.

Diverse customers have different expectations. Creating satisfaction requires paying close attention to various tastes and preferences. Many companies have created units to address specific groups. The variations in customer tastes and preferences are particularly challenging for large companies that want to gain high satisfaction scores. They still need to address each specific segment to achieve high ratings. Satisfaction scores have historically been higher for some foreign companies in this country, reflecting their attention to quality. This has helped them gain a market foothold. Now that U.S. companies also are stressing quality and satisfaction, their scores are improving in marketing to foreign countries.

Objective 5: Define quality and describe how it is obtained.

Quality can be assessed objectively and subjectively. Objective assessments indicate whether the product performs as designed. Subjective assessments indicate whether the product performs according to what customers want. Businesses must be careful not to focus only on static quality. The quality of change — dynamic quality — is also important. Both build value. Total quality management (TQM) is an organizational philosophy that focuses on quality. It includes several specific actions, such as continuous improvement, reduced cycle time and analysis of process problems. Benchmarking is also important. It refers to learning from organizations considered to be among the very best and assessing how well you perform relative to them.

REVIEW YOUR UNDERSTANDING

1. What is customer satisfaction? What is loyalty? What are four reasons for an organization to stress loyalty and satisfaction? Explain each.
2. How do you calculate the lifetime value of a customer?
3. What are customer expectations? Why do customers defect? Why are complainers often your most loyal customers?
4. What are the three elements that form the personal basis of relationships? Explain each. How do companies reward loyal customers?
5. What are companies doing to address satisfaction with diversified customers?
6. Why is satisfaction important in global marketing?
7. What is customer-delivered value? Explain.
8. What is the value chain? Explain.
9. What are objective and subjective assessments of quality? Static and dynamic quality?
10. What is TQM, and what are its four critical components?
11. What is benchmarking?
12. What are the Deming Prize and the Malcolm Baldrige National Quality Award?

DISCUSSION OF CONCEPTS

1. Why should companies focus on both satisfaction and loyalty? Why is satisfaction alone inadequate?
2. Imagine that you are the marketing director of a local company. How would you use the concept of customer-delivered value to improve the marketing for a product?
3. Discuss how connecting with customers through relationships relates to satisfaction and loyalty.
4. If you observed a large percentage of customer defections from a business, what might be the causes? How would you investigate?
5. Is complaining behavior good or bad? Should you encourage customers to complain?
6. What would you recommend for an organization that wishes to connect with customers through relationships?
7. What is the relationship between quality and customer value? How is quality attained?
8. Do you feel companies should allocate a great deal of effort to apply for the Malcolm Baldrige National Quality Award? Why or why not?

KEY TERMS & DEFINITIONS

1. **Analysis of process problems:** Methods designed to find and fix problems that could reduce quality.
2. **Benchmarking:** The systematic evaluation of practices of excellent organizations to learn new and better ways to serve customers.
3. **Best practices:** The competencies of industry leaders that other organizations use as benchmarks.
4. **Continuous improvement:** The enhancement process used by an organization to find the best ways of satisfying its customers.
5. **Cost structure:** The amount of money required to produce a specific amount of sales.
6. **Customer defections:** The percentage of customers who switch to another brand or supplier.
7. **Customer expectations:** Consumer beliefs about the performance of a product based on prior experience and communications.
8. **Customer loyalty:** A measure of how often, when selecting from a product class, a customer purchases a particular brand.
9. **Customer satisfaction:** A customer's positive, neutral or negative feeling about the value received from an organization's product in specific use situations.
10. **Customer satisfaction measurement program:** An ongoing survey of customers (and competitors' customers) for the purpose of obtaining continuous estimates of satisfaction.
11. **Dynamic quality:** Quality that results from a change that makes an existing standard obsolete.
12. **ISO 9001:** An inclusive set of standards established by the International Standards Organization (ISO) to ensure that quality requirements are met.
13. **Customer Lifetime Value (CLV):** The amount of profit a company expects to obtain over the course of the relationship.
14. **Malcolm Baldrige National Quality Award:** A program designed to raise quality awareness and practice among U.S. businesses.
15. **Objective assessment of quality:** An evaluation of the degree to which a product does what it is supposed to do.
16. **Quality:** The degree of excellence of a company's products or services.
17. **Quality function deployment (QFD):** A process that builds customer wants and desires into the final product offering.
18. **Reduced cycle time:** A TQM activity that helps a company move more rapidly from product inception to final delivery of the product to the marketplace.
19. **Satisfaction ratings:** Ratings provided by testing agencies that compare purchase satisfaction with specified brands or with how well products perform.
20. **Service quality:** The expected and perceived quality of all of

the services an organization offers.

21. **Static quality:** Quality that results when individuals or organizations perfect an accepted practice.

22. **Statistical quality control:** The use of statistics to isolate and quantify production line problems that may cause product defects.

23. **Subjective assessment of quality:** The degree to which a product does what consumers would like it to do.

24. **Supply chain:** All the activities that organizations undertake to deliver value to the customer, such as working with suppliers, and distribution through convenient channels.

25. **Total quality management (TQM):** An organizational philosophy that helps companies produce goods and services that deliver value to satisfy customers.

REFERENCES

1. www.ritzcarlton.com, website visited June 18, 2014.
2. Spreng, Richard, American Marketing Association, Conference Proceedings, Chicago: 1999, Vol. 10, pg. 208.
3. www.sprint.com, website visited June 22, 2014.
4. JoAnna Brandi, "The Real Costs of Losing Customers," http://expertaccess.cincom.com, website visited February 9, 2012.
5. "Customer Care Goes End-to-End," Information Week, May 15, 2000, pp. 55-61.
6. Gupta, Sunil, Lehmann, Donald R., Stuart, Jennifer Ames, "Valuing Customers," Journal of Marketing Research, Vol. 41, Issue 1, February 2004.
7. Baig, Edward, "Sprint customers get a handwritten thank-you note," USA Today, August 7, 2012.
8. "We Interrupt This Issue to Remind You That the Internet Is Big," Wired, www.wired.com, website visited April 15, 2014.
9. "Unexpected Starbucks Apology Overflows Your Rewards Card With Delicious Credits,", www.consumerist.com, website visited June 18, 2014.
10. "Beyond Satisfaction," CMA Management, March 2000, pp. 14-15.
11. Carr, Clay, Front Customer Service (New York: John Wiley and Sons, 1990), p. 31.
12. "2014 Temkin Loyalty Ratings", www.customermanagementiq.com, website visited July 20, 2014.
13. Carr, Front Customer Service, p. 19.
14. "A Public Relations Disaster: How saving $1,200 cost United Airlines 10,772,839 negative views on YouTube," www.sentium.com, website visited June 29, 2014.
15. "Press Release." J.D. Power and Associates. www.jdpower.com, website visited March 15, 2014.
16. www.theacsi.org, website visited June 17, 2014.
17. "Judges Panel of the Malcolm Baldrige National Quality Award," Federal Register, July 21, 2000.
18. www.harley-davidson.com, website visited April 7, 2014.
19. "Apple and the Environment," www.apple.com/environment, website visited June 16, 2014.
20. "Company Information." Coach Leatherware, www.coach.com, website visited June 16, 2014.
21. "Rebuilding Hope & Homes," The Home Depot, http://corporate.homedepot.com, website visited June 16, 2014.
22. "Do Rewards Really Create Loyalty?" Harvard Business Review, May-June 1995, p. 75.
23. www.starwoodhotels.com, website visited June 7, 2014.
24. www.starbucks.com, website visited June 7, 2014.
25. "What Price Loyalty," Customer Relationship Management, March 2005, Vol. 9, Iss. 3, pg. 14.
26. www.jollibee.com.ph, website visited June 6, 2014.
27. www.exfinity.comcast.net, website visited June 10, 2014.
28. Bill Saporito, "Toyota's Flawed Focus on Quantity Over Quality," Time, www.time.com, February 4, 2010.
29. "Consumer Perceptions of Price, Quality and Value: A Means-End Model and Synthesis of Evidence," Journal of Marketing, July 1988, p. 2; Vandermerwe, Sandra, "How Increasing Value to Customers Improves Business Results," Sloan Management Review, Fall 2000, pp. 27-37.
30. Czinkote, Michael R., Kotabe, Masaki, Mercer, David, Marketing Management, 1997, pg. 273.
31. "ACSI Utilities, Consumer Shipping, and Health Care Report 2014," May 6, 2014, pg. 6.
32. www.cat.com, website visited April 7, 2014.
33. "FedEx Express Canada Achieves Contact Center Employer of Choice® Certification For Tenth Consecutive Year," FedEx, http://news.van.fedex.com, July 19, 2013.
34. Malcolm Baldrige National Quality Improvement Act of 1987, report of the Senate Committee on Commerce, Science and Technology on HR 812 (Washington, DC: US Government Printing Office, 1987).
35. Malcolm Baldrige National Quality Program, "Criteria for Performance Excellence," 2010, pg. 1.
36. www.ritzcarlton.com, website last visited April 24, 2014.
37. www.quality.nist.gov, website visited March 12, 2014.
38. Deloitte CIO Journal Editor, "Using Analytics to Detect Retail Fraud," The Wallstreet Journal, March 17, 2014.
39. Naumann, Earl, Customer Value Toolkit (Boise, ID: Thomson Executive Press, 1994.)
40. Lee, Thomas, "Constraint-Based Ontology Induction from Online Customer Reviews," Group Decision and Negotiation, Vol. 16, May 2007, pg. 255, www.springerlink.com, website visited March 12, 2014.

Chapter 08

SEGMENTATION, TARGETING & POSITIONING

Small businesses are big business for Dell Computer, a leading personal computer company in the United States. Michael Dell was a pre-med student when he started selling PCs and components from his dorm room at the University of Texas in 1984. He dropped out of college when monthly sales topped $80,000 and founded Dell Computer to sell PCs and related equipment to consumers and businesses via direct marketing. Today Dell has 110,000 global team members and is relying on its direct sales model through the Internet to ring up more than half of its $50 billion in annual sales. Dell sells in several technology arenas, including high-powered workstations, notebook computers, servers, data storage systems, enterprise solutions, networking, and software.

Michael Dell and his team have long understood that different kinds of customers have different computing requirements. For example, many families buy lower-priced PCs for daily household needs such as homework and entertainment, whereas corporations need more sophisticated workstations to complete more complicated tasks. Similarly, an entrepreneur with a simple website does not need the high-end server that a large hospital requires to power its sprawling internal and consumer sites with vast database of information. With these differing needs in mind, Dell's marketers use geographic, demographic and behavioristic variables to segment the consumer and organizational markets for computers and servers.

Using the geographic variable of national boundaries, Dell has segmented the world market and created product offerings for dozens of countries. Each geographic area has a tailored website, presented in the local language, which features hardware, software, services and online content specifically geared to that market's interests and requirements. In addition, Dell divides its overall market into consumer, business, government and institutional segments. The consumer segment consists of consumers who buy for personal and home-office use.

Responding to stiff competition from HP, Lenovo, and Apple, Dell was forced to depart from its strictly direct-to-customer sales approach and begin selling its computers at Walmart. Now, Dell partners with retailers to sell its products at many locations worldwide, including Best Buy and Staples. However, the late transition to retail brick-and-mortar sales left Dell on the back-side of selling to new lucrative technology arenas like MP3 players, flat-screen televisions, tablets and smartphones.

Positioned as a company with great supply chain efficiencies to sell established technologies at low prices, Dell was lacking the research and development to be a truly innovative company like its thriving competitors — who were selling to new and emerging segments. To combat declining PC sales and razor thin margins on technology outsourced by Dell, Michael Dell shifted gears to target the prized big-business segment — customers whose annual hardware purchases may total millions of dollars — with even more emphasis on customized enterprise solutions with servers, networking, software, and services.

Other segments targeted by Dell are the health-care industry, government agencies, education and e-commerce. Dell has forged alliances with a number of specialized suppliers to offer a well-rounded menu of goods and services to large hospitals for staff and administrative use. Within the government market, Dell targets federal government agencies (in the United States and other countries) separately from state and local government agencies. Within the education market, Dell targets K-to-12 schools separately from administrators, faculty and students of colleges and universities. Within the world of e-commerce, Dell targets Internet service providers separately from companies that need goods and services for web-based sales.[1]

<< **Dell Headquarters -- Round Rock, Texas**

Learning Objectives

1. Understand the advantages of target marketing and how it differs from mass marketing and product differentiation.
2. Describe how to do market segmentation and select target markets.
3. Explore three basic target marketing strategies: undifferentiated, differentiated and concentrated marketing.
4. Know how to do positioning and describe several approaches marketers use to create valuable, lasting images of their products.

THE CONCEPT OF SEGMENTATION AND POSITIONING

In General Motors' (GM) early days, the company philosophy was "a different auto for every need." At that time, each GM division focused its creative energies and economic might on satisfying loyal customers in separate market segments. They connected with customers by targeting clearly designated groups of buyers defined primarily by social class. After the auto bailout by the United States Government in 2009, General Motors had to examine its brands of vehicles and decided to cut its brands in half, from eight to four: Chevrolet, Buick, GMC and Cadillac. Pontiac, Saturn, Oldsmobile and Hummer were all dropped.

Despite the downsizing of the company, GM's initial strategy is still playing into the upward mobility of the American social class. A typical young family may be attracted to the affordability and reliability of a Chevy. Years later, the family may have saved and stabilized enough to purchase a somewhat more luxurious Buick. Finally, after financial success, they can obtain a symbol of prestige among automobiles: a Cadillac. America is no longer defined largely by social class, so although the relative costs of GM models still reflect, to some degree, the pricing hierarchy of previous years, their target markets are vastly different.

Why would strong companies such as Pepsico and Kraft develop so many brands? Among other products, Pepsico markets five restaurant chains under its brand Yum![2] That brand specifically targets consumers looking for fast-food dining, a much different market than those targeted for Pepsico's Quaker brand product line of wholesome breakfast foods. A **market segment** is a homogeneous group of customers with similar needs, wants, values and buying behavior. Each segment is an arena for competition. Both Pepsico and Kraft have a tradition of building marketing strategies around strong brands that match the uniqueness of diverse segments. There is certainly some overlapping competition among a company's own products, but this is down-played and minor compared to competition with other companies.

Through **segmentation**, the market can be divided into several groups of people with similar characteristics. These divisions are by no means equal, with segments varying widely in size and the amount of opportunity they present. Because it may be difficult to appeal successfully to each segment, companies select certain ones that they attempt to cater to and satisfy better than competitors, which is called **target marketing**. For example, Great Lakes Crossing, an outlet mall with many entertainment destinations, was opened in Auburn Hills, Michigan. The mall appeals to the entire family, with stores such as Bass Pro Shop's Outdoor World and Neiman Marcus LAST Call. In addition to the shopping, the mall has family-oriented entertainment options including a movie theater, a carousel and Jeepers, an indoor amusement park and restaurant. It is targeting value-conscious families who want to make

Market Segment

A homogeneous group with similar needs, wants, values, and buying behavior.

Segmentation

Division of a market into homogeneous groups with similar needs, wants, values, and buying behavior.

Target Marketing

The selection of specific homogeneous groups (segments) of potential customers for emphasis.

shopping an experience enjoyed by all members.[3]

Positioning is the creation of an image, reputation or perception in the minds of consumers about the organization or its products relative to competition. Great Lakes Crossing has positioned itself as a one-stop destination with "something for everyone." The company appeals to customers in the target segments by adjusting products, prices, promotional campaigns, services, and distribution channels in a way consistent with its positioning strategy. Great Lakes Crossing has identified a segment of value-conscious families and positioned itself as a dominant retail outlet and entertainment destination, attracting customers from throughout the Midwest and Canada. This provides an advantage over competitors that offer only one of the many options available.

Segmentation, targeting and positioning give organizations the means to connect with customers by identifying and understanding their characteristics, by focusing resources to meet their needs and wants, and by establishing how customers will view the organization. Let us say a company simply compiles data on consumers, averages them, and tries to develop one brand that appeals to the average consumer. In the U.S. marketplace alone, there are over 318 million people.[4] You can find the average for certain demographic characteristics — age, gender, income, location, and so forth — but what about ethnic origin, home life or taste in music, clothing and food? The "average" American represents few, if any, real people. Efforts to connect with this mythical average consumer probably wouldn't have appeal for many customers, making an "average" in this sense rather useless to marketers. Instead, they use segmentation, targeting and positioning to define unique consumer groups, select those they wish to serve, and then integrate the marketing mix to establish a unified image of the product relative to the competition.

To be a leader, companies know that they must connect with customers by identifying, selecting and relating to them in innovative ways. That's why it is crucial to apply the above concepts in sequence, as shown in Figure 8.1. The activities a leading company would require to accomplish each stage are described in the sections that follow. Under market segmentation, we include descriptions of mass marketing and product differentiation as general marketing approaches that are contrasted with the more preferred segmentation methods. We also introduce several ways to identify diverse market segments. The section on target marketing describes how to select targets and focus resources where they will accomplish the most. The last section looks at positioning. It also describes how to reposition when things change.

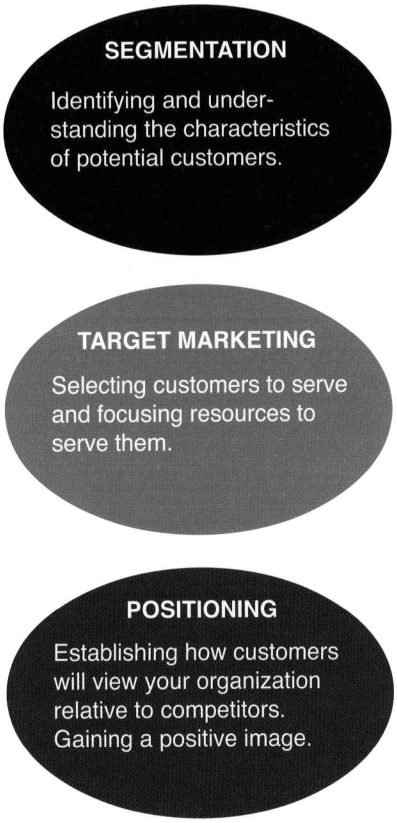

Positioning

Creating an image or perception in the minds of consumers about the organization or its products relative to the competition.

SEGMENTATION

Identifying and understanding the characteristics of potential customers.

TARGET MARKETING

Selecting customers to serve and focusing resources to serve them.

POSITIONING

Establishing how customers will view your organization relative to competitors. Gaining a positive image.

Figure 8.1   Connecting With Customers by Identifying, Selecting and Relating to Them

MARKET SEGMENTATION

Most modern leading-edge companies are very conscious about targeting specific market segments. Competitors can leave themselves vulnerable when their products or services lump together groups of customers with different needs or wants. Identifying key segments offers unique opportunities for marketing based on meeting specific customers' needs more precisely.[5] Historically, there has been a movement from mass marketing to product differentiation to market segmentation, targeting and positioning. In the following sections, you'll explore how these approaches differ.

SEGMENTATION VERSUS MASS MARKETING

We know from Chapter 1 that many companies once pursued mass marketing, which is the mass distribution and mass promotion of the product to all potential customers. The objective of mass marketing is to reach as many people as possible with the same marketing approach. Coca-Cola, introduced in 1886, pioneered this strategy and was successful in reaching most consumers with the same product formula, price, promotion and place (distribution) strategy.

Although mass marketing was useful decades ago, competition that appeals to consumer diversity prevents this from being a viable strategy for most organizations to use today. Segmentation is a much more effective way to market. Today, Coca-Cola's success depends on recognizing the tremendous diversity of the market. In an effort to expand its presence in the water and energy drink markets, Coke acquired Glaceau, maker of the popular Vitaminwater and Vitaminenergy, in a deal at the time valued at more than $4 billion.[6] The company also owns popular beverage options such as Illy Issimo coffee brand, which is a much different market segment.[7]

While tools are constantly being developed that can reach the mass markets, these tools must be used carefully to get the greatest benefit. For instance, there are more wireless subscribers in the United States than actual people residing there. In 2013, global mobile ad spending increased 105 percent to total $17.96 billion. In 2014, mobile spending is on pace to rise another 75.1 percent to $31.45 billion, accounting for nearly one-quarter of total digital ad spending worldwide.[8] Many consumers have already turned to their mobile devices as a primary way of web browsing, shopping and reading books. With a large consumer group invested in mobile devices, there is certainly an opportunity for mass marketing. However, what makes it interesting is that this group of wireless consumers contains unique qualities, many of which are not shared among every other member. These qualities can be organized into specific segments that can be addressed with varying approaches.

Be sure not to confuse mass marketing, discussed in Chapter 1, with mass customization. As will be explained later in this chapter, mass customization is actually a form of target marketing that takes advantage of technology and resources to provide customers unique services.

www.cocacolacompany.com

Coca-Cola is striving to create reusable packaging. Coke's sustainable packing strategy focuses on package design, community recycling programs and package material reuse. Check out its website to further explore each of these key areas.

SEGMENTATION VERSUS PRODUCT DIFFERENTIATION

Product Differentiation

A marketing strategy with which companies attempt to make their products appear unique relative to the competition.

Eventually, companies realized that mass marketing didn't provide enough variety and they began to follow a product differentiation strategy. **Product differentiation** makes a product appear unique relative to others, whether produced by the same company or the competition. This uniqueness is then used as a major factor in appealing to customers. The belief is that by offering choices, the company will attract more of the mass market. Notice that product differentiation implies recognition that consumers may want variety. But unlike market segmentation, the leading dynamic is a difference in the product, not in buyer characteristics. The pain-reliever market is dominated by product differentiation. Aspirin comes in plain formula or with caffeine, buffered or not, with or without sleep aids, with or without a cold remedy, and in standard or extra strength. You can also find it in caplet, liquid, tablet, chewing gum or capsule form, coated or noncoated, flavored or not. The objective is to offer an aspirin for every preference imaginable. This might go unnoticed by consumers, if companies didn't call attention to it through advertising.

It is important to keep the distinction between product differences and market segments in mind. Market segments are made up of people and organizations, not defined by product names. Consequently, market segments are described according to their distinguishing characteristics, not according to the products they buy. Misunderstanding this distinction is a common and often deadly flaw for the marketing strategist. For example, a marketing consultant once asked the chief engineer of an air-conditioning manufacturer to describe the company's target segments. The engineer responded with product categories: heavy, medium and light-duty units. When asked questions about the characteristics of current and potential buyers, the engineer had little knowledge. The consultant knew immediately that this client did not fully understand market segmentation, a key reason customers were buying fewer of the engineer's new products. When executives equate product categories with market segments, they tend to focus attention on what they want to make, which may not meet customer requirements. The result is often products that please the people who make them but disappoint customers.

SEGMENTATION VARIABLES

The market as a whole is **heterogeneous,** meaning it has many types of buyers. Market segmentation divides the total market into **homogeneous** subgroups or clusters with similar characteristics, which can then be studied individually. Without a well-focused picture of the market, it's virtually impossible to create a powerful marketing strategy. Essentially, segmentation allows marketers to focus on relevant aspects of potential buyers. It's a critical step in connecting with customers.

How is segmentation done? First, the marketer must select a way to categorize potential customers into subgroups. A **segmentation variable** is any descriptive characteristic that helps separate all potential purchasers into groups. Examples include gender, age and income. Variables are then subdivided into categories. For example, within the gender variable, the two categories are male and female. Categories may be very broadly or very narrowly defined. Income can be classified generally as low, moderate and high, or more specifically as, for example, up to $10,000, $10,001 to $30,000, $30,001 to $50,000, $50,001 to $70,000, and above $70,000.

Think about how colleges segment students for recruiting and admissions. Like companies, they do this to gain a better understanding of potential customers. At the most basic level, the segmentation variables are grade-point average in high school, SAT or ACT scores, and high school class rank. These variables can be subdivided into categories, as shown in Figure 8.2. The categories then can be grouped together in various ways to form several market segments, which often are named descriptively. For example, the market segment in the third categories column of Figure 8.2 might be called the "cream of the crop." Or students with above-average SAT/ACT scores but in the bottom of their class and with a low GPA might be the "underachiever" market segment.

Most colleges add other variables, and these can dramatically change the segmentation structure. For example, what seems to be a fairly uniform market turns out to be a lot of segments. From our example in Figure 8.2, 27 market segments emerge (three GPA catego-

Heterogeneous Group

Buyers with diverse characteristics.

Homogeneous Group

Buyers with similar characteristics.

Segmentation Variable

Any distinguished market factor that can vary, such as gender, age or income.

Variable	Categories		
High School GPA	Below 2.0	2.0–3.5	3.6–4.0
SAT/ACT Score	Below average	Average	Above average
High School Class Rank	Lowest 25%	Middle 50%	Top 25%

Figure 8.2 Segmenting the College Market

ries, three SAT/ACT categories, three class rank categories). Adding just two residence categories (in and out of state) would produce 54 segments.

Variables need to be chosen with care, because each segment must meet certain criteria in order to be useful to a marketer. Figure 8.3 outlines guidelines for effective market segmentation. Segmentation typically is based on geographic, demographic, diversity, psychographic and behavioristic factors as well as benefits sought. Figure 8.4 lists the variables and categories commonly used to segment consumer markets. Additional variables and categories that are primarily useful to segment business markets are provided in Chapter 6 on B2B marketing.

Effective Market Segmentation

→ Members should have similar needs, wants, and preferences, because these are what marketers want to understand and influence.

→ Members should have similar information-gathering and media usage patterns, because these allow marketers to communicate with the segment.

→ Members should have similar shopping and buying patterns, because marketers then can find efficient places to sell and service their products.

→ The number of members should be large, because marketers need to generate a profit.

→ Data about the segments should be available, because marketers need to know about customers in order to build marketing strategies.

Figure 8.3 Effective Market Segmentation

Geographic Segmentation
One of the most common ways to analyze a market is by geography. Geography can reveal interesting facts, such as this disparity between the size of men's suits. In New York, the most typical size is 42 regular; in Paris, 40 regular; in San Francisco, 38 regular; and in Chicago, a strapping 44 long.[9]

Global companies often segment their markets by city. Coke knows that soft-drink consumption relates to population size. With the exception of New York City and Los Angeles, all metropolitan areas of more than 10 million are located outside the United States, which is a simple reason for Coke to market globally. A city's population size alone doesn't always provide enough segmentation information, so marketers consider other factors. Some metropolitan areas are known for their industry expertise: In Hollywood, it's movies; in Silicon Valley, computer software; and in Philadelphia, pharmaceuticals. Auto components suppliers, such as Bosch and Eaton Corporation, know that virtually all major buying decisions by auto manufactures are made in fewer than 20 cities located in a handful of countries. A presence in Stuttgart, Detroit, Los Angeles, Wiesbaden, Paris, Osaka and Seoul gives the supplier substantial global coverage.

Computer techniques allow researchers to cluster consumers in groups based on numerous variables. Using a small number of variables to explain consumer purchases in product categories, organizations develop site strategies for grocery stores, drugstores, department stores, big-box retailers and apparel companies. An understanding of segments in regions is used to adjust merchandising and identify local challenges to customize product offerings.[10]

ZIP Code Segmentation

Division of a market into specific geographic locations based on the demographic makeup of the ZIP code area.

ZIP code segmentation divides the market according to the demographic makeup of the ZIP code area. Nielsen Claritas is a leader in the use of ZIP codes for consumer segmentation. It uses many customer characteristics to describe geographic locations even deep within ZIP codes in more specific neighborhoods and in some cases to individual households. As the population shifts, Nielsen Claritas and other similar firms adjust their data and the descriptive names they give to specific segments. For example, the most important city residents no longer are the older, mostly white "Urban Gold Coast" people in neighborhoods like Chicago's Lakeshore Drive and Boston's Beacon Hill. Instead, young, tech-savvy, highly educated singles and couples are driving the vitality of cities and live in places like sections of Chicago's Lincoln Park. These young professionals read less printed newspapers and magazines in favor or online content, so they are no longer called the "Young Literati." Now, they're called the "Young Digerati." According to Claritas, the three most affluent population segments are suburban homeowners: couples age 45 and older ("Upper Crust"), middle-age executives with children ("Blue Blood Estates") and middle-age couples, often entrepreneurs ("Movers and Shakers"). Claritas can tell you specifically which geographies, by ZIP codes, contain each market segment.[11] With ZIP code and geographic segmentation at their disposal, marketers for virtually any product can discover a segment to focus efforts on.

For even more specific segmentation, similar methods can be used to identify customers by city block based on street addresses. The LEXIS®-NEXIS® electronic database now provides a service called REZIDE, which segments customers by any variable the user requests (zip code, area code, city, and so forth) and supplies the information.

Demographic Segmentation Characteristics such

	Variable	Examples of Categories
Geographic	World region	Pacific Rim, Europe, North America
	Economic stage	Advanced, developing, subsistence
	Nation	U.S., England, Japan, Mexico
	City	Tokyo, Paris, Mexico City
	City size and density	Large and dense, small and spread out, suburban, rural
	Region	New England, Mid-Atlantic, South Atlantic, East South Central, Midwest, Mountain Pacific
	Climate	Northern Equator, Southern Equator
	Zip Code	10001, 10002, etc.
Demographic	Gender	Female, male
	Age	1–5, 6–11, 12–19, 20–34, 35–49, 50–64, 65–72, 721
	Income	Poverty, up to $15,000, up to $20,000, up to $30,0000, up to $50,000, up to $100,000, $100,0001
	Family size	1, 2, 3, 4, 5, 6
	Family life cycle	Young single, young married no children, young married with children (under 6), young married with children (over 6), older married full nest, older married empty nest, retired, middle-aged, single, divorced, sole survivor
	Occupation	Unemployed, homemaker, student, retired, clerical, blue collar, white collar, professional, proprietor
	Education	Grade school (or less), some high school, high school graduate, some college, college graduate, postgraduate degree
Diversity	Religion	Protestant, Catholic, Jewish, Muslim
	Race	Anglo, African, Asian, Hispanic, Native American
	Social class	Lower-lower, upper-lower, lower-middle (working class),middle, upper-middle, lower-upper, upper-upper
Psychographic	Lifestyle	Actualizer, Fulfilled, Achiever, Experiencer, Believer, Striver, Maker, Struggler
	Personality	Compliant, aggressive, detached, sensory, intuitive, thinking, feeling
Behavioristic	Readiness	Unaware, aware, interested, knowledgeable, desirous, intend to buy, trial
	Ability and experience	None, novice, expert, professional, nonuser, first-time user, regular user, former user
	Loyalty	Switcher, moderate, high
	Media and shopping habits	Magazine subscriber, cable user, mall, convenience stores
	Usage	Daily, weekly, monthly
	Rates	Heavy, medium, light
Benefit Sought	Delivery	Convenience, speed, flexibility
	Service	No questions asked, returns
	Price	Low, medium, high

Figure 8.4   Ways to Segment Consumer Markets
Source: Adapted from Philip Kotler, Marketing Management: Analysis, Planning, Implementation, and Control, 12th ed. ©2007. Adapted by permission of Prentice Hall, Inc., Upper Saddle River, NJ.

Demographic Segmentation

Division of the market according to such characteristics as gender, family life cycle, household type, and income.

as gender, family life cycle, household type and income are used in **demographic segmentation**. Demographics are very useful in categorizing different tastes and preferences, so this information is readily available. An added benefit is that it's relatively easy to project the composition and size of demographic segments for the next five, 10 or even 15 years. Consequently, this kind of segmentation is an excellent tool for long-range strategic planning as well as short-term marketing.

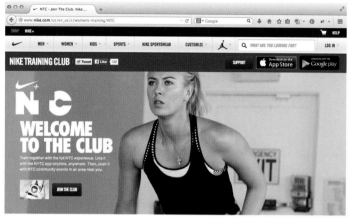

NikeWomen.com uses gender segmentation to market products geared toward female athletes.

Segmentation by Gender Men and women have different buying behaviors. Marketers need to be able to adapt their techniques in order to reach one particular gender. Nike does just that with Nike-Women.com, a website especially geared toward female athletes. Shoppers can sort by product category, sport, or featured articles such as bra and pant guides, seasonal style guides, news releases, and the Nike Training Club, where members benefit from an even more personal experience.[12] By focusing on the specific values and lifestyles that women have, marketers can more effectively reach an entire gender of the population. Even the auto industry has a long history of targeting women. A 1907 ad for a Franklin automobile showed women in long skirts behind the wheel and the caption, "Notice how much room there is to get in or out of the driver's side." In 1930, Chrysler research found women to be a "potent factor" in 75 percent of new car purchases, and themes focusing on them were credited with raising company sales by 33 percent. By 1948, all major automakers were advertising in Women's Home Companion, the No. 1 magazine targeted at women. The issue has never been whether to segment by gender — only how to address women. Chrysler formed a Women's Advisory Committee composed of 30 women from disciplines such as finance, manufacturing and marketing. The company pioneered driver's-side sliding doors and integrated child seats on its minivans.

Men also make unique purchases. Traditional products include sports tickets, hunting and fishing equipment, and auto supplies. Sometimes men buy products traditionally sold to women. Market researcher Marketwire expects the men's grooming market to reach $84 billion worldwide by 2014. A survey conducted by WSL Research showed that among men ages 18-55, 55 percent stated that they currently buy some skin-care products, and 16 percent said they were spending more than they did the preceding year.[13] The growth in these markets is attributed to a redefinition of masculinity and men's concern for their appearance.

Segmentation by Family Life Cycle Families pass through stages, from young single adults, to marriage, to childbearing, to later life. The next chapter describes the specific categories in depth, but for now, it is important to note that these family stages are excellent segmentation categories. Several of the wireless service providers market packages of multiple cellphones to families, particularly parents with teenagers. Being able to stay in touch with their children and knowing where they are is comforting to parents. But cellphones are used for much more than keeping in touch with parents. According to a study by Context, a company that uses anthropologists to study consumer trends, cellphones and smartphones have become a primary mode of socializing for teens. "Next time a teenager says, 'Mom, if I don't have a phone,' or 'Dad, if I don't have a phone, I'm going to be a nobody,' they are being serious," said Robbie Blinkoff, Context's principal anthropologist.[14]

Organic food manufacturers are also seeing the importance of targeting health-conscious parents by offering "fun" healthy meals for children. These companies target parents of babies, in hopes of keeping them as the children mature. Marketers like the Hain Celestial Group, of Melville, N.Y., hope that parents who start their infants on Earth's Best baby food will stick with Hain brands through the childhood years, including Arthur cookies and Earth's Best whole-grain bars. Gerber, based in Freemont, Michigan, recently added "first foods" in single flavors and "third foods" in toddler textures to its organic Tender Harvest line. Both Tender Harvest and Earth's Best are free of genetically modified ingredients. Fran's Healthy Helpings, of Burlingame, Calif., positions its Dino Chicken Chompers and Twinkle Star Fish in the gap between healthy products that kids deem disgusting and kid-oriented products full of additives, fat and sodium.[15] By directing attention specifically to families, these companies have gained leadership in this important segment.

Segmentation by Age Age cohorts are people of similar age and life experience. Heroes, music and even economic times are somewhat unique for each generation. Tastes, preferences, and product choices reflect those differences. Other generational similarities include physical capacity and earning power. You've probably heard of baby boomers and baby busters.

Recently, the baby boomers, the largest generation, are nearing 70 years old. Some notable baby boomers include Elton John, Bill Gates and former Presidents George W. Bush and Bill Clinton. There are currently about 76 million baby boomers, and approximately 61 million will still be living in 2029.[16] The precise year the baby boom began is debatable, but is generally estimated to be about 1946, when World War II had ended and an era of postwar prosperity arrived, through 1964. Population grew at an increasing rate, creating a large number of consumers with increasing incomes and standards of living.[17]

People with higher spending power, born before World War II, are sometimes called WOOFS (Well-Off Older Folks). This age cohort is often the target of major marketers. JCPenney has a clothing line called Easy Dressing, which uses Velcro fasteners instead of buttons and zippers. Barnes & Noble carries large-print paperbacks, and travel agencies market special trips for the elderly.

Bill Gates, born in 1955, is a prominent business person in the Baby Boomers generation.

As for Gen X, the baby busters, their purchasing power will peak around the time the boomers retire. A survey of 3,000 U.S. citizens has indicated that Generation X has saved more for retirement than previous generations. Part of this could be attributed to their lack of confidence in the social security system. In 1979, when the oldest Gen Xers were teenagers, 62 percent of workers relied on the traditional pension. Today, 63 percent of workers find themselves covered only by voluntary 401(k) plans.[18] Social security payments that baby boomers have made over the years have gone to pay benefits to current social security recipients, so little of what the boomers actually paid will remain when they retire. That issue is spurring efforts to change the social security system in the United States. Generation Xers have a lower net worth at the same stage in life than their parents had at the same age. Because of income limitations, this generation stays home more and spends less.[19] As the boomers retire, there is concern that the more frugal busters will consume less and will be burdened by the need to support the aging boomers, who will require retirement subsidies and help with health care.

Lady Gaga, born in 1986, is a prominent singer in Generation Y.

Generation Y, sometimes referred to as Millennials, are younger, smart, and sometimes viewed as brash but are largely becoming more accepted as older generations adopt many of their habits. They often come to work wearing flip-flops and listen to music at their desks. Members of this generation include Britney Spears, Shaun White, Lady Gaga and perhaps even you. Research suggests that Generation Y people get involved in social and civic issues, such as education, poverty and the environment. Thanks to their heavy connectivity through the Internet, this group is very aware of global issues.

Members of Generation Y likely grew up fairly affluent or witnessed affluence on televisions and in the movies. They are aware of huge incomes of athletes, some executives and coaches. Perhaps the biggest difference with this generation is that it grew up with technology and feels very comfortable around it. Consequently, marketers were able to connect with this segment through the web and social media for the first time.

With a population estimated at roughly 72 million, Generation Y is the most educated, diverse, tech-proficient, and largest generation.[20] Marketers have recognized the importance of targeting this savvy group of consumers, a segment that was largely ignored in the past. However, as some Gen Yers reach their mid-30s and increase their spending, the pressure is on for marketers to figure out how to capture this generation's attention due to their general distrust of traditional advertising. [21]

Generation Z represents the most multicultural age group to date and is growing at alarming rates. It is the first group to be born with complete technology: PCs, mobile phones, games, MP3 players and the Internet. This generation is very creative, highly collaborative and extremely adept at multi-tasking. They are more likely to live at home, rely on financial assistance from their parents, and trust their friends' opinions before believing traditional marketing methods. With a significant amount of income at their discretion, this group displays financial sophistication and is a prime target for marketers. This generation believes it is extremely important to invest in their future, with 84 percent of young adults striving to achieve at least $1 million in retirement before they stop working.[22]

Age is a useful segmentation variable for high-technology services. As you would expect, most Internet users have high levels of income and education. Women outnumber men online, and their habits vary by age. Women ages 24 to 35 spend most of their time on sites that provide information and advice, whereas girls ages 2 to 11 visit television and learning websites most often. The growth rate of the female population online has outpaced the overall online growth rate. All categories except females ages 18 to 24 saw a significant increase in their numbers online. Because of this shift in online usage, sites must start to target women, keeping in mind the age-specific differences in their use of the Internet. Comscore, Nielsen, MediaMetrix and Quantcast studies indicate that women are the driving force of social web, a trend marketers can't ignore. In e-commerce, female purchasing power is clear — Groupon reports 77 percent of its customers are women.[23]

Segmentation Based on Diversity

Some people hesitate to segment markets based on ethnic heritage, race or religious factors, but the world's tremendous diversity cannot be ignored. Marketers know that the character of many markets is dramatically influenced by these factors. What marketers need to consider is that a given ethnic group is heterogeneous.

African Americans, Hispanics and Asian Americans account for much of the current population growth in the United States. Within 25 years, each group will be approximately the same size — about 42 million people. Compared to the general population, African Americans will grow at about twice the overall rate, Hispanics at 4.5 times the rate, and Asians at more than eight times the rate. Whites will increase at about 60 percent the rate of other groups.[24] Many people will maintain their high ethnicity by living among and associating within these groups. High ethnicity results in attractive market segments.

CAREER TIP!

Interested in a career with PepsiCo? Visit the Pepsi website and learn more about the opportunities available in different geographic locations within the Frito-Lay North America, Pepsi Bottling Group, PepsiCo Corporate, Pepsi-Cola North America or Tropicana North America companies. You can perform a search of the job database and apply online.

Minorities represent approximately one-third of the U.S. population, and the Bureau of the Census estimates that figure will rise to nearly 64 percent by 2020.[25] Minorities are now a majority in one of every six U.S. cities. Most immigrants settle in urban areas along with people from their home country. This produces concentrations of new ethnic populations, as the examples in Figure 8.5 show.[26]

City	Origin
Atlanta	Vietnam, South Korea
Baltimore	South Korea
Chicago	Mexico, Philippines, South Korea
Denver	Mexico, Vietnam
Dallas	Mexico, Vietnam, India
Jersey City	Cuba
Los Angeles	Mexico
Miami	Cuba
Minneapolis/St. Paul	Laotians
New York City	all immigrants
Seattle	Philippines, Vietnam, South Korea

Figure 8.5 New Ethnic Populations in Selected Cities

Currently, the U.S. Hispanic market consists of approximately 50 million individuals, making up 16.7 percent of the U.S. population. With a 3.3 percent increase per year, it is also the fastest growing market. The second-largest group is blacks (40 million) followed by Asians (15 million), American Indians and Alaska natives (4 million) and Hawaiians/Pacific Islanders (1 million).[27] Total spending power of Hispanics is a considerable $670 billion, a number that is growing at twice the annual rate of non-Hispanics. Kellogg Co., the nation's most dominate cereal maker, recently boosted its marketing to Hispanics by 60 percent. Tony the Tiger's well-known shout, "They're g-r-r-reat!" has been changed to "G-r-r-riquisimos!" in Spanish language promotions.[28]

De-ethnicization occurs when a product heavily associated with one ethnic group is targeted at other segments. Products such as salsa and spring rolls have become favorites of many people other than those of Mexican or Chinese heritage. Kikkoman soy sauce was originally marketed to Chinese groceries and restaurants, but now that ethnic foods have become more mainstream, Kikkoman products are sold in grocery chains to consumers from many different backgrounds.

De-ethnicization

The result of targeting a product heavily associated with one ethnic group to other segments.

Psychographic and Lifestyle Segmentation Psychographic and lifestyle

segmentation links geographic and demographic descriptors with a consumer's behavioral and psychological decisions. Psychographic variables used alone are often not very helpful to marketers; however, they can be quite powerful when joined with demographic, geographic and other data. Lifestyle is a person's distinctive mode of living. It describes how an individual spends his or her time and money and what aspects of life he/she considers important. The choice of products, patterns of usage, and the amount of enjoyment a person gains from being a consumer are all part of lifestyle. Consider the difference between people who are physically fit from exercise and proper nutrition and those who are out of shape from high-fat diets, smoking and sedentary living. Messages such as "Just do it!" or "No pain, no gain" are received very differently by these two groups. Of course, since there are so many lifestyles, the trick is to identify them in the context of your company's marketing strategy.

Psychographics are marketing approaches and tools used to identify lifestyles based on measures of consumer values, activities, interests, opinions, demographics and other factors. Classifying lifestyles emerged from a Roper/Starch Worldwide survey of about 2,000 Americans for insights into views about money. Seven distinct profiles were discerned: hunter, gatherer, protector, splurger, striver, nester and idealist. The hunter takes risks to get ahead and equates money with happiness. The gatherer is better safe than sorry, a conservative investor. The protector puts others first and uses money to protect loved ones. The splurger is self-indulgent. The striver believes that money makes the world go around and equates it with power. The nester isn't very interested in money except to take care of immediate need. The idealist believes there is more to life than money; material things aren't all that important.[29]

There are many ways to define lifestyles using psychographics, so marketers must use a combination of research and creativity to develop useful segments. The best psychographic segmentation approaches are based on accepted consumer psychology and sound research methods. One of the most popular systems is SRI Consulting Business Intelligence's (SRIC-BI's) VALS™ systems. This second version of earlier research divides consumers into groups that think and act differently. VALS research found three major categories of consumers, each with a different primary motivation. Ideals-motivated consumers follow their own beliefs; achievement-motivated consumers are influenced by others; and self-expression-motivated consumers seek variety, action and risk-taking. In addition, VALS considers a consumer's resources, which are education, age, income, energy, self-confidence, eagerness to buy and health. Figure 8.6 illustrates the VALS segmentation system, and Figure 8.7 provides summary descriptions of the segments. The VALS battery of attitude items is used in survey research to discover the product choices, media preferences and leisure activities of each of the VALS consumer groups. Marketers, advertisers, media planners and new-product designers use VALS to discover who is naturally

Psychographics

Marketing approaches and tools used to identify lifestyles based on measures of consumers' values, activities, interests, opinions, demographics, and other factors.

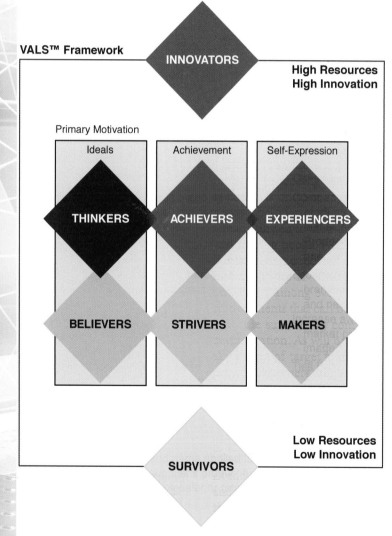

Figure 8.6   The VALS™ Segmentation System
Source: Printed with permission from SRI Consulting Business Intelligence (SRIC-BI), Menlo Park, California.

VALS™ Segment	Primary Motivation	Description	Portion of U.S. Adult Population
Innovator	Can express all three	High self-esteem, sophisticated, open to new ideas	10%
Thinker	Ideals	Information-seeking, reflective	13%
Believer	Ideals	Traditional, respect authority, risk-averse	16%
Achiever	Achievement	Goal-oriented, focus on career and family	13%
Striver	Achievement	Trendy, low self-esteem, resource constrained	11%
Experiencer	Self-expression	Stimulation-seeking, highly social	13%
Maker	Self-expression	Self sufficient in a hands on way, practical	12%
Survivor	No particular	Not active consumers, quiet, older	12%

Figure 8.7 Brief Descriptions of the U.S. VALS Groups
Source: SRI Consulting Business Intelligence (SRIC-BI); www.sric-bi.com/VALS

attracted to their product or service and then to design communication strategies, advertising and distribution plans that will be attractive to their particular consumer target. VALS refreshes its product media database twice a year. GeoVALS™ estimates the percentage of each VALS group living in each U.S. residential ZIP code. VALS systems have also been developed for Japan and the United Kingdom.

You can obtain your VALS profile at www.strategicbusinessinsights.com. If you answer the questions on the VALS questionnaire, you can find out whether you are an Innovator, Thinker, Believer, Achiever, Striver, Experiencer, Maker or a Survivor. Additionally, you can explore the types of media, products and services your profile prefers. This is just an example of how psychographic segmentation helps companies connect with customers.

Using sophisticated computer technology, GeoVALS allows marketers to profile a city, metropolitan area and ZIP code.[30] It has been adjusted for use in other countries. The Japanese version shows categories of buyers according to product adoption as well as the VALS two categories.[31]

Behavioristic Segmentation
Behavioristic segmentation groups consumers based on people's awareness, product and media uses, and actions. Past behavior is one of the best predictors of future behavior, so these variables require an understanding of what consumers have previously done. The variables include purchase volume, purchase readiness, ability and experience, loyalty, media habits and shopping behaviors.

Segmentation by Usage Rates
You have probably heard about the 80-20 rule: 20 percent of buyers purchase 80 percent of the volume of any product. It is amazing how true this is for many products. Heavy users can be extremely important to companies. Consequently, most marketers divide the market into heavy, moderate and light users, and then they look for characteristics that may explain why some people consume vastly greater amounts. It usually costs no more to reach heavy users than light users. Therefore, the marketing costs are lower per unit of sales.

Still, marketing strategists need to realize that competition for heavy users can be extreme. If medium or light users are being ignored, they may provide a marketing opportunity. Giants such as PepsiCo are always targeting the college crowd. For instance, the company created a campus campaign for its popular brand Mountain Dew. The "Dew Crew" was composed of campus representatives from major universities that held events and samplings and spread positive buzz about the brand on college campuses.[32] Royal Crown Cola avoids this segment altogether because of the stiff competition. Instead, it concentrates on older adults, who tend to be lighter users of cola.

Segmentation by Readiness For many products, potential users go through a series of stages that describe their readiness to purchase. These stretch all the way from being unaware of a product to those who are trying a product, leading up to brand loyalty. Readiness is a useful segmentation variable particularly for newer products. This scheme is often used in adjusting the communications mix.

Segmentation by Ability and Experience The performance of products is determined by the ability or experience of its user. Consequently, ability is an excellent segmentation variable for almost any skill-based product. For example, the marketing of skis, tennis racquets, golf clubs and most other sports equipment is often targeted to ability segments. As performance requirements increase, new technologies release products with higher performance capabilities that generally require more skill. Organizations selling sports equipment and apparel might consider targets in a range of skill levels from non-athlete to professional.

Many times organizations use product differentiation to satisfy the needs of customers with different abilities or experience. Bridgestone Golf produces a range of golf balls that can have an immediate impact on the performance of a golfer. Bridgestone's e5 model is engineered for moderate swing speeds, and its dimple technology helps combat hooks and slices common to amateurs. The e7 model provides a penetrating ball flight and unparalleled distance for golfers with higher swing speeds and more control of side spin.[33]

Segmentation by Loyalty As we have discussed, a key goal of firms is to create brand loyalty. Some consumers are naturally loyal to particular product categories. There are many ways to look at loyalty, but the most popular one segments consumers into three categories: switchers, moderately loyal and highly loyal. Switchers may select a separate brand with nearly every purchase. They may actually seek variety or they simply don't care which brand they buy. Moderately loyal customers have a preference for a brand but will switch if it is convenient to do so. Highly loyal buyers have strong preferences. Some buyers are not loyal to a single brand but will accept two or three brands of the same type. This type of segmentation may include more than the three categories described.

Segmentation by Media and Shopping Habits A broad range of media and shopping habits can also be used to categorize shoppers. For example, some people subscribe to cable, others don't; some prefer shopping in malls, others online; and so forth. These variables focus on the accessibility of target customers. Those who shop only in mall settings are accessed differently from those who prefer catalog or online shopping at home. Shopping habits in the United States changed dramatically with the advent of e-commerce. For example, the average shopper will go from spending two hours shopping online to spending closer to five hours online in the near future.[34] Online shopping will continue to increase as consumers become accustomed to larger selections, lower prices and the convenience of shopping from home. Another popular shopping habit marketers target is the likeliness of purchasing eco-friendly products. For example, Dell uses the "plant a tree for me" slogan to attract green-minded consumers to its products. This allows customers to make a donation while purchasing products. Dell will then plant a tree to offset CO_2 emissions.[35] A survey featured in the International Journal of Consumer Studies states that older consumers are more apt to take environmental issues seriously and hence be more skeptical of the contents of any green labeling.[36]

Segmentation by Benefit
Benefit segmentation divides the market into homogeneous groups based on the attributes consumers seek from a particular product class. Russell Haley popularized this method in the 1960s by dividing the toothpaste

market into segments based on whether the consumer wanted flavor, brightness of teeth, dental health or low price. A benefit segmentation of auto buyers might group them according to the importance they place on economy, performance, styling or reliability. When a lot is known about the attitudes and perceptions of buyers, it is possible to develop a benefit profile of what product attributes are considered most important. This can be a useful step in segmentation, because customers in a benefit segment are likely to have other identifiable characteristics. For example, people who desire convenience are likely to be members of a dual-career family or single-parent household.

When only benefits are addressed, this technique is not always consistent with good segmentation procedures. Because the benefits are often described according to product characteristics, we learn very little about the buyers themselves. For example, you could say that Apple addressed the user-friendly computer benefit segment. Then again, you could say that Apple products are user-friendly. A good rule of thumb is that segments should not be defined solely by product characteristics. In fact, when benefit segmentation is based on product attributes, it may be confused with product positioning, which will be discussed later in this chapter.

Nevertheless, benefit segmentation can be useful when it leads to descriptions of the consumers who prefer each benefit. In order to create these descriptions, researchers generally start with benefit segments and then use the other segmentation schemes to define each group. This way, the focus is ultimately on buyers, not products.

BUSINESS MARKET SEGMENTATION

Although the business market is segmented using procedures much like those used to segment the consumer market, its distinctive characteristics are used to categorize business consumers along different dimensions — by company demographics, geographic scope, buying approach, and product/technology — as outlined in Figure 8.8.

Basis	Example
Company Demographics	
Industry	food, mining, automotive, computer
Company size	large, medium, small
Financial stability and profitability	strong, medium, weak
Channel	distributor, OEM, first tier, second tier
Ownership	private, public
Industry leadership	leader, close follower, laggard
Geographic Scope	local, regional, national, international, global
Buying Approach	
Centralization	centralized, decentralized
Functional involvement	finance, marketing, manufacturing
Partnering approach	bid, relationship oriented, contracts
Product/Technology	
Level of technology	high, medium, low
Configuration purchased	components, modules, subsystem
Design source	internal, external

Figure 8.8   Segmenting the Business Market

Segmentation by Company Demographics In describing a company, we usually think first about its demographics: industry, size, financial stability, place in the distribution channel and ownership. Industry is defined by the company's products. Ford, GM and Honda are in the automotive industry, whereas Mack and International are in the heavy truck industry. Large companies may have strategic business units (SBUs) in different industries. Johnson & Johnson, for example, makes consumer health-care products as well as medical supplies for professionals. The federal government's Standard Industry Classification (SIC) codes can help identify a company's industrial category. Industry classification reveals a great deal about an organization — the types of problems it is likely to face, the kinds of products it purchases, its economic cycles and regulatory environment, and the types of competitive practices it is likely to encounter.

Company size is based on dollar amount or volume of sales, number of employees, or units produced. Size affects purchase procedures and requirements such as delivery schedules and inventory capacity. Large firms often do much of their own engineering, and their purchasing departments use formal buying arrangements. Medium-sized companies may be interested in value-added services a seller can provide. Small firms often use less formal procedures and may want the seller's help with tracking and restocking inventory.

Another demographic characteristic is financial stability and profitability. Marketing to a company in difficulty comes with risks, and if the investment is substantial, delays in payments can cause the seller financial hardship. The profitability of a company is often used as an indication of its ability to pay as well as other characteristics.

Channel membership refers to whether the organization is a distributor, original equipment manufacturer (OEM), or one of the tier suppliers. Each type has significantly different needs. Distributors acquire to resell, OEMs want to develop a final product, and tiers typically have unique needs as well.

Ownership influences how organizations buy. Since private companies can set policies as they see fit, we find many purchasing strategies. In the public sector, governmental units and utilities must follow very strict guidelines.

Segmentation by Geographic Scope
When we discussed geographic segmentation previously, it was in terms of locating clusters of targeted consumers. In the case of businesses, however, how they buy depends largely on the scope of their operations, whether local, regional, national, international or global. Pepsi has a global scope, so sellers must be able to think in terms of manufacturing plants around the world — and of reaching buyers who may come from various cultures.

Segmentation by Buying Approach
Organizations also can be differentiated according to their buying approach. This takes into account their degree of centralization, what functional areas are involved, and what kind of partnering arrangements they have. A centralized organization generally has one purchasing unit with very set policies, whereas a decentralized organization is likely to allow more favorable local buying decisions using various procedures and policies. Functional involvement refers to a company's orientation: Manufacturing firms use one set of criteria, whereas a financial institution or a consulting firm may use others. Partnering can range from simple bid purchases to a long- or short-term contract that may or may not contain detailed specifications and other requirements, such as an exclusivity clause.

> A centralized organization generally has one purchasing unit with very set policies, whereas a decentralized organization is likely to allow local buying decisions using various procedures and policies.

Segmentation by Product/Technology
Product/technology can affect purchasing in numerous ways, but three of the more important are level of technolo-

gy, configuration purchased and design orientation. First, firms vary dramatically in technological capability. This is primarily due to their hiring, training, retention and technical practices. A high-tech firm has very different expectations than a low-tech firm. Consequently, marketing to each group is different. Second, buying configurations differ. Some companies want to purchase only components and base their decisions on price and delivery specifications. Others buy modules that already combine many components and make it easier to add the supplier's product at the time of manufacturing. Still others prefer to purchase a system that enhances the functionality of their products, as when Chrysler buys traction-control products from Tevis. This variable is related in some ways to product design. Some organizations handle design in-house, some pay suppliers to take care of it, and others collaborate on it with suppliers. A company such as Delphi Automotive Systems has extensive design capabilities but sometimes relies on suppliers for the design of certain components, modules, and systems.

TWO COMMON SEGMENTING METHODS

Most markets are very complex, which can make the segmentation process difficult. There are many different types of customers and, as we have seen, literally thousands of variables can be used to segment them. Marketers typically use one of two approaches in selecting variables and grouping customers.

The **take-down segmentation method** starts with all consumers and seeks meaningful variables for subdividing the entire market. For example, the social media site Pinterest is primarily targeted to women. The virtual pinboard is significantly more appealing to women, who make up about 80 percent of the site's users. At least one-third of all women in the U.S. are using the platform and there is more than 70 million users globally. With an expanded test of ad products and targeting underway on Pinterest, users will likely see a lot more ads as the company aims at social media marketers. Various organizations like ABC Family, Expedia, Kraft and Target have realized the power of the platform and entered the market with paid advertisements called "Promoted Pins." These organizations are able to reach target consumers with extremely pertinent messaging, making Pinterest a valuable platform for advertising. Some analysts estimate these ads could generate $500 million in revenue for Pinterest by 2016.[37]

The **build-up segmentation method** starts with a single potential customer and adds others with similar characteristics. Anyone without those characteristics is placed in a new segment, and the process continues. In other words, rather than the whole market, the focus is on one segment at a time. For example, Fancl, a Japanese line of natural hair and skin care products, is extremely successful with environmentally conscious women in Japan. To expand, it began marketing to Japanese women living in the United States. Now, Fancl is targeting American women by marketing both the idea of using natural products and

Take-down Segmentation Method

Method that starts with a set of variables and assigns all consumers to one of them.

Build-up Segmentation Method

Method that starts with a single potential customer and adds others with similar characteristics.

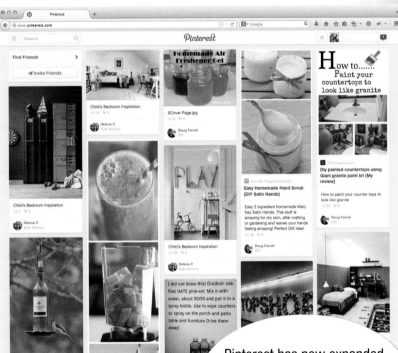

Pinterest has now expanded paid advertisements, which could generate as much as $500 million by 2016.

of providing benefits. Fancl has expanded its product line to include makeup free of additives and preservatives, suitable for all skin tones targeted for the environmentally concious women in Japan and America.[38] The build-up segmentation method is helping Fancl expand its business.

TARGET MARKETING

While segmentation is an analytical process, target marketing is a decision-making process. The company must choose the segment(s) on which it will focus its time and resources. At one extreme, a company will attempt to cover all segments, or at the other, it may choose only one. The Limited focuses on young, trendy women; Gerber on infants and young toddlers; McDonald's on families; and Lexus on quality-conscious, high-income adults. The Marketing Gazette feature on relationships (below), "Credit Card Co-Branding: New Shortcut to Hitting the Target Market," discusses a new spin on target marketing.

CREATING & CAPTURING VALUE THROUGH *Relationships*

Credit Card Co-Branding: New Shortcut to Hitting the Target Market

Credit card issuers are finding it a lot easier to target someone else's loyal customers than to inspire loyalty in their own. After all, with the flood of cut-rate cards filling mailboxes and the ease of transferring balances, consumers have little incentive to stick with a particular one. But what if a card gives something back? That's the principle behind credit card co-branding, a marketing strategy that's taken the business world by storm since it appeared in 1990.

Co-branding works like this: An issuer such as MasterCard or Visa teams up with a partner. It can be a retailer, a mail-order company, an airline, a university or a nonprofit group. In a typical co-branding program, the issuer develops a marketing campaign that targets the partner's customers. The issuer also contributes about one percent of its sales to the partner's reward program, which may be merchandise discounts, cash rebates, gift certificates or donations to a particular cause.

Co-branding flourishes because it's a win-win-win situation. The card issuer can easily target and reach a new base of customers and net a steady stream of revenue from transaction fees. The partner gains increased customer loyalty, higher average orders and more frequent purchases. And the consumer gets free toys, air miles or a host of other perks for using the co-branded card. Disney teamed up with Chase to offer a "Disney Rewards From Chase" Visa card. For every $100 spent, Disney rewards one "Disney Dream Dollar" that can be used to purchase theme park tickets, meals, and merchandise.

Of course, perks only draw customers if the brand appeals to them in the first place. The co-branding relationship taps into consumer loyalty or emotional ties to a co-brand sponsor, says Leslie Dukker Dory, Senior Vice President and Director of Marketing for Sun Trust BankCard of Orlando, Florida. "A well-established, well-identified, easily reached target, if provided the right perks," says Dory, "will gravitate to a card."

Kelly Shermach, "Cobranded Credit Cards Inspire Consumer Loyalty," Marketing News, September 9, 1996, p. 12.; https://disneyrewards.com, website visited July 1, 2014.

SELECTING TARGET SEGMENTS

How do companies decide which market segments to target? Once the segmentation scheme is developed, you need to describe, or profile, each group in more detail. The **market segment profile** compiles information about a market segment and the amount of opportunity it represents. The profile may include (1) the number of current and potential buyers; (2) the potential number of products these buyers may purchase; (3) the amount of revenue the segment may provide; and (4) the expected growth rate. In addition to size and growth, other criteria used to select targets include competitive factors, cost and efficiency factors, the segment's leadership qualities and the segment's compatibility with the company.

Market Segment Profile

Compiles information about a market segment and the amount of opportunity it represents.

Size and Growth Market segments vary considerably by size and growth rate. Although a segment must be large enough to generate revenues and profits, the biggest is not always the most attractive. The very largest segments may attract tougher competition. In the 1990s, Korean companies gained strong footholds in many countries (including the United States) by targeting smaller segments that other companies were ignoring. These were large enough to support sustained marketing efforts and included people whose spending power would increase over time.

Competitive Factors In general, the less competition within a segment, the better. Marketers must be aware not only of who is currently serving the segment but also of who is likely to do so in the future. A company may decide not to serve a particular segment in order to avoid particularly dangerous competitors. In other cases, a company may choose to challenge rivals. Church & Dwight decided to take on Procter & Gamble and Colgate-Palmolive by introducing its Arm & Hammer baking soda toothpaste, deeming the product just different enough to be successful with certain segments.

Cost and Efficiency Factors It is more efficient to target some segments than others. When Citibank set its sights on chief financial officers of several worldwide corporations, costs ran into the millions for research, product development, and personal selling. This sounds expensive, but it was a very efficient use of funds. This extremely compact segment consists of a few known and very influential people, so all the marketing dollars could be aimed directly at the targets. If the message reaches all sorts of consumers, then the result is higher cost and reduced efficiency. For example, alcohol abuse prevention advertisements are seen by responsible drinkers and non-drinkers, not just the target audience.

Segment Leadership Qualities Some segments set the trend for adopting new ideas and products. Professional sports teams influence the dress and equipment of college athletes, who, in turn, influence high school teams. Marketers often choose a target segment with leadership qualities, hoping that other segments will follow suit.

Compatibility Factors Companies often select segments they believe are particularly compatible with the company's vision, objectives and resources. Thus, to a significant degree, target segments reflect the qualities and character of the company. In the early 1980s, Honda recognized that Harley-Davidson was attracting customers who didn't appeal to much of the general population. Honda took advantage of this by targeting younger, well-educated buyers with the theme "You meet the nicest people on a Honda." This segment was consistent with Honda's image. Other Japanese motorcycle companies, such as Yamaha and Kawasaki, did the same and captured a large number of U.S. customers. In the past few years, Harley-Davidson has been trying to erase its Hell's Angels image.[39] Today the Harley-Davidson emphasis is on a lifestyle, and buyers include a broad range of responsible individuals. Harley-

Davidson executives make the point that "Nobody Needs a Harley," so they attempt to market all of the factors that promote the excitement of a Harley.

FINDING NEW MARKETS TO TARGET

A major innovation occurs when companies discover new market segments. You can probably think of many examples. Kajeet Inc. discovered a novel way to market cell phones. The phones are designed specifically for kids and tweens, and allowing parents to set security settings for their kids on the go. The parents can restrict incoming calls and text messaging and monitor cell phone use online. These phones can give parents piece of mind, assuring them that their that their children are always just a phone call away, while giving kids a sense of responsibility without the dangers of misuse that come with a normal cell phone. With a slightly altered approach, Kajeet broke into a new market.

TARGET MARKETING STRATEGIES

Targeting Strategy

The number of market segments and the relative amount of resources targeted at each.

A **targeting strategy** defines the number of target markets and the relative amount of resources allocated to each. Strategies usually fall within one of the three categories shown in Figure 8.9: undifferentiated marketing, differentiated marketing and concentrated marketing. Niche marketing and mass customization are two other targeting strategies.

Undifferentiated	**Differentiated**	**Concentrated**
Single mass market	Several well-defined markets	Single well-defined market
One approach for all	Different approach for each	One approach for the particular market

Figure 8.9   Target Market Strategies

Undifferentiated Marketing

A strategy that views all potential customers as though they are the same.

Undifferentiated Marketing Similar to mass marketing, **undifferentiated marketing** treats all customers the same. Companies look for desires that are common to most potential customers and then try to design products that appeal to everyone. By focusing internally on a single or a few products, companies can streamline manufacturing, distribution and even promotion in order to improve quality and gain cost efficiencies. But the standardized product may fail to meet individual customer needs. For years, United Parcel Service (UPS) used this strategy, with users and the company alike benefiting from its efficient operations. Users, however, became upset by the company's inability to fulfill unique customer requirements. UPS had to adapt to continue to thrive, as you will see in the next section.

As long as companies keep the price relatively low and competitive alternatives are unavailable, an undifferentiated marketing strategy can be successful, but with the tough, widespread competition of today, it is an extremely difficult strategy to implement. Companies that once thrived are being threatened by rivals that use more targeted approaches, such as differentiated or concentrated marketing.

Differentiated Marketing

Marketing to each of several segments with a marketing mix strategy matched specifically to its desires and expectations.

Differentiated Marketing **Differentiated marketing** serves each segment with marketing mix elements matched specifically to its desires and expectations. When Federal Express and others entered the market with differentiated strategies, UPS executives had to make a choice. Should the company settle for slowly eroding sales, or should it choose the risk, hard work and uncertainty of a new course? UPS decided on a differentiated marketing strategy. It carefully selected targets and designed services to meet their different needs. Some of its operations are applicable to all segments, such as its computerized tracking system and extensive aircraft fleet. Other elements differ, such as product mix, personal selling and pricing. This approach allows UPS to serve all its customers better.

The advantage of differentiated marketing is that needs and wants are better satisfied for each targeted segment. The disadvantage is that it may also cost more than undifferentiated marketing, because several marketing mix strategies are typically required. Differentiated marketing requires decentralized decision making. **Centralized decision making** involves a small group of executives who make all the major decisions for the whole company. **Decentralized decision making** permits numerous groups, each dedicated to a specific segment, to make the decisions for their particular segment. This gives marketers a lead role in the company, as they need to ensure that customers' needs and wants are considered in every decision. When UPS decided to engage in differentiated marketing, the first step was to strengthen its marketing capabilities. This meant educating large numbers of executives about the latest marketing techniques.

Concentrated Marketing

Focusing the organization's marketing mix on one or two of the many possible segments is called **concentrated marketing**. Companies must make sure they have a great deal of knowledge about their core market segment, as this major target is called. Although most of the marketing is aimed at the core, substantial revenues and profits may be gained from other segments. This is because concentrated marketing often targets segments with leadership qualities, in the hope that they will influence other segments' purchasing behavior. Ralph Lauren has used concentrated marketing successfully to target high-income, well-educated professionals and their families. Wanting to emulate them, consumers in the noncore segment are drawn to Lauren products as well.

Concentrated marketing has worked extremely well for new companies or companies entering new areas of the world. By gaining a foothold in a core market, a company can build the financial strength, experience and credibility needed for expansion. When Tower Records opened its first music store in Thailand, it concentrated on young people. Success in this segment is leading to further expansion in Thailand, including a host of additional outlets catering to listeners of all types.

Niche Marketing

A **niche** is a very small market that most companies ignore because they do not perceive adequate opportunity. For example, Mert's Meats in Okemos and Lansing, Michigan features Chairman's reserve beef from a Midwest distributor. The premium meat includes grass-fed ground beef and steaks, homemade sausages, freerange chickens, and duck. The seafood selection includes salmon, crab, shrimp and prepared selections such as stuffed clams and crusted tilapia. Decker Prescott, co-owner of Mert's Meats, says, "We can also bring specialty items in as customers ask and availability is there. We have the ability to fill a much needed niche." The store also stocks spices, sauces and limited local produce like asparagus, potatoes, and tomatoes. Mert's Meats has no desire to become a full-fledged grocer; it caters to the niche of consumers looking for premium and healthier cuts of meat. "We're just going to focus on meat —

Centralized Decision Making

Management process in which a small group of executives makes all the major decisions for the whole company.

Decentralized Decision Making

Management process in which numerous groups, each dedicated to a specific segment, make decisions about their segment.

Concentrated Marketing

Focusing the organization's marketing mix strategy on one or only a few of many possible segments.

Niche

A very small market segment that most companies ignore because they fail to see any opportunity.

that's what we're best at," she said. "We can't compete with Kroger or Meijer, but we can do something they can't by keeping our emphasis on quality and personal customer service."[40]

Mass Customization Probably the most important technological development for marketing is the personalization of mass merchandise. As mentioned previously, mass customization serves one or several markets while efficiently responding to the needs and desires of individual consumers. By creating a process that can respond to uniquely defined needs of targeted consumers, mass customization gives customers tremendous individualized attention. Companies can make affordable, high-quality products tailored to a customer's needs—but with the short cycle time and low costs associated with mass production.[41]

Nike has enjoyed success with mass customization. The company introduced Nike ID, unique shoes that consumers create on its website. The consumer starts with a basic shoe and works from there, choosing the base and the accent colors. In addition, Nike allows each person to put a personal "ID" on the shoe.[42]

ETHICAL DIMENSIONS OF TARGETING

It makes sense that manufacturers should want to target age segments, but this brings controversy upon some companies, such as those in the tobacco industry. When e-cigarettes hit the market, it was believed to be a safer alternative to traditional cigarettes, but recent indications show that companies are targeting the young adult market with fruity flavors and clever advertising. A recent Congressional Report calls on the FDA to assert its authority over e-cigarettes, suggesting that advertisements should not be allowed on radio and television, and that manufacturers should be banned from marketing in ways that are designed to attract minors. The report prioritizes a ban on all sales of e-cigarettes to anyone under the age of 18. Many manufacturers are fighting back claiming they are simply offering a safer alternative to traditional cigarette smoking, although no long-term studies exist to support that claim.[43]

The tobacco industry has come under intense fire for similar reasons. With more than 400 cigarette brands available in the U.S., many of the products could not survive without appealing to very specific consumer groups. For example, American Tobacco Company's Misty and Philip Morris' Virginia Slims are both geared toward women. These brands effectively target subsets of the larger population. When R. J. Reynolds introduced a menthol cigarette for African Americans called Uptown, the result was public scrutiny and condemnation by the U.S. secretary of health and human services and numerous African-American and community groups. There were demands that the government bar tobacco companies from designing and promoting cigarettes targeted at this market segment. The fight stopped short of litigation when Reynolds agreed to cancel the brand at an estimated cost of $5 million to $7 million. Not all businesspeople believe this should have happened. Caroline Jones, president of a New York advertising agency owned predominantly by African Americans, said that it is insulting to ignore the African-American community and not target it. "Marketers could and should advertise products to blacks, and that includes cigarettes and alcohol as well as bread and candy."[44]

Are there differences between products such as Uptown cigarettes and Kmart's line of private-label health and beauty care items aimed specifically at African Americans? There are varying opinions among consumer groups and industry manufacturers. One thing is certain: tobacco and alcohol companies find it increasingly difficult to introduce, position and market their products to ethnic consumers.

GLOBAL TARGETING

Major U.S. and foreign companies often reach carefully targeted market segments outside of domestic markets. They sometimes spend vast amounts of resources to create a presence in areas with potential for significant growth. Chinese companies are trying to leverage their advances in wind power by exploring prospects in markets in Europe and the U.S. China has several companies that rank in the world's top 10 turbine manufacturers, including Sinovel, Goldwind and Dongfang, who have seen rapid growth under Beijing's renewable energy law. Goldwind has already put several wind turbines on U.S. soil, with the first installed in Minnesota. Sinovel has an agreement with the Greek Public Power Corporation and Ireland's Mainstream Renewable Power to install wind turbines in their respective countries. While China's domestic wind turbine market remains strong, competition is fierce and has slower demand than supply. Global targets may make the difference on which of these companies will succeed.[45]

POSITIONING STRATEGIES

Once the segmentation process gives a clear picture of the market and the target marketing strategy is selected, the positioning approach can develop. Positioning is the process of creating in the mind of consumers an image, reputation or perception of the company and its products relative to competitors. Positioning aligns a marketing strategy with the way the marketer wants buyers in a given target market to perceive the value they will receive from the company's products.

Positioning helps potential customers understand what is unique about the company and its products relative to competitors. Most importantly, it helps buyers understand what a brand represents. **Product position** refers to the characteristics that consumers associate with a brand. For example, Snickers is positioned as the snack to give energy, while Milky Way provides comfort in every bar. BMW is positioned on prestige performance, while Mercedes projects prestige luxury.

Product Position

The characteristics consumers associate with a brand based on important attributes.

THE POSITIONING MAP

A **positioning map** is a diagram of how consumers in a segment perceive specific brand elements they find important, giving marketers a picture of how their products are viewed. Essentially, the idea is to graph where each brand falls regarding important attributes relative to other brands. To understand this, consider Figure 8.10, which depicts a positioning map of executives at a seminar asked to give their perceptions of talk shows (the product). The graph depicts the combined results, using

Positioning Map

A diagram of how consumers in a segment perceive specific brand elements they consider important.

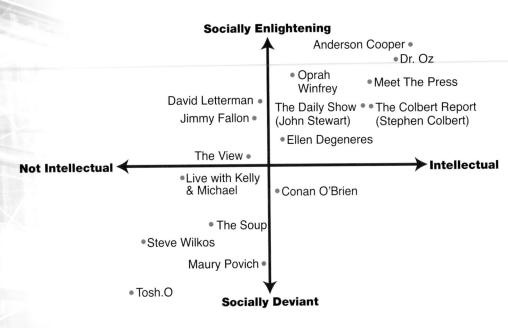

Figure 8.10   Examples of a Positioning Map: TV Talk Shows

social enlightenment and intellect as anchors. Take a moment to consider other talk shows and where you would place them relative to the ones listed in the figure.

Once the perceptions are plotted, most marketers want to know the consumer's ideal position. The ideal position is the one most preferred by each consumer. Oprah Winfrey faced a dilemma when she realized that her own show had migrated toward the lower left quadrant, which she felt was out of alignment with her own values. Oprah took action to move her show back to its original position in the upper right quadrant. Oprah's Book Club and health features, as well as showcasing her charitable contributions in South Africa, helped to cement her as educated and socially responsible in the minds of her viewers.

POSITIONING BUSINESS PRODUCTS

In addition to the same positioning methods used by consumer marketers, business marketers look at three other product classifications: commodity, differentiated and specialty. Commodity products, as seen in Figure 8.11, are distinguishable from each other primarily through price and delivery reliability. The differentiated position requires buyers to evaluate, compare and contrast the products from various suppliers. The specialty position is for a unique product that can be customized to user needs.

Delphi markets auto components to various GM groups such as GMC, Cadillac and Opel, as well as to manufacturers around the world, such as BMW and Renault. Depending on the product line and target segment, Delphi uses all three positioning strategies. In some cases it positions products as cost-efficient, standard commodities, such as simple wire harnesses that connect parts of the electrical system. Delphi also markets brake systems that are differentiated from those of competitors and require state-of-the-art technology. In order to produce unique specialty products, Delphi works closely with designers at other levels. For instance, the company markets engine fuel systems that are both up to code and tailor-made for a consumer by collaborating with drive train designers.

Category	Commodity	Differentiated	Specialty
Product Characteristics	No hidden qualities, similar to other suppliers	Comparisons with other suppliers show advantages	Unique
Technology	Standard	State-of-the-art	Customized

Figure 8.11   Positioning of Business Products

STEPS FOR POSITIONING

Consumers' perceptions are influenced by how marketers choose to categorize a product. Music, for example, is categorized as rock, country, jazz, classical and so forth, whereas other dimensions help differentiate one artist or group from another. Consumers also evaluate a brand relative to others based on their impression of how similar they seem. Finally, they look at a brand according to their preferences — or how close it comes to their ideal position. The following steps can be used to position a brand.

1. Identify the attributes or characteristics used by buyers in a segment to understand brands.
2. Diagram the most important dimensions on a grid (map).
3. Locate the brand relative to others based on how it is perceived by buyers.
4. Identify the ideal position for buyers in the segment.
5. Determine the fundamental way to position the product.
6. Develop the marketing mix that supports the positioning strategy selected.

BASES FOR POSITIONING

David Aaker and J. Gary Shansby, two noted marketing scholars, have identified the following seven fundamental bases that marketers can use to position products. Each base is described in more detail next.

Positioning by Benefit Benefits (attributes) can be used to describe the appeal of a product. For example, Procter & Gamble uses medical testimony to position Crest as a cavity-fighting toothpaste. Glad trash bags are positioned to be more durable than the competition. Fisher-Price toys are positioned as safe and educational. Energizer batteries are positioned to keep going and going.

You must carefully select the benefits to associate with your product. Describing benefits that satisfy wants tends to work better than merely describing product attributes, because consumers can relate the benefits to themselves.

Positioning by Price or Quality Sam Walton made $25 billion by identifying underserved geographical market segments and then positioning Walmart as being consistently lower priced than competitors. Other retailers, such as Neiman Marcus, position themselves as high priced to signal higher quality. Another typical example of price vs. quality is the pharmaceutical industry. Branded drugs (usually marketed by firms that first develop them) are priced much higher than generics (usually marketed by companies that copy drugs when the patent expires). While the generics are positioned on price and the branded products emphasize quality, the products are basically the same.

Positioning by Time of Use or Application Marketers frequently position products on the basis of how they are used or applied. Gatorade, Powerade, and All-Sport are positioned for drinking while exercising. Hot Pockets sandwiches and paninis are positioned as hot meals on-the-go.

Often sales can be increased by positioning a product for more than one use or application. For example, McDonald's discovered a huge opportunity when breakfast service was added. It recently expanded further by adding the McCafé coffee items to its selection.[46] Arm & Hammer increased baking soda sales by positioning the product as an odor fighter in the refrigerator, auto or cupboard, in addition to its uses in toothpaste, laundry and baking. V-8 juice, originally consumed at breakfast, is now infused with fruit and vegetable flavors to make it an "anytime" beverage.

Positioning by Product User or Spokesperson Sometimes a product is associated with characteristics of its spokesperson. For example, Garnier Nutrisse uses Sarah Jessica Parker to position its hair products as classy and chic.[47] Andre

Agassi and John McEnroe, both considered tennis rebels, were used to help position Nike athletic shoes as an alternative to the conservative models sold by competitors.

Sometimes spokespeople are not even real, such as Betty Crocker and Mr. Goodwrench. At other times, the person's area of expertise may be more significant than his or her identity as an individual. The Club, a device designed to prevent auto theft, was introduced in a national ad campaign by actual police officers.

Positioning by Direct Comparison

Nearly all customers develop impressions about a brand by comparing it to another, so marketers attempt to favorably influence impressions. In a few cases, competitors are named, although many marketers believe they should not be given "free" publicity. More often, the comparison is general — one brand is stronger, brighter and so forth than "the others." In a recent example some consider "classic," Apple created a series of commercials making direct comparisons to competitor personal computers. The "Hi, I'm a MAC" and "Hi, I'm a PC" skits between two actors portrayed as each operating system showcased direct comparisons between the system components, with popular Apple features coming out on top each time. Apple sold its system based on both its well-known and loved features as well as the perceived downsides of its primary competitor.

Positioning by Product Class or Category

Cereals can be categorized as natural or sweetened. Consumers are likely to position the natural cereals, such as All-Bran or Kashi, or sweetened cereals, like Frosted Flakes and Lucky Charms, relative to one another. But since they serve different purposes as breakfast, customers are not likely to compare Frosted Flakes and All-Bran. When a marketer is determining a positioning strategy, it is important that he or she understands how customers categorize products.

Positioning by Country of Origin

A company's image can be affected by the mental association people make with its country of origin. We think of German precision engineering, Japanese cost and quality, Italian fashion, French taste and U.S. technology. Certain countries are associated with certain products: the United States with movies, Germany with beer, Japan with electronics, Belgium with chocolate, France with wine, and Italy with shoes. Companies may create a subsidiary in a nation associated with a product, or they may use a brand name that sounds like it's from that country.

REPOSITIONING

Repositioning is important for the longevity of a brand. It often rejuvenates a brand that might otherwise fade from lack of appeal. For example, some beer brands like Pabst Blue Ribbon (PBR) have repositioned several times. It had a tough-guy persona for years until it repositioned in the 1950's to be "The Fashionable Beer." PBR advertising campaigns appeared in high-end magazines like The New Yorker and Vogue with the tag line "Pabst Makes it Perfect." In the 1970's PBR made a Southern expansion in the U.S. and was even featured in a hit country song "Rednecks, White Socks, and Blue Ribbon Beer," by Johnny Russell. This redneck image would prove to plague PBR until it repositioned again in the past decade to be the beer of choice by hipsters and other urban groups.[48]

P&G's brand Old Spice also found huge success by repositioning. It was long viewed as an old-timer's brand with many remembering the classic aftershave bottle on the back of their grandfather's sink. P&G cleverly leveraged the masculinity and age of the brand in the new slogan "Experience Is Everything," and created bold new advertisements to appeal to a younger generation. It further expanded to young audiences through successful marketing across social media channels including Facebook, Twitter and YouTube.

Repositioning may become necessary over time as competitive forces, customer preferences, and marketing environments change. It requires significant time and effort to replace past impressions with new ones. Whether a company is positioning a new product or repositioning an old one, the ultimate goal of its decision making is to persuade the targeted consumer to make a decision as well — the decision to purchase the product.

CHAPTER SUMMARY

Objective 1: Understand the advantages of target marketing and how it differs from mass marketing and product differentiation.

Mass marketing treats all customers as though they have the same needs and wants. A single marketing strategy is designed to appeal to all potential customers. This strategy does not generally work well, because customers with differing characteristics have different needs and wants. Product differentiation is a strategy that alters products to stress their uniqueness relative to competitors. It recognizes that customers have differing needs and wants, but it doesn't start with an understanding of them. Target marketing focuses on select groups of customers so marketers can more clearly understand their specific needs and wants and adjust accordingly.

Objective 2: Describe how to do market segmentation and select target markets.

Market segmentation separates potential customers into several groups or segments with distinctive characteristics. Customers within a segment should have similar needs, wants and preferences; they should have similar media habits and shopping and buying patterns; the group should be large enough to justify attention; and data about individuals in each segment should be available.

Typical segmentation variables are geographic and demographic factors, ethnic and other diversity-related factors, psychographic and behavioristic factors, and benefits desired. Two common segmenting methods are the take-down method and the build-up method. The take-down method begins by selecting segmentation variables and assigning customers to the category in which they fit. The build-up method starts with the unique characteristics of one potential customer. Each time someone with unique characteristics is discovered, a new segment is added.

Segments are selected as target markets based on such factors as their size and growth potential, competition, cost and efficiency, leadership qualities and compatibility with the organization.

Objective 3: Explore three basic target marketing strategies: undifferentiated, differentiated and concentrated marketing.

Undifferentiated marketing treats all customers alike and is similar to mass marketing. In order for this strategy to work, companies generally must have significant cost advantages. Differentiated marketing involves serving several segments but adjusting the marketing mix for each. It usually requires decentralized decision making. Concentrated marketing focuses on one segment or only a few. Companies can use all their resources to gain advantage within that group. Because differentiated and concentrated strategies consider customer needs and wants, they are far superior to an undifferentiated strategy.

Objective 4: Know how to create positioning and describe several approaches marketers use to establish valuable, lasting images of their products.

Positioning creates in the mind of consumers an image, reputation or perception of the company and its products relative to competitors. It helps customers understand what is unique about a company and its products. Marketers can use a positioning map to depict how customers perceive products according to certain characteristics. For business products, a commodity, differentiated or specialty positioning strategy can be used. Products are often positioned by benefit, by price and quality, by the time of use or application, by user or spokesperson, by direct comparison with a competitor, by product class or by country of origin.

REVIEW YOUR UNDERSTANDING

1. Define mass marketing, segmentation and targeting. How are they different?
2. What are the steps in segmentation, targeting and positioning?
3. What variables are used to segment markets? Give examples of each.
4. What are the three basic marketing strategies associated with segmentation?
5. What is VALS™ 2? What major categories of consumers does it profile?
6. What is the difference between the take-down and the build-up segmentation methods?
7. What characteristics are used to select target markets?
8. What is micromarketing, and how does it differ from mass customization?
9. What are positioning strategies? List three used in business markets.
10. What is a positioning map, and how do organizations use it to position products?

DISCUSSION OF CONCEPTS

1. Why do marketers use market segmentation to summarize information about large numbers of consumers? Why not just use averages?
2. Are segmentation techniques used by companies that follow a mass marketing strategy? A product differentiation strategy?
3. Imagine that you are the marketing manager for a company that wants to produce a new line of men's and women's dress shirts. Which segmentation variables would be relevant for this market? What categories would you use? Describe five or six market segments that may emerge.
4. What is a segment profile? Develop one for each market segment you listed in question 3.
5. Which segments in question 3 would you select as target markets?
6. Once target markets are chosen, what different strategies are available? Which would work best for your target markets?
7. Why is positioning important? What are some of the different ways to position dress shirts in your target markets?
8. Positioning is typically done relative to the competition. If you have no important competitors, then how can the concept still be useful?

KEY TERMS & DEFINITIONS

1. **Build-up segmentation method:** Method that starts with a single potential customer's characteristics and adds a segment for each new characteristic found in other customers.
2. **Centralized decision making:** Management process in which a small group of executives makes all the major decisions for the whole company.
3. **Concentrated marketing:** Focusing the organization's marketing mix strategy on one or only a few of many possible segments.
4. **Decentralized decision making:** Management process in which numerous groups, each dedicated to a specific segment, make decisions about their segment.
5. **De-ethnicization:** The result of targeting a product heavily associated with one ethnic group to other segments.
6. **Demographic segmentation:** Division of the market according to such characteristics as gender, family life cycle, household type and income.
7. **Differentiated marketing:** Marketing to each of several segments with a marketing mix strategy matched specifically to its desires and expectations.
8. **Heterogeneous group:** Buyers with diverse characteristics.
9. **Homogeneous group:** Buyers with similar characteristics.
10. **Market segment:** A homogeneous group with similar needs, wants, values and buying behavior.
11. **Market segment profile:** Information about a market segment and the amount of opportunity it represents.
12. **Niche:** A very small market segment that most companies ignore because they fail to see any opportunity.
13. **Positioning:** Creating an image or perception in the minds of consumers about the organization or its products relative to the competition.
14. **Positioning map:** A diagram of how consumers in a segment perceive brands based on specific elements they consider important.
15. **Product differentiation:** A marketing strategy with which companies attempt to make their products appear unique relative to the competition.
16. **Product position:** The characteristics consumers associate with a brand based on important attributes.
17. **Psychographics:** Marketing approaches and tools used to identify lifestyles based on measures of consumers' values, activities, interests, opinions, demographics and other factors.
18. **Segmentation:** Division of a market into homogeneous groups with similar needs, wants, values and buying behavior.
19. **Segmentation variable:** Any distinguishing market factor that can vary, such as gender, age or income.
20. **Take-down segmentation method:** Method that starts with a set of variables and assigns all consumers to one of them.

21. **Target marketing:** The selection of specific homogeneous groups (segment) of potential customers for emphasis.
22. **Targeting strategy:** The number of market segments and the relative amount of resources targeted at each.
23. **Undifferentiated marketing:** A strategy that views all potential customers as though they are the same.
24. **ZIP code segmentation:** Division of a market into specific geographic locations based on the demographic makeup of the ZIP code area.

REFERENCES

1. www.dell.com, website visited June 21, 2014.
2. Bradford, Harry, "These 10 Companies Control Enormous Number Of Consumer Brands," The Huffington Post, April 27, 2012.
3. www.shopgreatlakescrossing.com, website visited August 4, 2014.
4. www.census.gov, website visited June 24, 2014.
5. Raynor, Michael E., Weinberg, Howard, S., "Beyond Segmentation — Does your company want to satisfy a niche or gain a foothold in the market?" Marketing Management, November/December 2004.
6. Sorkin, Andrew, "Coca-Cola Agrees to Buy Vitaminwater," May 26, 2007, New York Times.
7. "Products," CocaCola, www.cocacola.com, website visited June 8, 2014.
8. "Driven by Facebook and Google, Mobile Ad Market Soars 105% in 2013," eMarketer, March 19, 2014.
9. Chicago, March 1996, pg. 22.
10. Rigby, Darrell K., Vishwanath, Vijay, "Localization: The Revolution in Consumer Markets," Harvard Business Review, April 1, 2006.
11. "PRIZM NE Segments", www.tretrad.com, website visited June 21, 2014.
12. Nike, www.nikewomen.com, website visited April 9, 2014.
13. "American Men Get More Savvy," Business and Industry, Vol. 22, No. 6, March 21, 2005, pg. 21.
14. Batista, Elisa, "She's Gotta Have It: Cell Phone," www.wired.com, May 16, 2003.
15. Everitt, Lisa, "What's Best for Baby? Parents go to four corners of the store to shop for their pride and joy," National Grocery Buyer, January/February 2003 Issue.
16. "Just How Many Baby Boomers Are There?," PRB, April 2014.
17. http://endoftheamericandream.com, website visited July 29, 2012.
18. "Debt-squeezed Gen X," USA Today, www.usatoday.com, website visited April 12, 2014.
19. Palmer, Kimberly, "Gen X-ers: Stingy or Strapped," U.S. News and World Report, www.usnews.com, website visited April 14, 2014.
20. Judith Aguino, "Gen Y: The Next Generation of Spenders," CRM Magazine, February 2012.
21. Ibid.
22. www.mybudget360.com, website visited April 14, 2014.
23. Lee, Aileen, "Why Women Rule the Internet," www.techcrunch.com, March 20, 2011.
24. U.S. Census Bureau, www.census.gov, website visited April 9, 2014.
25. U.S. Census Bureau News, May 10, 2006.
26. McDermott, Michael J., "Marketers Pay Attention! Ethnics Comprise 25% of the U.S.," Brandweek, July 18, 1994, pg. 26.
27. http://quickfacts.census.gov, website visited July 14 2012.
28. "Food Companies Targeting Hispanic Consumer," www.foxnews.com, website visited April 12, 2014.
29. Sullivan, Robert, "Americans and Their Money," Worth, June 1994, pg. 60.
30. "The Best 100 Sources for Marketing Information," American Demographics, January 1995, pg. 29.
31. Winters, Lewis C., "International Psychographics," Marketing Research, September 1992, pp. 48-49.
32. "Highlighted Campaigns," RepNation, www.repnation.com, website visited June 8, 2014.
33. Bridgestone e5, e6, and e7 Ball Review, www.thesandtrap.com, website visited June 8, 2014.
34. Burns, Enid, "Shoppers Shift to Online," ClickZ Network, www.clickz.com, website visited April 9, 2014.
35. www.dell.com, site visited April 13, 2042.
36. D'Souza, Clare, Mehdi Taghian, Peter Lamb, and Roman Peretiatko. "Green decisions: demographics and consumer understanding of environmental labels." International Journal of Consumer Studies 31 (2007): 371.
37. Matt Kapko, "Pinterest Pins Revenue Plans on Ad Targeting," CIO, May 30, 2014.
38. www.fancl.com, website visited April 8, 2014.
39. Associated Press, "Biker Sues Harley-Davidson for Trying to Yank Business," The State News, April 10, 1996, pg. 6.
40. Allan I. Ross, "New in town," Lansing City Pulse, May 21, 2014.
41. Weiss, Michael J., The Clustering of America (New York: Harper & Row), pg. 1.
42. "What is Nike+?", www.nike.com, website visited April 9, 2014.
43. Irvin Jackson, "E-Cigarette Ads Aimed At Underage Smokers: Congressional Report," www.aboutlawuits.com, April 15, 2014.
44. Dagnoli, Judann, "RJR's Uptown Targets Blacks," Advertising Age, December 18, 1989, pg. 4.
45. Sarah Murray, "Wind power in China: Turbine talent seeks overseas outlets," www.ft.com, September 28, 2011.
46. Zachary, G., "Strategic Shift," Wall Street Journal, June 13, 1996, pg. A1.
47. Aaker, D., and Shansby, J., "Positioning Your Product," Business Horizons, May-June 1982, p. 56
48. www.pabstblueribbon.com, website visited June 28, 2014.

Chapter 09

BRAND MANAGEMENT & PRODUCT DECISIONS

Birthday Girl

Over the years, Sir Richard Branson's name has become synonymous with innovation, money and global appeal. Knighted by the Queen of England for his entrepreneurship, he is best known for Virgin Records, a label that signed such acts as the Rolling Stones, the Sex Pistols and Janet Jackson. In 1970, Branson founded Virgin Group and has since formed more than 200 companies, employing over 50,000 people in 34 countries. Virgin has been successful in a variety of markets, including mobile phones, transportation, travel, media, music and financial services. It has even dabbled in businesses such as bridal wear, soda, vodka, cars, cosmetics, vacations and condoms. Each area of business is under the umbrella of a core category: Lifestyle, Media & Mobile, Money, People & Planet, Music, and Travel.

Virgin's eclectic and broad business portfolio is well planned through extensive research and analysis. According to Virgin, it focuses on putting itself in the customer's shoes to see what can be improved. Each new customer-centric venture demonstrates the company's devotion to picking the right market and the right opportunity. Virgin is known for building great marketing strategies with excellent teams of executives.

Virgin understands that customers want fun and innovative choices that are high in quality and affordability. In the mid-'80s, Virgin Atlantic Airways was created to make transatlantic flights more appealing. The airline revolutionized the industry by extending passenger legroom and installing individual TV screens. Most major competitors followed years later.

Virgin Atlantic's mission states: "Virgin Atlantic wants to be a profitable airline where people love to fly and where people love to work." For Virgin Atlantic, flying is less about getting from one place to another than about being able to relax in a comfortable atmosphere and enjoy exceptional passenger service.

Virgin Galactic was founded with a lofty vision to provide space flights to the paying public. The planned spacecraft will be robust and affordable enough to send eight passengers to 70,000 feet for a short sub-orbital journey to experience true weightlessness. The company is offering this groundbreaking opportunity so high-end consumers can become some of the initial civilian astronauts. The first 450 seats are already booked with Virgin Galactic at a cost of $200,000 each, but Virgin plans to eventually make the price more affordable to the general public.

Virgin also recognizes that taking care of the planet is as important as taking care of customers. That is why it has committed to sustainability goals that include using bio-fueled planes, serving only fair-trade tea and coffee onboard, and reducing off-aircraft landfill wastes by 50 percent. Branson has dedicated all profits from his travel business to research and development for finding alternative renewable fuels. Through Virgin Green Fund, the company is investing in renewable energy and resource efficiency.

Virgin's commitment to customers, employees and the environment is the catalyst for its success. Its marketing plans aim at exceeding customer expectations through innovation and fun. Thanks to Branson's vision, Virgin will continue to inspire and capture value for its customers.[1]

<< Richard Branson with Virgin Atlantic Flight Attendants

Learning Objectives

1. Describe the major dimensions used by marketers to differentiate products from competitors. Understand bundling and unbundling.
2. Understand consumer and business product classifications based on how and why products are purchased and consumed.
3. Know how organizations make product line decisions that determine what will be sold, including the degree of standardization chosen for global markets.
4. Recognize that branding and brand strategies are important aspects of building and maintaining a brand name.
5. Know how to create brand equity — the value associated with a product's name.
6. Discuss the many legal and ethical issues surrounding brand and packaging decisions.

THE CONCEPT OF PRODUCTS

When Harley-Davidson recently announced its radical new electric motorcycle prototype, dubbed Project LiveWire, a lot of skepticism surrounded the product as Harley traditionalists spoke out. "It's not going to make any noise," said Gigi Beaird, Chapter Director of Women on Wheels in the DeKalb County area. "I was surprised Harley was testing an electric model because it's the polar opposite of what they're known for."[2] Indeed, Harley has long been known for its size and sound, not for its sportiness and eco-friendly silence. Ashley Lambert, the marketing director at Woodstock Harley-Davidson says, "There is something to be said about sitting on a Harley-Davidson and hearing that 'pop-pop-pop-pop-pop' vibration underneath you and the sound and the roar of the bike."[3] The new bike is certainly a risk for Harley-Davidson, but the company also understands that great risk can produce great rewards. Harley just might have the name and brand to bring legitimacy to the electric motorcycle industry, which is often regarded as a fad for a few niche buyers. It could also tap into a hard-to-reach market -- younger, progressive, thought-leading buyers. The jury may still be out for some, but for others the electric motorcycle has finally been validated.[4]

The Harley-Davidson Project LiveWire is shaking up the industry and could be the future of cycling.

Product strategies provide an exciting challenge to marketers, since they affect nearly every aspect of a business. This chapter describes how products are managed from a marketer's perspective with particular attention to brand management, which is critical for many organizations. The next chapter focuses on service, which is a special case, and Chapter 11 addresses new-product development.

Technically, a product is either a good or a service. For our purposes, however, a **product** is any physical object, service, idea, person, event, place or organization that can be offered to satisfy consumers' needs and wants. Products can be combined

Product

Any physical object, service, idea, person, event, place, or organization offered to satisfy consumers' needs and wants.

to perform important functions for individuals, families or organizations. In the broadest sense, anything that is purchased or sold can be considered a product. Corn, cornflakes and Kellogg's Corn Flakes are all products. A movie, a baseball game and an airplane trip are also products. For many people, the term *product* refers to a tangible item, but services are considered products as well. Services represent more than 68 percent of U.S. G.D.P., and about four out of five people in the U.S. are employed in service industries, such as restaurants, lodging, health care and law.[5]

Figure 9.1 presents the topics covered in this chapter. First we explore the three dimensions of a product, discuss product classifications and consider global product line decisions. We will then take a look at branding, packaging and labeling. The chapter concludes with a discussion of ethical issues surrounding product safety and liability.

Most marketing experts describe products in terms of three dimensions: core, branded and augmented.

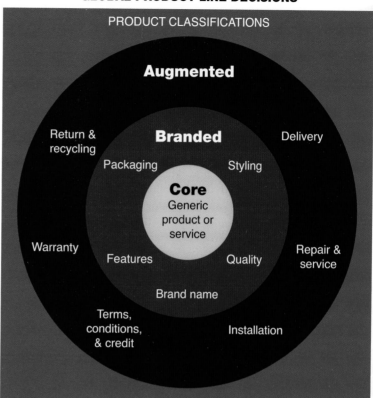

GLOBAL PRODUCT LINE DECISIONS

Figure 9.1   Concept of a Product

CORE PRODUCTS

A **core product** is associated with the basic function a consumer receives in the form of a physical item or intangible service. It could be a tennis racket, a subcompact automobile, a bowling center, a life insurance policy or a physical examination. The core product does not include the brand name, styling features, packaging or any other descriptive aspects.

A core product is often called the *generic product,* which means it conforms to the basic description. While some bicycles are suited for different terrains and activities, all of them have two wheels and function as a mode of non-motorized transportation. Another common example is generic pharmaceuticals, which refers to drugs sold without reference to a particular manufacturer. When the patent on an invented drug expires, other companies can simply copy the pharmacological formula and sell it as a generic drug. It usually costs much less than the branded drug since its price doesn't have to reflect the research or marketing costs associated with developing and introducing a new drug.

Core Product

The essential physical item or intangible service that the customer receives.

BRANDED PRODUCTS

A **branded product** is the core product plus characteristics organizations use to differentiate it from similar products. Most important is the brand name, although styling, quality, features and packaging are additional ways to distinguish brands. The branded product also can be called the identified product, because branding confers an identity just as a rancher's brand identifies a herd. Branded products not only carry the value of the core product but also have a distinctiveness that allows consumers to recognize and recall experiences with them. Nearly every global con-

Branded Product

The core product plus the characteristics that allow the consumer to differentiate it from similar products.

sumer recognizes the name Apple. In a recent international readers survey, Apple was ranked the brand with the most global impact. With its unique emphasis on innovation, simplicity and style, Apple-branded products have captured the eyes and dollars of consumers worldwide.[6]

Some branded products are identified purely by the need for the function they perform, such as Morton's salt. Distinctive style, such as the lines of a Porsche or a Corvette, can be an identifying point. Volkswagen confused the marketplace when it dropped the popular Beetle model styling, and its reintroduction of the swoop-back Beetle was met with public approval. Brands like Maytag, which is now owned by Whirlpool Corporation, attempt to create identification through a product benefit such as reliability. For many decades, Maytag has successfully promoted its reliability by depicting a lonely repairman who never gets to visit a customer. Packaging can also distinguish a product, such as the instantly identifiable "Coke" bottle form and script, or the Tic Tac case. Finally, a symbol like the enormously popular Nike swoosh carries instant brand identification.

AUGMENTED PRODUCTS

Augmented Product

Product with characteristics that enhance its value beyond that of the core and branded products.

An **augmented product** has characteristics that enhance value beyond that of the core and branded products. Delivery methods, warranty conditions and credit terms are ways to augment a product. A dishwasher from Sears can be delivered, installed, covered by a limited warranty and paid off on credit. Many products also require extensive installation, such as an in-ground swimming pool, which may require maintenance or repair after some use. That's why warranty conditions and the availability of service are significant in augmenting products.

Bundling Strategy

A strategy in which several products are combined into a single offering.

Another aspect of augmentation is product **bundling strategy** that combines many products into a single offering. Stereo equipment, for example, can be sold as a system or as individual components. Maybe in the purchasing process, you find that Bose speakers sound better, but you prefer the Pioneer receiver, prompting you to purchase the components separately. Sony's strategy is to market an entertainment system with components specifically designed to work together, such as a Blu-ray player, speakers, TV and receiver.

As online shopping continues to increase, privacy and security are becoming very important ways to augment a product. Patagonia, for example, recognizes its customers' concern about confidentiality issues while shopping on its website. The company takes the initiative to ensure its customers' safety through high-security measures, making the consumer feel safe about shopping for its products online.[7]

The movement toward green marketing is a form of augmentation. In particular, there is increasing demand for products that can be returned or recycled after their usefulness to the initial buyer has ended. A common example of recycling is automobiles that flow to the used car market and eventually into reclamation centers, where usable parts are extracted and raw materials such as metal and rubber are recycled. In order to promote its brand as environmentally conscientious, Toyota's Harmony commercial features a car built from nature. As the commercial continues, the car fades back into the scenery in perfect harmony with the environment. A voiceover states that Toyota believes, "The best way to have an impact on the environment is to have as little impact as possible."[8]

CONSUMER PRODUCT CLASSIFICATION

Marketers divide products into the five categories listed in Figure 9.2.

Classification	Repurchase Planning	Number of Comparisons Made	Frequency of Purchase	Location of Purchase	Examples
Unsought	None	Few or none	Seldom	At buyer's home or at store checkout	Cemetery plots Pet rock
Emergency	Unexpected need	None	Very rarely or once	Closest to emergency	Ambulance Towing service
Convenience	Little	Several (but over many purchases)	Often and regularly	Close to home, travel, work	Soft drinks Chewing gum Fast food
Shopping	Moderate	Many	Infrequent	In areas with many similar products	Automobiles Televisions Appliances Furniture Clothing
Specialty	Extensive	Few	Infrequent	Buyer travels to merchant's location	Fine watches Gourmet restaurants

Figure 9.2   A Product Classification Based on Consumer Purchase Behavior

Unsought Products

Unsought products are not thought about frequently nor perceived as very necessary. The desire is usually felt just briefly before purchase, such as novelties, T-shirts or "over the hill" gag gifts. They also include items that are important but unpleasant for many buyers to think about, such as cemetery plots. In any case, consumers don't seek information about these products, so it is essential for marketers to effectively promote them. In some cases, heavy promotion efforts, such as advertising and point of sales materials, may be required to persuade potential buyers to consider the item.

Impulse items make up a special category of unsought products, which as the name suggests, are often purchased on a whim. In most cases, impulse items are relatively inexpensive and have little to do with need fulfillment, other than the buyer's immediate enjoyment at the time of purchase. How many times have you been grocery shopping and tossed a box of Chips Ahoy! or Twinkies into your cart?

Emergency Products

Emergency products are purchased when an unexpected event takes place and the consumer has an urgent need for a product. When an ambulance or tow truck is needed, the buyer is unlikely to compare prices and probably has little choice about the supplier. From the marketer's standpoint, it's crucial to have telephone numbers and other means of access available to buyers when an emergency occurs. A good example is the 911 service that local police, fire and ambulance agencies promote. American Express provides consumers with phone numbers that allow lost traveler's checks to be replaced immediately. Many automo-

Unsought Product

An item that consumers don't think about frequently and for which they don't perceive much need.

Emergency Product

A product purchased due to an unexpected event and for which the consumer has an urgent need.

bile companies also provide toll-free numbers for emergency roadside service.

Convenience Product

A relatively inexpensive item that consumers purchase frequently and with minimum effort.

Convenience Products

Convenience products are relatively inexpensive items that consumers purchase frequently and with minimum effort. Often they are referred to as staples, because people always need them — milk, toilet paper, gum, bottled water and so on. Convenience items are usually bought close to home, work or travel routes. Typically they are purchased only when the consumer's supply is low, like when you notice the last tube of toothpaste is nearly empty so you buy some more on your way home from work.

Branding is very important for convenience products; buyers don't spend a lot of time selecting their purchases, so they gravitate toward the brands they know. The national drugstore chain CVS caters to purchasers' desire to obtain these products quickly by providing a one-stop shopping center for a multitude of consumers' convenience needs. CVS also offers its own brand, which reduces purchase decision time as well as cost. Marketers must ensure that convenience items are widely distributed and prominently displayed with eye-catching packaging so they are quickly noticed and easily purchased.

Shopping Product

A purchase generally made only after the consumer has compared several alternatives.

Shopping Products

Shopping products are generally purchased only after the consumer has compared the style, features, pricing, packaging and quality of several alternatives. Buyers compare prices to select the product providing the best value. Shopping products typically cost more and are purchased less frequently than convenience items; they include automobiles, televisions, appliances, furniture and clothing. Although people may do some pre-purchase planning at home, they are likely to visit stores to examine shopping goods, a desire that companies accommodate by often establishing stores near competitors. There may be several shoe stores in the same wing of a shopping mall, or several automobile dealerships not far apart on the same street. This makes it easier for consumers to draw comparisons and increases the chance that one of the outlets will make the sale.

Because shopping goods tend to be relatively durable, consumers don't want to be stuck with an unsuitable purchase for a long time. Selecting just the right piece of furniture to complement a room or finding an item of clothing that coordinates with one's wardrobe can require extensive shopping. Many people take along friends or family to help with the decision, and many do not feel comfortable making a major purchase without speaking with a salesperson. Many retailers and manufacturers recognize this and train their salespeople to identify buyers' needs and help them find exactly the right item.

Because comparisons are made among shopping goods, many manufacturers market several similar products at different price points. Apple continually launches a range of new-generation MP3 players. The iPod Touch allows users to watch movies, listen to music and surf the Internet. Apple also offers the iPod Classic, Nano and Shuffle, which all have different features and storage capacities. The four units give customers more choices at multiple price points.[9]

Specialty Item

A product with unique characteristics that provides unusual value to the purchaser.

Specialty Products

Specialty items have unique characteristics that provide unusual value to the purchaser, such as an association with the buyer's self-image. Consequently, customers are brand loyal and willing to travel long distances rather than settle for a substitute. Some examples are Movado watches, Gucci purses, Godiva chocolates, Louis Vuitton luggage and Armani suits. A lobster and filet mignon dinner, a dress from Saks Fifth Avenue, a stay at the Plaza Hotel or a luxury cruise also can be considered specialty items.

Most consumers spend a considerable amount of time on pre-purchase planning for specialty items. Because of the typically high cost of these items, both purchaser and retailers need to be highly involved to ensure that an ultimately satisfying purchase is made. To justify the expense of this service, marketers work hard to create customer loyalty. Repeat purchases generate enough profit over time to offset the cost of the first sale.

Service professionals often try to achieve the status of a specialty provider. There are physicians who practice only internal medicine, oncology or cosmetic surgery. The specialty classification signifies a great deal more value to most customers, which prompts certain types of lawyers, architects, consultants and accountants to charge more than their non-specialized counterparts. Buyers often seek these suppliers not only for their status but also because of the unique qualities of the product or service they provide.

BUSINESS PRODUCT CLASSIFICATION

Business products are purchased by an organization for its own use. The seven types listed in Figure 9.3 are grouped into three categories according to function. These are the products needed to start a company and maintain it for the long term.

Category and Type	Description	Examples
Capital Products		
Installations	Facilities that contain operations	Office buildings, factories, stores, distribution centers
Equipment	Items used to manufacture products and support the business	Drills, computers, desks, robots, lifts, trucks, airplanes
Production Products		
Raw materials	Substances in natural state	Crude oil, sand, gas, water
Processed materials	Basic substances used to manufacture products	Refined oil, steel, plastic, aluminum
Component Parts and Subassemblies		
Operations products	Products that are elements of other products	Brakes, transmissions, computer chips, switches, lights, cords
Operating services	Activities purchased to help run the business	Consulting, accounting, waste removal, employee food service
Operating supplies	Consumable items used by the business	Paper, pens, file folders, cleaning products

Figure 9.3   A Classification of Business Products

Capital Products **Capital products** are costly items that last a long time but are not part of any finished product. They usually are built or used to manufacture, distribute or support the development of other products. For accounting purposes, these items are depreciated over several years. Capital products are subdivided into installations and equipment.

Installations refer to house operations, and can also include office buildings, factories and distribution centers. Because they have a high cost and are intended to last for a considerable time, they are carefully selected by top management, and the involved salespeople possess technical expertise. Marketing generally requires a team approach, an understanding of the prospective client's business, and customization of the product to meet the unique requirements of each customer. Providers range from a small construction firm that may put up an office for a local dentist to companies such as Bechtel, a huge multinational. It has offices in most world regions and relies on marketing skills to find opportunities and win construction business globally.

Equipment is movable capital goods, such as drills, computers and forklifts,

Capital Product

A costly item that lasts a long time but does not become part of any finished product.

used to manufacture or maintain other products. ABB and AO Smith sell robotics designed for specific tasks to many types of manufacturers. General Motors (GM), Nissan and Toyota have purchased thousands of robots for welding alone; other functions include sorting, lifting and inspecting. Of course, products that bring information to businesses represent a huge equipment marketing opportunity. Companies such as Sun Microsystems sell computerized workstations for professional and clerical workers. These products are connected through elaborate networks that allow personnel around the globe to tie into the company system. Airline reservations in Japan, France, the United States and the Czech Republic are likely to be made this way. It is not unusual for equipment systems like these to be priced at hundreds of millions of dollars.

Production Products

Production products — which include raw materials, processed materials, component parts and subassemblies — become part of other goods. Few manufacturers extract the raw materials or make all the components for a finished product. Instead, they rely on external suppliers to perform at least part of the task. Raw materials are basic substances used in the manufacture of products, such as ore to produce steel, or cotton and wool for textiles, oil for plastics, and soybeans for food products. Companies such as Archer-Daniels-Midland (ADM) claim that they "feed the world" because their agricultural products go into so many food items. Headquartered in Decatur, Illinois, the company's 31,000 employees work with crops such as oilseeds, wheat and soybeans. The harvested products are converted into food ingredients, animal feeds, chemicals and alternative fuel options. ADM serves as a vital link between farmers and the global community.[10] Processed materials undergo an intermediate treatment — such as refining, chemical combination, purification, crushing or milling — before reaching the manufacturer.

Courtesy of Archer Daniels Midland Company

Component parts and subassemblies are manufactured goods that are elements of other products (like brake lines, components of antilock brake systems). Since these have several components and are part of still another product — vehicles — they are called subassemblies. Companies such as Eaton and North American Rockwell make components and subassemblies. Although each component is relatively inexpensive, manufacturing companies are likely to purchase large quantities at one time, numbering thousands or even millions of units.

Quality control and delivery of component parts can be very complicated, so successful companies must perform these operations at a high level of precision. Marketers stress this aspect of their product when selling to businesses, which usually is done by highly trained sales representatives.

Operations Products

Operations products are purchased to help run the business but are not included in finished products. These range from very inexpensive items, such as paper clips, to an expensive product like nuclear waste removal from power plants. Operations products are subdivided into supplies and services. **Supplies** are consumable items that may seem relatively unimportant, but in total they can involve large sums. In banks, printed business forms alone often cost several hundred thousand dollars a year. Items such as pens, folders and cleaning products

---

Production Products

Raw materials, processed materials, component parts, and subassemblies that become part of other goods.

Operations Products

Products purchased to help run a business and are not included in finished products.

Supplies

Consumable items used for business operations.

can contribute significantly to company costs. Even with the increased use of the Internet and more offices going paperless, Xerox found that the world prints about 2.8 trillion pages each year, with 45 percent of them read only once.[11]

Operations services are activities purchased to help run the business. Examples are legal, accounting, advertising and billing services. Accenture and McKinsey & Company all compete for lucrative contracts involving R&D, tactical and strategic plans and design of information systems, while companies like ARAMARK supply food services. Many companies subcontract other companies to help handle customer service; for example, if your Toshiba laptop computer needs to be repaired, UPS will pick it up, repair it and return it to you within four days. By having a third party (UPS) handle its customer service, Toshiba was able to greatly reduce the repair turnaround time and increase customer satisfaction.[12]

PRODUCT LINE DECISIONS

Product lines must be configured for domestic and global markets. Decisions about how many lines to carry, how many products will be in each line and the degree of standardization across markets shape the overall offering of an organization. A product line consists of closely related products marketed by a single organization. A company may have one line or several, but a single line usually focuses on the same type of benefit, such as hair care. An **item** is a specific version of a product within a product line. Each item, in turn, consists of several units, which refers to the specific product amount, container type and formula. Retailers call these stock keeping units (SKUs) to identify the variations they regularly have on their shelves.

Consider a line of products in the hair-care category made by Procter & Gamble: Pantene, which includes several items — mousse, styling gel, hair spray and shampoo. Pantene's 40-SKU shampoo product line consists of five different categories based on the consumer's desired style (basic, volume, smooth, curl and color care). Each category has a shampoo, a conditioner, two hairsprays and various other styling aids. Procter & Gamble carefully manages the entire line, and Pantene is the market leader in shampoo and conditioner.

Product Depth and Breadth Most companies need to consider how broad and deep their product lines should be, as described in Figure 9.4. The **depth** of a product line refers to the number of items it is composed of. Since the Pantene shampoo product line consists of many items, it is said to be deep. **Breadth** of product lines refers to the number of different lines a company markets. General Electric markets household products to consumers and nuclear power plants to foreign governments, as well as hundreds of other product lines, classifying it as very broad.

Hershey's candies can be considered a narrow and deep product line. Its products fall into a single category, candy, and there is a wide variety of items. Hershey's produces everything from their gourmet CaCao Reserve chocolate bar to Bubble Yum. Organizations such as Domino's Pizza have a broad and shallow product line. Domino's menu offers a wide variety of products that include pizza, salads and drinks, with only a few choices within each category.

Most companies with a broad product line are large, although there are exceptions. Small organizations usually lack the resources for competing across diverse product categories. Brunswick is a large company that uses a broad and deep product line strategy. Its brand

Product Line

Closely related products marketed by the organization.

Item

A specific version of a product within a product line.

Depth

The number of items in a product line.

Breadth

The number of different lines a company markets.

	PRODUCT LINE BREADTH	
	Narrow	Broad
Shallow	Few product lines with a few items in each	Many different product lines with a few items in each
Deep	Few product lines with many items in each	Many different product lines with many items in each

PRODUCT LINE DEPTH

Figure 9.4   Product Line Depth and Breadth

name, Sea Ray, represents the product line of recreational boats, which range from 12 to more than 80 feet in length. It also owns Brunswick Bowling & Billiards, which markets a line of products ranging from alleys with automatic pinsetters to bowling balls and other equipment. Another Brunswick product line is fishing equipment, marketed under the Zebco brand name, with several types of rods, reels and related items. Brunswick also markets a number of other product lines with several items in each.

Now think about 7-11. It carries a broad product line, but the variety of items within each is limited. In other words, 7-11 carries a broad and shallow product line, including beverages, cleaning supplies, food, over-the-counter pharmaceuticals, snack foods, auto supplies, cosmetics and energy bars.

It is entirely possible for companies to overextend their resources and make product lines too deep or broad, so they need to be adaptable and ready to restructure if necessary.

7-11 caries a broad and shallow product line.

GLOBAL PRODUCT DECISIONS

The globalization of business creates several product-related dilemmas. Among the most critical is determining the optimal amount of standardization for individual products and lines across market regions. Different areas of the world vary greatly in terms of consumer and business purchasing approaches, media exposure, tastes and preferences. In addition, product standards and regulations, measurements and calibration systems, and economic factors vary immensely. Despite these differences, many firms like to standardize products to achieve economics of scale in R&D, production and marketing.

Standardization plays a major role in global company strategy. Companies often start by standardizing their suppliers to consolidate worldwide supply purchasing, improve material quality and reduce costs. By purchasing from a few similar suppliers, companies reduce product variations from region to region and develop relationships with their suppliers that enhance customer satisfaction.

Although product modifications usually center around conforming to local needs, the costs can be very high. Europe and the United States use different interfaces for electronics, so products made for one market simply will not work in the other. R&D costs to conform to standards run into the hundreds of millions for companies such as Siemens in Germany.

The depth and breadth of a product line have a lot to do with successful global competition. Pepsi and Coca-Cola continually compete with each other to expand their product lines. Some believe Coke's global strategy of carrying a narrow, deep product line focused strictly on beverages, with geographic variations, is one reason for its success. Pepsi, in contrast, has a broader line that includes convenience food chains and has standardized its beverage line globally. Clearly, product line breadth and depth doesn't determine why one company outsells another, but the issue is important in developing global strategy. Although Coca-Cola remains the No. 1 beverage company with a deep product line, Pepsi is gaining in popularity through its other products. Pepsi recently acquired the South Beach Beverage Company, makers of SoBe, and Quaker Oats, maker of Gatorade, deepening its beverage offerings to include fruit blends, teas and energy drinks, in addition to its already-held Aquafina,

All Sport, Lipton's Ice Tea and Frappuccino. Coca-Cola has responded to Pepsi's expansion by purchasing Planet Java coffee, selling its own energy drink KMX, and experimenting with children's milk drinks. Coca-Cola also has its own brands of bottled water, sports drink, and root beer, in addition to other brands sold around the world. With Pepsi deriving 65 percent of its profits from its snack food line, including products such as Doritos, Cheetos and Sun Chips, Coca-Cola must continue to promote its beverage products in ways that capture buyers in order to retain its lead.[13]

Even some companies with deep domestic product lines find additions are necessary to compete internationally. Newell Rubbermaid, known for its large number of products, has its product lines divided to include products marketed globally, which account for approximately 28 percent of total revenues. Newell Rubbermaid implemented a global group product line strategy with four distinct product lines: cleaning, organization and decor; office products; tools and hardware; and home and family. The focus is to invest in strategic brands, reduce supply chain costs, strengthen the portfolio and streamline non-strategic selling, general and administrative (SG&A) expenses.[14] Experience with a deep and broad product line in the consumer, industrial and health care fields will be important as companies seek to connect with the needs and tastes of consumers in diverse regions.

Emerging economies such as China present their own problems from a product standpoint because large and risky investments in design and manufacturing are often necessary. For example, Caterpillar Inc. has 16 manufacturing facilities in China, with nine more under construction; however, its first-quarter sales for 2012 plunged by $250 million, a far cry from the expected growth of 5 to 10 percent. Mike DeWalt, the head of investor relations, admitted the company had "too many finished goods on the ground" in China and was planning to divert about a fifth of its excavator production to other countries.[15]

BRAND MANAGEMENT

Brand

A distinguishing name or symbol to identify and differentiate products from those of competitors.

A **brand** is a distinguishing name or symbol that identifies and differentiates products from those offered by competitors.[16] Take a moment to try to name the top 10 brands in the world (check Figure 9.5 when you're done). No matter what criteria are used in creating such a list, the same brands tend to emerge as leaders.

Brands are very powerful concepts in business. They send strong signals about what a company represents, signals that can make or break a reputation. To a consumer, a trusted brand promises high quality, but a "tainted" reputation means poor quality or bad service. One study by Pricewaterhouse-Coopers found that 80 percent of online shoppers say that their purchasing decisions are strongly influenced by the need to buy brand-name products.[17]

Rank	2000	2013
1.	Coca-Cola	Apple
2.	Microsoft	Google
3.	IBM	Coca-Cola
4.	Intel	IBM
5.	Nokia	Microsoft
6.	General Electric	General Electric
7.	Ford	McDonalds
8.	Disney	Samsung
9.	McDonald's	Intel
10.	AT&T	Toyota

Figure 9.5   Top 10 Brands Worldwide
Source: Interbrand & Business Week — Best Global Brands 2013

Today, brands do far more than identify the manufacturer. They have become "personalities" with a character much greater than the products they represent. An early example of successful branding is Ivory soap, introduced in 1879 by Harvey Procter. With its claim of "99.44 percent pure," it has long been the leader of the soap market. Estimates suggest that the Ivory brand has brought more than $3 billion in profit to Procter & Gamble over the years. In some cases the brand name becomes the product itself to many people: Xerox, Band-Aid, Kleenex and Post-It Notes are synonymous with their functions. And such brands as Nabisco, Kellogg's, Kodak, Gillette, Campbell's and Goodyear have all outlived the specific items they represented when introduced. Although the products themselves may have changed due to technology, customer preferences and modernization, the brand name has remained consistent.

Historically, brands were used to identify a product's manufacturer. They also protected both the customer and the producer by ensuring that the products met certain quality standards and came from a reputable source. Companies with early success in building brands include Procter & Gamble (P&G), IBM, McDonalds, Sony, American Express, Volkswagen, American Airlines, Pepsi and Kodak. Such companies created a brand perceived by consumers as having more intrinsic value.

In the 1960s, strategy was simple: The greater the perceived value, the greater the sales. This strategy is still used today, but companies must work hard to ensure that the products themselves provide the added value communicated by the name. Brand strategies help businesses such as Coca-Cola, Disney, Gillette and Intel develop and retain credibility with customers, and that shows no sign of changing. According to TNS Media Intelligence, a leading provider of market information, most advertising expenditures are brand related.[18]

TRADEMARKS

Trademark (Brand Mark)

A distinctive form or figure that identifies the brand.

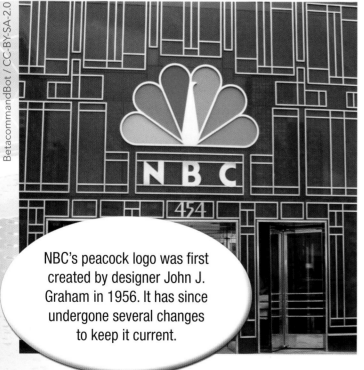

NBC's peacock logo was first created by designer John J. Graham in 1956. It has since undergone several changes to keep it current.

People tend to use the words "brand" and "trademark" interchangeably, but there are some notable differences. The brand name is the wording attached to the product. Adidas, Levis and Chiquita are brand names. The **trademark (brand mark)** is a word, phrase, symbol, or design that identifies and distinguishes the source of a good/service. The term "trademark" is often used to refer to both trademarks and service marks.[19] A picture is called a trademark symbol, such as McDonald's golden arches; distinctively shaped letters are called a logo: IBM, HBO, GE. Other examples are NBC's peacock, Adidas's three stripes and Chrysler's five-pointed star.

An identifying mark, slogan or set of words can provide immediate recognition and credibility even when applied to products owned by other companies. FAFSA is commonly known as Free Application for Federal Student Aid, though it is not a trademark. When a company began running a website called FAFSA.com, offering financial aid forms online and by phone to students, the Department of Education protested, claiming that the site deceived customers by associating itself with the government organization and implying that fees were required for financial aid services. The site's operator says that he is not trying to trick students into paying for services, while the Department of Education claims that it should have the rights to the FAFSA.com site by common law. Now, the site contains a disclaimer that it is not affiliated with the Department of Education. Though not explicitly involving trademarks, this issue demonstrates the effectiveness of name-brand association.

TRADEMARK PIRACY

The brand name and trademark symbols or logos are protected by law if they are registered. That gives the owner sole right to use them any way he or she chooses. Just as most people want to protect their reputation, companies are careful to protect a brand from imitators or competitors. For example, a federal court in Milwaukee ruled that the Hog Farm, a motorcycle parts and repair shop, had infringed on the rights of Harley-Davidson, whose motorcycles are widely known as "hogs."

Apple secured a massive patent that could have turned the smartphone industry upside-down. It was granted a series of patents that include almost all of the user interface elements in smartphones, including the multi-touch system developed for its iPhone. Tim Cook, Apple's CEO, stated "From our point of view, it's important that Apple not be the developer for the world. We can't take all of our energy and all of our care and finish the painting, then have someone else put their name on it". While Apple wants proprietary standards, Google advocates the broadening of Standards Essential Patent (SEP) product category of patents, making these popular features that consumers know and love shared industry standards.[20]

Securing trademarks globally can be very tricky. People throughout the world recognize Mickey Mouse and Donald Duck as Disney characters, but a court in Indonesia ruled that the duck's picture could be used by a local company. This situation occurs frequently, particularly in developing countries where more pressing problems command government attention. In advanced economies, trademark protection is considered essential for sound competitive industrial policy. Elsewhere trademarks may be viewed as merely a tool to stimulate commerce. No single world policy has yet been developed that takes into account the perspectives of all nations.

No one knows exactly how big the market for counterfeit goods is, but trade associations generally agree that it is an estimated $750 billion-a-year business. About 80 percent of consumers worldwide regularly purchase counterfeit products.[21] Counterfeiting has become so widespread that *Fortune* has coined the term "brand-napping" for copying products and affixing illegal labels. This represents huge losses to legitimate owners of the brands. Pirated products range from computer software and designer goods to soap and candy. Packaging closely resembles that of the American-made counterpart, and often stolen logo designs are used. Individual firms may or may not choose to file an international suit against offenders.

Many problems with brand counterfeiting are occurring in China. In fact, China accounts for nearly two-thirds of all counterfeit goods. Recent raids in China have turned up everything from fake Sony PlayStation game controllers, Sharpie markers, Cisco Systems router interface cards, even counterfeit elevators. When these components leave China, they sometimes end up in the product's legitimate supply chain, and can force companies to initiate expensive recalls. However, many fakes today are getting so good that even company executives say that it takes a forensic scientist to distinguish them from the real thing.[22] For instance, the popular baby carrier brand Ergobaby has been fighting counterfeit versions of its carriers, which are often sold through online auction sites such as eBay. The company has released lists of known or suspected sellers of counterfeit carriers, along with suggestions for how to spot fakes.[23]

Unfortunately, some fakes can have very serious consequences. For example, it is estimated that in a single year, fake drugs led to the deaths of 192,000 patients in China who were given ineffective treatments. According to the World Health Organization, counterfeit drugs account for more than 10 percent of the total global supply and can run as high as 50 percent in parts of Africa and Asia. Merck, a large pharmaceutical company, exclusively funded Global Pharma Health Fund (GPHF) in an effort to derail the counterfeit drug market. The organization will work in conjunction with various governmental and world health agencies.[24] U.S. trade negotiations have lessened the occurrence of infringements, but developing countries have little incentive to enforce laws. Efforts continue through such organizations as GATT (General Agreement on Tariffs and Trade) and the United Nations to develop international norms.

BRAND STRATEGIES

There are a number of brand strategies, as shown in Figure 9.6. In addition to a generic or nonbranded approach, the most common types are individual, family, manufacturer (national), private and hybrid.

Generic Brand Strategy

Strategy in which no brand name is used.

Generic Strategy   A **generic brand strategy** uses no brand name whatsoever. Firms generally select this approach when they want to gain a low-cost commodity market position. As mentioned before, pharmaceutical companies often adopt

Type	Description	Reasons for Use	Examples
Generic	No brand name is used.	Lower cost. Commodity position.	Pharmaceuticals Vegetables
Individual	Unique brand name for each major product or line.	Company has dissimilar products. Each product is matched to a segment. Products compete against one another.	Procter & Gamble's Tide, Bold, Cheer, Dreft, Era, Gain, Ivory, Oxydol, and Solo laundry detergents.
Family	Umbrella name covers all products in the line.	Economical way to create one brand identity for all existing and new products. Increase awareness and market presence by using one image for all.	Dole Sony Campbell's Sara Lee Black & Decker
Manufacturer (national)	Brand name synonymous with the owner.	Ties R&D, manufacturing, and company reputation to the product.	McDonald's Kodak Fisher-Price Johnson & Johnson General Motors General Electric
Private (labels)	Brand name applied to supplier's product by wholesaler or retailer.	Lower cost. Builds on and enhances reputation of firm. Enhances firm's buying power.	Meijer A&P: Aunt Jane Wal-Mart: Sam's American Choice ACE Hardware IGA Stores Spartain Stores Sears: Kenmore
Hybrid	Two or more approaches are used.	Merger and acquisition. Gain benefits of all approaches.	Kraft

Figure 9.6   Types of Brand Strategies

this strategy. Some grocery stores devote entire aisles exclusively to generic products, packaged in plain black and white. Many consumers prefer generics because they cost less than name brands.

Individual Brand Strategy

An **individual brand strategy** assigns a unique brand name to each major product or product line. There are three situations in which this approach is likely to be used. First, companies may have different product lines that compete against one another. For example, Ford Motor Company builds market share with several individual brands such as Mazda, Lincoln and Mercury. Second, products within one line may be matched with unique market segment needs. For example, Procter & Gamble's nine laundry detergents appeal to different segments. Third, a company may make highly dissimilar products. For example, Kellogg markets breakfast cereals under its name, toaster pastries under the Pop-Tarts brand and pies under the Mrs. Smith's label.

Individual Brand Strategy

Strategy in which there is a unique name for each major product or product line.

Family Brand Strategy

A **family brand strategy** uses a single brand name for the entire group of products in the company's line(s). This can be very cost-effective, because advertising, promotion and distribution resources can be focused to create a single image in the marketplace. The result is increased consumer awareness of the company and its products, such as Black & Decker tools.

The family brand strategy is used when products are similar. Dole markets more than 20 mainstream fruits and vegetables as well as numerous exotic fruits under one name. The Sony name covers hundreds of products, from high-priced stereos to inexpensive alarm-clock radios. The family brand approach has allowed Sony to introduce and eliminate products fairly rapidly while almost guaranteeing that its new products will at least be tried. Both Dole and Sony have sought to make their names synonymous with quality, regardless of the specific product.

Family Brand Strategy

Strategy in which a single brand name covers the entire group of products in the company's line(s).

Manufacturer's Brand Strategy

Manufacturer's brands (national brand), as the term implies, are named after the maker. Sometimes they are called national brands or global brands, since the products often are found throughout the country or world. We've already mentioned a few in this chapter, such as Kodak and General Electric, but manufacturer's brands also can be local, such as Hanover pretzels. The company's reputation is closely tied to the product. Benetton, McDonald's and Johnson & Johnson use public relations, advertising and other means to ensure that the public connects their products with the policies of the firm. Usually this means creating a singular image for the company and the products it makes. Kodak's brand name revolves around imaging; Fisher-Price is known for products that relate to child development and safety; and Gerber is famous for baby food.

Manufacturer's Brand (National Brand)

Brand named after the manufacturer.

Private Brand Strategy

When wholesalers or retailers place their own name on a product, it's called a **private brand (private label)**. Since these are promoted locally rather than nationally, they can be sold at a lower price than manufacturer's brands. Private labels allow the reseller to build and enhance its own reputation. By carefully selecting suppliers and developing quality control mechanisms, Meijer can promote its line of private brands by exceeding the quality of national brands at a lower price. Meijer also offers specialty labels such as Meijer Gold, Organics and Naturals, which give consumers more options for their specific needs.[25] In addition, private brands enable retailers and wholesalers to differentiate themselves from competitors.

Companies that use private labels attempt to understand consumers better than national marketers in several key respects, especially in their knowledge of local or regional consumer needs and shopping habits. Although they do not have the resources to innovate far beyond current brands, their goal is to increase in-store brand sales, which may carry strong margins. For their national brand competitors, the challenge is to persuade consumers not to be drawn by the low prices. Some compa-

Private Brand (Private Label)

The name wholesalers or retailers attach to products they resell for numerous suppliers.

nies like Home Depot present particular challenges to manufacturers. It markets its own private brands, yet Home Depot is the major retail outlet for many manufacturers' brands. Essentially, these manufactures must cooperate with Home Depot while competing against its increasingly popular private brands.

The "battle of the brands" rivalry between in-store and national products is intense. The private label market is growing in supermarkets as consumers become more cost-conscious and as private label brands rival the quality of national brands. The "battle" started when large manufacturers gained power by selling products through a broad range of distribution channels, and their size allowed them to place many demands on retailers. Large retailers countered by creating private labels.

Hybrid Brand Strategy

A combination of two or more brand strategies.

Hybrid Brand Strategy Many firms employ a **hybrid brand strategy**, which is a combination of two or more approaches. Often this happens when mergers and acquisitions join organizations that employ different strategies. In these cases, executives must decide whether to blend the acquired brands into the company's portfolio or let them maintain their identity.

BRAND EQUITY: THE VALUE OF A SUCCESSFUL BRAND

Brand Equity

The assets linked with the brand name and symbol that add value to the product.

Brand equity refers to the assets linked with the brand name and symbol that add value to the product or service.[26] It indicates (in both denotative and connotative lights) how valuable the brand is to the parent company. It denotes (identifies) what the brand is, such as Head & Shoulders or Selsun Blue shampoo. It also connotes (produces an image of) the brand's relationship to the consumer's lifestyle. Connotative meanings, if properly supported, can strengthen over time. Names such as Gillette, Morton's Salt and Betty Crocker predate your grandparents. When people invest in a home and gradually purchase it from the mortgage company, we say that they are earning or gaining equity. In a similar fashion, companies must invest in developing brands. Through sustained communication of the brand's connotative qualities, value is increased. Brand equity is an intangible asset with five dimensions, as shown in Figure 9.7. Let's look at each dimension in more detail

Brand Awareness

The extent to which consumers recognize the brand and are likely to include it among the set of brands they consider.

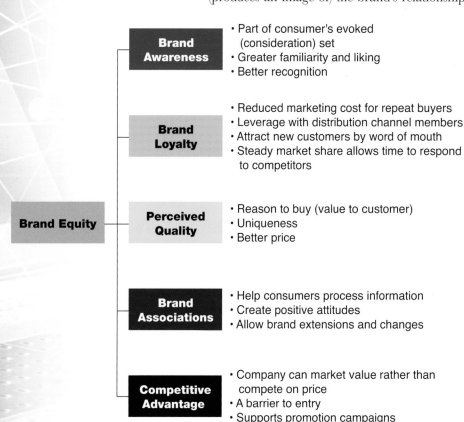

Brand Awareness Brand awareness is the extent to which consumers recognize the name and are likely to include it among the set of brands they consider. If consumers are familiar with a brand and like it, they will have positive attitudes about the product(s) with that name. Consider the warmth and reli-

Figure 9.7   The Five Dimensions of Brand Equity
Source: Adapted from David A. Aaker, Managing Brand Equity (New York: The Free Press, 1991), inside cover.

ability of the Betty Crocker mother figure or Pillsbury's Poppin' Fresh baker. Because strong brands are often global, they may be recognized around the world and provide traveling consumers with ready access to a familiar item. High brand awareness also represents the commitment of the company to maintaining long-term standards of excellence for the consumer.

Even established companies work to sustain brand awareness. One way Kraft does this is through its website, www.kraftfoods.com, which provides information on nutrition, cooking for specific occasions, mealtime tips, a personal recipe box and recipes customized to suit the user's available ingredients. Customers can also download apps to their smart phones and tablets that allow them to gain access to recipes and Kraft inspired games on the go. Online customers who choose to add their address to a marketing list will receive product information, promotions, a quarterly magazine and coupons through the mail.[27] This increased accessibility to Kraft's brand name is intended to heighten brand awareness.

Brand Loyalty

Brand loyalty occurs when consumers select a particular brand over others on a regular basis. Brand loyalty leads to lower overall marketing costs because it's much less expensive to persuade repeat buyers than to create new ones. Distribution channel members are more likely to provide a good location within their outlet for the sale of an item with high brand loyalty. Furthermore, companies with faithful customers tend to be less susceptible to economic downturns or new competitors. Loyal buyers are not immediately inclined to look at other options, staying with the product even in times of economic hardship.

> **Brand Loyalty**
>
> A dimension of brand equity that causes consumers to choose one brand over others available.

Brand loyalty is highest among more mature segments, who tend to find a brand they like and stick with it, whereas younger generations are more willing to experiment with various brands. However, studies show that brand loyalty may begin as early as the age of 2. The 9-10 age group, usually referred to as "tweens," is the transitional generation, when "collective individualism" is a big trend; the 13-15 age group is more aware of what is "cool" and less affected by other advertisers.[28] Loyalty produces sales that enhance the earning power of the company. Cheerwine, created in 1917, is a nonalcoholic, carbonated drink produced by Carolina Beverage Corporation and sold mainly in the Southeast. Although Cheerwine does not even register in national market-share polls, it has established itself as a Southern icon and has found its way of creating a niche of loyal customers. Carolinians are so loyal to the drink that those who relocate often write the company asking where they can find Cheerwine near their new location. Loyalists

tell others about their favorite brand, often referred to as the "Nectar of the Tarheels" and the "Legend."[29]

Even Mother Nature's own fruits have been branded — bananas by Chiquita and oranges by Sunkist. While there is no critical difference between them and other bananas and oranges, consumers recognize and prefer the brand names. For a brand to be valuable to a company, a significant number of customers must prefer it over competitive brands.

Brand Insistence

A dimension of brand equity that makes consumers unwilling to accept substitutes for the brand.

Perceived Brand Quality

The degree to which a brand consistently produces satisfaction by meeting customer expectations.

The best kind of loyalty for a company is when consumers insist on the company's brand. **Brand insistence** occurs when consumers are unwilling to accept substitutes, an enviable position for the corporation, especially in the long run. This degree of loyalty is more likely for specialty items, such as polo shirts or branded pharmaceuticals, but in recent years, some unlikely products have gained brand insistence status. It used to be that technology products, such as electrical components, did not have much brand awareness, to say nothing of brand loyalty. Intel Corporation, the pioneering semiconductor company, gave technology branding a boost. It has persuaded consumers to insist on Intel microprocessors in their PCs and mobile devices. Apple has done the same; if you like your iPhone, you probably have - or want - an apple computer. You likely use iTunes and FaceTime with friends. Most Apple users are not only brand loyal, they are also brand insistent.

Perceived Brand Quality The third dimension of brand equity is **perceived brand quality**, the degree to which brands consistently produce satisfaction by

CREATING & CAPTURING VALUE *Globally*

UGG Brand Boots: Function or Fashion?

From the beaches of Australia to nearly every college campus in the U.S., those bulky, fur-lined boots known as UGGs have become a staple in many wardrobes year-round. The makers at UGG have found a way to establish traditional sheepskin as one of the most luxurious kinds of footwear.

The UGG journey began when Australian surfer Brian Smith came to California with a sack full of sheepskin boots. The style spread fairly quickly on the West Coast, but didn't make its way across the U.S. until 1998, after company was acquired by Deckers Outdoor Corporation. Using a premium marketing strategy, UGG Australia went straight for distribution at high-end department stores. Those working for UGG pride themselves on their lavish and relatively pricey products.

There are plenty of imitation UGG boots out there, found anywhere from Payless to Nordstrom's, but nothing quite compares to the quality of the UGG Australia brand. Almost all of its products use Grade-A sheepskin; even some of the brand's flip flops feature a sheep-

skin footbed. This material is naturally thermostatic, which keeps feet at normal body temperature no matter what the outside thermometer says. This versatility makes UGGs popular on both the sandy beaches of California and during the frigid temperatures of a Midwestern winter. And UGGs are available for the whole family in boundless colors and styles.

UGG has definitely proven that luxurious footwear doesn't have to come in the form of 5-inch stilettos. UGGs can be worn with a bathing suit, snow pants, jeans, leggings — the list goes on. But what this means for the average person is that you can be sexy and fashionable without sacrificing comfort and functionality.

Deckers Outdoor Corporation understands how to market its products, building several of its niche brands into global market leaders. Teva, Simple and UGG footwear brands are certainly attracting customers, through both function and fashion.

www.uggaustralia.com, website visited March 7, 2012.

meeting customer expectations. This is one of the most important reasons consumers buy a product. The high or unique quality of a brand is directly related to what consumers are willing to pay and to whether the firm can charge a premium. For example, having and using a major accounting firm is associated with premium audit fees. However, a number of companies are willing to pay higher fees for the perceived higher quality of a Big Four audit, even though another firm could provide the identical service at a lower price.

Brand Associations Brand equity also involves establishing **brand associations** that evoke positive attitudes and feelings in consumers' minds. This enables firms to create messages that gain consumers' attention more easily and extends the company's good reputation to additional products. For instance, Procter & Gamble marketed only 13 advertised brands in 1950. By 1991, there were more than 100, and there are more than 300 today. Twenty-five of these brands are called its Billion-Dollar Brands, each generating more than $1 billion in annual sales. [30] In a hard-hitting campaign against Yamaha motorcycles, Honda used brand associations with its automobiles. It quickly produced a great number of motorcycles of every type in an effort to crowd Yamaha out of the market. This was a feasible strategy because consumers already had a positive feeling about the Honda brand name.

> Brand associations also can facilitate product changes. For example, Tide gradually altered its detergent from a bulky powder to concentrated powder and liquid forms. Since 1985, Patagonia has donated more than $31 million to grassroots environmental activists and more than 1,000 organizations through its Environmental Grants Program. As a member

of One Percent for the Planet, it contributes one percent of all sales to grassroots efforts. While encouraging a green lifestyle, Patagonia has also created affirmative brand awareness.[31] Positive brand associations help consumers make the transition to an altered product or a similar one with new features.

Competitive Advantage Finally, brand equity can lead to **competitive advantage**, since a company can sell value rather than compete on the basis of price alone. The firm can charge a premium for many of the intangible dimensions associated with the brand. Brand equity also creates competitive advantages by serving as a barrier to entry. In other words, it may be too risky or expensive for another company or brand to compete in the same market. In the 1980s, a battle of the brands among beer companies created an environment in which only the strong survived. Within only 10 years, hundreds of small and local breweries were put out of business by such companies as Anheuser-Busch, Stroh's, Miller and Coors. Nearly every beer company that relied on product processing and procedures rather than building brand equity fell out of contention.

MAINTAINING BRAND VALUE

How many times have you requested a Coke in a restaurant and been asked whether a Pepsi would be okay? Coca-Cola has gone to great lengths to make sure that the Coke brand does not become a generic name. Believe it or not, aspirin, escalator, kerosene, nylon and zipper were all brand names at one time. To prevent brand names from falling into the public domain, a company must continually announce and defend its exclusive ownership. Consequently, Coca-Cola waged court battles against retailers who substituted Pepsi when Coke was ordered. Without such efforts, Coke could have lost its trademark exclusivity.

Brand Associations

The positive attitudes and feelings a brand evokes in consumers' minds.

www.yamaha.com

Yamaha has six principles that guide its approach to environmental stewardship. Learn more about how Yamaha applies these principles across its many products by visiting its website.

Competitive Advantage

A dimension of brand equity that permits the product to be sold on a value basis rather than a price basis and may serve as a barrier to entrance against competitive products.

Often, the first manufacturer of a new technology or product becomes synonymous with the entire product class. Did you grow up believing that Kleenex was another name for facial tissue? Do you ask for a Band-Aid when you want an adhesive bandage? Many people say they are going to Xerox something, but they may be using a Canon or some other brand of copier. To avoid the loss of its exclusivity, Xerox runs advertisements explaining that "Xerox" is its registered trademark and should be used only when referring to the company and its products as opposed to a general process.

DEVELOPING A SUCCESSFUL BRAND NAME

Choosing a brand name may not be easy. Americans file more than 500,000 trademark applications each year, a number that continues to increase. To keep pace, the U.S. Patent and Trademark Office staff includes more than 400 trademark-examining attorneys.[32] This poses a challenge to companies that want a memorable and meaningful brand name. Name Lab Inc., a specialist in this area, recommends choosing names that eliminate cultural associations or linguistic borders and can therefore succeed globally uninhibited. Names like Sony, Kodak and Acura do not show bias toward a particular language or region, and are also memorable, unique and distinctive.[33]

Some firms have chosen brand names that communicate product attributes or benefits. For example, Wheaties describes the ingredients of the cereal. When "Breakfast of Champions" is added, we get an image of wholesomeness or goodness. The name Weight Watchers communicates a direct consumer behavior, and it carries strong associations with weight control and health.

Brand names must represent quality and commitment. That's why extensive research is usually conducted to identify whether the name is appropriate and can be used internationally. Standard Oil tested Exxon in multiple languages and foreign markets before making a final decision. Marketers must be acutely aware that not all brand names carry the same meaning when translated. For example, in the early 1990s, General Mills introduced a cereal called Fingos that was designed to be eaten with your fingers; however, it translated into a less than appetizing word for Hungarians. Also consider Chevy Nova, which in Spanish-speaking countries meant "no va," or "no go."

Some brand names are successful because of what they say about the user. Many convey a personality trait that makes the connection directly. Magazines such as GQ, Cosmopolitan and Vogue represent attributes that readers consider desirable.

Joint Marketing

Cooperation between two companies to sell their products, which tend to be complementary.

JOINT MARKETING OF BRANDS

Joint marketing is cooperation between two companies, often two goods manufacturers, to sell their brands. Since coupons and short-term promotions (such as refund certificates) often cause disloyalty and confusion among customers, replacing those tactics with joint marketing can build business for the cooperating companies. It is important for marketers to understand how a consumer perceives the way a product, brand and the corporations fit together. Even more so, it is crucial to create a positive impression before marketing a co-branded product.[34] An example of this can be found in the partnership between the National Basketball Association (NBA) and YouTube which has led to the creation of a channel where NBA fans can watch videos of their favorite athletes online as well as post videos of themselves doing NBA moves for the potential to be shown on a weekly TV segment. The NBA also posts select, behind-the-scenes features on its channel to give fans a personal look into their favorite sports teams.[35]

When you buy concert tickets at Ticketmaster.com, you may be offered free Apple iTunes downloads. By establishing this partnership, Ticketmaster.com was encouraging customers to purchase tickets through its venue by promoting iTunes. This type of cooperation is expected to become more frequent.[36] Starbucks has also partnered with Apple. Many Starbucks locations offer free iTunes of selected artists in conjunction with a beverage purchase. Joint marketing efforts such as these are usually successful when the consumer has a positive image of both companies.

PACKAGING AND LABELING

"People don't buy spray paint, they buy spray paint cans." That statement was made in a marketing research report for a major manufacturer in the industry to dramatize the importance of packaging. The research found that most buying decisions were made at the point of purchase. By looking at the color and design of the cans and by reading labels, consumers quickly determined which spray paint would best suit their needs.

Packaging and labeling once served simply to protect and identify the product inside. Arnold Palmer, golfing legend, has long been associated with his favorite refreshment, a mixed drink of half iced tea and half lemonade. Now the "Arnold Palmer" can be found at many golf pro shops, and on courses nationwide, recognizable in its distinctive bottle with the golf ball cap and Arnie's picture prominently displayed. Packaging has seven functions:

- Contain and protect items.

- Be environmentally friendly.

- Communicate messages to customers.

- Contain product codes.

- Make the product more convenient to use.

- Protect against misuse.

- Facilitate product storage.

The **labels** on a package inform consumers and help promote the product. The Fair Packaging and Labeling Act of 1966 requires that consumer products carry clear and easily understood labels, displaying the brand name and symbol, the manufacturer's name and address, the product content and amount, and recommended uses. The law also requires adequate information when value comparisons are made among competitive products.

In 1990, Congress passed the Nutritional Labeling and Education Act, which applies to food.[37] Excluded are meat, poultry and eggs (covered by U.S. Department of Agriculture regulations) as well as restaurants, delicatessens and infant formulas. Additional legislation that year required the FDA to develop standard definitions of terms commonly found on products, such as reduced calories, high fiber and low fat.[38] These laws affect about 15,000 U.S. food packagers as well as many importers. Food labels are required to display fat, saturated fat, cholesterol, carbohydrates, protein and the percentage of daily vitamin requirements contained. European standards on "diet" claims are even stricter. Research shows that the people most likely to read food labels are educated women who live with others, are relatively knowledge-

Labels

Information printed on a product's package to inform consumers and help promote the product.

able about nutrition, are concerned about the quality of food they purchase, and believe that current dietary recommendations are important to their health, while less educated men are the least likely to take a look.[39]

The Labeling of Hazardous Art Materials Act (LHAMA) of 1990 addresses another product category. The U.S. Public Interest Research Group (PIRG) lobbied for this legislation because it believed that a wide variety of suppliers inadequately warned consumers of chronic and long-term health risks related to certain chemicals used in their products.[40]

Marketers must take care to ensure that packages are properly labeled. They benefit from this along with their customers, particularly when health and safety issues are involved.

ETHICAL ISSUES SURROUNDING PRODUCT SAFETY AND LIABILITY

The Consumer Product Safety Act of 1972 created the Consumer Product Safety Commission (CPSC) to police consumer goods. It has broad authority over the end product, can demand recalls and redesigns, and even inspects production facilities. For example, a massive toy recall was recently issued for high lead content in the paint on children's toys imported from China. In response, toymakers such as Mattel instated a comprehensive safety protocol for all of its products.[41] Of particular significance is the commission's ability to bring criminal charges against companies and individuals who develop unsafe products.

Product Liability

The responsibility of marketers and manufacturers for injuries and damages caused by a faulty product.

Product liability refers to the fact that marketers and manufacturers are held responsible for injuries and damages caused by a faulty product. In one case the CPSC found that more than 7,000 people were being injured monthly on three-wheel all-terrain vehicles (ATVs), most of them made by Honda and Kawasaki. Although the number of accidents was well known to dealers and distributors, only when the CPSC applied pressure did the makers agree to stop marketing the product in the United States. Many people believe consumers had the right to know about the ATV injuries. Clearly, wider publicity about the hazards would have meant lost sales.

The liability issue involves the right to safety and the manufacturer's responsibility for designing safe products and for informing the public about any dangers. Most companies fulfill this obligation through the product warranty and, in extreme cases, product recalls.

PRODUCT WARRANTIES

Warranties

Written or implied expectations about product performance.

Warranties are written or implied expectations about product performance. An express warranty is a written statement about the content or quality of a product and the manufacturer's responsibility to repair or replace it if it fails to perform. For example, an express warranty may indicate that an item is handcrafted in the United States, or may use such general terms as "unconditionally guaranteed" or "fully guaranteed," or may be a technical description of the goods. In the past, when consumers made claims under a warranty, some unethical manufacturers made it very difficult for them to receive satisfaction, rendering many general warranty statements meaningless.

To address this problem, Congress passed the Magnuson-Moss Warranty–Federal Trade Commission Improvement Act in 1975. Essentially, the law requires that express warranties be written in clear language and indicate which parts or components are covered and which are not. If repair is included in the express warranty, it must occur within a reasonable time, free of charge. A full warranty states that either the merchandise will be repaired or the purchase price will be refunded if the product does not work after repair.

Many retailers pressure their suppliers to take back any product a customer returns for any reason. Companies such as Walmart have a very liberal return policy, allowing them to receive feedback on product performance and build good customer relations, which in turn helps to gain market share.

An implied warranty is an unwritten guarantee that the product or service will do the job it is intended to do. All products, even if not accompanied by a written statement, have an implied warranty based on the Uniform Commercial Code (UCC). Adopted in 1952, the UCC is a federal statute affecting the sale of goods and giving consumers the right to reject a product if it does not meet their needs. Many individual states also have laws protecting consumers.

PRODUCT RECALLS

Product Recall

The withdrawal from the market, by either a manufacturer or the federal government, and repair, replacement, or discontinuation of a potentially harmful product.

A **product recall** is the withdrawal of a potentially harmful product from the market, by either a manufacturer or the federal government, for its repair, replacement or discontinuation. The Consumer Product Safety Commission (CPSC) is the federal agency responsible for protecting consumers from product-related injuries. It establishes standards for product design and requires that products meet those standards during testing. Manufacturers and retailers are required by law to notify the CPSC if they find a defective product that may result in injury.

When a manufacturer realizes a product is defective, its response can inspire consumer confidence and actually promote sales. In Chapter 2, we described the actions of Johnson & Johnson during the Tylenol scare in 1982. The unprecedented recall brought tremendous positive publicity to the company. When Tylenol was returned to store shelves, consumers made it the top-selling pain reliever.

Just because a company issues a recall does not guarantee that consumers will take action or that they will see the company in a positive light. Sometimes they aren't even aware of a recall if they didn't complete and return a product registration card after purchase. Sears sent a letter to registered owners of a particular dishwasher that was being recalled. The letter used large red letters for these words: "Important Safety Notice. Dishwasher Rework — Potential Fire Hazard. Please Give This Your Immediate Attention." After three days the response rate was only 20 percent.[42]

Even when a company meets its legal obligations, consumer awareness and other factors may have a lot to do with ethical considerations that must be addressed. It may be more devastating for a company to resist recalling a faulty product. Toyota recalled 4.3 million vehicles, including Avalon, Camry, Corolla, Highlander, Matrix, Prius, RAV4, Sequoia, Tundra and Venza models. Owners were experiencing sticking gas pedals that could cause unwanted acceleration. In less than 4 months, Google had more than 10 million hits about the situation. The first sites tended to be created by Toyota itself in efforts to manage the negative fallout from customers with concerns. In addition to experiencing one of the largest recalls in auto history, Toyota was confronted by angry shareholders who claimed the company misinformed the public, causing the stock price to rise initially and then fall, costing shareholders millions of dollars. Several class-action lawsuits claimed that Toyota publicly dismissed the seriousness of design flaws, knowing that public knowledge of the problems might have resulted in a large sell-off of Toyota shares. The suits claimed that initially the company blamed acceleration problems on floor mats, leading many consumers to believe that the problems were not as serious as the design problems that were identified later. The company eventually acknowledged that the problem existed without floor mats.[43]

Throughout this chapter, we have explored a wide range of strategies — from bundling products into special value units to assuring product safety — that marketers employ to build strong brand equity and give appeal to existing products. In Chapter 10, we will take a look at the characteristics of goods, services and nonprofit marketing.

CHAPTER SUMMARY

Objective 1: Describe the major dimensions used by marketers to differentiate their products from competitors. Understand bundling and unbundling.

Products can be core, branded and augmented. The core product represents the most basic functions and benefits. Some call this the generic product. The branded product adds characteristics that help consumers differentiate it from others. The augmented product includes such features as delivery, warranty and customer service. A bundling strategy combines several products into one offering and sold together. When products are bundled, they provide more value to the buyer than if each were sold separately.

Objective 2: Understand consumer and business product classifications based on how and why products are purchased and consumed.

Five categories are used to classify consumer products. Unsought products are bought on the spur of the moment. They include novelty, impulse and low-involvement items. Emergency products are bought because of unexpected events, such as an accident or theft. Convenience products are inexpensive and are usually purchased near home. Brand name and wide distribution are very important for these items. Shopping items are selected after comparisons are made. They tend to be carefully chosen and are kept for a long time. Specialty products have unique characteristics and value. They are often high-involvement purchases.

Business products are divided into capital, production and operations products, depending on their primary use. Capital products include installations, such as offices and factories, and equipment, such as delivery vans and computers. These products last for a long time. Production products become part of other products. This category includes raw and processed materials, components and subassemblies. Operations products help run the business. These include services such as accounting and waste removal, and office supplies such as business forms and cleaning products.

Objective 3: Know how organizations make product line decisions that determine what will be sold, including the degree of standardization chosen for global markets.

A product line may be comprised of one item or a number of related products. Companies may have one or more product lines, each with many or few items. The term depth refers to the number of items in a product line; the term breadth refers to the number of lines the company offers. Most companies with broad lines are relatively large; those with narrow lines may be large or small. The degree to which products should be standardized is a major consideration for global firms. Some organizations pursue standardization to benefit from the resulting economies of scale, whereas others use a local strategy to respond to local needs.

Objective 4: Recognize that branding and brand strategies are important aspects of building and maintaining a brand name.

A brand is distinguished from the product in general or other brands. Brands signify the "personality" of a product. The brand name and trademark can provide immediate recognition and credibility. Consequently, companies must register and protect trademarks. This is particularly challenging in global markets because stolen brand names and counterfeit products are so prevalent. There are several brand strategies. The generic approach involves no brand name. The individual strategy uses a unique name for each product line. The family brand is one name that covers all products in the line. Manufacturer brands are synonymous with the company that owns them. Private label brands are names used by wholesalers or retailers for products supplied to them. Combining two or more of these strategies is called a hybrid approach.

Objective 5: Know how to create brand equity — the value associated with a product's name.

A strong brand name is extremely valuable, but developing that name is not simple. First, the name must be selected with care. It should be acceptable globally, represent quality and commitment, and be protected legally. A good brand can easily be extended to additional products as they are developed. Second, brand equity must be created by devoting ompany resources to each of its five dimensions: brand awareness, rand loyalty, perceived quality, brand associations and competitive advantage. Third, care must be taken to protect the brand so it does not ecome a generic name for the product.

bjective 6: Discuss the many legal and ethical issues surrounding brand and packaging decisions.

ederal laws and codes require that labels clearly identify the brand nd manufacturer and warn consumers of safety hazards associated vith use. Product liability holds marketers responsible for injuries and damages caused by a faulty product. Warranties refer to how products perform when used. In many cases, manufacturers are legally obligated to replace or repair faulty products. Express warranties are written. An implied warranty is unwritten. Essentially, a product should perform as it was designed. A product recall is instituted by the government or manufacturer to withdraw or modify a product. This occurs when a product is defective, especially if the potential for injury exists.

REVIEW YOUR UNDERSTANDING

1. What is a product? Give several examples.
2. What are core, branded and augmented products?
3. Explain bundling and unbundling?
4. What are five categories of consumer products? What are three categories of business products? Give examples.
5. Define product line, unit and SKU.
6. What is a broad and deep product line? What is a narrow and shallow product line? Give examples.
7. What are global products and brands?
8. What is joint marketing of products? Give an example.
9. What is brand equity? How is it developed?
10. Why is it important to secure trademarks?
11. Name and describe five brand categories.
12. What are the functions of packaging?
13. What is product liability?

DISCUSSION OF CONCEPTS

1. Imagine that you are a marketing manager at IBM responsible for the sale of personal computers to individual consumers. How would you describe your product in terms of core, branded and augmented characteristics? Which of these do you feel is most important?
2. What are some advantages of a bundling strategy over an unbundling strategy? Disadvantages?
3. Name the five categories of products based on consumer buying behavior. Why is it so important for marketers to understand the category of their product?
4. Discuss the differences between product line breadth and depth. What are some advantages and disadvantages of each combination of breadth and depth?
5. Classify each of the following companies in terms of product line breadth and depth and explain your reasoning: Sears, 7-Eleven, Hallmark, Walmart, Kmart, Victoria's Secret.
6. If you were the marketing manager at a company with a broad product line, which of the six brand strategies would you likely select? What factors would affect your decision? What if the product line were narrow?
7. What are the most important activities involved in developing a successful brand name? Once the name is developed, how is brand equity formed?
8. Name the key functions of packaging. Which do you feel is most important? Does this vary by product?
9. The Consumer Product Safety Commission is a government entity with the power to bring criminal charges against companies and individuals who develop and market unsafe products. Is it fair to consider marketers criminals if consumers are injured by their company's products? Why or why not?

KEY TERMS & DEFINITIONS

1. **Augmented product:** Product with characteristics that enhance its value beyond that of the core and branded product.

2. **Brand:** A distinguishing name or symbol to identify and differentiate products from those of competitors.

3. **Brand associations:** The positive attitudes and feelings a brand evokes in consumers' minds.

4. **Brand awareness:** The extent to which consumers recognize the brand and are likely to include it among the set of brands they consider.

5. **Branded product:** The core product plus the characteristics that allow the consumer to differentiate it from similar products.

6. **Brand equity:** The assets linked with the brand name and symbol that add value to the product.

7. **Brand insistence:** A dimension of brand equity that makes consumers unwilling to accept substitutes for the brand.

8. **Brand loyalty:** A dimension of brand equity that causes consumers to choose one brand over others available.

9. **Breadth:** The number of different lines a company markets.

10. **Bundling strategy:** A strategy in which several products are combined into a single offering.

11. **Capital product:** A costly item that lasts a long time but does not become part of any finished product.

12. **Competitive advantage:** A dimension of brand equity that permits the product to be sold on a value basis rather than a price basis and may serve as an entry barrier to competitive products.

13. **Convenience product:** A relatively inexpensive item that consumers purchase frequently and with minimum effort.

14. **Core product:** The essential physical item or intangible service that the customer receives.

15. **Depth:** The number of items in a product line.

16. **Emergency product:** A product purchased due to an unexpected event and for which the consumer has an urgent need.

17. **Family brand strategy:** Strategy in which a single brand name covers the entire group of products in the company's line(s).

18. **Generic brand strategy:** Strategy in which no brand name is used.

19. **Hybrid brand strategy:** A combination of two or more brand strategies.

20. **Individual brand strategy:** Strategy in which there is a unique name for each major product or product line.

21. **Item:** A specific version of a product within a product line.

22. **Joint marketing:** Cooperation between two companies to sell their products, which tend to be complementary.

23. **Labels:** Information printed on a product's package to inform consumers and help promote the product.

24. **Manufacturer's brand (national brand):** Brand named after the manufacturer.

25. **Operations products:** Products purchased to help run a business that are not included in the finished products.

26. **Perceived brand quality:** The degree to which a brand consistently produces satisfaction by meeting customer expectations.

27. **Private brand (private label):** The name wholesalers or retailers attach to products they resell for numerous suppliers.

28. **Product:** Any physical object, service, idea, person, event, place or organization offered to satisfy consumers' needs and wants.

29. **Product liability:** The responsibility of marketers and manufacturers for injuries and damages caused by a faulty product.

30. **Product line:** Closely related products marketed by the organization.

31. **Product recall:** The withdrawal from the market, by either a manufacturer or the federal government, and the repair, replacement or discontinuation of a potentially harmful product.

32. **Production product:** Raw materials, processed materials, component parts and subassemblies that become parts of other goods.

33. **Shopping product:** A purchase generally made only after the consumer has compared several alternatives.

34. **Specialty item:** A product with unique characteristics that provides unusual value to the purchaser.

35. **Supplies:** Consumable items used for business operations.

36. **Trademark (brand mark):** A distinctive form or figure that identifies the brand.

37. **Unsought product:** An item that consumers don't think about frequently and for which they don't perceive much need.

38. **Warranties:** Implied or written expectations about product performance.

REFERENCES

1. www.virgin.com, website visited July 22, 2012.

2. Allison Goodrich, "Harley-Davidson's electric bike gets mixed reactions," Northwest Herald, June 24, 2014.

3. Ibid.

4. Hannah Elliott, "If Harley-Davidson Makes An Electric Motorcycle Does That Make It Okay?," Forbes, June 23, 2014.

5. www.ustr.gov, website visited June 12, 2014.

6. "Best Global Brands 2013," Interbrand, www.interbrand.com, website visited June 12, 2014.

7. Patagonia, www.patagonia.com, website visited June 23, 2014.

8. "Toyota Harmony TV Commercial," YouTube, www.youtube.com, website visited June 23, 2014.

9. www.apple.com/ipod, website visited June 23, 2014.

10. "Overview," Archer Daniels Midland, www.adm.com, website visited June 26, 2014.

11. Waller, Dave, "Dave's Eco-nomics: Stop the paper chase," Management Today, February 2008.

12. "UPS Helps Toshiba Shrink Service Time from 2 Weeks to 4 Days," www.thenewlogistics.ups.com, website visited June 26, 2014.

13. www.pepsico.com, website visited June 26, 2014.

14. http://ir.newellrubbermaid.com/annuals/cfm, Annual Report, 2009.

15. "China Crushes Caterpillar," Forbes, www.forbes.com, May 6, 2012.

16. Aaker, David, A., Managing Brand Equity, (New York: The Free Press, 1991), pg. 7.

17. Jones, Glenda, S., "Your New Brand Image," Catalog Age, July 2000, pp. 175-178.

18. www.tns-mi.com, website visited April 4, 2014.

19. www.uspto.gov, website visited June 26, 2014.

20. Karen Haslam, "Many Apple Technologies Should be Shared Standards, Google Says," www.pcworld.com, July 23, 2012; Lou Hattersley "Massive Apple patent win could kill off Android completely," www.macworld.com, website visited July 19, 2012.

21. "Study shows most consumers buy counterfeit goods with little remorse," International Chamber of Commerce, www.iccwbo.org, December 2, 2009.

22. "Fakes!" Business Week cover story, www.businessweek.com, website visited April 16, 2014.

23. http://store.ergobaby.com/Content/AboutUs_Counterfeits, website visited August 5, 2014.

24. www.gphf.org, website visited April 16, 2014.

25. www.meijer.com, website visited April 17, 2014.

26. Managing Brand Equity, pg. 4.

27. www.kraftfoods.com, website visited June 30, 2014.

28. Gray, Rob, "Stages of Youth," Campaign, May 5, 2006, pg. 4-5.

29. www.cheerwine.com, website visited June 30, 2014.

30. Weilbacher, William M., Brand Marketing (Illinois: NTC Business Books, 1993), pg. 51; P&G Corporate Biographical Information, www.pg.com, website visited April 14, 2014.

31. "Environmental Grants Program," Patagonia, www.patagonia.com, website visited April 15, 2014.

32. www.uspto.gov, website visited April 4, 2014.

33. www.namelab.com, website visited April 12, 2014.

34. Helmig, Bernd, Huber, Jan-Alexander, Leeflang, Peter, "Explaining Behavioral Intentions Toward Co-Branded Products," Journal of Marketing Management, Vol. 23, No. 3-4, April 2007, pp. 285-304.

35. NBA, www.youtube.com, website visited June 30, 2014.

36. www.ticketmaster.com, website visited June 30, 2014.

37. Baum, Chris, "NLEA Compels Food Packagers to Redesign," Packaging, May 1994, pg. 21.

38. Dorfman, Andrea, "Less Bologna on the Shelves," Time, November 5, 1990, pg. 79.

39. Demetrakakes, Pam, "Packaging Field Gears Up for New Labeling Rules," Packaging, January 1993, pg. 3.

40. Hartley, Mark. "For the Sake of Invisible Ink," Occupational Health & Safety, December 1993, pg. 4.

41. Collins, Josephine, "Safety Zone: Massive Toy Recalls Have Rocked the Industry This Year — But Is Some Good Coming Out of the Bad?", License, www.licensemag.com, website visited April 16, 2014.

42. Recall letter from Sears, on file with authors.

43. DailyFinance: Betsy Schiffman, "Toyota's Second Shoe Drops: Shareholders Sue," www.dailyfinance.com, website visited March 22, 2014.

Chapter 10

GOODS, SERVICES
& NONPROFIT
MARKETING

College Summit is not an average nonprofit organization. With branches all over the United States, College Summit provides national services to train principals, teachers and students to boost college enrollment and create a college-going culture in their schools. It also provides workshops and classes to high school students to teach them how to get a jump start on college academics and application processes. Students work with writing coaches and college counselors free of charge to complete a quality college essay and a universal college application. Through College Summit's services, colleges benefit from diverse and talented students who might have otherwise been overlooked.

College Summit is extremely valuable to school districts to achieve education standards set by the federal law "No Child Left Behind," which requires school districts to show a certain degree of improvement. If a school district fails to show that it has been successfully educating students to federal standards, the district must change its curriculum or personnel, or bring in outside education experts to oversee progress and make recommendations. As a result, many local school districts partner with College Summit to obtain higher college attendance rates. College Summit participants enroll in college at a rate 20 percent higher than students who do not participate. About 700 teachers and counselors are trained each year to work with more than 50,000 students.

Over the years, College Summit has generated revenue in a number of ways, including federal grants and partnerships with businesses. Noteworthy companies such as Google, Wells Fargo, Citi Foundation and Deloitte support College Summit with a good portion of the organization's funds. Many of these donor companies have donated more than $1 million at a time to the nonprofit organization.

In a recent issue of the New York Times, College Summit's Chairman of the Board stated that the organization "held a series of roadshow meetings with finance executives to share the organization's objectives and seek their support." By doing this, College Summit raised $15 million in just nine months.

College Summit was also awarded $125,000 of President Obama's $1.4 million Nobel Peace Prize award, which supports students in communities across the country on the path to higher education. "College Summit is privileged that President Obama has made this commitment to our students and school partners," said J.B. Schramm, founder and C.E.O. of College Summit. "We believe ensuring that the next generation is ready to create, thrive and compete in 21st Century jobs is the single best way to advance innovation, prosperity and peace."

These types of support allow College Summit to continue to operate with great success as a nonprofit organization focused on providing services to give students a path to a higher education.[1]

<< Student participating in College Summit

Courtesy of College Summit

Learning Objectives

1. Identify the forces that have produced and will continue to create tremendous growth in the service economy.
2. Understand which characteristics of services must be adjusted for successful marketing.
3. Know how to develop the service mix.
4. Explore the expanded concept of services.
5. Appreciate the importance of nonprofit marketing and the uniqueness of this important marketing arena.

THE CONCEPT OF SERVICES

Service

An idea, task, experience, or activity that can be exchanged for value to satisfy the needs and wants of consumers and businesses.

Products can be either be goods (physical objects), or **services** (intangible ideas, tasks, experiences, performances or activities). A major difference between a service and a good is that services generally involve suppliers connecting directly with consumers for performance of the service. Your barber, your doctor and your professor all form a personal connection with you in order to perform their services. When you think about it, even goods are more valuable when accompanied by excellent service. Consequently, goods and services often go hand-in-hand.

To serve means to benefit a receiving party through personal acts. The marketing of services, by its very nature, concerns the development of beneficial relationships. Interpersonal skills are critical, because for a service to be performed well, these skills must help support the customer relationship. Marketers need to emphasize how well their company's service embodies these skills.

For more than a quarter century, the dollar volume of services in the U.S. economy has grown at nearly four percent annually with no sign of decline, approximately double the growth rate for products. Developed countries such as the United States rely on the marketing of services for domestic growth.

Burger King in Shenyang, the most populated city in Northeast China.

Services are also very important globally, representing about 60 percent of all trade among nations. The U.S. has emerged as the leader of services, with foreign countries spending more on American services than America spends on foreign ones.[2] Global marketing, therefore, is particularly important for many U.S. service providers. Burger King is already in many global marketplaces like Russia, Europe, the Middle East and Africa, and is now rapidly expanding in China. It is clearly focused on the global market; four-fifths of its new restaurants are opening outside America.[3] Western companies like Burger King have a unique advantage in marketing themselves as brands of choice for younger Chinese. Helen H. Wang, Award-winning author and expert on China's middle class, writes: "Sometimes, by simply keeping the locations clean, brightly lit, and air-conditioned, they can set themselves apart from competitors. This is one of the major reasons that many young Chinese have their first dates at Starbucks and hold their weddings at KFCs."[4]

As you can see in Figure 10.1, this chapter begins by looking at forces that will continue to produce explosive growth for services. Following this is an in-depth look at services, which shows how they are differentiated, their relationships to goods, the attributes consumers use to judge them, and elements of service quality. Next, we will describe the aspects marketers consider when developing the

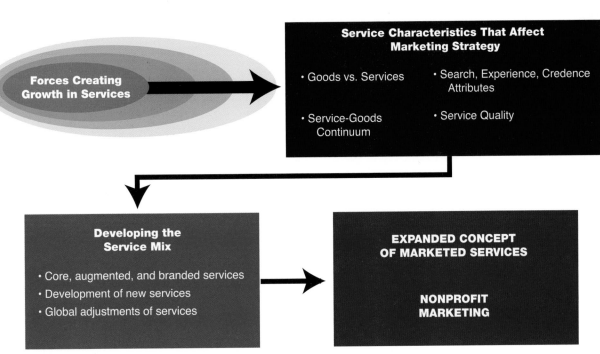

Figure 10.1 The Concept of Services

service mix. You will extend what you learned in Chapter 9 to services by looking at core, augmented and branded services with the development of new offerings. Keep in mind that services are as important in business-to-business marketing as they are in consumer marketing. Such traditional services as health care, insurance, energy, telecommunications, garbage and snow removal, accounting and tax preparation, auto service and restaurants have been the backbone of the service economy for a long time. Finally, we will discuss the importance of nonprofit service marketing.

GLOBAL FORCES CREATING GROWTH IN SERVICES

The service economy is not unique to the United States. As a nation develops and becomes more sophisticated, more and more of its total economic well-being is based on services. The Industrial Revolution brought about productivity gains through the substitution of machines for human and animal labor. The technology revolution that followed went far beyond that, seeing the creation of products that exceeded human and animal capabilities. A century ago, who would have imagined that millions of business travelers would routinely fly six miles above the earth and use plastic cards to charge phone calls while in flight? Air transportation and telecommunications, including the explosion of the Internet as a means of global communication, are examples of services that have brought the concept of a global community closer to reality. Figure 10.2 depicts the global forces that are influencing growth in services.

Figure 10.2 Global Forces Creating Growth in Services

TECHNOLOGY

Until recently, even advanced nations were dedicated to the production of goods. However, technology is producing more sophisticated services rapidly, and today's technologies generally require highly trained professionals to educate consumers. Smaller percentages of the population are now able to produce greater quantities of more valuable goods, thereby shifting the emphasis to value-added services. Some of these services in the consumer sector include entertainment, travel, health and education, while consulting and environmental controls have risen to prominence in the B2B sector.

The technological revolution is making an information revolution possible, which facilitates nearly every human endeavor. Computer and web-based technology is increasing exponentially. An array of devices let "lifeloggers" record nearly every aspect of their lives, from their sleep (with the Zeo) to their exercise (Fitbit and Motoactv) to their travel (just about any smartphone), then upload it, sync it or share it with PCs, social media sites and more.[5] Each generation of microprocessors is replaced by technologies that operate millions of times faster, continually altering the commercial landscape. Technology continues to eliminate the need for face-to-face interaction between a buyer and seller. For example, according to the Federal Deposit Insurance Corporation, the number of commercial banks has declined from 12,343 in 1990 to about 5,800 today.[6] This is partially due to consumer preferences for automated teller machines, online banking and other services. Yet, the same technology has provided greater personalization through one-to-one connections. Electronic banking allows consumers the freedom to sit in their favorite coffee shop and conduct all of their banking, including making real-time communications with customer service representatives. At tax time, the same systems provide financial information categorized for seamless integration into tax reporting programs.

Online shopping is putting added pressures on traditional brick-and-mortar stores. Online sales increased by more than double the rate of brick-and-mortar sales during the 2013 holiday season, and foot traffic is steadily declining. Retailers saw only about half the holiday traffic in 2013 as they did just three years earlier.[7] According to a CoStar Group study, the amount of new retail space opened in 2013 was 43.8 million square feet, down from over 300 million square feet just five years earlier.[8]

QUALITY OF LIFE

Quality of life is defined more by how people feel and experience life than by how much they consume. For example, our thinking about basic services such as health, education and mobility has expanded dramatically. Health once meant the absence of sickness, but today's perception of health has expanded to include fitness, increased physical performance and enhanced mental well-being. Education, once the domain of the elite few, has become accessible to a significant percentage of the population, particularly in emerging nations like China and India. Today people find expenditures at a theater as valuable as the purchase of a microwave oven was in the 1970s. In fact, a patron of a Broadway play can be expected to spend more on a single performance than the cost of a microwave at Home Depot. Mobility, expressed in the 1950s by a high-performance car, now includes psychological mobility provided by movies, cellular phones and the Internet. Internet cafes illustrate yet another change in the quality of life, providing customers with two popular services in one — specialty coffees and wireless access.

The fast pace of life has placed a tremendous premium on services of all types. Most people would prefer to spend precious leisure time on activities other than shopping and cooking. Nearly all women who entered the workplace in the last three decades have joined the service sector, corresponding with the increasing demand for services. Today, Americans' eating patterns are changing from three square meals a day to five smaller meals, some of which are often consumed on the road. This has led to an explosion of services catering to on-the-go consumers.

GOVERNMENT DEREGULATION OF SERVICES

Another factor profoundly influencing growth in services is industry deregulation that has occurred over the past 20 years. This trend, started in the United States, has now spread throughout Europe and Asia. Understanding that competition provides vast opportunities for economic growth, legislators have deregulated many services that were traditionally controlled by government agencies. As expected, numerous private companies have stepped in to seize and create opportunities. For example, the spectacular growth in personal communication devices was stimulated by deregulation of the telephone industry, which led to competitive (and productive) phone wars. Some of the smaller companies, however, bought each other out to emerge as larger, more consolidated telecommunications companies. With more resources at their disposal, they were able to compete with older companies for customers. Most of these companies, such as Verizon, sell services as a part of a total package, a "bundle" that appeals to a particular group, such as business customers. Due to deregulation, the telecommunications industry has become one of the three fastest-growing industries in the United States. Worldwide, telecom revenue is expected to grow from $2.1 trillion in 2012 to $2.7 trillion in 2017."[9] But consumers should eventually emerge as winners in the midst of increasing competition due to improved services and lower prices. Major deregulation also has occurred in:

> **Spectacular growth in personal communication devices was stimulated by deregulation of the telephone industry, which led to competitive (and productive) phone wars.**

- **Transportation** — air freight, airlines, trucking and shipping.

- **Finance** — banking, securities and insurance.

- **Telecommunications** — radio, television and telephones.

- **Energy** — electricity and gas.

Competition stimulated by deregulation results in a better selection at a better price, which improves demand and creates jobs. For example, when the government deregulated the airline industry, companies expanded the number, location and pricing approaches of flights, among other changes. The result has been better prices, better schedules and overall improved service levels for consumers. Increased competition has made it necessary for companies to deliver greater value to consumers, which in turn has stimulated demand for these services.

COMPETITION IN PROFESSIONAL SERVICES

Not long ago, doctors, lawyers and other professionals were prohibited from marketing their services in the media. They could subvert this only with subtle means, such as sponsorships or word of mouth. All of this changed in 1974, when the Supreme Court ruled that a ban on lawyer marketing was unconstitutional. Today, nearly every profession engages in some form of marketing. Health care is a good case in point.

Hospitals, preferred provider organizations and health maintenance organizations compete vigorously for patients, and there are elaborate educational campaigns designed to teach doctors how to market services. The availability of information via technology has enhanced marketers' opportunities to promote health-care services. Users are able to access medical specialists and information as well as interact with visuals and audio. Since the health-care industry is complex and often confusing, consumers usually know very little about products and services offered. Without this knowledge and expertise about the industry, consumers must rely, to some degree, on marketers to inform them, making it extremely important that marketers provide truthful and reliable information, even with well-known and trusted websites such as WebMD. The recent explosion of drug companies advertising on television has caused some problems. The FDA regulates drug advertising and requires that advertisers name at least one approved use for the drug, the generic name of the drug and all the risks of using it.[10] For example, Pfizer and Pharmacia Corporation, the makers of Celebrex, an arthritis drug, were ordered to pull a TV advertisement by the FDA. The ad showed "Bill," a person with "arthritic knees," zipping around a park on a scooter. The FDA claimed that this ad overstated to consumers the actual efficacy of the drug.[11] The pharmaceutical industry claims that its advertisements serve to inform customers. In reality, ads often tug at emotions, and it is impossible to gain comparable knowledge to what a doctor would share by processing the information in a 30-second drug commercial.[12]

PRIVATIZATION

Privatization occurs when government services are contracted to private organizations for them to manage. The concept originated in the United Kingdom as an effort to revitalize the economy by shifting many bureaucratic services: railroad,

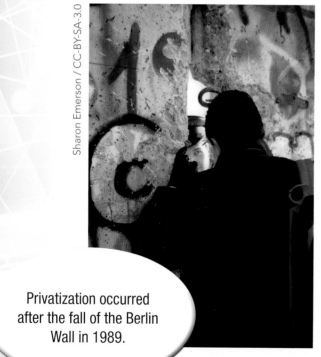

Sharon Emerson / CC-BY-SA-3.0

Privatization occurred after the fall of the Berlin Wall in 1989.

telecommunications and transportation industries, among others, to aggressive private firms. Privatization also occurred in East Germany when the Berlin Wall came down and in Russia when the Soviet Union was dissolved. Both countries immediately began to transfer ownership of huge, government-controlled service institutions to private companies. Consulting organizations from the United States, Europe and Japan worked diligently to help these private companies succeed. In Greece, in the wake of the country's economic collapse, Prime Minister Antonis Samaras plans to privatize the country's train network and power company. The country's creditors say that taking these money-losing companies off its balance sheet will help stabilize Greece's finances and help its economy in the long term.[13]

In the United States, there is a definite trend toward privatization of local, state and federal government services. Private companies now operate many hospitals and jails, which were once the responsibility of city and county governments. A recent milestone in the privatization movement occurred when Los Alamos, the birthplace of the atomic bomb and oldest national laboratory, was handed to a private contractor.[14]

THE NEED FOR SPECIALIZATION

Specialization occurs when an organization chooses to focus its resources on core business activities. In order to utilize resources and build strength in the core business, many organizations rely on service providers for basic support of their business. Most companies find it economical to farm out some of the services they previously performed themselves. Personnel agencies hire and assess employees, accounting firms do the books, systems consultants set up the computers and so forth. Accenture provides management consulting, technology services and outsourcing to other businesses. Corporations can hire Accenture to integrate sustainability approaches into their business strategies, industrialize application development or maximize IT security, for example. Companies realize that just as they specialize in a certain aspect of business, there are service providers who do the same.

GROWTH OF FRANCHISING

A **franchise** is a contractual agreement in which an entrepreneur pays a fee and agrees to meet operating requirements in exchange for the franchise name and marketing plan. Franchising is another major trend influencing the service industry, with fast food, fitness and auto service sectors experiencing particularly aggressive growth, due to their ability to sustain many different locations. Subway, for instance, operates 42,057 restaurants in 107 countries. All of its stores are franchises.[15]

Another area of franchise growth is in the distribution channels for car sales. Since customers value pressure-free shopping when purchasing an automobile, online car sales have become increasingly popular. These alternatives have taken a fixed-price approach without aggressive sales tactics. However, customers rarely make the final sale without being able to see, touch and drive the car firsthand.

Franchise

A contractual agreement whereby an entrepreneur pays a fee for the franchise name and agrees to meet operating requirements and use the organization's marketing plan.

SERVICE CHARACTERISTICS THAT AFFECT MARKETING STRATEGY

Marketers have to consider several aspects of service when developing strategies. First, services can be clearly contrasted from goods in several ways. Second, services should be looked at from the perspective of a service–goods continuum, not simply as services. Some products are all service, others are a combination of each and still others are pure goods. Third, consumers evaluate a service by looking at its attributes to find clues about its expected performance. Fourth, service quality plays a key role in success.

CONTRASTS BETWEEN GOODS AND SERVICES

When marketers refer to products, they are talking about both goods and services. In general, companies' products consist of a mix of the two, and marketing strategies for one generally work for the other. Even so, there are six sharp distinctions between the two. The uniqueness of services lies in their intangibility, the relationship with the consumer, the importance of the service encounter, their simultaneous production and consumption, their perishability and the type of quality controls required for services.

Marketing Intangibles
Physical goods have form and mass; they can be seen and touched. Prior to sale, services exist primarily as an offer or promise of some experience that will occur in the future. They don't become "real" until performed. Insurance, for example, simply offers a description of promised benefits that the policy contains. Only when the consumer suffers a loss is the product delivered — in the form of money or a replacement for an insured item.

www.subway.com

Subway understands it's the small things that can make a big difference, such as using napkins made from 100 percent recycled fiber. Learn more about how Subway franchises are going green on its website.

Many services take shape in unexpected ways over time. With a home security system, for instance it may be weeks, months or even years — hopefully never! — before the potential benefit is realized. This intangibility makes it difficult to assess the value of services or compare alternatives prior to purchase. After the service is performed, it is too late to change the decision. Paragliding is another example. By the time you are in the position to experience the thrilling sensation, it is too late to reject the service.

Relationship of Provider to Customer
Services are performed on customers personally or entities in their care — children (day care, youth sports camps), animals (vets, stables, feedlots), property (lawn care, car wash, auto repair), and so forth. Whereas most goods are manufactured at a plant far from customers, most services are created in their presence or with their personal knowledge of how they were performed, creating an inseparable bond between provider and customer. In some cases this interaction may be very personal, such as the relationship between parents and the provider of their child's care. Consumers can develop strong preferences for the work of a particular service provider, be it a doctor, dentist or hairdresser. As with loyalty to quality brands, they may even be willing to pay more to receive service from their trusted providers.

Service Encounter

The interaction between the consumer and the seller.

The Service Encounter Connection
One of the most important aspects of service marketing is the **service encounter**, the contact between the consumer and the seller. An early proponent of service as a strategy, Jan Carlzon, former president of Scandinavian Airline Systems (SAS), spoke of service encounters as "moments of truth." Carlzon led SAS toward a strong customer focus, pointing out that the airline came face-to-face with consumers 65,000 times each day. He estimated that each passenger had contact with five SAS employees over the course of a year. Although the typical service encounter lasted only about 15 seconds, the outcome of each one ultimately translated into success or failure for the company. His fervent conviction has made SAS one of the most customer-oriented carriers in the industry.

The service encounter concept reinforces the importance of customer relationships in marketing a service. Employees not only must have the interpersonal skills to treat consumers well but also must be oriented toward solving the customer's problem. At the most elementary level, service providers need to be cordial and gracious. At a more fundamental level, they have to be helpful in discovering and meeting service needs during the encounter. Each moment contributes to the customer's experience with the service.

At SAS, Carlzon realized that in order to satisfy a customer in 15 seconds, his system needed to give frontline personnel the tools and authority to solve a wide range of consumer problems. Managers, who typically hold power and responsibility, became supporters for those employees. Walmart took up a similar policy, and the company receives letters daily from customers pleased with their service encounter, which may include an associate who remembers their name or carries out a purchase for them. Some customers write letters in appreciation of a simple smile. Sam Walton, the company founder, insisted that associates practice "aggressive hospitality" in order to offer better service, and the People Greeter program at Walmart is one example of this. The greeters have the job of handing out shopping carts, greeting customers with a smile as they enter the store, and letting them know they're glad they came to Walmart.

Walmart greeters are a product of Sam Walton's insistence on "aggressive hospitality."

Simultaneous Production and Consumption
The fact that many services are made and used at the same moment creates interesting situations. First,

the buyer and seller have to cooperate, which often involves recognition of power dynamics. When you tell your stylist how you want your hair cut, you accomplish a managerial act. Second, since buyers vary and services depend on the recipient, the same service may be dramatically different from one situation to the next. A provider may operate one way with one consumer and then adjust the service considerably to meet the needs of another. A personal fitness trainer, for instance, must create a training program to suit each client's individual desires and condition. Finally, since the buyer must be present in order for at least part of the service to be performed, consumers invest time. This places a premium on the speed of delivery and the importance of correct performance the first time. For example, whether a car being serviced is ready when promised, or if the wait in a crowded physician's office is relatively short, may have as much to do with satisfaction as the performance of the specific service.

No Storage and Inventory Although goods can be stored until needed, services can be extremely **perishable** — their value exists for a short time. When an airplane takes off with several empty seats, those fares can never be recovered. Therefore, accurate forecasting and the need to match supply with demand are important. When the demand for a service is stable, there is little difficulty in meeting supply requirements, but most services have erratic demand. For example, on very hot days, almost all consumers turn on their air conditioners, creating a surge in energy demand. Should the utility company build enough capacity to supply its peak load or its average load? In the first case, there will be many periods when resources are unused; in the latter case, blackouts can result. When you call on Mother's Day or Thanksgiving, it may be difficult to get through right away because of an unusually high demand. At peak hours of Internet demand, the speed at which you can access information might decrease significantly. Similarly, cell phone use is often a problem while tailgating at major sporting events, when a large number of people in one location try make calls. If the service provider cannot meet the peak load, then customers are likely to go elsewhere.

Perishable

The temporal nature of services, whose value exists for only a short time.

Service Quality Control The quality of goods is usually monitored by human inspectors or the electronic eye of machinery, which is much more difficult to do with services. Unique quality control techniques, which are discussed in detail later in the chapter, are necessary for services. For now, it is important to remember that many services cannot be performed again if a mistake is made. An 18-year-old who emerges from high school poorly educated is unlikely to start all over again. In addition, because services are so people-intensive, quality can depend directly on service suppliers.

Service quality control is monitored by trained observers during and after service delivery. Chances are that you have called a company and heard a recording saying the call may be monitored for training purposes. This type of feedback, used by companies such as Amazon.com, lets the organization know whether service is being performed consistently as intended. Amazon also encourages feedback through its "contact us" page, which lets users choose to talk to a customer service representative via email, phone or online chat.[16] When there are difficulties, most customer-oriented service providers give employees additional training, supervision and help.

THE SERVICE–GOODS CONTINUUM

Although there are differences in marketing goods and services, there are also many similarities. In fact, few organizations market only one or the other. Most purchases fall somewhere along the continuum between almost pure goods and almost pure services, as illustrated in Figure 10.3.

Notice the word *almost* at each end of the continuum. Even in their purest

ALMOST PURE GOODS	GOODS WITH SERVICES	HALF GOODS, HALF SERVICES	SERVICES WITH GOODS	ALMOST PURE SERVICES
Physical products that are purchased and consumed with little or no service	Products supported with repair, maintenance, add-ons, and advice	Products that consist of both goods and services	Intellectual property or equipment to make goods work	Experiences that are consumed during delivery
Groceries Gasoline (self-serve) Steel	Autos Auto repair Video games	Restaurants Bookstores Movie theaters Prepared food delivery	Rental movies Training books Software Electronic mail Fax service	Health clubs Medical care Consulting Legal services Day care

Figure 10.3   Continuum of Goods and Services
Source: Valarie A. Zeithaml, "How Consumer Evaluation Processes Differ Between Goods and Services," in Marketing of Services, eds. James H. Donnelly and William R. George.

form, goods and services still contain some aspect of the other. Almost pure goods are physical products that can be described by their form, mass and function. There are thousands of types, ranging from computer chips to ocean liners. A gym supplies several different products that can be considered almost pure goods, such as clothes, equipment and health food.

Next along the continuum are goods with services. These are physical products accompanied by the supportive services required to make them work. For example, technology plays a major role in our economy not only because of its sales revenue but also due to the services it requires. Dell remains a very profitable computer company because of the extensive technical service it offers to support customers.

Half goods and half services are products that require both elements almost equally to succeed. Restaurants provide a certain level of service, which includes the wait staff, and goods such as food and beverages. Customers want to anticipate as well as enjoy their dining experiences, so marketers appeal to customer expectations about entertainment, a unique atmosphere or opportunities to interact with others. Dusty's Tap Room, an upscale Pub in Okemos, Michigan, is known for its food as well as wait staff who make it a point to know the names of loyal customers. Bookstores provide not only products (books) but also guidance in seeking unique topics. In addition, their spatial arrangement, background music and atmosphere all contribute to the "feelings" that sell. Coffee and beverage shops have been added to most leading bookstores to encourage customers to spend hours on a self-actualizing experience. A popular example of this is Barnes and Noble's exclusive partnership with Starbucks.[17]

Services with goods often entail intellectual properties and equipment required to make goods work. Examples include rental movies and software. A particular consideration with software is not only if it will run, but how well it will run. Microsoft once touted its Windows 8 operating system as designed to run on all hardware that can handle Windows 7, but beta testers noted that "Windows 8 is less kind to older, low-end graphics hardware" and "You should be using at least double the recommended amount [of RAM] to ensure headroom for additional programs and background services."[18] Beyond hardware issues, many people struggled with the new operating system's lack of familiarity to other upgrades. However, the newest operating system in development, Threshold (or what ultimately may be called Windows 9), Microsoft will attempt to shorten development cycles, offering more frequent releases that may be less dependent on hardware updates.[19]

Almost pure services provide customers with experiences that are consumed during the delivery process. Among the many items in this category are health clubs, legal services and education. Although a haircut is considered the classic example of a pure service, even that ordinarily takes place in an establishment selling styling and beautification products. Services such as air and train travel involve such goods as meals and soft drinks as well as tickets that can be exchanged. Even though Southwest Airlines does not offer meals or assigned seats, consumers still have a reasonable perception of quality and service value, usually citing the good service, such as frequent departures, on-time arrival, friendly employees and low fares. According to statistics reported to the Department of Transportation (DOT), Southwest Airlines has consistently received the lowest ratio of complaints per passengers boarded of all Major U.S. carriers.[20] This is an almost pure service that passengers value highly, which contributes to customer loyalty at Southwest.

CONSUMER EVALUATION OF SERVICES

Products can be viewed as having three types of qualities — search, experience and credence — that affect consumer evaluation. Search qualities can be evaluated prior to purchase. Experience qualities can be assessed only during or after consumption. Credence qualities are almost impossible to evaluate even after purchase and consumption. As Figure 10.4 illustrates, most goods are high in search and experience qualities, whereas most services are high in experience and credence qualities.[21]

Search Qualities Search qualities are found mostly in goods. They make it easy for consumers to judge one product relative to another. People can use their senses

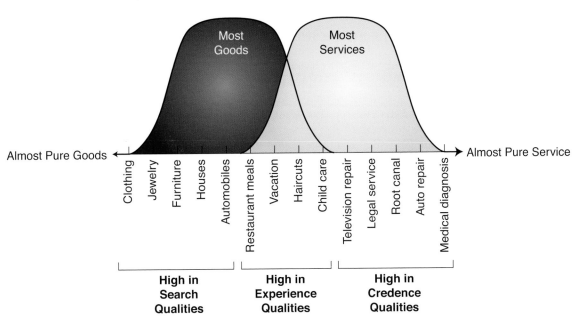

Figure 10.4   Search, Experience and Credence Qualities of Goods and Services
Source: Valarie A. Zeithaml, "How Consumer Evaluation Processes Differ Between Goods and Services," in Marketing of Services, eds. James H. Donnelly and William R. George.

of smell, hearing, sight, touch and taste to note differences in attribute quality. Many products are compared and studied in detail before a selection is made. For example, if you are shopping for new stereo speakers, you can listen to different models at the retail store to decide which pair sounds best. Similarly, you can test-drive different cars or try out a pair of in-line skates in the store parking lot. Even after purchase, items high in search qualities allow the consumer to assess their value. Best Buy, the nation's leading volume specialty retailer, offers demonstrations of video games and other products in their stores. Since Best Buy offers a number of items high in search qualities, its format enables consumers to compare and contrast products easily.

Experience Qualities The combined categories — goods with services, half goods and half services, and services with goods — are high in experience qualities. Consumers cannot assess the amount of pleasure until they try them. Then they can decide whether the product meets or exceeds their expectations and can describe desired improvements or changes. As the name suggests, products high in experience qualities involve the customer, and promotional efforts usually show people taking part in the experience. For instance, photos on the Crystal Cruises website show travelers relaxing in a deluxe stateroom, families snorkeling and adults taking complimentary golf lessons onboard. Consumers can assess their experience only after the cruise has ended, but many are apparently satisfied — Crystal Cruises received the 2013 World's Best Award in Top Large-Ship Cruise Lines in a Travel + Leisure reader survey.[22]

Credence Qualities Credence refers to a person's belief that something is true or trustworthy. The credence qualities are found only in services and cannot easily be evaluated before, during or after consumption. A medical diagnosis, for example, is almost impossible for consumers to assess, since most people have little or no knowledge of pathology and must trust the ability of others. The outcomes of credence qualities are largely unobservable to the customer until indirect benefits emerge, such as feeling better after being treated by a doctor. Of course, there can also be negative effects from the service, such as continued or worsening symptoms. The more intangible the result, the higher the credence qualities involved. In other words, customers must have a high degree of confidence that the exchange has been worthwhile.

Consumer Evaluation and Buying Behavior
Because services are high in credence qualities, consumer buying behavior tends to be different for services than for goods. Specific differences, described next, range from the more personal nature of the information sources relied upon to the fact that the customer is often a competitor of the service provider.

The Personal Factor Services tend to be personal, so it's not surprising that buyers rely more on information from personal sources than anything else when selecting a service provider. Suppose you are going to court in an important lawsuit. Would you select your lawyer from an ad on television or a recommendation from a knowledgeable friend? Consumers not only relate better to personal information sources but also give them more credence.

Post-Purchase Evaluation Because services are not easily evaluated before purchase, most assessments are made during or after the fact. Reputable lawn care companies are careful not only to do a good job of mowing and trimming but also to clean away the clippings, leaving a well-manicured look with very little for the consumer to criticize.

Surrogates for Judgment When a product is high in credence quality, consumers use surrogate cues to make judgments. Many people equate high-priced services with greater value, for example. Another cue is physical features, such as how the service provider dresses or the location of offices. Some consumers may judge a car dealership by a detail like the cleanliness of the restrooms. An inefficiently run physician's office with new furniture may send off more positive cues than one that is better run but has poor lighting, outdated furniture and clutter. In this case, the cues are used to make judgments about the quality of medical treatment the consumer will receive, and the office decor is a surrogate for measuring the skill and success of the physician.

Small Sets of Acceptable Brands or Suppliers Because services are personal and difficult to judge, consumers are likely to consider a small set of providers when seeking a service. Since services have no search qualities, consumers will not benefit from elaborate comparisons. Furthermore, their personal sources of information are likely to yield relatively few options. Once consumers find a reliable provider, they tend to be loyal. For example, most of us use only one or perhaps two dry cleaners all the time. The same is probably true for hairstylists, tailors, party planners and other types of providers. Some business travelers limit their choice when selecting a hotel, booking only Marriott or Sheraton because they are brand loyal and confident they will receive acceptable service.

CAREER TIP!

ARAMARK is the world's leading managed services provider, with a portfolio of career opportunities in nearly every service area. Since ARAMARK has units in thousands of locations, it can offer companywide, nationwide and worldwide opportunities. Check out current employment listings and submit your qualifications online at www.aramark.com/careers.

Slow Adoption Because pre-purchase evaluation is almost impossible, the risk of buying a service is greater than for goods. Therefore, new services take time to catch on, with most consumers waiting for word from the few adopters to hear how the service performs. Many consumers were initially reluctant to use the e-deposit feature many banks offer for depositing checks via a smartphone. They anticipated problems such as faulty deposits or theft and preferred contact with a human being or ATMs. With time, these fears are diminishing, and many consumers now e-deposit without hesitation. Shopping on the Internet caused similar security concerns among consumers, but web developers and credit card companies developed security measures to ensure better consumer safety while shopping online.

Strong Brand Loyalty Services have a built-in loyalty factor. People show greater loyalty to other people than to things, and due to the participatory nature of services, they may blame an unsatisfying experience at least partially on themselves. For example, if your hairdresser cuts your bangs too short, you may think you were not explicit about what you wanted. Furthermore, the high degree of credence qualities in services makes it difficult to know whether the provider has done a poor job unless something goes wrong, such as your car failing to start the day after it was repaired. Without a negative signal, consumers are likely to assume that the provider did at least a good job. In general, there is less complaining behavior from consumers about services as opposed to goods. We know from earlier chapters, however, that it is very important to seek out and respond to consumer complaints about any type of product.

The Customer as Competitor Services usually involve activities that consumers can do for themselves. Parents may elect to stay home with their young children or have relatives take care of them, in which case, they are "competing" with day care centers. People can mow their own lawns, clean their own cars or homes, prepare their own tax returns, or prepare food for their own parties. In many instances the trade-off is between time and money, which is why so many providers stress the amount of time their services will save consumers. For example, the United States Postal Service now offers Pickup On Demand, a time-specific service giving customers the opportunity to conveniently schedule a pickup at their home or office on its website.[23]

SERVICE QUALITY

Since service quality plays a significant part in the purchase decision for most consumers, it is crucial for marketing success. One study shows that service is "irrelevant" to customer perception of quality in only 15 percent of markets.[24] The Marketing Science Institute, through international conferences and research with major corporations, has identified how consumers assess overall service quality. The results, outlined in Figure 10.5, indicate that assessments have three aspects: dimensions of service quality, consumer factors and quality perception. Dimensions of service quality are elements that consumers are most likely to perceive when making judgments, such as reliability and responsiveness. Consumer factors refer to customer needs and information acquisition, and quality perception depends on how closely the buyer's expectations are matched (or exceeded) by the service actually delivered, a concept very similar to customer satisfaction. Each of these is discussed next.

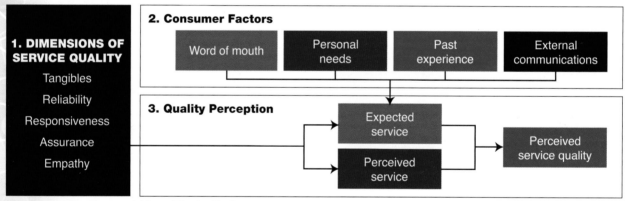

Figure 10.5   The Customer's View of Service Quality
Source: Adapted from Valarie A. Zeithaml, A. Parasuraman and Leonard L. Berry, Delivering Quality Service, Balancing Customer Perceptions and Expectations (New York: The Free Press, 1990), p. 26.

Dimensions of Service Quality The dimensions of service quality fall into five categories: tangibles, reliability, responsiveness, assurance and empathy. It's important for marketers to consider each of these as they evaluate the quality of the services they provide to consumers.

Tangibles It has been noted already that services are intangible but often are associated with physical facilities, equipment, personnel and promotional materials. These tangibles have a very significant effect on customers. Organizations that provide tangibles of high quality communicate an impression of their intangible offerings as well. For example, the way an office is designed and equipped, its cleanliness and the personal appearance of employees all play a major role in conveying quality.

Reliability The ability to perform the promised service dependably and accurately is critical to service quality. Reliability involves performing activities precisely as outlined, such as sticking to the script in training programs, producing credit card statements free of errors and doing a task correctly the first time. Research has shown that having car repairs completed when promised is more important to consumers than the quality of the work itself.

Responsiveness The willingness of providers to be helpful and give prompt service is very important to buyers. Waiting time is critical to buyer satisfaction and evaluation of service quality. It is important to respond in a timely manner (from the customer's perspective) to customer requests and needs. Are salespeople willing to answer questions about what to expect from a service? Do they help resolve difficulties if they arise? Cisco SMARTnet Service solves customer problems soon after they take place. This technical support system is an award-winning service that allows customers to access Cisco's top engineers at any time with any problems. Cisco SMARTnet Service is technologically advanced and was designed to help maximize the efficiency of communication with its customers.[25]

Assurance The knowledge and courtesy of employees and their ability to convey trust and competence are essential for services that have high credence qualities. It is very important that employees display credibility — evidence that they are proficient at a job — while always showing the customer respect. Assurance is related to security, the belief that the services will be performed safely and confidentially and that a free exchange of ideas between the provider and the consumer is possible. Providing assurance is a major component in a company's ability to build and maintain customer relationships.

Empathy The caring, individualized attention that a firm provides its customers encompasses a number of dimensions. It is through providers' ability to listen, communicate clearly and relate well to the client that they transmit empathy. This is often called a physician's "bedside manner," which has a lot to do with the patient's evaluation of the effectiveness of treatment. The same is true of a marketing consultant working with a client who needs advice about specific problems.

Consumer Factors Factors that influence the consumer's view of service quality include word of mouth, personal needs, past experience and external communication. Word of mouth is particularly important because services are not readily observable and must be described verbally, often with friends who have required the service in the past. It is also important that the service delivers what the consumer expects and needs. Past experience refers to what consumers have learned through personal interaction with a service provider. This is particularly important in shaping expectations, which is discussed below. The final element is external communication, that is, such marketer-dominated sources as personal selling and advertising. How a service is positioned and what is communicated through paid messages can influence consumer perceptions.

Quality Perception Because perceptions of service quality depend on a service meeting or exceeding customer expectations, service providers must take care in shaping those expectations. Since the product is intangible and people cannot readily observe what to expect, the messages and examples from service providers form a customer's expectations. To ensure high perceived quality and a loyal customer base, providers need to be accurate and reasonable about what they lead customers to expect. They also need to do a good job in the areas of tangibles, reliability, responsiveness, assurance and empathy. Because the personal nature of services makes them very difficult for competitors to emulate, companies that invest resources and energy into building strong service quality are most likely to be winners. Steak 'N' Shake, recognizing consumer interest in quality service, promotes the atmosphere of its restaurants as a higher-quality, more personal alternative to "fast-food" establishments. The friendly, prompt service encourages revisits.

DEVELOPING THE SERVICE MIX

Services, like goods, usually occur as a mix that relies on branding to communicate uniqueness. At the same time, several qualities must be considered when developing a new service. These include the service itself, the brand and factors that enhance the fundamental service. This section explores those dimensions in detail.

CORE, AUGMENTED AND BRANDED SERVICES

Core Service

The basic benefit delivered.

Services, like all products, have core, augmented and branded dimensions. We can use the example of a baby's birth in a hospital, as depicted in Figure 10.6. The **core service** is the basic benefit and main objective, in this case delivery of a healthy baby and safety for the mother. But, in today's competitive health-care arena, the augmented and branded product also plays a key role. The augmented service is the package of bundled goods and services that differentiates one provider from another. It has a great deal to do with how well service providers connect with customers. Since the core service is the same for all providers, the augmented features are critical.

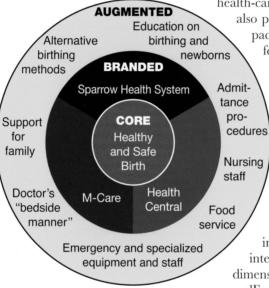

Figure 10.6 Example of a Core, Augmented and Branded Service

Because a service is intangible, a customer comes to know its value through the symbols and cues around it. McDonald's has achieved name recognition not only because of the reliability of its products but also because of its customer service, personnel management, cleanliness, child-oriented image and so forth. Its brand equity reflects the interactive service element as well as the functional dimensions of the physical goods sold. Consider FedEx Office, with more than 1,900 branches worldwide and 400 centers open 24 hours a day, 7 days a week.[26] Others provide copy services, but FedEx Office has become synonymous with a customer-oriented philosophy. It has expanded services to computer rental and Internet access, packing and shipping, convention center services, and marketing products such as banners, posters and signs. Customers rely on the FedEx Office's name for value and service.[27]

Marriott extended its branded line by developing three chains with lower complexity than the original service. Courtyard has become an identifiable service mark associated with high-quality accommodations and limited services. Fairfield Inn is positioned as the least complex, no-frills part of the chain. Residence Inn caters to extended stay guests, such as business travelers and families who are relocating. With these three brand names, the company has developed services consistent with the target markets for which each is intended.

Functional Element

What a service is supposed to accomplished.

Interactive Element

The personal behaviors and atmosphere of the service environment.

DEVELOPING NEW SERVICES

Certain functional and interactive elements are important when new services are created. The **functional element** is about accomplishing what is intended. (Does the orthodontist straighten a patient's teeth? Does an accountant prepare a client's tax return?) The **interactive element** involves the personal behaviors and physical atmosphere of the service environment.

Functional Elements in Service Development

The functional element is influenced by the complexity and divergence of the service. **Service complexity** is the number and intricacy of steps involved in producing a service. The service a defense lawyer provides to a murder suspect is much more complex than what a real estate lawyer provides to a new home buyer. **Divergence** is the amount of routine procedure involved. A very customized service has high divergence, such as a consultant who tailors staff development advice to each person in a company. Fred Pryor Seminars Inc., a standardized service provider, gives a set presentation on various topics to groups representing many organizations, keeping divergence to a minimum. Crowd Management Strategies tailors strategic planning services for a broad range of clients in the entertainment industry, requiring consultants competent to deal with high complexity. The company focuses on addressing crowd management issues at concerts, festivals and other public assembly events through risk assessment, event planning assistance, crowd management training, on-site safety reviews and more.[28]

Figure 10.7 illustrates complexity and divergence for four services. Since most local hair salons do approximately the same thing, and cutting hair is not highly complicated, divergence and complexity are very low. Dentistry has low divergence due to standardized procedures, but it tends to be high in complexity. House cleaning is highly customized (divergent) but low in complexity, whereas litigation tends to be high in both divergence and complexity.

		COMPLEXITY (Degree of Intricacy)	
		Low	High
DIVERGENCE (Degree of Standardization)	Low	Local barber	Dentistry
	High	House cleaning	Litigation

Figure 10.7 Complexity and Divergence in Services

Service Complexity

The number and intricacy of steps involved in producing a service.

Divergence

The degree to which a service involves customization beyond routine or standardized procedures.

Interactive Elements in Service Development

The interactive element is often more important than the functional aspect in creating service excellence. Walt Disney Enterprises has attempted to produce a strong interactive service by using a stage (the environment) with actors (Disney employees) to involve the audience (consumers). Through extensive role-playing, the Disney organization has learned to connect in a way that produces strong customer satisfaction. One part of this interaction is simply to provide an enjoyable and entertaining experience for Disney guests.

Many companies use atmospherics, the environment in which the service is performed, to enhance the interactive element.[29] Originally applied to retail stores, atmospherics has important implications for all types of services outside the consumer's home. Such features as color, music and layout are all part of the atmosphere. They not only influence the selection of a service provider but also, and more importantly, they determine if service outcomes are satisfying.

The physical components of atmosphere have an emotional dimension. The mood created greatly influences whether consumers want to enter and explore the environment, communicate with personnel and gain satisfaction from the service encounter.[30] Retail stores such as Abercrombie & Fitch and Victoria's Secret emphasize music as a way to increase sales. DMX, a service provider to many retailers, researches the demographics and psychographics of a store's customers and then creates suitable sound. The music is designed to encourage customers to shop longer, and it also creates an atmosphere for each retailer.[31] The next time you visit an H&M, 24 Hour Fitness or DKNY location, note the music program created especially to appeal to you.

Structuring New Services The functional and interactive aspects of services affect how organizations structure new offerings. Marketers determine where each new service attribute fits on the continuum from low complexity/divergence to high complexity/divergence. Figure 10.8 shows an example of structural alternatives in the restaurant business. The standard restaurant would fall in the middle, and restaurant marketing managers can choose to move in one of two directions for each area shown: more upscale (higher complexity/divergence) or more downscale (lower complexity/divergence). By conducting this type of analysis, the organization can make clear choices in developing new services.

CREATING & CAPTURING VALUE THROUGH *Sustainability*

PepsiCo Promises to Perform With a Purpose

After several years of discussion about climate change and the adverse impact of humans on the environment, many companies have taken to increasing sustainability. PepsiCo is a leader in this area. It is in the midst of an enormous campaign called "Performance with Purpose." In this campaign, PepsiCo breaks sustainability into three segments: human, environmental, and talent, each of which it considers to be essential to performing with a purpose.

PepsiCo believes that building up and sustaining our world all starts with people. In order for humans to care for the health of the environment, they must first take care of their own health. For this reason, PepsiCo has made it a major goal to provide a wide variety of healthier and more wholesome foods across the globe. It starts with the children of today who will be the decision makers of the future. PepsiCo has implemented a policy for beverage sales in schools which is focused on providing the students with low calorie drinks such as water, milk, and juice. PepsiCo promotes human sustainability through great products, responsible marketing, accurate nutritional labeling, and community services.

This human sustainability leads up to environmental sustainability. PepsiCo recognizes that natural resources need to be protected. The company is constantly searching for new and innovative ways to produce and recycle products in order to conserve these resources, such as its "waste to wealth" programs. PepsiCo describes one such program in India as "an award-winning, income-generating partnership to manage domestic solid waste in an environmentally friendly manner" and the company states that it has "provided a clean environment to thousands of households through projects at seven locations in India." PepsiCo also participates in endeavors such as sustainable farming, biodiversity, solar energy solutions, and energy reduction...all of which are changing the way food and beverages are produced and distributed.

Finally, PepsiCo participates in talent sustainability. By implementing learning and development programs for its employees and associates, PepsiCo can continue to learn, teach, and grow in its sustainability efforts. These programs also include training on health, safety, and human rights.

Because PepsiCo is the world's second largest food and beverage company, all of these efforts have made an enormous impact on the environment. They have also strengthened customer relations. PepsiCo has set the bar extremely high when it comes to sustainability, and other companies are following its example.

PepsiCo Inc. "Purpose.", www.pepsico.com/Purpose.html, website visited July 28, 2012.

Lower Complexity/Divergence	Current Process	Higher Complexity/Divergence
No reservation	← Take reservation →	Specific table selection
Self-seating; menu on blackboard	← Seat guest, give menu →	Recite menu; describe entrees and specials
Eliminate	← Serve water and bread →	Assortment of hot breads and hors d'oeuvres
Customer fills out form	← Take orders; prepare orders →	Taken personally by maitre d' at table
Prepared; no choice	← Salad (4 choices) →	Individually prepared at table
Limited to 4 choices	← Entree (15 choices) →	Expand to 20 choices; add flaming dishes; bone fish at table; prepare sauces at table
Sundae bar; self-service	← Dessert (6 choices) →	Expand to 12 choices
Coffee, tea, milk, and sodas	← Beverage served (6 choices) →	Add exotic coffees; wine list; liqueurs
Serve salad and entree together; bill and beverage together	← Serve orders →	Separate course service; sherbet between courses; hand-grind pepper
Cash only; pay when leaving	← Collect payment at table →	Choice of payment, including house accounts; serve mints

Figure 10.8   Structural Alternatives in the Restaurant Business
Source: Adapted with permission from G. Lynn Shostack, "Service Positioning through Structural Change," *Journal of Marketing* 51 (January 1987): 34–43.

AN EXPANDED CONCEPT OF SERVICES

In addition to the traditional offerings, service marketing is used to promote people, entertainment and events, places, political candidates and ideas, and different causes. It can even be used within an organization, through internal marketing, to promote one group's capabilities to another. The following sections describe additional types of service marketing.

PERSON MARKETING

Person marketing involves promoting an individual's character, personality and appeal, which in turn may be used to promote a service or product. Ashton Kutcher, the model turned actor, has transformed himself into a social media mogul, using his own brand as a springboard. The "That '70s Show" star founded Katalyst, a production company that is a merger of three industries: film, TV and web. Kutcher uses his brand image to leverage his company through Twitter and Facebook. His Twitter feed, @aplusk, is among the most-followed on Earth, topping 16.2 million in July 2014. Ashton's irresistible charm and fun-loving attitude have caught the attention of corporations such as Nikon, whose cameras he endorses, as well as Kellogg's and PepsiCo, who have both teamed up with Katalyst on social media projects through

Person Marketing

Promoting an individual's personality, character, and appeal, which in turn may assist in the promotion of a product.

Twitter. Twitter was used as an interaction portal, urging users to post short commercials filmed with their Coolpix cameras.[32]

Many celebrities have agents who help market their exceptional appeal to various companies and to consumers. While celebrities and athletes are admired for their skill or character, a great deal of their popularity is due to service providers marketing their personalities. Person marketing is often a two-way process, in which promotion of the individual increases his or her value as a product endorser. Public exposure that enhances reputation leads to more lucrative endorsement contracts, and vice versa.

ENTERTAINMENT AND EVENT MARKETING

This summer, "Transformers: Age of Extinction" broke multiple box-office records in China in its first weekend of release and appears to be on track to displace "Avatar" as the top-grossing film ever on the mainland. Paramount Pictures cast several Chinese actors in the film, shot in Hong Kong and other cities, established multiple product-placement deals with Chinese consumer brands, and booked a snazzy premiere in Hong Kong. The clever marketing helped the film gross more abroad than it did domestically.[33]

Television and radio also thrive on sophisticated marketing. Mark Burnett, creator and producer of "Survivor" and "The Apprentice," has a knack for marketing. His programs are successful because viewers can relate to the people cast as participants as well as the dramatic individual and team tasks that separate winners and losers. His shows are heavily promoted to inform viewers about each new series, and careful monitoring ensures that a show consistently reaches its target demographic.

Event marketing is the promotion of an event in order to generate revenues and enhance the reputation of an organization. It has become a huge factor in the entertainment world, with sporting events at the forefront. Ohio State University characterizes its athletic department as being in the entertainment business; the university has an annual athletics budget exceeding $100 million.[34] College athletics comprise a multibillion-dollar industry, generating revenue from game attendance, television and radio ratings, concessions, sponsorships and merchandising. Many universities earn several million in royalties annually.

Event Marketing

Promoting an event in order to generate revenues and enhance the reputation of an organization.

One of the most successful event marketers is the National Basketball Association. Although most NBA games are played in the United States, the All-Star Game is broadcast in over 215 countries in more than 47 languages.[35] The NBA has assisted in basketball-themed movies as well: "Coach Carter" starring Samuel L. Jackson, "Finding Forrester" starring Sean Connery, "White Men Can't Jump" starring Wesley Snipes, "Space Jam" starring Michael Jordan and "Kazaam" starring Shaquille O'Neal.

Another event marketer, FIFA (Fédération Internationale de Football Association), is responsible for the organization of soccer tournaments like the World Cup, held every four years. It is also responsible for its promotion, which generates revenue from sponsorship. FIFA generates revenues of over 1.3 billion U.S. dollars, for a net profit of 72 million, and had cash reserves over 1.4 billion U.S. dollars.[36] The 2014 World Cup, held in Brazil, experienced a massive surge of viewership in the United States. ESPN reported record household ratings and aver-

BRAZIL 2014
Heroic Howard earns global praise
Wednesday 2 July 2014

aged 3.7 million viewers per match. The increasing popularity of the sport domestically is nothing short of incredible. Viewership in 2014 rose 26 percent from 2010, and surged 116 percent from 2006.[37] Univision, a Spanish language broadcast television network in the United States, reported 10.4 million viewers during the Mexico vs. Netherlands match. The game was not only the most watched soccer game ever on Univision, but also the most watched telecast ever for the broadcaster -- besting ESPN's broadcast of the match by 57 percent.[38] There is no shortage of excitement for a sport that is sweeping the nation.

PLACE MARKETING

Place marketing enhances a location in order to appeal to businesses, investors and tourists. Vacation places receive tremendous marketing attention, which countries, states and cities are all eager to encourage. Michigan branded "Pure Michigan" to promote tourism with ads focusing on the state's 3,000 miles of shoreline, beautiful autumn colors and more than 100 lighthouses, among other highlights. The brand's 2014 national campaign launched with a $13 million dollar budget. Television commercials are aired on 20 cable channels along with NBC, CBS and ABC. Tim Allen, a Michigan native, narrates the 30-second spots. Its website, www.michigan.org, allows users to explore all the state has to offer, with featured destinations, special events, outdoor activities and package deals.[39]

Place Marketing

Promoting a geographical location in order to appeal to businesses, investors, and tourists.

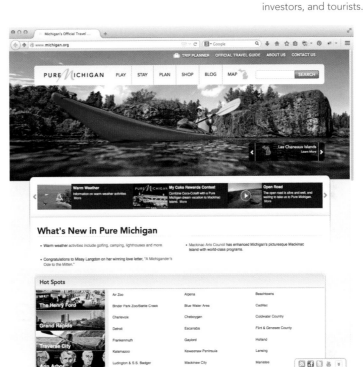

POLITICAL MARKETING

Political marketing involves the promotion of an individual or idea with the aim of influencing public policy and voters. Politicians use political marketing in order to present themselves and their ideas in the best possible way. Sophisticated political campaigns make efficient use out of virtually every marketing tool. The Internet has provided an outstanding venue for political communication, often called web campaigning. As the 2008 presidential campaign began to heat up, new candidates like now-President Barack Obama developed an outstanding web presence. During the 2012 re-election campaign, Obama's website showed a "Romney tax calculator" to highlight the difference between Obama and Mitt Romney's tax plans; links where supporters could make campaign donations; volunteer opportunities; blog posts; videos; and more. Submitting a $3 donation on Mitt Romney's website would automatically enter you in a promotion for the chance to meet "America's Comeback Team."[40]

Political Marketing

Promoting an individual or idea motivated by the desire to influence public policy and voters.

CAUSE MARKETING

Cause marketing involves gaining public support and financing for a cause in order to bring about a change or a remedy. You are familiar with many of the marketing campaigns to combat AIDS, drunk driving, drugs, domestic violence, and smok-

Cause Marketing

Gaining public support and financing in order to change or remedy a situation.

ing among teens, as well as campaigns to prevent animal cruelty and to encourage the use of seatbelts. Cause marketing is used for blood drives, Community Chest drives and charities that feed and clothe the homeless or combat various diseases. The overall objective is to remedy a situation by gaining public support for change.

Cause marketing is challenging because it usually confronts two very difficult tasks: raising money and providing help to those in need. For example, Walgreens won a 2014 Gold Halo Award for its "Give a Shot. Get a Shot" campaign. Partnering with the United Nations Foundation's Shot@Life program, it successfully drove flu shot volumes up through its pharmacy. For every flu shot administered in Walgreens, it donated the value of the vaccine to children in developing countries.[41]

Eyewear company Warby Parker has a "Buy a Pair, Give a Pair program;" for every pair of glasses purchased, the company provides funds for glasses to a nonprofit partner such as VisionSpring. Warby Parker also works with nonprofits to train low-income entrepreneurs and help them start their own businesses selling glasses in their home countries.[42]

INTERNAL MARKETING

Internal Marketing

The marketing of a business unit's capabilities to others within the same firm.

Internal marketing occurs when one part of an organization markets its capabilities to others within the same firm. For example, imagine that you are a human resources manager. Your job, among other responsibilities, is to provide training and career development for employees in all the company's different divisions and departments. Using familiar marketing concepts can effectively achieve this; you're just aiming them at your own employees, rather than the target consumers of your organization's final product. This is not the same as internal communications, which are also important; internal marketing uses all the tools of the marketing mix, as well as techniques to insure customer satisfaction and loyalty.

THE MARKETING OF NONPROFIT SERVICES

Nonprofit Marketing

The activities performed by an organization not motivated by profit in order to influence consumers to support it with a contribution.

Marketing of nonprofit services is a huge area. According to the National Center for Charitable Statistics, there are more than 1.5 million nonprofit organizations in the United States.[43] **Nonprofit marketing** is performed by an organization that is not motivated by profit and is exempt from paying taxes on any excess revenues over costs. Churches, museums, foundations, hospitals, universities, symphonies and municipalities, among other institutions, regularly create marketing plans in an effort to gain funds and public support. Nonprofit organizations often use person marketing, entertainment and event marketing, and place marketing. Nearly all political and cause marketing, as well as marketing of the arts, fits the nonprofit description. Most nonprofit organizations have begun advertising and soliciting donations as well as volunteers on the Internet, in an effort to maximize fundraising at little cost.[44]

TYPES OF NONPROFIT SERVICE PROVIDERS

Figure 10.9 shows several categories of nonprofit service providers and gives examples of each. As you can see, marketing skills are required by a very broad range of nonprofit organizations. For example, your university probably has a fairly elaborate marketing plan, and chances are that many of the administrators have attended American Marketing Association seminars on how to promote higher education. Many athletic directors and university presidents are currently being advised to view their positions as similar to that of a CEO of a major corporation.

Category	Example	Product
Arts/Culture/Humanities	Metropolitan Museum of Art, New York Chicago Symphony	Exhibits Musical programs
Education/Instruction	Michigan State University Executive Education University of Southern California Undergraduate Program	Executive programs Classes, degrees
Environmental Quality/ Protection/Beautification	Smokey the Bear (U.S. Forest Service) Greenpeace	Fire safety Saving the environment
Animal Related	San Diego Zoo People for the Ethical Treatment of Animals (PETA)	Species preservation Animal rights
Health	Listening Ear Alcoholics Anonymous (AA)	Cure for AIDS Stop alcoholism
Consumer Protection	Consumer Hotline	Legal aid
Crime Prevention	Neighborhood Watch Crime Tip Hotline	Discourage criminals Catch criminals
Employment/Jobs Public Safety	U.S. Army State of Michigan State of Florida	Volunteer recruitment Drive safely Wear seat belts
Recreation/Sports	Silverdome American Youth Soccer Organization	Football Youth sports programs
Youth Development	Boy Scouts of America Big Sister/Big Brother programs	Scouting jamborees Companionship and role models
Community/Civic	Bring Your Company to . . . Kiwanis Club	Community enhancement Economic development
Grant Agencies	Rockefeller Foundation Robert Wood Johnson Foundation	Arts development Medical research
Religious Organizations	Catholic Church Evangelists	Membership Spirituality
Other Cause-Based Groups	National Organization of Women (NOW) American Civil Liberties Union (ACLU)	Women's rights Individual rights

Figure 10.9   Types of Nonprofit Service Providers

THE NEED FOR EXCESS REVENUES

Nonprofit service organizations are usually tax exempt and may appear to be less concerned about pricing and cost structures, but they still have several reasons to generate more revenue than cost. First, their revenues (money for services and from contributions) tend to fluctuate from year to year. For example, the Museum of Fine Arts in Boston relies on blockbuster shows every few years to boost revenues. For its all-star game, the NBA partners with local schools and youth serving community-based organizations in the host city to raise money. Tying a nonprofit event to a profit-making organization, especially a well-known one such as the NBA, can provide fund-raising opportunities.[45]

Second, organizations can't raise money if they are not solvent. The United Way wants the organizations it supports to have at least a three-month safety net, requiring the stern task of earning and setting aside a full quarter's worth of expenses. Fundraising operations must be run in a financially sound manner in order to gain support from large donors. That requires efficiency and documentation identifying the costs of items as well as the revenues received.

Third, nonprofits hire professionals to help the organization grow. Similar to any business, growth generally requires capital and the ability to access funds from financial institutions. Lenders look at nonprofits much the same way they look at any other organization. The Red Cross operates with positive cash flows (more revenues than expenditures), which not only attracts managerial talent but also affords the company access to lenders and all the services required by a for-profit company.

FUNDRAISING AND REVENUE GENERATION

Nonprofit organizations may raise revenues in two ways. First, they acquire funding from third parties, such as governments, private and public agencies and individual contributors. Second, they may expand into a number of business operations.

A considerable amount of funding comes from donations by individuals, families or businesses. Microsoft CEO Bill Gates is recognized for making substantial contributions to non-profits. The Bill & Melinda Gates Foundation works to reduce inequities and improve lives around the world.[46] Less well known is Microsoft co-founder Paul G. Allen, who has given more than $1.5 billion towards the advancement of science, technology, education, wildlife conservation, the arts and community services in his lifetime.[47]

Understanding donor profiles helps nonprofit groups target fundraising efforts. There are six categories of donors: Communitarians, Devout, Investors, Socialites, Repayers and Dynasts. The largest group is made up of communitarians, who believe in supporting their community. As government has decreased its support of social services and the arts, nonprofits in these areas must compete against one another for private dollars. Just as new ventures need a well-honed marketing strategy and innovative approach to entice venture capitalists, new nonprofits need to do the same to capture the attention of donors besieged by requests. For example, Shoestring bills itself as "the nonprofit's agency" and offers help with branding, media relations, strategy and more.[48]

Microsoft's co-founder, Paul G. Allen, has donated over $1.5 billion to various organizations.

In addition to fundraising, many organizations develop business ventures that provide substantial revenues. These are often unrelated to the basic nature of the core activity. Your high school band, drama club or sports team probably used some type of retail operation at one time or another — a car wash, a food stand at the local fair or a candy sale — to raise money for uniforms or a special trip. In fact, these activities often compete with the for-profit sector. Because the service labor is donated, the price charged by the nonprofit group can be substantially lower than the normal retail price, and the nonprofit group's cause often attracts consumer loyalty. In some cases, for-profit businesses simply cannot compete while a fundraiser is going on. Can you think of when nonprofits are customers of for-profit businesses?

Sometimes the revenue-generating venture fits nicely with the core activity of the nonprofit. For example, private schools and universities have bookstores and other merchandising operations. Museums and musical organizations (symphonies, opera companies) may have shops and mail-order catalogs. Some groups license their name or logo for a fee. Zoos, museums, sports teams and others often charge admission.

Finally, membership fees represent a large source of revenue. Most associations are formed for the benefit of members, whether individuals or organizations. For example, a member of the American Marketing Association pays $210 annually to the AMA in addition to chapter dues. This entitles the member to obtain AMA publications and attend conferences at substantially reduced rates. The AMA is the world's largest professional society of marketers, with more than 30,000 members worldwide; there are 78 professional chapters in the U.S. and Canada and dozens of collegiate chapters. The association works to promote education and assist in career development among marketing professionals.[49]

Most professions have a similar organization, and in many cases companies can be members. For example, firms interested in service quality are likely to join the Center for Services Leadership (CSL) at Arizona State University, North America's leading university-based program for the study of services marketing and management. The center conducts research, offers specialized education and training and works to provide firms with applicable principles, concepts and tools.[50]

PROVIDING POSITIVE SOCIAL BENEFITS

Another challenge for nonprofits is to provide maximum positive social benefits to their constituency. This can be difficult, because constituents may have differing objectives and needs. For example, the San Diego Zoo must balance the public's desire to see certain animals with the interests of environmentalists in species preservation. Expenses to house, care for and in some cases help rare animals reproduce can be very high. Likewise, groups concerned with spouse or child abuse must allocate funds to serving families as well as to promoting their cause.

Matthew Field / GFDL

The nonprofit San Diego Zoo is the most successful zoo in terms of panda reproduction.

Having a good understanding of constituent needs is not always easy, but the Internet is a useful marketing tool for nonprofit groups. Many use it to communicate, share information, educate, collaborate and interact. It is an excellent format for publishing, sharing perspectives on issues, assisting in community development and increasing participation.

A good example of the importance of serving constituency needs can be found in the arts. These include a long list of services — museums, theaters, opera, symphonies, dance companies, exhibitions, public radio, public television and others. A major indicator of the quality of life in many communities is the availability of the arts. Numerous cities have a symphony orchestra, which can be an important factor in attracting businesses and people to the area.

Customers for the arts are called patrons. Attracting them is a critical aspect of marketing the arts, but that is only part of the challenge. Equally important is finding sponsors of all types, since revenues from ticket sales seldom generate enough money for sustained success. Yet patrons may have many choices about which arts events to attend, and sponsors may have a broad range of requests for donations. Ultimately, successful organizations are those that can clearly demonstrate the benefits they bring to their constituents.

ETHICAL ISSUES SURROUNDING NONPROFIT ORGANIZATIONS

Today, many types of organizations claim nonprofit status, which entitles them to tax exemption. While a majority of these benefit society, a growing number have little or no resemblance to traditional charities. In fact, of the 45,000 new organizations that apply for tax-exempt status each year, many make a considerable profit, which raises the question of whether it is ethical for money-making nonprofits to pay no taxes. The Journal News of New York state found that there were 33 private golf and country clubs in Westchester, Putnam and Rockland counties organized as tax-exempt nonprofits and thus not liable for federal income taxes. Initiation fees at some of the courses ranged from $35,000 to $200,000, and annual dues were $10,000 and $20,000.[51]

Although nonprofits are taxed on income from businesses unrelated to their function, fewer than five percent report such income. Nonprofit executives say they have shifted toward profit-making schemes, such as investments and business operations, in order to survive. Many others feel that there are too many nonprofits taking advantage of tax-exempt status, but efforts to change the law have failed repeatedly in Congress.

You may be familiar with many nonprofit organizations, such as the National Geographic Society, the Academy of Motion Picture Arts and Sciences (which presents the Oscars) and the Humane Society of the United States. Nonprofits are not limited to charity, and many can be found in retail, restaurant, hotel, insurance and even laundry services. Most nonprofits do not pay taxes on investment income either. Competitors of these organizations are at a clear financial disadvantage, and

several find the tax exemptions unfair and unethical. Consider the difference between a nonprofit hotel operated by a university and tax-paying hotels in an area. The Nittany Lion Inn, owned by The Pennsylvania State University, sits on one of the most valuable pieces of land on the university campus, within walking distance of nearly every event on campus from football and basketball games to lectures by outstanding educators and business leaders. Supported by the vast resources of the university, the hotel can develop marketing programs and charge prices that maximize occupancy regardless of costs. The nation's nonprofit sector generates amazing revenues every year and controls a large percentage of all assets. While these organizations directly benefit their constituents, their tax-free status remains an ethical issue.

CHAPTER SUMMARY

Objective 1: Identify the forces that have produced and will continue to create tremendous growth in the service economy.

The service economy is growing at about twice the rate of the sale of goods. First, technological advances and the accompanying information revolution are creating vast opportunities in the service sector. Technology often can only be used with the help of service specialists who have the necessary knowledge and skills. Second, the quality of life is being measured by how people feel and experience life. Third, governments around the world have deregulated services. Fourth, professional service providers such as lawyers are turning to marketing as a way to conduct their business operations. Fifth, privatization of government functions is opening up service opportunities. Sixth, there is a need for outside specialists by companies that want to concentrate resources on their core business. Finally, there is a strong growth in franchising, which tends to focus on service-based products.

Objective 2: Understand which characteristics of services must be adjusted for successful marketing.

Services are differentiated from goods on several key dimensions that must be considered in successful marketing. First, services are intangible, so evidence of benefits may occur long after purchase and may be difficult to assess. Second, there is a unique relationship between the service provider and customers, who are either present when the service is performed or have knowledge of how it was performed. Third, the service encounter is a crucial point of connection between provider and consumer, in which each moment must contribute to meeting customer needs. Fourth, since production and consumption often occur simultaneously, the same service may be different each time it is performed and may be adjusted to the unique circumstances of each consumer. Fifth, because there is no storage or inventory with a service, demand forecasting is important so that service providers are ready when needed. Finally, service quality control is extremely important, but it is complicated. It requires thorough training of personnel and careful monitoring.

Most products contain elements of both goods and services and can be placed on a service–goods continuum. Consumers tend to evaluate services differently from goods. Generally, services are high in credence qualities, which means it is difficult to evaluate them even after they have been consumed. Therefore, consumers tend to rely on personal references for information, engage in postpurchase evaluation, develop surrogates for judging quality, select providers from a small set of choices, and actually serve as a competitor to the service provider. They are slow to adopt new services but eventually develop strong brand loyalty. Judgments of service quality usually have three aspects: the dimensions of service quality, consumer factors and quality perceptions. The dimensions of service quality include tangibles, reliability, responsiveness, assurance and empathy. Customer factors — word of mouth, personal needs, past experience and external communication — help form customer expectations. Quality perception is based on the difference between what is expected and what is received.

Objective 3: Know how to develop the service mix.

Service mix development requires understanding in two areas. First, services have core, augmented and branded dimensions similar to goods. Brand equity is equally if not more important for services than for goods. Second, when developing new services, marketers must give careful consideration to both functional and interactive elements. The functional element is influenced by the complexity and divergence of a service, which must provide benefits that match customer needs and wants. The interactive element involves such concerns as the consumer's personal behaviors and the atmosphere in which the service will be performed.

Objective 4: Explore the expanded concept of services.

There are many types of service marketing including person marketing, entertainment and event marketing, place marketing, political marketing, cause marketing and internal marketing. Person marketing promotes an individual, often a sports figure or movie personality, who in turn generally helps market another product. Entertainment marketing promotes movies, television programming and the like. Event marketing, like that for sporting events and concerts, is a major category. Through sponsorships of events, companies also market other products. Place marketing promotes a geographic location, such as a city, state or country. It is often connected to investment or travel products. Political marketing promotes politicians or political ideas and policy issues. Cause marketing attempts to gain support for a cause, such as research on HIV and AIDS. Internal marketing occurs when one business unit markets its capabilities to others within the same firm.

Objective 5: Appreciate the importance of nonprofit marketing and the uniqueness of this important marketing arena.

Nonprofit marketing accounts for more than seven percent of economic activity in the United States and is growing. It is performed by organizations that are tax exempt, such as churches, museums, foundations, hospitals, universities and orchestras. Even nonprofits need revenues in excess of their costs. These revenues provide service continuity from year to year and allow nonprofits to access the talent and funding required to serve their constituents. Consequently, fund-raising and revenue generation from donors, patrons and members are often a focal point. At the same time, nonprofits must provide benefits to all constituents, which can be difficult, because different parties have varying expectations and needs. Ethically, there is a question about tax-exempt status for at least some nonprofits, especially when they compete with for-profit organizations.

REVIEW YOUR UNDERSTANDING

1. List the seven forces that are producing explosive growth in services. Very briefly describe each.
2. What are the differences between goods and services?
3. What is the service–goods continuum? What are the categories of the continuum?
4. What are search, experience and credence attributes of services? List a product example in each attribute category.
5. What are the five dimensions of service quality, the four consumer factors, and the three elements of quality perception that shape the customer's view of service quality?
6. What are the functional and interactive elements of services?
7. List three examples of person marketing.
8. What is entertainment and event marketing?
9. Give an example of cause marketing.
10. What is internal marketing?
11. What differentiates nonprofit services from other services?
12. Why do nonprofit organizations need more revenues than costs?

DISCUSSION OF CONCEPTS

1. List three of the seven forces driving the explosive growth of the service economy. How will each force influence the nature of college education?
2. Select two differences between services and goods and detail how each affects marketing strategy development.
3. Do you think it is possible for a product to be either a pure good or a pure service? Why or why not?
4. What are the differences between search, experience and credence qualities of products? How does each affect marketing strategy development?
5. Name a service high in credence quality. What type of buyer behavior would you expect to encounter?
6. Imagine that you are the marketing manager for a major hotel chain. What steps would you recommend to help ensure success in each of the five dimensions of service quality?
7. Select a target market and design the core, augmented and branded aspects of a restaurant.
8. Do you consider it appropriate for politicians to develop sophisticated marketing campaigns in order to be elected to office?

KEY TERMS & DEFINITIONS

1. **Cause marketing:** Gaining public support and financing in order to change or remedy a situation.
2. **Core service:** The basic benefit delivered.
3. **Divergence:** The degree to which a service involves customization beyond routine or standardized procedures.
4. **Event marketing:** Promoting an event in order to generate revenues and enhance the reputation of an organization.
5. **Franchise:** A contractual agreement whereby an entrepreneur pays a fee for the franchise name and agrees to meet operating requirements and use the organization's marketing plan.
6. **Functional element:** What a service is supposed to accomplish.
7. **Interactive element:** The personal behaviors and atmosphere of the service environment.
8. **Internal marketing:** The marketing of a business unit's capabilities to others within the same firm.
9. **Nonprofit marketing:** The activities performed by an organization not motivated by profit to influence consumers to support it with a contribution.
10. **Perishable:** The temporal nature of services, whose value exists for only a short time.
11. **Person marketing:** Promoting an individual's personality character, and appeal, which in turn may assist in the promotion of a product.
12. **Place marketing:** Promoting a geographical location in order to appeal to businesses, investors and tourists.
13. **Political marketing:** Promoting an individual or idea motivated by the desire to influence public policy and voters.
14. **Service:** An idea, task, experience or activity that can be exchanged for value to satisfy the needs and wants of consumers and businesses.
15. **Service complexity:** The number and intricacy of steps involved in producing a service.
16. **Service encounter:** The interaction between the consumer and the seller.

REFERENCES

1. www.collegesummit.org, website visited July 2, 2014.

2. World Trade Organization, www.wto.org, website visited April 7, 2012.

3. Helen H. Wang, "How Burger King Can Recover in China," Forbes, March 4, 2013.

4. Ibid.

5. "Dear digital diary – lifelogging in the Internet age," The Guardian, www.guardian.co.uk, August 12, 2012, website visited August 13, 2012.

6. "Federal Deposit Insurance Corporation — Number of Institutions, Branches and Total Offices," FDIC Balance Sheet, www.fdic.gov, website visited June 13, 2014.

7. Shelly Banjo "Stores Confront New World of Reduced Shopper Traffic," Wall Street Journal, January 16, 2014.

8. Ibid.

9. "Report: Global telecom industry revenue to grow at 5.3% annually," RCR Wireless, www.rcrwireless.com, January 5, 2012.

10. "Do Prescription Drug Ads Belong On TV?" The People's Pharmacy. www.peoplespharmacy.com, site visited April 7, 2012.

11. "Prescription Drug Advertising: Questions and Answers," FDA, www.fda.gov, website visited August 13, 2012.

12. "Do Prescription Drug Ads Belong On TV?" The People's Pharmacy. www.peoplespharmacy.com, site visited April 7, 2012.

13. "Greece faces difficult odds with privatization," Washington Post, www.washingtonpost.com, August 3, 2012.

14. "Privatization Gets an Endorsement from Smart Folks," Knight Ridder Tribune Business News, June 6, 2006, pg. 1.

15. Subway, www.subway.com, website visited June 13, 2014.

16. www.amazon.com, website visited January 16, 2012.

17. "The Book Superstore." Barnes and Noble, www.barnesandnobleinc.com, website visited April 21, 2012.

18. "Refining the recommended system requirements for Windows 8," Ars Technica, www.arstechnica.com, May 31, 2012.

19. Dave Altavilla, "Microsoft Learns From Windows 8 Backlash, Plans Windows Threshold Catering To Device Types," Forbes, June 30, 2014.

20. "Corporate Fact Sheet," Southwest, www.swamedia.com, web site visited June 13, 2014.

21. Zeithaml, Valeria A., "How Consumer Evaluation Processes Differ Between Goods and Services," Marketing of Services, (Chicago: American Marketing Association, 1981).

22. www.travelandleisure.com, website visited June 13, 2014.

23. www.usps.gov, website visited June 17, 2014.

24. Bharadwaj, Sandar G.; Menon, Anil, "Determining Success in Service Industries," Journal of Services Marketing 7, no. 4, 1993, pp. 19-40.

25. Cisco, www.cisco.com, website visited June 19, 2014.

26. "FAQ," FedEx Office, http://www.fedex.com, website visited June 14, 2014.

27. "Office Services," FedEx Office, http://www.fedex.com, website visited June 14, 2014.

28. www.pryor.com, website visited April 7, 2014.

29. Kotler, Philip, "Atmospherics as a Marketing Tool," Journal of Marketing 40 (Winter 1973-74, pg. 50).

30. Mehrabian, M.; Russel, J.A., An Approach to Environmental Psychology (Cambridge, Massachusetts: MIT Press, 1974).

31. www.dmx.com, website visited June 6, 2014.

32. McGirt, Ellen, "Want a Piece of This?" Fast Company, January, 2010; www.twitter.com, website visited June 6, 2014.

33. Julie Makinen, "'Transformers' breaks box-office records in China," Hollywood Reporter, Los Angeles Times, June 30, 2014.

34. Weinbach, John, "Inside College Sports' Biggest Money Machine," October 19, 2007, Wall Street Journal.

35. "Fans worldwide to enjoy NBA 2014 All-Star Game," NBA News by Official Release, www.nba.com, February 12, 2014.

36. "FIFA Financial Report 2013," FIFA.

37. Matt Yoder, "2014 World Cup viewership up 26% versus 2010, up 116% versus 2006," Bloguin, June 21, 2014.

38. Nancy Tartaglione and Dominic Patten, "World Cup Ratings Update: Univision Hits Highest Viewership Ever With Mexico Vs. Netherlands Game," Deadline, June 30, 2014.

39. www.michigan.org, website visited June 14, 2014.

40. www.barackobama.com, website visited August 6, 2012; www.mittromney.com, website visited August 6, 2012.

41. "2014 Halo Award - Best Health Campaign," Halo Awards, causemarketingforum.com, website visited June 14, 2014.

42. Warby Parker, www.warbyparker.com, website visited June 14, 2014..

43. National Center for Charitable Statistics, http://nccs.urban.org, website visited June 15, 2014.

44. Bianchi, Alessandra, "The New Philanthropy," Inc., October 2000, pp. 23-25.

45. www.nba.com, website visited June 19, 2014.

46. www.gatesfoundation.org, website visited June 19, 2014.

47. Paul G. Allen, Philanthropy, www.philanthropicpeople.com, website visited June 19, 2014.

48. www.shoestringagency.org, website visited June 19, 2014.

49. www.marketingpower.com, website visited June 19, 2014.

50. http://wpcarey.asu.edu/csl, website visited June 19, 2014.

51. "(Loop) hole in one: 33 elite, private golf clubs do not pay federal taxes," Journal News, www.lohud.com, June 23, 2012.

Chapter 11

INNOVATION & PRODUCT MANAGEMENT

Google™

"Google it" is a common way to refer to a web search — but that may not have been the case had Larry Page and Sergey Brin not met in 1995 at Stanford University. The two men set out to create what we know today as Google, arguably the most robust Internet search engine available. While the company has made numerous upgrades and added dozens of products over the years, the core principles that originally defined Google remain the same.

Today, Google is a solid global leader in four major technology industries: search, ads, apps and mobile. The success of the company represents what Google set out to be: the ultimate search engine. Larry Page remarks, "The perfect search engine would understand exactly what you mean and give back exactly what you want." The speed and consistency in which Google answers web queries has drastically changed the way we interface with the World Wide Web. And with the site accessible in over 110 languages, the entire world has the ability to utilize the power of Google.

Google rests on a foundation of 10 principles; they include items such as "focus on the user and all else will follow" and "fast is better than slow." These principles, combined with Google's corporate culture, have repeatedly landed Google in the top spot in lists of the best companies to work for. By creating comfortable work environments and multiple onsite benefits, the Google culture is one that gives to get. This culture transcends the workplace and trickles down into product offerings, making Google more useful and unique.

Google's product line continues to grow as new technologies and needs are identified. Today, Google offers more than 100 different products, including YouTube, Picasa, Blogger, Chrome and Earth. With just one Google account, consumers are able to access Gmail, Google Docs, Google Calendar and Google Video. Each of these apps allows collaboration across the Internet's data cloud, storing files and data on the Google servers, so users can access them from almost any device with an Internet connection. Google adapts quickly and adds new products often. One upcoming offering is Google Fiber, a new Internet and TV service coming to selected cities and promising speeds up to 100 times faster than the average household can currently run.

Google Fiber will require a monthly fee, but many of the company's products are free — so how does Google make any money? Through ads! Google's extensive AdWords and AdSense business units provide allow companies to advertise through Google's search engine. Businesses simply select keywords that they believe their customers are searching for and create a simple text ad to appear when those words are searched. The ad may be displayed many times in a given day, though the business will only pay if the consumer clicks on the ad. The cost per click ranges from a few cents to several dollars and is based on an auction related to popularity of keywords and phrases. AdWords allows users to customize their budgets to set caps on how many clicks or how much to spend per day. For many small businesses with low ad budgets, Google AdWords is an easy way to advertise online.

Consider how many times you've said "Google it," and you'll appreciate the innovation and product management of this extraordinary company. If you couldn't search for information on Google, what would you do? The company continues to reward its stakeholders from employees to advertisers to end users to shareholders.[1]

<< Google offices from around the globe

Courtesy of Google

Learning Objectives

1. Provide a framework to evaluate the extent to which existing or new products are marketed to existing or new market segments.
2. Understand how the characteristics of innovation influence the speed with which product innovations are accepted.
3. Know the steps used to develop new products from the initial idea through commercialization.
4. Show how the product life cycle concept can be used to build and adjust marketing strategies over time.
5. Recognize how innovations are adopted by consumers by being spread from group to group.

THE CONCEPTS OF INNOVATION AND PRODUCT MANAGEMENT

A winning company doesn't rest — it innovates. New products invigorate organizations. They create enthusiasm among employees even before they excite the market. They are absolutely essential to competitive advantage. Companies that fail to innovate usually fail, period. Even those slower than competitors will find their customer connections strained or broken as leading-edge organizations step in and step ahead. At the same time, winning companies don't prematurely abandon their existing products. They nurture and support them like old friends. Organizations make direct connections with customers through products. Without these, no relationship can exist. Products form the fundamental substance of all business exchanges. Whether these connections remain solid depends largely on the ability of marketers to introduce and manage products. This chapter explores how long-term, tight connections are made through technological innovations and product management that fulfill market potential.

Speed and responsiveness — the ability to develop products quickly — is extremely important in gaining a competitive advantage. Companies are compressing the amount of time required to turn an idea into a marketable product. This vastly increases the number of products companies can offer, but also shortens the life of each product to make room for accelerated R&D. Because of these trends, executives are emphasizing the firm's **product mix** — the collective entirety of product lines and products a company offers. They are also adjusting the depth and breadth of product lines in response to rapidly changing market forces. Excellent product management is considered essential for creating superior customer value.

Organizations must be able to balance the management of existing products and the ability to identify, find or create new ones. In a classic study, the consulting firm of Booz, Allen & Hamilton found that 28 percent of company growth comes from products introduced in the past five years. This statistic makes new-product development look like an extremely valuable endeavor, but it comes with a great deal of risk and cost. About 56 percent of introductions fail within five years, and about 45 percent of new-product development resources are spent on failures. In fact, companies usually have to come up with 13 new-product ideas before they hit on one that works.[2] With the right strategy, products can generate profits necessary to reach the organization's objectives and cover the costs of cultivating new products.

The main objective of product management is to ensure a steady flow of products that support the company's mission. Important elements to consider in product development and management are shown in Figure 11.1. This chapter begins with a

Product Mix

All the product lines and products a company offers

look at how organizations focus on the product mix in order to create growth. Next, we explore types of innovations and factors that affect how rapidly potential customers accept them. Once a company decides the role of new products for accomplishing objectives, it employs a new-product development process. We explore a successful process — from formulation of new-product strategy to product launch. A section follows on product management approaches, particularly the policies and organizational structures that foster innovation. Finally, we examine how the product life cycle and the diffusion process relate to decisions, ranging from introduction to discontinuation.

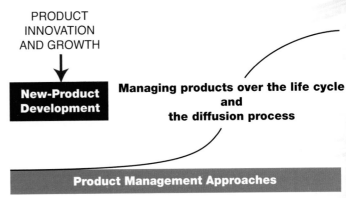

Figure 11.1 The Concepts of Product Development and Management

PRODUCT PLANNING AND TYPES OF INNOVATION

PRODUCT PLANNING

Every business needs to develop a product plan consistent with its overall marketing strategy. **Product planning** outlines the focus given to core businesses (current products in current segments), market development (new segments for current products), product development (new products for current segments) or diversification (products totally new to the company for new segments).

Product planning decisions are influenced by market segment strategies. Marketers must decide how to balance development of the existing product lines and segments with that of new products and markets. Figure 11.2 depicts these fundamental choices.

Core Business Focus A core business focus emphasizes the marketing of existing products to existing market segments. While this focus does not involve the risk and expenses of creating new products, it still requires careful decisions about whether to maintain, expand or eliminate current products, depending on market conditions, the age of the product and competitive factors. Firms that do not make these adjustments are often forced to downsize, consolidate or withdraw from some market altogether.

Product Planning

The focus given to core businesses, market development, product development, and diversification.

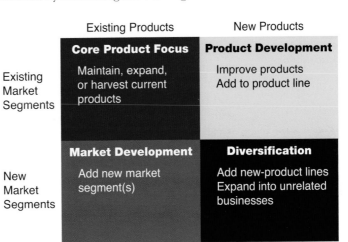

Figure 11.2 Product Planning Options

Many strong companies achieve success by focusing on their core products and market segments. This does not mean to develop the core exclusively; rather, a successful core can generate revenues to support other ventures. Sometimes companies extend their core business to take advantage of additional product offerings supported by a unique competency. For example, Nikon opened in 1918 as a manufacturer principally of binoculars. It later expanded to cameras, microscopes, surveying instruments, measuring instruments and ophthalmic lenses. Today, its products range from imaging software to film scanners to cameras for everyone from kids to professional sports photographers.[3]

Market Development

Market Development

Offering existing products to new market segments.

Market development occurs when existing products are offered to new segments. Firms may sell directly to these or use new channels of distribution. They also may expand from local markets to regional, national, international or global markets. Many clothing companies and department stores are diversifying their product lines with plus-size clothing for women. I.N.C. label clothing, sold in Macy's and Bloomingdale's, is offering plus-size clothing that is designed exactly like regular-sized clothing, as well as styles designed to provide more coverage. Ralph Lauren has extended its products to include marketing to big and tall consumers through the Rochester Big and Tall retailing outlets.[4]

Product Development

Product development occurs when companies make new products for existing market segments. This may take the form of simple improvements to older products or extensions of the product line. Most companies are continuously introducing improved versions.

Whether in the consumer or business market, product lines are continuously expanding. Pizza Hut is always developing new products, many focused on stuffing, double-stuffing, even triple-stuffing cheese into crusts and breads in every way imaginable. Its most recent innovation is an old school throwback to traditional hand-tossed pizzas. The new hand-tossed pizzas feature a lighter, airier texture and contain imperfections in an attempt to appear more artisan, a trend popular with millennials.[5] Developing new products that are closely related to existing ones is called a **line extension**. In one recent example of a line extension, Dr Pepper rolled out its Dr Pepper TEN line, featuring 10 calories per serving. The soda was so successful the company has now come up with ten-calorie versions of its other core brands, like 7-Up, Sunkist, A&W, and Canada Dry.[6] Line extension is not limited to physical products: web-based companies frequently expand their product lines to keep up with a growing market.

Diversification

Diversification occurs when new products are introduced into new market segments. Sometimes this is done with extensions of the current business, and sometimes it occurs with new ventures. Nintendo engaged in product diversification through the release of the Wii. With more powerful processors and impressively realistic graphics, competitors Microsoft and Sony went after their existing market of established gamers. Nintendo went in another direction, focusing on simplicity and creating a system drastically different from any video-game console on the market. Rather than requiring a complex controller with multiple buttons, the Wii's wireless, motion-sensitive controllers allow users to mimic real movements.[7] Nintendo went a step further into expanding its market with the Wii Fit balance board. Wii Fit is meant to make fitness more fun for all ages and includes balance and aerobic games, and even yoga positions.[8] With accessibility and the ability to perform exercise while playing, the Wii has proven

Product Development

Offering new products to existing market segments.

Line Extension

A new product closely related to others in the line.

popular among markets that were previously not experienced gamers. The Wii successor, Wii U, brought the revolutionary new Wii U GamePad controller with a second window into your gaming world.[9]

Another incredibly effective case of diversification was Apple's introduction of the iPod, iPhone and iPad. Apple ventured away from the computer arena and into uncharted territory. The result has been dramatic. Because of these ventures, Apple is growing exponentially and gaining significant ground on Microsoft.

Wii U Spotlight

TYPES OF PRODUCT INNOVATION

Marketers classify innovations according to the effect they are likely to have on consumers. **Continuous innovation** is a minor change to a familiar product, such as a new style or model that can be easily adopted without significant alterations in consumer behavior. For example, Adobe continually adds new features to its software products. Photoshop CS6 brought Content Aware tools to scale and improve aspect ratios in images, digital noise reduction tools, advanced 3D and video editing capabilities, and more.[10] Photoshop Creative Cloud 2014 added a load of new mobile features and two new features of the most interest to professional and aspiring photographers — path-based blurs and focus-based selections.[11]

A **dynamically continuous innovation** endows a familiar product with additional features and benefits that require or permit consumers to alter some aspect of their behavior. When auto companies introduced the antilock braking system (ABS), consumers needed to relearn how they had been taught to react in an emergency. On slippery terrain, pumping the brake was the advised way to regain control, but brakes equipped with ABS work best when fully compressed. Manufacturers were careful to educate drivers about the benefits and requirements of ABS so that reaction to the new system would be positive. Another example is the transformation of music devices over time. From records to eight-track and cassette tapes to CDs to digital MP3s, each new device created a shift in how we listen to music.

A **discontinuous innovation** is an entirely new product with new functions. Sometimes called "new to the world," these products require behavioral changes by users. The high degree of novelty gives early potential adopters a great deal of costs and benefits to consider before making a decision. Examples include cellular phones, satellite-transmitted maps for autos, and heart pumps. When automobile airbags were introduced, buyers had to evaluate the benefits carefully before committing the additional funds for the optional purchase. Eventually airbags, became standard equipment and were included in the vehicle price.

The advent of the laptop computer is another example. Laptops created an opportunity for work to be done outside of the office, whether in a café or on an airplane. They have become almost obligatory for college students and are preferred over desktop computers for general use. Laptops are also becoming increasingly portable, as companies like Acer are decreasing the size and weight of their products. The Acer Aspire S7 weighs just 2.79 pounds and is only 12.9 millimeters thick — hardly even noticeable in a backpack.[12]

Continuous Innovation

A minor alteration in an existing product, such as a new style or model, that can be easily adopted without significant changes in consumer behavior.

Dynamically Continuous Innovation

A familiar product with additional features and benefits that require or permit consumers to alter some aspect of their behavior.

Discontinuous Innovation

An entirely new product with new functions.

WHY INNOVATIONS SUCCEED

Research reveals that novelty itself is not as important as a new product meeting consumer needs.[13] Several specific factors influence consumer acceptance of new products: relative advantage, compatibility, complexity, trialability and observability.

Relative Advantage Relative advantage is the amount of perceived superiority the new product has in comparison to existing ones. Marketers must make it easy for consumers to recognize the benefits of switching from the old product, while making clear that any costs can be overcome. A new word-processing program may be easier to use but requires additional training. If consumers aren't convinced that the additional training will pay off, they are unlikely to purchase the new product.

In Apple's pursuit to gain market share over PCs, it is important to create a relative advantage over all other players in the industry. One way Apple attracts customers is through its claim of no-hassle software and ease of use, a claim that is demonstrated through its website. Visitors can not only review product information, but also access guided online tours demonstrating Apple products, such as how to download iTunes for use with an iPod. Apple.com also provides a wide array of support services and resources, so the customer can research and purchase products, and revisit the site for support later.

Compatibility Compatible products fit easily into the consumer's current thinking or system. Successful products are aligned with their consumers' thoughts and values, and are designed to meet their needs, not create problems. This is one reason many organizations now have 800 numbers to answer questions.

Most people consider safety important when deciding to purchase an automobile. Several companies understand the value of this and are working on high-tech ways to make driving safer. For example, GM's Delco division has created blind-spot radar to warn drivers when it's unsafe to change lanes. Texas Instruments has developed a thermal-image camera that eliminates glare from oncoming headlights. Since the products are included in the vehicle purchase, the issues of installation and additional purchase are avoided. Apple is especially successful at compatibility; its products synch so customers have their information and music on all their Apple devices.

Complexity Complexity is the degree to which a new product is easy to understand and use. Apple's Macintosh computers achieved great success by making personal computers accessible to anyone. Many people have sat down at a Macintosh, followed the simple instructions, and quickly learned to use elaborate programs. It wasn't until Microsoft developed its Windows interface that the DOS platform provided similar ease of use.

Facebook makes social media easy to use even for the less-technically inclined. On Facebook, "liking," "commenting" or "sharing" a post is a simple click away. A search bar at the top invites users to "search for people, places and things," and another area invites users to share their status updates by asking, "What's on your mind?" The site is self-explanatory enough that 49 percent of seniors use it, according to a recent study by Forrester. YouTube also makes its site easy to navigate, with "channels" to choose from, such as trending videos, music, entertainment, sports and comedy. Select a video, and after it plays YouTube will recommend related videos you may enjoy.

Trialability Trialability refers to the ease with which potential users can test a new product at little or no expense. New-product acceptance can be sped up through free samples, low-cost trials, interactive showroom techniques or loaners. Computer retailers usually place equipment on display so consumers can interact with it. Nearly every car buyer test-drives an automobile before purchasing it. General Motors offers an overnight test drive option on almost all of its vehicles to qualified drivers, providing the consumer doesn't drive more than 100 miles or leave the state. This promoted increased trialability of its products in a setting that's comfortable for the consumer.

Trialability is critical for software vendors, because only through use can potential buyers understand the features they would gain; software companies such as Adobe frequently offer free 30-day trials of their products. In the magazine world, free trial issues are common. Food companies often provide free samples in supermarkets.

Observability Observability means that a consumer can obtain a full appreciation for a product's features by watching someone else use it. When a new product has obvious benefits, it can usually be marketed at a rapid pace. When benefits are subtle, it's more difficult to gain acceptance. When the iPod was created, Apple realized it had low observability, because the device was frequently inside users' pockets or bags. To offset this, Apple made all of the iPod accessories white to create a dif-

ferentiation in the market. When you see someone wearing white earbuds, the Apple iPod comes to mind even though the actual device cannot be seen. The white accessories help Apple increase the observability of its products.

The benefits of smartphone cameras have exploded into the cellular phone market. The continued growth of camera phones has been driven by improvements in imaging functions like flash, zoom and auto focus, and optics. The easily observable benefits of taking and instantly sharing a picture wirelessly, along with convenience and ease of use, are among the reasons these products have become so successful. Not to mention, the world's affection of taking and sharing selfies.

PD-USGov

Bill Nye, Barack Obama and Neil deGrasse Tyson selfie taken using a smartphone.

THE NEW-PRODUCT DEVELOPMENT PROCESS

Success with new products depends on translating the organization's core competencies into goods or services that provide superior value to the customer. The competitiveness of most markets requires a stream of new products, processes and ventures. It's difficult to pinpoint exactly why some organizations are more innovative than others, but researchers suggest the following concepts help innovation succeed:

- A champion who believes in the new idea.
- A sponsor high enough in the organization to provide access to major resources.
- A mix of creative minds (to generate ideas) and experienced operators (to keep things practical).
- A team process that moves ideas through the system quickly so that they get top-level endorsement, resources and attention early in the game.
- A focus on customers at every step.

Executives must be objective about the chances of product success. Since the costs of new product development increases as the product moves toward com-

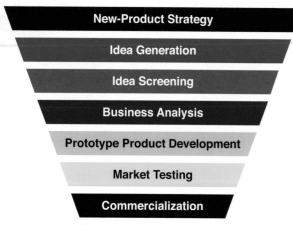

Figure 11.3   The New-Product Development Process

mercialization, companies will often implement a stage-gate method to prevent further investment into a product likely to fail.[15] Figure 11.3 describes the elements in the new-product development process.

NEW-PRODUCT STRATEGY

Leading companies have a strategy for new-product development. In forming that strategy, top executives must answer a number of questions: Will the organization be a market leader, close follower or also-ran? Will it have broad or deep product lines? How rapidly must the product stream flow, given competitive conditions and market expectations? How much will be invested in R&D over time? The business vision discussed in Chapter 2 is the starting point, since most company missions require that new technologies and innovative processes be used to create superior customer value. Shiseido's R&D vision, below, is a core part of its overall business strategy.

SHISEIDO Research and Development Vision

Our R&D people combine their scientific and sensory skills to innovate cosmetics that deliver new values to our customers.

We propose a "new value" to our customers, which integrates "functionality" that realizes beautiful and youthful skin, "sensitivity" that leads to comfort, and "safe and reliable quality."

We develop products with a high quality of international standards and tailored to the various regional characteristics by creatively integrating the power of research and development of our R&D bases around the world.

We try to give our customers the best satisfaction by integrating and synergistically increasing the knowledge, skills, abilities, and drive of each and every person involved in research and development.

We provide a wide variety of solutions that make our customers" dream about "beauty and health" come true.

Companies that do the best job of new product development have excellent market knowledge, including an understanding of customers and the competition.[16] They also use cross-functional collaboration among marketing, research and development, and other areas of the company.[17]

Fulfilling the company mission requires that marketers have the courage to bring out newer and more advanced technologies. The value statements of many corporations recognize the social responsibility of providing more functional, cost-effective, environmentally sound and safe products. How do those goals become a reality?

IDEA GENERATION

Idea Generation

The gathering of suggestions for new products from a number of sources using a range of formal and informal methods

Organizations need idea-generation systems to find an adequate number of significant new-product ideas. **Idea generation** is the use of a range of formal and informal methods to stimulate new product concepts from a number of sources.[18] Among the many possible sources are employees, customers, technology analysis, distributors and suppliers, competitors, R&D, environmental trend analysis and outside consultants. Marketers often provide incentives to individuals who make significant contributions to idea generation.

A system based on four general principles seems to work quite well:

- Systematically seek and ask for new-product ideas.
- Make sure that all ideas, no matter how trivial or elaborate, reach the individual or group responsible for collecting them.
- Provide timely feedback to all people contributing ideas.
- Build rewards and recognition into the organization scaled according to the number and quality of ideas.

Good marketers will continually encourage employees to submit ideas. After, all employees have a great deal of experience working with the products, and can probably identify at least minor improvements that could be made. The 3M Company has several policies that create a culture of creativity. For instance, it demands that at least 40 percent of its profits come from products developed within the last four years. It also allows flexibility and individuality among employees, encouraging each to try different positions within the company and dedicate at least 15 percent of his or her time to brainstorming new products.[19] Company salespeople are in the field where they can learn about new trends or ideas that may lead to the development of a new product.

Customers are a logical source of new-product ideas. This is particularly true in business-to-business marketing, since customers rely on suppliers to improve their own products and processes. By training salespeople to explore customer problems and creating a system for feedback (such as surveys and focus groups), companies are likely to discover many new concepts.

A technology analysis forecasts the speed and applicability of advances. The ideal result is a novel product that improves the standard of living. Any number of products have changed the way people live, from indoor plumbing and telephones to four-wheel-drive automobiles and MP3 players. True innovations such as the Internet are rare, but in the consumer and services sector, they tend to be in areas where the bulk of exploration is focused, such as electronics or pharmaceuticals. Also, the push for environmentally safe products has urged companies to innovate. The automotive industry as a whole has been making moves to reduce its carbon footprint. The European Union implemented the End-of-Life Vehicle Directive, which set a target for car manufacturers to be able to reuse and recycle 85 percent of vehicle weight by 2015.[20] Lexus has responded to this Directive by manufacturing its HS250h hybrid, made with sustainable materials like castor seeds used in the seat cushions.[21] On the other side of the Atlantic, General Motors engineered an "extended-range electric car," the Chevy Volt. The car runs on electric power, but is also equipped with a small gas engine for longer trips.

Distributors and suppliers have a personal interest in the number of products a company makes. They are often asked to serve on the council that many organizations establish to generate new-product concepts. At semiannual meetings, these councils exchange ideas and develop concrete lists of innovations and new approaches. Sun Microsystems involves suppliers at the idea stage and allows them to qualify as providers of the new product. These suppliers help Sun introduce new technology into its own workstations.[22]

Competitors can be a major source of ideas. Leading marketers observe the competition on many levels, analyzing market trends and how they will react to it. For example, by recognizing progressive changes in miniaturization, Allen-Bradley Corporation has been able to surpass competitors and develop new robotics that leapfrog entire generations. Japanese firms often imitate and improve on the products of U.S. companies rather than develop original products.

For R&D personnel — scientists, engineers, designers and others — new-product development is a major component of the job. Companies that encourage innovation make sure they provide ample opportunity for scientists to explore on their own. When a percentage of their time is free from routine tasks, an R&D staff will often forge major breakthroughs. The 3M Corporation not only allows employees to work on projects they choose, but it urges them to seek new-product ideas from everywhere, even failed experiments. The classic example, Post-it notes, came about from failed attempts to produce strong adhesive.

An environmental trend analysis estimates how major social forces may affect

www.3m.com

At the 3M website, learn how the company's innovative products are protecting the environment.

an industry. The organization can then use the results to project ways in which it can offer timely products. One example is to identify pollutants in a current product, find substitute ingredients and components, and develop a new version that will appeal to "green" consumers. Seventh Generation is a company that sells bathroom tissue made from 100 percent recycled paper rather than trees, as well as many other eco-friendly household products. The company's website states, "We create household and personal care products that are effective and safe for the air, the surfaces, the fabrics, the pets and the people within your living home."[23]

Consultants make up a business that thrives on generating ideas that their consumers, other companies, can use. They use a broad range of techniques to help companies develop concepts: surveys, brainstorming, focus groups and others. Each method provides a structured way of discovering innovative products. The consulting firm Booz, Allen & Hamilton has gained a global reputation for its ability to identify commercially viable solutions to customer problems.

IDEA SCREENING

Idea Screening

Identifying the new-product ideas that have the most potential to succeed.

A good system will provide hundreds of new-product ideas each year. The **idea screening** process identifies those with the strongest potential for success. Each company applies its own criteria to judge concepts, which can fall into several categories: the market, competition, required resources, technology, the environment, legal and liability issues, and financial factors.[24] Multiple scales measure how well a product performs on each dimension.

Usually, a cross-functional team examines the limited information about the idea, using both experience and subjective judgment. The team may weigh certain factors more than others, and a summary total is provided with qualitative comments to support the evaluation. Once this is completed, the team decides which products to develop further by how the evaluation scored them. The team then provides feedback to everyone who contributed an idea, including an explanation of why it was accepted or rejected. The various team members take different responsibilities over the course of a new-product project. Involving several functions at the idea stage greatly increases the likelihood of picking the best ideas and developing a great product. Each member of the team has specific skills (engineering, marketing, manufacturing) that contribute to product success.[25]

BUSINESS ANALYSIS

Business Analysis

Assessment of the attractiveness of the product from a sales, cost, profit, and cash flow standpoint.

Product Concept

A product idea that has been refined into written descriptions, pictures, and specifications.

Concept Testing

Testing the new-product concept to evaluate the likelihood of its success.

A **business analysis** assesses the attractiveness of a product from a sales, cost, profit and cash flow standpoint. Business analysis starts with the **product concept**, which refines the idea into written descriptions, pictures and specifications. Marketing and R&D work diligently to define the benefits, form, features and functions the product will have. The product concept is then presented to consumers, distributors and retailers, who provide input regarding the product's potential as well as its description and visual representations. In the process, the description is likely to undergo changes. **Concept testing** helps identify the facilitators and inhibitors to a product's success. While testing concepts to sell its new cake batters, Duncan Hines stumbled on the theme of moistness. After hundreds of hours of concept testing, one homemaker said the cake was so moist, it stuck to the fork, a phrase that inspired a successful campaign.

Once the concept has been fully defined, an initial marketing strategy is developed. Success depends not only on the product but also on the strategy for marketing it, including examining the opportunities for segmentation, product positioning and other aspects of the marketing mix. It's also important to look at production and materials acquisition needs as well as the time required before launch. A key feature of strategy development is to project long-term profitability under different scenarios.

At this point, the likelihood of success or failure becomes more apparent. Doubtful products must be weeded out before costs start mounting up in subsequent stages.

PROTOTYPE PRODUCT DEVELOPMENT

A prototype is a working model of the product, usually created by a team of marketing, manufacturing, engineering and R&D personnel. Prototypes are typically made by hand, and can be vastly more expensive than the final product. Although costly, these models are necessary for the all-important next step, market testing. Openness among team members and a clear sense of direction, led by a product champion, greatly increase the chances for prototype success regardless of the competitive situation.[26]

Among the difficulties of developing new products is changing customer preferences and uncertainty about competitive products. When there is high uncertainty, organizations need to maintain flexibility in defining specific product characteristics. Often a core team of professionals is used to create product descriptions and supervise frequent interactions with customers, which help evolve product prototypes to meet latest marketing needs.[27]

MARKET TESTING

Test marketing is a limited trial of the strategy for the product under real or simulated conditions. Up to this point, champions may be able to push a weak product through the system. Now reality sets in. A **test market** is a small geographical area, with characteristics similar to the total market, where the product is introduced with a complete marketing program. Test marketing allows companies to implement the product strategy on a limited basis under real conditions. In fact, a test may involve trying two or more marketing strategies in separate areas to identify which works better.

In carefully designed test marketing, consumers are unaware that they are part of an experiment. Retailing, distribution and promotion activities are similar to what would occur at the national or international level. When the results are in, marketers can forecast how long it will take for the product to be adopted in the general market.

Marketers choose test market sites very carefully to represent the segments that eventually will be targeted. For example, manufacturers testing toys would avoid Sarasota, Florida, which has a large elderly population, and snowshoes would get a better reception farther north. Boise, Idaho is a particularly popular site, hosting tests that range from kitchen towels and oven mitts before they hit supermarkets. Audit services in more than 125 cities throughout the United States monitor test market results. Figure 11.4 lists the top 20 test markets with a population of 50,000 or more.

By the time an organization enters a test market, substantial funds have been spent on the new venture. There is a very strong probability of committing to a full-scale product launch at this point — unless the test is a total failure. The results rarely make or break the product; they simply help predict adoption rates among consumers and channel members. Testing products are very beneficial to companies that do not have large amounts

Test Market

A small geographic area, with characteristics similar to the total market, in which a product is introduced with a complete marketing program.

Rank	Place	Population Rank
1.	Albany, NY	56
2.	Rochester, NY	46
3.	Greensboro, NC	36
4.	Birmingham, AL	54
5.	Syracuse, NY	59
6.	Charlotte, NC	33
7.	Nashville, TN	38
8.	Springfield, OR	123
9.	Wichita, KS	77
10.	Richmond, VA	50
11.	Davenport, IL	114
12.	Lexington, KY	85
13.	Charleston, SC	76
14.	Macon, GA	124
15.	Jacksonville, FL	45
16.	Greenvill, SC	51
17.	Little Rock, AR	73
18.	Evansville, IN	131
19.	Harrisburg, PA	66
20.	Cincinnati, OH	23

Figure 11.4 Top 20 Test Markets
Source: Kristen Bremner, "Albany Ranked No. 1 Test Market in Acxiom Study," DM News, May 24, 2004.

of money to spend on research. Experiments also help identify factors that facilitate or hinder product adoption and may yield surprises about who the users will be.

There are several drawbacks to using test markets. First, it takes time, and product development costs rise with every delay in a full-scale launch. Second, marketers sacrifice secrecy and surprise, exposing their products to potential competitors. Sometimes a rival will jump in with a similar product or use tactics that spoil the results. For example, when a competitor test-marketed a new item, Vicks pulled all its similar products off the shelves, leaving no basis for judging whether the test was successful. Other tactics are flooding the market with unusual promotions, point-of-purchase displays and price cuts. Third, it's impractical to use test marketing for many products, like automobiles, because prototypes are too costly. Fourth, it is extremely expensive to make the trial products, stock stores, train salespeople, run ads and so forth.

Controlled Test Market

Consumer panels or other technique to gain similar information obtained from real test markets.

A **controlled test market** uses consumer panels or other techniques to attempt to gain the same type of information obtained from real test markets. AC Nielsen's Scantrack and IRI's BehaviorScan monitor consumer behavior on new products. By combining information about consumer demographics and TV viewing behaviors with purchase data, it is possible to forecast product success. A controlled test market is often less expensive than conducting regular test marketing.

Simulated Product Test

Experimentation with the marketing strategy in artificial conditions.

A **simulated product test** is an experiment in artificial conditions. This may be done before or instead of a full test. GHI, the most authoritative product-testing center in Great Britain, performed tests on vacuum cleaners by cleaning carpets and hard flooring covered with measured amounts of a sand and flour mixture that simulated actual conditions.[28] Such simulated product testing helps identify flaws and provides feedback. It can also be used to make evaluations against competitors. The food industry often sets up a replica of a supermarket, asks consumers to shop as if they were in a natural environment, and interviews them afterward. Although simulations are not as effective as a test market, they do provide useful information at dramatically reduced costs. Furthermore, competitors are less likely to find out about a company's plans prior to product launch.

COMMERCIALIZATION

Commercialization

Final stage in the new-product development process, when the product is introduced into the market.

During the final stage of the process, **commercialization** introduces the product to the market. Launching consumer products requires heavy company support, such as advertising, sales promotions and often free samples. Consider the $30 million commercialization of Frito-Lay's SunChips brand, which included television spots and the company's largest ever direct-mail sampling program to more than 6 million households. After a decade of development, SunChips breezed through test marketing in six months, indicating to Frito-Lay executives that this multigrain snack had the potential for overnight success. In the snack food industry, new products rarely achieve even $40 million in sales, but SunChips topped $100 million in the first year and continues to bring in huge profits. Years later, Frito-Lay continues to develop the market for SunChips, attempting to prevent consumers from considering them "junk food." David Radar, executive vice president and chief financial officer, spoke at the University of Texas at Austin, stating that SunChips, which contain whole grains, can be considered a healthy product.[29] Frito-Lay has also engineered an environmentally friendly, 100

percent compostable bag for SunChips that will naturally decompose in about 14 weeks.[30]

THE ETHICS OF PRODUCT IMITATION

Some argue that since companies make substantial investments in new products, they should be the only ones allowed to market them, which intellectual property and patent laws address. Others argue that imitation forces market leaders to keep up with technology, contend with lower-priced substitutes, and respond to smaller and faster challengers — in short, providing healthy competition. Organizations that want to remain competitive are responsible for keeping pace with an ever-growing and changing market, which in many cases calls for emulating competitors' innovations.

Since product imitation has become a recognized business strategy, it is increasingly difficult for a firm to protect its products from emulation. Software development giant and market leader Microsoft has greatly benefited from the inventions of others. Its Windows operating system is considered very similar in accessibility and visual format to Apple's operating system. But it goes both ways; Apple's newest iOS 7 is certainly inspired by Microsoft's Windows 8 "flat design," a term given to a style of design in which elements like icons lose any type of stylistic characteristics that make them appear as though they lift off the screen.

Microsoft is credited for popularizing flat design, a shadowless counterpart to competitors attempting to make a 2D surface look 3D.

Not all imitations are created equal. Some are illegal duplicates of popular products, and some are truly innovative products merely inspired by a pioneering brand.[31] The makers of knockoffs or clones often copy original designs but may leave off important attributes. Clones are legal because protective patents, copyrights and trademarks are absent or have expired.

Some copies play on the style, design or fashion of a popular product. This type of imitation is common in the automobile industry. In the 1980s, several Japanese automakers introduced lines to challenge Mercedes-Benz and BMW. Toyota's Lexus, Nissan's Infiniti and Honda's Acura closely mirror the design and features of the German luxury cars. When technical products are copied, reverse engineering is often used to learn how the original was designed or made. Today, Hyundai is using the same approach but is now copying Toyota and other Japanese models.

Creative adoptions innovate beyond an existing product. These may occur as a technological development or as an adaptation to another industry. Initially, DuPont developed Teflon for the nose-cones of spacecrafts but soon extended its uses to coatings for consumer products. W.L. Gore, who was researching Teflon uses, left DuPont in 1958 and eventually developed Gore-Tex Fabrics, whose products are best known for being wind and waterproof. Gore-Tex fabric is frequently used in high-end sports clothing and has become the industry standard for outerwear comfort and protection.[32]

ORGANIZATIONAL STRUCTURES AND PRODUCT MANAGEMENT

Simultaneous new-product development occurs when people from a number of functional areas work together. Marketing coordinates the team, which usually represents R&D, engineering, production, procurement, legal and human resources, financing and so on. This approach has many advantages over the old technique of **sequential new-product development**, which passes responsibility from one functional area to the next. Companies can produce better products at lower cost and gain returns more quickly when operating simultaneously, which is why the marketers should do their best to ensure all units of the business are working together effectively.

RECENT ORGANIZATIONAL TRENDS

There are many ways to manage existing and new products. Today, companies make creative use of computer and communications technologies to support a flexible organizational structure. This enables them to respond quickly to buyer demands. It also provides access to global technologies and the ability to adapt to competitive forces. There are three notable organizational trends.

1. **Downsizing:** Several product lines are brought under a single management team, or product offerings are reduced to those that generate strong and increasing revenues.

2. **De-layering:** The number of personnel and positions between top executives and those who manage market activities is reduced.

3. **Fewer functional silos:** When one function works in isolation from others, it is called a functional silo. Organizations are stressing cross-functional synergy and personnel with experience in multiple areas.[33] It is just as important that marketers and accountants be able to work with each other as it is with those in their own department.

FUNDAMENTAL STRUCTURES

There are many acceptable organizational structures. Today, most companies prefer a structure that supports strategy changes. As strategies alter to meet new challenges, organizational structures need to change with them. The most fundamental structures for new-product development are the product or market manager, the new-product department, the new-product committee and the venture team. Companies may combine elements of several of these and may use consulting organizations as well.

Product or Market Managers
Some of the most successful organizations have used the product manager or market manager structure. **Product managers** oversee one or several products targeted at all market segments. **Market managers** are responsible for one or several similar product lines targeted at defined mar-

---

Simultaneous New-product Development

People from all functional areas work together to develop products.

Sequential New-product Development

People from various functional areas work on different stages of product development.

Product Managers

A manager who oversees one or several products targeted at all market segments.

Market Managers

A manager responsible for one or several similar product lines targeted at specific market segments.

ket areas. In either case, the manager works closely with individuals from a range of functions to build integrated strategies. The system was pioneered by Procter & Gamble, which developed teams of experts loosely tied but headed by a very strong manager. Each team was responsible for building the equity of a given brand. Product managers compete almost as strongly with other teams in the organization as they do with competitors on the outside. For example, the Crest product manager is in competition with the Gleem product manager. However, since each product is positioned to address a particular benefit — Crest for tooth decay prevention and Gleem for brightness — competition may not be direct.

Product managers or market managers have the following specific responsibilities:

- Achieve the sales, profit, market share and cash flow objectives for the product line.
- Develop the market strategy for the product.
- Prepare a written marketing plan, develop forecasts and maintain timely updates of progress.
- Integrate all functions necessary to implement a synergistic marketing strategy.

One difficulty with this system is that the manager has responsibilities beyond the traditional lines of authority. The product manager can be described as the hub of a wheel. Think of the spokes as all the functional areas that help make a good marketing strategy work. Product managers have no formal authority over these people, who report directly to managers in their own functional area.

What makes the system work? First, the product or market manager must have the necessary interpersonal and business skills to gain the team's respect without exerting too much authority. In this system, team play and networking are the most valued qualities of all involved, and strong product or market managers can use them to tap into very specialized talents from a range of people. Second, the manager must report to someone high enough in the organization to obtain the status required. Although unable to govern the activities of team members, product and marketing managers can make their presence felt through communication with top executives and across functional areas of the company.

The system's strength is also its weakness. Product managers must rely on functional managers from various areas of the organization to help them build a strong team, and if everyone is not on the same page, this can lead to miscommunication or a lack of productivity. Experience has shown that without proper attention by top management, the product or marketing manager may be relegated to relatively mundane tasks. When there is appropriate executive leadership, the system can be a flexible way to address numerous market situations.

CAREER TIP!

3M says: "We foster an individual, entrepreneurial spirit that leads to the development of innovative processes and products. We encourage the exchange of ideas, teamwork across different functions, and empowerment of our employees with the freedom to take risks." 3M is famous for its product development and innovations. You can get a detailed look at the company's employment opportunities online. The company's website will fill you in on the varied career opportunities and corresponding job requirements. You can also obtain an application online, or send an email directly from the site for further inquiries. Check it out at www.3m.com.

> **Product managers must rely on functional managers from various areas of the organization to help them build a strong team, and if everyone is not on the same page, this can lead to miscommunication or a lack of productivity.**

New-product Department

The organizational unit responsible for identifying product ideas and preparing them for commercialization.

New-product Committee

A group of key functional personnel who are brought together periodically to develop new products.

Venture Team

A group formed for a set period to accomplish a set objective.

Product Life Cycle

The four stages a product goes through: introduction, growth, maturity, and decline.

New-Product Department

The **new-product department** is responsible for identifying ideas, developing products and preparing them for commercialization. The members generally report directly to top executives and include individuals with experience in many aspects of the business. This structure separates the responsibility of new-product development from the rest of the organization. It also helps eliminate redundancies that occur when the same ideas are developed in different product areas. These personnel have a firm grasp of the methods and risks involved in developing new products. In reality, these departments are often formed with great expectations, but some quickly become a functional silo neglected by top management. This is particularly the case when top management is preoccupied with current products or when the new-product department does not set aggressive goals regarding potential commercial products. Such a department usually operates best when it has strong executive involvement and concentrates its efforts on finding strategies to make product ideas successful.

New-Product Committee

The **new-product committee** consists of key functional personnel who are brought together from time to time to develop new products. Because this activity is often not considered a strong factor in building a career, participants may give it less attention than required. Furthermore, the committee often lacks the authority to make things happen. However, it is flexible, allowing different people throughout the organization to contribute ideas and expertise, and committee members can come and go as needed in a project's development.

Venture Team

A **venture team** (sometimes called a task force) is a group formed for a set period to accomplish a set objective. A venture team is headed by a manager who reports to someone very high in the organization. The manager selects team members from various areas of the company, and each is given release time so they may give the assignment their full attention. The very specific objectives and limited time frame are great incentives for the team to focus on completing its task. Strong leadership and decision-making power allow the team to commit resources in a timely fashion. Unfortunately, in many organizations, managers are unwilling to permit their best people to participate. In addition, the teams only remain assembled for the duration of the assignment, and a new team may be put together when another objective arises, stunting cohesive experience. Hewlett-Packard used a venture team to develop the first low-cost laser printer.

Consulting Organizations

Organizations will sometimes hire full service or specialty consulting firms to set up new-product development systems, facilitate the process or conduct the development task to some degree. In many cases, consulting groups have outstanding talent with experience in the area of new products. Because of that experience, companies can save vast amounts of time and money in the innovation process. Unfortunately, some companies leave their employees out of the decision-making process, which in turn can make the employees resentful and reluctant to implement the firm's ideas. Consulting organizations such as Booz, Allen & Hamilton and McKinsey and Company often make strong efforts to involve their clients in all phases of their new-product consulting.

PRODUCT LIFE CYCLES

One of the oldest and most useful concepts for marketers is the product life cycle, depicted in Figure 11.5. Like living organisms, products move from birth through infancy, adolescence, maturity, old age and on to death. The **product life cycle** consists of four stages: introduction, growth, maturity and decline. It's important to recognize that this is only a conceptual tool, and not all products move through a complete life cycle. Some marketers question the usefulness of the idea, but it remains one of the most common notions in marketing strategy. It has been applied to generic products, suppliers, industries and individual brands.

Figure 11.5 illustrates the sales and profits for a typical product as it moves through its life cycle. Before introduction, large sums are likely to be expended on development. The average pharmaceutical company spends at least $4 billion to develop a new drug, and that can soar as high as $11 billion. The cost accounts for failures, because only one drug of every 10 that makes it to human clinical trials succeeds, leaving the small fraction of drugs that actually make it to the market responsible for offsetting R&D costs.[34]

STAGES IN THE PRODUCT LIFE CYCLE

Each of the four stages in the product life cycle is associated with its own opportunities, costs and marketing strategies. In this section, we examine each stage in more detail.

Stage 1: Introduction

During the introductory phase of the product life cycle, sales slowly take off and grow. Shipments from the factory may be high, and channels of distribution are filled as wholesalers and retailers stock the item. Since the product is new, marketers organize everything from heavy advertising campaigns and samples to educational sales techniques in order to create consumer awareness. During this critical period, marketers attempt to build share quickly to gain first-mover advantages. As numerous studies have shown, whoever introduces a product is likely to become the future industry leader in that area. Chrysler was the first to introduce minivans in the early 1980s, and its Chrysler Town & Country continues to be a market leader today.

Typically, there are few competitors during introduction, so marketers attempt to sell consumers on the new, unfamiliar concept, not focusing too intently on their own brands. When car phones were introduced, most advertising focused on selling the idea. Later advertising attempted to distinguish the various products from one another. Most organizations introduce only one or two items in a new-product line so they can gain experience and monitor progress. Furthermore, global markets offer such vast opportunities for new products that some rivals may elect to avoid confrontations by selecting an untapped area.

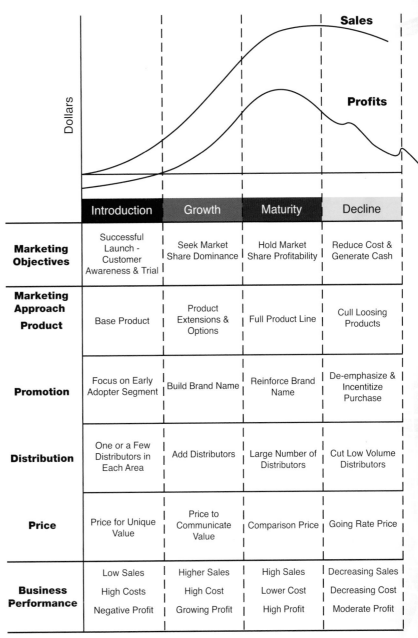

	Introduction	Growth	Maturity	Decline
Marketing Objectives	Successful Launch - Customer Awareness & Trial	Seek Market Share Dominance	Hold Market Share Profitability	Reduce Cost & Generate Cash
Marketing Approach Product	Base Product	Product Extensions & Options	Full Product Line	Cull Loosing Products
Promotion	Focus on Early Adopter Segment	Build Brand Name	Reinforce Brand Name	De-emphasize & Incentitize Purchase
Distribution	One or a Few Distributors in Each Area	Add Distributors	Large Number of Distributors	Cut Low Volume Distributors
Price	Price for Unique Value	Price to Communicate Value	Comparison Price	Going Rate Price
Business Performance	Low Sales High Costs Negative Profit	Higher Sales High Cost Growing Profit	High Sales Lower Cost High Profit	Decreasing Sales Decreasing Cost Moderate Profit

Figure 11.5   Traditional Life Cycle Curves and Marketing Approaches

As a rule, introductions represent advances in technology, manufacturing and service. Firms should make sure, however, that the design does not sacrifice accessibility. It's also important to have flexible manufacturing that can match production to highly uncertain demand. Distributors don't want to be left with unsold units, but if they don't produce enough to meet demand, consumers may lose interest or go to

CREATING & CAPTURING VALUE THROUGH *Technology*

IDEO Innovating for the Future

Can smart design change the way we act? Tim Brown thinks so. As the President and CEO of IDEO, Brown and his team fuse design, business and social studies to develop carefully researched ideas that create high-impact products. "Design thinking is a human-centered approach to innovation that draws from the designer's toolkit to integrate the needs of people, the possibilities of technology, and the requirements for business success," said Tim Brown.

Ford launched a hybrid edition of its popular Fusion model with an estimated 41 miles per gallon (mpg) city and 36 mpg highway. The critics, eager to see if the claims were true, tested the car and reported an interesting outcome. They achieved mpg ratings higher than Ford claimed; nine more miles per gallon, to be exact.

Why? Because the Fusion contains the Ford SmartGauge, an instrument panel designed collectively by IDEO and SmartDesign. In addition to displaying current speed and fuel level like a traditional instrument panel, the full-color LCD screen's graphics and animation provide feedback on the vehicle's energy efficiency at any given moment, which encourages better driving. The display actually trains drivers to increase performance and reduce fuel consumption.

Using "Design Thinking," IDEO uses the designer's sensibility and methods to match people's needs with what is technologically feasible and viable in terms of business strategy. In the case of the SmartGauge, IDEO conducted research on hybrid owners and tested the idea of offering performance feedback. When it proved popular, IDEO turned the concept over to SmartDesign, which developed a successful product.

This isn't the first success for the pre-mier design company. Fast Company Magazine reports that in the last 30 years, IDEO has delivered a needle-free vaccine for Intercel, built a better Pringle for Procter & Gamble, revitalized the bicycle for Shimano, and revised airport-security checkpoints for the TSA. With more than 1,000 patents since 1978 and 350 design awards since 1991, the company is leading the way for product innovation and generating nearly $100 million in annual revenue.

IDEO's success comes from radical collaboration. When Proctor & Gamble approached IDEO to reinvent its Pringles product line, IDEO designers didn't retreat to their offices and emerge five months later to reveal a brand-new product. Instead, they consulted with Pringles employees at every step of the process and eventually created Pringles Prints. This variant of the popular snack displays an amusing message or interesting fact on each chip. The idea was so successful that Proctor & Gamble teamed up with Trivial Pursuit and other companies in co-branding efforts.

Radical collaboration is a powerful practice that helps IDEO drive product innovation. Clients are deeply involved in the process, which IDEO encourages, as long as the final product satisfies both them and their customers.

www.ideo.com, website visited June 30, 2014.

"Hybrid Electric Vehicle Dashboard Interaction for Ford Motor Company," Case Studies, IDEO, 2009.

"Pringles Prints for Proctor & Gamble," Case Studies, IDEO, 2005.

Tischler, Linda, "Ideo's David Kelley on 'Design Thinking'," Fast Company, www.fastcompany.com, January 14, 2009.

Walker, Alissa, "Ford's SmartGauge Improves Fuel Efficiency Through Better Instrument Design," Fast Company, www.fastcompany.com, March 20, 2009.

competitors' equivalents. Finally, customer service efforts must seek out and correct problems.

Profits may be negative during all or most of the introductory phase. Sales usually grow slowly, and consumers need to be made aware of the product's existence, which requires relatively expensive promotion. It can also be costly to develop distribution channels and to educate people about the product's use.

Stage 2: Growth

During the growth stage, the pace of consumer acceptance and sales quickens. This is an especially critical time because rivals, noticing the increase in sales, will develop competitive products and aggressively pursue distribution channels. Consumers begin to make comparisons among the various products, so companies (especially powerhouses like Microsoft or Apple) attempt to gain preferred status and brand loyalty. Many organizations believe that if they don't emerge from the growth stage as No. 1 or 2, then they should abandon that line of business. Honda, an automobile company which began in 1946 as a company to create 2-cycle motorbike engines, has continued to grow beyond its original product line. Honda is now famous for its automobiles, motorcycles, power equipment, marine motors and even jets.[35]

Honda has grown substantially since its 1947 introductory Model A motorbike engine.

Product technology often enters its second generation during the growth stage. The first-generation technology applied to the original products is improved as companies gain experience, both costing the customer less and providing greater functionality. The first car phones had to be mounted permanently, and an antenna was attached to the outside. The next generation included bag phones that could be transferred from vehicle to vehicle. Now, mobile phones fit in your pocket, and some cars include Bluetooth integration that allows you to talk hands-free while driving.

With growth comes product designs that differ substantially from one manufacturer to the next. Building on the technology of short-range wireless connections and electronics, many companies have developed devices with Bluetooth or other wireless capabilities, allowing data to be transferred from mobile phones, computers and networked peripheral devices such as printers and scanners.

Manufacturing processes undergo change during the growth phase. The flexibility of the previous stage gives way to assembly lines and more automation. Higher sales volumes mean that standardized production can be used to achieve economies of scale and cost savings. Since markets are more predictable, just-in-time delivery and advanced quality control systems are possible.

Promotion and sales take on a whole new dimension during growth. Aggressive, head-to-head competition forces organizations to show their uniqueness, and the augmented product becomes extremely important. It remains critical that companies be cooperative with installation and training in product use, so they don't give any reason to go to the competition. Advertising shifts to substantive messages that describe the benefits, functions and features of the product relative to competitors' offerings.

The companies that emerge as leaders tend to provide uncompromising customer service. They build trust in the distribution channel and with end users. Sometimes repeat purchases are based more on service satisfaction than on product performance and styling. Most consumers will forgive, and even expect, a problem with any product; it is the way the organization handles the situation that really impacts consumer relations. If service is performed correctly the first time, then consumers are likely to feel an affinity toward the supplier. In fact, loyalty may be strengthened when problems occur and are handled well.

Stage 3: Maturity
As products mature, sales level off and may remain flat for long periods. Overall market growth is relatively small, so a sales increase for one company usually comes at the expense of another, which is why firms with loyal buyers tend to have the greatest longevity. Yet, loyalty also indicates that consumer interest in the product is subsiding, which makes it very difficult and costly to build market share. Most firms are happy if they simply hold their own in this phase. Weaker competitors are likely to lower prices, while stronger rivals may sacrifice market share to maintain a satisfactory profit level. Strong rivals also engage in dramatic cost containment to preserve profits. Often this results in a standardized product design with less costly components and more efficient manufacturing.

At maturity, weaker rivals may drop out and use resources on more promising products. Even strong companies may exit if profit margins suffer too much, as GE did with its consumer line of light bulbs. The maturity phase may last several months, years or even decades, and a low-cost position is critical for long-term success. This is particularly true if low-cost foreign competitors enter the business.

Product line size becomes especially important during the mature phase. Companies need to drop products with low-volume sales, high production costs or little competitive viability. But many buyers want to deal with a supplier who offers a full product line. This leads many organizations to employ outsourcing; that is, they purchase certain items from other companies and affix their own label. In this way they continue to mass-produce the lower-cost standardized items while depending on smaller firms to make the rest. Competitors may even buy from one another during the mature stage in order to gain an overall cost advantage, sometimes called co-competition.

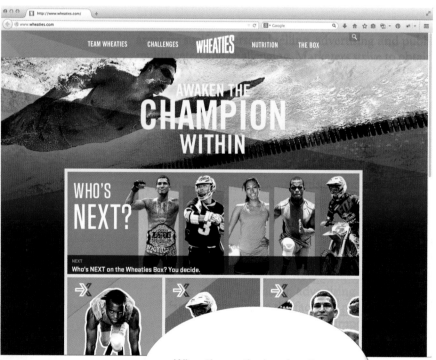

Wheaties actively advertises "the next" box cover athlete on its website.

The technology used for mature products tends to be older. Many firms have invested so heavily in past technology that they resist committing more resources to an aging product, focusing instead on streamlining and improving the manufacturing process. For example, some organizations move from assembly-line and batch-oriented production to a continuous-flow system. This integrates people, paperwork, computerization and manufacturing into a seamless operation that maintains production at the greatest level of efficiency.

Promotional campaigns focus more on reminder advertising than on new themes, since most buyers are now loyal to a particular brand or company. Sometimes companies resurrect messages that were used to build the brand's name. By adding a novel twist, the firm can keep its product in the forefront. For example, Wheaties, the traditional "Breakfast of Champions," regularly updates its package to show the latest sports superstars or to pay tribute to past champions. The objective is to create a link to younger consumers while maintaining its strong brand identity.

Service usually is standardized for mature products. In many cases, new service firms are formed to specialize in a particular product area. Even though Otis or Westinghouse installs most of the elevators we use, it is private service companies that keep them in optimal condition. Many organizations elect to hire local service firms to perform repairs. The marketing of replacement parts may become extremely profitable at this stage, especially during recessions, where consumers often prefer to repair an existing product than to replace it. In the United States, movable furniture systems from such companies as Steelcase, Herman Miller and Haworth have entered the maturity phase. Local firms are now purchasing and refurbishing the units for resale.

The rapid sales increase in the growth stage peaks during early maturity. Profits are likely to decline because of price competition, both domestically and internationally. Industries that would endure high costs to end a line of business (in other words, have a high exit barrier) are especially likely to run into this. Since it is costly to stop making the product, the companies often lower prices to maintain demand, sometimes using point-of-purchase sales or discounts. By the end of the maturity phase, a product may be losing money or have a very thin profit margin because of low demand.

Stage 4: Decline

In the decline stage of the product life cycle, sales of new units diminish. For some products, such as earlier models of computers, the decrease may be very rapid. For others, it may be slow and steady, as with black-and-white television sets. Or it may be slow and then rapid, which was the case with vinyl records. Their sales dropped gradually and then plummeted as more and more titles became available on CDs. The speed of decline is related to the types and value of substitute products.

Most companies with a declining product want to maintain the lucrative replacement market but are willing to give up market share in exchange for earnings. Fierce price wars are likely to result in losses for all competitors. Low-cost producers that minimize new activities and standardize product design are in a much better position than high-cost competitors. Changes are intended to reduce the cost of components, which helps the company maintain earnings.

Companies are likely to return to a more shallow product line at this stage, focusing on the products that generate adequate cash flow. Old technology is kept in place, and manufacturing runs are limited, which frees up production capacity for more profitable items. To keep costs down, services are usually turned over to independents and very little promotional activity occurs, so buyers may have to seek out the product themselves. Because replacement parts still generate a profit, the firm is likely to maintain a supply that affords some level of earnings.

The profit life cycle implies that companies should have products in all stages at all times. Firms with only mature and declining products can expect dwindling profitability. A company with only products in the growing and mature stages will enjoy large profits, but they'll have to develop new products eventually, which will absorb a good deal of that profit. Strong companies, and ones that rely on patented products, plan ahead and add products at various stages in the life cycle to ensure a viable business. Pfizer faced a challenge when the patent on its biggest drug, Lipitor, expired in 2011, opening the door for generics. Analysts speculated that the company didn't have enough new drugs in the pipeline to offset the sales decline that would occur. Pfizer is awaiting Federal Drug Administration approval on several drugs, including the anticlotting drug Eliquis, in hopes they will fill the sales void left by the company's mature products.[36]

VARIATIONS IN PRODUCT LIFE CYCLES

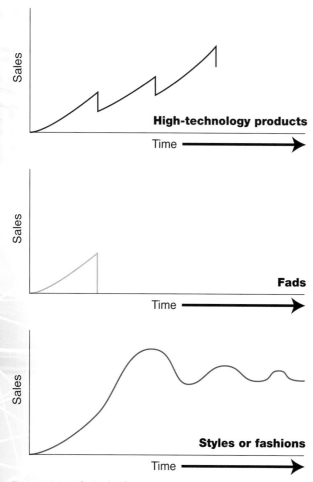

Figure 11.6   Life Cycles for Various Types of Products

By looking at extinct products, we know that several kinds of life cycles are possible as depicted in Figure 11.6. By understanding the different types, marketers can make general predictions about the challenges they face. The first curve is typical of high-tech products, such as computer software. Just when sales achieve a healthy pace, another generation hits the market. General acceptance of the product grows with each wave, however, which explains the successively higher peaks. Each generation usually lowers the cost to consumers.

The second curve illustrates the life cycle of a fad. Sales rise sharply in the introductory and growth phases and then quickly fall. Marketers of such products realize they are likely to be passing windfalls and are careful not to base the longevity of their company on one or two items. The overwhelming success of the young-adult trilogy "The Hunger Games" sent publishers on a search for more novels about teens facing grim futures. However, just as this trend replaced the "Twilight"-inspired vampire craze, it will inevitably fade as well.[37]

Clothing fashions follow yet another kind of curve. When a style is first introduced, it is likely to experience relatively fast growth and then trail off, only to be resurrected a few years later. The width of neckties has gone from narrow, to medium, to wide, and back to narrow. Skirt lengths rise and fall. Marketers of these products must be aware of constantly changing consumer preferences and build strategies accordingly.

Although the product life cycle gives marketers a rule of thumb, it is not an exact science. To obtain more precise forecasts, researchers have developed mathematical and statistical models that examine market size, the number of initial buyers, and the time between first and repeat purchase. These can be very useful, particularly for products that behave similarly to those modeled.

EXTENDING THE PRODUCT LIFE CYCLE

Firms that resist change sometimes keep products going far beyond their usefulness, but sometimes extending a product's life cycle is good business. The four most common ways to do this are to sell to new market segments, to stimulate more frequent use, to encourage more use per occasion, and to promote more varied use.

Selling to New Segments
One way to give a product a new lease on life is to find new buyers. For example, in-line skates originally targeted primarily males, who typically wanted to simulate ice hockey, but now they have been adopted widely by females. Cosmetic surgery used to be thought of as primarily for celebrities and socialites, but middle-class moms are actually among the biggest buyers, opting for breast lifts, implants, tummy tucks and liposuction. The "mommy makeover" generally costs around $15,000 and isn't covered by insurance, but, as Dr. Jeffrey Ditesheim of Charlotte, North Carolina says, "Women don't want to look like pretty moms, they want to look like pretty women."[38]

Stimulating More Frequent Use After a decade of declining sales nationwide, the milk industry needed a marketing campaign to stimulate use. From this, the well-known "Got Milk?" campaign was born. Research indicated that the product played only a peripheral role in people's lives, with most only giving it a second thought when they ran out. The campaign theme chosen was "milk deprivation" — a man agonizing over a milk-free bowl of cereal, deciding whether to rob his baby's bottle or his cat's dish, or Santa entering a home, eating a brownie, finding no milk and taking the Christmas presents away. The ads also have featured such celebrities as Nina Dobrev, Salma Hayek and the cast of "Modern Family." These award-winning ads not only heightened awareness of milk by more than 90 percent but also increased the sales of milk.[39]

Encouraging More Use Per Occasion Have you ever purchased a Snickers bar offering 20 percent more candy for free? That is one way to encourage more use per occasion. Many companies promote on this basis. For years, McDonald's offered a "Super Sized®" meal, with a larger order of French fries and a larger beverage. Recently, McDonald's has shifted away from supersizing, perhaps because of public obesity concerns. Coca-Cola encourages greater consumption with 20-ounce sizes in vending machines. Claussen, a division of Campbell's, sells a giant crinkle-cut pickle slice to "blanket" hamburgers. Americans who enjoy pickles on their burgers have a bigger option.

Promoting More Varied Use Arm & Hammer dramatically extended the life cycle of baking soda by using it as an ingredient in toothpaste, laundry products, room fresheners and deodorant. Furthermore, ads recommend it for absorbing odors in refrigerators and closets. Once used only for cooking, today baking soda has far more applications. Even when it is being disposed of, it helps sanitize the drain. Another example is the "I could have had a V-8" campaign, which popularized the traditional breakfast drink as a refreshment for any time of day. Yellowstone Park, traditionally viewed as a summer attraction, now advertises snowmobile trips in the winter.

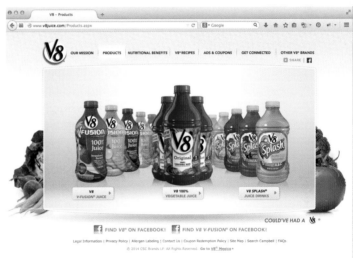

THE PRODUCT LIFE CYCLE IN INTERNATIONAL MARKETS

A product's stage in the life cycle has important implications for international trade, not only in terms of marketing but also in terms of design and manufacture.

New products tend to be designed, manufactured and sold first in advanced economies, where there is sufficient wealth to underwrite development costs, and where markets accept innovation more readily. For example, personal computers were developed largely in the United States and sold primarily in the more upscale U.S. and Western European markets. As sales grew, however, Pacific Rim manufacturers developed clones, produced them with lower-cost labor, and became important competitors in Western markets. The lower prices that resulted in turn opened up new international markets in less advanced economies such as Russia and Eastern Europe.

A product at the peak of its popularity, with many brands competing for market share, may be manufactured far from its primary market if it can gain a competitive advantage through lower manufacturing costs. Athletic shoes, for example, were pioneered in the United States — which remains their largest single market. But as product sales burgeoned and new competitors entered the market, both Nike and Reebok moved their production to low-wage countries to reduce costs.

Maturing products tend to be exported to less advanced economies looking for lower-priced goods. As these markets grow, companies are likely to establish production facilities there, using their already standardized processes. We see this in Mexico, where both Nissan and Volkswagen have assembly plants that produce for the local market — and export to the United States as well. As manufacturing skills and processes are absorbed locally, the local companies may set up their own plants and begin producing for the home market, eliminating the need for foreign-owned manufacturing plants and thereby increasing competition.

Products that have reached the end of their life cycle in one economy may still be needed in another. Few U.S. households still do their laundry with washboards and tubs, but in other parts of the world, particularly in rural areas that have no access to electricity, such products remain useful and desirable.

Some countries are more suitable markets early in a product's life and others are more suitable later. Where products are made and marketed depends on their stage in the life cycle and on the economic characteristics of the location.[40]

The last of the Type 1 VW Beetle produced in the world rolled off the production line at Puebla, Mexico, in 2003.

CONSUMER ACCEPTANCE OF INNOVATION

ADOPTION PROCESS

Adoption Process

The steps an individual consumer goes through in making a product choice.

The **adoption process** refers to the five steps that consumers go through in making a product choice: knowledge, persuasion, decision, implementation and confirmation. First, the consumer becomes aware of the product and learns about it. Second, the person forms a favorable or unfavorable attitude toward the product. Third, the consumer chooses or rejects the product. Fourth, the consumer tries the product. Fifth, experience confirms or refutes the wisdom of the choice and whether the item will be purchased again.[41]

The speed of adoption depends on buyer characteristics and other factors, but it usually takes time. Because people are different, it is possible to categorize them according to how long it will take them to adopt an idea. We know, moreover, that product acceptance is passed from one group of consumers to the next. To explain this path, marketers have developed the diffusion process.

DIFFUSION PROCESS

The **diffusion process** describes the spread of innovations from one individual or group to another over time. Marketers are keenly aware of how diffusion affects the introduction and long-term adoption of goods and services. We know that sales are influenced dramatically by the interaction of buyers, through word of mouth, as well as by promotions and messages from marketers. Often managers focus only on developing new or improved products, but they must also keep consumers' evaluations of these products in mind. Otherwise even very beneficial products may not be diffused throughout the market.[42]

Figure 11.7 illustrates the five groups of consumers who can be expected to purchase a product over time. The approximate distribution is 2.5 percent innovators, 13 percent early adopters, 34 percent early majority buyers, 34 percent late majority buyers and 16 percent laggards. The illustration is based on standard deviations, but the proportions may differ with various products.

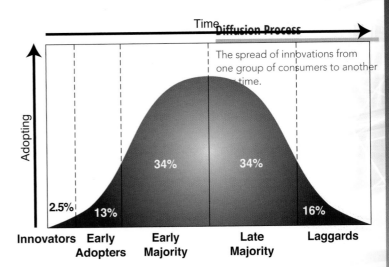

Figure 11.7   The Product Diffusion Cycle

Innovators   The first consumers to purchase a new product are **innovators.** As you can guess, they are more adventurous than most of the population. They are technically competent and in some cases are almost obsessed with the details of new products, sometimes to the point of being eccentric. This small group has only minor influence over others, but their adoption provides proof that the product functions properly. Marketers can point to that experience in attempting to educate other buyers. The marketer of a new computerized vision system for detecting manufacturing flaws first installed the system at a small innovative firm that makes electronic parts. The company later cited successful use in selling the product to a leader in the industry.

Early Adopters   **Early adopters** are the second group to purchase new products and are critical to marketers. They have higher incomes, so they can afford to try relatively expensive introductions. They are the key to good word-of-mouth publicity and wider acceptance. They are well respected in their community, so other categories of buyers are likely to emulate them.

Early Majority Buyers   **Early majority** consumers tend to be more risk-averse than innovators and early adopters. They wait to see how something new works for others before purchasing it themselves. They also tend to read extensively about various products and compare different brands before reaching a decision. For the most part, these consumers are followers rather than leaders. For this reason, early majority consumers are likely to wait for new products to work out potential drawbacks before adopting them.

Late Majority and Laggards   The more skeptical consumers tend to fall into the **late majority** group. They have little faith in new products, so they wait until half the population has purchased them before they do. However, even more resistant to new products is the last group of consumers to purchase, the **laggards**; little, if anything, can be done to convince laggards to purchase a new product.

U.S. farmers can be viewed using the diffusion cycle. Innovators and early adopters stay current on all developments in agriculture. They go to trade shows and

Innovators

The first group of consumers to purchase a new product.

Early Adopters

The second group of consumers to purchase new products.

Early Majority

The third group of adopters, who are more risk averse in purchase decisions than innovators and early adopters.

Late Majority

The more skeptical consumers who purchase products after the early majority.

Laggards

Consumers who resist new products the longest.

read everything they can get their hands on. These consumers are the first to buy a new piece of equipment or pesticide. At the other extreme lie the laggards. They feel "if it ain't broke, don't fix it" and tend to stay brand oriented, influencing little to none of the market. Marketers have used different strategies to reach each group. The innovators and early adopters prefer advertising with a lot of good information or copy. Laggards, on the other hand, need attention-grabbing ads and coupons as an incentive to purchase new products.[43] Since laggards often have low incomes and form a relatively small group, many marketers simply avoid marketing to them completely. The fact that they have low education and low income often makes them bad credit risks as well.

Here is an example of applying the diffusion cycle to the pharmaceutical industry. A pharmaceutical firm introduced a new pain reliever. Salespeople were asked to identify physicians who fit the early adopter profile: younger, heavy prescribers, on hospital boards, with modern offices and equipment. Special attention was given to these physicians through direct mail, sampling and sales calls. Because early adopters are more cosmopolitan than average, they are more inclined to accept information and interact with innovative firms. They agreed to test and evaluate the new product, quickly gave it their support and set in motion rapid diffusion throughout the medical community.

When we think of product innovation and new-product introductions, our tendency is to think in terms of manufactured goods. Remember that services, too, are products — as you are aware from the marketing definition in Chapter 1 and the many examples of services encountered thus far.

CHAPTER SUMMARY

Objective 1: Provide a framework to evaluate the extent to which existing or new products are marketed to existing or new market segments.

Every organization needs to develop a product mix consistent with its overall strategy. It must match current and new products with current and new segments. This produces four basic options for marketing mix management. A core business focus maintains, expands or harvests current products in current markets. Market development seeks new market segments for existing products. Product development improves or adds new products for sale to current segments. Diversification introduces new products into new market segments. Organizations can use this framework to help allocate resources to obtain the best overall performance.

Objective 2: Understand how the characteristics of innovation influence the speed with which product innovations are accepted.

Product innovations are of three types. Continuous innovations are minor changes in existing products that require no alterations in how consumers use them. Dynamically continuous innovations have added features and benefits that require minor changes in behavior. Discontinuous innovations are new to the world and may require major changes. How rapidly a product is accepted depends on several factors. If its relative advantage over other products is high, then faster acceptance can be expected. If the product is compatible with current thinking then quick adoption is likely. Also, less complex products and those that can be easily tried are more readily accepted. Finally, if the product can be observed in use by others, then it is more likely to be adopted rapidly.

Objective 3: Know the steps used to develop new products from the initial idea through commercialization.

The new-product development process has seven steps. First, a strategy is outlined by top management. This indicates the importance of new products to the organization. Second, idea generation provides a list of possibilities. These can come from numerous sources, especially if they are actively sought. Third, idea screening narrows the list to those most compatible with the organization's need. Several criteria are used in screening. Fourth, business analysis develops a product concept and performs a financial analysis to assess feasibility and estimate profitability under numerous assumptions. Fifth, prototype product development involves all the steps leading up to and including the creation of a working model. Sixth, test marketing provides a limited trial of the marketing strategy under real or simulated conditions. The objective is to see whether the strategy will work or needs to be refined before full-scale launch. Seventh, commercialization occurs when the product is formally introduced into the market.

Objective 4: Show how the product life cycle concept can be used to build and adjust marketing strategies over time.

Products can be viewed as moving over a life cycle with several stages. In the introduction phase, sales usually take off slowly despite heavy promotion. Marketers concentrate on getting consumers to be aware of and accept the product class. During the growth stage, sales increase, and product technology often enters its second generation. Manufacturing and promotion are adjusted. Leading producers focus on customer service. At maturity, sales begin to slow and level off. Gains in market share for one company come at the expense of another. A few companies exit at this point. Low cost really counts now in manufacturing and marketing. The decline stage is marked by a downward sales trend. Although a good replacement parts market may exist for some products, many companies choose to exit or harvest.

Objective 5: Recognize how innovations are adopted by consumers by being spread from group to group.

People go through a series of steps in adopting a new product. The speed depends on personal characteristics. Individuals can be grouped into five categories that comprise the diffusion process. Innovators are the first to adopt. They are usually a small group and tend to be eccentric. Early adopters, a larger group, are next. They have high income and education levels, and others respect them. This group is key to the success of new products. The third category is early majority buyers, a larger segment that generally follows the leadership of the early adopters. The last two categories, late majority buyers and laggards, are the last to adopt. The late majority group is numerous, so it is important.

REVIEW YOUR UNDERSTANDING

1. What are the four product mix options? Describe each.
2. What are the three product innovation categories? What are the characteristics of each?
3. What product characteristics speed the adoption of an innovation?
4. What are the steps in new-product development? Describe each.
5. What are test markets?
6. List five organizational structures for new-product development.
7. What are the differences between simultaneous and sequential methods of new-product development?
8. What is the difference between a product manager and a market manager?
9. What are the stages in the product life cycle? Identify and describe each .

DISCUSSION OF CONCEPTS

1. Explain the differences among continuous innovation, dynamically continuous innovation and discontinuous innovation. What are the main activities for marketers when introducing each type?
2. Assume you are senior vice president of marketing for General Electric. What four product mix management options might you consider? Give specific examples of each.
3. Describe the typical profit scenario as a product moves through its life cycle. Do you think it's important for companies to have products in all stages? Why or why not?
4. What are some problems with using the product life cycle concept to make marketing decisions? Why do you think so many compa-

nies use the concept?
5. What are some ways to extend the product life cycle? Can you think of any companies that have used these techniques?
6. Many marketers use the diffusion cycle concept and the product life cycle concept. How are they different?
7. When introducing a new product, how may a marketer facilitate consumer acceptance?
8. Describe each organizational structure for new-product development. What factors would influence your decision to select one structure over another?

KEY TERMS & DEFINITIONS

1. **Adoption process:** The steps an individual consumer goes through in making a product choice.
2. **Business analysis:** Assessment of the attractiveness of the product from a sales, cost, profit and cash flow standpoint.
3. **Commercialization:** Final stage in the new-product development process, when the product is introduced into the market.
4. **Concept testing:** Testing the new-product concept to evaluate the likelihood of its success.
5. **Controlled test market:** Consumer panels or other techniques to gain similar information obtained from real test markets.
6. **Continuous innovation:** A minor alteration in an existing product, such as a new style or model, that can be easily adopted without significant changes in consumer behavior.
7. **Diffusion process:** The spread of innovations from one group of consumers to another over time.
8. **Discontinuous innovation:** An entirely new product with new functions.
9. **Dynamically continuous innovation:** A familiar product with additional features and benefits that require or permit consumers to alter some aspect of their behavior.
10. **Early adopters:** The second group of consumers to purchase new products.
11. **Early majority:** The third group of adopters, who are more risk averse in purchase decisions than innovators and early adopters.
12. **Idea generation:** The gathering of suggestions for new products from a number of sources using a range of formal and informal methods.
13. **Idea screening:** Identifying the new-product ideas that have the most potential to succeed.
14. **Innovators:** The first group of consumers to purchase a new product.
15. **Laggards:** Consumers who resist new products the longest.
16. **Late majority:** The more skeptical consumers who purchase products after the early majority.
17. **Line extension:** A new product closely related to others in the line.
18. **Market development:** Offering existing products to new market segments.
19. **Market manager:** A manager responsible for one or several similar product lines targeted at specific market segments.
20. **New-product committee:** A group of key functional personnel who are brought together periodically to develop new products.
21. **New-product department:** The organizational unit responsible for identifying product ideas and preparing them for commercialization.
22. **Product concept:** A product idea that has been refined into written descriptions, pictures and specifications.
23. **Product development:** Offering new products to existing market segments.
24. **Product life cycle:** The four stages a product goes through: introduction, growth, maturity and decline.
25. **Product manager:** A manager who oversees one or several products targeted at all market segments.
26. **Product mix:** All the product lines and products a company offers.
27. **Product planning:** The focus given to core businesses, market development, product development and diversification.
28. **Sequential new-product development:** People from various functional areas work on different stages of product development.
29. **Simulated product test:** Experimentation with the marketing strategy in artificial conditions.
30. **Simultaneous new-product development:** People from all functional areas work together to develop products.
31. **Test market:** A small geographic area, with characteristics similar to the total market, in which a product is introduced with a complete marketing program.
32. **Venture team:** Personnel from various areas of the company who are given release time to work on a specific assignment.

REFERENCES

1. Google, www.google.com, website visited July 2, 2014.
2. Christopher Power, "Flops — Too Many New Products Fail. Here is Why — And How to Do Better," Business Week, August 16, 1993, pp. 76-82.
3. Nikon, www.nikon.com, website visited July 2, 2014.
4. www.rochesterclothing.com, website visited July 2, 2014.
5. Maureen Morrison, "Pizza Hut Rolls Out 'Game Changer': Pie With Imperfections," AdAge, January 15, 2014.
6. Jane Wells, "Dr Pepper Thinks 10 Is the Magic Number'," CNBC, April 30, 2013.
7. "Nintendo Wii: A Gesture Toward Broader Entertainment," PC Magazine, Nov. 1, 2006, 25(21), p. 1.
8. www.wiifit.com, website visited April 22, 2014.
9. www.nintendo.com, website visited April 22, 2014.
10. Adobe, www.adobe.com, website visited August 13, 2012.
11. David Cardinal, "Creative Cloud and Photoshop 2014: Adobe piles on the goodies for photographers," ExtremeTech, June 18, 2014.
12. www.acer.com, website visited April 22, 2014.
13. Calantone, R.J.; DiBenedetto, C.A.; Bhoovaroghaven, S., "Examining the Relationship Between Degree of Innovation and New Product Success," Journal of Business Research 30, 1994, pp. 143-148.
14. "Consumers Now Take More Than a Quarter of All Photos and Videos on Smartphones," NPD Group, www.npd.com, December 22, 2011.
15. Schmidt, Jeffery B.; Calantone, Roger, "Are Really New Product Development Projects Harder to Shut Down?", Journal of Product Innovation Management, 1998, pp. 111-123; Schmidt; Calantone, "Escalation of Commitment During New Product Development," Journal of the Academy of Marketing Science, Spring 2002; Power, "Flops"; Schlossberg, Howard, "Fear of Failure Stifles Product Development," Marketing news, May 14, 1990, pp. 1, 16.
16. Calantone, Roger; Schmidt, Jeffery; Song, Michael, "Controllable Factors of New Product Success: A Cross-National Comparison," Marketing Science, 1986-1998.
17. Luca, Luigi M. De; Atuahene-Gima, Kwaku, "Market Knowledge Dimensions and Cross-Functional Collaboration: Examining the Different Routes to Product Innovation Performance," Journal of Marketing, January 2007, Vol. 71, Issue 1, pp. 95-112.
18. Griffiths-Hemans, Janice; Grover, Rajivl, Journal of the Academy of Marketing Science, Winter 2006, Vol. 34, Issue 1, pp. 27-39.
19. A Century of Innovation: The 3M Story, 3M Company, 2002.
20. www.lexus.eu, http://ec.europa.eu/environment/waste website visited April 22, 2010.
21. www.lexus.com/hs, website visited April 22, 2010.
22. Carbone, James, "Sun Shines By Taking Time Out," Purchasing, September 19, 1996, pp. 34-35.
23. "Seventh Generation, Inc.," Marketing News, April 25, 1994, pg. E8. www.seventhgeneration.com, website visited April 22, 2014.
24. Calantone, Roger; Schmidt, Jeffery; DiBenedetto, C. A., "Using the Analytic Hierarchy Process in New Product Screening," Journal of Product Innovation Management, 1999, pp. 65-76.
25. Calantone, Roger; Vikery, S.; Droge, C., "Business Performance and New Product Development Activities: An Empirical Investigation," Journal of Product Innovation Management 12, June 1995, pp. 214-223.
26. Haggblom, T.; Calantone, R.; DiBenedetto, C.A., "Do New Product Managers in Large or Hi-Market Share Firms Perceive Marketing R&D Interface Principles Differently?" Journal of Product Innovation Management 12, September 1995, pp. 323-333.
27. Bhattacharya, Shantanu; Krishnan, V.; Mahajan, Vijay, "Managing New Product Definition in High Dynamic Environments," Management Science, November 1998, Vol. 44, No. 11, Part 2, pp. S50-S54.
28. "Consumer: Suck It and See: Dyson Has Triumphed Over Hoover in the Great Vacuum Cleaner Legal War, but Which Are the Best Dust-Busters?" The Guardian, October 5, 2000.
29. Lawrence, Jennifer, "The SunChip Also Rises," Advertising Age, April 27, 1992, pg. S2; Lawrence, Jennifer, "Big Push for SunChips," Advertising Age, February 24, 1992, pg. 2; Taylor, Sandie, "Changing Perceptions of Frito-Lay Products Biggest Strategic Opportunity, Says Rader," Presentation at University of Texas at Austin, September 21, 2006.
30. www.sunchips.com/healthier_planet, website visited April 23, 2014.
31. Schnaars, Steven P.; Managing Imitation Strategies (New York: The Free Press, 1994), pg. 5.
32. W.L. Gore & Associates, Inc., Hoover's Company Records, March 15, 2008.
33. Song, X.M.; Montoya-Weiss, M.; Schmidt, Jeffery, "Antecedents and Consequences of Cross-Functional Cooperation: A Comparison of R&D, Manufacturing, Marketing Perspectives," Journal of Product Innovation Management, 1997, pp. 35-47.
34. " The Truly Staggering Cost of Inventing New Drugs," Forbes, www.forbes.com, February 10, 2012.
35. www.honda.com, website visited March 31, 2014.
36. "Pfizer's Cost-Cuts Offset Loss of Lipitor," Wall Street Journal, www.wsj.com, website visited August 7, 2014.
37. "Spurred By Success, Publishers Look For The Next 'Hunger Games'," NPR, www.npr.org, March 6, 2012.
38. "More moms opting for 'Mommy Makeovers'," WBTV, www.wbtv.com, July 16, 2012.
39. Mergenhagen, Paula, "How 'Got Milk' Got Sales," American Demographics, www.marketingpower.com, website visited April 23, 2010; www.milkmustache.com, website visited August 7, 2012.
40. Vernon, Raymond, "International Investment and International Trade in The Product Life Cycle," Quarterly Journal of Economics, May 1986, pg. 199.
41. Rogers, Everett M., Diffusion of Innovations, 3rd ed. (New York: The Free Press, 1982), pp. 164-175.
42. Ohlshavsky, R.; Spreng, R., "An Exploratory Study of the Innovation Evaluation Process," Journal of Product Innovation Management 13, November 1996, pp. 512-529.
43. Blake, Brian F., "They May Be Innovative, But They're Not the Same," Marketing news, April 15, 1991, pg. 12.

Chapter 12

INTEGRATED MARKETING COMMUNICATIONS

Placing customers in "Good Hands™" is something that the Allstate Corporation does every day. Allstate provides a wide range of services including auto, home and life insurance. Allstate is the nation's largest publicly held personal lines insurer. It employs more than 38,000 professionals and serves approximately 16 million households.

Allstate's marketing team has the challenge of advertising an intangible product. The marketing team, along with agency partners such as Leo Burnett, Starcom, IMG and Octagon, create a seamless, integrated marketing communications (IMC) platform that combines national and local advertising as well as sponsorship activities to connect with customers. One way that Allstate implements its IMC strategy is through the consistent use of a spokesperson to represent their brand. Dennis Haysbert, most commonly known for his role as President Palmer from the TV series "24," has been the spokesman for Allstate since 2003 and has become a voice synonymous with the brand.

The company has won numerous awards for its philanthropic, employee volunteerism and diversity efforts. It's newest LGBT (lesbian, gay, bisexual, and transgender) campaign is on the front end of an era where companies are no longer afraid to include LGBT content. The "Safe in My Hands" commercial is a touching story featuring an original song by Eli Lieb. A little boy with an abnormally large hand is depicted as he grows up feeling self-conscious and judged because he is different...until one day he finds another person like himself. The two cartoon men reach for each other, hold hands and begin to walk into the sunset while the cartoon fades to two real-life men holding hands. The words "Being visible should never leave you feeling vulnerable," and "**Everyone** deserves to be in good hands" appear as the screen fades to black. You can learn more about the campaign, download Eli Lieb's "Safe in My Hands" song for free, and see the commercial at www.allstate.com/LGBT.

In combination with TV commercials and print ads, Allstate holds an extensive sponsorship portfolio that includes the Mexican and U.S. national soccer teams, the FIFA World Cup, the U.S. Olympic Team, and 65 college football teams. Each of these sponsorship deals contains multiple assets that Allstate is able to leverage to communicate its branding and messaging to consumers.

Allstate's presence in college football has been building over the last few years with the "Good Hands™" field goal nets in stadiums across the U.S. During a field goal attempt, the kicker will actually kick the football into the hands of an Allstate-branded net. Televised football games display the nets for several seconds, showing them to the millions watching the game on TV. In addition to the sponsorship of 65 colleges, Allstate also owns the naming rights to the Allstate Sugar Bowl®, held annually in New Orleans, Louisiana.

Beyond advertising and public relations efforts, Allstate also funds and promotes corporate advocacy campaigns, including promoting the Allstate Foundation and initiatives supporting new legislation regarding automobile safety. However, one of the company's largest campaigns pertains to safe teen driving, which is why it created a Parent-Teen Driving Contract, where parents can start a conversation with their children about driving safely. Allstate even commissioned the group Lifehouse to produce a song used in one of their most memorable TV spots, titled "Tail Lights."

"It's time to make the world a safer place to drive — that's Allstate's stand. Are you in Good Hands™?"[1]

<< Allstate provides insurance to about 16 million households.

Learning Objectives

1. Understand the objectives of integrated marketing communications.
2. Learn how the communication process provides the intended information for the market.
3. Learn about the communication mix, including personal selling, advertising, sales promotion, sponsorships and public relations.
4. Know the factors that influence the communication mix.
5. Describe the steps in developing an integrated marketing communication plan.
6. Learn how to address diversity, ethics and technology in communications.

THE CONCEPT OF INTEGRATED MARKETING COMMUNICATIONS

Which do you think would sell better — a poor product supported by great marketing communication or a great product supported by poor marketing communication? Actually, the product probably would not do well in either case. A good product that is poorly communicated is unlikely to be perceived well by consumers. A poor product, no matter how well it is promoted, will quickly become known for its lack of value. Social media and personal interactions help to spread people's reaction to a product.

Marketers need to ensure that all elements of the marketing mix — product, price, promotion and place — are working together. This chapter deals with communication, a broad concept that encompasses promotion. Recall from Chapter 5 that a product's position is its image relative to competition in the minds of consumers. It would not make sense for Payless shoe stores to carry expensive brands. Nor would it make sense for Campbell's to charge less for its premium soup than its regular soup. Both would seem inconsistent in the minds of consumers.

Nearly everything about a product communicates something to consumers. The gold label on Campbell's premium soups communicates quality. Even where you buy a product implies something; the very name *Payless* means inexpensive shoes. Think of a doctor's waiting room; if you feel uneasy in it, you may decide to leave or change physicians altogether. That's why medical centers often hire interior decorators to include carpeted patient areas, art and other elements that communicate a professional and caring environment.

Communication is the process of sending and receiving messages. It is an exchange of meaning between parties which involves sharing points of view and connecting with others to form relationships. **Promotion,** the process designed to influence consumers, can be used to inform, educate, persuade, remind and reinforce through communication. Although most marketing communications are aimed at consumers, a significant number also address shareholders, employees, channel members, suppliers and society. In addition, we will see that effective communication is a two-way street: receiving messages is often as important as sending them.

Integrated marketing communication (IMC) is the coordination of advertising, sales promotion, personal selling, public relations and sponsorships to reach consumers with a powerful, unified effect. These five elements impact and enhance each other, and should be viewed as components of one whole. The strategic use of television, newspaper, radio, direct mail and the Internet can produce an extremely successful communication. The Coca-Cola Company uses nearly every form of media including television, print ads and the Internet to market its products.

Communication

The process of sending and receiving messages.

Promotion

The process marketers use to inform, educate, persuade, remind, and reinforce consumers through communication.

Integrated Marketing Communication (IMC)

The coordination of advertising, sales promotion, personal selling, public relations, and sponsorship to reach consumers with a powerful effect in the market.

It also maximizes brand awareness, especially in growing markets, through sponsorships such as the Olympic Games.

The IMC concept has three parts, as depicted in Figure 12.1. First, it is important to consider the objectives of IMC, which are related to the overall marketing strategy. Second, marketers utilize the communication process characteristics to improve communications. Third, each type of communication in the plan accomplishes a unique task. Using each effectively requires planning, budgeting, implementation and feedback. After outlining these three components of IMC, the chapter concludes with a look at diversity, ethics and technology issues pertaining to IMC.

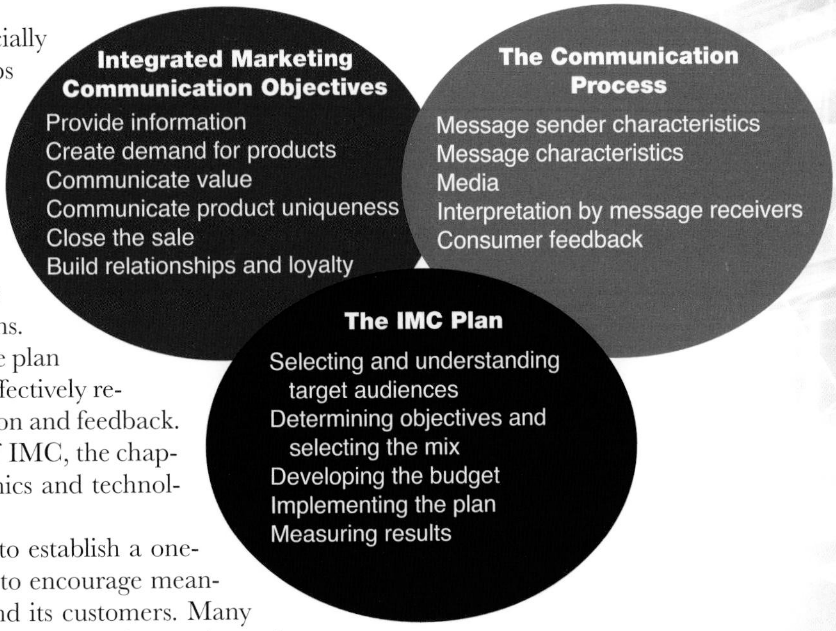

Two important goals of IMC are to establish a one-on-one relationship with consumers and to encourage meaningful communication between a firm and its customers. Many companies try to achieve these goals by orchestrating various elements of the promotion mix and creating a brand experience that directly impacts consumers. Oprah Winfrey created exceptional experiences that forged valuable connections with millions of customers via her talk show, website and multimedia empire. Oprah's Angel Network opened 55 schools in 12 countries, created scholarships, as well as funded women's shelters and the building of youth centers and homes.[2]

Integrated Marketing Communication Objectives

Provide information
Create demand for products
Communicate value
Communicate product uniqueness
Close the sale
Build relationships and loyalty

The Communication Process

Message sender characteristics
Message characteristics
Media
Interpretation by message receivers
Consumer feedback

The IMC Plan

Selecting and understanding target audiences
Determining objectives and selecting the mix
Developing the budget
Implementing the plan
Measuring results

Figure 12.1 The Concept of IMC

OBJECTIVES OF INTEGRATED MARKETING COMMUNICATIONS

Integrated marketing communications has numerous objectives. The most notable are to provide information, create demand, communicate value and product uniqueness, close the sale and build loyal customer relationships.

PROVIDE INFORMATION

Ultimately, all communication is designed to provide some form of information. Proper marketing communication gives consumers what they need to know to make informed choices within a reasonable time frame. Depending on how familiar the target audience is with the product in question, communication can be dedicated to different degrees of explanation. Often this communication introduces consumers to the product's benefits and uses. When it is working most effectively, information helps consumers make the buying decision. It provides data on a broad range of topics, including product characteristics, uses, availability, prices and methods of acquisition. Marketers need to be aware, however, that a consumer has many sources of information about a given product, so they need to select the most appropriate method for their situation. In many cases, information is purely descriptive. For example, AT&T's "It Can Wait" awareness campaign focuses on the dangers of texting while driving." The company runs ads featuring young people who have suffered permanent disabilities or families who have lost loved ones because of texting-related accidents; it also has a Facebook page where drivers are asked to pledge not to text and drive, then share the pledge with their friends and ask them to sign too. It had collected 4,754,260 pledges as of July 1, 2014. In addition, the AT&T site features a downloadable tool kit with public service announcements, advertisements and educational materials for schools and companies.[3] Marketers are challenged to create communications that contribute to the consumer's search for value in the marketplace or marketspace. Consequently, communications should be designed with consumer information needs in mind.

CREATE DEMAND FOR PRODUCTS

Communication helps create demand for products in global and domestic markets. It stimulates people to desire what they do not have and inspires them to earn the money to acquire items that improve their standard of living. Communication helps assure that products will be purchased in sufficient quantities to justify their development, production and distribution. Today, the speed of communication allows companies to obtain worldwide demand in a short period. Many products marketed globally have coordinated IMC campaigns supported by high-tech information systems. The Internet and corporate networks make it possible for companies to see what demand is being created by communication in different geographical areas and to adjust product availability accordingly. For example, smartphones and tablets have created a growing demand for wi-fi connectivity. Boingo recently acquired wi-fi advertising company Cloud Nine Media in an effort to add sponsored access to its managed wireless hotspots, which reach more than 1.4 billion people each year in such locations as airports, malls, restaurants and stadiums.[4] Communication infrastructures provide growing platforms for messages that build demand within society.

COMMUNICATE VALUE

The search for value is complicated because consumers need to assess the benefits of a product relative to thousands of others. Marketers compete to provide value in keeping with consumers' willingness to pay. Consequently, a great deal of communication focuses on conveying a product's benefits in a memorable way. For example, Eaton Corporation technical sales representatives are trained to learn the various features and benefits of sophisticated electronics products, as well as how best to communicate those features to consumers. However, they first need to know how the customer intends to use the product. A contractor, for instance, would be installing equipment in a building. The sales representative can then point out cost-saving product attributes due to easy installation and reliable design.

Advertisers are often careful to depict scenes of consumers clearly benefiting from products. Beats by Dre "The Game Before The Game" short film cleverly communicates value by depicting athletes using the product in pregame situations. Brazilian soccer star Neymar Jr., uses Beats by Dre headphones to help prepare for a game on the world's biggest stage, the 2014 FIFA

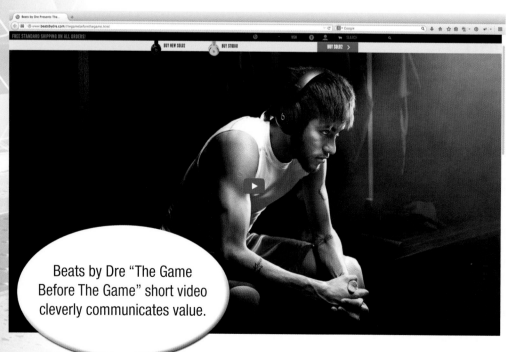

Beats by Dre "The Game Before The Game" short video cleverly communicates value.

World Cup. Neymar says, "Without Music, my preparation is not complete," communicating the impact Beats by Dre headphones has on his career. The five minute commercial, found on www.beatsbydre.com and YouTube, features cameos of Nicki Minaj, LeBron James, ESPN's Stuart Scott, Lil Wayne, Serena Williams, and music by Jay-Z.[5] Ironically, Beats by Dre headphones were banned from the tournament. FIFA's licensing agreement with rival Sony prevents players from wearing them inside stadiums or at media events. Despite Sony's efforts, even providing each player with a set of Sony headphones, players were spotted wearing Beats by Dre almost everywhere else.[6] Traditionally valued for sound quality and style, Beats by Dre added to its perceived value by suggesting that users could enhance their athletic performance.

COMMUNICATE PRODUCT UNIQUENESS

Marketers attempt to communicate uniqueness in order to differentiate their product from others. Burger King is broiled; McDonald's is fried; Southwest Airlines is less expensive because it has no frills; Titleist is used by more professional golfers than any other ball; and so on. Marketers also use persuasive communication to convince consumers to switch from one brand to another. Typical advertising messages compare a product's features, functions and benefits to those of the competition. In all of these cases, the ultimate goal is for marketers to illustrate their brands' unique qualities to build preference in their target markets.

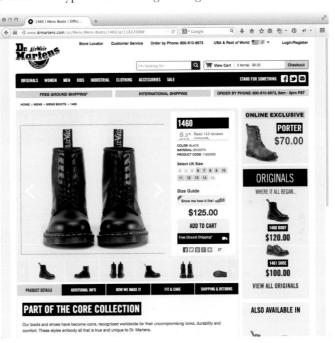

Dr. Martens, an iconic boot manufacturer, has a historic culture of being different. Dr. Klaus Martens, the founder, injured his foot while skiing. He then invented a rubber-soled shoe that provides comfort to people who are on their feet all day. His shoes and boots quickly gained a reputation for being solid in construction and durable for years. Youth subcultures for decades have championed the brand: skinheads, punks, hardcore, psychobilly, goth, industrial, grunge, Britpop, and emos have all sported the working-man boot. Perhaps the next brave group of youths daring to be different will do so in a pair of Dr. Martens.

CLOSE THE SALE

Communication also helps close the sale. If purchasing a product leads to a good experience for the consumer, chances are that consumer will purchase it again or recommend it to others. IMC seeks to move buyers to action the first time and then reinforce their positive experience so they will become repeat customers. Today, customers are selective when they want to receive communications, and often that is just prior to purchase. Many people use the web to look up ads that contain extensive information necessary to make an informed first purchase. Current newspaper, magazine and television ads often include website information so consumers can learn more or refresh their memory of what they have seen. These websites are interactive, so communication is more personal and involves the consumer. Purchasing is made easy when customers are told just where and how to buy.

BUILD RELATIONSHIPS AND LOYALTY

Once consumers have tried a particular brand, marketers remind them why they chose it in the first place, reinforcing that behavior. Reminder communications reinforce the popularity of existing goods by reassuring loyal customers that they have made the correct choice. Because consumers tend to pay more attention to ads for products that they currently use, advertising is often meant to reinforce, which can bolster brand loyalty. For example, American Express builds loyalty and relationships with their cardholders by establishing "rewarding relationships" with them.

THE COMMUNICATION PROCESS

The basic communication process is outlined in Figure 12.2. As you can see, messages move from the sender (marketer) to the receiver (consumer). Traditionally, communication has been seen as a one-way process. With the advent of one-to-one marketing through technologies such as the Internet, it is more useful to envision a two-way or continuous flow. Marketers need to start with a clear understanding of the target market, the objectives of the communication, and how to meet those objectives. They should also be aware that proactive customers have their own objectives and use the same process in reverse.

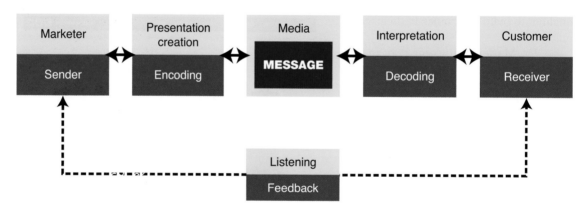

Figure 12.2   The Communication Process

Let's look at the process. Effective communication can be difficult, because consumers are bombarded daily by thousands of conflicting messages. Once marketers decide what to communicate, they must encode the message for the target market. It can be spoken, written, illustrated through pictures or diagrams, set to music or conveyed by a combination of these. The encoded message is then sent to consumers via one or more media: television, radio, newspapers, magazines, telephone, fax, personal contact, the Internet and others.

Customers must decode, or interpret, the message that marketers send. Each customer's reaction will depend on personal background and experiences. One of the most important aspects of the communication process is feedback from the target audience. For example, if a campaign is designed to encourage product awareness, then positive feedback is an increase in the number of consumers who know about the product, and negative feedback is a flat or declining awareness. Such information is vital because it helps marketers judge whether the message accomplished its goal or needs to be adjusted.

One final element marketers should consider when communicating to consumers is noise, which can refer to anything that interferes with a message being received. For example, after talking to a salesperson about a new sports car, you may want to buy it. But then a friend says, "It's a piece of junk." Your friend obviously interferes with the marketer's message. Noise can also occur if you are distracted from receiving the message or if you're not sure who sent the message.

THE MESSAGE SENDER

Once marketers have determined that communication is in order, they initiate the process by formulating a message. As the sender, it is the marketer's responsibility to make sure the message is received by the targeted audience, is understood as intended, helps the audience become knowledgeable and elicits an appropriate response.

> **As the sender, it is the marketer's responsibility to make sure the message is received by the targeted audience, is understood as intended, helps the audience become knowledgeable, and elicits an appropriate response.**

Communications take valuable time from the receiver, so it is up to the sender to provide relevant information. Generally, a series of contacts is required. Once a relationship is created between the two parties, communication is much easier for two reasons: The sender learns the most useful information to supply, and the receiver is more inclined to listen. Effective communications obtain consumer responses that contribute to a company's goals. In some cases, the message simply identifies the product so potential customers are more likely to include it in their set of possible choices. In other cases, it may move consumers to act immediately.

The reputation of the sender — whether a person, a company or some other organization — influences how consumers receive a message. In fact, when several sources communicate precisely the same message, it is received differently depending on the source, which is why the selection of the right spokesperson for a message is very important. Recently, Weight Watchers signed a multi-million dollar deal with singer, actress and new mom of two, Jessica Simpson, to promote the company as she loses her pregnancy weight. Different consumers have different beliefs and standards, so finding a single spokesperson that has high credibility with everyone is nearly impossible. Even within one segment, it's difficult to identify a single spokesperson to whom everyone relates. That is why the famous "Got Milk?" mustache appears on so many famous faces.

What makes a source credible with a target audience? Generally, spokespersons are judged according to their expertise, trustworthiness and attractiveness.

Expertise Consumers attribute expertise to a spokesperson for many reasons. They may believe he or she has specialized training, a great deal of experience or exceptional knowledge. Some companies hire engineers for industrial sales positions, believing that their academic degrees lend special credibility. Doctors are highly credible spokespersons in messages for pain relievers. Children's Tylenol, for example, is promoted as "the first choice of pediatricians." Robitussin notes that it is recommended by physicians, pharmacists and "Dr. Mom." Both campaigns are based on the credibility of their sources.

Consumers also tend to rely on someone with a lifestyle similar to their own, which accounts for the surge in advertising that features average, everyday people. "Real people" advertising uses "regular" people (not actors) who appreciate the products or services about which they are advertising. This creates instant credibility for the average consumer looking to purchase the products or services. Nike, like many companies, count on star appeal, and sign large endorsement deals with the world's best athletes. Michelle Wie, a recent women's major golf champion, has endorsements from Nike, McDonalds, Kia Motors, and Sony.[7]

Trustworthiness Organizations such as the Underwriter's Laboratory, American Medical Association, American Dental Association, Good Housekeeping Institute and Consumer's Union have gained a great deal of credibility because of their trustworthiness. Not only do they have considerable technical knowledge, but most consumers perceive them as unbiased. People tend to discount messages from sources that stand to benefit in some way, but trust those from sources that appear "objective." Imagine that you are purchasing an MP3 player and the salesperson constantly emphasizes the importance of an extended warranty. If you know the salesperson gets a commission on warranty sales, you are less likely to believe what he or she is telling you. If no commission is involved, you are more inclined to trust the person.

Attractiveness (Personal Demeanor and Appeal) It's not surprising that many successful spokespersons are attractive, pleasant and likable. Attractiveness is not about good looks; a source is more attractive if he or she is reliable, pleasant to be around and helpful.

Often celebrities gain credibility in areas outside their careers, such as movie stars who have influenced political campaigns. When famous endorsers are also informed, their power can be substantial. Actor George Clooney has been a longtime advocate of ending violence in Darfur and the Sudan, traveling to the region repeatedly, co-founding charities, and meeting with heads of state, including President Barack Obama. He even owns a private spy satellite that hovers over Sudan, tracking movements of the war criminal Omar Al-Bashir.[8] It's important to note that attractiveness involves all aspects of the source, from a company's reputation to its sales personnel to any others who represent the organization.

PRESENTATION CREATION: ENCODING

Encoding is the process of translating a message into terms easily understood by the target audience. We know from Chapter 6 that information processing is a complex but very important aspect of the purchase decision. Marketers must encode messages so they are interpreted appropriately by the people for whom they are intended. For example, marketers of fine jewelry have traditionally encoded their messages to reach men — once the main purchasers of engagement rings and other gems as gifts. Today, however, women have higher disposable incomes, and purchasing jewelry has become less associated with only special occasions. Generational encoding is also important: As the baby boomers reach milestone anniversaries and birthdays, jewelers expect them to celebrate with the purchase of jewelry. The De Beers Jewelry website allows visitors to create their own diamond engagement rings, encoding the message that buyers can be actively involved in creating their own dream jewelry.[9]

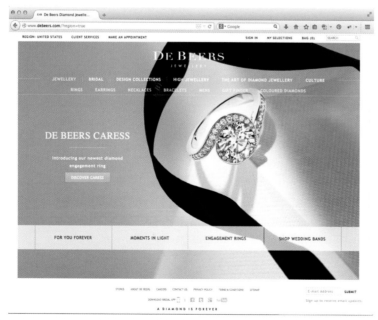

Consumers screen out many messages. Although some people seek information on their own, it is often up to the sender to stimulate the consumer's interest in receiving a message. This involves grabbing attention and keeping it while the information is processed. Consumers are really good at tuning out messages that are boring, lack stimulation or are irrelevant. In order to facilitate consumer information processing, communications should limit the amount of information conveyed at one time. We know that consumers take in only a fraction of information presented to them, and that comprehension is aligned with their life circumstances and experiences. Consequently, structuring messages in a context relevant to the target audience is critical.

MESSAGE CHARACTERISTICS

There are countless ways to communicate a given message: One viewpoint or several can be presented. Recommendations or conclusions may or may not be included. Key points can be made at the beginning, middle or end. Humor or fear can be used. The product being described may or may not be compared with a competitor's.

One-Sided and Two-Sided Messages
A **one-sided message** presents only aspects favorable to the source. A **two-sided message** recognizes the elements against a position and often provides the recipient with reasons why those arguments are invalid. For example, a message for a fast-food chain might mention only the positive aspects of the ingredients and cooking methods, or it might address a competitor's charge as well. When the source and receiver have relatively similar views, a one-sided message is more appropriate. When there is disagreement, a two-sided message often is more useful.

One-sided Message

A message that presents only arguments favorable to the source.

Two-sided Message

A message that presents arguments that are unfavorable as well as favorable to the source.

CAREER TIP!

The web is an abundant source for information regarding advertising, public relations, personal selling and other career opportunities. You'll have an opportunity to explore your career of interest or research a specific company. You will also discover links to networks that allow you to post a resume, receive daily news briefs or access a job information service. Popular career sites include www.monster.com and www.careerbuilder.com, or search within your desired industry for professional associations that post jobs in a particular field.

Recommendations or Conclusions
A message can make recommendations, draw conclusions or leave those tasks to the receiver. Messages with conclusions are more easily understood, but those that allow the audience to draw their own conclusions are more likely to gain acceptance, particularly if the audience is highly educated. Repeated exposures give the target audience an opportunity to reach its own conclusions. If the marketer wants the message to have immediate effect, then the communication probably should draw direct conclusions. Rubbermaid launched a now-classic campaign in response to smaller competitors that were rapidly gaining market share. Since Rubbermaid wanted to influence consumers quickly, its ads were designed to focus on the numerous solutions its products provide to everyday problems. The company reinforced the campaign with an 89-page booklet, "1001 Solutions for Better Living."[10] Today, Rubbermaid's website, www.rubbermaid.com, provides a "Tips & Solutions" tab containing information to help customers organize with Rubbermaid products, an "Ask the Organizer" section, video tips and a blog. Customers can also register for the Rubbermaid Club to receive coupons, tips and new product announcements.[11] This type of promotional effort presents the conclusions about product benefits directly to customers.

Order of Presentation
The placement of the key point of a communication affects how the message is interpreted and later recalled by buyers. People are more likely to remember messages at the beginning and end of a message, so advertisements often open and close with strong statements, leaving weaker arguments for the middle.

Humor

Humor is effective when viewers find it novel and enjoyable, but it should not obscure the message. There are several things for marketers to keep in mind:

- Be sure to mention the brand name within the first 10 seconds. Otherwise, the communication runs the risk of inhibiting recall of key selling points.

- Subtle humor is more effective than bizarre humor.

- Humor must be relevant to the brand or the key selling point. Without this linkage, recall and persuasion are diminished.

- It is best not to use humor that belittles or makes fun of the potential user. Jokes about the brand, the situation or the subject matter are usually more effective.[12]

Evidence is still inconclusive as to whether a humorous approach is more effective than a serious one. Although humor tends to increase attention, it also may distract from or decrease acceptance of the message. TBS runs an annual special in which it counts down the funniest advertisements of the year from around the world. Its www.veryfunnyads.com website allows users to stream the nominees and offers additional ad exposure for companies.

Humor is constantly utilized to create a viral message. The intention of humor is to make people laugh enough to tell their friends, which is an efficient way to pass around the message. Budweiser's "Whassup" campaign from 1999 to 2002 is one of the legendary paragons of advertising gone viral. It captured the essence of greeting friends with the popular "what's up?" to the point that many found themselves saying "Whassup?," or even "Whassuuuuup?" Today, widespread high-speed Internet access and social media sites like YouTube facilitate the rapid growth of online viral advertising. Toyota's "Swagger Wagon," a recent YouTube sensation, is a perfect example of how social media and a little humor can be a powerful combination.

Toyota's viral YouTube video "Swagger Wagon" attempted to make parenting, and vans, "cool."

Fear Appeals Marketers sometimes use fear to gain the attention and interest of their audience. Campaigns by the American Dental Association warn that poor dental hygiene can result in tooth decay, gum disease and loss of teeth. In some instances, advertisers play on fear for the safety of loved ones. A Michelin spot shows a baby floating in a tire and reminds parents, "You have a lot riding on them." An advertisement for seat belt use by the Michigan Association for Traffic Safety pictures a wheelchair: "It's your choice."

In many instances, fear appeals are very effective. They can create higher attention and interest in the message. By Petty and Cacioppo's theory of persuasion, fear appeal works more successfully in a high-involvement product than in a low-involvement product. Furthermore, the reaction from audiences tends to be more uniform than reactions to other messages, since fear is a basic human emotion.[13]

Comparative Messages In the 1970s, the Federal Trade Commission began allowing advertisers to name competitors in ads, something companies wasted no time in taking advantage of. There have been sneaker wars, hamburger wars, beer wars and cola wars. In each case, claims and counterclaims have been used in comparative messages. Burger King ran an unusual comparative ad against McDonald's, depicting the King breaking into McDonald's headquarters to steal the McDonald's Sausage McMuffin with Egg sandwich recipe. A voice-over in the ad proclaims, "It's not that original but it's super affordable" — Burger King offers the sandwich on its dollar menu, while McDonald's has a higher price. While these techniques draw attention, they do not guarantee success. Even though comparative messages allow marketers to present clear, objective arguments in favor of their products, many companies hesitate to use the technique. References to the competition may inadvertently cause the consumer to recall that product at the time of purchase. In addition, competitors may legally challenge claims of superiority or respond with comparative ads of their own. McDonald's has chosen to ignore the Burger King comparative ad, which is often the case with a market leader who does not want to give the contender's brand any ad time.

In general, comparative messages may be more useful for companies with a lower market share, since they have little to lose by confronting the leader. For them, the potential gain in consumer awareness outweighs the likelihood that a large competitor will launch a counterattack.

MEDIA

Media are the means for transmitting messages from the sender to the receiver. There are three categories — personal, mass and mixed — each with its advantages and disadvantages, as summarized in Figure 12.3.

Media

The channels through which messages are communicated.

	Examples	Advantages	Disadvantages
Personal Media	Face-to-face Telephone Television Radio	Two-way communication Allows for creative problem solving Flexible tailoring of messages Immediate response Messages can be developed prior to sending Low cost	Expensive Time-consuming Parties must be brought together at one time Messages tend to be one-way
Mass Media	Magazines Newspapers Billboards Brochures	Many media choices Reaches most customers inexpensively	Preparations are expensive Harder to obtain feedback
Mixed (personal and mass combined)	Fax Internet Answering machine	Delayed or interactive Two-way communication Low cost	Receiver needs technology Lack of consumer experience

Figure 12.3   Media Advantages and Disadvantages

Personal media channels involve direct contact, such as face-to-face communication or telephone conversations. These two-way exchanges allow for creative solutions to the consumer's problem. Each party can assess characteristics of the other, granting opportunity for relationships to form. Although the phone does not provide physical contact, it has dramatic cost advantages over personal encounters. It also offers hotlines, which provide customer support after a sale. They not only help when problems arise with a product but also offer all kinds of advice that ultimately can maintain customer loyalty. GoDaddy customers have access to technical support 24/7/365 via phone, through an email ticket system, or by real-time online chat.[14] The disadvantage of personal media is its expense. Each representative can only have a limited number of conversations, and the costs associated with hiring, training and motivating people can be very high.

Mass media channels include television, radio, magazines, billboards, brochures and one-way Internet. Services are readily available to help plan for and acquire space in most markets around the world. CIO Communications Inc., for instance, offers a resource center on the web to assist with media planning.[15] Messages can be developed prior to being communicated through a range of nonpersonal sources. With so many methods available to send a message, just about any customer can be reached at a reasonable cost. The downside of using mass media is the lack of interactive or two-way communication. Because it is impossible to get quick feedback, significant resources are spent beforehand on research to understand the customer. Furthermore, ad preparation can be expensive and take a long time.

The mixed media approach combines personal and mass communication channels and has many of the benefits of both. First, material can be developed well in advance and offered in both print (fax) and audio (via Internet) formats. Many companies have adopted social media into their marketing mix, urging customers exploring Facebook or Twitter to follow them. For example, Ellen DeGeneres promotes her program, The Ellen Show, through her Twitter account. She often gives away tickets and other offers as an incentive for users to continue to follow and connect with her. Sponsored Tweets, a company with expertise in social media promotion, is one of many places companies and advertising agencies can get help with a Twitter advertising campaign. Because Twitter is a free social networking service that allows users to send and read each other's updates, known as tweets, companies can engage large numbers of consumers in semi-orchestrated message campaigns. These can be stand-alone campaigns or more often part of a mixed media approach. Second, because mixed media can reach large numbers simultaneously, the technique is very cost-effective. Social media provides an outlet for companies to personally reach out to a wide base of consumers at once. However, it can only connect with customers who have the necessary technology andability to use those sites.

INTERPRETATION BY RECEIVERS: DECODING

Strong communications begin with an understanding of target audiences. People are not passive receivers of communications. In fact, they resist persuasion by refuting arguments, attacking the source, distorting messages, rationalizing and tuning out. Many consumers regard marketing messages as "tricks" to make them purchase a particular product.

Refuting arguments is one way consumers resist persuasion. Weak messages may backfire as consumers create stronger counter-arguments in their own minds. Another defense mechanism is to attack the source. If a consumer doesn't trust an automobile, that person may reject all of its claims, whether they address comfort, prestige or gas mileage. Attacking the source rather than the ideas being communicated is common in politics. When politicians don't have a very convincing case, they are likely to strike out at the people who reject their arguments.

Intelligence and self-esteem have a lot to do with susceptibility to persuasion. Highly intelligent people are more likely to be influenced by logical, precise and complex information. Others have to be very carefully led through an argument. Depending on the audience, marketers should let some people draw their own conclusions. Unsurprisingly, people with low self-esteem are more likely to be easily persuaded by the suggestions of others. Messages designed for such people should avoid complex arguments.[16]

CONSUMER FEEDBACK

Listening is an important way to learn what consumers think. Feedback is essential to a customer-focused company, and it helps the marketer adjust communications. Today, leading organizations consider listening to be the first step in the communication process, even before the message is created. By listening to the consumer, they determine needs and wants, as well as how to structure communication.

THE COMMUNICATION MIX

TYPES OF COMMUNICATION ACTIVITIES

The six main types of communication activities are personal selling, sales promotion, advertising, public relations and sponsorship. Figure 12.4 describes some characteristics of each type.

	Personal Selling	Sales Promotion	Advertising	Public Relations	Sponsorship	Social Media
Focus	Person-to-person interaction	Support of sales activity	Mass communication directed at target segments	Unpaid publicity that enhances the company and its products	Cash or resources in support of an event	Individual and group interaction through web-based technologies
Objective	Develop business relationship resulting in loyal customers	Obtain immediate sale and remind after the sale	Position the product and/or increase sales	Gain a favorable impression	Be associated with influential groups	Gain awareness and knowledge in real-time
Example	Pharmaceutical salesperson	Point-of-sale displays	Billboards	Press releases	Team sponsorship	Facebook promotion
	Computer and tele-communications sales	T-shirts with company name	TV ads	Charitable projects	Sport tournaments	LinkedIn job search
	Retail sales Consulting sales	Special sales 2-for-1 offers	Magazine ads Direct mail	Civic leadership Company spokesperson gives association speech	Arts events Association events	Community and association connectivity
Appeal	Personal	Move buyer to action	Mass	Mass	Market segment	Personal
Cost per customer	Very high	Low	Low to high	Very low	High to low	Extremely Low
Amount and speed of feedback	A lot and immediately	A little and fairly fast	A little and delayed	A little and fairly fast	A lot and fast	A lot and immediately

Figure 12.4 Communication Mix Characteristics

Personal Selling

Face-to-face or other individual communication between a buyer and a seller.

Personal Selling **Personal selling** requires person-to-person communication between buyer and seller. Generally, this occurs face-to-face, although it also may involve the telephone, video conferencing or interactive computer/mobile linkages. Despite its relatively high cost, personal selling continues to be the most important part of business-to-business marketing and is also significant in sales of big-ticket consumer items, such as autos, computers and housing. The objective of most personal selling is to build loyal relationships with customers that result in profitable sales volume. For example, physicians say that pharmaceutical salespeople are the most effective when they develop personal relationships and build rapport through their personal selling techniques. Since personal selling provides two-way communication, it is possible to engage in a dialogue that leads to problem solving, consulting and relationship building. Because this is generally the most expensive form of contact, salespeople are trained to do the best possible job of helping a customer find solutions through use of their goods and services.

Advertising

Paid communication through non-personal channels.

Advertising **Advertising** is paid, impersonal communication from an identified sponsor using mass media to persuade or influence an audience. It includes newspapers, television, radio, magazines, direct mail, billboards, the Internet and point-of-sale displays. It is considered mass communication because the same message is sent throughout the targeted audience as to the rest of the market. Advertising usually features the same basic theme regardless of where it is displayed. Depending on audience size, cost per consumer can be very low. In 2014, it was estimated that 111.5 million people watched Super Bowl XLVIII, making it the most-watched program in U.S. television history.[17] Companies paid as much as $4 million for a 30-second ad, or $133,333 a second. However, these figures average out to a bargain low cost of 3.6 cents per viewer.[18] Additionally, the Super Bowl is a unique arena for advertising on television since the dawn of the TiVo. A recent survey found that 78 percent of viewers look forward to Super Bowl commercials more than the game itself.[19] The best ads often gain additional viewers when they are shared through social media. Because advertising plays a supportive role, it is sometimes difficult to determine just how well it works, in relation to other parts of the marketing mix. For example, the effects of accompanying shifts in product distribution and pricing are often felt more quickly.

Anthony Quintano / CC BY-SA 2.0

Sales Promotion

A communication designed to stimulate immediate purchase using such tools as coupons, contests and free samples.

Sales Promotion **Sales promotion** is communication designed to stimulate immediate purchases using tools such as coupons, contests and free samples. Since the approach generally is designed to stimulate immediate purchases, its effectiveness can be easily measured. For example, Stride, "The Ridiculously Long Lasting Gum," is promoting its brand on college campuses. Major colleges, such as Michigan State University, have Stride Brand Ambassadors that sponsor events in order to create buzz about its products and pass out free samples.[20] Sometimes sales promotion is meant to remind customers of the organization after the sale, which contributes to relationship building. For example, a box of cookies may contain a discount coupon for the next box. Sales promotions usually last a short time.

Public Relations

Public relations (**PR**) is the use of publicity and other unpaid forms of communication designed to present the firm and its products positively. Because they are not paying for space, companies do not have total control over what is disseminated. The most common public relations channel is the news media. Of course, publicity can be negative. The presence of Internet search engines and new social media makes it more complex to handle negative publicity. About a decade ago, news media broadcast negative information about the Ford Explorer when Firestone tires failed on the vehicle. Ford executives launched a massive public relations campaign, issuing statements to counteract the negative press after the recall of more than 6 million tires. Despite the PR campaign, Ford decided to launch a paid-for national mail campaign to assure owners of the vehicles' safety.[21] When Toyota recently recalled over 4 million vehicles because of acceleration surges, social media and Google made the situation much more complex to handle. If you Google "Toyota," you will get some company information about the recall, which is followed just a few clicks away by hundreds of news reports about the company's faulty accelerators linked to 19 deaths. Toyota's relatively slow and measured response to issues caused consumers deep concern about the company. In a public relations effort, Jim Lentz, Toyota's President of U.S. Sales, went on "The Today Show" to counter the negative news from media and owners alike.

Public Relations (PR)

Unpaid promotion designed to present the firm and its products in a positive light in the buyers mind.

Sponsorships

A major form of communication is sponsorships, which are reaching 10 to 15 percent of promotion budgets. A **sponsorship** is the exchange of money (or some other form of value) in return for a public association with an event. Automobile companies sponsor many Professional Golfers' Association tournaments. PGA Tour events bear such titles as Wendy's 3-Tour Challenge, The Honda Classic and Hyundai Tournament of Champions.[22] Coca-Cola, PepsiCo, General Motors, Anheuser-Busch, United Parcel Service and Nissan are among the largest sponsors of sports. Corporate sponsorship is everywhere in NASCAR, from sponsors of individual drivers to official NASCAR products. One interview with a NASCAR fan had a die-hard stating, "I can tell you right now I wouldn't walk into Lowe's if I had a hole in my roof. ... So I will go to Home Depot and support Joey Logano as much as I possibly can."[23] Who knows if that person stayed a loyal customer after Home Depot dropped Joey Logano in 2012, but for a time the sponsorship had dramatic impact on the consumer. Virtually all sporting events are sponsored now by either major products or corporations. The college football bowl season features games such as the Tostitos Fiesta Bowl, the Allstate Sugar Bowl, the Discover Orange Bowl and the Rose Bowl presented by Vizio, each explicitly showcasing its sponsor's name.

Sponsorship

The exchange of money (or some other form of value) in return for a public association with an event.

NASCAR fans have a very strong loyalty to sponsors.

Sponsorships are usually integrated with all other aspects of the communications mix. General Motors takes its key dealers and business customers to the NASCAR racing events it sponsors, features the races in its magazine ads and cites testimonials from NASCAR drivers. This benefits both parties of the sponsorship.

SOCIAL MEDIA Social media provides a platform for companies to get and stay in touch with targeted and diverse audiences. Several social media platforms such as Facebook, Twitter, YouTube and LinkedIn can be integrated to form a powerful mechanism for customer activity. Social media strategies, tools and analytics are important elements in today's marketing campaigns. As an example, many companies use websites like LivingSocial to market outstanding deals for restaurants, spas, fitness centers, and other experiences in cities around the world; more specialized deal sites aim at a smaller target market, such as Zulily, which advertises items for children and moms. Many services also provide easy ways for users to share deals with their friends on social sites such as Facebook or Pinterest. Other, more traditional companies like Nike are heavy players on Twitter and share comments by company spokespersons and paid athletes. It also gives them a platform to allow customers to RSVP for new products, eliminating the long lines and need to camp out at Nike stores to get the coveted new release.

FACTORS AFFECTING THE COMMUNICATION MIX

Marketers must consider several factors in selecting the communication mix. The most important are whether the audience is the business-to-business or consumer market, whether a push or pull strategy is desirable, the product's stage in the life cycle and whether opinion leaders will play a role.

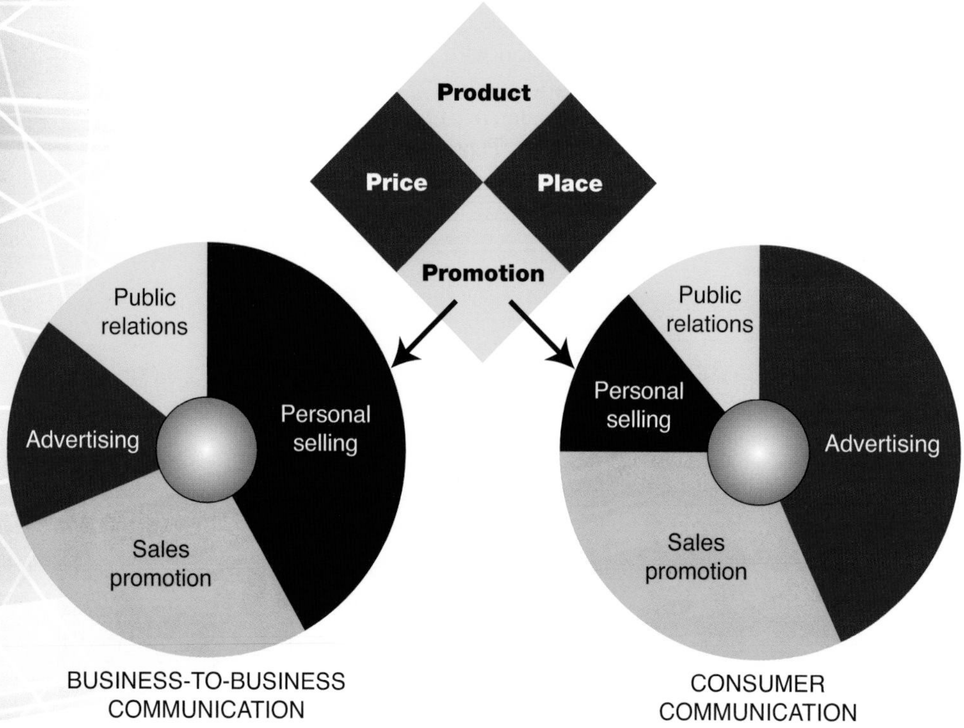

Business Versus Consumer Markets

All aspects of the communication mix can be applied to both business-to-business (B2B) and business-to-consumer (B2C) marketing, but different aspects are emphasized depending on the client category (Figure 12.5). Personal selling is most important in marketing to businesses, whereas advertising dominates in the consumer products arena. Sales promotion is equally important to both and outweighs advertising in business markets, while public relations is a relatively lower priority in both.

Figure 12.5 Communication Mix for Business vs. Consumer Markets

Weighing costs against revenue reveals a lot about these differences. Per exposure, television advertising can cost less than a few cents; a print ad slightly more; direct mail, a dollar or two; a telephone call, about $10; and face-to-face personal selling in a B2B business, more than several hundred dollars. Although public relations involves few such expenditures, it cannot compare to the other forms in terms of effectiveness and the degree of message control.

Pull Versus Push Strategies

Marketers attempt to influence the market through either a push or pull strategy (or both), as illustrated in Figure 12.6. A **pull strategy** attempts to influence consumers directly. Communication is designed to

Pull Strategy

An attempt to influence consumers directly so they will "pull" the product through the distribution channel.

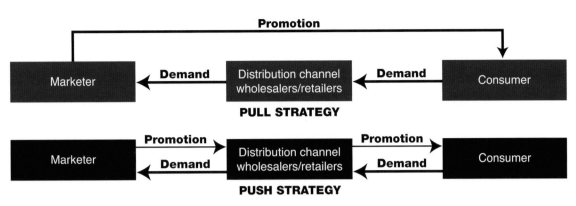

Figure 12.6   Pull vs. Push Strategies

build demand so consumers will "pull" the product through the channel of distribution. In other words, consumer demand is high, so retailers want to carry the product, who in turn ask wholesalers, who in turn contact the manufacturer. Many service firms use price discounts as pull strategies. But effectiveness of price discounts as a pull strategy has been suspicious.[24] For an airline company, dynamic pricing was proven to be the starting point for a competent pull strategy.[25]

Although pull strategies tend to be used often for consumer products, they also have a place in business-to-business marketing. For example, marketers of electrical control and distribution equipment often target the purchasing agent with their messages. Sales representatives call on design firms, which then specify that particular electrical equipment in the engineering design.

The **push strategy** involves communicating to distribution channel members, which in turn promote to the end user. This is particularly common in industrial, business-to-business or retail marketing. Marketers often train distribution channel members on the sales techniques they believe are most suited to their products. For example, many manufacturers who sell to Home Depot, such as cabinet manufacturers, train Home Depot in-store salespeople on the best way to sell their brand. They provide sales aids and literature to help Home Depot representatives entice consumers to their brands.[26]

Often, a **push-pull strategy** is appropriate. The combination approach markets directly to both the channel and end user, speeding adoption and the overall flow through the channel. This combination also helps address conflict that may arise between marketers and retailers. Retailers want to stock the most profitable products, which may not be marketers' biggest brands. Using a pull strategy to create strong demand at the consumer level makes channel members more willing to handle the product.

Product's Stage in the Life Cycle
The appropriate use of the communication mix is related to the product's stage in the life cycle. Consumers need to be informed and educated about new products, whereas they may need to be persuaded to purchase during growth and early maturity. When a product is mature or in decline, consumers often need reminders and reinforcements in order to be convinced that it is reliable and time-tested, not on its last legs. Many products, such as clothes, have cycles that depend on the time of year, in addition to a general life cycle. Most department stores or clothing stores do not advertise or promote swimwear in the winter, nor do they promote wool coats in July. Other products also have life cycles, and advertisers adapt their methods to the cycles. In a classic case of a must-have holiday toy, the Tickle Me Elmo doll began to sell out in stores at the height of its popularity; Tyco temporarily pulled its television ads. Later, the product succumbed to less advertising again, as its life cycle greatly declined, and it was eventually replaced by updated versions of the toy. In other words, communications were adjusted to match the stages of the product life cycle.

Push Strategy

Communication to distribution channel members, which in turn will promote or "push" the product to the end user.

Push-pull Strategy

Marketing directly to the channel and to the consumer or end user.

One-step Communication

Communication in which all audience members are simultaneously exposed to the same marketing message.

Opinion Leadership Marketing communications reach consumers directly and indirectly (Figure 12.7). In **one-step communication**, all members of the target audience are simultaneously exposed to the same message. **Multiple-step communication** uses influential members of the target audience, known as **opinion leaders**, to filter a message before it reaches other group members, modifying its effect positively or negatively for the rest of the group.[27]

CREATING & CAPTURING VALUE THROUGH
Relationships

Multinationals Target China's "Little Emperors"

In urban areas, where a government policy of one child per family is strictly enforced, the one and only child exerts a lot of influence on household purchasing decisions, especially if that child is a boy. These "little emperors," born after 1979, are also beneficiaries of the "six-pocket syndrome," with as many as six doting adults — parents and grandparents — to indulge every whim. It has created a new culture of cash-wielding teens, known as singletons, asserting self expression and individuality with what they wear, what they eat, and what they listen to. Little emperors, as a target market, are typically considered to be 10 to 23 years old, who are still supported by their parents. This generation has not experienced an economic downturn, only sustained growth and prosperity. Because of this, the Chinese youth have developed a mind-set of "if you've got it, flaunt it."

It is easy to understand why multinational companies took aim at this demographic. Western goods from brands like Nike, Coca-Cola, Procter & Gamble, Apple and Adidas have exploded on the mainland. In fact, 13 of the top 20 brands in China are U.S. companies. Only one Asian brand exists on the list, Samsung, a company headquartered in South Korea. The fast food industry is largely dominated by KFC and McDonald's.

The Chinese covet Western goods. Nike shoes and blue jeans are seen as status symbols by kids. As the first generation to grow up in a consumer society, they are tuned in to messages of Western ads and do not want to "buy Chinese." Still, as consumer culture develops, companies need to differentiate their products and market them successfully through the right communication mix, rather than just feature a "Western" label.

Chinese youth spend a lot of their free time in front of technology. According to Steve Blackman, CEO of OMD in Asia-Pacific region, "China's youth are incredibly tech savvy and sate their appetite for all things new via ecommerce. They are much more likely to spend time online, and connect to the internet more often than not by their mobile phones. Consequently, they are increasingly difficult to reach via traditional media, spending almost double the time on the internet that they spend on TV. And their affinity to tech, especially mobile, is more than double that of TV."

Understanding the Chinese culture is the key to a company's success in that marketplace. The market is changing quickly and companies need to learn to keep up. McDonald's says "Everyone is learning about how they need to work with changing social attitudes and continuous aspirational trade-ups, even the Chinese themselves...Never assume what works for your mature markets will work for China. Success comes for those who stay relevant to the needs of the Chinese consumer." Developing and sustaining a strong IMC strategy is critical to the short-term and long-term success of any organization in China.

Ian Rose, "How to win in China: Top brands share tips for success," BBC News, July 24, 2013.

Steve Blakeman, "From 'little emperors' to big spenders: How a new wave of marketing optimism is sweeping China," The Drum, July 10, 2013.

Because of their important role, opinion leaders have often been called gatekeepers, to indicate the control they have over ideas flowing into the group. Competitive marketers make it a priority to identify opinion leaders. Opinion leaders tend to be well-informed on a wide variety of subjects, often as a result of research and direct communication with involved parties (in the case of marketing, salespeople). They can have a sort of multiplier effect, intensifying the strength of the message if they respond positively and passing it on to others. Consequently, the resources used to gain support from opinion leaders are probably well spent.

Public figures are often opinion leaders. In one campaign video for Barack Obama, singer Beyonce reads a letter she wrote in praising first lady Michelle Obama as "the ultimate example of a truly strong African-American woman."[28] Clint Eastwood supported Mitt Romney, telling supporters, "Now more than ever do we need Gov. Romney. I'm going to be voting for him."[29]

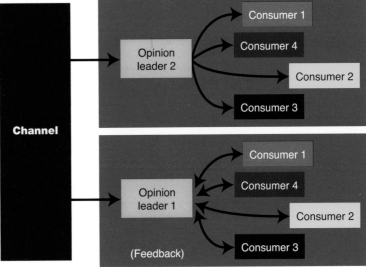

Figure 12.7 Opinion Leadership

DEVELOPING THE INTEGRATED MARKETING COMMUNICATIONS PLAN

Now that we have examined the factors influencing the process, let us see how an integrated marketing communication plan is built. The steps are outlined in Figure 12.8. The IMC plan should never be developed in isolation from the strategic marketing plan. It's the responsibility of strategic marketing personnel to define the role of communication in the overall marketing strategy. The IMC plan is designed to position the organization and its products in a manner consistent with that strategy.

STEPS IN THE IMC PLAN

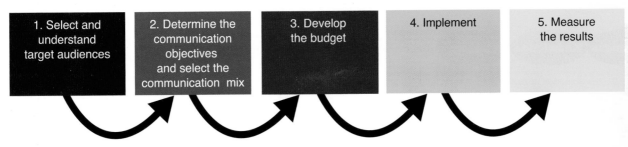

Figure 12.8   Developing the Communication Plan

SELECTING AND UNDERSTANDING TARGET AUDIENCES

As we have discussed many times, selecting target markets is a critical step in nearly every aspect of marketing. The same thing is true regarding the development of an integrated marketing communications plan. Coke and Nike have outstanding communication programs that reach a very large portion of the population. However, these two leading edge marketers carefully segment markets and tailor specific integrated marketing communications for each target segment. For every target audience, communications experts generally have data to help understand key aspects of consumer behavior: where, how and why they obtain information. When market data and information are unavailable, for example in developing markets, companies sometimes use trial and error to get a grasp on media and buying habits. However, experimentation is expensive when a company doesn't know if it will hit the wrong audience, miss` high potential customers or simply fail to resonate with the appropriate people.

DETERMINING OBJECTIVES AND SELECTING THE IMC MIX

Consumers move from a lack of awareness about brands to purchase and hopefully loyalty. This process of increasing involvement can be described by hierarchical models. The most straightforward of these is AIDA, which stands for attention, interest, desire and action.[30] Figure 12.9 depicts AIDA and a more detailed version that includes awareness, knowledge, liking, preference, conviction and purchase. For example, imagine you sit down to study but are distracted when you notice a friend's new Beats by Dre headphones (awareness). You ask how he likes them, then observe others wearing them around campus (knowledge). Perhaps you borrow a pair and are so amazed by the clarity and comfort over your stock iPod ear buds that you consider purchasing a pair of your own (liking). By talking to friends and reading ads, you decide you like Beats by Dre (preference). In-store displays and product guarantees convince you to buy the particular brand (conviction). Finally, you decide to put the headphones on your credit card (purchase).

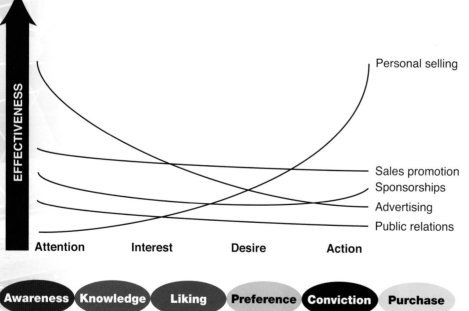

Figure 12.9 Effectiveness of Main Types of Communication at Different Stages in the Consumer Buying Process

As marketers plan communication activities, the objective must be foremost in mind. Is it to create awareness, build brand preference or encourage purchase? The IMC mix will vary considerably depending on the objective. To create awareness and product knowledge, advertising is very effective. It gains attention and even can lead to liking and brand preference. Once desire is created, however, sales promotion may be more useful. At this point the customer is more influenced by personal selling, sales promotions and sponsorships. Attending a sponsored event could make the product so immediately prominent that the consumer decides to buy. Sales promotions involving coupons, price incentives or in-store samples may move buyers to action by reinforcing their conviction to try the brand. The effectiveness of personal selling increases dramatically in the later stages of the buying process. This is especially true for high-priced items in consumer markets, but in some business markets, personal selling may be necessary just to gain attention. Although public relations appears to be least useful — because it tapers off after the attention stage and remains low compared to the others — keep in mind that it has a lower cost. Other than the fairly minor expense of creating the public relations message, there is no cost for delivering it.

DEVELOPING THE COMMUNICATION BUDGET

The communication budget falls within expenditures for the entire marketing mix. Consequently, establishing the specific amount for IMC requires an understanding of the overall marketing strategy, the financial resources available and the contribution communication is expected to make. When allocating IMC money, organizations must remember that some activities can be started or stopped quickly, such as advertising and sales promotion. They often have to adjust personal selling more slowly, since time is required to hire, train and deploy the sales force.

The IMC budget is usually determined in two steps. First, the total allocation is decided. Second, the amount for each type of communication is assigned.

Determining the Overall Budget The first issue is how much it will cost to accomplish the objective. Generally, for existing products communication objectives are established once a year. Two-thirds of advertising budgets for the following year are submitted to top marketing management during September or October, and nearly 80 percent are approved by November.[31] Most IMC budgets are based on one of the following: percentage of sales, competitive budgeting, payout plan or cost of tasks that must be performed to accomplish objectives.

Deciding precisely how much to invest in communication requires many financial calculations. It is important to establish the contribution of IMC to volume objectives and determine resulting profits and cash flows. By completing these calculations, most organizations forecast sales levels based on total expenditures. The latter include all costs that can be realistically allocated to the communication campaign such as special training and compensation for the sales force. The forecasts are based on marketing research about consumer responses to communications, expected IMC spending by competitors, and product demand estimates. The percentage of sales method simply estimates the sales level and then allocates a certain percentage of sales to communications. This percentage is commonly set at the industry average, but will sometimes be based on the previous year's sales. In either case, the problem is that sales are used to create the communications budget, whereas IMC should be used to create sales. Because the method is very easy to administer, however, it is used widely.

Competitive budgeting involves determining what rivals are spending and setting the budget accordingly. For example, when auto companies introduce new car models, a benchmark for spending is set against historic and current expenditures by competitors also launching similar models. Ford, Toyota, GM and Nissan monitor each other's spending on a daily basis by subscribing to third-party data services. One of these companies, IHS Automotive, offers products that help automakers analyze competitors' products, technology, market and manufacturing strategies.

The payout plan method is generally used for new products that require high communication expenditures. The marketer estimates future sales and establishes the budget required to gain initial acceptance and trial of the product. Generally,

IMC costs are very high relative to sales, in some cases even greater. The early expenditures are deemed reasonable because of the payback expected in later years. This is similar to investing money in product development.

The task method sets specific sales targets or other objectives and then determines what activities and amounts are required to accomplish them. This approach can be very complex and tends to be used by large organizations in highly competitive environments. Marketers must have very accurate information and considerable experience in order to develop the extensive models necessary to guide the method. The task method is superior to the others because so much detailed attention is paid to how IMC contributes to accomplishing objectives.

Allocating the Budget Communication works synergistically. In other words, investments in one type of communication may help other types accomplish their objectives. A salesperson benefits tremendously from awareness created by advertising and from purchase incentives due to sales promotion. The integrated aspect of marketing communication needs to be kept in mind when deciding the allocation for each activity. This process requires considerable and continuous dialogue among marketing team members. In many cases, data are fed into computer simulations that help determine the best allocations. In other cases, the team simply estimates what is required. In companies with major brands, many executives are usually involved, including senior management media and advertising staff, marketing personnel, brand marketing management and sales personnel. The allocations may be determined by very specific objectives. When Westinghouse process control wanted to increase name recognition, it shifted resources from the sales force to advertising.

IMPLEMENTATION

Implementation of an IMC plan tends to be done by functional specialists with considerable experience in their field. There are ample career opportunities in these areas — such as personal selling, advertising and public relations — because each is multifaceted and challenging. Marketers strive to obtain uniquely talented employees and suppliers to carry out communication programs. Even the best of plans will fail if not implemented by creative and professional team members.

The first decision is how much to do in-house and how much to outsource. For example, personal selling can be done by company personnel, manufacturer representatives (private salespeople) or distributors. Likewise, companies must decide whether to do their own advertising and sales promotion or hire outsiders. Most large and medium-sized firms outsource much of their IMC implementation. Often representatives from these advertising and promotion agencies work on-site with the client's marketing executives and personnel.

MEASURING IMC RESULTS

It was John Wanamaker, a famous 19th-century retailer, who first said: "I know that half of the money I spend on advertising is wasted, but I can never figure out which half." He was referring to the fact that many messages may never reach much of the target audience. This highlights two important questions to consider. First, who is reached by a communication? And, second, what does it accomplish relative to the goals established in the plan?

Why is it difficult to estimate the results of communication? The major problem is isolating the effects of one part of the IMC plan to determine its relative influence on product performance. Most marketers start by identifying criteria or measures. Performance measures are variables or factors that tell us how well the organization or product is doing. Common measures are market share, sales level and profitability. Other factors are often used, such as number of loyal customers, amount of brand recognition, brand image and knowledge of the product.

Once performance measures are selected, the task of assessing IMC influence can begin. Very seldom is only one part of the IMC mix adjusted at a time, and competitors' activities are virtually never stable, so determining the precise effect of communication is rarely possible. When Nike introduces a new model, how much of its success can be attributed to pricing, product distribution, customer service or promotion? Still, by monitoring IMC expenditures and performance measures for a large number of companies and then applying statistical analysis, researchers can get a good idea of the overall effect of IMC. This information is very useful in determining whether objectives are being met and whether changes are required.

ISSUES IN COMMUNICATION

DIVERSITY

Effective communications are carefully targeted. The vast differences among consumers create opportunities for a wide variety of promotions to meet their needs. For example, 54 million Americans have some form of disability, and marketers are changing the way they communicate with these consumers. Long ignored, they represent several substantial target segments.[32] Marketers now have a new vehicle for communicating with many of these consumers — the Internet.

Until recently, the web was not very user friendly for people with limited vision or dexterity. The American Federation for the Blind (AFB) and Interliant Inc. recently redesigned the AFB's website, www.afb.org, to better accommodate Internet users with disabilities. Previous assistive technologies such as screen magnifiers or screen readers did not properly read site content, but the new site allows for a more thoroughly accessible site. Graphics are now labeled with text that can be read by screen readers, and all audio on the site is now available in text form so that it can be read by the hearing impaired. The AFB's site serves as a model for other government sites, which are required by the 1998 Rehabilitation Act to make the information they provide accessible to those with disabilities.[33]

LD OnLine is the world's leading website for learning disabilities and ADHD, serving more than 200,000 parents, teachers, and other professionals each month.[34] Visitors to the site can find relevant news articles, information on technology that can make living easier, issues related to schools and child disabilities, and health and medical information. In addition, site visitors can find stories about other people with disabilities who continue to lead fulfilling lives. Visitors can also become members of the site and receive e-mail updates and articles based on their interests. The site aims to assist people with disabilities who live independently.

Promotions in general are becoming more inclusive by depicting people with disabilities. Public tolerance of insensitivity toward people with disabilities is decreasing. When Nike ran ads that claimed its trail-running shoes would prevent a jogger from running into a tree and becoming a "drooling, misshapen, non-extreme-trail-running husk of my former self," it was met with swift opposition, and Nike removed the advertisement with a formal apology.

ETHICS

Marketers must be careful about how they communicate. The American Marketing Association Code of Ethics states that acceptable standards include "avoidance of false and misleading advertising, rejection of high-pressure manipulations or misleading sales tactics, and avoidance of communications that use deception or manipulation." Despite these guidelines, the ethical boundaries for promotion are not always clear.

Communications targeting children have long faced public scrutiny. Under pressure from consumer groups and the federal government, R. J. Reynolds agreed to stop using the Joe Camel character in its tobacco advertisements. Philip Morris Company pulled its tobacco ads from magazines with teenage readership. This decision removed ads from *Sports Illustrated* and *Rolling Stone*. The alcohol industry has also been accused of knowingly pushing products to minors. The Federal Trade Commission issued a report asking that beer, liquor and wine companies stop the promotion of alcohol in ads that would appeal to minors, including "promotional placement" in PG and PG-13 films, TV programs aimed at younger audiences and on college campuses. At the same time, Anheuser-Busch launched its "We All Make a Difference" campaign, which salutes those who have made a difference in fighting alcohol abuse.

Americans have voiced much concern about violence being marketed to children either through gun companies, video games, movies or television. Former U.S. Surgeon General David Satcher found that exposure to violent entertainment in childhood leads to aggressive behavior throughout life.[35] In response to attacks on the entertainment industry for marketing violence to children, ABC launched public service announcements featuring stars of the network's television series urging children to avoid violence.

TECHNOLOGY THAT BUILDS RELATIONSHIPS

In communication, marketers often use technology to reach consumers and establish relationships. Advances like the Internet and cell phones make it possible to connect with customers quickly. Almost every company has developed its own website to give consumers information about itself and its products, and also to use effective promotions. Today, email is an essential new form of personal communication. Email communications can be targeted more directly to a select audience, providing information that will be useful for making a purchase. Microsoft invented its own email advertising application in a frantic race to catch Google's online advertising revenue with its own software.[36] However, a survey showed that 63 percent of people erase email advertising without reading it, and 56 percent think they receive excessive amounts of email promotions.[37] Therefore, marketers must be aware that sending messages indiscreetly may have a negative effect.

Smartphone communication can also be aimed directly to consumers, especially appealing to younger generations. For example, a message containing a special discount coupon can be sent on a consumer's birthday, creating a positive company impression and helping to build relationships. Mobile advertising continues to grow rapidly in the United States; spending reached $17.7 billion in 2014, up 83 percent from 2013.[38]

Social media also has opened new doors for marketers; on Facebook, for example, marketers can "choose the location, gender, age, likes and interests, relationship status, workplace and education of your target audience."[39] For example, a Facebook user who has "liked"

George R.R. Martin's novel "Game of Thrones" may get ads from Audible.com advertising a free download of the audio version of the book. Clearly, the Internet offers exciting new targeting opportunities that will affect the way marketers combine and orchestrate various communication activities to create the most effective IMC mix.

CHAPTER SUMMARY

Objective 1: Understand the objectives of integrated marketing communication.

Integrated marketing communication (IMC) is the coordination of all information to the market in order to provide consistent, unified messages. Since each aspect of IMC — personal selling, advertising, sales promotion, public relations and sponsorships — tends to work synergistically, integration is very important. Marketing communication has six objectives. First, it should provide useful information that improves customer decision making and consumption. Second, it creates demand to ensure that products will be consumed in sufficient quantities to justify their development, production and distribution. Third, it supplies knowledge about the value of products, such as their benefits, features and functions. Fourth, it helps differentiate products by describing their uniqueness. Fifth, it helps close the sale by moving customers to action. Finally, it is critical in building the all-important relationship with customers and in securing their loyalty.

Objective 2: Learn how the communication process provides the intended information for the market.

Traditionally, communication was seen as a one-way process — from seller to buyer — without a feedback loop. Today, a two-way process is more realistic. The sender needs to specify objectives, as discussed previously. The sender's characteristics are important determinants of how well messages will be received. Source credibility is determined by expertise, trustworthiness and attractiveness (or appeal). Encoding requires translating the message into terms that will be easily understood. Since message interpretation depends on consumer life experiences, a thorough comprehension of consumer behavior is required to do an adequate job of encoding. Message characteristics also play a major role. Marketers need to decide whether a one-sided or two-sided message is better; whether to supply conclusions; the order in which information will be presented; whether to use humor or fear appeals; and whether to use comparative messages. The choice of media — mass, personal or mixed — also influences communications. Today, mixed media channels such as the Internet are becoming more important. Audiences are not passive receivers; they interpret information by processing it. Their intelligence and self-esteem are important factors here.

Objective 3: Learn about the communication mix, including personal selling, advertising, sales promotion, sponsorships and public relations.

The communication mix has five major components. Each has particular advantages. Personal selling involves face-to-face contact or two-way technology linkages, such as the telephone or Internet. This allows dialogue and interactive problem solving. Advertising is paid, nonpersonal communication. It reaches all members of the audience with the same "mass" message. Sales promotion uses a one-way message to motivate purchase, usually in the form of short-term incentives to buy. Sponsorship is paid support of an event. It associates the sponsor with the event and its participants. Public relations is nonpaid communication (publicity) about a company and its products. These messages are sometimes broadcast by sources considered to be unbiased so they can have considerable credibility.

Objective 4: Know the factors that influence the communications mix.

The communication mix is influenced by several factors. First, business-to-business and consumer markets use different mixes. The former are dominated by personal selling, whereas the latter are dominated by sales promotion and advertising. Second, marketers use a push or pull communication strategy. A push strategy communicates to channel members, who in turn communicate to end users. A pull strategy communicates with end users, who in turn demand products from channel members. Third, communications must be suited to the product's stage in the life cycle in order to have the greatest effectiveness. Finally, marketing communications do not always work directly on consumers. There is often a two-stage process whereby opinion leaders filter information before it reaches others in the market.

Objective 5: Describe the steps in developing an integrated marketing communication plan.

The IMC plan is an outgrowth of the marketing plan. It has five steps. First, select and understand target markets. Second, determine communication objectives and select the IMC mix. Third, develop the IMC budget in line with the overall strategic marketing plan. Fourth, implement the plan. Fifth, measure communication results and adjust accordingly.

Objective 6:   Address diversity, ethics and technology in communications.

Many media are not accessible to physically impaired individuals, and other avenues must be used. One is the Internet, especially through innovative software. Marketers must be careful not to cross ethical boundaries in their communications. They should avoid false and misleading ads and sales tactics as well as high-pressure manipulation. Targeting children is a questionable practice, because they may easily be misled or manipulated. Communication technology is providing better ways to connect with consumers and create relationships; email is one example. Fortunately, today's software makes interactive communication much easier and more rapid than ever before.

REVIEW YOUR UNDERSTANDING

1. What is integrated marketing communication?
2. What are the six objectives of integrated marketing communication?
3. What is the one-way communication process? How does it differ from the two-way process?
4. What are message sender characteristics, and why are they important?
5. What is encoding?
6. What message characteristics should be considered? How does each influence effectiveness?
7. What are personal, mass and mixed media? What are the characteristics of each?
8. What factors influence how messages are interpreted? Describe each.
9. What are the main categories in the communication mix?
10. What factors influence the communication mix? Describe each.
11. What are the steps in building an integrated communication plan?
12. How does diversity offer an opportunity and a challenge to communication?
13. What aspects of communication are covered by the American Marketing Association Code of Ethics?
14. Name one way that communication technology is helping to build relationships with consumers.

DISCUSSION OF CONCEPTS

1. Describe the various goals of communication. What helps determine communication objectives?
2. Why is it so important for marketers to understand the communication process? How does that process affect the development and implementation of a campaign?
3. The way in which a message is communicated to consumers is critically important to its success. Name some of the issues involved in developing a message.
4. How do consumers distort messages? Have you ever distorted a message directed at you? How can marketers combat this problem?
5. Why is the source of a message so important? What are the three characteristics of a good spokesperson? Do you think one spokesperson can communicate effectively with the entire market? Why or why not?
6. Briefly describe the five steps in developing a communication plan. How are the plan and the company's overall marketing strategy related?
7. List the pros and cons of each type of communication activity: personal selling, sales promotion, advertising, sponsorship and public relations. What factors help determine the appropriate one to select?

KEY TERMS & DEFINITIONS

1. **Advertising:** Paid communication through nonpersonal channels.

2. **Communication:** The process of sending and receiving messages.

3. **Encoding:** Translating a message into terms easily understood by the target audience.

4. **Integrated marketing communication (IMC):** The coordination of advertising, sales promotion, personal selling, public relations and sponsorship to reach consumers with a powerful effect in the market.

5. **Media:** The channels through which messages are communicated.

6. **Multiple-step communication:** Communication in which opinion leaders filter messages and modify positively or negatively their effect on the rest of the group.

7. **One-sided message:** A message that presents only arguments favorable to the source.

8. **One-step communication:** Communication in which all audience members are simultaneously exposed to the same marketing message.

9. **Opinion leader:** Influential member of a target audience who first screens messages sent by marketers.

10. **Personal selling:** Face-to-face or other individual communication between a buyer and a seller.

11. **Promotion:** The process whereby marketers inform, educate, persuade, remind and reinforce consumers through communication.

12. **Public relations (PR):** Unpaid promotion designed to present the firm and its products in a positive light in the buyer's mind.

13. **Pull strategy:** An attempt to influence consumers directly so they will "pull" the product through the distribution channel.

14. **Push-pull strategy:** Marketing directly to the channel and to the consumer or end user.

15. **Push strategy:** An attempt to influence the distribution channel, which in turn will "push" the product through to the user.

16. **Sales promotion:** Communication designed to stimulate immediate purchases, using tools such as coupons, contests and free samples.

17. **Sponsorship:** The exchange of money (or some other form of value) in return for a public association with an event.

18. **Two-sided message:** A message that presents arguments that are unfavorable as well as favorable to the source.

REFERENCES

1. www.allstate.com, website visited July 1, 2014.
2. www.oprah.com, website visited July 1, 2014.
3. www.itcanwait.com, website visited July 1, 2014.
4. "Boingo Acquires AWG, Combining Airport Industry's 2 Largest Wi-Fi Providers," AirportRevenueNews.com, August 26, 2013.
5. www.beatsbydre.com, website visited July 1, 2014.
6. Chris Harris, "Well This Is Awkward: FIFA Has Banned Beats by Dre Headphones From the World Cup," www.complex.com, June 17, 2014.
7. Patrick Rishe, "Michelle Wie, At Long Last A Major Champion, Should See Greater Endorsements," Forbes, June 22, 2014.
8. "If George Clooney has a spy satellite, who else has one?," The Telegraph, August 30, 2013.
9. www.adiamondisforever.com, website visited July 1, 2014.
10. Narisetti, Raju, "Rubbermaid Opens Door to TV, Hoping to Put Houses in Order," Wall Street Journal Interactive Edition, February 4, 1997.
11. www.rubbermaid.com, website visited July 2, 2014.
12. Ross Jr., Harold L., "How to Create Effective Humorous Commercials Yielding Above Average Brand Preference Change," Marketing News, March 26, 1976, pg. 4.
13. Cochrane, Lucy; Quester, Pascale, "Fear in Advertising: The Influence of Consumers' Product Involvement and Culture," Journal of International Consumer Marketing, Vol. 17, 2005, pg. 7.
14. www.support.godaddy.com, website visited July 3, 2014.
15. www.cio.com, website visited July 3, 2014.
16. Zelner, M., "Self-Esteem, Self-Perception, and Influenceability," Journal of Personality and Social Psychology 25, 1973, pp. 87-93.
17. "Super Bowl 2014 ratings set new record" CBS News, February 3, 2014.
18. "The rising costs of Super Bowl ads in one chart," USA Today, February 1, 2014.
19. "Buzz Meter: Many just watch the Super Bowl for the ads," USA Today, January 15, 2014.
20. Stride, www.stridegum.com, website visited July 3, 2014.
21. Wenske, Paul, "Reaching Out to Customers," The Kansas City Star, January 10, 2001, pg. C1.
22. www.golf.com, website visited July 3, 2014.
23. "NASCAR Fans Have Unparalleled Awareness of Sport's Sponsor New Study Finds," February 7, 2005.
24. Hu, Hsin-Hui; Parsa, H.G.; Khan, Maryam, "Effectiveness of Pric Discount Levels and Formats in Service Industries," Journal of Servi Research, July 2006, pg. 17.
25. Burger, Beat; Fuchs, Matthias, "Dynamic pricing — A future airline bus ness model," Journal of Revenue and Pricing Management Leader, p 39.
26. www.homedepot.com, website visited July 3, 2014.
27. Sheth, Jagdish N., "Word-of-Mouth in Low Risk Innovations," Journa of Advertising Research 11, 1971, pp. 15-18.
28. Jessica Derschowitz, "Beyonce reads her letter to Michelle Obama i new campaign video," CBS News, July 16, 2012.
29. Steve Peoples, "Clint Eastwood Endorsing Romney's Presidential Bid, Associated Press, August 3, 2012.
30. Strong, E.K., The Psychology of Selling (New York, McGraw-Hil 1925).
31. Russell, J.T.; Lane, Ronald; King, Karen, Kleppner's Advertising Proce dure, ed. 17, 2007, (Prentice Hall).
32. www.ncd.gov, website visited April 5, 2014.
33. www.afb.org, website visited April 5, 2014.
34. www.ldonline.org, website visited April 5, 2014.
35. Leeds, Jeff, "Surgeon General Links TV, Real Violence Entertainment, Los Angeles Times, January 17, 2001, pg. A1; "Youth Violence on th Decline but Surgeon General Warns of Complacency," The Hartfor Courant, January 18, 2001, pg. A10.
36. Nick Buchan, "Global dispatches," B&T Weekly (Sydney), June 9, 200(pg. 11.
37. Greg Brooks, "Overcrowded Inbox," Marketing (London), July 13, 200 pg. 40.
38. "Mobile ad spending expected to jump 83% this year," CNET, July 2014.
39. www.facebook.com/advertising, website visited July 3, 2014.

Chapter 13

MASS COMMUNICATIONS:
ADVERTISING
SALES PROMOTION
& PUBLIC RELATIONS

Advertisements during the Olympic Games might not be as glitzy as the coveted Super Bowl commercials, but they are watched during a global event that draws millions of viewers over the course of weeks, instead of only a few short hours. While Super Bowl ads might offer creativity and humor to be talked about the next day at work, the Olympics offer an opportunity to tap into human sentiment, spirit and achievement. Tone is an extremely important aspect to advertising, sales promotion and public relations. Learning when to use humor and when to use emotion in advertising is no different than in everyday life.

It is important to understand that the Olympic Games offer more to organizations than a single television commercial. They offer repetitive exposure, which can be extremely powerful when a brand is seen worldwide through television, events, consumer goods, gear and apparel. Sponsors earn an exclusive right to place the Olympic rings on products and packaging, which can make a brand stand out from the competition. In return, sponsors provide support for the staging and operations of the Olympic Games in the form of products, services, expertise, and staff. They also provide support for the training and development of Olympic athletes around the world. Finally, an Olympic sponsorship positions organizations to appear patriotic, supportive, and inspiring.

The extensive media coverage of the Olympic Games, through television, online and social media, provides a perfect vehicle for mass communication - particularly for sponsors and their advertising. Procter & Gamble communicated a touching message with its "Proud Sponsor of Moms" campaign, honoring not just the Olympic athletes but also the mothers who sacrificed to help their kids realize their Olympic dreams. The ads were not only named the best of the Olympics by London research firm Ace Metrix, but they were the social media winner by a mile; the ad videos were shared over 2.5 million times.

Interestingly, many consumers seem to misplace sponsors for other leading brands. A recent online survey found that 24 percent of respondents correctly identified Adidas as a sponsor, while 37 percent incorrectly believed Nike had sponsored the games. Some believe this is due to Nike's global brand prowess for sporting events and premier athletes. Certainly a good number of athletes on the U.S. Basketball Team could be quickly associated with Nike with or without the infamous "swoosh" on their apparel. Other companies were getting undeserved credit as well: 28 percent believed Pepsi was a sponsor and 19 percent believed Burger King was a sponsor. Even Google was recognized by 16 percent of respondents, even though they have never sponsored the games. Perhaps this is an indication that consumers are leaning on Google to provide relevant and timely Olympic news.

Whether an Olympic sponsor or not, it is clear that the Olympics provide a powerful influence on the world as a whole, providing a unique opportunity for all types of mass communications to flourish.[1]

Learning Objectives

1. Understand the concept of mass communications, including the relative use of advertising, sales promotion and public relations.
2. Learn how technology, globalization and ethics are playing major roles in mass communications.
3. Know the objectives, advantages and disadvantages of advertising, as well as the sequence of steps in creating an advertising campaign.
4. Understand sales promotion objectives and what types of promotions are used to stimulate sales in business, trade, retailer and consumer markets.
5. Understand the use of public relations in marketing.

THE CONCEPT OF MASS COMMUNICATIONS: ADVERTISING, SALES PROMOTION & PUBLIC RELATIONS

Today, mass communication helps companies connect with customers by providing information in exciting and creative formats. The ability to inform large groups of people about available products in the global market is extremely important. It's so pervasive that most of us are exposed every few seconds to a message designed to influence our behavior.

Spending in the United States for mass communication is about $628 billion, with growth of 7 percent annually. Most of the spending is on sales promotion (about $366 billion), with advertising second (about $262 billion) and public relations a distant third. The U.S. accounts for about one third of the planet's spending on mass communication. Mass communication in the rest of the world totals about $1.2 trillion, for a combined global figure of nearly $2 trillion. About two-thirds is devoted to consumer products, and one-third is spent by businesses marketing to other businesses (B2B).[2]

Much of the increase in mass communication is due to competitive factors, particularly the battle for brand strength. Familiar examples are Coke vs. Pepsi, Kellogg vs. General Mills, Proctor & Gamble vs. Unilever, Verizon vs. AT&T, and Staples vs. Office Max. Although the battle of the brands started in the United States, it has become global. Burger King and McDonald's no longer just compete at home but also in most cities around the world, while Pepsi and Coke are notorious for their vigorous rivalry in Brazil, Taiwan and France.

Mass communication is composed of advertising, sales promotion and public relations, as shown in Figure 13.1. Historically, techniques have changed according to advances in technology. Another recent influence is the need for standardization in global markets. And because mass communication is

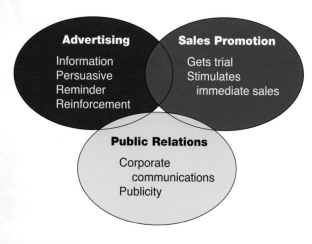

Figure 13.1   The Concept of Mass Communication in Marketing

persuasive and powerful, marketers need to be very considerate of ethical issues. This chapter looks at advertising and its purposes. We describe its categories, the agencies that create and place it, and the media that carry it to the consumer. Next, sales promotion is described as a means to run trials, stimulate immediate sales and build customer relationships. Finally, a section on public relations and publicity addresses those roles in corporate communications.

ADVERTISING

Advertising is paid, impersonal communication from an identified sponsor using mass media to persuade or influence an audience. The word is derived from the Latin advertere, "to turn toward."[3] Notice that advertising is paid for by an identified sponsor, so the audience knows the source of the message. In addition, it is a form of impersonal communication through mass media, such as newspapers, magazines, radio, television and the Internet, which each grant access to relatively large audiences. Traditionally there was no opportunity for the receiver to ask questions or for the advertiser to obtain immediate feedback. Advertising on the Internet has changed that by allowing potential customers to directly contact sponsors with questions and in some cases make orders for goods and services. Consequently, planning is extremely important in traditional advertising in order to create a successful ad the first time.

Advertising

Paid communication through non-personal channels.

www.unilever.com

A core element of Unilever's corporate responsibility strategy is uniting environmental sustainability with economic and social concerns worldwide. Learn more about its corporate responsibility strategy on its website.

THE FOUR OBJECTIVES AND PURPOSES OF ADVERTISING

Although advertising itself is powerful, it also plays an important support role for other forms of communication. In a famous McGraw-Hill Publishing Company ad, a grumpy purchasing agent stares directly at the viewer, saying: "I don't know who you are. I don't know your company. I don't know your company's product. I don't know what your company stands for. I don't know your company's customers. I don't know your company's record. I don't know your company's reputation. Now — what was it you wanted to sell me?" The ad goes on to explain that the sales effort starts before a salesperson calls — with business publication advertising. Whether alone or in support of other promotion methods, advertising can be invaluable. There are four objectives in advertising, each of which accomplishes a different purpose: to inform, to persuade, to remind or to reinforce.

Informative Advertising **Informative advertising** is designed to provide messages that consumers can store for later use. For example, an art museum may place an informative advertisement to make the community aware that a particular exhibit is on display. Often, the more information an ad provides, the better the response will be. A 6,450-word ad for Merrill Lynch brought 10,000 inquiries from interested investors. An 800-word ad for Mercedes-Benz was headlined: "You give up things when you buy the Mercedes Benz 230S. Things like rattles, rust and shabby workmanship." Sales rose from 10,000 to 40,000 cars. Many consumers want to be provided with as much information as possible about items that interest them. Today, the Internet provides a very effective format for informative advertising. An online ad can link customers to various pages that offer additional information they desire.

Informative Advertising

Messages designed to provide information that consumers can store for later use.

Persuasive Advertising

Messages designed to change consumers' attitudes and opinions about products, often listing product attributes, pricing, and other factors that may influence consumer decisions.

Reminder Advertising

Messages that keep the product at the forefront of the consumer's mind.

Reinforcement Advertising

Messages that call attention to specific characteristics of products experienced by the user.

Persuasive Advertising

Persuasive advertising is designed to change consumers' attitudes and opinions about products as well as create attitudes where none exist. These ads often list the product's attributes, pricing and other factors that influence the buying decision. They attempt to make the product choice important so consumers will think about the subject. In this way, the message recipient is asked to form an attitude first and then buy. For example, a Chevy Volt ad features an exasperated car owner explaining to aliens examining his car that the vehicle is electric but also has a gas tank that allows it to go farther when necessary. The consumer can draw the conclusion that the driving a Volt won't leave him or her stranded if the charge runs out, because the car also runs on gasoline.[4]

Reminder Advertising

Reminder advertising keeps the product at the forefront of the consumer's mind. In some cases, these ads simply draw a connection between the brand and some aspect of life. The ideal result, however, is to inspire action by the consumer. One major medium for reminders is outdoor advertising. McDonald's tried to move consumers into its restaurants with the slogan "You deserve a break today." The next campaign phrases asked, "Have you had your break today?" and "Did somebody say McDonald's?" "I'm lovin' it" is the most recent reminder slogan.[5] Product placement in television and movies is becoming a popular form of reminder advertising. Millions of viewers see "American Idol" judges sipping Cokes, and Apple products have been featured on "Modern Family" and "30 Rock," to name a few.

Reinforcement Advertising

To encourage repeat buying behavior, **reinforcement advertising** calls attention to specific characteristics of products experienced by the user. The key here is to communicate with the consumer about product features that created the greatest amount of satisfaction. These ads also reassure customers that they made the right choice. For example, classic ads for Dial asked, "Aren't you glad you used Dial … don't you wish everyone did?"

ADVANTAGES OF ADVERTISING

Advertising has many advantages. By controlling what is said, how it is said and where it is said, marketers can develop standardized campaigns that run for extended periods. Over time, these help build a strong brand equity position. Moreover, advertising is a very cost-effective way to reach large audiences. For example, one 30-second network TV spot in prime time would currently cost less than one cent per customer and reach on average 12 million households. No other promotional method comes close to accomplishing that kind of exposure at such low rates.

The availability of such advertising media as television, radio, newspapers, magazines, social media and billboards makes it easy to reach most audiences. Because advertising is used so much, it's easy for marketers to find excellent agencies that can help research markets, develop campaigns and manage the entire process. The advantages of

Evert F. Baumgardner - National Archives and Records Administration

During the 1950s, television became the primary medium for molding public opinion.

advertising can be summarized as follows:

- Controls the content, presentation and placement of messages.

- Builds brand position and equity over time.

- Is cost-effective for large audiences.

- Serves many communication needs — awareness, information, reminder.

- Is easy to reach most audiences.

- Is easy to find professionals to create effective advertising.

Advertising does have a downside. It's difficult to direct an ad at only the target audience — many others will be exposed to it. Because consumers often distrust ads and try to avoid them, advertising campaigns may need to run for a long time, repeating the message so it is eventually absorbed. It is not unusual for some companies or industries to spend hundreds of millions of dollars on advertising. The disadvantages of advertising can be summarized as follows:

- Reaches many nonusers.

- Has high level of audience avoidance.

- Contains brief one-way messages.

- Can be costly in long run.

CATEGORIES OF ADVERTISING

Advertising falls into various categories depending on its objectives, target audience and type of message. Most marketers use one or more of the eight types described in Figure 13.2.

National or brand advertising, as the name implies, focuses on brand identity such as Delmonte or Pepsi, and positioning throughout the country. The

National or Brand Advertising

Advertising that focuses on brand identity and positioning throughout the country.

Category	Description
National and Global (Brand) Advertising	Focuses on brand identity nationwide (globally). Aims to develop a distinctive brand image.
Retail (Local) Advertising	Focuses on local retail areas. Emphasizes positive attributes of retail outlets.
Directory Advertising	Company listings in a directory. Important to most businesses and retailers. Uses a short differentiating message.
Business-to-Business Advertising	Directed at professionals. Often communicates technical content. Common media include business publications and professional journals.
Institutional Advertising	Communicates corporate identity and philosophy. Describes social and ecological responsibilities of a company.
Direct-Response Advertising	Appeals directly to individual consumers. Usual delivery methods are telephone and mail.
Public Service Advertising	Supports public issues. Usually created for free and media donate space and time.
Political Advertising	Aimed at obtaining votes for issues or political candidates.

Figure 13.2   Categories of Advertising

Retail (Local) Advertising

Advertising that focuses attention on nearby outlets where products and services can be purchased.

Directory Advertising

A listing of businesses, their addresses, phone numbers and sometimes brief descriptions in a publication.

Business-to-Business Advertising

Advertisements to businesses and professionals.

Institutional Advertising

Messages designed to communicate corporate identity and philosophy as opposed to product information.

Direct-response Advertising

Targets individual consumers to get immediate sales.

Public Service Advertising

Free advertising that supports societal issues.

Political Advertising

Advertising to influence voters.

Advertising Agencies

A business that develops, prepares, and places advertising for sellers seeking to find customers for their products.

---

aim is to develop a distinctive brand image in the mind of the consumer. While often known as national advertising, the same strategy can apply to a global market.

Retail (local) advertising attempts to draw attention to relatively nearby establishments, such as local restaurants. The emphasis is on attributes that will stimulate people to shop there, such as price, location, convenience or customer service.

Directory advertising is a listing of businesses, their addresses, phone numbers and sometimes brief descriptions in a publication such as the Yellow Pages. A short, differentiating message can be critical, since so many competitors also advertise there. Businesses usually consider directories extremely important because most consumers turn to them only when they have made the decision to buy a product.

Business-to-business advertising sends messages, often providing technical information, to a variety of organizations ranging from healthcare providers to accountants, lawyers and manufacturers. In the health-care field, for example, publications such as the *Journal of the American Medical Association* carry extensive advertising of pharmaceutical products of all types.

Institutional advertising is designed to communicate corporate identity and philosophy rather than messages about individual products. It describes the company's social and ecological responsibilities. The Environmental Working Group works to protect health and the environment; for example, its website features a "take action" tab where visitors can contact the FDA to protest bisphenol A being allowed in cans and bottles; support the Local Farms, Food and Jobs Act; and sign a petition for safer cosmetics.[6]

Direct-response advertising targets individual consumers with the intent of obtaining immediate sales. Sales are stimulated through appeals by telephone, mail and the Internet, and TV infomercials; the product is then delivered to the customer's home or business. Companies such as Federal Express and UPS have helped facilitate the dramatic increase in sales from direct-response advertising.

Public service advertising support societal issues like smoking cessation or the prevention of child abuse. These announcements are usually created free by advertising agencies, and the space or airtime is donated by the media. Sometimes they are partially supported by charitable organizations or the government. The Ad Council and the Free to Be Foundation recently teamed up for a new series of anti-bullying ads urging parents to "teach your kids how to be more than a bystander." The campaign uses television, print and online ads to convey its message.[7]

Political advertising is aimed at influencing voters in favor of individuals or particular ballot issues. It has come under harsh criticism for mudslinging, negative and sometimes false accusations against political candidates, and the lack of focus on substantive issues.

ADVERTISING AGENCIES

Advertising agencies are independent businesses that develop, prepare and place advertising in the appropriate media. Most companies, even large, established corporations, outsource some or all of these services. In fact, more than 90 percent of all advertising is placed through outside agencies. The cost-effectiveness of outside agencies makes this a good choice for most companies. There are more than 10,000 ad agencies in the U.S. alone, and as in any industry, some are very large any many are small. Big companies, such as WPP Group (UK) or Omnicom, have offices in nearly every major country to provide the services required for global marketers.

In addition to full-service agencies, many specialize in certain advertising functions or in selected industries. For example, Creative Boutiques focuses primarily on developing ideas for advertising. In many cases, industries have certain unique needs. The health-care industry is a good example. Durot, Donahoe and Purohit of Rosemont, Illinois, is an expert in that kind of advertising, which requires knowledge of extensive regulation of health-care ads by the Federal Drug Administration.

Some agencies focus on certain target groups. L3 Advertising Inc. has expertise in the growing Asian market. It has helped major companies like Verizon and Pepsi to successfully reach the Asian demographic.[8] Other advertising agencies specialize in various minorities.

THE ADVERTISING PLAN

The six major steps in developing a strong advertising plan are outlined in Figure 13.3. The process begins by setting objectives and determining the budget. Marketers then develop their message and a theme (creative concept) to convey it. Next, they select the media that would most effectively showcase their message and set a schedule. At this point, they actually create the ads. Once they have had time for audiences to recognize them, the company evaluates their effectiveness.

Set the advertising objectives

↓

Develop the Advertising Budget

↓

Develop the theme and message

↓

Select media, set the schedule, and buy space

↓

Create the ads

↓

Assess advertising effectiveness

Figure 13.3   Steps in the Advertising Plan

SETTING OBJECTIVES

Each objective should be developed in such a way that its accomplishment can be measured. Remember that advertising should support the communications plan, which in turn supports the strategic marketing plan. As Figure 13.4 suggests, the goals of informing, persuading, reminding and reinforcing should be accompanied by specific objectives, such as: increase sales, establish brand position, increase awareness, support the sales force or distributors, maintain awareness or introduce a new brand.

DEVELOPING THE ADVERTISING BUDGET

As we mentioned before, advertising can be expensive in total, although quite cost-effective on a per-person basis. In setting the budget, the first question to answer is how much will it cost to accomplish the objective? Most advertising budgets are determined using one of the following methods: percentage of sales method, competitive budgeting method, payout plan method or task method.

The **percentage of sales method** for developing the advertising budget involves simply estimating the desired sales level and then allocating a certain percentage of sales to advertising. Often this percentage is equal to the industry average.

In some cases, the percentage of sales method is performed by taking a percentage of the previous year's sales and allocating it to advertising. The problem with this method is that sales are used to create the advertising budget when, in fact, advertising should be used to create sales. However, the method is used widely because it is very easy to administer.

The **competitive budgeting method** involves determining what competitors are spending and setting the advertising budget accordingly. Large companies use this method to maintain a strong presence in the eye of the consumer.

Percentage of Sales Method

Allocating a percentage of estimated sales to advertising.

Competitive Budgeting Method

Setting the advertising expenditures relative to what competitors spend.

GOALS
Inform
Persuade
Remind
Reinforce

Are Fulfilled to Meet →

PRIMARY OBJECTIVES

Increase sales

Establish brand position (Product image)

Increase awareness

Support sales force/distributors

Communicate a price or distribution change

Introduce a new brand

Increase loyalty

Figure 13.4   Advertising Objectives

Payout Method

Setting the ad budget to gain initial acceptance and trial.

Task Method

Setting the advertising budget based on activities required to accomplish objectives.

Creative Strategy

The strategy that governs and coordinates the development of individual ads and assures that their visual images and words convey precisely and consistently what the advertiser wants to communicate.

Advertising Campaign

A series of advertisements with a main theme running through them.

Exposure

The process of putting the ad in contact with the customer.

Stopping Power

The ability of an ad to gain and hold the consumer's attention.

The **payout method** is generally used for new products that require high advertising expenditures. In this case, the marketer estimates future sales and establishes the advertising budget required to gain initial acceptance and trial of the product. Generally, these expenditures are very high relative to sales and in some cases even exceed sales. The large expenditures are deemed reasonable because of the payback that occurs in later years. This is similar to investing money in product development.

The **task method** sets specific sales targets or other objectives and then determines what advertising activities and amounts are required to accomplish those objectives. This approach can be extremely complex. Advertisers who use the task method rely on accurate information experience and extensive models developed for the purpose. It tends to be used by large organizations in highly competitive environments. It's superior to the other methods because so much attention to detail is given in determining how advertising contributes toward accomplishment of objectives.

DEVELOPING THE THEME AND MESSAGE

Once objectives are in place and the budget has been established, it is time to develop the theme and message — the **creative strategy** — that will govern and coordinate the development of individual ads and assure that their visual images and words convey precisely and consistently what the advertiser wishes to communicate. Be careful not to confuse this overall strategy with the creative work in putting a specific ad together. The message is a fairly straightforward outgrowth of the marketer's understanding of consumer behavior, information processing and the advertising objectives.

An **advertising campaign** is a series of different ads with the same creative strategy. Because one ad tends to have very little effect, campaigns are required to sustain the message and accomplish the objectives. There is usually an element of continuity across a campaign, with ads featuring recurring music, settings or characters, such as the pink Energizer bunny that keeps going and going through any number of ads. Other examples are Charmin's bears and Kellogg's Tony the Tiger commercials for Frosted Flakes. To be effective, an advertising campaign's theme and message must reach the consumer and be creative, understandable and memorable.

Reaching the Consumer
Before an ad can benefit a company at all, it must reach its target audience. **Exposure** is the process of putting the ad in contact with the market. Once that is done, it's up to the ad's content to communicate the message. A good advertisement addresses nearly every aspect of consumer behavior in a package that captures interest and keeps it until the message is absorbed. Exposure does not ensure attention. As we learned in Chapter 5, the perceptual process filters out a great deal. The ad must have what marketers call **stopping power** — the ability to gain and hold attention. Ads with stopping power demand attention so effectively that they interrupt whatever the person is doing. The best ads gain and hold attention because the consumer finds them interesting and relevant to his or her lifestyle. Sometimes catchy music, humor or an association with a celebrity works. Some phrases may gain immediate attention from certain people: lose weight, quick cash, retire early, pay off debts, work at home, free, new, amazing, now and easy. On the other hand, some catch phrases have been so overused by advertisers that many people immediately tune out messages containing them.

Creativity
Originality and uniqueness are very important in advertisements. On one hand, ads that are too unusual may not work, because people have difficulty relating to them. On the other hand, creative, humorous, upbeat ads that provide some novelty tend to gain more attention than the same old thing. Coca-Cola also captured viewers with its computer-animated polar bears, which people considered to be heartwarming, creative and upbeat."

Once a consumer gives an advertisement his or her attention, he or she is likely to become aware of the message and internalize it. **Pulling power** holds the interest of the consumer to the end of the message. Most advertisers insist that the message must relate to some aspect of the recipient's life. Celebrities, for instance, have reference group appeal. "Proactiv" acne skin-care system ads in recent years featured entertainers such as Adam Levine, Katy Perry and Justin Bieber.[9]

Pulling Power

The ability to maintain the interest of the consumer to the end of the advertising message.

CAREER TIP!

Leo Burnett once said, "Creative ideas flourish best in a shop which preserves some spirit of fun. Nobody is in business for fun, but that does not mean there cannot be fun in business." While the advertising industry can mean long hours and meeting deadlines, those who have the work ethic and creativity thrive in that environment. Typical jobs in an advertising agency may include account managers, producers and copywriters. Leo Burnett Worldwide, a Publicis company, operates from Bangkok to Berlin, Chicago to Cairo. Visit the Leo Burnett website (www.leoburnett.com) to learn more about its work and its locations globally.

Understandability

Although most ads don't attempt to say everything about a product, it's important that the information selected for communication be clearly understood or it will not be remembered. Procter & Gamble communicated the benefits of its portable stain-removal pen, "Tide to Go," through a series of ads featuring "immediate results with a remarkable handy touch." Viewers have a clear understanding of what the product can do when the items are shown stain-free from the application of "Tide to Go."[10]

Memorability

It's important that ads be memorable so that they are retained for some time. A high initial effect is useless if forgotten before the consumer actually purchases the product. One way to achieve this is through repetition. An ad usually must be seen at least three times before it moves into long-term memory. Jingles, slogans and tag lines also help ensure recall. How many of the popular slogans listed in Figure 13.5 do you recognize?

Slogan	Product or Brand
Now That's Better*	Wendy's Restaurants
Mobilizing Your World*	AT&T
Welcome In*	American Express
Just Do It	Nike
Live for Now	Pepsi
Innovation That Excites*	Nissan
Breakfast of Champions	Wheaties
Imagination at Work	General Electric
I'm Lovin' it.	McDonald's
Zoom Zoom	Mazda
Good to the Last Drop	Maxwell House
Obey Your Thirst	Sprite
Sometimes You Feel Like a Nut	Almond Joy
Let's Fly Together	United Airlines

*Used for 2 years or less

Figure 13.5   Modern Advertising Slogans

SELECTING AND SCHEDULING MEDIA

Media Options

Media are the channels through which messages are transmitted from the sender to the receiver. Each medium has unique advantages and disadvantages, as described in Figure 13.6.

Media

The channels through which messages are transmitted.

Newspapers A highly credible and flexible medium, newspapers offer wide exposure to upscale adults. Many newspapers have prestige because of their positive impact on communities, and newspapers can also facilitate coordination between local and national advertising. Recently, however, newspapers have lost ground to television and the Internet, so their effectiveness has declined. Daily circulation has declined 30 percent from 1990, to approximately 45 million today.[11] Newspaper companies have attempted to adapt by selling advertising on their websites and by sometimes requiring users to subscribe to access online articles.

	Advantages	Disadvantages
Newspapers	Wide exposure for upscale adults. Flexible; timely; buyers can save for later reference. High credibility.	Few ads are fully read. Young adults don't read them. Costs are rising. Alternate media are becoming more important news sources.
Television	Creative and flexible. Cost efficient. Credible.	Message is quickly forgotten. High production cost. Difficult to get attention.
Radio	Selective targeting possible. Mobile—goes with listeners. Low production costs.	No visual content. High frequency is required to reach many people. Audience research has traditionally been difficult.
Magazines	Target narrowly defined segments. Prestigious sources. Long life—can be passed along.	Audiences declining. Long lead times to develop ads. Need to use many different magazines to reach a lot of buyers.
Outdoor Ads	Low cost per exposure. Good to supplement other media. With color, lighting, and mechanization gets attention.	Can't communicate much. Difficult to measure results.
Internet	Considerable potential. Medium for relationship marketing. Customer driven and dialogue oriented. Increasing number of users.	Relies on consumers accessing the necessary technologies. Revenues still small. Difficult to target a specific audience. Difficult to measure results.
Social Media	High for relationship marketing. Quickly growing. Message can go viral and spread rapidly.	Rapidly changing and evolving. Few guarantees for advertisers. Must conform to rules set by privately owned companies.
Mobile	Growth in technologies offer greater flexibility. Excellent means to reach younger generations.	Potential to annoy consumers. Few standardizations in technologies.

Figure 13.6   Advantages and Disadvantages of Various Media

Television Television is also a credible source and is extremely cost-efficient per person. It provides the creative flexibility to use both video and audio, allowing an unlimited range of spokespersons and themes. The disadvantages are high production costs and low recall of messages. Television is filled with advertising, which makes competition for the viewer's attention fierce and many consumers change the channel when commercials air. Additionally, with more people owning DVRs, the ability to bypass commercials altogether is compelling. Consequently, television ads need to be rerun often to be effective.

Radio Very low production costs make radio an attractive medium. Furthermore, marketers can be extremely selective in targeting U.S. consumers, because each market area averages 30 stations, each aimed at a specific audience. In the past, radio advertising has been limited by difficulties in researching its effectiveness, but new computer systems are changing that. Software is available to assist with post-purchase analysis so that ad agencies can estimate the ratings for stations and specific airtimes. Lacking visual content, radio spots require more repetition than television ads. As methods for audience rating improve, however, it should be possible to use fewer spots and more accurately evaluate each ad's effect on selected segments. Even online radio can be a medium — for example, Pandora, which allows users to customize their own radio stations, features ads between every few songs.

Magazines Magazines also target well-defined consumer segments, and professional journals reach very specific groups. Although about 93 percent of adults read magazines, overall magazine readership is declining. However, magazines still carry about $20 billion worth of advertising, and more than three-quarters of Americans have purchased a product after seeing or reading about it in a magazine.[12] In the past few years, many "small" magazines have been introduced to appeal to unique tastes, which makes more finely tuned targeting possible. The disadvantages of magazines are long lead times and high production costs for ads. In efforts to target more finely, new techniques for producing special ads are being designed that will bring costs down. Magazines that focus on particular hobbies and interests allow advertisers to get very close to unique markets.

Outdoor Advertising Outdoor advertisements, primarily billboards, are very inexpensive per exposure, so they provide an attractive supplement to other media. With color, lighting and mechanization, some billboards have fantastic stopping power. Even though advertising in general has been declining, outdoor advertisements have increased steadily. Moreover, digital technology has been applied to outdoor advertising ,and this medium is expected to broaden vividly for several years. Digital outdoor advertising is managed by the Internet and benefits from ads that can be changed in a short period of time; therefore, it is expected to be more useful than standard outdoor advertising to do strategic promotions.

The 2014 Tour de France began with Prince William, Prince Harry and the Duchess of Cambridge, Kate Middleton, cutting the ribbon to start a three-day tour of the United Kingdom, ending in front of Buckingham Palace. Transport for London (TfL) effectively used colorful outdoor advertisements to bring attention to the event while also warning Londoners about road closures and areas that would be affected. It also encouraged the use of its website, where travelers could plan and

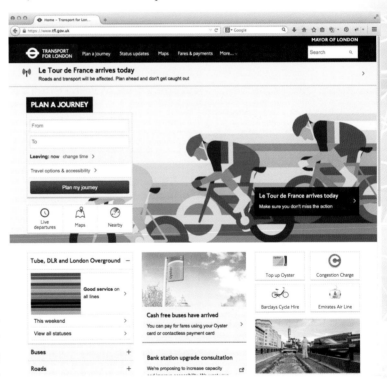

map out their trip. Miranda Leedham, head of marketing operations at TfL, said: "As well as capturing the excitement of such an iconic event, we also wanted to ensure the city is prepared for its arrival by informing our customers of the travel options available to them. This communication helps to build our reputation for hosting major sporting events by ensuring the city is ready for the impact on travel."[13] According to the NBC Sports Network broadcast, the event attracted nearly five million people to watch the race in person.[14] Despite their flashiness, outdoor ads can't communicate a great amount of information, because people move past them so quickly. It's often difficult to measure the results of outdoor advertisements.

The Internet The Internet provides a medium that is both customer-driven and dialogue-oriented. More than three-quarters of the U.S. uses the Internet, and research of the products on the Internet controls almost half of all retail purchases. This gives companies another way to develop relationships with customers through websites that provide many messages about their products or services, and other information that builds a good, solid relationship with customers. Oral-B's website has a learning center section; customers are able to access not only product information but tips for good oral care habits and so on.[15] The Internet allows advertising to occur in forms of banners, pop-up ads, pop-under ads and interstitials (web pages displayed before or after an expected content page).[16] Google Analytics and Google AdWords are two services that track visitors on a company's website and online banner advertisements, determining what keywords attract the most desirable prospects, what advertising copy pulled the most responses and what landing pages and content make the most money for a client.[17]

A major disadvantage of Internet marketing is low click-through rates, as us-

Viral Marketing

Diffusing a marketing message across people.

ers ignore banner ads for the most part. However, the Internet is the key tool in **viral marketing**, or diffusing a marketing message across several groups of people. Marketers can extend their message in a very limited, extremely cost-efficient format, ensure that a few people receive it and allow them to spread it through word-of-mouth discussion. As viral marketing develops, it becomes increasingly important to find an accurate method of tracking its effectiveness, which is what marketers are still attempting to discover.[18] Ford created a viral campaign for the Ford Fiesta with Fiesta Movement, an online competition in which 100 winners were given free gas and a brand-new Fiesta for six months, long before its release date. Winners were given a camera and a monthly challenge to complete and document in their Fiesta. Mission themes included travel, entertainment, social activism and adventure. Contestants submitted their videos to the Fiesta Movement website as well as their own YouTube pages. Ford has generated great promotion with this viral campaign and has helped to position the Fiesta as a fuel-efficient car for the hip and adventurous. Four thousand entrants submitted videos to Ford explaining why they were perfect for the Fiesta Movement challenge, and the winners have collectively generated millions of hits through their YouTube pages and the Fiesta Movement website.[19]

Social Media Many companies have recently taken advantage of marketing through social-media sites like Facebook, Twitter and LinkedIn. Although social media has millions of participants, there are no guarantees for advertisers, many of whom have not yet found an effective method of cutting through the clutter. Some companies opt to scan sites like Facebook and Twitter looking for positive and negative mentions of their companies or brands. Many companies opt to use social media as a way of advertising, and some use it as a way of running contests and promotions, as well. Detroit's Faygo Beverages, Inc. introduced its newest flavor, Faygo Cotton Candy in 2014, with a summer contest using Instagram. Faygo fans are encouraged to photograph themselves and upload it to Instagram using hashtag, #FaygoCottonCandy. The top three photos that generate the most "likes" will win prizes including Cedar Point tickets and a bicycle, valued at $699 from its promotion partner, Detroit Bikes.[20]

Mobile Mobile advertising means delivering text and video messages of ads to cell phones. Marketers are expecting to extend their messaging from offline to online and mobile handsets. Many Internet advertisers have already tried mobile messaging marketing. According to eMarketer, mobile ad spending will grow faster than any other ad channel in the US this year, an 83 percent increase to reach $17.7 billion.[21] This trend is likely to continue as people spend more time on smartphones and tablets. If predictions are correct, mobile advertising will become the second-largest ad channel in 2018, behind only television.[22] Marketers expect this medium will be especially valuable for targeting younger generations.

Media Popularity
Which media do the major advertisers select? Figure 13.7 illustrates a distribution of global advertising expenditures for 2013 and projected 2016. TV advertising is most popular, followed by newspapers, Internet, magazines, radio, outdoor and mobile respectively. You will notice that the projected growth in mobile will most likely come at the expense of newspaper and magazine advertising.

The Media Schedule
Media scheduling can be viewed as a plan within the advertising plan. This very exact work involves a number of considerations: target audience analysis; reach, frequency and continuity balance; media timing; and budgeting.

Target Audience As you know, the marketing plan is always directed at specific market segments. Marketers have developed very detailed methods for defining their targets. For example, Claritas Corporation created PRIZM, which uses such variables as socioeconomic status, ethnicity, family life cycle, education, employment,

Distribution of global advertising expenditure in 2013 and 2016, by media

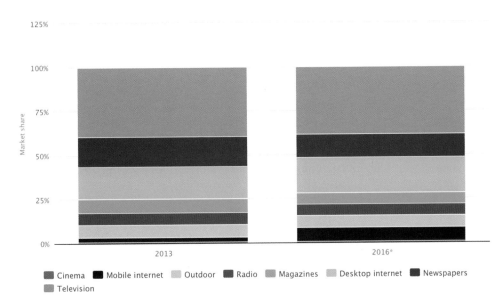

Figure 13.7 Distribution of Global Advertising Expenditure in 2013 and 2016, by Media.
Source: ZenithOptimedia, © Statista, 2014.

type of housing and location of housing to describe 40 audiences. In turn, these data are correlated with media usage patterns. The information helps determine which media are likely to influence the respective segments at various times and locations.

Media scheduling usually is done geographically and demographically. For example, Taco Bell, McDonald's and Burger King all compete for the fast-food dollar in the United States, but Taco Bell targets males aged 19 to 24, whereas the other two include families with children.

Once decisions are made about target audience and geographic considerations, media planners calculate the cost of communicating with the audience through various media. Media costs are generally expressed in units of cost per thousand, abbreviated as CPM (M is the Roman numeral for 1,000). The CPM for reaching the target audience is calculated as follows:

$$CPM = \frac{Advertising\ cost \times 1,000}{Cirulation\ to\ target\ audience}$$

Suppose we are interested in reaching women with children younger than 2. We know that McCall's has 600,000 readers in this category, and an advertisement there will cost $60,000. The CPM of reaching our target audience is $100 ($60,000 times 1,000 divided by 600,000 = $100). We can then determine the cost per person by dividing CPM by 1,000. In this case it is $0.10 ($100 divided by 1,000 = $0.10).

Reach, Frequency and Continuity Balance Once media planners know the target audience and the cost of reaching it, they consider the reach, frequency and continuity of the advertising campaign. **Reach** is the number of consumers in the target audience who can be contacted through a given medium. In the preceding example the reach through McCall's is 600,000. **Frequency** is the number of times the audience is contacted during a given period, usually over four weeks. **Continuity** is the length of time the advertising campaign will run in a given medium. It is important to select a medium with enough reach, frequency and continuity to gain the desired effect. At the same time, agencies do not want to waste funds. **Overexposure** refers to reaching a prospect either after a purchase decision has been made or so frequently that the campaign actually wastes money.

Media Timing Products may be seasonal or purchased more frequently on cer-

Reach

The number of consumers in the target audience who can be contacted through a given medium.

Frequency

The number of times the audience is reached in a given period, usually per day or per week.

Overexposure

Continuing to reach a prospect after a buying decision has been made or to the point that the campaign becomes tedious and actually turns off some potential buyers.

Continuity

The length of time the advertising campaign will run in a given medium.

tain days of the week. For example, sunblock is bought mainly during the summer and especially on weekends. Products such as soaps and cosmetics are purchased frequently all year round and may require constant advertising. Consider the importance of media timing for advertising weight-loss products. Companies such as Weight Watchers, Curves and Jenny Craig Inc. spend millions of dollars on television and print ads every January, since about half of all dieters initiate a program between January and April.

To complicate matters, it's important to look at the activity of competitors. Depending on the resources of the company, it may be necessary to counteract the competitions' campaigns or take advantage of times when they tend to promote less. Tactics include selecting media that competitors are not using or making adjustments to the scheduling, timing and frequency of various advertisements.

Media Budget Generally, the media budget is set according to the strategic marketing and communication plans. Marketers attempt to maximize the advertising effort within budget constraints, using one or a combination of media to achieve the most influence in the market. As part of the media plan, it's important to determine whether messages will be visual, verbal or both. The amount of information to be communicated will influence the choice of media and, consequently, the budget. Recently, the costs of all forms have been escalating, so careful attention must be paid to the trade-offs among them. Fortunately, media competition helps temper rising costs, since the media themselves have marketers that each hope to make their medium more attractive. To accommodate clients, they are willing to provide help in media selection and scheduling.

CREATING ADS

This step in the ad plan involves both science and art. Creating ads can be as complicated as making a movie. The key is to know your objectives and the constraints imposed by the media, scheduling and budget. As with any creative process, it's difficult to determine precisely what people will like and remember. To help answer that question, Marketing, a British journal, conducts a survey each month called "ad watch." British consumers are asked whether or not they remember a specific advertisement.

There are certainly many classics. The California raisins who "heard it through the grapevine" combined humor, visual novelty and a great rock beat that caught the attention of millions in the 1980s. Most of the older generations still remember Mikey, who willingly ate Life cereal. And nearly everyone (if old enough) can recall the little boy sharing his Coke with Mean Joe Greene of the Pittsburgh Steelers after a game.

When diverse segments are part of the target audience, the advertisement must be created in such a way that it appeals to various tastes and preferences. Marketers also need to be aware of language differences, acceptable behaviors, ethnicity and cultural norms. Many current promotional efforts are aimed at a global audience, and that means communicating in a huge number of languages and dialects. To avoid costly mistakes, it is critical for marketers to research and understand the language(s) of a target market segment before advertising to it. In Italy, a campaign for Schweppes tonic water referred to the product as Schweppes toilet water, Kentucky Fried Chicken's slogan in China became "eat your fingers off" rather than "finger-lickin' good."[23]

Of course, not all diversity is ethnic or linguistic. Gays and lesbians, for example, may be unresponsive to ads that employ only heterosexual couples to represent the warm, loving relationships associated with use of the product. The diversity feature discusses advertisements targeting gays and lesbians.

ASSESSING ADVERTISING EFFECTIVENESS

The effect of advertising can be assessed at two different points: before running the ad campaign and afterward. This kind of measurement is extremely important to determine what does and doesn't work so that the campaign can be adjusted.

Individual ads and campaigns may be tested to evaluate effectiveness before committing more funds. Various recall and recognition tests are used on the sample audience to determine whether the ad content has been stored in the consumer's memory. One test asks the audience what it remembers about an ad after a limited run in a particular medium. These tests usually attempt to measure two types of recall. **Unaided recall** asks the viewer to identify any advertisements he or she can recall, such as "What commercials do you remember seeing for automobiles?" **Aided recall** refers to content that can be remembered without seeing the particular ad. An example is: "Do you recall seeing a commercial for Honda?" By questioning several respondents, researchers determine both the unaided and aided recall scores. These tests may be conducted immediately following exposure to the ad or up to several days thereafter.

Recognition means that you remember the ad when you see it again. This kind of remembrance is typically adequate for low-involvement products such as chewing gum or soup. To test recognition, audience members are shown an ad and later are asked if they remember it. In other words, the ad is a stimulus during the testing procedure. One of the most popular types of recognition test is the Starch test, which is usually conducted after an ad has been run. Respondents leaf through a magazine containing the ad and are then asked if they remember seeing it. Next, a series of questions determines whether they associated the ad with the advertiser's name or logo and whether they read at least half of the copy. Because Starch tests have been run on so many ads, marketers can compare the scores of their ad to similar types.

When persuasion is the objective of the advertisement, it is very important to go beyond simple memory tests and determine whether the ad influences attitudes or behavior. For this, marketers use persuasion tests, which essentially measure attitude change. For example, respondents may be asked to preview a particular television show with ads embedded in it. They are then questioned about the program itself as well as brand preferences. Comparing the answers to measures taken beforehand, it's possible to determine the amount of attitude change.

Unaided Recall

The viewer is asked to identify any advertisements he or she can remember.

Aided Recall

The viewer is given some specific piece of information about the ad before being asked if he or she recalls having seen it.

SALES PROMOTION

Sales promotion is communication designed to stimulate immediate purchases using tools such as coupons, contests and free samples.[24] It is used frequently by most companies and it accounts for about $366 billion in annual expenditures in the United States.[25] Notice that the definition focuses on immediate results and changes in the behavior of consumers or other channel members. In addition to its value as a short-term incentive, there is no doubt that sales promotion for many brands has a lot to do with long-term brand equity, particularly frequently purchased items like Coke and Pepsi. Sales promotion plays an important role in reinforcing continuous usage and offsetting gains made by competitors. When brand switching occurs, sales promotion is a valuable way to regain consumer loyalty.

Sales promotion also stimulates trial. Many times buyers are reluctant to try a new product because it may not perform as well as their existing one. Sales promotion reduces the risk by lowering the price or creating other incentives. Car dealers are usually expected to offer test drives, and many food-based companies provide free samples.

Whereas advertising and public relations increase awareness, sales promotion prompts people to action, resulting in immediate sales. By either increasing the per-

Sales Promotion

Communications designed to stimulate immediate purchases using tools such as coupons, contests, and free samples.

ceived value of a product or reducing its price, sales promotion motivates customers to make an immediate purchase decision. A promotion can increase value by providing a complimentary gift, an unusual warranty or other rewards. Price may be lowered directly, with an introductory offer, or through coupons and rebates. These concepts can also be combined by "bundling" products together for a price cheaper than purchasing them separately. In any case, the consumer recognizes an immediate opportunity and acts on it.

Although sales promotion generally has an immediate result, its long-term effects are less clear. It is most commonly used in conjunction with other forms of promotion, such as advertising, public relations campaigns or personal selling. Consequently, it is usually seen as part of the total promotion package designed by the marketing communication strategists.

TYPES OF SALES PROMOTION

Consumer Promotions

Offer designed to pull the product through the retail establishment.

Figure 13.8 depicts four different types of sales promotion: business-to-business, consumer, trade and retailer promotions.

Figure 13.9 lists typical activities in each category. Business-to-business promotions usually involve trade shows, conventions, sales contests and specialty deals, such as volume discounts and price sales. Manufacturers use two basic approaches to influence the consumer — the sales pull and the sales push. **Consumer promotions** are manufacturer incentives offered directly to consumers, largely bypassing the retailer. They are designed to pull the product through the retail establishment with coupons, rebates and other means that the manufacturer can control from headquarters.

Trade promotions are provided by manufacturers to distribution channel members. The objective is to give wholesalers and retailers an incentive to sell the manufacturer's brand. Essentially, these promotions make it worthwhile for the channel member to push the product to the consumer. Common incentives are advertising allowances and price reductions. For example, Ralston Purina may offer a three percent discount on Cat Chow to retailers, in hopes that retailers will pass the savings on to customers so more items are moved.

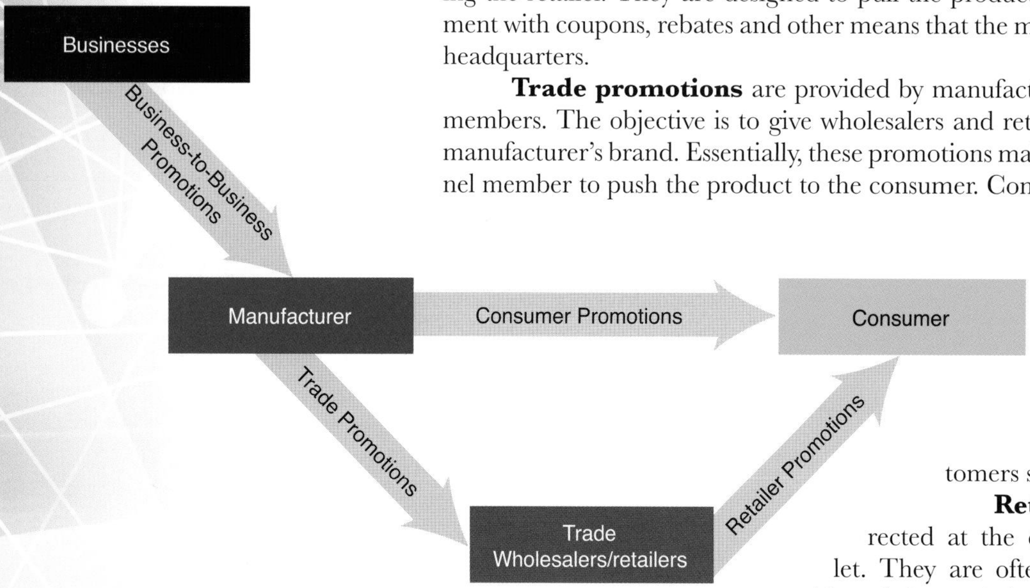

Retailer promotions are directed at the consumer by the retail outlet. They are often confined to a local area, although large chains such as Best Buy may run many of the same promotions at all locations. This provides a sales level sufficient to obtain quantity discounts from suppliers, which enables prices to be kept low.

Figure 13.8   Types of Sales Promotions

Trade Promotions

An offer from a manufacturer to channel members, such as wholesalers and retailers.

Retailer Promotions

An offer to the consumer that is sponsored by a retailer.

Normally, the push and pull elements of the sales promotion strategy should work hand-in-hand. The sales force works to persuade customers (retailers or wholesalers) to purchase greater volume and push to consumers through retailer promotions. At the same time, the marketers are coordinating consumer promotions with ad messages about coupons and point-of-purchase displays tied into the advertising theme. This kind of one-two punch can produce dramatic results.

THE SUCCESS OF SALES PROMOTION

Sales promotion has become increasingly successful due to changing consumer life-

Business-to-Business Promotions	Manufacturer Trade Promotions	Manufacturer Consumer Promotions	Retailer Consumer Promotions
Trade shows	Discounts	Coupons	Price cuts
Conventions	• off invoice	Rebates (refunds)	Displays
Sales contests	• off list	Samples	Free goods ("trials")
Specialty items	Allowances	Price packs ("cents off")	Retailer coupons
Virtual trade shows	• advertising	Value packs ("2 for 1")	Feature advertising
	• display	Premiums (gifts)	Patronage awards
	Financing incentives	Sweepstakes (prizes and contests)	
	Contests	Point-of-purchase displays	
	Spiffs	Cross-promotion	
		Continuity programs	

Figure 13.9   Major Types of Sales Promotion Activities

styles, improving technology and the changing structure of the retail industry. Stores need to present themselves as destinations.[26] Today's busy consumers are looking for ways to simplify purchase choices in order to save time. In addition, they want value, and they view sales promotion as a way of getting more for their money.

Technology helps marketers target sales promotions more precisely than ever before. Checkout scanners can instantly identify a brand being purchased, sorting machines can trace the origin of coupons and other redemption items, and tracking devices identify the location and consumer involved in a purchase. It's now very easy for marketers to measure the effect of specific promotion activities on unit sales and profitability. The Internet has also begun to track consumer spending patterns.

Another influence on the use of promotions is the changing structure of the retail industry. As large establishments such as Walmart gain market power, they can compete more effectively with manufacturers' brands. To counteract this power, manufacturers use sales promotion to create a pull through the channel to maintain their customer base. At the same time, they are engaged in competitive battles to maintain market share. A company that wants to hold onto market share is almost required to use sales promotions commensurate with those of other major competitors, whether retailers or other manufacturers.

CREATING CUSTOMER RELATIONSHIPS AND LOYALTY THROUGH SALES PROMOTION

Sales promotion is an excellent tool for organizations that want to connect with customers through relationships. The purpose of relationship marketing is to create loyal, satisfied customers. Consumers can be very fickle, however, and marketers must keep that constantly in mind. Relational marketing and customer relationship management have received considerable attention by managers. One study finds that, among business managers, relationship marketing is becoming institutionalized. That is, relationship marketing has been so widely discussed that managers now perceive it is a standard practice to implement it in business-to-business exchange relationships.[27] Figure 13.10 describes the four main categories of buyers and strategies for marketing to each group.

Current Loyals   As the name implies, current loyals are presently purchasing a company's brand. They range from intensely loyal users who buy because of their relationship with the company to people who are loyal because of simple convenience or price factors. In either case, it is difficult to persuade this group to switch

brands. One strategy used to maintain these customers is to reward their loyalty with personally targeted one-to-one promotions. This encourages them to continue using the brand, further forges a unique relationship with them, and reminds them about the product they have been purchasing. Many retail establishments send out e-newsletters and coupons, particularly for special occasions such as birthdays. Others will provide loyalty cards that reward the customer for making purchases.

Loyal consumers also may respond to sales promotions by buying a product in larger quantities or at a time when they normally do not purchase. For example, loyal users of Cheerios will likely view a promotion as an opportunity to stockpile the product. Users of Starkist tuna may buy several cans when the brand is on sale. If they have the product available at home, they are likely to use it more often.

When a manufacturer owns two or more brands, current loyal customers are excellent candidates for **cross-selling**, promoting another of the brands or using one product to boost sales of another, often unrelated product. In many cases the customer doesn't know they are the recipient of cross-selling. When you go to Mc-

CREATING & CAPTURING VALUE THROUGH *Diversity*

Targeting Gay, Lesbian, Bisexual & Transgender Consumers

Since 1991, Atlantis Events has been serving the GLBT (gay, lesbian, bisexual and transgender) market by customizing exclusive vacations for 25,000 gay and lesbian travelers each year. Outreach efforts representing the West Hollywood, California-based travel company's cruises and resort getaways have always included editorial opportunities in a variety of gay-media outlets. It is estimated that the GLBT market in the U.S. has reached $830 billion, with more than 15 million GLBT adults.

Not long ago, the number of mainstream advertisers openly targeting the gay and lesbian market was rather low. But today, companies recognize the significant purchasing power of the segment and are now more willing to risk boycotts and consumer backlash in order to gain favor with GLBT buyers.

According to a study from Packaged Facts, a division of MarketResearch.com, more than 90 percent of gay and lesbian consumers are more likely to purchase from companies that market directly to them. As a result, companies have become more sensitive to use words like "partner" and "sexual orientation" instead of "husband" and "preference."

Delta has long been a Seattle PRIDE Festival sponsor, supporting diversity that extends well beyond its airports. "Delta embraces its position as a global corporation — from the places we fly to the community events and organizations we support that reflect the diverse interests of our customers and Delta people," said Cherie Caldwell, Delta's Director of Global Diversity. "Delta's sponsorship of PRIDE and Gay Days is one example in which Delta Employee Networks involve themselves annually."

Marriott International has consistently earned a perfect score on the HRC Corporate Equality Index as one of the Best Employers for LGBT people, and also has been a supporting member of the National Gay & Lesbian Chamber of Commerce. It recently launched its #LoveTravels campaign to convey the company's inclusion and celebration of the LGBT community.

"Delta, Official Airline of 2007 U.S. PRIDE Festivals, Supports Diversity," New York Beacon, Jun 7-Jun 13, 2007, 14(23), p. 22; Atlantis Events, Company Overview, www.atlantisevents.com, site visited May 01, 2014; "America's LGBT 2013 Buying Power Estimated at $830 Billion," Witeck Communications, November 18, 2013; Jay Pulitano, "Marriott launches #LoveTravels campaign for Pride Month," www.glaad.org, June 4, 2014.

Donald's and you are asked, "Would you like that 'super-sized'?" or, "Do you want to make that a 'meal deal'?" you are experiencing cross-selling in its most basic form. Amazon uses very sophisticated cross-selling techniques. When a visitor clicks on an item or adds it to a shopping cart, additional related products are displayed for purchase.[28]

ALL CONSUMERS

Current Loyals
• Reinforce existing behavior
• Increase usage
• Cross-sell

Switchers
• Show availability
• Better value
• Occasional use
• Variety (novelty) seeker

Price Buyers
• Little income
• Best price oriented

Nonusers
• Increase involvement
• Gain trial
• Impulse purchase

Figure 13.10   Types of Buyers

Switchers Switchers purchase a number of different brands. In recent years, this category has increased in size as the amount of loyals declined. Consequently, many manufacturers and retailers focus on this group. In many cases, switchers cut their overall expenditures by finding the best deal at the time. They may switch regularly or only when they see an opportunity to increase value or decrease price.

Switchers are not likely to wait for an out-of-stock brand, so they respond well to trade promotions that are designed to maximize inventory levels and store space. Since they are interested in price and value, they respond to even fairly complex purchase offers. For example, several units of the same product can be bundled together, the amount of product can be increased for the same price, or the price can be reduced.

Some switchers are simply seeking novelty or variety and change brands to alleviate boredom or monotony. Sales promotions work particularly well on them, since they are responsive to new purchase opportunities. If the product is noticed at the precise time the variety seeker is interested in buying, then the manufacturer benefits. 7-Up positioned itself in a way that distinguishes it not only from colas but also from other non-colas. A new Tropical flavor is in limited edition tall cans, and only available for the 2014 summer.[29]

Price Buyers The price buyer's only concern is cost. Most consumers in this category want low prices, but a few choose only the most expensive brand, equating price with quality. People in the latter category tend to ignore nearly all sales promotion, and they consider clipping coupons a total waste of time. In contrast, buyers after low prices are likely to purchase opportunistically, when they have funds and the product is on sale. They respond very well to price promotions: cents-off, two for one, buy a second one for a penny, limited-time offers and so forth.

Nonusers Nonusers do not currently purchase a particular brand. Sales promotions are designed to create involvement, which may stimulate purchase. Again, cross-selling supplies a trial opportunity. For instance, many Barnes & Noble bookstores have Starbucks cafes inside, encouraging nonusers to try a new drink. Some companies mail samples to nonusers, who will often at least try a free product with no strings attached. In other cases, nonusers are supplied a trial under captive circumstances. An example is the complimentary snacks offered on airlines, such as branded peanuts, pretzels and sodas.

BUSINESS-TO-BUSINESS PROMOTIONS

The four main types of business-to-business promotion are trade shows, conventions, sales contests and specialty items. Often volume discounts and price sales occur in conjunction with these four activities.

Trade Shows Trade shows are designed to bring marketers and customers together at a given location for a short period. They occur around the world and provide opportunity for companies to display existing and upcoming product lines in ways that are convenient for customers. The majority of large firms use trade shows as a major promotion mechanism. On average, business-to-business marketers spend about 20 percent of an annual marketing budget on trade shows.[30]

JMPerez / CC BY-SA 3.0

Companies set up booths that are staffed by key personnel and salespeople, and it's not unusual for retailers and distributors to select the merchandise they will carry during the coming year. Since they play such an important role in future activity, business marketers may invest a large percentage of their promotional budget in trade shows. Specific shows are very cost-effective ways to meet a great number of potential purchasers.

Today, trade show information is accessible and heavily promoted on the Internet. The Biz Trade Shows website is the largest directory of business events and trade fairs on the Internet. Companies can quickly identify and select the event that will be the most beneficial in reaching potential customers.[31]

> Trade shows account for about 20 percent of the annual marketing budget in B2B companies.

Conventions Conventions provide another opportunity for marketers and buyers to meet. They are often sponsored by professional groups, such as the American Hospital Association, the American Medical Association or the International Association of Certified Public Accountants. It is important to note that conventions are held around the world, giving marketers the chance to assess the level of global competition and gather ideas for new strategies. Although companies attend primarily to stimulate immediate sales, they also can take the opportunity to do long-range assessments of customer and industry trends. Marketing researchers often attend conventions and trade shows because so many qualified buyers are concentrated in one place. This provides a pool of readily available respondents, and schedules often permit in-depth interviews, focus groups and surveys. These events are considered prime opportunities for data collection.

Sales Contests

Sales contests for salespeople and dealers offer prizes for accomplishing specific goals. Most companies sponsor some type of sales contest from time to time and award trips, gifts or cash, often at an annual sales convention. Volkswagen, for example, rewards top sellers of its featured models with free trips to vacation spots.[32] This type of sales promotion is designed to elicit immediate action by giving short-term rewards for short-term behavior. When incentives are tied to measurable and achievable sales objectives, they can be highly motivating. Sales contests are frequently tailored to specific product lines or market segments and are integrated into the company's overall selling and promotion strategy.

Specialty Items

Specialty items are gifts for customers, usually sent through the mail or handed out by salespeople, with the organization's name imprinted on them. These are typically small office supplies or clothing items and do not require a purchase. Specialty items create goodwill with customers and allow brand exposure in a variety of places.[33]

TRADE PROMOTIONS

Trade promotions are offered by the manufacturer to wholesalers or retailers. The Dubai World Trade Centre in the United Arab Emirates has become a focal point for international trade promotions, which are becoming increasingly common, by hosting a range of industry events including the Middle East International Motor Show.[34] You can expect nearly every type of trade promotion to be offered by the suppliers. Five common types are discounts, allowances, financing incentives, sales contests and spiffs.

Discounts

One of the most popular trade promotions is discount or price-off arrangements, which reduce either the invoice or the list price. The invoice price is what the manufacturer charges to the distributor, whereas the list price is what the end customer is charged. If distributors choose to pass the price cut on to consumers, demand may increase. If not, distributor profit margins increase. Like all trade promotions, discounts encourage distributors to handle more of the company's product and to stimulate sales to consumers

Allowances

Allowances are funds given to retailers and wholesalers based on the amount of product they buy. Two typical allowances are for advertising and display purposes. For example, a retailer who purchases $5,000 worth of product may receive a $500 allowance to help pay for advertising. Display allowances work the same way, except that the funds must be used for point-of-purchase displays in the retail outlet.

Financing Incentives

Financing incentives help reduce the retailer's inventory carrying cost. This is commonly referred to as financing the "floor plan," which is the retailer's stock of inventory. For example, in the automobile business, dealers do not have to pay immediately for all the cars shipped to them, instead paying a fee for having them in their showroom. Financing incentives come in many forms, but all are designed to get the manufacturer's product into the retail establishment.

Sales Contests and Spiffs

Two other types of trade promotion are sales contests and "spiffs." In this context, sales contests reward the retailer for selling a certain

Sale Contests

A competition for salespeople and dealers that awards prizes for accomplishing specific goals.

Specialty Items

Gifts with the organization's name that are provided to customers, usually given through the mail or by the sales force.

Allowances

Funds given to retailers and wholesalers based on the amount of product they buy.

Financing Incentive

An offer to finance the retailer's inventory prior to its sale.

level of product and often extend to the salespeople within the retail establishment. Spiffs are like a commission paid to salespeople in retail outlets who sell the manufacturer's product rather than a competitor's brand. These cash incentives are not uncommon for such items as cameras, televisions, mobile homes and cell phones. Many people consider spiffs unethical because they encourage the promotion of one brand over others regardless of its value to the customer. Because consumers are not aware of the spiff, they may believe the salesperson's motives are more "pure" than is actually the case.

RETAILER PROMOTIONS

Retailer promotions are directed specifically at the end customer and originate within the retailing organization. They encourage consumers to purchase a product from a given location. Consequently, retailer promotions are often in-store or specific with regard to where the promotion can be exercised. Manufacturers may help with retailer promotions, as Sony did with "Modern Rock Live," one of the biggest promotions ever undertaken by the company. It was helpful for consumers and a great sales builder for retailers, because Sony provided kits to help outlets develop local tie-ins to the national promotion campaign by using TV, radio, print ads and consumer websites.

The most common type of retailer promotion is cutting prices. Retailers are likely to use price cuts regularly to stimulate sales of certain product lines or to reduce inventory of older products. They will also direct attention to particular goods with display promotions. Large national retailers are likely to send teams on a seasonal basis to work with local outlets in developing similar displays across the country. Gap takes this approach for displays. Some retailers will promote their products with free trials, hoping to draw in future repeat customers. Retailer coupons are used relatively frequently and are often placed in local newspapers. Also popular is radio or television advertising that highlights discounted items, such as automobiles and mobile homes. Finally, patronage awards are very useful promotions. Generally, a card is punched or stamped each time the consumer shops at the retail outlet. When the card is filled, it's redeemed for free merchandise. Some coffee shops redeem not only their own loyalty cards but also those of competitors as a way to get new trials. Patronage awards, which stimulate loyalty to a given outlet, are particularly useful in local markets for creating a bond between regular customers and the retailer.

CONSUMER PROMOTIONS

Manufacturers use consumer sales promotions to influence their market share across all retailing outlets. There are several popular forms: coupons, rebates, samples, sweepstakes, price and value packs, point-of-purchase displays and continuity programs.

Coupon

Certificate that entitles a consumer to an incentive to buy the product, usually a price reduction or a free sample.

Coupons **Coupons** are certificates that entitle a consumer to an incentive, usually a price reduction or free sample. Trade coupons are redeemable only at a particular store or chain, whereas manufacturer coupons are redeemable at any outlet. They are particularly appealing to manufacturers because they can make a direct connection with consumers. Since manufacturers' coupons create work for retailers, they may be given incentives for handling them.

Coupons are one of the most popular forms of consumer sales promotion. Some consumers purchase a large percentage of their nondurable products through coupons and many plan their shopping lists around them. Other consumers do not want to take the time to search for and cut coupons, especially those who are loyal to particular brands and stores.

Coupons are generally distributed as freestanding inserts (FSIs) in newspapers or magazines, but don't be surprised if someone tweets a coupon to you. They can also be sent in special mailings or as bill stuffers. Another technique is an on-shelf dispenser at the retail outlet, placed near the manufacturer's brand. Only about 2 percent of regular coupons are redeemed, while checkout coupons see 8.5 percent redeemed, electronic coupons 9.8 percent and on-shelf coupons 13 percent. Marketers try to identify the level of price reduction that will stimulate coupon use. If a 25-cent incentive will do as much as a 50-cent reduction, then the 25-cent incentive should be used.

Rebates

Rebates are refunds given to consumers for the purchase of particular items. Psychologically, rebates make a larger impression than price reductions. For example, an automobile manufacturer offers a $1,500 rebate or a 10 percent reduction in price for a $15,000 car. Although the discount may be precisely the same, consumers are likely to see the rebate as greater, since the price discount from $15,000 to $13,500 is a perceptually smaller decrease than the $1,500 rebate. Since consumers usually have to mail a form to the manufacturer to get the rebate, they often will not bother if the amount is small. They also may lose or forget about the rebate, allowing the company to close the sale without paying the incentive. Another advantage of rebates is that they leave higher margins for intermediaries.

Rebates tend to be particularly effective in stimulating trial of brands that are priced higher than those of competitors. Hewlett-Packard frequently runs rebate offers on its printers and other electronic devices. To get the rebate, customers have to submit a completed rebate coupon in addition to a proof-of-purchase sticker. They receive their rebate six to eight weeks after the purchase.

Rebate

Refunds given to consumers for the purchase of particular items.

Samples

Generally, samples are distributed via direct mail, door-to-door or in stores. Sometimes coupons may be redeemed for free samples. This method is effective with new products or when targeted at people who lack experience with the brand. Occasionally, manufacturers attempt to renew an older product by providing samples. American Sampling Inc. sends gift packs to 3.8 million new mothers annually, and companies such as Market Source provide samples to college freshmen.

This kind of sales promotion requires very careful attention to detail, because the cost of samples is high. One study found that 51 million coupons for a free product distributed through freestanding inserts (FSIs) cost $7 per thousand, whereas 5 million samples distributed through direct mail cost $80 per thousand. But the FSIs only converted 367,200 people ($0.97 per convert), whereas the mail samples converted 800,000 ($0.50 per convert.)[35]

Sweepstakes

A sweepstakes is a contest in which participants' names are pooled, and the winner is drawn randomly. Most of you have experienced a twinge of anticipation upon receiving an envelope stating that you may have won millions of dollars. The objective of the contest is to get buyers to purchase the products included in the sweepstakes offer, although laws prevent the sponsor from requiring a purchase in order to participate. Sweepstakes promoters must provide full disclosure of the requirements for entering as well as the probabilities of winning. Visa offers a sweepstakes for users of its credit cards, with the prize of lifetime trips to the Olympic Games. To enter, all you have to do is use your credit card during the games.[36]

Price and Value Packs

Price and value packs are cents-off or two-for-one offers. The cents-off variety is easier to administer and receives a great deal of attention. The value pack, while more difficult to administer, gets more product in the hands of the consumer in a shorter period. Both are very flexible and relatively easy sales promotions to consumers. Value packs are different from premiums or gifts, which may not be related directly to the product. For example, in real estate sales, it's not uncommon for the purchaser of a home to receive a free airline ticket to a vacation spot.

Point-of-Purchase Displays

Point-of-purchase (POP) displays exhibit products at retail locations. Since up to 70 percent of purchase decisions are made in a store, the displays can be very important. Companies spend huge amounts annually on POP. More than 52 percent of carbonated beverage sales, 26 percent of candy/mint sales, and 22 percent of beer/ale sales have been attributed to such displays.[37] They work best when tied directly to other messages or advertising campaigns. Generally, POP displays need to have a lot of attention-getting power and must focus the consumer's interest on the sales promotion and product at hand.

Many stores are using POP to connect with customers in an interactive and exciting environment. For example, customers at Niketown will hear the sounds of bouncing tennis balls and squeaking tennis shoes. Displays of gear even mimic what you might see in a locker room, further connecting with consumers of the goods.

© BrokenSphere / Wikimedia Commons.

Some Niketown POP displays resemble what you might expect to see in a locker room.

Continuity Programs

Continuity programs reward people for continued and frequent use of a particular product. A good example is the frequent flyer miles offered in the airline industry. Although these usually don't stimulate more air travel, they are an incentive for a purchaser to continue to travel with a particular carrier. The programs are also recognized tools for increasing customer satisfaction. Nearly every airline offers frequent flyer miles, and most hotel chains now have similar programs. Hyatt, for example, offers free room stays after a certain number of regular stays. Continuity programs tend to run longer than other types of sales promotion because their basic objective is to promote long-term usage.

PUBLIC RELATIONS AND PUBLICITY

PUBLIC RELATIONS

Public Relations

The use of publicity and other nonpaid forms of communication to present the firm and its products positively.

Public relations (PR) is the use of publicity and other nonpaid forms of communication designed to present the firm and its products positively. It is often confused with advertising, but, in fact, PR is very different. A company controls its advertising; it can only influence its PR. For example, a company can determine when to issue press releases and hold events, but it cannot control the press that independently decides whether to run the communication. Gatekeepers — editors and news reporters — screen company-issued communication to ensure its accuracy, so the public can have some confidence that the information it receives through public relations is truthful. In addition, PR provides editorial-type messages in language that can break through advertising clutter, which is usually visual. Public relations can be used to establish the social responsibility of a good corporate citizen; it builds trust because it must be earned, whereas advertising builds exposure that a company buys. Furthermore, there are few legal restrictions on PR activities, making it a way to address numerous issues in a more balanced light than may be possible with advertising.

Public relations is likely to focus on many publics, including employees, shareholders, community members, news media and government. Rather than directly promote a particular product or brand, most PR messages have the appearance of objectivity. Many PR promotional campaigns center on social issues, taking local markets into account. For example, Avon supports breast cancer awareness in the United States, the prevention of violence against women in Malaysia, child nourishment in China, and AIDS prevention in Thailand. Recently, Kentucky Fried Chicken ran its Buckets for the Cure campaign. The company's red buckets were changed to pink, and the chain donated 50 cents to the Susan G. Komen Foundation for every bucket sold, raising $1.9 million in the first week alone.[38] These cause marketing campaigns are generally supported by major PR activities including visibility of company executives and other spokespersons.

Public relations supports the marketing function in several ways:

- *Corporate communication.* Messages promote a better understanding of the organization among employees, shareholders and other relevant publics.

- *Media relations.* Newsworthy information, such as new activities and personnel promotions, are provided to the media on a timely basis.

- *Lobbying.* Communication with legislators and government officials to promote or defeat legislation is a major activity for heavily regulated industries.

- *Product publicity.* Newsworthy innovations or new attributes of products can be promoted at little cost through the media.

PUBLICITY

Publicity is what is communicated about an organization in the public news media. Negative publicity detracts from the organization's image and can have serious effects on its market position. Most PR groups attempt to generate positive publicity through news stories and public service announcements. The more common avenues are press releases, news conferences and event sponsorship. The Internet is increasingly being used by marketers, both to spread publicity and to respond to crisis situations.

Press Releases and News Conferences
A **press release** is a statement written by company personnel and distributed to various media for publication at their discretion. It includes information about the organization or product that marketers believe will be of interest to the public. The advantage of a press release is that the marketer has control over what information is provided. Many large organizations issue press releases regularly. Organizations will use them almost invariably when negative publicity needs to be countered. Rather than leave it to the media to track down the facts, companies provide the same information to all members of the press simultaneously. Press releases must be accurate, to the point and based on hard evidence. If not, then the media will become skeptical about any material the company issues.

News or press conferences occur when reporters are invited to a meeting at which company officials make a public statement and usually respond to questions. As with press releases, companies have some control over news conferences.

Sponsored Events or Activities
A very popular type of publicity is sponsored events or activities, especially for local promotion. Many companies sponsor rock or symphony concerts, sports teams or youth groups. This gets the company's name into the public while contributing to the community. Sponsors of the 2014 Wimbledon tennis tournament in London included organizations like IBM, Ralph

Press Release

A statement written by company personnel and distributed to various media for publication at their discretion.

The Wimbledon website, featuring 2014 winner Novak Djokovic, also features sponsor IBM in the upper-right corner.

Lauren, Evian, and HSBC. Peak viewership for the championship game between Novak Djokovic and Roger Federer was 10 million viewers — giving sponsors a massive amount of publicity in exchange for their funding.[39] IBM provides technology to the event in addition to funding. A team of 48 IBM analysts capture data, from ball speed to player statistics, to provide insights in real time. The data is then pushed to broadcasters so TV graphics are updated instantly. Match analysis DVDs are given to coaches and players for more detailed stats on their performance.[40]

The Internet The Internet can be an ideal medium for publicity, having already spawned a new group of PR companies. Edelman Public Relations Worldwide is a leading creator of websites. Its services can be especially helpful when companies need to minimize negative publicity. For example, less than three hours after several bottles of Odwalla apple juice were found to contain E. coli bacteria, Edelman created a site to provide consumers with information. Ford has also utilized the Internet to aid in the recall of defective tires.

Marketers who skillfully blend public relations and publicity into their communications mix can underscore and intensify the positive feelings created by other mass communications activities. In Chapter 18 we will turn our attention to the most personal and individualized form of marketing communication — personal selling. Although one-on-one relationship building is key to effective personal selling, mass communication provides important support. It lays the groundwork for personal sales by creating deeper receptivity toward the company and its products.

TECHNOLOGICAL PERSPECTIVE

The history of mass communication mirrors a number of technological advances. Before the age of printing, street criers shouted merchants' messages, and shop signs often used pictures to identify their trade to a largely illiterate public. Movable type was invented around 1440, helping to spread literacy, and 32 years later an advertisement for a prayer book was tacked to church doors. The word advertisement appeared in about 1665, when it was used as a header to describe announcements of commercial significance. By the mid-1700s, newspapers were popular and carried publicity and ads.

By the 1800s, mass communication through newspapers and handbills was abundant. When the magazine was introduced in the mid-1800s, it provided an excellent way to communicate commercial messages. The birth of magazines provided a medium for the professions of copywriting and advertising to develop. By the mid-1930s, great ad agencies such as J. Walter Thompson, Rubicam and BBDO were successful. During that era, the growth of radio provided yet another medium for promotion and quickly surpassed magazines as the leading vehicle.

Although television came along in 1939 when NBC was established, it did not surpass radio as the primary promotional medium until the '50s. Once marketers adopted it, they were able to take advantage of the combination of video and voice, addressing consumers with famous spokespersons, such as actor (and later president) Ronald Reagan. Television now dominates, but magazines, newspapers, radio and the Internet still carry a significant proportion of promotional messages. In recent years, marketers have been budgeting fewer advertising dollars to traditional media and more to Internet advertising. This increased popularity is due in part to the fact that online advertising is easier to measure than traditional means. Better measurement allows for more efficient assessment and adjustment, leading to a higher marketing ROI. eMarketer recently released a study showing that online ad spending is expected to surpass TV spending in 2018, for the first time in U.S. history.[41] Whereas the traditional media revolutionized advertising and public relations, they have taken a back seat in recent years as computer technology has allowed for information systems that contribute dramatically to sales promotion. Computers have made it possible to track product sales globally, enhancing the usefulness of all forms of sales promotion. Clearly, the Internet has shaped communication in even more exciting ways — as a two-way exchange of value, it is doing for mass communication what the telephone did for interpersonal communication.

GLOBAL MASS COMMUNICATIONS

Global advertising, sales promotion or public relations occurs when a marketing team standardizes key elements of these activities across national boundaries. Since campaigns are usually used to support global brand strategies, companies such as Coca-Cola, PepsiCo, Procter & Gamble, BMW, Nike, Toyota and Nestlé are leaders in this arena. Today, all the large advertising agencies have offices worldwide to support clients who seek global coordination. Due to cultural differences, marketers need to assess the benefits of standardized versus localized promotion. Sometimes global strategies require some adjustment at the local level to appeal to different segments of a diverse market.

Because standardization provides numerous economies, the cost of developing creative promotions can be shared across many markets. For example, when Gillette introduces a new product, a worldwide campaign often uses the same actors dubbed in various languages. Using LeBron James' fantastic slam dunks to promote Nike costs millions, but they have the same appeal in Italy or Russia as in the United States.

Global standardization works best when customers, not countries, are the basis for identifying segments and when the product is compatible across cultures. It is also important for the firm to have similar competitors and an equivalent competitive position in most of the markets. Finally, promotion management should be somewhat centralized so that global marketing can occur.[42] Since every culture has a different view of marketing, global standardization cannot be applied to every concept. Although this attitude is changing, Singaporeans tend to regard promotion negatively, whereas Russian consumers are even more positive about it than Americans.[43]

Sales promotion and publicity often have a very local flavor. Each country has a unique promotional style, and most have legal as well as other restrictions. For example, Procter & Gamble (P&G) found it was legal to mail free samples to consumers in Poland, a practice prohibited in many countries. What surprised P&G's marketers was that thieves stole the samples from mailboxes before they reached intended recipients. In Germany, however, the government regulates the size of samples sent through the mail; another law prohibits advertising via personal letter.[44] In England, Hoover Ltd. gave away free round-trip airplane tickets to New York or Orlando with the purchase of £250 in merchandise. The company underestimated demand and spent several million pounds more than it had budgeted.

ETHICAL ISSUES IN ADVERTISING, SALES PROMOTION AND PUBLIC RELATIONS

The most serious ethical issue surrounding advertising, sales promotion and public relations is deception. These communication methods are designed to be persuasive,

Deception

When a false belief is created or implied and interferes with the ability of consumers to make a rational choice.

but too much of the wrong type of persuasion can be misleading.

Deception occurs when a false belief is created or implied and interferes with the ability of consumers to make rational choices.[45] Purely descriptive information is seldom deceptive, but what about embellishment or omissions? At what point does it become deception? Marketers must use a great amount of judgment to avoid being deceptive. An ad may show Michael Jordan soaring hundreds of feet to make a slam dunk in his Nikes, but no one is likely to believe that shoes make this possible. The exaggerated message is that Nike shoes will significantly improve the performance of the common athlete. But Nike lets you know that playing basketball well is also based on ability, training and skill building. Nike campaigns have featured athletes as role models for children, not as superstars. By depicting the athletes as serious, compassionate and hardworking, Nike is able to convey that being an athlete is about more than just the sport. How exciting would it be to see Nike or Reebok simply describe the materials and design for their shoes? Most would not consider Nike's more outlandish "fluff" to be deceptive, and many see it as creative or clever.

Marketers must walk a fine line between producing creative, stimulating messages and being deceptive. Even company slogans can come into question when they evoke strong emotions or make comparative comments. Verizon reminds us, "We never stop working for you." Navy recruiting ads say, "It's not a job. It's an adventure." Is Verizon really at our beck and call 24 hours a day? Does joining the Navy really involve zero work? While they are not necessarily true, consumers probably would not think these slogans seriously interfere with their ability to make informed choices. Are these catchy phrases provocative or misleading?

When false information or exaggerated claims are used, deception is clear — and illegal. Kentucky Fried Chicken (KFC) used deceptive communication by leaving some information out: The FTC charged that KFC provided false information about the relative nutritional value and healthiness of its fried chicken in a national television advertising campaign. KFC publicized that its fried chicken, in particular two Original Recipe fried breasts, was healthier than a Burger King Whopper, due to less total fat and saturated fat. However, its product has more than three times the trans fat and cholesterol, more than twice the sodium, and more calories.[46]

CHAPTER SUMMARY

Objective 1:   Understand the concept of mass communication including the relative use of advertising, sales promotion and public relations.

Mass communication helps companies connect with customers around the world. It adds value by providing information about the goods and services available. Expenditure on mass communication — advertising, sales promotion and public relations — is increasing at about 7 percent annually in the United States and at a slightly higher rate globally. Roughly the same amount is spent on sales promotion and advertising, but sales promotion is slightly ahead and is growing at a faster rate. Public relations is a distant third.

Objective 2:   Learn how technology, globalization and ethics are playing major roles in mass communication.

The history of mass communication coincides with the development of communications technology, particularly print, radio and television. Today, the Internet is adding an interactive medium. Global mass com-

munication occurs when key elements of messages are standardized across regions and nations. Standardization has cost advantages when the same customer segments are found in many countries, but it has several limitations. The primary ethical issue in mass communication is deception. Puffery may be used to make a point, but care must be taken not to be deceptive. Some countries have very strict legislation that does not allow exaggerations of any sort.

Objective 3:   Know the objectives, advantages and disadvantages of advertising, as well as the sequence of steps in creating an advertising campaign.

Advertising is highly controllable and works over time to build brand equity. It is cost-effective for reaching large audiences. Its primary objective may be to inform consumers, to persuade them to buy, to remind them of the product or to reinforce buying behavior and positive feelings about the brand. Advertising media are readily available, and it's easy for marketers to find help in creating effective campaigns. But advertising reaches many people outside the target audience, encounrs a high level of avoidance and can be costly. It also can communi-te only brief, one-way messages. There are several different types of dvertising: national, retail (local), directory, business-to-business, insti-tional, direct response, public service and political. Generally, there e six steps in developing the advertising plan: set objectives, establish e budget, create the theme and message, select and schedule media, eate the ads, and assess effectiveness.

bjective 4: Understand sales promotion objectives and hat types of promotions are used to stimulate sales in usiness, trade, retailer, and consumer markets.

ales promotion is used to prompt consumers to action, resulting in nmediate sales results. It is generally used with other forms of promo-on, such as advertising, public relations or personal selling. There are ur types of sales promotion: business-to-business, trade, retailer and onsumer. Business-to-business promotions include trade shows, con-entions, sales contests and specialty deals. Trade promotions, which re offered by manufacturers to wholesalers or retailers, include dis-ounts, allowances, financing incentives, sales contests and spiffs. Re-

tailer promotions, offered to consumers, include price cuts, displays, free trials, coupons and patronage awards. Consumer promotions are manufacturers' offers, including coupons, rebates, free samples, sweep-stakes, price and value packs, POP displays and continuity programs.

Objective 5: Understand the use of public relations in mar-keting.

Public relations activities are used primarily to influence feelings, opin-ions, or beliefs about a company or its products. An attempt is made to develop messages that at least have the appearance of objectivity. PR supports the marketing function in the following ways: corporate communication, press relations, lobbying and product publicity. Com-mon publicity-generating activities are press releases, news conferences and sponsorship of events or activities. Because public relations mes-sages are placed through public channels, the messages tend to be more credible and believable than advertisements. They also tend to break through the advertising clutter and are relatively low in cost. Public relations can publicize the social responsibility of a good corporate citi-zen.

REVIEW YOUR UNDERSTANDING

1. Why is global standardization of mass communication useful?
2. How do deception and puffery relate?
3. What is advertising? What is its overriding goal?
4. What are the four objectives of advertising? Describe each.
5. What are some of the advantages and disadvantages of advertising?
6. List the eight types of advertising. What is the focus of each?
7. Name the six types of advertising media. What are the advantages and disadvantages of each?
8. What is sales promotion? How is it different from advertising?
9. Briefly describe the four different types of sales promotion. What are the most common promotional activities within each category?
10. How does sales promotion help build relationships?
11. What is public relations? How is it unique from other forms of mass communication such as advertising and sales promotion?
12. What are the pros and cons of public relations?

DISCUSSION OF CONCEPTS

1. Describe the five steps in developing an advertising plan. On which ones would you most enjoy working? Least enjoy? Why?
2. Why is it important to develop a creative strategy before creating specific ads?
3. Which techniques are most commonly used to determine the ad-vertising budget? Which one do you believe should be used and why?
4. What are the critical issues in selecting and scheduling the appro-priate advertising media?
5. As with any creative process, it's difficult to determine precisely what people will like. When it comes to developing an advertise-ment, what are some of the characteristics that will tend to make the ad successful? Why?
6. In business, it's important to measure how well the organization performs certain tasks in order to make adjustments as necessary. How do marketers measure the effectiveness of advertising cam-paigns?
7. Marketers sometimes divide consumers into four categories of buyers. Briefly describe each type and the promotional activities that are likely to be successful with each.
8. List the most popular types of trade promotions. When is each type appropriate?
9. How do the advantages and disadvantages of public relations compare to those of other forms of promotional activities?

KEY TERMS & DEFINITIONS

1. **Advertising:** Paid communication through nonpersonal channels.

2. **Advertising agency:** A business that develops, prepares and places advertising for sellers seeking to find customers for their products.

3. **Advertising campaign:** A series of advertisements with a main theme running through them.

4. **Aided recall:** The viewer is given some specific piece of information about the ad before being asked if he or she recalls having seen it.

5. **Allowances:** Funds given to retailers and wholesalers based on the amount of product they buy.

6. **Business-to-business advertising:** Advertising to business and professionals.

7. **Competitive budgeting method:** Setting the advertising expenditures relative to what competitors spend.

8. **Consumer promotion:** Offer designed to pull the product through the retail establishment.

9. **Continuity:** The length of time the advertising campaign will run in a given medium.

10. **Coupon:** Certificate that entitles a consumer to an incentive to buy the product, usually a price reduction or a free sample.

11. **Creative strategy:** The strategy that governs and coordinates the development of individual ads and assures that their visual images and words convey precisely and consistently what the advertiser wants to communicate.

12. **Cross-selling:** Promotion in which the manufacturer of one brand attempts to sell another brand to the same customers, or the purchase of one product is used to stimulate the selection of another, often unrelated product.

13. **Deception:** When a false belief is created or implied and interferes with the ability of consumers to make a rational choice.

14. **Directory advertising:** A listing of businesses, their addresses, phone numbers and sometimes brief descriptions in a publication.

15. **Direct response advertising:** Targets individual consumers to get immediate sales.

16. **Exposure:** The process of putting the ad in contact with the consumer.

17. **Financing incentive:** An offer to finance the retailer's inventory prior to its sale.

18. **Frequency:** The number of times the audience is reached in a given period, usually per day or per week.

19. **Informative advertising:** Messages designed to provide information that consumers can store for later use.

20. **Institutional advertising:** Messages designed to communicate corporate identity and philosophy as opposed to product information.

21. **Media:** The channels through which messages are transmitted.

22. **National or brand advertising:** Advertising that focuses on brand identity and positioning throughout the country.

23. **Overexposure:** Continuing to reach a prospect after a buying decision has been made or to the point that the campaign becomes tedious and actually turns off some potential buyers.

24. **Payout method:** Setting the advertising budget to gain initial acceptance and trial.

25. **Percentage of sales method:** Allocating a percentage of anticipated sales to advertising.

26. **Persuasive advertising:** Messages designed to change consumers' attitudes and opinions about products, often listing product attributes, pricing and other factors that may influence consumer decisions.

27. **Political advertising:** Advertising to influence voters.

28. **Press release:** A statement written by company personnel and distributed to various media for publication at their discretion.

29. **Public Service Advertising:** Free advertising that supports societal issues.

30. **Public relations (PR):** The use of publicity and other non-paid forms of communication to present the firm and its product positively.

31. **Pulling power:** The ability to maintain the interest of the consumer to the end of the advertising message.

32. **Reach:** The number of consumers in the target audience who can be contacted through a given medium.

33. **Rebate:** Refunds given to consumers for the purchase of particular items.

34. **Reinforcement advertising:** Messages that call attention to specific characteristics of products experienced by the user.

35. **Reminder advertising:** Messages that keep the product at the forefront of the consumer's mind.

36. **Retail (local) advertising:** Advertising that focuses attention on nearby outlets where products and services can be purchased.

37. **Retailer promotion:** An offer to the consumer that is sponsored by a retailer.

38. **Sales contest:** A competition for salespeople and dealers that awards prizes for accomplishing specific goals.

39. **Sales promotion:** Communications designed to stimulate immediate purchases using tools such as coupons, contests, and free samples.

40. **Specialty items:** Gifts with the organization's name that are provided to customers, usually given through the mail or by the sales force.

41. **Stopping power:** The ability of an ad to gain and hold the consumer's attention.

42. **Task method:** Setting the advertising budget based on activities required to accomplish objectives.

43. **Trade promotion:** An offer from a manufacturer to channel members, such as wholesalers and retailers.

44. **Unaided recall:** The viewer is asked to identify any advertisements he or she can remember.

45. **Viral marketing:** Diffusing a marketing message across people

REFERENCES

1. "Some post-Olympics social media numbers," The Day, www.theday.com, August 13, 2012; Wentz, Laurel, "Consumers Don't Really Know Who Sponsors the Olympics," Ad Age, July 27, 2012; Derek D. Rucker, "Olympic Ads Won't Win Any Medals, but Marketers Should Take Note," Bloomberg Businessweek, February 12, 2014.

2. Projected based on Murphy, Ian P., "Yearly 7% Growth Seen for Communication Spending," Marketing News, October 7, 1996, pg. 8; "Marketing Communications and Promotion Strategy," www.pcola.gulf.net, website visited on February 20, 1997; Cassino, Kip D., "A World of Advertising," American Demographics, November 1997, pp. 57-60; Coen, Robert J., "Ad Revenue Growth Hits 7% in 1997 to Surpass Forecasts," Advertising Age, May 18, 1998, pg. 50.

3. Wells, Burnett, and Moriarty, Advertising, pg. 10.

4. www.youtube.com/user/Chevrolet, website visited July 5, 2014.

5. McDonald's, www.mcdonalds.com, website visited July 5, 2014.

6. "Get Involved: EWG's Action Center," www.ewg.org, website visited August 14, 2012.

7. www.adcouncil.org, website visited July 5, 2014.

8. C2 Advertising, www.c2advertising.com, website visited May 12, 2010.

9. Proactiv, www.proactiv.com, website visited August 8, 2012.

10. http://business.maktoob.com, website visited May 12, 2009

11. www.naa.org, website visited June 8, 2014.

12. "Testimony from Hearst's Ellen Levine on the Postal Crisis," Association of Magazine Media, www.magazine.org, website visited June 30, 2014.

13. Gillian West, "Transport for London warns commuters of possible disruption with Tour de France creative," The Drum, July 9, 2014.

14. "2014 Tour de France," NBCSN, Stamford, Connecticut. July 9, 2014. Television.

15. www.oralb.com, website visited June 30, 2014.

16. Huang, Chun-Yao; Lin, Chen-Shun, "Modeling the Audience's Banner Ad Exposure for Internet Advertising Planning," Journal of Advertising Vol. 35, Summer 2006, pg. 123.

17. www.google.com/analytics, website visited June 30, 2014.

18. Watts, Duncan J.; Peretti, Jonah, "Viral Marketing for the Real World," Harvard Business Review Vol. 85, May 2007, pg. 22.

19. www.fiestamovement.com; www.youtube.com, websites visited July 2, 2014.

20. Kathy Blake, "Detroit's Faygo now offering cotton candy flavor," Oakland Press, July 3, 2014.

21. Ben Fox Rubin, "Mobile ad spending expected to jump 83% this year," CNET, July 3, 2014.

22. Ibid.

23. "International Marketing Nightmares," Marketing Update Newsletter, www.exton.com, website visited August 15, 1996.

24. Bennett, Peter D., Dictionary of Marketing Terms (Chicago, American Marketing Association, 1988), pg. 179.

25. Projection based on "Marketing Communications and Promotion Strategy."

26. "The changing face of retail," Deloitte, www.deloitte.com, February 2012.

27. McNally, Regina C.; Griffin, Abbie, "An Exploratory Study of the Effect of Relationship Marketing Institutionalization and Professional and Organizational Commitment in Business-to-Business Exchanges," Journal of Business-to-Business Marketing, 2005, 12(4), pp. 1-39.

28. "Examples of Cross-selling," http://crossselling.org, website visited July 5, 2014.

29. 7-Up, www.7up.com, website visited July 5, 2014.

30. Alex Kantrowitz, "B2B Marketing Budgets Set to Rise 6% in 2014: Forrester," Ad Age, January 21, 2014.

31. www.biztradeshows.com, website visited July 5, 2014.

32. Alonzo, Vincent, "Showering Dealers with Incentives," Sales and Marketing Management, October 1999, pp. 24-26.

33. Hernandez, Andrea, Free Gifts Work as a Marketing Tool, McClatchy-Tribune Business News, December 18, 2007.

34. Bawaba, Al, Dubai World Trade Centre Receives Trade Promotion Award, November 28, 2007.

35. Lefton, "Try It: You'll Like It."

36. www.visa.com, website visited July 5, 2014.

37. Heath, Rebeca P., "Pop Art," Marketing Tools, April 1997.

38. "Cause & Effect," Department of Business Administration, College of Business at Illinois, http://business.illinois.edu, February 2012.

39. Susanna Lazarus, "Wimbledon beats British Grand Prix and Tour de France on TV's super sporting Sunday," RadioTimes, July 7, 2014.

40. www.ibm.com/innovation, website visited July 7, 2014.

41. "Digital Will Surpass TV In Ad Spending By 2018," The Wall Street Journal, March 13, 2014.

42. Jain, Subhash C., "Standardication of International Marketing Strategy: Some Research Hypotheses," Journal of Marketing 53, January 1989, pp. 70-79.

43. Darley, William K.; Johnson, Denise M., "An Exploratory Investigation of the Dimensions of Beliefs Toward Advertising in General: A Comparative Analysis of Four Developing Countries," Journal of International Consumer Marketing 7, No. 1, 1994, pp. 5-21; Andrews, J.C.; Durvasula, Srinivas; Netemeyer, Richard G., "Testing the Cross-National Applicability of U.S. and Russian Advertising Belief and Attitude Measures," Journal of Advertising 23, March 1994, pg. 21.

44. Wessel, David, "Memo to Marketers: Germany Wants to Import American Junk Mail," Wall Street Journal, December 10, 1999, pg. B1.

45. Boatright, John R., Ethics and the Conduct of Business (Upper Saddle River, New Jersey, Prentice Hall), 1997, pg. 277.

Chapter 14

PERSONAL SELLING
& SALES FORCE
MANAGEMENT

AVON

Avon Products, Inc. is one of the largest direct-selling companies in the world. Since its inception in 1886, when the company began with one Representative in New Hampshire, it has grown to a multinational corporation with more than 6 million Representatives in over 100 countries. Through the years, Avon has tightly embraced its founding principles and its five corporate values of trust, respect, belief, humility and integrity. It continues to dedicate resources to the support of women through beauty, health, fitness, self-empowerment and financial independence. Its website home page declares: This is the company that... puts mascara on lashes and food on tables. That fights wrinkles with one hand and breast cancer with the other. That knows the value of a perfect lip, but still opens its mouth and speaks out against domestic violence and for women's financial independence. This is the company that not only brings beauty to doors, but also opens them...This is Avon. The company that for more than 125 years has stood for beauty, innovation, optimism and above all for women.

Avon's direct sales strategy has continued to evolve -- as social, economical, and technological changes take place. In the 1970s, more women began working outside of the home, so Avon created sample packets that could be left on doorknobs. In the 1980s Avon started selling in the workplace, and in the 1990s it launched its Sales Leadership Program, enabling Representatives to make additional money by recruiting and training others. This model, sometimes called multi-level marketing, has allowed some Representatives to create multimillion-dollar businesses. In the 2000s Avon developed its revolutionary online ordering system, called "intelligent ordering." Representatives can prompt customers with reminders, promotions, and other marketing materials, and customers can make purchases at their leisure. The company remains dedicated to threading its direct selling benefits through to on-line customers with exceptional service.

Traditionally, Avon's core customer base has been women 35 and older, but in 2003 the company developed a product line called 'mark.', targeted at women 16 to 24 years old. At its inception, former president of Avon Future, Deborah Fine, explained, "The 'mark.' brand will leverage Avon's core equities of relationship marketing and empowerment and help the company to reinvent direct selling by creating an entirely new beauty experience for young women," said Ms. Fine. "Many recent news reports and studies show that there is a shortage of viable employment options for this demographic. The 'mark.' brand will help fill this gap and provide young women with entrepreneurial choice, an earnings opportunity, and a platform for developing the skills needed to run their own business."

This summer, international tennis sensation Maria Sharapova joined the Avon fragrance family as the face of Avon Luck, two new fragrances: one for men and one for women. According to an Avon press release, "Avon Luck scents celebrate life's good fortunes, amazing events and infinite possibilities. As a renowned athlete, businesswoman and humanitarian, Sharapova perfectly embodies the spirit of having luck on your side, captured by these two new scents." The decision to bring Sharapova onboard Avon was a smart one – Maria's charitable work is a great fit for the image of Avon and she was 2013's most searched athlete on Bing.

Avon's commitment to supporting women by forging unique connections through direct selling and philanthropy is inspiring. A quick look at Avon's press release page on its website provides a snapshot of some of its most recent charitable activities. "Avon Walk for Breast Cancer," "Avon Foundation for Women," "Avon Breast Cancer Crusade," "#SeeTheSigns of Domestic Violence," and "Avon Speak Out Against Domestic Violence" are all incredible programs designed with women, the heart of the company, in mind. With its solid management and its focused commitment to women, customers, employees, Representatives, local and worldwide communities, it's easy to understand how Avon generates $10 billion in annual revenue.[1]

<< **Maria Sharapova joins the Avon fragrance family as the face of Avon Luck.**

Avon Products, Inc.

Learning Objectives

1. Understand the evolution of selling with a focus on relationships and the elements that result in strong customer relationships.
2. Know the responsibilities of salespeople and sales managers.
3. Identify and understand the steps in personal selling.
4. Learn the characteristics of strong salespeople.
5. Understand how to develop a diverse sales organization.
6. Explore how to implement sales actions from setting quotas and compensating salespeople to evaluating and adjusting plans.

THE CONCEPTS OF PERSONAL SELLING AND SALES MANAGEMENT

Successful people usually manage to "sell" their ideas. Broadly speaking, any time one party attempts to motivate the behavior of another party through personal contact, some form of selling takes place. When was the last time you tried to influence someone by expressing your point of view? Did you try to convince a friend to go to a movie you wanted to see or to a restaurant you wanted to visit? While this kind of communication is not always considered personal selling, they share many characteristics. It is through interpersonal contact that leaders influence the behavior of others. What makes personal selling a profession and not just interpersonal influence? It focuses on creating the economic exchange that is at the center of marketing. Salespeople often sell customers on products in very similar ways to how you sell your friends on your desired movie.

Personal selling is one of the most prevalent and highest-paid occupations in the United States. For every person employed in advertising, there are many more jobs in sales; about 11 percent of American workers are employed in sales in some capacity.[2] Furthermore, personal selling pays well, and compensation is rising dramatically. Income varies according to industry and position, but the median salary of top sales executives is $235,034 a year.[3] It is not unusual for salespeople to make hundreds of thousands--sometimes more than a million dollars annually.

Whether you are planning a professional sales career or simply want to sell your ideas more effectively, you'll find this chapter very helpful. We begin by describing the different types of sales personnel and selling situations. Next, we emphasize the importance of relationship selling by comparing various selling approaches. We follow this with a section on the responsibilities of the salesperson, both to the customer and to the company. We then explore each of the steps involved in personal selling — from planning and prospecting to closing the sale and providing follow-up service. The final personal selling section, which describes the four characteristics of strong salespeople, may help you determine if sales would be a good career choice for you.

Although a salesperson in a small start-up company may work fairly independently, as a company grows, its management must begin to think in terms of a sales force, sales teams and sales managers. Good sales force management is needed to coordinate and inspire the efforts of these personnel, as well as to integrate them with the overall marketing plan. In the second half of the chapter we examine the five key functions of sales management: organizing the sales force, developing diverse sales teams, preparing forecasts and budgets, implementing sales actions, and overseeing sales force activities.

PERSONAL SELLING

Figure 14.1 diagrams the topics in personal selling. We will examine each of these in turn.

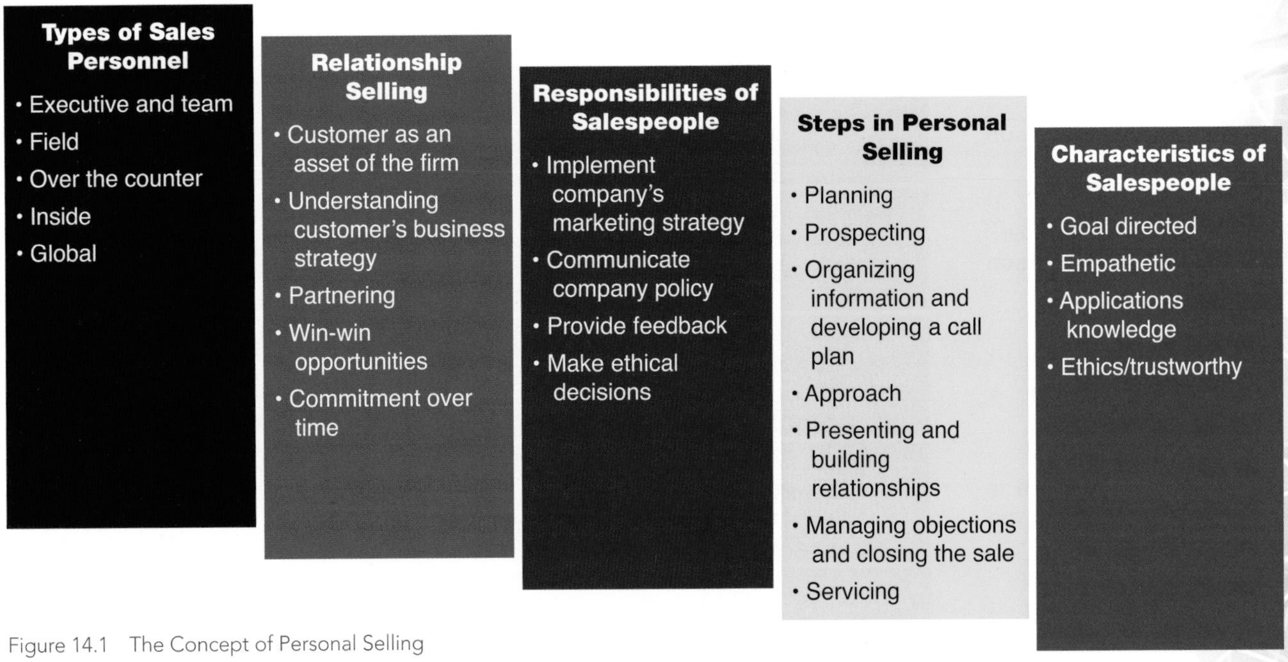

Types of Sales Personnel
- Executive and team
- Field
- Over the counter
- Inside
- Global

Relationship Selling
- Customer as an asset of the firm
- Understanding customer's business strategy
- Partnering
- Win-win opportunities
- Commitment over time

Responsibilities of Salespeople
- Implement company's marketing strategy
- Communicate company policy
- Provide feedback
- Make ethical decisions

Steps in Personal Selling
- Planning
- Prospecting
- Organizing information and developing a call plan
- Approach
- Presenting and building relationships
- Managing objections and closing the sale
- Servicing

Characteristics of Salespeople
- Goal directed
- Empathetic
- Applications knowledge
- Ethics/trustworthy

Figure 14.1   The Concept of Personal Selling

TYPES OF SALES PERSONNEL AND SELLING

The many titles for sales positions tend to describe the type of activity performed: sales executive, sales engineer, sales consultant, sales counselor, representative, account executive, account representative, territory representative, management representative, technical representative, marketing representative, agent and sales associate. Many times the title of vice president is conferred on top-level salespeople who have important sales responsibilities but may have few if any people reporting to them.

Some common categories of salespeople are described in Figure 14.2. **Direct sales** occur when a salesperson interacts with a consumer or company in order to make a sale. **Missionary sales** are made by people who do not take orders but influence purchase by recommending or specifying a product to others. For example, textbook salespeople influence professors, who then require students to purchase a particular book for a class. Likewise, physicians prescribe drugs, golf professionals endorse a brand of clubs and travel agents help select vacation packages.

The circumstances in which selling occurs can be categorized as executive and team selling, field selling, over-the-counter selling, inside sales and global sales. Because each category involves a different setting, the activities of salespeople differ accordingly.

Executive and Team Selling
Although many people are employed in personal selling, the statistics don't count the numerous individuals with non-sales titles who spend much of their time on sales activities. Many executives, regardless of their departments, view personal selling as one of their primary functions. They not only communicate with the board of directors and employees in order to "sell" corporate

Direct Sales

Sales that result from the salesperson's direct interaction with a consumer or company.

Missionary Sales

Sales made indirectly through people who do not obtain orders but influence the buying decision of others.

	ACTIONS	EXAMPLE
Telemarketing Representative	Uses telephone to contact customers to receive orders.	People who respond to callers of 800 numbers (Gateway 2000).
Inside Sales Support	One-to-one contact with customers via the internet or telephone.	IBM salesperson who sells without traveling to a customer's site.
Field Salesperson	Meet face-to-face with customers.	Nike salesperson calling on retail sporting goods chain.
Technical Salesperson	Meets face-to-face with customers to sell very technical products.	Square D salesperson (engineering background) calling on an electric utility.
Detail Person	Meets with people who influence the sale of a company's products but may not purchase directly.	Eli Lilly salesperson who calls on doctors to increase prescription rate for Lilly products.
Service Salesperson	Sells intangible products, such as insurance and real estate, to a broad range of customers.	Prudential salesperson who sells a life insurance policy.
Retail Salesperson	Associates or clerks selling items in a retail outlet.	Saturn salesperson working in showroom.

Figure 14.2   Types of Sales Personnel

Team Selling

Selling that involves people from most parts of the organization, including top executives, working together to create a relationship with the buying organization.

policies but also frequently interact with major customers and suppliers.

Team selling involves people from most parts of the organization, including top executives, who work together to create relationships with the client's buying organization. Boeing recently won a $14.7 billion order for 150 737 jets for United Airlines, and in late 2011, the company had a record $22 billion sale of 230 737 models to Indonesia's Lion Air.[4] Many top corporate executives were deeply committed to the effort, although most of the responsibility still remained with the sales force. In a high-technology business such as aircraft manufacturing, nearly every function gets involved in the sales process. At Boeing it is the salesperson's job to coordinate contact between the company and the technical, financial and planning personnel from the airline. Even if the CEO is brought in, it is not unusual for the salesperson to remain in charge of the sale, using the CEO when appropriate. The salespeople perform the leadership function because they know all aspects of their customers' business. They also must be thoroughly familiar with Boeing's services. This includes cost-per-seat calculations, computerized route simulations and many other analysis tools Boeing uses to show how it can fulfill customer needs.[5]

Field Selling
Field selling occurs at a customer's place of business. Field representatives spend most of their time, as the name implies, away from their company and near customers. Their job is to discover prospects, make contacts and create relationships. By working with customers in their own environment, field reps have ample opportunity to understand the customer's circumstances in depth. The best performers in field selling are often skilled at learning about the customer's situation and problems. Field sales in consumer markets (B2C) include products such as real estate, home building and remodeling, landscape maintenance and even computers.

Field selling to businesses (B2B) is also common. It is used for nearly every imaginable industrial product, for pharmaceutical sales to physicians and hospitals, and for services such as consulting, accounting and business management services to manufacturers and retailers. Merck, a leader in health-care products, sends sales reps to hospitals, clinics, government agencies, drug wholesalers and retailers, among others. In the 2013 fiscal year, Merck salespeople sold $44 billion in goods and services to other businesses and organizations including hospitals, physician clinics and pharmacies.[6]

www.boeing.com

Learn more about the world's leading producer of commercial airplanes and its successful team-selling effort. Also read about how the company is trying to reduce its carbon footprint.

Over-the-Counter Selling Sales that take place in retail outlets (such as clothing, furniture or jewelry stores) are examples of over-the-counter selling. Customers are drawn to the salesperson by the attraction of the store itself or by advertising and sales promotion. Salespeople need to be skilled at identifying customers' requirements quickly, often in a single encounter, and at providing the appropriate service at the point of sale. Providing first-time consumers with quality service entices them to return, which creates the opportunity to gain a loyal customer. It also creates positive word-of-mouth, which attracts friends and relatives of satisfied customers. Successful over-the-counter salespeople tend to build loyal relationships by working with customers multiple times over a long period and becoming knowledgeable about their unique tastes.

Inside Sales Inside sales involve one-to-one contact with a customer via the telephone and Internet. Mail-order companies are a good example. At Nordstrom, sales representatives know the products, how they fit, how to ship them quickly, how to care for them and how to expedite repairs if necessary. The section of the company website called "Nordstrom Live Help" offers customers an opportunity to chat with knowledgeable salespeople. Customers are given three options regarding the type of online assistance needed: customer service representative, beauty specialist and designer specialist. Nordstrom's website provides customers with a helpful, pleasant experience so that they will be likely to use the service again.[7] Another example is the banks of telephone sales representatives who take orders in response to advertisements and infomercials. Sometimes they perform only a clerical function, since the consumer already is sold on the product, but many of these people do an excellent job of answering questions and selling additional items. Telephone marketers perform similar tasks, either attempting to sell a product or arrange a home visit for field salespeople.

Another form of inside sales is to work with established clients primarily by phone. Stock brokerage firms conduct much of their business this way. Many manufacturers and distributors have field reps and inside salespeople who work together with large customers. The reps solicit business at the customer's site, and inside sales personnel are ready at all times to provide technical support and take orders via the phone. This form of inside sales can be critical for industrial companies.[8] These inside sales people are increasingly educated and trained about products, acting more as consultants for the customer. This position requires crucial skills for recruiting and retaining customers, and can serve as a first job for many technical salespeople, since they learn about company policies and products while receiving help with their first customer contacts. Once experience is gained inside, these people often take a field sales position.

Global Sales It is difficult to overstate the importance of personal selling in global markets. Many of these sales involve millions or even billions of dollars. Kathy Sacks, Vice President of Communications for Infusionsoft, compares selling to dating and says, "You have to attract leads by playing up your positives; you have to differentiate yourself from the competition; and you have to spend time building meaningful relationships — ultimately choosing one person for what you hope will be lifelong wedded bliss."[9] Even as today's communication becomes increasingly more technological, many cultures adhere to personal relationships as the foundation of business.

In the domestic arena, companies and their representatives often become accepted in a short period, but this may take years in a foreign environment. To overcome this resistance, many companies use domestic personnel from the host country to represent them, but if that culture does not consider personal selling a prestigious occupation, this is not an ideal solution. Furthermore, finding and training qualified people can be challenging and expensive. As a compromise solution, companies often rely on nationals to provide information and make initial customer contact, but then they send salespeople from headquarters on regular visits to establish relationships and negotiate larger contracts. For tips on global etiquette, see the global diversity feature, "A Few Do's and Taboos for the 'Round-the-World Rep."

RELATIONSHIP AND OTHER SELLING APPROACHES

All employees are important in building and maintaining customer relationships, but salespeople are critical, because that is their primary responsibility. There is a growing trend to move from building short-term sales to building long-term satisfaction and loyalty. By establishing personal, long-term and loyal relationships with customers, salespeople can increase customer retention and repeat sales, furthering their company's competitive advantage. If salespeople do not have the skills and desire to build relationships one customer at a time, then no amount of support from all the other company employees will compensate.

Business strategies should focus on creating relationships rather than simply selling products. Companies are entering into joint activities in record numbers, and selling organizations must work closely with customers to help them accomplish their goals. Sellers must understand the consumer's lifestyle or how the customer's business works. Consequently, sales organizations are shifting from traditional ways of doing business to a new emphasis on building relationships. The three basic sales approaches are shown in Figure 14.3 — traditional sales, consultative sales and relationship selling.

Traditional Sales Approach

Emphasizing persuasive techniques to convince consumers to buy a company's products.

The Traditional Sales Approach The **traditional sales approach** focuses on persuading consumers to buy a company's products, thereby raising sales

	Traditional Sales	**Consultative Sales**	**Relationship Selling**
Focus	Understand your product	Understand customer's problems	Understand customer's business or lifestyle
Role of the customer	Prospect	Target	Asset of the business
Salesperson focus	Persuasion	Problem solving	Partnering
Salesperson role	Obtain sales volume	Advise customers	Building win-win circumstances
Objective	Profit through sales volume	Profit through problem solving	Profit through strategic relationships and customer satisfaction

Figure 14.3 Major Sales Approaches

volume. Remember that the Industrial Revolution produced goods in record quantities, much more quickly than demand could keep up with. During the first half of this century, the purpose of personal selling was to stimulate sales. Firms were focusing on selling more in order to keep up with increased production. The salesperson's focus was on pushing the company's products, especially features and functions, to persuade prospects to buy them and increase the sales volume. Techniques for persuasive selling, which taught salespeople how to negotiate, were often the dominant subject of sales training courses. Essentially, sellers and buyers tried to see who could get the best deal.

The Consultative Sales Approach

For many organizations, the traditional sales era continued well into the 1990s. As the marketing function became more important, however, the sales function also took on new responsibilities. Marketing began to focus on serving customers, and selling had to change with it. **Consultative selling** means working closely with customers to help solve problems. Salespeople are expected to advise customers on how their company's products can solve problems rather than beat a competitor's price. In order for this type of selling to be successful, salespeople must work closely with the customer over an extended period. Customers on all levels, from individuals to businesses, are extending the buying cycle through spending more time in the decision-making process.[10] At some companies, salespeople act as consultants to their customers and may even suggest a competitor's product if it would better suit the customer. Consultative selling stops just short of relationship selling.

Consultative Selling

An approach to selling in which sales personnel work closely with customers to help solve problems.

Relationship Selling

Relationship selling attempts to forge bonds between buyers and sellers in an effort to gain loyalty and mutual satisfaction.[11] Because it promotes loyalty, it is in tune with the strategic nature of marketing, recognizing that sellers and buyers benefit from one another's success. In today's consumer markets, people want to buy based on relationships with companies that can be counted on to enhance their lifestyle. Businesses, meanwhile, are looking for partners who will help them compete. Relationship selling recognizes that the salesperson's role is to create value for the customer as well as the company. Typically, a great deal of work on both sides goes into building and maintaining relationships.

Relationship Selling

Forging bonds between buyer and seller to gain loyalty and mutual satisfaction.

Understanding the Customer's Business Strategy

The focus of relationship selling is to uncover strategic needs, develop creative solutions and arrive at mutually beneficial agreements.[12] Salespeople must recognize that companies buy products to help them run their businesses more efficiently. By understanding the customer's business, salespeople are more likely to communicate in meaningful ways with the potential buyer. Dow Chemical Company, a supplier of plastics and adhesives to the global automotive industry, "lends" technical sales engineers to assist clients with product and program development. They help create product strategies and are very familiar with confidential aspects of the client's business, effectively becoming a core part of the customer's marketing team. Cisco Systems demonstrated its customer-focused structure when it entered into a deal with Wachovia, the parent company of the nation's fourth-largest bank and third-largest brokerage firm. Wachovia wanted to improve its key business drivers, which included business growth, higher productivity and employee engagement. Cisco provided its TelePresence system to Wachovia to enhance collaboration by providing ultra-high-definition "in person" virtual communications, ultimately saving on travel

expenses and increasing individual productivity.[13]

The Customer as an Asset Loyal Customers should be viewed as an asset by the firm. Long-term contracts and repeat sales produce predictable sources of revenue. In fact, the worth of many businesses can be calculated by the size of the customer base, such as the number of subscribers of a cellular phone company. Companies with foresight do not treat customers as prospects for a single sale, but as partners in a long-term relationship. In the highly competitive hotel industry, Marriott International restructured its sales program to make it possible for individuals to earn reward points at one hotel and then take their families on vacation at another. After implementing the program, customer loyalty and frequency of stays increased.

Partnering Under the traditional approach, salespeople use persuasion to obtain orders, whereas consultative selling emphasizes the ability to solve customers' problems. In contrast, relationship selling focuses on partnering. Some partnerships are contractual, established through long-term written agreements. Some are non contractual; that is, the buyer and seller enter into an implied agreement to do business together over time. In either case, a sharing of power occurs. In traditional sales, the balance of power is typically with the salesperson; in consultative selling it is with the customer. Relationship selling involves a symmetrical relationship — both parties have equal authority and responsibility. Both share information to help the other party succeed.[14]

Relationship selling replaces short-term thinking with a perspective that ensures value long after the sale is made. Consequently, just as much work is needed after the sale as before. A strong follow-through makes certain that partnerships are honored.

Building Win-Win Circumstances Historically, buying and selling have involved negotiation. **Negotiation** can be defined as discussions by two or more parties to arrange a mutually beneficial transaction, with some degree of compromise. To some it means that each party tries to maximize its own benefit relative to the other through a power position obtained during the interaction. To others, negotiation is a way to build relationships. Instead of being seen as conflict or struggle, negotiations can be regarded as information sessions that lead to win-win opportunities.[15]

Figure 14.4 describes the negotiating possibilities. When any party loses, the foundation for building a relationship diminishes greatly. When one party gains a great deal more than the other, a relationship will not grow or will dissolve over time. A sound relationship requires that each party perceives it has gained value; the best negotiations are win-win situations. Even in early meetings with customers, both parties need to win.

Negotiation

Discussion between two or more parties to arrange a transaction.

	Buyer Gains	Buyer Loses
Seller Gains	Win-Win	Buyer negotiates poorly
Seller Loses	Seller negotiates poorly	Lose-Lose

Figure 14.4 Buyer-Seller Negotiations

Managing Strategic Relationships Account management refers to the activities of a salesperson or sales team to build and support the relationship with a customer. To become more customer-focused, many companies assign an account manager to each large customer. Consulting firms, advertising agencies and manufacturers often have account managers. Delphi assigns them to work with the Ford, Toyota, Volkswagen and BMW accounts as well as with GM assembly divisions. These managers concentrate their energies on maintaining the bonds between Delphi and the client. Account managers are particularly effective when the product supplied is important to the overall strategy of the buying company. For example, Delphi's components are critical to their customers' product designs. For some auto brands, Delphi produces most of the electrical systems, brake systems and other components. Account managers spend considerable time with customers and carefully monitor satisfaction with products and delivery.

Walgreens Health Systems sells pharmacy benefit programs, home health-care and specialty pharmacy programs to employer groups, managed-care organizations, hospitals and government agencies. Some clients want basic services such as an on-site pharmacy and others want complete benefit programs. According to Katie Lestan, Walgreens regional vice president of sales: "In the health-care industry, which is rapidly changing, many services such as contracting for retail pharmacy service are being viewed as commodities. Most clients are looking for the best services at the lowest cost. Our Strategic Account managers are trained to help customers to align their business priorities with the requirements needed and the criteria in which to measure their success. If the customer and Walgreens can align priorities with the proper solutions, everybody wins. Our goal is to provide the best services that meet the needs of the client at the lowest net cost." Win-win occurs when both parties accomplish its objectives. Generally this requires careful understanding of the other party's needs, cooperation and compromise.

CAREER TIP!

At Hewlett-Packard, field sales trainees are responsible for attending formal training classes and performance of appropriate projects. They develop sales through customer presentations, demos, trade shows and territory management, as well as conduct customer and competitive research. Hewlett-Packard offers worldwide employment opportunities as well as leadership and development programs geared toward high-performing, high-potential sales professionals. If you think you might be interested in a sales career at Hewlett-Packard, connect to its website at www.jobs.hp.com. You will have an opportunity to learn about the company's recruiting process, events and internships.

THE RESPONSIBILITIES OF A SALESPERSON

Salespeople do not simply increase sales volume. Today, most view themselves as the marketing manager of a territory. This can be a geographical area, such as a city or region or a single large account. Essentially, a **sales territory** is all the actual and potential customers for whom the salesperson has responsibility. As marketing manager of a territory, the salesperson has several functions. He or she must implement the company's marketing strategy in that territory and communicate company policy to clients and potential customers. The salesperson must also provide the company with feedback about the marketing environment, including the competition and customer needs and wants. Finally, salespeople must operate ethically.

Sales Territory

All the actual and potential customers, often within a specified geographic area, for which the salesperson has responsibility.

Implement the Marketing Strategy In order to translate the company's marketing strategy into action, the sales force needs to have a basic understanding of all marketing functions. In many companies, salespeople have considerable flexibility in applying the entire marketing mix to their territory, including which products to emphasize, which prices and discounts to offer, and which promotional materials to distribute. In other words, although their primary responsibility is to carry out the company's strategic marketing plan, they can use their own judgment in determining *how* to do it. Constant communication between sales teams and marketers is essential to success. Salespeople are able to provide the customer with information gathered by the marketing team's surveys and focus groups. Sales calls are often made by representatives from both marketing and sales divisions.

Communicate Company Policy As agents of their organization, salespeople are responsible for communicating company policies to customers. A policy is a guide or set of rules the company uses in conducting business. For example,

Urban Outfitters allows customers to return or exchange any unworn, unwashed or defective merchandise. Within 30 days, their original method of payment will be refunded; after 30 days, they receive a merchandise credit.[16] Although company policies are relatively straightforward in most consumer sales situations, they can be extremely complex in business-to-business selling. For example, pharmaceutical sales representatives usually educate doctors about the proper use of certain drugs or medical equipment, and sometimes they are present when surgeons operate in order to answer questions about products should the need arise.

Companies are likely to specify exactly what salespeople can communicate. Also common are policies on appropriate product use, warranty issues, delivery and pricing. By communicating such policies and enforcing them, salespeople help shape customer expectations, create goodwill and maintain positive customer relationships.

Provide Feedback

Another important role of the sales force is to provide their company with information about customers, competitors and market conditions. Salespeople are in constant contact with the market, and many companies have formal systems for collecting their information rapidly. Examples are portable personal computers with elaborate, user-friendly programs or arrangements with customers to contact their computer systems directly.

Most salespeople have an array of sophisticated communication capabilities, including voice mail, email, fax and satellite linkages, cell phones, and social media. This keeps them in touch 24 hours a day, seven days a week. Customer inventory levels (stock on hand), purchase orders, price quotations, shipping data and promotional offers can be transmitted in both directions online. In addition, salespeople usually help forecast opportunities by describing the plans of current and potential customers that may affect future sales. Many times these estimates require careful analysis of a client's strategic plan.

Salespeople also provide valuable information about competitors. By collecting and assembling this input from around the globe, Lear Corporation can identify nearly every initiative competitors make. Let's say a salesperson in Germany identifies a rival's product introduction, new promotional campaign or altered pricing strategy in that territory. The information can be evaluated at Lear Corporation headquarters to determine the likelihood that markets elsewhere will be affected. Because auto suppliers like Lear need to develop automotive systems to sell to global auto companies like Ford, Suburu and Toyota, this type of feedback is critical.

Make Ethical Decisions

Salespeople rarely have many restrictions on what they do and say, so it falls to them to use sound ethical judgment. Because performance evaluation frequently is tied to sales levels, there are strong pressures to put their own interests ahead of those of customers. Salespeople are likely to face ethical dilemmas regarding the company they represent and the customers they serve. It helps immensely if their company's philosophy is value creation for the customer as well as the organization.

Why does independence from supervision pose ethical issues? The company usually goes to great expense to hire, train and support a salesperson. If he or she does not work hard, then the company may be denied sales. The amount of time spent selling is an issue of personal ethics. Most employers recognize that the job may require spending time on evenings or weekends with customers or doing paperwork. To compensate, there tends to be some flexibility regarding working hours, but an unethical salesperson may take advantage of the situation. For example, it may be relatively easy to shorten the workweek without being missed or to play golf repeatedly with clients, with more concern for stroke count than for building a relationship. A salesperson may take on another job rather than devote full energy to the primary employer. What about taking an MBA class during work hours without telling the company?

Other ethical issues arise with regard to performance objectives. Most salespeople are evaluated at least partially on sales volume or profitability. This creates several temptations, including overstocking, overselling or pushing brands that yield higher commissions. Overstocking occurs when customers purchase more than is required for a given period, which results in unnecessary inventory-carrying charges. Imagine that you are a few thousand dollars short of your monthly sales objective. Suppose there is a distributor who relies on your estimates to restock inventory. If you put in an order for more than is needed, then you may gain a better performance evaluation, but you have acted unethically. Overselling occurs when customers request a lower-priced product that suits their needs and budget, but the salesperson supplies a much more expensive and profitable product. Similarly, some companies offer spiffs for selling their product rather than a competitor's. Another unethical practice is to promise delivery when the salesperson knows the product will be late. The customer is prevented from ordering a competitor's brand, and when the delay becomes apparent, it is too late to obtain a substitute.

What salespeople communicate can also be an ethical issue. Puffery, or sales rhetoric so obviously excessive that customers recognize it as such, may not be in good taste but rarely is considered dishonest. Misrepresentation is far more serious. Salespeople are unethical when they give incorrect information, such as claiming their product is the same as another when it is not. Selling often involves verbal communication, and there may be little documentation other than an invoice after the sale, so actions like this can be difficult to prove. Whether spoken or written, intentional misrepresentation is illegal and can result in criminal or civil suits. Unintentional misrepresentation is at best a sign of incompetence in the salesperson and is grounds for canceling a contract. Ethical salespeople say, "I don't know, but I'll find out," rather than guess at the facts.

THE STEPS IN PERSONAL SELLING

Personal selling can be divided into seven stages, as outlined in Figure 14.5 and explained below.

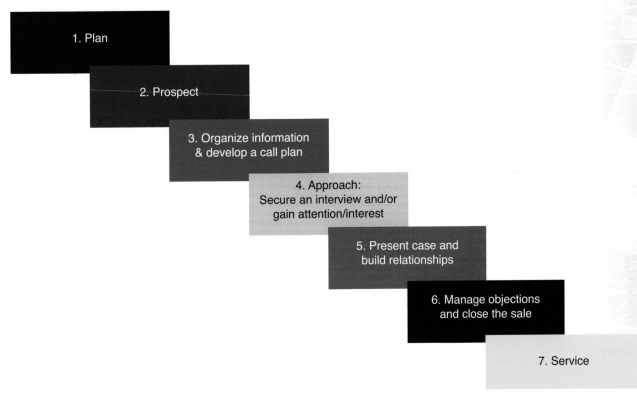

1. Plan
2. Prospect
3. Organize information & develop a call plan
4. Approach: Secure an interview and/or gain attention/interest
5. Present case and build relationships
6. Manage objections and close the sale
7. Service

Figure 14.5   Steps in Personal Selling

Planning

Sales planning translates the company's marketing strategy into territory plans and account plans. Territory management is extremely important. Salespeople must determine how the company's target marketing and positioning can best be applied in their territory. Because each area is different, it is important to make adjustments based on local conditions. Exceptional sales skills are of little use if calls are not made on the appropriate accounts with the right frequency and intensity. **Territory planning** determines the pool of customers, their sales potential and the frequency with which they will be contacted about various products. The fundamental objective is to allocate sales time and use company resources to obtain the best results. Territory management is so important that many companies calculate, to the minute, how their salespeople should use their time.

Account planning establishes sales goals and objectives for each major customer, such as the sales volume and profitability to be obtained. Increasingly, account objectives include customer satisfaction, often measured by loyalty (repeat business). Account plans are based on an understanding of the customer's business and how the seller's products contribute to it. Elaborate account plans for major customers are common. For example, the AT&T sales team responsible for Ford Motor Company has a detailed description of its entire communication picture. This required a massive effort to develop, but the millions of dollars generated in revenues make it worthwhile. The plan provides all the information necessary to build and maintain the AT&T relationship with Ford.

Prospecting

As the name implies, **prospecting** is looking for potential customers within the company's target markets. As illustrated in Figure 14.6, it involves three steps: obtain leads, identify prospects and qualify them. **Leads** are the names of all those who might have a need for the product, a large pool that must be nar-

Territory Planning

Identifying potential customers, their sales potential, and the frequency with which they will be contacted about various products.

Account Planning

Establishing sales goals and objectives for each major customer.

Prospecting

Looking for potential customers within the company's target market.

Leads

Names of all those who may have a need for a company's products.

Figure 14.6 Potential Customers

Prospect

A potential customer interested in the seller's product.

Qualifying

Examining prospects to identify those with the authority and ability to buy the product.

Qualified Prospect

A potential buyer interested in the seller's product who possesses the attributes of a good customer.

Cold Calling

Contacting a lead for the first time.

rowed down to the most likely buyers. **Prospects** are potential customers who have an interest in the product. They may currently buy from a competitor, are former customers or have shown interest in some way. **Qualifying** is the process of determining which prospects have the authority and ability to buy the product, as well as whether they are desirable customers. A **qualified prospect** is a potential buyer interested in the product and likely to be a reliable customer.

A number of methods are used in prospecting: cold calls (canvassing), referrals, exhibiting at trade shows, networking, telemarketing, secondary data, and coupons and ads. These are shown in Figure 14.7.

Cold calling (canvassing) is contacting the lead for the first time, either by telephone, fax or in person. The salesperson has no idea whether the person will be interested. A few prospects are likely to be found, some of whom may be qualified. Cold calling is warranted when there is little information about the market or when the product is likely to have universal appeal. Many consumer products are sold door-to-door, and cold calling is also used in business-to-business selling. It is not very popular with customers, but it can be a useful method if not abused.[17]

Cold Calls (Canvassing)	Going door-to-door
Center of Influence	Identify opinion leaders and contact them for leads.
Referrals	Get customers or prospects to provide names of others.
Exhibitions and Demonstrations	Exhibit at trade shows or give speeches.
Networking	Contact friends, relatives, and associates to obtain leads.
Telemarketing	Phone people on lists.
Secondary Data	Obtain lists from companies such as Dun & Bradstreet.
Coupons and Ads	The prospect responds to an ad or redeems a coupon.

Figure 14.7 Prospecting Methods

A variation of cold calling is the **center of influence** method, which identifies leads by contacting opinion leaders. Opinion leaders are open to communications with salespeople and are considered reference group models. It is common knowledge that the pharmaceutical industry has profiled every physician in the country according to opinion leadership. The leaders are more open to new products and also are more likely to influence colleagues.

Referrals are names of leads provided by a qualified prospect. This method can be very effective, since qualified prospects tend to associate with those who have similar attributes. Furthermore, compared to cold calling, the referral is likely to be receptive when the salesperson mentions the name of someone they both know.

Exhibitions and trade shows are an important way to obtain leads. About 85 percent of attendees significantly influence buying within their firm. It also costs 70 percent less to close a sale with these leads than with others.[18] In 2014, more than 800,000 people attended the North American International Auto Show in Detroit.[19] More than 1.2 million are drawn to North America's largest auto show, held in Chicago. Participants include both domestic and foreign automakers as well as specialty manufacturers and retailers.[20] Nearly every industry sponsors a trade show. Large halls such as Madison Square Garden in New York City, the Omni in Atlanta, and McCormick Place in Chicago provide facilities for thousands of organizations to display their products and obtain leads. Though networking through the Internet is increasing, there is no substitution for the human element of exhibitions and trade shows.[21]

Networking involves contacting friends, relatives, previous customers and associates to obtain leads. Successful salespeople in most fields find this an important part of their business. Amway Corporation, a part of the Alticor family of companies, has had great success obtaining sales through networking. The company uses a system of independent agents who sell home care products directly to consumers. The agents ask customers for names of additional leads to contact. Amway is an incredible global success, with distributors in Asia, Africa, Latin America and North America. Its worldwide sales are more than $11.8 billion annually.[22]

Telemarketing uses phone calls to contact lists of leads provided by marketing services and various directories. Organizations, such as Dun & Bradstreet and Information Resources Inc., provide listings of nearly every private and public organization as well as the name and title of executives, managers and buying influencers. Many marketing services contact these leads to determine the types of products they purchase and other information. These interviews are then turned into lists of prospects and sold to various

Center of Influence

An opinion leader who can be quickly qualified as a potential customer because of his or her standing in the community.

Referral

A lead provided by a qualified prospect

Networking

Contacting friends, relatives, and associates to obtain leads.

Telemarketing

Making telephone calls to leads provided by marketing services or from other lists.

©iStockphoto.com/Zsolt Nyulaszi

marketing organizations. For example, AT&T has its own staff of telemarketers to find small business prospects for its products. Increased use and accessibility of the Internet are changing the nature of telemarketing. Marketing services still make phone calls, but many also use real-time Internet conversations and email responses to consumer inquiries.

Secondary data sources can provide thousands of lists. Categories of secondary data can range from local libraries to company databases. Today, the information highway provides access to the names of nearly all U.S. companies and most international organizations. By using database technologies, companies can effectively filter to find qualified prospects. In some cases, the selling organization manages the database, but this is a highly specialized field. Because of the very costly technology and expertise required, most secondary data searches are outsourced.

Coupons and ads form another method for obtaining leads. Generally, coupons are placed in newspapers or magazines or sent through the mail. People who take the time to respond tend to be very interested and may have the attributes of a qualified prospect. A trend in magazine advertising is response cards that consumers mail in for free information after circling a number that corresponds to a specific ad. These cards give the seller a list of leads to pursue.

Organizing Information and Developing a Call Plan **Preapproach**

Preapproach

Preparation by the salesperson for the initial meeting with a prospect.

refers to preparing for the initial meeting by learning about the prospect. For consumers, just their address can yield socioeconomic information, such as the likelihood of sufficient income to purchase the product and even some general idea of tastes and preferences. Columbia TriStar Home Video has developed its own software for its sales force to use in learning about the large retail chain outlets they visit. In the case of businesses, the salesperson can obtain copies of the organization's literature and annual reports. These contain data on the firm's financial strength, organizational structure, objectives, plant locations and sometimes even its purchasing philosophy. The salesperson's goal is to obtain enough information to develop an initial strategy for each call.

Once the preapproach phase is completed, a call plan is developed to save time and minimize travel expenses. The **routing schedule** identifies which prospects will be called on and when. Companies sometimes form routes with computerized programs, or they can elect to do it informally.

Routing Schedule

A travel plan for calling on prospects that is developed to save time and minimize expenses.

Approach

The salesperson's first formal contact with the potential customer.

Approach The **approach**

is the salesperson's first formal contact with the potential customer. The objective is to secure an initial meeting and gain customer interest. It's usually a good idea to schedule an appointment; it will save time, and it puts the prospect in the frame of mind for a sales call. Many times, a letter of introduction before calling to schedule will help in obtaining the first appointment.

Many techniques have been developed for the initial approach. The most successful ones focus on the potential customer's business, such as a brief explanation of how or why the seller's product can help. It is also important to determine not just when the meeting will take place but how long it will last and its objective. Organizations with a strong reputation generally have an advantage in the approach stage. For example, Xerox or Kodak salespeople will have more success gaining an initial interview than will representatives of an unknown company.

Presentation

A two-way process in which the salesperson listens to the customer to identify needs and then describes how the product will fulfill them.

Making the Case and Building Relationships The sales **presentation**

is a two-way process: The salesperson listens in order to identify customer needs and then describes how the company will fulfill them. It is often said that successful selling is 90 percent listening and 10 percent talking. Unfortunately, many salespeople do not place proper emphasis on the importance of listening and believe their role is to tell prospects about products. However, by asking questions, they empower the customer to participate and demonstrate that they have the customer's best interest in mind. The first contact is the first opportunity to connect with a customer.

Few people are naturally good listeners; effective organizations train their sales force to listen properly. The training identifies ways to learn about the prospect's situation. It also teaches how to show that the salesperson is listening and is concerned about the customer's needs and wants. **Empathy** occurs when a salesperson understands precisely how the prospect feels. Only when prospects know that the seller understands their needs and wants are they receptive to solutions the salesperson offers.

A popular technique for interfacing with customers is SPIN selling. It stands for situation, problem, implication and need payoff.[23] The approach resulted from research into what makes people successful at large sales. Companies such as Xerox and IBM supported the study, which investigated more than 35,000 sales calls, and have used the system successfully for years. Considerable training is required for people to become proficient with the technique. Essentially, it employs a sequence of probing questions that enlighten the salesperson and the client at the same time.

Situation questions help discover facts about the buyer's condition. Much of this can be learned before the interview, so these questions should be limited. Problem questions identify dissatisfaction with the current circumstances.[24] For example, the salesperson may ask: "What makes it difficult to use this type of product?" Implication questions follow, and these are crucial. They unearth the consequences of current problems and are likely to reveal important needs. For example, in response to questions about product safety, one customer began to realize that high insurance costs, low morale and ethical issues were consequences or hidden costs.[25] Need payoff questions then explore why it is important to solve the problem. In the SPIN process, the buyer and seller establish the need for a product and the benefit of its ownership.

The first contact not only is an opportunity for the salesperson to make a case for a product but also may be the first step in building a relationship. Although sales are sometimes made on the first visit, most occur later. Over time, the salesperson assumes different roles as the relationship develops.

Managing Objections and Closing the Sale

One of the most important sales skills is the ability to overcome a buyer's objections. These may be raised subtly in many cultures. In the United States, for example, they are often disguised questions. A consumer may say, "I can't afford to purchase that automobile," but he or she is really asking about what financing is available, or how much it costs, or about the trade-in terms. Assertive salespeople do not let the first objection stop the dialogue; they use it to advance the discussion. Most organizations have training programs to teach salespeople how to manage objections.

Closing means getting the first order. In many cases this is simple, such as asking directly if someone wants to buy the product or whether they will use cash or credit. In other cases, it involves elaborate contracts. Good salespeople know how important it is to help the buyer toward the final decision. You have probably tried on a suit or dress and heard the salesperson say, "Shall I have that measured for alterations?" or "Shall I wrap that for you now?" In business-to-business situations, the salesperson may ask if the purchaser is ready to make a decision or would like to discuss the issue more thoroughly.

> **Good salespeople know how important it is to help the buyer toward the final decision.**

It is important to use caution in regards to closing.[26] If a buyer is not ready to make the commitment, then asking for an order prematurely can make the salesperson appear pushy and unconcerned with the buyer's needs. A great deal of sensitivity is required to accurately read the buyer's state of mind.

Service

There is a big difference between making a sale and gaining a customer. One sale equals one sale. The word "customer" implies something more than a

---

Empathy

An interpersonal connection in which the salesperson understands precisely how the prospect feels and communicates that understanding.

Closing

The point at which the salesperson obtains the first order from the customer.

single sale. In order to maintain relationships, salespeople spend significant time servicing accounts. They make sure products are delivered on schedule and operate to the buyer's liking. When there is a problem, the salesperson makes sure that it is resolved quickly and satisfactorily.

Follow-up occurs when a salesperson ensures after-sale satisfaction in order to obtain repeat business. If a salesperson effectively provides information that supports the purchasing decision, it can alleviate buyer's remorse. If that evidence is not forthcoming, then customers may quickly become dissatisfied, especially with more expensive purchases. Follow-up also offers a way to identify additional sales opportunities. After the first step is taken, the second is easier. The salesperson who continues to work closely with the buying organization can uncover other needs to fulfill. Good service builds strong customer loyalty, which is the goal of partnership selling.

Follow-up

After-sales service to ensure customer satisfaction in order to obtain repeat business.

CHARACTERISTICS OF STRONG SALESPEOPLE

Hundreds, perhaps thousands, of studies have been done to determine what makes a good salesperson. Figure 14.8 describes the characteristics noted most often: goal direction, empathy, strong knowledge of applications and ethics.

Figure 14.8 Characteristics of Successful Salespeople

First, strong sales performers tend to be goal directed. They spend focused time on planning and then work according to those plans. They use their time effectively, which allows them to manage their territory efficiently. They are also highly competitive and obtain results in the face of stiff competition.

Second, because strong salespeople are empathetic, they are aware of the concerns and feelings of others. This means they can understand buyer behavior and see things from the customer's perspective. Most have very good listening and questioning skills that help them get this information.

Third, strong salespeople know how their products apply to the customer's situation. This requires technical competency as well as a good understanding of the customer's business. That combination allows the salesperson to creatively solve problems for the customer. Since each customer has a specific set of needs, each requires special attention. A salesperson must customize or assemble a mix of products that best addresses the specific customer's needs. In essence, the strong salesperson works with the customer to tailor a solution.

Fourth, salespeople must be ethical. The nature of the job often places them in difficult situations. Since good salespeople build relationships, they must be viewed as trustworthy. They find the appropriate information when they don't know the answer to a question. They provide pertinent information and don't waste a customer's time with irrelevant information. They try to help customers solve problems, whether or not a sale is involved. They have a reputation for keeping customers informed, for admitting mistakes and for promising only what they can deliver.

Relationship selling requires that salespeople be more versatile, creative and visionary than ever before. A strong salesperson works to harness all company resources for the customer's benefit.

SALES FORCE MANAGEMENT

The sales organization places great emphasis on forging personal relationships with customers. Managers develop and guide the sales organization to make sure connections are made in the right ways with the right customers. They lead others in order to carry out the overall personal selling portion of the communications mix. **Sales force management** is the marketing function involved with planning, implementing and adjusting sales force activities. It is a tremendously important function for companies that stress customer relationships. Nearly every dimension of how salespeople behave with customers is influenced by how they are managed. Sales management teams keep this in mind when they recruit, train and motivate salespeople. And sales force management helps salespeople create lasting connections with customers by directing company resources to support relationship building.

Sales managers are responsible for the leadership and management of salespeople in order to accomplish the sales objectives established in the marketing plan. Sales managers are more than very good salespeople. They are vital in implementing the marketing strategy in companies such as General Electric, Intel, Xerox, Kodak, Eaton Corporation and thousands of others. Many marketing executives, especially in technology-driven firms, have made their way up through the sales manager route. To be effective, sales managers need a full understanding of the marketing strategy and planning, each aspect of the marketing mix and personnel management, in addition to the principles of selling and sales management.

Sales managers need to handle their teams with care, however. One study published in the Journal of Marketing showed that, especially when selling a new product, it's more important to focus on "strengthening a salesperson's selling intentions by creating positive attitudes about the launch and heightened feelings of self-efficacy" and treating sales staff as the first "customers," rather than merely exhorting them to sell. Perceived pressure by management can actually reduce a salesperson's ability to influence buyers.[27]

Sales force managers perform many functions in support of the marketing strategy. Figure 14.9 describes the most important ones: organize the sales force, develop sales teams, prepare sales forecasts and budgets, implement sales actions and oversee the sales force. These functions may be performed alone in a smaller organization or by a team of people in a larger company. The sales management team is composed of representatives from personnel, who help with recruiting, training and personnel records; from marketing (management) information systems, who provide necessary sales data; and from customer service, who connect the sales force and their customers with manufacturing and logistics. Yet the overall responsibility for all the functions described in Figure 14.9 belongs to sales management.

Sales Force Management

The marketing function involved with planning, implementing, and adjusting sales force activities.

Sales Manager

The person responsible for the leadership and management of salespeople in order to accomplish the sales objectives established in the marketing plan.

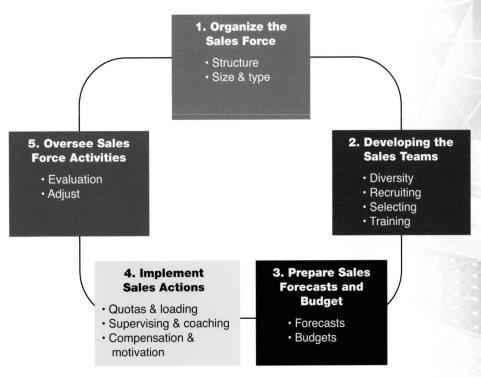

Figure 14.9 Sales Management Functions

CREATING & CAPTURING VALUE THROUGH *Diversity*

A Few Do's and Taboos For the 'Round-the-World Rep

Many selling skills that work in the United States also work overseas, but knowing how to act in certain cultures can make the difference in closing a sale. For instance, the simple thumbs-up sign that Americans use every day may offend a customer in the Middle East. And while health nuts often sip seltzer at a U.S. business lunch, in Japan it is bad manners to refuse a stronger drink. Here are a few global p's and q's gathered from a number of international business experts:

China
• Negotiating is an art, and there is no such thing as a quick sale.
• The more sales reps know about the culture, the better. Foreigners who exert themselves to learn about Chinese society are more accepted by Chinese business people.
• Chinese regard modesty as a moral virtue and part of their integrity. They may display modesty by humbling or downplaying themselves, which does not mean they are not professional.

Japan
• Business is about relationships. Japanese may prolong the relationship building time until they reach consensus, so clinching a deal in Japan is a time-consuming affair that may take months or even years.
• Gift giving at a first meeting is the norm; business cards should be presented with both hands and a slight bow, and the card received should be scrutinized carefully.
• The Japanese will rarely say no. Instead, they will say, "Maybe" or "That would be very difficult" — both of which essentially mean no.

France
• When at dinner, never mention business before discussing the menu and choosing the wine. Better still, hold off until after the second or third course of the dinner.
• The traditional elite networks are powerful. Once a foreigner taps into such networks, doors will open.
• Hierarchy is important. The more formal "vous" remains the rule with any boss, often addressed as Mr. Chairman even after several years.
• Group meetings are not for decisions, for it is hard for French to compromise. The only way to get things done is to have one-on-one meetings.

United Arab Emirates
• Punctuality is not considered a virtue but often treated casually. Be patient in waiting before or during meetings; take time to chat and establish good working relationships.
• Business is frequently conducted over lunch or dinner, often in a lavish hotel or restaurant, and it is polite to return the invitation.
• Foreigners are expected to abide by local standards of modesty, but not expected to adopt native clothing; traditional clothes on foreigners may be considered offensive.

Tony Fang, "Negotiation: the Chinese Style," The Journal of Business and Industrial Marketing, 2006, 21 (1), p. 50-60; Daniel D. Ding, "An Indirect Style in Business Communication," Journal of Business and Technical Communication, Jan 2006, 20 (1), p. 87-100; Mariko Sanchanta, "Japanese Value Relationships and Quality Time," Financial Times, Apr 2, 2007, p. 4; Peggy Hollinger, "Business Etiquette: Excuse My French, But Pleasure Before Business?" FT.com, Feb 13, 2007; Abigail Stevens, "When in Rome ... A Glimpse of Global Business Etiquette," Accountancy Ireland, Feb 2007, 39(1), p. 70-71; Robert Eugene DiPaolo, "Doing Business in Brazil Is First of All an Adventure," Brazzil, Sep 11, 2006.

ORGANIZING THE SALES FORCE

The characteristics of sales managers and the chain of command are important considerations in organizing the sales force. These and other concerns are of particular importance in global settings. Both the structure and the size of the sales group have a lot to do with sales coverage.

Sales Manager Types The sales manager position can be executive, mid-level or first line, depending on responsibilities and scope of operations. At the top are national and international sales executives, often with the title of vice president. They usually report to the top marketing executive. In most companies, only one or a few people are in this position. Their management scope covers several products across a broad territory. In large companies, executive sales managers may have several other sales managers reporting to them and they ultimately are responsible for several thousand salespeople. Mid-level managers, called regional managers when the sales force structure is geographic, supervise several other managers in a large area, such as all of the states in New England or the southwestern U.S. First-line managers oversee several salespeople who handle certain products or types of accounts in a limited geographic area. First-line managers who supervise field reps and retail salespeople usually have a sales force of eight to 12; those who supervise inside sales or telemarketing personnel are likely to have more. As a first assignment, some sales managers supervise only three or four people.

Sales Force Structures A **sales force structure** is the organization of the reporting relationship between sales managers and salespeople. Sales organizations can be structured by geography, product or division, by market segment, or by individual account. In some cases, all four are used. Figure 14.10 shows a typical geographical structure, topped by a general sales manager who reports to the vice president of marketing. Sales managers in the various geographical areas report to the general sales manager. Below them may be sales managers at the regional and district level, then territory representatives (salespeople).

Sales Force Structure

The organization of the reporting relationship between sales managers and sales people.

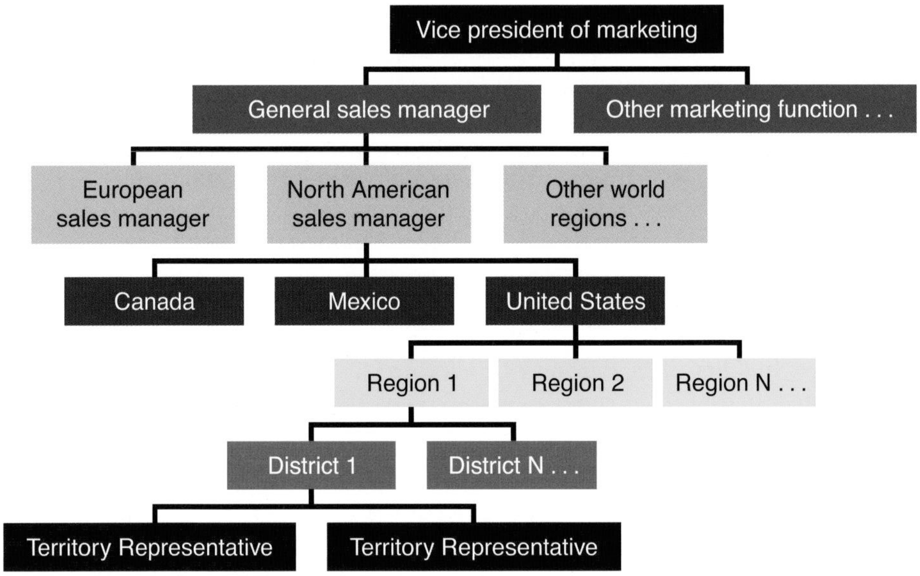

Figure 14.10 A Geographic Sales Force Structure

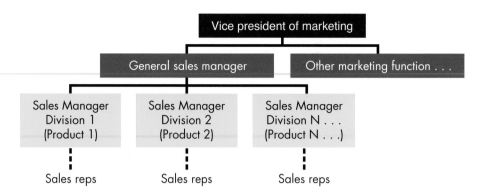

Figure 14.11 A Division or Product Line Sales Force Structure

Figure 14.11 illustrates the division or product line structure. Many companies are organized into divisions, and each may have a sales organization. Companies with very technical products are likely to use this sort of structure. For example, companies within the auto industry often have a sales organization structured according to the components of an automobile: interior, exterior, electronics and so forth. Each area requires a great deal of interaction among salespeople, designers, manufacturing personnel and individual customers.

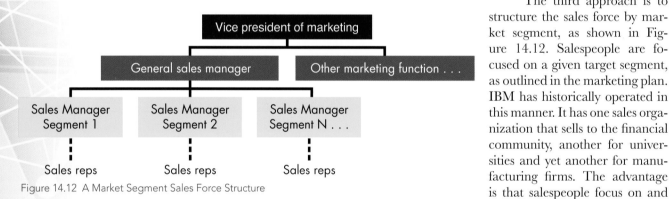

Figure 14.12 A Market Segment Sales Force Structure

The third approach is to structure the sales force by market segment, as shown in Figure 14.12. Salespeople are focused on a given target segment, as outlined in the marketing plan. IBM has historically operated in this manner. It has one sales organization that sells to the financial community, another for universities and yet another for manufacturing firms. The advantage is that salespeople focus on and truly understand the needs of a particular market segment. A company with a limited product line that has differing applications by segment would prefer this arrangement.

Many companies have a few customers who represent extremely large volume, called key accounts, house accounts, national accounts or global accounts, depending on how they are managed. Major accounts may fit the 80-20 rule: About 80 percent of a company's sales volume comes from only 20 percent of its accounts. Although the percentages may differ considerably, the point is that major accounts are large, usually have unique sales needs and are so important to volume and profitability that they require special emphasis. Major accounts are often managed by a separate sales group of a few very experienced people who report to the top sales executive. In other cases, they may be allocated to the mid-level area in which they are located. In some companies, major accounts are assigned to sales managers who split their time between these customers and their management duties.

DEVELOPING THE SALES TEAM

In order to develop the sales team, a good sales force must first be recruited, selected and trained. Recruitment is the activity of attracting qualified prospects for the sales job. Selection involves choosing the strongest recruits for employment in the sales force. Training provides education and disbursement of equipment/tools so salespeople are prepared for the job. In the United States it is a manager's responsibility to comply with the federal Equal Employment Opportunity Act. Hiring discrimination based on age, sex, race, national origin, religion, ethnic background and physical handicap is strictly forbidden. Many countries have similar requirements.

Diversity in the Sales Force Although the structure and size of the sales force are important, nothing is more critical for relationship marketing than the diversity of the sales organization. A sales force that represents various groups has a greater ability to be sensitive to the needs of more individual customers, which improves the company's relationship-building capacity. A diverse sales force provides a variety of insights, ideas and perspectives, all of which make it easier to accommodate a dynamic and multicultural customer base.[28] Strong managers consider diversity in all stages of their sales force development, particularly during recruitment, selection and training. Whirlpool, for example, recruits many of its new sales reps from colleges or related sales-education programs. In the company's "Real Whirld" program, the recruits live and learn together in a nine-bedroom house dedicated to their new careers. The program helped Vice President of Sales Sam Abdelnour recruit a more diverse sales force; 60 percent are women or minorities.[29]

Although men traditionally have dominated the sales profession, many managers are finding that women have excellent relationship skills and often are more successful at selling. The mostly male readership of *Sales and Marketing Management* was asked: "Who is better at sales, women or men?" Although 70 percent ranked the sexes as equal, 17 percent said women were better, compared to 13 percent who ranked men higher. Gender-balanced sales forces were the focus of a more recent study that concluded few gender differences existed.[30]

Recruiting Effective recruitment attracts a qualified pool of candidates to fill the sales positions. The first step is to develop a job description specifying activities and qualifications. This written document spells out organizational relationships, responsibilities and duties of the position.

The convenience of the recruiting site is important, which is why college campuses are often chosen. Strong organizations devote time to finding experienced candidates through recruiting companies. Many companies have increased college hiring with aggressive e-recruiting through the Internet. Some companies also offer mock interviews, career fairs and resume critiques on university campuses. To learn more, contact your college placement office or visit company websites directly.

Selecting Because good sales talent is in high demand, strong candidates have some choice in where they work. Sales managers must demonstrate sound judgment in selecting from a broad range of talent, and they need to sell top candidates on opportunities with their organization. FedEx sales managers see recruitment and selection of sales candidates as one of their most important functions. FedEx is considered to have one of the best global sales forces, selecting candidates who can build relationships with a dynamic customer base spread over 220 countries.[31]

Although there is no definitive list of attributes that define those likely to become successful salespeople, the attitudes, skills and knowledge of some individuals set them apart. Important personality traits include empathy, which allows a salesperson to understand problems from another's perspective; ego drive, which ties self-image and identity to job performance; and resilience, which allows a salesperson to bounce back from defeat. Also important is the ability to communicate, think analytically and effectively organize and manage time. Knowledge of and experience with a product, industry, competitor or company territory are also valuable qualities. Others include self-discipline, intelligence, creativity, flexibility, self-motivation, persistence, a personable nature and dependability.

Training Even the most qualified salespeople need continuous education. New hires need the most, but seasoned veterans also can benefit from advanced training and formal practice. Many sales executives believe training is critical for developing individual and team skills. Many companies find that it increases morale, reduces turnover, improves relationship-building skills and develops a stronger sense of team-work, all of which combine to increase sales dramatically. Total U.S. training expenditures were $55.8 billion in 2013 according to Training magazine's 2013 Training Industry Report.[32] Training programs are usually conducted regarding company policies and procedures, product and customer applications knowledge, sales skills and territory and account planning.

Company policies and procedures can be very elaborate, specifying the exact relationship that salespeople are expected to have with customers. Policies range from mundane matters, such as sales account and entertainment budgets, to complicated issues, such as the types of special customer requests the company will honor. In today's sales environment, procedures are often highly complex. Among other things, they may involve understanding how to enter orders, how to service accounts and how to create and maintain reporting systems between the selling and buying organizations.

Training is necessary to understand the product's attributes and benefits. In technical sales jobs, products are often very sophisticated. In some cases, training builds background information, such as knowledge of electricity for electrical products or pharmacology for drug products. Salespeople learn not only about the technologies behind the product but also about how the product works. Teaching salespeople about new items is critical to the success of a pharmaceutical company such as Merck. There is very little time between a product's FDA approval and its introduction to customers.

Most organizations train new hires in basic relationship-selling skills and experienced salespeople in more advanced techniques. The objective is to help the sales force do a better job of working with customers, listening and finding ways to develop profitable relationships for each party. There are companies that specialize in sales training that provide sales certification programs to enhance the skills and credibility of a sales force. In this form of training, salespeople must attend classes or in some cases take distanced learning courses offered over the Internet. Certificates are given according to the competency level attained. More than 50 percent of managers believe that a certification program would benefit their company, and 66 percent of consumers believe certified salespeople are more credible, skilled and competent. Although such training is expensive, many organizations consider it a good investment.[33]

SALES FORECASTING AND BUDGETING

Forecasting and budgeting are important steps in allocating sales resources. The forecast estimates the potential sales demand based on likely responses of buyers to future market conditions, sales force and other promotional activities and marketing actions. Sales force budgets are generally set with the sales forecast in mind. Accuracy in the forecast and budgets is important, since production is scheduled to meet demand. When forecasts are lower than actual demand, customers go unserved. When they are higher than demand, high inventory-carrying costs dramatically reduce profitability. Estimation methods vary from elaborate computer programs to fairly simple questioning of potential buyers. Even small companies, which are known for their ability to adjust quickly, depend on accurate forecasts.

Sales Forecasting Most companies go through three basic steps in estimating demand — an environmental forecast, an industry forecast and a company sales forecast. The **environmental forecast** examines the economic, political and social factors likely to affect the level of spending for a product. Factors include un-

Environmental Forecast

An estimate of the economic, political, and social factors likely to affect the level of spending for the types of products or services being forecasted.

employment, consumer spending, interest rates, business investments and inventory levels. In general, information of this type helps determine whether economic conditions for the company's products are likely to be positive or negative. Environmental forecasting can estimate not only global, international, national and regional trends but also very localized trends. Every year, Sales and Marketing Management prints a "Survey of Buying Power," a tool that helps marketers predict sales of products based on environmental conditions, consumer age, wealth and distribution channels.

Sales forecasts often use the industry outlook as a key element. An **industry forecast** estimates the amount of overall demand expected based on such factors as the industry business condition, amount of spending, number of new products and communications budgets anticipated for competitors. In other words, this forecast projects the level of sales and marketing activity for the industry as a whole as well as for competitors likely to affect the company most directly.

The **company sales forecast** is based on the overall marketing strategy. It forecasts unit sales and must be in line with marketing, financial and operations plans. If not, then the company must adjust the sales forecast. The marketing plan is particularly critical. For example, a product positioned as a high-priced specialty item may have a low expected sales volume. For a product positioned as a low-priced commodity, the sales volume estimate will probably be higher. In addition, in order to do a good job of developing objectives, it is important to estimate demand with other departments in mind. Sales managers communicate about forecasts with many areas of the company to reconcile any differences. Since various departments may have specific objectives, such as cost containment, brand growth and financial targets, this interaction is necessary. Estimates may be made for the entire company, a particular product, a geographic region, a market segment or on some other basis.

It's important to remember the more dynamic the situation, the more difficult the prediction is likely to be. Consequently, businesses in new fields may have to spend more time estimating demand than do businesses with mature product lines. Yet, even in innovative, highly competitive industries, it is important to obtain reliable forecasts.

Some marketers mistakenly associate good forecasting with strong marketing. In fact, there are many examples of organizations that have forecast low sales volume and created less aggressive marketing strategies. Although they met their forecasts, they probably would have reached much higher sales levels if they had pursued an aggressive strategy. Most organizations recognize that perfect sales projections may mean the company is operating much too conservatively. Whirlpool Corporation believes a perfect forecast is possible only when a marketing group is performing below potential.

Industry Forecast

An estimate of the amount and type of competitive activity likely to occur in an industry.

Company Sales Forecast

A prediction of unit or dollar sales for a given period, in total or broken down by product, segments, or other categories, and based on the marketing strategy that will be put in

©iStockphoto.com/Francesco Ridolfi

Forecasts are very important in deciding how to allocate company resources. Divisions that foresee high levels of sales are often given ample resources, such as additional salespeople, large advertising and promotion budgets, and lots of attention from product development and manufacturing. Consequently, the forecast can become a self-fulfilling prophecy. When forecasts are low, fewer resources are provided, and lower sales result.

Sales Force Budgets   One of the most important tasks of the sales manager is to create and administer the sales budget. The three most common methods for setting the budget are: as a percentage of overall sales, relative to competitors' budgets, and as projected costs for the sales tasks. The first method establishes the sales budget as a percentage of the historical sales level. Although simple to use, this method has a major flaw. The estimated increase over past sales results in a larger sales budget, but perhaps the situation should be the reverse: A larger sales budget should result in improved sales volume. Despite this problem, many sales organizations base the budget on past performance.

> **The three most common methods for setting the budget are: 1) as a percentage of overall sales, 2) relative to a competitor's budget, and 3) as projected costs for the sales tasks.**

Essentially, a sales force that produces more is rewarded with increased resources in the future for its past success. A variation on this is to use the sales forecast to establish the budget. This is more acceptable because it looks at the future rather than the past.

The second way to determine the sales budget is through comparison with a competitor's budget. Industry data provide the number of salespeople and sales offices as well as sales expenditures for other companies. The sales budget is then set accordingly. One advantage of this method is that it emphasizes competitive activity in the marketplace. A disadvantage is that it is not based on an understanding of the actual costs of one's own sales activities.

Finally, task-based budgeting looks at the tasks salespeople must perform in order to accomplish objectives. Careful thought is given to each aspect of the sales process and to estimating the associated costs. The items usually considered are salaries, recruiting, training, travel, sales promotion, staff and clerical expenses, dues and supplies.

IMPLEMENTING SALES ACTIONS

Once the sales forecast and budget have been established, sales activity can take place. Sales managers set quotas, measure performance, determine compensation and supervise, coach and motivate the sales organization in such a way that objectives are accomplished.

Quotas

Quantitative objectives used to direct sales force activity and evaluate performance.

Sales Volume Quotas

Unit or dollar objectives, usually set by market segment, product or service line, and average volume per customer.

Quotas   **Quotas** are quantitative performance standards used to direct sales force activity. They also provide a way to evaluate performance. Whereas forecasts estimate results, quotas provide guidelines. They are one of the most important methods sales managers use to set and meet objectives. When quotas are exceeded, the sales force has produced beyond objectives; when quotas are not met, the sales force has fallen short of objectives. Overall, quotas are set in line with the strategic marketing plan. Most sales organizations use one of three types: sales volume, profit or activity quotas.

Sales volume quotas establish unit or dollar objectives. Usually these are set for a market segment, product or service line, and average volume per customer. Typically, a quota for the entire sales organization is determined and then divided among the various sales regions and salespeople. During this process, salespeople and others are likely to provide feedback to sales executives regarding potential in their territory, the level of competition and what goals they think are realistic. That information is combined with the sales forecast.

Sales profit quotas establish profitability objectives for customers, products and market segments. Rather than volume, the focus is on the overall profit that can be made. This kind of quota is particularly important when sales actions such as price negotiations or the ratio of repeat to new customers influence profit. It is also important when different products yield different profits.

Activity quotas encourage salespeople to engage in certain tasks, such as prospecting calls, service calls, sales calls, demonstrations and visiting new accounts. The focus is on customer contacts that will allow the company to implement its overall marketing strategy.

Quotas are generally used to determine some portion of a salesperson's compensation. The simplest procedure is to set the same quota (such as amount of sales) for all salespeople and provide bonuses to those who exceed it. This tends to be inequitable, however, because sales potential and competition are likely to differ from one sales territory to another. Consequently, sales quotas usually vary for different parts of the organization and different salespeople. Compensation is covered in more detail in a later section.

Sales Profit Quotas

Profitability objectives for customers, products, and market segments.

Activity Quotas

Action objectives that encourage salespeople to engage in certain tasks, such as prospecting calls, service calls, sales calls, demonstrations, and visiting new accounts.

Performance Measures

Volume, profit and activity quotas can be combined to measure performance, as shown in Figure 14.13. In this example the quota is based on sales volume, profit margin percentage, number of new accounts obtained, percentage of accounts retained, level of customer satisfaction and number of new leads. Each factor is weighted in terms of importance. At the end of the sales period, the percentage of quota reached in each category is multiplied by the weight

	(1) Weight	(2) Quota	(3) Performance	(4) % of Quota	(5) Contribution to Total Quota: (4) 3 (1)
Sales in dollars	40%	$500,000	$525,000	105%	42%
Profit margin	20%	30%	33%	110%	22%
Number of new accounts	15%	25%	20%	80%	12%
Number of accounts retained	20%	100%	120%	120%	24%
Number of new leads	5%	25%	50%	200%	10%
					TOTAL: 110%

Figure 14.13   Quotas as a Measure of Performance

to determine the contribution of that category to achieving the total quota. In the example, sales are weighted at 40 percent, the quota is $500,000, and performance is $25,000 above that, leading to 105 percent of quota on that item. Multiplying by the weight, we get a 42 percent contribution to the total quota. Notice that when all these items are put together, this particular salesperson achieved 110 percent of quota (exceeded objectives by 10 percent). Performance exceeded the quota in all areas except the number of new accounts.

The performance measurement shown in Figure 14.13 can be used for several purposes. First, this person maintains loyal customers but seems to do little to increase the number of new accounts. The sales manager should discuss the situation to see whether training is needed or whether the territory has minimal potential for new customers. Second, since quotas can be used to motivate the sales force, the salesperson could be compensated for performing so well. Third, although the example provided here focuses on dollar volume, organizations often use this method to emphasize certain products or market segments consistent with their overall marketing strategy and positioning plan.

Compensation

Compensation A well-designed compensation plan should be geared toward the needs of both the company and the sales force. It should be developed with the overall sales strategy in mind. A compensation system not only helps motivate salespeople but is also important in keeping loyal employees. Satisfied employees are less likely to leave the company and will probably work harder to develop loyal customers. It is almost impossible to build customer loyalty with a dissatisfied sales force.

The three basic elements of sales force compensation are salaries, commissions and bonuses. A **salary** is a fixed amount paid regardless of specific performance. Salaries are usually based on education, experience, longevity and overall professionalism. A **commission** is an amount paid in direct proportion to the accomplishment of specific short-term sales objectives. It usually is given for meeting or exceeding a broad range of criteria, including volume and profit by product, or according to customer type and loyalty. A **bonus** is a percentage of salary or fee paid in addition to other compensation for meeting long-term or unique goals. Bonuses are often given to the entire sales team for an outstanding effort, usually quarterly or annually. Compensation plans can be based on salary only, commission only, or both, and sometimes bonuses as well.

Supervision and Coaching

Supervision and Coaching Supervision and coaching are face-to-face interactions between the sales manager and a salesperson. Most managers spend considerable time working with their people in the field. Good managers communicate well and help salespeople determine appropriate sales actions. They provide guidance to keep the sales force operating according to the company's philosophies, policies and marketing plans.

The three components to central coaching are: "supervisory feedback, role modeling and salesperson trust in managers."[34] Essentially, sales coaching occurs when the manager assists in the development of skills. Similar to a voice coach or athletic coach, the sales manager gives advice and demonstrations that enable salespeople to do a better job. Feedback should be objective and balanced, and positive incentives should be used as progress is made. Coaching usually involves visits with customers by the manager and salesperson. The sales manager observes and gives pointers afterward on sales techniques. Good coaches also address all aspects of selling — from time management to customer sales support to interaction with other company employees, sometimes involving role-playing. Henry Mueller, former vice president of new business partnerships at American Express, said: "The sales manager's role is to add value, whether it's with the customer or whether it's helping your salespeople prepare for their next round of sales calls. It's keeping an eye out for those common problems and opportunities that are coming up. ... You're always coaching, coaching, coaching."[35]

There are many appropriate coaching styles, but good coaches usually don't simply take over. They observe, ask questions and listen. They communicate clearly and provide positive reinforcement for the activities that salespeople carry out well. Feedback from sales managers is invaluable because it helps salespeople understand their strengths and weaknesses.

Motivation

Motivation Most top salespeople are motivated by the very nature of the job. They find selling fascinating and want to excel in a competitive environment. Still, good sales managers can add to motivation by providing a positive organizational climate as well as financial and career incentives. Since many salespeople spend little time under direct supervision, the systems for motivation must work well without the constant presence of the sales manager. A positive organizational climate exists when salespeople feel good about their opportunities and rewards. A positive climate also

---

Salary

The fixed amount of compensation paid regardless of performance.

Commission

A form of sales force compensation in which the amount paid is in direct proportion to the accomplishment of specific objectives.

Bonus

A percentage of salary or a fee paid in addition to other compensation for meeting long-term or unique goals

helps salespeople perform at the highest professional level.

Many companies use financial incentives. Money is a strong motivator, but companies are increasingly incorporating different forms of incentives. Carlson Marketing Group's (CMG) employee motivation and loyalty programs include employee rewards to each other, seminars on personal growth and day-care facilities. CMG's program "Ovation" personalizes a sales target for each salesperson, which provides incentive without creating an atmosphere overly competitive with coworkers.[36]

Ethical Issues in Motivation and Compensation

In striving to produce peak performers, sales managers may use several motivational approaches. If they push too hard in the wrong ways, salespeople may be pressured to compromise ethical standards. When performance is poor, rewards may be withheld, or in extreme cases punishment may be used. Proper motivational techniques generally reward people for good performance. A key part of the management job, however, is to establish expectations not only in terms of sales volume but also regarding acceptable behavior. When managers focus exclusively on sales volume objectives, they are telling salespeople that the ends justify the means.

> **Proper motivational techniques generally reward people for good performance.**

This lack of attention to appropriate behavior in combination with pressure to perform can be considered unethical in itself. Let's look at three questionable practices.

- *Family pressure*: Salespeople are required to attend the annual sales meeting with their spouse (and perhaps other family members). Those performing well are rewarded publicly with free trips, gifts or a large bonus. For the others, it is obvious to the family that they are low producers. Essentially, the company is interfering in family relationships with the intent of elevating sales.

- *Peer pressure*: The sales manager broadcasts performance results to all salespeople or, in announcing sales contest winners, points out a few low producers. Rather than private communications between the manager and the salesperson, overt peer pressure is being used to gain behavior changes. This would be like posting student names along with grades in the student newspaper. Is that an ethical way to motivate you to learn? Could this increase the pressure on students to cheat?

- *Termination*: All salespeople are rank ordered, and the lowest performers are asked to leave, even though they may be performing very profitably for the company. This keeps all salespeople pushing for fear of losing their job. Since termination is devastating for most people, to avoid it they may put undue or unscrupulous pressure on buyers.

Even quotas, though less extreme than these scenarios, can be troublesome. They are generally considered useful tools, but some sales managers believe they lead to high-pressure tactics and thus are harmful to relationship building.

OVERSEEING SALES FORCE ACTIVITIES

Once sales operations are in effect, management needs to take the final steps of its process: evaluation and adjustment. Sales activities nearly always can be improved. In fact, some of the strongest sales organizations are very flexible in meeting business challenges and competitive situations, an especially useful attribute in industries subject to rapid change. In general, most evaluation programs look at efforts and results, assess the company's influence in supporting performance, identify problems and opportunities and take corrective action.

Salesperson performance can be evaluated behaviorally or by outcome. Behavioral performance is based on skills and the ability to meet the demands of the job. This includes such aspects as sales presentation, planning, teamwork, relationship selling and technical knowledge. Outcome performance is measured by such customer-related factors as sales volume, market share, customer loyalty and satisfaction and number of new accounts.[37]

In addition to evaluating individual salespeople, managers must regularly assess the entire sales force. This tells whether overall performance is strong. It may result in territory shifts, the addition of people or other adjustments. The process gives both field reps and management an opportunity to learn whether the level of activity has produced the expected results. This often means doing productivity analysis to determine whether sales volumes have been reached, market shares have been accomplished, and the appropriate product mix has been sold to targeted segments. Usually, good evaluation requires looking behind the numbers to determine where the strongest and weakest results occurred and under what conditions.

Today, many companies use 360-degree evaluations; that is, salespeople are asked to evaluate their sales managers as well. This supports the team concept and helps break down the old barriers to joint progress. It is instrumental in helping sales managers improve. Since managerial success depends on working through others, this type of feedback is seen as absolutely critical in many companies.

CHAPTER SUMMARY

Objective 1: Understand how selling evolved to a focus on relationships and what elements are involved in building them.

Personal selling techniques have moved through three distinct modes: the traditional persuasive approach, consultative selling and relationship selling. The latter is strategic in nature and involves developing long-term relationships that are mutually beneficial for buyer and seller. It requires that the selling organization understand the customer's business or lifestyle and treat loyal customers as assets of the firm. Typically this leads to partnering that creates value for the customer and the selling organization. The objective of relationship selling is to create steady profit through customer loyalty and satisfaction. Interactions with customers focus on win-win situations.

Objective 2: Know the responsibilities of salespeople and sales managers.

Most professional salespeople view themselves as the marketing manager of a territory. As such, they are responsible for implementing the company's marketing strategy within the territory. They also communicate company policy to customers and potential customers. They are important sources of feedback and have a responsibility to convey this information to their organization. Salespeople must have excellent ethical judgment since they often operate without much direct supervision, are under pressure to boost volume and have flexibility in what they say to customers.

Sales force management is the marketing function involved with planning, implementing and adjusting sales force activities. First, sales managers work with others in their company to organize the sales force, including its structure, size and type. Second, they develop diverse sales teams through recruiting, selecting and training. Third, they prepare forecasts and budgets. Fourth, they implement actions by establishing quotas, assessing performance, determining compensation and supervising, coaching and motivating the sales force. Finally, they evaluate sales activities and make any necessary changes.

Objective 3: Identify and understand the steps in personal selling.

The seven steps in personal selling are planning, prospecting, organizing information and developing a call plan, approaching a prospect, presenting a case and building relationships, managing objections and closing, and service. Sales planning translates the company's marketing strategy into territory and account plans. Prospecting involves looking for new customers within the company's target markets. Next, sales personnel organize information and develop a call plan. To do this, they learn about prospects and prepare a routing schedule to identify which prospects will be called on and when. The approach is the first formal contact with the customer. The objective is to secure an initial meeting and gain customer interest. The next step is making the case and building relationships. This is done through the sales presentation. Sales personnel then manage objections and close the sale. One of the most important sales skills is the ability to overcome business objections. Closing means getting the first order. Service follow-through is essential for developing customer loyalty.

Objective 4: Learn the characteristics of strong salespeople.

First, strong salespeople are goal-oriented. They use time well, manage their territory efficiently and like to compete to obtain results. Second, they are empathetic; they understand buyer behavior, are customer-focused and possess excellent listening and questioning skills. Third, they have applications knowledge. They are technically competent, know their customers' business and are good at creative problem solving. Fourth, excellent salespeople are ethical and trustworthy; they are honest, seek additional information when they don't know the answer and make reliable partners.

Objective 5: Understand how to develop a diverse sales organization.

Once the sales structure is determined, the sales organization is developed. Diversity is one of the most important aspects of a sales force because of its role in building relationships with multicultural customers. Strong attention must be paid to diversity when recruiting, selecting and training salespeople. Recruitment seeks a pool of exceptional candidates and often takes place on college campuses. Selection is a choice process for the company and candidates alike, as both seek a good match. Training involves educating salespeople about company policies and procedures, product and customer application knowledge, relationship selling skills, territory and account planning, and diversity.

Objective 6: Explore how to implement sales actions, from setting quotas and compensating salespeople to evaluating and adjusting plans.

Implementing sales actions involves several steps. Quotas establish the sales volume, profit and activities expected from each salesperson. They are used to direct action and evaluate performance. Supervision and coaching, which involve working with salespeople to improve performance, build self-esteem and skills. Motivation is also part of the sales manager's job. It depends on a positive organizational climate in which employees feel rewarded for the effort they make. Sales force compensation is developed with the overall marketing strategy in mind. It is designed to support the development of loyal salespeople, who in turn help create loyal customers. Salaries, commissions, and bonuses are used singly or in combination. Several significant ethical issues surround motivation and compensation. Managers must be careful not to use techniques that lead to unethical actions by salespeople. The final step in sales force management is evaluation and adjustment. Organizations must be flexible in order to maintain competitive advantage. This requires an assessment of individual salespeople and each part of the sales organization. Companies are beginning to use 360-degree feedback techniques to evaluate sales managers as well as the sales force.

REVIEW YOUR UNDERSTANDING

1. List several types of personal selling situations. Give an example of each.
2. What is relationship selling?
3. List the responsibilities of a salesperson.
4. What are the seven steps in personal selling?
5. What characterizes a strong salesperson?
6. What does closing mean?
7. Give three reasons why ethics are important to salespeople.
8. What are the five sales management functions?
9. List the types of sales forecasting. Briefly describe each.
10. What are three methods for setting a sales force budget?
11. What are quotas?
12. What is coaching?
13. What are three ethical issues surrounding sales force management?

DISCUSSION OF CONCEPTS

1. What are the key differences among the traditional, consultative and relationship sales approaches? Which do you feel is most appropriate in a majority of circumstances? Why?
2. List the seven types of sales personnel. Under what circumstances would it make sense to have each type?
3. Why is it important for the salesperson to support the company's strategic marketing plan?
4. What is most important about each of the seven steps in personal selling? How do they form a process?
5. Describe some of the ways salespeople find new customers. Under what circumstances might each be appropriate?
6. Do you have the characteristics of a strong salesperson? Do you believe people are born with these, or can they be learned?
7. The job of the sales manager is to support the strategic marketing and communications plan of the organization. What are the key responsibilities of a sales manager?
8. Describe the methods a sales manager can use to set the sales budget. Which one do you feel is most effective? Why?
9. Training is now considered one of the most important factors in developing a strong sales team. What are the four major areas of a training program?
10. Is it acceptable to use family pressure to motivate salespeople? Why or why not?

KEY TERMS & DEFINITIONS

1. **Account planning:**   Establishing sales goals and objectives for each major customer.
2. **Activity quotas:**   Action objectives that encourage salespeople to engage in certain tasks, such as prospecting calls, service calls, sales calls, demonstrations and visiting new accounts.
3. **Approach:**   The salesperson's first formal contact with the potential customer.
4. **Bonus:**   A percentage of salary or a fee paid in addition to other compensation for meeting long-term or unique goals.
5. **Center of influence:**   An opinion leader who can be quickly qualified as a potential customer because of his or her standing in the community.
6. **Closing:**   The point at which the salesperson obtains the first order from the customer.
7. **Cold calling:**   Contacting a lead for the first time.
8. **Commission:**   A form of sales force compensation in which the amount paid is in direct proportion to the accomplishment of specific objectives.
9. **Company sales forecast:**   A prediction of unit or dollar sales for a given period, in total or broken down by product, segments or other categories, and based on the marketing strategy that will be put in place.
10. **Consultative selling:**   An approach to selling in which sales personnel work closely with customers to help solve problems.
11. **Direct sales:**   Sales that result from the salesperson's direct interaction with a consumer or company.
12. **Empathy:**   An interpersonal connection in which the salesperson knows precisely how the prospect feels and communicates that understanding.
13. **Environmental forecast:**   An estimate of the economic, political and social factors likely to affect the level of spending for the types of products or services being forecast.
14. **Follow-up:**   After-sales service to ensure customer satisfaction in order to obtain repeat business.
15. **Industry forecast:**   An estimate of the amount and type of competitive activity that is likely to occur in an industry.
16. **Leads:**   All those who may have need of a company's product.
17. **Missionary sales:**   Sales made indirectly through people who do not obtain orders but influence the buying decision of others.
18. **Negotiation:**   Discussion by two or more parties to arrange a transaction.
19. **Networking:**   Contacting friends, relatives and associates to obtain leads.
20. **Preapproach:**   Preparation by the salesperson for the initial meeting with a prospect.
21. **Presentation:**   A two-way process in which the salesperson listens to the customer to identify needs and then describes how the product will fulfill them.
22. **Prospect:**   A potential customer interested in the seller's product.
23. **Prospecting:**   Looking for potential customers within the company's target markets.
24. **Qualified prospect:**   A potential buyer interested in the seller's product and with the attributes of a good customer.
25. **Qualifying:**   Examining prospects to identify those with the authority and ability to buy the product.
26. **Quotas:**   Quantitative objectives used to direct sales force activity and evaluate performance.
27. **Referral:**   A lead provided by a qualified prospect.
28. **Relationship selling:**   Forging bonds between buyer and seller to gain loyalty and mutual satisfaction.
29. **Routing schedule:**   A travel plan for calling on prospects that is developed to save time and minimize expenses.
30. **Salary:**   The fixed amount of compensation paid regardless of performance.
31. **Sales force management:**   The marketing function involved with planning, implementing and adjusting sales force activities.
32. **Sales force structure:**   The organization of the reporting relationship between sales managers and salespeople.
33. **Sales manager:**   The person responsible for the leadership and management of salespeople in order to accomplish the sales objectives established in the marketing plan.
34. **Sales profit quotas:**   Profitability objectives for customers, products and market segments.
35. **Sales territory:**   All the actual and potential customers, often within a specified geographic area, for which the salesperson has responsibility.
36. **Sales volume quotas:**   Unit or dollar objectives, usually set by market segment, product or service line, and average volume per customer.
37. **Team selling:**   Selling that involves people from most parts of the organization, including top executives, working together to create a relationship with the buying organization.
38. **Telemarketing:**   Making telephone calls to leads provided by marketing services or from other lists.
39. **Territory planning:**   Identifying potential customers, their sales potential and the frequency with which they will be contacted about various products.
40. **Traditional sales approach:**   Emphasizing persuasive techniques to get consumers to buy a company's products.

REFERENCES

1. www.avoncompany.com, website visited July 8, 2014; "Avon's New Business for Reaching Young Women Set to Launch in August 2003," PRNewswire-FirstCall, NEW YORK, March 28, 2003; "Maria Sharapova Named the Face of Avon Luck Fragrances for Him and Her," Avon Press Release, June 11, 2014.

2. "Occupational Employment and Wages News Release," Bureau of Labor Statistics, www.bls.gov, website visited August 10, 2012.

3. www.salary.com, website visited July 10, 2014.

4. "Boeing Commercial Airplanes Achieves 2009 Delivery Target, Maintains Strong Backlog," http://boeing.mediaroom.com, January 7, 2010.

5. "Boeing wins $14.7 billion jet order from United," CNN Money, http://money.cnn.com, July 12, 2012.

6. "2013 Annual Report on Form 10-K" Merck, February 27, 2014.

7. "Live Help," Nordstrom, http://shop.nordstrom.com, website visited July 10, 2014.

8. Boyle, Brett A., "The Importance of the Industrial Inside Sales Force: A Case Study," Industrial Marketing Management, September 1996, Vol. 25, Issue 5, pp. 339-348.

9. "Five Relationship Blunders to Avoid in Your Sales and Marketing," MarketingProfs, www.marketingprofs.com, February 14, 2011.

10. Graham, John R., "Successful Selling: Learn the Customer's Buying Cycle," The American Salesman, March 2000, Vol. 45, Issue 3, pp. 3-9.

11. Chapman, Joe; Rauck, Stephanie, "Relationship Selling: A Synopsis of Recent Research," Developments in Marketing Science, no. 18, ed. Roger Gomes (Coral Gables FL, Academy of Marketing Science, 1995), pg. 163.

12. Del Gaizo, Edward R.; Corcoran, Keven J.; Erdman, David J., The Alligator Trap (Chicago, Irwin Professional Pub) 1996, pg. 21.

13. "Wachovia Chooses to Innovate With Cisco TelePresence," CiscoNews Release, www.newsroom.cisco.com, June 4, 2007.

14. Ellram, Lisa M., "Partnering Pitfalls and Success Factors," International Journal of Purchasing and Materials Management, April 1995, Vol. 31, Issue 2, pp. 35-44.

15. Foster, Dean A., "Negotiating and 'Mind-Meeting,'" Directors and Boards, Fall 1992, Vol. 17, Issue 1, pp. 52-54.

16. "Returns and Exchanges," Urban Outfitters, www.urbanoutfitters.com, website visited July 10, 2014.

17. Astarita, Mark J., "Cold Calling Rules and Procedures," 1995, www.se-claw.com/coldcall.htm, website visited July 10, 2014.

18. Peterson, Roger S., "Go Modular, Be Flexible to Control Exhibit Costs," Marketing News, December 2, 1996, Vol. 30, Issue 25, pg. 11.

19. "Snowy Sunday Brings NAIAS 2014 to Successful Finish," NAIAS News Release, January 26, 2014.

20. "Chicago Auto Show Attendance Record Signals Continued Market Strength," PR Newswire, www.prnewswire.com, website visited July 10, 2014; Chicago Auto Show Press Kit, January 2009, www.chicagoautoshow.com, website visited July 10, 2014.

21. Karen E. Klein, "Wring the Most Out of a Trade Show", Bloomberg Businessweek, April 12, 2012.

22. "Amway reports record sales of USD $11.8 billion," Amway Press Release, http://globalnews.amway.com, February 4, 2014.

23. Rackham, Neil, SPIN Fieldbook: Practical Tools, Methods, Exercises, and Resources (New York, McGraw-Hill) 1996.

24. Ibid, pp. 11-12.

25. Role-playing with executives witnessed by the author.

26. Hawes, Jon M.; Strong, James T.; Winich, Bernard S., "Do Closing Techniques Diminish Prospect Trust?" Industrial Marketing Management, September 1996, Vol. 25, Issue 5, pp. 349-360.

27. Frank Q. Fu, Keith A. Richards, Douglas E. Hughes and Eli Jones, "Motivating Salespeople to Sell New Products: The Relative Influence of Attitudes, Subjective Norms, and Self-Efficacy," Journal of Marketing, Vol. 74 (November 2010), pgs. 20-21.

28. Labich, Kenneth, "Making Diversity Pay," Fortune, September 9, 1996, Vol. 134, Issue 5, pp. 177-179; Wah, Louisa, "Diversity at Allstate: A Competitive Weapon," Management Review, July/August 1999, Vol. 49, Issue 3, pp. 24-30.

29. "How One Enterprise Sales Force Works With Channel Partners to Maintain and Build Sales," Selling Power, June 27, 2012.

30. Moncrief, William C., et al., "Examining Gender Differences in Field Sales Organizations," Journal of Business Research, September 2000, Vol. 49, Issue 3, pp. 245-257.

31. Brewer, Geoffrey; Galea, Christine, "Best Sales Forces: The Top 25," www.fedex.com, website visited June 26, 2010.

32. "2013 Training Industry Report," Training, www.trainingmag.com, website visited July 12, 2014.

33. Honeycutt, Jr., Earl D.; Attia, Ashraf M.; D'Auria, Angela R., "Sales Certification Programs," Journal of Personal Selling and Sales Management, Summer 1996, Vol. 16, Issue 3, pp. 59-65.

34. Rich, Gregory A., "The Constructs of Sales Coaching: Supervisory Feedback, Role Modeling, and Trust," The Journal of Personal Seslling and Sales Management, Winter 1998, Volume 18, Issue 1, pp. 53-63.

35. Brewer, Geoffrey, "Meeting of the Minds," Sales and Marketing Management, November 1996, Vol. 148, Issue 11, pp. 72-74.

36. Kaydo, Chad, "A Motivation Master Class," Sales and Marketing Management, August 2000, Vol. 18, Issue 1, pp. 88-91; www.carlsonmarketing.com, website visited June 27, 2010.

37. Grant, Ken; Cravens, David W., "Examining Sales Force Performance in Organizations That Use Behavior-Based Sales Management Processes," Industrial Marketing Management, September 1996, Vol. 25, pp. 361-371.

Chapter 15

SUPPLY CHAIN MANAGEMENT & CHANNELS

Lbrands

Shopping malls wouldn't be the same without L Brands. With a range of stores including Bath & Body Works, Victoria's Secret, Pink, La Senzam, and Henri Bendel, L Brands sells women's apparel, lingerie, beauty, and personal care products through more than 2,600 stores.

L Brands, like many companies, outsources its manufacturing. Its transformation began by recognizing the need for greater visibility of the supply chain. A supply chain is basically a system of all parties involved in moving a product or service from supplier to customer, including distributors, transporters, storage facilities, and retailers. Visibility pertains to collecting and understanding data, creating intelligence, and improving the process. The company evaluated not only its internal operations but also its global network. .

For retailers like L Brands, it is important to keep the customer focus firmly in mind while developing and implementing a sophisticated supply-chain solution. The first step for L Brands was to change procurement from a transportation-based activity to a tactical one. The company consolidated procurement for its many brands into one function.

The second step was to obtain the right technology. As a result of acquiring many stores and brands, L Brands had a complex assortment of information-technology systems and software, many of them redundant and on different platforms. The company started consolidating IT by integrating its suppliers online so they could all access data. It also gained the ability to track customer information from store to store. The system was user-friendly, easily accessible, high speed, and most importantly, it was contained in a central database. L Brands did not just address the problem of information access; it capitalized on the opportunity to improve all aspects of its business.

Integrating suppliers was no small task for L Brands. It buys merchandise from more than 1,000 suppliers and sells through multiple channels- retail stores, Internet, catalog, and third party. Radio-frequency identification technology will continue to play a significant role in deeper collaboration and transport-cycle reduction time.

Aside from integrating suppliers with technology, L Brands encourages environmental stewardship, inclusion, and moral choices. The core values that drive the company directly correlate the strength of its business model with supply-chain excellence. Believing that effective management is established through the thoughtful procurement of suppliers, L Brands insists on lean and recyclable packaging as well as fuel-efficient transportation from them.

Continually investing in its state-of-the-art supply chain will help L Brands realize its goal to build a family of the world's best brands by offering rewarding customer experiences that drive long-term loyalty and deliver sustained growth. As L Brands Chairman and CEO Leslie Wexner states, "We don't sell products, we sell experiences. We are L Brands. We are a segment leader. Forward thinking. People focused. Responsible. And influential." A supply chain that begins and ends with the customer is key.

<< Bath & Body Works is a staple at most shopping centers

Learning Objectives

1. Understand supply chain management activities and objectives and how they improve business performance.
2. Learn why companies frequently use intermediaries to reach targeted customers.
3. Attain insight into how channel relationships should be managed over time.
4. Appreciate the economic importance of wholesalers.
5. Identify what physical distribution entails and why it is critical for any business organization.
6. Learn the steps in the order management process.

THE CONCEPT OF SUPPLY CHAIN MANAGEMENT AND CHANNELS

Supply chain management helps companies link upstream suppliers of raw materials, components and expertise required to make a product — and all of the downstream distribution of products by wholesalers, retailers and other organizations. Historically, marketers focused primarily on marketing channels used to distribute products. Today, information systems provide the data required to manage the entire supply chain to create outstanding customer value. For example, as soon as you buy a product from Walmart, a supplier from as far away as China knows the product has left the store — and all other members of the chain that produce and ship that product get the same information. This allows the product to be replaced in the quickest and most efficient way possible.

Figure 15.1 illustrates supply chain management and channels in the most elementary way. Notice that supply chain management deals with the total chain, while channels are a very important part of the chain. The idea of a value chain presented in Chapter 6 is useful to discussions about supply chain management. We will use the same idea in this chapter extending it to include the consumer. Channels is included in two places in figure 15.1 because channel strategies are equally important in B2B (business-to-business) and B2C (business-to-consumer) marketing.

It is useful to look at the value chain depicted in Figure 15.2, which shows the linkage of actions performed by suppliers, producers and all channel members to create and deliver value to customers. Members of the value chain extend from the environment, including all of the natural resources, to society, which consumes and disposes of products. Members include extractors, suppliers, OEMs, distributors, providers and users. At each link in the chain, marketing helps connect the specific organizations by forming beneficial relationships. These are the value added interfaces along the chain. The types of organizations that are linked for a particular product form the supply chain for the product's industry. An individual company generally refers to its supply chain as that part of the value chain which is most important to its overall business. In some cases it only refers to upstream elements, but both upstream and downstream members are critical.

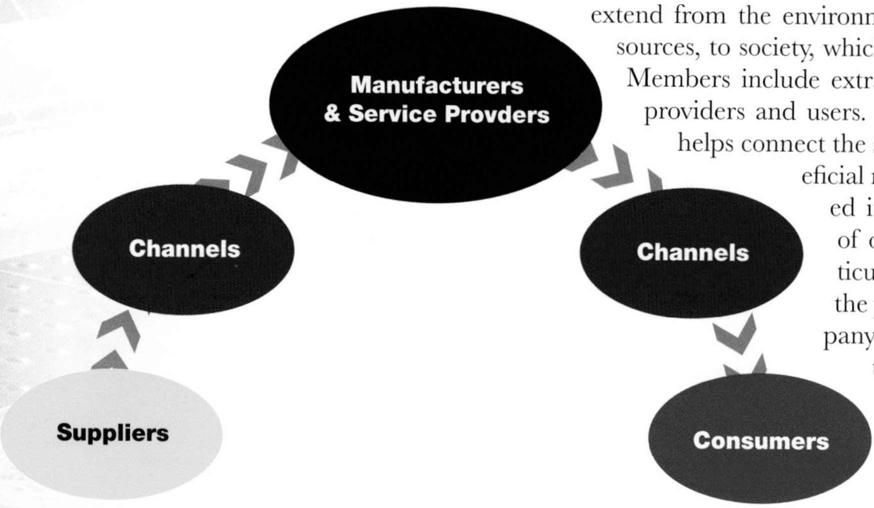

Figure 15.1 Supply Chain Management & Channels

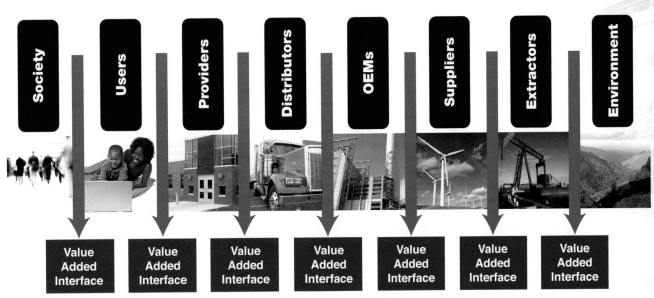

Figure 15.2 Elements of a Value Chain

SUPPLY CHAIN MANAGEMENT, LOGISTICS AND PHYSICAL DISTRIBUTION

Supply chain management incorporates all of the activities concerned with planning, implementation and control of sourcing, manufacturing and delivery for products and services.[2] The development of a network of supply and distribution organizations involved in acquiring and moving products, as well as the flow of information about these activities within and across different firms, is important because these business activities impact customer satisfaction and profitability. First, we will discuss supply chain management. We will then cover integrated logistics management, which deals mostly with the physical management of raw materials, components and finished products. Finally, we will address physical distribution in detail.

SUPPLY CHAIN MANAGEMENT

Excellent supply chain management can typically lower a company's costs by three to seven percent and increase cash flow as much as 30 percent.[3] One important aspect of supply chain management is the development of a supply network. The **supply network** consists of the organizations from which components, semi-finished products and services are purchased. It is important to develop a network of suppliers that can provide the support required to develop excellent products. For example, Ford has a supply network of more than 2,000 companies, not including a large set of independent Ford dealers.

Firms employ different strategies to obtain a competitive advantage in supply chain management; many firms form strategic alliances with suppliers and distributors to optimize performance and increase customer satisfaction.[4] Raytheon, a leading contractor of defense and commercial electronics, uses a program to help its suppliers reduce costs and increase efficiency. This may or may not lead to a larger profit margin for Raytheon, but it invariably results in a lower cost for its end customers, which encourages customer loyalty.[5]

Supply Chain Management

Incorporation of all activities concerned with planning, implementation, and control of sourcing, manufacturing, and delivery of products and services.

Supply Network

All of the organizations from which components, semi-finished products, and services are purchased.

Vertical Integration

Ownership or control of suppliers by a buying company.

Some companies use vertical integration to control the supply chain. **Vertical integration** occurs when a company controls or owns the supplier or customer, which gives the organization a lot of control over the supply chain but is expensive to maintain. General Motors spun off Delphi, the world's largest auto supplier, and Ford spun off Visteon, the nation's second-largest auto supplier. Now General Motors and Ford have no direct management responsibilities for these spin-offs and as a result can focus their attention on other aspects of the company.

Supply Chain Management Activities and Objectives Figure 15.3

shows supply chain management activities, objectives and business performance elements. The activities are movement of products and information management, while objectives include increased efficiency and improved customer service. The resulting business performance improvements are described in the four cells.

Supply Chain Management Objectives

Supply Chain Management Activities

	Movement of Products	Information Management
Low Cost (Efficiency)	Improved profit	More relevant information which improves coordination and decision making
Customer Service (Effectiveness)	Rapid product delivery which improves customer satisfaction and loyalty	Better understanding of customer needs to satisfy unique customer requirements

Figure 15.3 Supply Chain Activities, Objectives and Business Performance Improvements

Business Performance Improvement Overall, there are four types of business performance improvements: decreased costs, which improves profit; more relevant information, which improves coordination and decision making; rapid product delivery, which improves customer satisfaction and loyalty; and better understanding of customer needs to satisfy unique customer requirements.

Activities — Movement of Products and Integration of Information The movement of goods in the supply chain starts with raw materials and ends with the final consumption of the product. An important part of this process is the selection of suppliers. In the case of cereal, the chain would start with the farmer and end with the family that finally consumes the cereal. Information management includes the collection, storage and processing of data from different departments and across firms to provide real-time knowledge of the flow of goods from all sources. It also provides feedback on whether schedules are being met, potential obstacles and their remedies. This information links all parties; therefore, integration provides consumers with what they want, when they expect it, in a location that is most convenient and at a reasonable cost.

Objectives — Efficiency and Customer Service Better efficiency occurs when unnecessary steps are avoided, delays are eliminated and the actions of all companies are coordinated at the lowest cost while supplying the customer with precisely what is intended. Customer service is all of the actions taken to meet customer expectations, including rapid and satisfactory resolution of any problems. A firm that focuses on customer service is dedicated to its customers and their needs. The initial increase in costs to the firm to meet those needs will allow it to capture greater rewards in the future through customer loyalty.

Logistics

The movement of raw materials, components, and finished products within and between companies.

LOGISTICS

Logistics is the movement of raw materials, components and finished products within and between companies. Physical distribution is the part of logistics that involves only finished products. **Integrated logistics management** coordinates all parts of the process. If the movement of inputs is not properly managed, then physical distribution to customers will be hindered. Coordination is equally important when goods move between plants, distribution centers, warehouses, wholesalers and retailers. A firm must excel at integrated logistics management to have superior supply chain management.[6] Integration requires effective communications among companies, departments and people whose decisions affect logistics. Any company is subject to internal problems, and proper communication can address or even circumvent these issues. Salespeople may be so worried about late deliveries that they pad their forecasts. Concern about costs may lead firms to make conservative sales projections. In many companies, the people deepest in the organization and farthest from the customer — production planners — develop the final estimates used to hire workers and build inventory.[7]

Integrated logistics management is only as strong as a company's understanding of its customers and the ability of its people to work together. Cross-functional teams in purchasing, production-warehousing, marketing and sales often produce excellent results. By sharing information on purchasing, production schedules, marketing and sales plans, customer service standards and customer preferences, the team can make logistical decisions that are truly integrated and beneficial to the company. Even without teams, integration can occur if communication from and about customers flows throughout the company in the form of market research reports, sales activity, forecasts and orders. This information can be refined into specific purchasing and manufacturing plans.

Integrated Logistics Management

The coordination of all parts of the logistics process.

PHYSICAL DISTRIBUTION

Physical distribution is the movement of finished products to customers. Although the concept is simple, accomplishing this task effectively and efficiently is often complex. The primary objective of physical distribution is to get the right products to the right locations at the right times at the lowest total cost. An effective distribution system can contribute to customer satisfaction and, in turn, increased sales revenues, while a poor performance will alienate customers and may even drive them to switch allegiance to competitors.[8]

While revenue generation is important, no less significant is careful control of the costs of processing orders, maintaining warehouses, carrying and handling inventory, and shipping products. Physical distribution can account for up to 40 percent of total cost and more than 25 percent of each sales dollar.[9] Achieving high customer service levels at the expense of company profitability makes no sense. Therefore, physical distribution management involves a delicate balance between effective customer service and efficient operations.

Physical Distribution

The movement of finished products through channels of distribution to customers.

> **The primary objective of physical distribution is to get the right products to the right locations at the right times at the lowest total cost.**

Toyota's Lexus division is an excellent example of striking the right balance. The typical car dealer has more than $200,000 in parts inventory, a heavy financial burden. At the same time, stockouts frequently occur. Understanding this, Lexus designed a system that better serves the company, its dealers and its customers. Lexus requires dealers to have AS400 computers and satellite dishes that connect them to company headquarters in Torrance, California. Specialized inventory control software helps dealers keep track of which parts they need on hand. If an item is unavailable in inventory, then it can be ordered electronically one day and received by air freight the next. Although Lexus dealers have only $100,000 tied up in parts inventory, there are few stockouts, and customer satisfaction levels are higher.[10] The system-wide costs of computers, satellite dishes, software and air freight are more than offset by lower inventory costs and increased sales through better customer service.

Order Management refers to how the company receives, fills and delivers orders to customers. The design of the physical distribution system — including order processing, warehousing, materials handling, inventory control and transportation functions — determines how well the company manages orders, as outlined in Figure 15.4. New technologies, such as electronic data interchange and bar coding, have had a remarkable effect on system design, which in turn has improved the effectiveness and efficiency of order management. **Electronic data interchange (EDI)** is an intercompany computer-to-computer exchange of orders and other business documents in standard formats.

Customer service standards will have a major bearing on the design of a physical distribution system. Companies that want high marks on order fill rate, order cycle time, delivery reliability and invoice accuracy must be prepared to invest heavily in network design. Often, managers find they must lower desired standards somewhat because the costs of achieving an ideal level are prohibitive. One approach is to recognize that all customers are not equal. As a general rule, a small percentage of a company's customers, often 20 percent or less, provide over 80 percent of its revenues. This is often called the Pareto Principle, after Italian economist Vilfredo Federico Damaso Pareto, who noticed 80 percent of the land in Italy was owned by 20 percent of the population. After realizing 80 percent of his peas were produced by 20 percent of the pea-pods, he concluded this noteworthy ratio applied to many areas of life.[11] Customer service standards can be set higher for the firm's most important customers. Scarce resources can be saved by lowering customer service standards, at least to some extent, with less important customers.

Order Management

The means by which a company receives, fills, and delivers orders to customers.

Electronic Data Interchange (EDI)

Intercompany computer-to-computer exchange of orders and other business documents in standard formats.

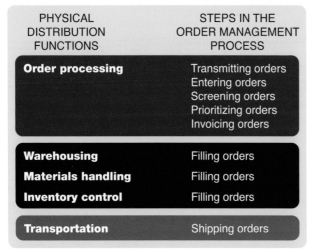

Figure 15.4 Order Management

Order Processing

The distribution of products cannot begin until the company receives an order. Order processing includes all the activities and paperwork involved in transmitting and entering, screening and prioritizing and invoicing orders.

Orders received from customers, channel members or company personnel are entered into the company's record-keeping system. Traditionally, salespeople wrote the orders by hand and delivered them to the office in person or by mail, phone or fax. New technologies have dramatically changed all that. EDI connects many companies directly with customers, who key in the order and submit it electronically, significantly cutting down cycle time. Furthermore, invoices are more accurate, because only the customer needs to enter his or her information. Labor and material costs for printing, mailing and handling paper-based transactions are lower. Companies such as Marshall Industries and Motorola supply their outside salespeople with laptop computers. They can access price information instantly rather than check price lists or call the office. They can enter an order, connect to the Internet and transmit it electronically. Inside salespeople input telephone orders directly into the system. Order cycle time, invoice errors and order-processing costs are all reduced.

Caller ID integrated with computer IT systems enables an inside salesperson to know who is calling before picking up the phone. A variety of information about the caller appears on a computer screen, including payment history and credit information. If a problem is apparent, then the salesperson can notify the customer before entering the order, which saves time on everyone's part. After screening, many companies prioritize orders based on the importance of the customer or the order cycle time requested. For example, often customers can request same-day delivery on orders at a premium price. The computer system transmits these orders to distribution ahead of next-day orders. Bills are prepared once it is known how much of the order can be filled from available inventory.

Warehousing

Warehousing is the storage of inventory in the physical distribution system. Many companies perform this function with a mix of distribution centers and warehouses. **Distribution centers** are where the bulk of a company's finished-goods inventory is maintained before being routed to individual sales outlets or customers. There are two types: **Private warehouses** are fixed costs owned and operated by the company, and **public warehouses** are variable costs -- rented space to store products. Preferences for fixed versus variable costs help determine a company's mix of private and public warehousing.

With technology, many companies can provide better customer service with fewer warehouses. Benetton Group, Italy's integrated fashion manufacturer and retailer, ships 150 million items each year directly to more than 6,000 shops in 120 countries. The company does so with its unique Automated Distribution System. Spanning more than 20,000 square meters, this system can handle 40,000 incoming and outgoing boxes per day and has a total capacity of 400,000 boxes. The Automated Distribution System operates efficiently, employing 24 people to take on what would traditionally require a workforce of 400.[12]

Cross-docking involves sorting and reloading an incoming shipment from a supplier for delivery to customers without its being stored in any warehouse. The method is used most frequently in truck transport. EDI and specialized information systems allow for the close coordination that makes cross-docking efficient. This practice is on the rise because it reduces inventory carrying costs and order cycle time. Furthermore, the fewer times the product is handled, the lower the potential for damage. Jacobson Co. is an example of a transportation company that specializes in cross-docking. The company can build a custom-designed plan for its customers in order to enhance the bottom line.[13] The technique affects warehousing design; larger parking lots are needed for transferring products from truck to truck, and buildings are smaller.

Materials Handling

Materials handling is the moving of products in a warehouse while filling orders. Traditionally, the facility manager would receive the paperwork and assign it to a worker. With a handcart or motorized forklift, the worker would go through the warehouse, picking up products and checking them

Mikael Jansson/Benetton

UNITED COLORS OF BENETTON.

Chloe Nørgaard, the model known for her colorful hair, was selected for a Benetton ad campaign.

Warehousing

The storage of inventory in the physical distribution system.

Distribution Centers

A location where inventory is maintained before being routed to individual sales outlets or customers.

Private Warehouses

A storage facility owned and operated by the company.

Public Warehouses

A storage facility owned and operated by businesses that rent space.

Cross-docking

Sorting and loading an incoming shipment from a supplier for delivery to customers without it being stored in any warehouse.

Materials Handling

The moving of products in and around a warehouse in the process of filling orders.

off on the order forms. If some were unavailable, that would be noted on the form, and the facility would produce a back order, filling and shipping it when a new supply arrived. New technology is significantly reducing the time it takes to find the inventory. Kiva Systems, a Massachusetts-based robotics company, has created small robots that transport inventory shelves to workers. The person processing the order pushes a button, and moments later, the shelf with the needed product is within reach. When multiple robots operate at the same time, products from all corners of the store can be brought to one place simultaneously instead of one worker going through the entire warehouse. Zappos and Walgreens both use these revolutionary and time-saving robots.

Bar codes, radio frequency technology and handheld scanning devices have remarkable effects on materials handling. Bar code labels for identification purposes can be placed on everything from cardboard boxes to plywood sheets. Handheld scanners with display panels receive orders directly from the mainframe computer through radio waves and guide workers to the appropriate locations. Workers then scan in the bar codes to make sure the right product and quantity are selected. If not, the scanner will beep. This system reduces errors and order cycle time, while filling back orders much more quickly. It is a must for any company interested in boosting quality control and customer satisfaction.

RFID, or radio-frequency identification, is one of the most useful automatic identification methods. It is used in supply chain management because it allows users to store and retrieve data remotely, saving them a great deal of time and preventing errors from re-entering data. Volkswagen uses RFID in its supply chain to improve the flow of supplies. The company worked with IBM to strategically place RFID tags in shipping containers. Information is collected by RFID readers at key locations throughout the entire supply chain.[14]

This RFID chip is used by Walmart on label cases and pallets.

Inventory Control

Management of stock levels

Economic Order Quantity (EOQ) Model

A method of determining the amount of product to be ordered each time.

Inventory Control

Inventory control is the management of stock levels. For each product, company management must decide how much inventory will be carried in each distribution center and warehouse. Carrying too little inventory leads to poor order fill rates, too many back orders and poor customer service. Carrying too much leads to higher than necessary costs. Many companies fail because they have too much capital tied up in inventory; this reduces cash flow, which means that bills cannot be paid.[15]

Inventory levels are often determined with the help of the ABC classification approach. Stockkeeping units (SKUs) are divided into three categories based on their sales volume and profitability. Inventory levels are kept relatively high for the A category, moderate for B, and relatively low for C. The trap to avoid is a large inventory of less profitable SKUs purchased by fringe or non-core customers.

Part of inventory control is to determine reorder points and order quantities. A reorder point is the inventory level at which a replenishment order is generated. The standard formula is:

Reorder point = Demand or usage rate x order cycle time + safety stock

In other words, there should be enough inventory to supply customers during the time required to get more stock, plus a margin of safety. More formally, safety stock is the inventory kept on hand in case of forecasting error or delayed delivery of replenishment stock. For example, if the average daily demand rate is 50 units, order cycle time is 4 days, and safety stock is 20 units, then the reorder point is $(50 \times 4) + 20 = 220$ units. Whenever inventory drops to that level, a replenishment order should be made.

The **economic order quantity (EOQ) model** is a method for determining how much product to order each time. It compares ordering costs to inventory carrying costs, with the objective of minimizing total costs. The standard formula is:

$$EOQ = \frac{2 \times CO \times D}{CI \times U}$$

CO = Cost per order
D = Annual sales volume in units
CI = Annual inventory carrying cost
U = Unit cost

The cost per order is calculated by determining purchasing costs, computer costs, and accounts payable costs associated with placing individual orders. Annual inventory carrying costs are calculated by summing expenses associated with warehouse space, insurance, taxes on inventory, obsolescence and shrinkage, materials handling (including wages and equipment) and costs of money invested. The lower the cost per order relative to inventory carrying costs, the lower the order quantity.

The EOQ method should be used only as a guideline. It works particularly well for products with consistent demand patterns throughout the year. For seasonal items or for products on which suppliers give discounts at certain order quantities, EOQ estimates need some adjustment. A just-in-time (JIT) system also skews the EOQ method. In a JIT system, the necessary unit is delivered in the necessary quantity at the necessary time. The fundamental objective is to eliminate waste of all sorts, especially excess inventory. Products are delivered in just enough quantity to cover demand for a short period. Shipments are made frequently and are scheduled precisely; 100 percent delivery reliability is sought because little safety stock is carried. Emphasis is placed on total cost of ownership; per-unit price is less important than the costs associated with extra handling, warehousing and inventory management. JIT requires companies to meet specific deadlines, supply exact quantities and adjust deliveries and quantities to meet changing needs, all with a minimum of paperwork. Strong relationships between the companies, including high trust, are critical to the success of such systems.

Transportation In a physical distribution system, transportation is the movement of goods to channel members and customer locations. It is the largest distribution expense for many manufacturers, especially if heavy, bulky products are involved, since transportation fees are charged by the pound. The cost of transporting weight-training equipment and exercise bicycles, for example, might approach the cost of the equipment itself. Deregulation of the transportation industry increased competition among carriers, which has led to greater efficiency and real cost savings

	Trucks	Railroads	Air	Water Carriers	Pipeline
Transportation cost	high	average	very high	very low	low
Door-to-door service	high	average	average	low	high
Speed of service	high	average	very high	very low	low
Dependability in meeting schedules	high	average	very high	average	high
Availability in different locations	very high	high	average	low	very low
Frequency of shipments	very high	low	average	very low	high
Need for intermodal transfer for door-to-door service	no	often	almost always	often	often
Primary advantage	door-to-door service and speed	low cost for long hauls of bulk commodities	fastest and highest quality	low cost for long hauls of bulk commodities	low cost and dependability

Figure 15.5   Comparison of Different Modes of Transportation

for U.S. manufacturers, wholesalers, retailers and consumers.

The methods for moving products are motor vehicles, railroads, airlines, water carriers and pipelines. Figure 15.5 contrasts the advantages and disadvantages of the various modes of transportation. Managers choose among them based on customer service versus cost trade-offs. Different modes can be used to serve different clients. For example, orders to core customers may go via fast, reliable air service, whereas orders to non-core customers may be delivered by less expensive ground transportation.

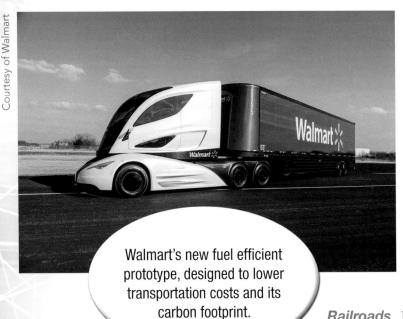

Courtesy of Walmart

Walmart's new fuel efficient prototype, designed to lower transportation costs and its carbon footprint.

Trucks The major advantages of trucks are door-to-door service and speed. Trucks also are dependable and widely available, making frequent shipments possible. Their major disadvantage is cost. Given these characteristics, trucks are ideally suited for high-value manufactured products. Companies can purchase and operate their own fleet of trucks or use the services of independent companies. The trade-offs have to do with level of control and fixed versus variable costs. When uncertainty is high, the use of independents is preferable. Walmart recently debuted a very futuristic truck to improve the overall fuel efficiency of its fleet and lower the company's carbon footprint. Walmart trucks log millions of miles every year, so sustainability and fleet efficiency are taken very seriously by the company.[16]

Railroads Railroads represent the most efficient mode of land transportation for bulky commodities, such as chemicals, coal, grain, iron ore, lumber, sand and steel. Major U.S. railroads haul more than 40 percent of all freight, more than any other mode of transportation. Coal is the most distinct commodity carried by rail, accounting for more than 70 percent of the coal used by power plants.[17] The major disadvantages of railroads are transit time and lack of door-to-door service, although rail spurs can reach some customer locations. Unit trains are known for running back and forth between a single loading point, such as a coal mine, and a single destination, such as a power plant, to deliver one commodity. Leading U.S. companies providing rail transportation include Burlington Northern, CSX and Union Pacific.

Air Transport Air transport is offered by the airlines and cargo service companies. Relative to other modes of transportation, it provides great speed and reliably adheres to schedules. Air is the most costly transportation method, however. Fashion merchandise, fragile and highly perishable items, emergency shipments and expensive industrial goods account for the majority of products shipped as air freight.

Water Carriers Water carriers include transoceanic ships as well as barges used on inland waterways. Their transportation cost is the lowest among the various options. However, they are relatively inaccessible, and only channel members and customers in port cities can be reached directly. Water carriers are used for bulky commodities, such as cement and petroleum. Ore barges, for example, are a common sight on the Great Lakes. This mode also is used to carry mass-produced goods, such as automobiles and toys, overseas.

Pipelines Pipelines transport natural gas and petroleum by land from production fields to refineries. Up to 40 different grades of product can be shipped through the same pipeline simultaneously and separated at destination points. Pipelines are very dependable and offer door-to-door service. They are the least labor-intensive of any mode, and maintenance expenses are low. They can be used only for a narrow range of products, however, and delivery speed — less than five miles per hour — is slow.

Intermodal transportation **Intermodal transportation**, the combination of two or more modes in moving freight, is gaining popularity. The objective is to exploit the major advantages of each. Piggybacking truck trailers on rail cars, for example, joins the benefits of long-haul rail movement with the door-to-door service of trucks. Express delivery often uses trucks and air to rush shipments from source to destination. Federal Express, the pioneer in overnight delivery, has developed a thriving business running transportation services for such clients as National Semiconductor, Laura Ashley and Vanstar. Other companies offer a variety of intermodal options. For example, CNF Transportation, headquartered in Palo Alto, California, owns and operates Conway Transportation Services, which focuses on trucking services, and Emery Worldwide, which offers global air freight, ocean transport and air charter.

Intermodal Transportation

The combination of two or more modes in moving freight.

CAREER TIP!

Texas Instruments, a leader in semiconductor and computer technology, is a Fortune 500 company, ranked by Fortune Magazine as a Top 100 Company to work for, and on AMR Research's Supply Chain Top 25. Job opportunities range from engineering and technical marketing to finance and accounting; they even have a tool that helps you find the career that's the best fit for your skills and interests. Check out current employment listings and benefits of a career at Texas Instruments, and learn more about the company, at http://:///careers.ti.com.

The transportation modes used by companies are sometimes influenced by laws and government pressure. Some companies use three-wheeled motorbikes for deliveries in Shanghai, China, because truck use is restricted during daylight hours. New York City, Tokyo and many metro areas have strict laws about truck deliveries because of extreme traffic congestion. Many companies use bicycles to deliver products in Europe because of pollution concerns, and a few cities in the United States have begun delivering goods this way for the same reason.

New technologies are having a major influence on transportation. Progressive trucking companies install on-board computers in vehicles. UPS, which provides transportation services to companies globally, gives its drivers electronic data that informs the driver exactly where to go, which route to take, and how much time to spend getting there.

Satellite communication systems also have an important role, providing a fast and high-volume channel for information movement around the globe. Many companies use a real-time global positioning system in their fleets of delivery trucks. The drivers and dispatchers can contact each other while the truck is in transit, and dispatchers always know where a truck is on the delivery route. The real-time interaction provides up-to-date information to customers regarding location and delivery time. Furthermore, dispatchers can redirect trucks in response to need or traffic congestion. Federal Express, UPS, Roadway and DHL are among the many companies that track shipments electronically to ensure that all customers remain fully informed about deliveries.

Efficient Consumer Response (ECR) Programs

Programs to improve the efficiency of replenishing, delivering, and stocking inventory in the distribution channel, while promoting customer value.

Efficient Customer Response **Efficient consumer response (ECR) programs** are designed to improve the efficiency of replenishing, delivering and stocking inventory while promoting customer value. Enhanced cooperation among channel members in order to eliminate activities that do not add value is a primary goal. A study found that excellent ECR could yield as much as $24 billion in operat-

ing cost reductions and $6 billion in financial savings. Potential savings ranged from about three percent for manufacturers to 12 percent for retailers.[18]

Traditionally, retailers and wholesalers have used professional buyers to decide what and when to order from suppliers. Suppliers frequently offered buyers price deals. Forward buying became commonplace: a large order for a product at a special price per carton and then a long delay until the next order, which resulted in inconsistent order patterns for manufacturers and general uncertainty. Because of inefficiencies, stockouts occurred much too frequently, even though inventory levels for many products were high throughout the channel.

ECR requires a change in the roles played by channel members. Wholesalers and retailers give up some of their buying authority. On a daily basis, they send information on stock levels and warehouse shipments to their suppliers over EDI networks. Personnel in the supplier organizations use this information to decide what and when to ship. Order quantities are determined with the objectives of providing sufficient safety stock, minimizing total logistics costs and eliminating excess inventory in the channel. Before shipments go out, wholesalers and retailers can review and edit orders if they desire via EDI. Fewer special prices are offered by suppliers to reduce the incentive for forward buying, which is disruptive to ECR. Instead, everyday low pricing may be used.

If administered effectively, ECR can reduce inventory costs and stockouts in the channel. Furthermore, wholesalers and retailers can reduce the number of professional buyers they employ, since suppliers assume more ordering responsibilities.

GLOBAL PHYSICAL DISTRIBUTION

Any challenge that domestic business presents is multiplied when taken abroad. Uncertainty increases because of greater transport distances, longer lead times and complex customs requirements and trade restrictions. The most important factor from a physical distribution perspective, however, is a country's infrastructure, which influences how products are stored and transported.

Due to its extremely high economic growth rate, China is now the world's second-largest economy after the United States. Many foreign companies have established supply relationships with China. The Chinese government has spent billions of dollars building and updating road and rail access, as well as water treatment plants. Moreover, the government has established very advanced e-commerce and business-to-business links, making China a huge market opening for non-Chinese businesses.

Freight Forwarders

Service companies specializing in the movement of cargo from one point to another, often country to country.

Of course, a major challenge for many companies is moving products into other countries. Organizations will often use cargo specialists, or **freight forwarders**. Domestically, they pick up partial shipments at the customer location, consolidate all of these into truckload or carload size, and arrange for delivery at destination points. Their gross margin is the difference between the rates they charge customers and what they pay carriers. Many exporters rely on freight forwarders to handle the documentation, insurance and other aspects of delivery abroad. For example, they ensure that letters of credit are issued at the buyer's bank and properly transferred into the seller's

account. Leading global freight forwarders include Nippon Express and Kintetsu World Express (Japan), Schenker (Germany), Lep International and MSAS (United Kingdom) and Burlington Air Express. The trend in air freight has been consolidation into a few large companies.

Regardless of geographic location, the ultimate goal of distribution is to make the product readily available to the consumer or end user. For the majority of consumer products, this has traditionally meant delivering goods to the retail outlets where consumers shop. Today, however, direct marketing — including sales via the Internet — is a growing force in consumer as well as business-to-business sales.

MARKETING CHANNELS

A **marketing/distribution channel** is a set of interdependent organizations that help make a good or service available for purchase by consumers or businesses. The distribution channel serves to connect a manufacturer, such as Coach, or a service provider, such as AT&T, with consumers or users. In simple terms, a distribution channel is a pipeline or pathway to the market.

Distribution channels are needed because producers are separated from prospective customers. Mattel's star product, Barbie, is made available to consumers in countries around the world through a host of different retail establishments. Walmart, Toys "R" Us and Target account for nearly 45 percent of Mattel sales.[19] These retailers are members of Mattel's distribution channel, and they are customers of Mattel.

Mattel brings back the 1966 classic game of boxing robots, sold through Walmart, Toys "R" Us and Target.

A distribution channel consists of at least a producer and a customer. Most channels, however, use one or more intermediaries to help move products to the customer. **Intermediaries** are independently owned organizations that act as links to move products between producers and the end user. The primary categories are brokers, wholesalers (distributors) and retailers. **Brokers** do not purchase the goods they handle but instead actively negotiate their sale for the client. A familiar example is real estate brokers, who negotiate the sale of property for their customers. Companies have more control over the activities of brokers, including the final price to the customer, because brokers do not own the goods they sell. **Wholesalers** (also referred to as distributors) take title to products and resell them to retail, industrial, commercial, institutional, professional or agricultural firms, as well as to other wholesalers. A good example is Ingram Micro Inc. The company, based in Santa Ana, California, is the world's largest technology distributor and logistics company for the IT industry worldwide. With approximately 190,000 customers, Ingram Micro distributes to retailers such as Walmart, Staples and Office Depot.[20] **Retailers** take title to products for resale to the ultimate consumer. These range from discounters such as Walmart and large department stores to specialty chains such as Victoria's Secret and local boutiques.

Marketing/Distribution Channel

A set of interdependent organizations that help make a good or service available for purchase.

Intermediaries

Independently owned organization that acts as a link to move products between the producer and the end user.

Brokers

A firm that does not take title to the goods it handles but actively negotiates the sale of goods for its clients.

Wholesalers

A firm that takes title to products for resale to businesses, consumers, or other wholesalers or distributors.

Retailers

A firm that takes title to products for resale to ultimate consumers.

CHANNEL STRUCTURE, DYNAMICS AND FUNCTIONS

Direct Channels

A distribution channel in which the producer uses its own employees and physical assets to distribute the product directly to the end user.

Indirect Channels

A distribution channel in which the producer makes use of independent organizations to distribute the product to end users.

Channel Levels

The number of distinct units (producers, intermediaries, and customers) in a distribution channel.

Direct and Indirect Channels
There are two fundamental types of channels. In **direct channels** (also called integrated channels) companies use their own employees (i.e., salespeople) and physical assets (i.e., warehouses and delivery vehicles) to serve the market. For example, IBM's sales force sells information technology systems directly to large companies such as Bank of America. Sherwin-Williams owns and operates a majority of the outlets where its paint is sold. In **indirect channels** (also called nonintegrated channels) companies make use of independent agents to serve markets. General Motors sells aftermarket components through a variety of channels such as independent parts distributors, auto body repair shops and independently owned dealerships.

Distribution channels can be described by the number of **channel levels** or the number of distinct units (producers, intermediaries and customers) in a distribution channel. A direct channel has two levels: the producer and its targeted customers. Indirect channels are longer, with at least three levels. Figure 15.6 illustrates common channel arrangements for consumer goods, business-to-business goods and services.

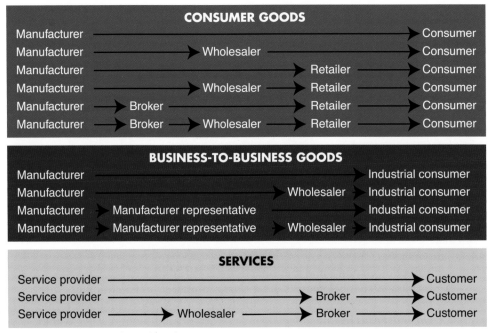

Figure 15.6   Common Channel Configurations

Companies must decide whether to use direct channels or intermediaries. Direct channels are more attractive when the following conditions apply:

- Customers and orders are large, especially if concentrated in a few geographical areas.

- Resource constraints are not severe.

- Environmental uncertainty is low to moderate.

- Investments in direct distribution will produce a high return.

- Significant value-added activity is required in the channel, including specialized investments.

- Customers prefer or demand to deal directly with manufacturers, Walmart being a prime example.

Many markets are simply too small to make it economically feasible for companies to establish a direct channel. Consider independently owned convenience stores, whose average order from a company such as Procter & Gamble would be tiny relative to supermarket or discount chains. The manufacturer's costs of selling, processing orders and delivering products to mom-and-pop stores would be larger than the revenues generated. The problem is intensified because convenience stores are so geographically dispersed.

Intermediaries assemble merchandise from a variety of manufacturers and sell in smaller lots at a regional or local level. Therefore, an order from a small convenience store represents a relatively larger sale to a wholesaler than to an individual manufacturer. Moreover, wholesalers often have greater cost efficiencies than manufacturers due to their smaller size (lower overhead) or proximity to customers (lower selling and logistics costs). The result is that wholesalers can make money serving smaller customers whereas manufacturers cannot. The same rationale applies to retailers. Figure 15.7 shows that four manufacturers selling directly to 10 retailers would need to make 40 contacts to conduct business, compared to four contacts if they do business with one wholesaler, who in turn makes 10 contacts with the retailers for a total of 14. Establishing each contact requires resources, so this is a significant difference.

Intermediaries tend to require less of the company's resources. They make investments in inventory, offer credit to customers and manage accounts receivable. They also pay for sales personnel and other employees, allowing the producer to avoid these costs. More and more companies such as General Electric, Intel and Texas Instruments are relying on the use of intermediaries rather than company-owned or direct channels.

The use of intermediaries is attractive to companies when it is difficult to make accurate predictions about the future. This lowers the risk level for the company because the intermediary is sharing the investment burden. Adapting to change is also easier, since companies have less fixed investment and, therefore, more financial flexibility. For instance, if a company owns its own warehouse facilities and the economy flounders, the company incurs a significant toll dealing with building, equipment and personnel costs.

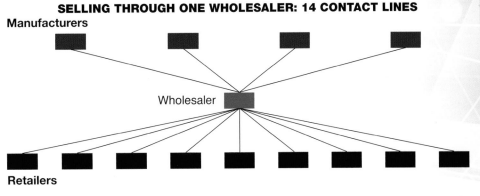

Figure 15.7   Contractual Efficiency
Source: Louis Stern, Adel El-Ansary and Anne Coughlan, Marketing Channels, 6th ed. © 2001.

Multiple Channel Systems

Often, manufacturers want to connect with customers in as many ways as possible. **Multiple channel systems** make use of more

Multiple Channel Systems

The use of more than one channel to access markets for the same product.

Reverse Channel

A distribution channel that flows from the end user to the wholesaler or producer.

Conventional Channel System

A channel system in which efforts to coordinate the actions of channel members are seen as unimportant.

Vertical Marketing System (VMS)

A system in which channel members emphasize coordination of behaviors and programs.

Administered Channel System

A vertical marketing system in which channel members devote effort to coordinating their relationships.

Contractual Channel System

A vertical marketing system in which relationships among channel members are formalized in some fashion, often with a written contract.

Retail Cooperative

An alliance of small retailers for wholesaling purposes.

Wholesaler-Sponsored Voluntary Chain

A group of retailers who have been united by a wholesaler.

Franchise System

A type of distribution channel in which the franchiser holds the product trademark and licenses it to franchisees who contract to meet certain obligations.

than one channel to access markets for the same product. For example, Ben & Jerry's distributes its premium ice cream through company-owned stores, wholesalers that resell to supermarkets and convenience stores, and franchised outlets. Most distribution channels flow from the manufacturer to the end user, but goods sometimes move in the opposite direction. A **reverse channel** flows from the end user to the wholesaler or the manufacturer. An example is the recycling of bottles and cans.

CHANNEL ALIGNMENT

In a **conventional channel system,** efforts to coordinate actions are seen as unimportant by channel members. Loosely aligned and relatively autonomous manufacturers, wholesalers and retailers bargain aggressively with one another over each transaction.[21] Once a deal is reached, there is not much concern about what others in the channel are doing. Most giftware, furniture and motion pictures move through conventional channels, where channel members tend to follow traditions.

In contrast, **vertical marketing systems** (VMS) are networks that emphasize channel coordination. VMS have grown in importance over the past two decades, as more and more companies realize that customer satisfaction is impossible without efficient and effective distribution. There are three types of VMS: administered, contractual and corporate.

Administered Channel Systems
Members of an **administered channel system** coordinate with others in the channel and facilitate activities. Marketing programs, such as cooperative advertising and sales training, are developed and offered to channel members.[22] Black & Decker, General Electric and Sealy (the mattress company) are among the manufacturers known for their administered channel systems. Among retailers, Walmart is among the heaviest investors in coordinating relationships with suppliers. The Internet has selling spaces in which companies and wholesalers can develop strong relationships, such as the shopping sites in Yahoo! or America Online. When channel members have roles that are rather complex and challenging, greater coordination is needed.

Contractual Channel Systems
In a **contractual channel system**, relationships are formalized, often with a written contract. Retail cooperatives, wholesaler-sponsored voluntary chains and franchises are three common forms.

A **retail cooperative** unites a group of small retailers into a wholesaling operation to increase buying power. Compare a hardware retailer who buys 20 Black & Decker power drills a year to 100 stores that buy 2,000. Obviously, the group will have more clout in negotiating price. Ace Hardware and SERVISTAR are major retail cooperatives. The grocery industry is a common ground for cooperatives, such as Associated Grocers and Topco Associates.

In a **wholesaler-sponsored voluntary chain**, a wholesaler takes the initiative to unite a group of retailers. Again, enhanced buying power is the main objective. Such channels are prominent in the automotive accessory market (Western Auto), the grocery trade (Independent Grocers Alliance, Red and White, and Super Value), and the hardware arena (Pro, Sentry). More than one-third of all U.S. pharmaceuticals used each day are delivered by McKesson Drug Co., a wholesaler of pharmaceuticals and health-care products.[23]

In a **franchise system**, a formal contract ties the franchiser to franchisees. The franchiser holds the product trademark and licenses it to franchisees. They pay royalty fees and promise to conform to standards and guidelines laid out in the contractual agreement. This usually covers such issues as the fees required, rights and responsibilities of both parties, transfer of the franchise and grounds for termination.

There are two types of franchise systems. In product and trade-name franchising, the franchisee acquires some of the identity of the franchiser. Automobile dealerships, gas stations, motorcycle dealerships and soft-drink bottlers are a few examples. Business format franchising involves not only the product and trademark but also the entire business concept — marketing, strategy, training, merchandising and operating procedures.[24] This is especially prevalent in the service arena: fast-food restaurants (McDonald's and Burger King), hotels and motels (Holiday Inn), diet programs (Nutrisystem), real estate (Century 21), travel services (Uniglobe) and vehicle rental (Hertz).

About 760,000 franchise outlets in the United States account for more than $1.5 trillion in annual sales. About 40 percent of all U.S. retail sales flow through a franchise system, and a new franchise is opened every eight minutes of every business day.[25] Business format franchising is growing at a particularly phenomenal rate. U.S. franchisers have been very successful in establishing indirect channels in global markets. For example, Coca-Cola has a long relationship with independent franchised bottlers in each market, who buy the syrup concentrate and then carbonate, package and sell the product to retailers. Its anchor bottlers, a breed of regional intermediaries, have deep local ties, huge capital budgets and finely tuned distribution systems. On a broader scale, McDonald's has developed an excellent program for recruiting and developing a diverse mix of franchisees.

Coca-Cola has a long relationship with independent franchised bottlers.

©istockphoto.com/koshtu

In a **corporate channel system**, the corporation runs and operates organizations at other levels in the channel. It is very similar to a direct channel, and great emphasis is placed on coordinating activities.

Corporate Channel System

A vertical marketing system in which a company owns and operates organizations at other levels in the channel.

INTENSIVE, SELECTIVE AND EXCLUSIVE DISTRIBUTION

The number of locations through which a company sells its products in a given market area is an important strategic consideration. There are three strategic options. **Intensive distribution** uses many outlets in each geographical area. **Selective distribution** uses several outlets per area. **Exclusive distribution** uses only one outlet in each trading area.

The choice is driven to some extent by the nature of the product. Many consumer and business-to-business products are relatively low in price and are purchased frequently, requiring little value-adding activity in the channel. Commonly referred to as convenience goods, they require intensive distribution. Numerous sales outlets per trade area will minimize travel time and acquisition costs for customers. Examples are most brands of coffee, detergent, chewing gum, motor oil, soft drinks and toilet tissue. Other products, referred to as shopping goods, require some search on the part of the customer. Different brands are compared on price, quality and other features at the time of purchase. Selective distribution is appropriate for these goods, which include bicycles, cameras and motorcycles. Finally, specialty goods, or luxury items, have unique qualities that induce high customer loyalty. Since people are willing to exert considerable effort to find and purchase them, exclusive distribution can be used.

The brand strategy of the company also will influence the decision. Different brands of the same product can have widely differing distribution patterns. High-priced brands that are intended to be high in quality require more selective distribu-

Intensive Distribution

Making the product available through every possible sales outlet in a trade area.

Selective Distribution

The use of a limited number of sales outlets per trade area.

Exclusive Distribution

Distributing a product through only one sales outlet in each trading area.

CREATING & CAPTURING VALUE THROUGH *Technology*

UPS: Logistics To Shrink The World

The United Parcel Service was founded in the U.S. in 1907 as a messenger company. Striving to enable commerce around the globe has led UPS to become the world's largest package delivery company and a leading global provider of specialized transportation and logistics services. Presently, UPS manages the flow of goods, funds and information every day in more than 200 countries and territories worldwide.

UPS is constantly working to increase efficiency while making moves to decrease its environmental impact as the booming company grows. UPS uses RFID (radio frequency identification) technology to automatically identify goods by simply scanning a tag. RFID allows UPS to track items at every stage of the supply chain, while allowing customers to track their packages online.

One of the goals in package process management, according to its VP, Mark Hopkins, is addressing the question, "How can we simplify these tasks?" Instead of relying on the memory and experience of its drivers, UPS now tries to rely more on technology that provides greater access to the most relevant information. Drivers carry a delivery information acquisition device, or DIAD, that contains the day's itinerary and displays the most efficient route for each stop. The resulting routes shaved 28.5 million driving miles from UPS' 95,000 vehicle fleet while minimizing idle time in left-turn lanes, which saved three million gallons of fuel and 69 million pounds of carbon emissions. This system saves the drivers time, the company money and the environment large amounts of carbon emissions. Other green ventures include offering carbon offsets on packages to customers at five cents per package and setting an ambitious goal to cut an additional 20 percent of carbon emissions from its airborne fleet by 2020. Furthermore, UPS recently announced it has deployed 245 new delivery trucks powered by compressed natural gas in Colorado and California, a number that it intends to expand.

A significant and sometimes overlooked part of UPS is its service sector, which helps other businesses run their companies more efficiently. UPS Supply Chain Solutions offers a full range of small package, freight and health-care shipping options to aid in efficient shipping and supply-chain consolidation. UPS Supply Chain Solutions also allows companies to outsource its supply chain tasks such as repairs and assembly. For instance, UPS is responsible for packaging Nikon cameras along with their corresponding instruction manuals and accessories. And when you send your Toshiba laptop in for repair, engineers at UPS Supply Chain Solutions are the ones repairing it. Services like these have sped up the turnaround for repairs and have resulted in customer satisfaction. Although largely invisible to end consumers, this UPS subsidiary gains approximately $9 billion annually along with its freight service, while representing an opportunity for its clients to become faster, more efficient and more competitive.

www.ups.com, website visited January 13, 2014; "Demystifying RFID in the Supply Chain," UPS Supply Chain Solutions White Papers, United Parcel Service of America, Inc., www.upsconsulting.biz; Schwartz, Ariel, "For Pennies, UPS Offers Carbon Offsets for Your Packages," Fast Company, www.fastcompany.com, October 6, 2009; Dillow, Clay, "UPS Sets High-Flying Efficiency Goal for Airliner Fleet," Fast Company, www.fastcompany.com, July 7, 2009; James, Geoffrey, "The Next Delivery? Computer Repairs by UPS," CNN Money, July 4, 2004.

tion, because broader markets may be swayed by lower-priced competitors.[26] Generally, the more prestigious the brand, the fewer the number of outlets used by the manufacturer.

When a company uses independent wholesalers and retailers in its channel system, selective and especially exclusive distribution breeds considerable loyalty. For example, Caterpillar uses only 178 independently owned dealers worldwide. They are like extensions of Caterpillar, willing to support the company in any way they can. Recently, Caterpillar recognized that many of its dealers have been missing important new opportunities, which it believes is costing the company between $9 and $18 billion. Because of this, Caterpillar is giving dealers until the end of the year to develop a three-year plan identifying how they will capture those lost sales.[27]

Companies that use independent intermediaries must be careful in moving from a selective to a more intensive strategy. The loyalty of traditional channel members can quickly vanish. For example, Vidal Sassoon hair care products used to be distributed only in beauty salons. When the company decided to distribute through major supermarket and drugstores, the salons dropped the line in a flash. Calvin Klein sued licensee Warnaco for selling goods bearing his name to discount outlets such as Costco; he was trying to prevent his own brand from being devalued in a similar fashion. Wider distribution is also likely to invite price competition, reducing profit margins of current channel members.

STRATEGICALLY MANAGING CHANNEL RELATIONSHIPS

Companies must think strategically about relationships with intermediaries. Interdependence, trust and support are important elements in managing channel relationships. Figure 15.8 outlines these guidelines for channel management.

Interdependence Each channel member depends to some degree on other channel members to achieve desired goals. This need is high when a large amount of a channel member's sales and profits can be attributed to the arrangement.[28] High interdependence means that each has the potential to influence the decisions of another. Gaining attention and support is easier in that case because each party has a vested interest in continuing the relationship. For example, Pepsi and Walmart have a highly dependent relationship, and both commit considerable effort and resources to ensuring that it works smoothly.

When a channel relationship is unbalanced, one firm is more dependent on the other for success, granting a power advantage to one of them. If the producer has the advantage, then the buyer is likely to be very receptive to its salespeople and their plans. In the semiconductor industry, Intel has that kind of power over wholesalers such as Arrow Electronics and Hamilton-Hallmark. When the supplier is dependent, because a particular buyer purchases the majority of its output, for instance, the supplier must be willing to make concessions. The buyer is likely to demand very low prices.

When dependence is low for all parties,

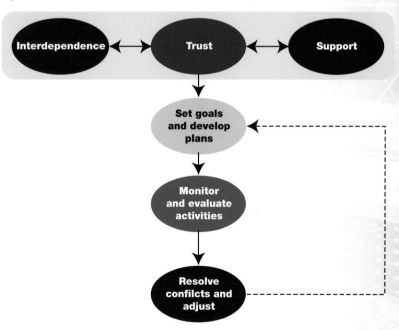

Figure 15.8   A Process for Managing Channel Relationships

each lacks power in the channel relationship, and they are unlikely to offer each other much support. Therefore, producers need to establish channel systems in which the dependence of associated firms is reasonably high.

Trust Another important factor in channel relationships is trust, or confidence in the reliability and integrity of channel members.[29] High trust is the belief that another's words and promises can be relied upon. Each member of the channel relationship has no need to question others' credibility, so coordination is much smoother. Lack of trust creates serious problems. When Anthony Conza, a cofounder of Astor Restaurant Group, discovered he was losing the trust of many of his 600 Blimpie franchisees, he responded by improving communications. He established a franchisee advisory council, a newsletter called No Baloney News and a toll-free hot line for franchisees. These changes increased trust — as well as sales growth and franchisee satisfaction.[30]

Support A company may lack power with an intermediary because of low dependence, but it can grab attention with the right kind of support. Cooperative advertising is a common means. The producer reimburses intermediaries for expenses when they submit proof of the ad along with media invoices, if the ad meets certain standards. For example, motorcycle manufacturers do not reimburse dealers if ads mention more than one brand. For eligible ads, half the expense is normally reimbursed, although limits are set on the amount per year, which are ordinarily based on the intermediary's percentage of annual sales for a product. Many manufacturers supply prepared advertising material to ensure quality.

Another form of support is to invite intermediaries to sales conferences to mingle and attend sessions devoted to new products or marketing techniques. Although some business is conducted at these events, the main purpose is to socialize and build personal relationships. As another way to foster goodwill, many companies help fund sales conferences sponsored by intermediaries. Support also may be offered through inventory management and sales training programs, hotlines and toll-free numbers.

Set Goals and Develop Plans Channel management is facilitated when members meet formally to set joint goals and develop plans for the coming year. This works best when interdependence and trust are high. During these sessions, intermediaries make a commitment to a set of goals, often including accounts and products that will get special emphasis. Specific business plans are developed regarding the activities and investments intermediaries will make to help achieve the goals. At the same time, the producer agrees to assist intermediaries through support programs and marketing efforts.

Monitor and Evaluate Performance Once the business plan is in place, company sales personnel must keep abreast of the marketing and selling efforts of each intermediary. Deviations from the plan must be noted. How well the intermediary is doing in reaching the goals established must be constantly evaluated.

For example, McDonald's has company personnel visit franchisee locations and order food as a regular customer. They rate the facility on a variety of dimensions, including friendliness of the staff, quality of the food and cleanliness. Similarly, Holiday Inn evaluators stay overnight and rate performance. Monitoring such as this gives a company leverage in channel relationships.

Conflict Resolution Channel conflict occurs when members disagree about the course of their relationship. It often arises due to business pressures, policy changes and the use of coercion. Some conflict is inevitable. Channel members recognize that some policies will not be changed and get on with their business. Sometimes company sales personnel can help by explaining policies to intermediaries. In other cases, companies recognize they made a mistake and try to correct it.

LEGAL AND ETHICAL ISSUES IN CHANNEL MANAGEMENT

U.S. antitrust laws and other regulations designed to promote competition and consumer welfare affect distribution practices. Legislation in other countries varies widely.

Resale Price Maintenance Resale price maintenance is an attempt by companies to compel channel members to charge certain prices. The practice is illegal when title to the product changes hands. Since wholesalers and retailers normally purchase the products they sell, they can charge any price they choose. If manufacturers cross the line between persuasion and coercion, then legal problems can arise. For example, a manufacturer should never threaten to take a product line away if prices are not raised.

Collusion among channel members to pressure a wholesaler or retailer to charge higher prices is against the law, so company personnel should never consult with channel members to find out whether any are discounting prices. They also should not solicit the support of intermediaries in persuading another channel member to maintain a certain price level.

Differential Pricing and Support Programs A company must give prices and support programs on proportionally equal terms to competing channel members unless two conditions are met. First, a price differential is justified if it costs less to serve one channel member versus another. Costs are usually lower in dealing with large distributors and retailers due to economies of scale, so quantity discounts are justified in those cases. Second, variations are legal if they are required to meet a competitive offer.

Companies can provide differential pricing and support programs to intermediaries who are not in competition. For example, a computer manufacturer can charge one price to a local wholesaler in San Diego and another to a local wholesaler in Seattle. Whether this makes good business sense is another matter.

Territorial and Customer Constraints A territorial constraint exists when a company assigns an intermediary a specific geographic area in which to sell its products. That is, it can sell there but nowhere else. Such constraints are legal, as they are seen as protecting the investment of all neighboring intermediaries who sell the company's products.

A class-of-customer constraint is a company limit on the customer groups to which an intermediary can sell its product. For example, a manufacturer of medical equipment may direct a wholesaler to sell to physicians and nursing homes in New York City but not to hospitals. This constraint is illegal, as the courts have found that it limits competition and harms consumer welfare. A company is allowed to suggest that an intermediary focus on certain targets: "We are looking for you to cover primarily these customer groups."

Exclusive Dealing Exclusive dealing occurs when a company restricts intermediaries from carrying competitive lines. Such constraints are legal, unless they are proved to be a substantial limit on competition in the marketplace. Furthermore, terminating intermediaries for failure to perform can be difficult if exclusive dealing is a requirement. The intermediary may have passed up opportunities to add other lines and may be very dependent on the channel relationship as a result.

Exclusive Dealing

Restricting intermediaries from carrying competitive lines.

Tying Arrangement

The purchase of a superior product is conditioned on the purchase of a second product of lower quality.

Full-line Forcing

Requiring intermediaries to carry and sell the company's complete line.

Tying Arrangements and Full-Line Forcing   A **tying arrangement** exists when a company conditions the purchase of a superior product on the purchase of a second and less desirable product. For example, a copier company may refuse to sell a high-quality machine unless the customer buys a service agreement. Such arrangements are illegal.

Full-line forcing occurs when a company requires intermediaries to carry and sell its complete line. This practice has been generally upheld in the courts, especially when it is common within an industry. It may be challenged, however, if it entails quantities to be purchased and inventory levels to be maintained. It also may be challenged as an illegal tying arrangement if it involves unrelated product lines.

Intermediary Termination   In many channel systems, agreements commonly allow either party to terminate the relationship with 30 days' notice. In franchise systems, contracts are more complex. Whatever the case, companies need to document the reasons for termination. Usually, the intermediary fails to meet standards or is a poor credit risk. The termination may be challenged if based on intermediary noncompliance with illegal restraints on trade.

Ease of termination varies considerably by state. Wisconsin has a very strict law. If a company's product comprises 12 percent or more of an intermediary's sales volume, then the company cannot terminate it. This has led many manufacturers to establish direct channels in Wisconsin, though they generally use indirect channels elsewhere.

Ethics   It is illegal for companies to impose certain constraints on channel members. Other practices may not be against the law but are ethically questionable. For example, franchisers often confront the issue of how close to place outlets. Market coverage improves with a greater number, but existing franchisees may be hurt. They have committed time and money to building their business, and they do not want to be crowded out by competition from their own company.

Another ethical issue arises when companies set territorial constraints and then choose to ignore them. They lack the courage to confront large intermediaries for selling outside their assigned territory. Such intermediaries often claim they will drop the product line and switch to competitors if they cannot broaden their market area.

Every company must take a deep look at itself. Competitive pressures aside, what is good, ethical business practice and what is not must be carefully spelled out to all employees. Companies must recognize that short-term sales increases make no sense if they weaken existing channel members. To maintain the integrity of the entire channel system, companies must enforce policies and terminate violators.

CHAPTER SUMMARY

Objective 1: Understand supply management activities and objectives, and how they improve business performance.

Supply chain management involves acquiring suppliers and moving products, as well as the flow of information about these activities within a firm and across different firms. The movement of goods in the supply chain starts with raw materials and ends with the final consumption of the product. An important part of this process is the selection of suppliers. Information management includes the collection, storage and processing of data from different departments within and across firms to provide real time knowledge of the flow of goods from all sources. The objectives of supply chain management are low cost and customer service. Business performance improvements include better profit, more relevant information, rapid product delivery and better understanding of customers.

Objective 2:   Learn why companies frequently use intermediaries to reach targeted customers.

Indirect channels involving independent intermediaries are frequently used, especially when the targeted market is small and geographically dispersed, companies face severe resource constraints, environmental uncertainty is high, the anticipated return from investments in direct channels is low, the level of value-added activities is low, and customers prefer dealing with intermediaries. Deciding whether to use direct or indirect channels in foreign markets is especially challenging, but culture, market structure, entrenched channels and legal regulations have a significant effect on the choice.

Objective 3: Attain insight into how channel relationships should be managed over time.

Coordinating relationships within the distribution channel is a challenge. The company must think strategically and develop a management plan. Interdependence, trust and support will influence the success of coordination. Joint goal setting and planning, monitoring, the use of influence, conflict resolution and performance appraisals are steps that need to be taken.

Objective 4: Appreciate the economic importance of wholesalers.

Wholesalers are intermediaries who take title to the products they carry and make the majority of their sales to businesses. Wholesalers purchase large amounts of merchandise from a variety of suppliers and offer it for resale in smaller quantities. They often provide credit, extensive information on product benefits, training on product use, and technical assistance. They are needed because small to medium-sized companies in many industries do not buy in sufficient quantity to deal directly with manufacturers. Many large companies also buy from wholesalers because of convenience, lower personnel costs and better customer service.

Objective 5: Identify what physical distribution entails and why it is critical for any business organization.

Physical distribution, the movement of finished products through channels of distribution to end customers, entails order processing, warehousing, materials handling and transportation. The primary objective is to get the right product to the right customer location at the right time at the lowest total cost. Physical distribution management involves a delicate balance between effective customer service and efficient operations. Order fill rate, order cycle time, delivery reliability and invoice accuracy are four commonly used measures of customer service proficiency.

Objective 6: Learn the steps in the order management process.

Order management is concerned with how the company receives, fills and delivers orders to customers. New technologies have dramatically changed the way orders are transmitted, entered, screened, prioritized, invoiced and filled. Many orders are now sent electronically. Handheld scanners with display panels often are used by warehouse workers in filling orders. There are automated distribution centers with mechanized picking equipment controlled by computers in conjunction with conveyor systems. Inventory control is essential to assure maximum fill rates at minimum cost. In transporting orders to customers, the major advantage of trucks and airplanes is speed, but they are relatively costly. Railroads and water carriers are the most efficient modes for the movement of bulky commodities. Gaining in popularity is intermodal transportation, the combination of two or more modes in moving freight. Efficient consumer response programs attempt to eliminate activities that do not add value in distribution channels. Wholesalers and retailers give up some of their buying authority. They send daily information via EDI to their suppliers on stock levels and warehouse shipments. Personnel in the supplier organization then decide what and when to ship.

REVIEW YOUR UNDERSTANDING

1. What are intermediaries? List three primary categories of intermediaries.
2. What is a reverse channel? Give an example.
3. What is a conventional channel system? Give an example.
4. What do members of an administered channel system do?
5. List three common forms of contractual channel systems. Briefly describe each.
6. What are the guidelines for managing channel relationships?
7. What is a wholesaler? Briefly explain why wholesalers are important.
8. What is integrated logistics? What is physical distribution? Name the primary objective of physical distribution.
9. What is order management? Name a technological advance that has improved its effectiveness and efficiency.
10. What is warehousing? Name two types of distribution centers.
11. What is economic order quantity? What is its formula?
12. List five modes of transportation used in a physical distribution system.
13. What is efficient consumer response?
14. Name an important factor in global physical distribution.

DISCUSSION OF CONCEPTS

1. What is a distribution channel? Why are distribution channels so important to companies and consumers?
2. How do direct channels differ from indirect channels? Under what conditions are indirect channels preferred to direct channels?
3. Why do channels vary in length or number of levels? What are multiple channels? Why are they being relied on by more and more companies today?
4. What are vertical marketing systems? Discuss the three types of VMS.
5. Describe the three distribution intensity options available to companies and give examples of each.
6. What is interdependence? Why is it such an important concept in managing channel relationships? What role do support programs play in the distribution channel?
7. Explain how conflicts can be resolved in channel relationships.
8. What is EDI? How is it influencing the effectiveness and efficiency of order processing?
9. Explain how bar codes, radio frequency technology and scanning devices are improving the effectiveness and efficiency of the materials handling function.
10. How are efficient consumer response programs changing the way business is conducted between manufacturers and retailers?
11. What is the major challenge to integrated logistics management? How can companies overcome this challenge?

KEY TERMS & DEFINITIONS

1. **Administered channel system:** A vertical marketing system in which channel members devote effort to coordinating their relationships.
2. **Broker:** A firm that does not take title to the goods it handles but actively negotiates the sale of goods for its clients.
3. **Channel levels:** The number of distinct units (producers, intermediaries and customers) in a distribution channel.
4. **Contractual channel system:** A vertical marketing system in which relationships among channel members are formalized in some fashion, often with a written contract.
5. **Conventional channel system:** A channel system in which efforts to coordinate the actions of channel members are seen as unimportant.
6. **Corporate channel system:** A vertical marketing system in which a company owns and operates organizations at other levels in the channel.
7. **Cross-docking:** Sorting and loading an incoming shipment from a supplier for delivery to customers without its being stored in any warehouse.
8. **Direct channel:** A distribution channel in which the producer uses its own employees and physical assets to distribute the product directly to the end user.
9. **Distribution center:** A location where inventory is maintained before being routed to individual sales outlets or customers.
10. **Distribution intensity:** The number of locations through which a company sells its product in a given market area.
11. **Economic order quantity (EOQ) model:** A method of determining the amount of product to be ordered each time.
12. **Efficient consumer response (ECR) programs:** Programs to improve the efficiency of replenishing, delivering and stocking inventory in the distribution channel, while promoting customer value.
13. **Electronic data interchange (EDI):** Intercompany computer-to-computer exchange of orders and other business documents in standard formats.
14. **Exclusive dealing:** Restricting intermediaries from carrying competitive lines.
15. **Exclusive distribution:** Distributing a product through only one sales outlet in each trading area.
16. **Franchise system:** A type of distribution channel in which the franchiser holds the product trademark and licenses it to franchisees who contract to meet certain obligations.
17. **Freight forwarders:** Service companies specializing in the movement of cargo from one point to another, often country to country.
18. **Full-line forcing:** Requiring intermediaries to carry and sell the company's complete line.
19. **Indirect channel:** A distribution channel in which the producer makes use of independent organizations to distribute the product to end users.
20. **Integrated logistics management:** The coordination of all logistical activities in a company.
21. **Intensive distribution:** Making the product available through every possible sales outlet in a trade area.
22. **Intermediary:** Independently owned organization that acts as a link to move products between the producer and the end user.
23. **Intermodal transportation:** The combination of two or more modes in moving freight.
24. **Inventory control:** Management of stock levels.
25. **Logistics:** The movement of raw materials, components and finished products within and between companies.
26. **Marketing/distribution channel:** A set of interdependent organizations involved in making a good available for purchase.
27. **Materials handling:** The moving of products in and around a warehouse in the process of filling orders.
28. **Multiple channel systems:** The use of more than one channel to access markets for the same product.
29. **Order management:** The means by which a company re-

ceives, fills and delivers orders to customers.

30. **Physical distribution:** The movement of finished products through channels of distribution to customers.

31. **Private warehouse:** A storage facility owned and operated by the company.

32. **Public warehouse:** A storage facility owned and operated by businesses that rent space.

33. **Retailer:** A firm that takes title to products for resale to ultimate consumers.

34. **Retail cooperative:** An alliance of small retailers for wholesaling purposes.

35. **Reverse channel:** A distribution channel that flows from the end user to the wholesaler and producer.

36. **Selective distribution:** The use of a limited number of sales outlets per trade area.

37. **Supply chain management:** Incorporation of all activities concerned with planning, implementation, and control of sourc-

ing, manufacturing, and delivery of products and services.

38. **Supply network:** All the organizations from which components, semi-finished products and services are purchased.

39. **Tying arrangement:** The purchase of a superior product is conditioned on the purchase of a second product of lower quality.

40. **Vertical Integration:** Ownership or control of suppliers by a buying company.

41. **Vertical marketing system (VMS):** A system in which channel members emphasize coordination of behaviors and programs.

42. **Warehousing:** The storage of inventory in the physical distribution system.

43. **Wholesaler:** A firm that takes title to products for resale to businesses, or other wholesalers or distributors, and sometimes consumers.

44. **Wholesaler-sponsored voluntary chain:** A group of retailers that have been united by a wholesaler.

REFERENCES

1. References: "A Clothes Call," Baseline. New York: April 2006, Vol. 1, Iss. 57; pg 1; William Hoffman, "Managing a Logistics Makeover," Traffic World. Newark: February 6, 2006. Pg 1; Lamont Wood, "Adding Visability to the Demand Chain," Chain Store Age. New Your; May 2006; www.limitedbrands com, site visited August 16, 2012.

2. Bowersox, Donald J.; Closs, David J.; Cooper, M.B., Supply Chain Logistics Management, (McGraw-Hill), 2009.

3. Ibid.

4. Bowersox, Donald J.; Closs, David J.; Stank, Theodore P., 21st Century Logistics: Making Supply Chain Integration a Reality, Council of Logistics Management, 1999, pg. 6.

5. Reeves, Collin, Raytheon, from a talk given on March 12, 2001, at Michigan State University.

6. Bowersox, Donald J.; Closs, David J.; Cooper, M.B., Supply Chain Logistics Management (McGraw-Hill), 2009.

7. Shapiro, Benson; Rangan, V.K.; Sviokla, John, "Staple Yourself to an Order," Harvard Business Review, July/August 1992, pp. 113-122.

8. Bowersox, Donald J.; Closs, David J., Logistical Management.

9. Stern; El-Ansary; Coughlan, Marketing Channels, pg. 119.

10. Reichheld, Frederick F.; Teal, Thomas; The Loyalty Effect; The Hidden Force Behind Growth, Profits, and Lasting Value, (Harvard business school press) 2001, pg. 263.

11. Bryan Eisenberg, The Pareto Principle: Applying the 80/20 Rule to Your Business, www.clickz.com, March 11, 2002.

12. "Distribution," Benetton Group, www.benettongroup.com, website visited July 13, 2014.

13. "Cross Docking," Jacobson Companies, www.jacobsonco.com, website visited July 13, 2014.

14. "Volkswagen drives RFID use through its supply chain," Computing. Co.UK, www.computing.co.uk, March 24, 2009.

15. Graham, Distributor Survival; Reichheld, Frederick F.; Teal, Thomas, The Loyalty Effect; The Hidden Force Behind Growth, Profits, and Lasting Value, (Harvard business school press; 2001), pg. 25B.

16. "Walmart Debuts Futuristic Truck," Walmart Press Release, March 26, 2014.

17. "Overview of America's Freight Railroads," American Association of Railroads, April, 2014.

18. Stern, El-Ansary, and Coughlan, Marketing Channels, pg. 119.

19. Hoover's Company Records, July 13, 2014.

20. Ingram Micro, www.ingrammicro.com, website visited July 13, 2014.

21. Davidson, William, "Changes in Distribution Institutions," Journal of Marketing, January 1970, pg. 7.

22. Rosenbloom, Bert, Marketing Channels, 8th ed., (Cincinnati, South-Western College Pub.), February 1, 2007.

23. www.mckesson.com, website visited July 13, 2014.

24. Coughlan, Anne; Anderson, Erin; Stern, Louis W., Marketing Channels, 7th ed., (Upper Saddles River, NJ, Prentice Hall), December 29, 2005.

25. International Franchise Association, www.franchise.org, website visited July 13, 2014.

26. Frazier; Lassar, "Determinants of Distribution Intensity."

27. James B. Kelleher, "From dumb iron to Big Data: Caterpillar's dealer sales push," Reuters, March 20, 2014.

28. Gundlach, Gregory; Cadotte, Ernest, "Exchange Interdependence and Interfirm Interaction: Research in a Simulated Channel Setting," Journal of Marketing Research 31, November 1994, pp. 516-553.

29. Morgan, Robert; Hunt, Shelby, "The Commitment-Trust Theory of Relationship Marketing," Journal of Marketing 58, July 1994, pp. 20-38.

30. Touby, Laurel, "Blimpie Is Trying to Be a Hero to Franchises Again," BusinessWeek, March 22, 1993, pg. 70.

Chapter 16

RETAILING
DIRECT MARKETING
& WHOLESALING

Retail giant IKEA has a retailing formula geared for growth. Its concept of "offering a wide range of well-designed, functional home furnishing products at prices so low that as many people as possible will be able to afford them," has over 590 million annual visitors purchasing more than $26 billion in products each year. As one of the world's top furniture retailers, IKEA sells home furnishings in 40 countries. To keep prices affordable, IKEA uses flat packaging and customers assemble the products at home. There are more than 330 IKEA locations worldwide, with 38 in the U.S., and their average size is 300,000 square feet, roughly five football fields.

Targeting the global middle class, IKEA has found success by creating a culture built for a community of trendy shoppers. Using clever promotions, IKEA creates a frenzy with each new store opening, becoming a global phenomenon. Before the Atlanta opening, IKEA managers accepted essays from local customers describing why they thought they deserved $2,000 in store vouchers. Five winners would each receive $2,000, but only after they lived in the store for three days before the opening. IKEA's press generated enough buzz to draw in even more shoppers than expected on opening day.

The company continues to expand around the world; it recently asked India for permission to begin retail operations and plans to invest $1.9 billion in the nation. IKEA also expects to expand operations into China and Russia.

IKEA's commitment to the environment has aided its impressive growth. The company uses renewable, biodegradable products whenever possible. It's very selective in obtaining timber, refusing to buy materials logged from intact natural forests and from others it considers to have high conservation value. Unused wood from the creation of one product is used in the production of other ones. IKEA also promotes energy-efficient light bulbs, which use 80 percent less energy than traditional incandescent lights and last up to 10 times longer. IKEA's "Bag the Plastic Bag" campaign aims at reducing the use of plastic bags in stores by 50 percent. The company charges five cents for every "throw-away" plastic bag and donates the proceeds to American Forest, a nonprofit conservation organization.

Selling products through its huge superstores is not the only way IKEA reaches its target market. Catalogs are used as a primary marketing channel, produced in 27 different languages and distributed to more than 198 million homes worldwide. IKEA also uses the Internet effectively to reach even more potential customers.

IKEA has achieved success in the U.S. market despite early challenges. Steen Kanter, a former IKEA employee, said, "We got our clocks cleaned in the early 1990s because we really didn't listen to the consumer." U.S. managers were not paying close enough attention to details. "Americans want more comfortable sofas, higher-quality textiles, bigger glasses, more spacious entertainment units," says Pernille Spiers-Lopez, head of IKEA North America. There is no doubt, with revised products in the U.S. and closer attention to other regional markets, consumers will continue to make IKEA one of the most successful retailers in the world.

The company is also planning to launch a chain of 150 budget hotels across Europe. The chain will incorporate the IKEA philosophy of "good quality at a reasonable price," said Harald Muller, Business Development Manager of Inter IKEA's Holding Services. In order to enter the market, IKEA teamed up with Marriott, to create a brand called Moxy. In a press release announcing the brand, a Marriott executive clarifies that Moxy was created for "the next generation traveler, not only Gen X and Y but people with a younger sensibility." [1]

<< IKEA has over 590 million visitors a year

Learning Objectives

1. Appreciate the important role retailers play in our economy and society.
2. Understand strategy issues confronted by retailers when making marketing decisions.
3. Recognize the diverse array of retailers that compete with one another.
4. Learn what direct marketing entails, its value, and how it differs from mass communication.
5. Be familiar with the different types of direct-response media.
6. Understand the marketing decisions made by direct-marketing companies.
7. Know the different types of wholesalers and the distinct roles they play.

THE CONCEPTS OF RETAILING, DIRECT MARKETING & WHOLESALING

www.ikea.com

Check out how IKEA effectively sells on the Internet by visiting its website. Also learn how the company uses innovative packaging to reduce waste!

Retailing, direct marketing and wholesaling touch our lives daily. Retailing is involved whenever you purchase a burger at McDonald's, select a cell phone at Verizon or buy a pair of jeans at The Gap. Direct marketing is involved whenever you receive a catalog from IKEA, watch QVC on TV, or place an order for Maroon 5's latest single on iTunes. Wholesalers enter the picture by supporting retailers and direct marketing with product assortments that match the needs of the vast array of target customers. Retailers, direct marketers and wholesalers help connect us with the goods and services that support our diverse lifestyles.

Operating a retailing organization in today's fast-paced world is challenging. Competition is intense, with different types of sellers vying for many of the same customers. Retailers must make decisions about target markets, service levels, pricing, merchandise assortment, store locations, image and the use of direct marketing, among other things. They must stay abreast of new technologies that affect the efficiency and effectiveness of store operations. Increasing numbers of retailers are entering into exciting global markets.

More and more companies like Apple and Best Buy are using direct marketing to connect with customers. Direct marketing plays an important role in selling to consumers as well as in the business-to-business market. As technologies continue to advance, direct marketing will increase in importance.

Wholesalers are important because they take title to products from a broad range of manufacturers and sell them to retailers and direct marketers. They help retailers and direct marketers by delivering products where and when needed to satisfy their customers' requirements.

RETAILING

Retailing

The activities involved in selling of products to end users for use and consumption by the purchaser.

Retailing refers to the selling of products to end users for use and consumption by the purchaser. It does not include the sale of products to other resellers, which is the domain of wholesaling. Best Buy sells primarily to consumers, while retailers like Staples have a large business clientele. Home Depot does significant business with each group. Typically, a retailer is a firm that makes the majority of its sales to consumers, although many also sell to small businesses. Home Depot sells a large percent of its volume to independent contractors such as builders, painters, plumbers and electricians. Many discounters and warehouse clubs sell to small businesses as well, such as restaurants and small independent stores. OfficeMax and Staples are also examples of retailers that have a significant amount of sales to business customers.

Retailers generally use direct mail and catalogs to supplement their store sales. Texas-based Neiman Marcus sends out a Christmas Book every October to its credit card customers. Over the years it has included exotic products such as camels, his-and-her airplanes, mummy cases, windmills and submarines. A study by technology and market research firm Forrester projects that online retail sales will reach $327 billion in 2016. Clearly, it is a key part of most retailing businesses.[2] Companies can increase customer profits through add-on services that encourage multi-channel shopping. For example, customers who order a product online but pick it up at a store location are exposed to multiple services and therefore expected to be more satisfied.[3]

THE IMPORTANCE OF RETAILERS

Retailers are vital to our economy. Retail sales in the United States represent about two-thirds of our gross domestic product annually. Retailing also is one of the largest U.S. employment industries — about 14.4 million people work in retailing.[4]

Retailing is the final stage in the distribution channel for the majority of products sold to consumers...everything from chewing gum to insurance to automobiles. As retailing practices develop and become more refined, better products are provided to consumers at better prices in more creative ways. Retailers perform a variety of functions described in Figure 16.1 that increase the value of products to consumers. Similar to wholesalers, they play two critical roles in the mix of goods. They perform an allocation function by purchasing products in large quantities from suppliers (manufacturers, wholesalers, or brokers) for resale to consumers in smaller quantities. They also perform an assortment function by purchasing merchandise from a variety of suppliers and offering it for sale in one location. Therefore, retailers make a broad variety of goods available to consumers in amounts they can afford and effectively handle.

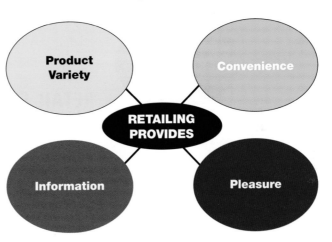

Figure 16.1 Functions of Retailing

Although packaged goods such as cereal, detergent, milk and toothpaste are purchased off the shelf by consumers, retailers still provide information about such products through advertising, displays and unit prices posted on the shelves. Other consumer products, especially durable goods and services such as insurance, require retailers to use salespeople who can provide information and answer questions about product benefits.

Well located stores increase the convenience of shopping for customers through physical locations and integrated web-based e-tailing. Furthermore, many retailers facilitate transactions by investing in scanner technology and offering credit. They also may customize products, as do clothing retailers who alter suits or insurance agents who develop specialized packages. Repair services are provided by retailers such as Sears, Best Buy and Radio Shack.

Without retailers, acquiring basic necessities would be difficult in terms of both time and money. Retailers bring convenience to customers by supplying them time, place, possession and form utilities.

Some manufacturers, such as Sherwin-Williams in the paint industry and Liz Claiborne in the apparel industry, own their outlets, at least in part. Others sell directly to consumers, bypassing retailers. For a majority of consumer good manufacturers, however, retailers are essential for product distribution. Most producers cannot afford to access consumer markets themselves. Their capital is tied up in operations, and it makes no sense for even large manufacturers such as Procter & Gamble to open up outlets. Retailers do this for them, investing in land, buildings, fixtures and personnel. Furthermore, retailers typically take title to the goods they resell, incurring the inventory carrying costs and sales risks otherwise held by the manufacturer. Retailers often sell goods to consumers on credit, assuming the risks associated with accounts receivable and bad debts, and many facilitate credit card purchases, shifting risk and payment services to credit card companies. Retailers also promote the products they carry. In other words, they make it economically feasible for manufacturers of consumer goods to operate.

Wheel of Retailing

A descriptive theory about how retailers emerge, evolve, and sometimes fade away.

The **wheel of retailing** is one way to describe how retailers emerge, evolve and sometimes fade away. According to the theory, new retailers locate their no-frills stores in low-rent areas to keep costs down. When they experience success, they add more services, move to more expensive real estate, upgrade facilities and raise prices. This makes them vulnerable to new low-price entrants, and the wheel goes round and round. If a retailer carefully develops and implements a strategy to satisfy its target market, it can escape the wheel. Upgrading services, locations and prices is justified only if that is what the target market demands.

RETAIL STRATEGY

The steps in formulating a retail strategy are shown in Figure 16.2. Invariably, successful retailers have a sound retail strategy.

Target Markets and Positioning Like any business, retailers must understand their customers to be truly successful. As a first step, they carefully analyze the general market and decide the segment or segments to target. For example, Autozone, based in Memphis, is an auto parts retailer that targets lower-income consumers who repair their own cars. Nordstrom's, headquartered in Seattle, is a department store chain that targets middle- to high-income households desiring superior service. Wet Seal Inc., based in Foothill Ranch, California, operates 532 apparel stores in 47 states and Puerto Rico with a target market of young women ages 13 through 18.[5]

Whatever the overall targeting strategy, individual outlets may face different mixes of customers. The primary trade area is the geographic territory in which the majority of a store's customers reside. The trade area can vary in circumference from less than one mile for a convenience store to 20 miles for a specialist such as Toys "R" Us. Each store manager must understand primary trade areas and operate ac-

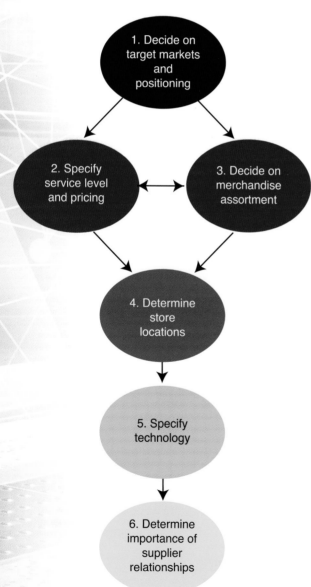

Figure 16.2 Developing a Retail Strategy

cordingly. For example, Walmart uses AC Nielson and census information to locate stores in areas with large multicultural populations and tailors merchandise for these locations specifically to the customer base.[6]

Retailer positioning is the mental picture consumers have of the retailer and the shopping experiences it provides in relation to competitors. Retailers decide what image they want to establish with customers — high prestige, superior service, friendly atmosphere, low prices, etc. Then they must determine how to instill this image in the minds of their customers. Decisions on service level and pricing, merchandise assortment, and store location all influence the retailer's image.

Service Level and Pricing

There are three different strategies that relate to service level and pricing, and which one a company chooses to use is influenced by its target market and positioning. Many retailers follow a discount-oriented strategy, offering products and service of acceptable quality at low prices. The objective is to keep service costs and overhead down in order to make prices competitive. Lucky Stores is a supermarket chain in southern California that offers low prices and few amenities. Walmart and Kmart have a discount-oriented strategy. Crown Books offers a standard 10 percent discount in addition to discounts up to 40 percent on New York Times hardback bestsellers.

A service-oriented strategy emphasizes quality products and value-added functions with prices to match. It is successful to the extent that this is what the target market wants. In the jewelry business, Italian jeweler Bvlgari offers unique jewelry, and its well-trained sales force caters to the specific needs of each customer. Nordstrom is well known in the Northwest for its quality of service, such as ironing shirts for customers immediately after purchase. A store's environment can also contribute to its success in competing against large competitors.

Other retailers follow a hybrid strategy, combining quality products, value-added services, and low pricing in some manner. Autonation, Carchoice and Carmax offer huge inventories of used cars marked with low, no-haggle prices. Their stores have such amenities as child care centers, coffee bars and touch-screen computers. The well-known booksellers Barnes & Noble offers more services than just selling books. The stores also feature coffee shops, sell music and toys, have special promotions and host in-store special events. The company also offers the Barnes & Noble membership program to enhance customer loyalty and distinguish Barnes & Noble from its competition.[7]

Merchandise Assortment

Retailers must take great care in deciding what merchandise to offer. Those with the right assortment have greater sales revenues and customer satisfaction. Merchandise breadth, the variety of product lines offered, and merchandise depth, the number of products available within each line, must be determined. Department stores have considerable breadth but only moderate depth, while retailers such as Best Buy have limited breadth but great depth.

A **scrambled merchandising** strategy means that the product lines carried seem to be unrelated. The goal is to facilitate one-stop shopping for customers and achieve competitive advantage. For example, Kmart introduced "Super Kmart" stores to combine its traditional goods with typical supermarket products. Meijer, a chain in the Midwest, has used this strategy since its inception.

Part of the assortment of many retailers is **private label merchandise**. JCPenney's St. John's Bay jeans and Sears' Canyon River Blues jeans are two examples. Private labels are especially common in the apparel, food, home appliance and drug industries. In apparel, private labels serve to build the image of the retailer rather than the manufacturer. Ann Taylor and Gap have taken this a step further, designing, manufacturing and marketing their own products in their own stores. Private label sales are growing quickly in supermarket chains that feature their own products. Notice the Kroger brand orange juice placed next to the popular Tropicana brand with the prices clearly displayed. Once supermarket retailers realized custom-

Scrambled Merchandising

A retail strategy that entails carrying an array of product lines that seem to be unrelated.

Private Label Merchandise

Products with brand names owned by the retailer.

ers would buy private label products if they believed they were of good quality, the quality and marketing of these products improved. A Nielsen Company study shows that private label sales in U.S. supermarkets total about $77 billion, 15.9 percent of total sales.[8] Globally, private label products represent more than 20 percent of grocery sales and are expected to grow to 30 percent by 2020.[9]

Store Location The location decision is very important for any retailer. Among other things, it affects how convenient shopping will be for customers. The target market dictates the choice to some degree. Autozone, for example, places its stores directly in low-income neighborhoods.[10] In contrast, specialty toy stores and clothing boutiques locate in well-to-do suburbs or high-end urban shopping districts such as the Gold Coast Magnificent Mile in Chicago. The location decision can be a source of competitive advantage if it preempts competitors from moving to an area with high sales and profit potential. Walmart's strategy was to establish stores in small towns that could not support more than one large discount operation. It froze out competition while building a strong sales base. Once it had this firm foundation, Walmart spread to larger suburban areas.[11]

> The location decision can be a source of competitive advantage if it preempts competitors from moving to an area with high sales and profit potential.

Some retailers use a destination location strategy; that is, stores are put in low-rent areas off highways and some distance from other retailers. Because the store is off the beaten path, consumers make it their destination when they want to shop there. In contrast, a competitor location strategy puts stores near those of major competitors, rationalizing that more consumers drawn to the area results in more likely to shop at any store there. Wherever you find McDonald's you are very likely to see Burger King. Diamond merchants cluster along 47th Street in New York City, antique stores line the Place du Grand Sablon in Brussels, and a Planet Hollywood usually can be found near a Hard Rock Cafe. In general, retailers with large stores, a large amount of merchandise, and attractive pricing can use a destination location strategy effectively. Retailers selling goods that consumers want to compare for quality and price are usually wise to locate close to competitors.

Of course, many retailers choose a local or regional shopping mall rather than a freestanding location. A shopping mall or center is a group of retail stores in one place marketed as a unit to shoppers in a trade area. Shopping malls, especially regional ones, provide a wide array of merchandise and immense pulling power. Merchants can pool resources to provide entertainment, such as pianists or clowns or even a supervised indoor playground, as at the huge Mall of America in Minneapolis. This supermall has 2.5 million square feet of retail space, equivalent to four regional shopping malls, features more than 520 specialty stores and brings in more than 40 million visitors annually, including many of whom charter flights from all over the world. It also has development rights for up to an additional 5.6 million square feet of mixed-use space.[12]

Supplier Relationships Developing strong relationships with suppliers is a strategic imperative for many retailers. Partners go out of their way to serve one another. Supplier loyalty pays off when the retailer gets the goods it needs in a quick and efficient manner. Walmart has long been known as a retailer that values close partnerships with its major suppliers.[13] Whatever the strength of a relationship, tough bargaining issues are likely to arise between suppliers and retailers.

Cost and pricing issues are the most common areas of friction. Retailers have a targeted **markup**, the difference between merchandise cost and the retail price. For example, if Wet Seal buys blouses from California Concepts, a manufacturer in Gardena, at $12 each and prices them in stores at $20 each, the markup is $8, or 40 percent of the selling price ($8 / $20 = 0.40). Goods that do not sell as expected re-

Markup

The difference between merchandise cost and retail price.

quire a **markdown**, a reduction in the original retail price. Wet Seal may sell some of the blouses at $20 but then lower the price to $15 in order to sell the rest. The markdown in this case is $5, and the markdown percentage is 25 percent ($5 / $20). The retailer typically goes back to the supplier and asks for markdown money, a credit to the retailer's account to adjust for the unanticipated price reduction.

Markdown

A reduction from the original retail selling price of a product.

TYPES OF RETAILERS

There are several ways to classify retailers. Form of ownership distinguishes between small independents (often called mom-and-pop stores) and **chain stores**, which are groups of centrally owned and managed retail outlets that handle the same product lines. Level of service can be used, whether full, limited or self-service. Price level can be used as well. However, the most informative classification is based on the merchandise assortment, whether retailers sell a limited line or general merchandise. Within each category, different types of retailers exist based on their service level and pricing strategy, as outlined in Figure 16.3. A number of successful companies have stores of more than one type, such as Macy's and Walmart.

Chain Store

One of a group of centrally owned and managed retail stores that handle the same product lines.

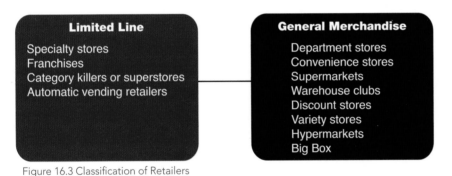

Figure 16.3 Classification of Retailers

Limited-Line Retailers Limited-line retailers focus on one product category. The four types are specialty stores, franchises, superstores and automated vending retailers.

   Specialty stores offer merchandise in one primary product category in considerable depth. Examples are Wet Seal, The Limited, Florsheim, Women's Foot Locker, Champ's Sports, and Roller Skates of America. Goods are of moderate to high quality. Prices tend to be high and comparable to department stores.

   Many specialty stores are run by franchisees, who sign a contractual agreement with a franchiser organization to represent and sell its products in particular retail locations. Examples include Blockbuster Video stores, the vast majority of fast-food restaurants (some outlets are company-owned) and automobile dealerships.

   Superstores, sometimes called category killers, focus on a single product category but offer huge selection, low-to-moderate service levels and low prices. Examples include Barnes & Noble, Home Depot, IKEA, Staples and Office Depot. Superstores have been particularly successful in taking business away from traditional discount stores as well as wholesalers.

   Automated vending retailers use machinery operated by coin or credit card to dispense goods. The placement of machines is critical, and airports, hospitals, schools and office buildings are among the most popular locations. Traditionally, vending has focused on beverages, candy, cigarettes and food, but the industry is expanding into new areas, such as life insurance policies in airports, movie rentals in supermarkets, and lottery tickets. ARAMARK and Canteen Corporation are two leading automatic vending retailers.

   In Japan, vending machines are more important in retail trade. Homes and apartments have little storage space, and consumers often travel on foot or by mass

Specialty Store

A retailer offering merchandise in one primary product category in considerable depth.

Superstore

A retailer that focuses on a single product category but offers huge selection and low prices; also called a category killer.

Automated Vending

The use of machinery operated by coins or credit cards to dispense goods.

transit. The convenience of location, wider variety of products, and small quantities are appealing. Roboshop Outlets allow customers to look through displayed items, punch in the desired product's number, and then receive their purchases through a trap door. More than a dozen of these shops exist in Tokyo alone, and the Vending Machine Manufacturers Association of Japan reports that there is one vending machine for every 23 people in Japan. These vending machines sell everything from alcohol to pagers to underwear.[14]

General Merchandise Retailers

General merchandise retailers carry a number of different product categories. There are seven types: department stores, convenience stores, supermarkets, warehouse clubs, discount stores, variety stores and hypermarkets.

Department stores carry a broad array and varying depth of merchandise, and the level of customer service is relatively high. Merchandise is grouped into well-defined departments. Both soft goods, such as apparel and linens, and hard goods, such as appliances and sporting goods, are normally sold. The intention is to provide one-stop shopping for most personal and household items. While often situated in downtown areas at a stand-alone location, department stores also are prevalent in shopping malls, where they are considered anchor tenants that draw customers.

Target markets and pricing strategies vary considerably among department stores. Some seek the upscale customer, such as Bloomingdale's, Neiman Marcus and Saks Fifth Avenue. Their decor is plush, with an ambience and prices to match. Others, such as Kohl's and Target, appeal to a somewhat broader middle-income clientele and focus on mainstream tastes, increasingly offering popular brands at lower prices.[15] Still others, such as JCPenney and Sears, seek an even broader array of customers. Specialty stores provide the most competition to upscale department stores, while discounters pose a threat to lower-end department stores.

Convenience stores are small and have moderately low breadth and depth of merchandise. Sandwiches, soft drinks, snack foods, newspapers and magazines, milk, and beer and wine are among the most popular products carried. They are open long hours, prices are high, and their location is their primary advantage. Some are part of large corporate chains, including Circle K and Dairy Mart. Some large oil companies have established their own operations, such as Arco's AM/PM stores and Texaco's Food Mart. Many convenience stores are mom-and-pop businesses, family-owned and operated.

Supermarkets are large, departmentalized, food-oriented retail establishments that sell a wide variety of foods and beverages, as well as many non-food items, typically cosmetics and toiletries. Many have in-store bakeries and delicatessens. Merchandise breadth and depth are moderately high. Since gross margins are generally low, supermarkets attempt to maximize sales volume. In the United States, regional chains dominate, such as Kroger, Safeway, and Winn-Dixie.

Recently, the east-coast regional supermarket Wegmans ranked in the No. 33 spot on Fortune's Best 100 Places to Work List. Operated in New York, Pennsylvania, New Jersey, Maryland, and Virginia, Wegmans' 75 supermarkets cater to those who want a complete upscale shopping experience. Wegmans stocks more than 60,000 products, including specialty cheeses, fine dinnerware, and ready-to-cook entrees.[16]

Warehouse clubs are large, no-frills stores that carry a revolving array of

---

Department Store

A retailer with merchandise of broad variety and moderate depth with a relatively high level of customer service.

Convenience Store

A small retailer with moderately low breadth and depth of merchandise.

Supermarket

A large, departmentalized, food-oriented retail establishment that sells beverages, canned goods, dairy products, frozen foods, meat, produce, and such nonfood items as health and beauty aids, kitchen utensils, magazines, pharmaceuticals, and toys.

Warehouse Club

A large, no-frills store that carries a revolving array of merchandise at low prices.

merchandise at low prices. They are typically 60,000 square feet or more. Consumers must become members before shopping in these clubs. Brands carried vary by day and week, depending on the deals arranged with suppliers, so product selection is somewhat limited. By carrying only the most popular items in a merchandise category, clubs strive for high asset turnover (net sales divided by total assets) with gross margins as low as 8 percent. There are approximately 4,000 warehouse clubs and superstores in the United States, accounting for $410 billion in annual revenue. A recent First Research Industry Profile reveals that the U.S. industry is highly concentrated: the top four companies hold over 90 percent of sales.[17] These retailers give supermarkets stiff competition.

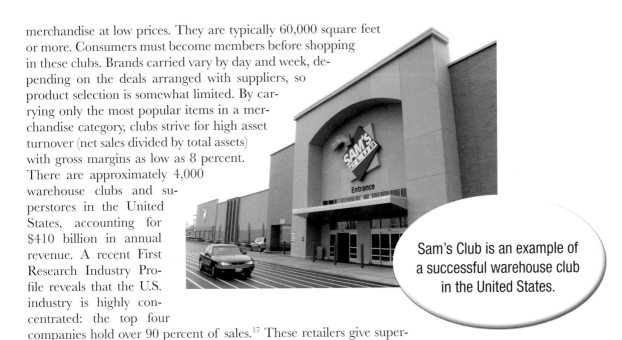

Sam's Club is an example of a successful warehouse club in the United States.

Discount stores offer a broad variety of merchandise with limited service and low prices. Merchandise depth is low to moderate. Service levels are minimal. Operating costs, including payroll, are normally 20 percent or less of total sales.[18] Discounters concentrate on low- to middle-income consumers, and their goal is asset turnover and sales volume per store. Walmart and Kmart are the major U.S. discount stores.

There are two specialized types of discounters. **Off-price retailers** sell brand-name clothing at low prices. Their inventory frequently changes as they take advantage of special deals from manufacturers selling excess merchandise. Examples are Loehmann's, Marshall's, Men's Warehouse and T. J. Maxx.

Variety stores offer an array of low-priced merchandise of low to moderate quality. There is not much depth. These retailers are becoming more scarce because of intense competition, mainly from larger discounters. Examples of variety stores are Everything's A Dollar and Pic'N'Save.

Hypermarkets are giant shopping facilities offering a wide selection of food and general merchandise at low prices. They have at least 100,000 square feet of space, some of them three times that. The concept was developed by a French company, Carrefour, which is very successful throughout Europe and Latin America. Hypermarkets have not thrived in the United States, partly because there is so much competition. Furthermore, consumers often complain about the required amount of walking and limited brand selections. The costs of operating the giant facilities are high.[19] Nevertheless, hypermarkets might become more popular in the United States because they offer one-stop shopping. Existing hypermarket operations include Kmart Super Centers.

Big Box Retailers Big box stores — large retail establishments, usually part of a chain, that focus on high sales volume — boomed in the 1990s, with chains such as Walmart, Costco, Home Depot and Best Buy expanding across the United States. Many stores, such as Target, offer one-stop shopping; you can get groceries, clothes and a new camera all in one location. In addition, big box stores often make it easy to find an item locally that smaller stores may not stock. Looking for a new Samsung Galaxy tablet? You can visit Best Buy's site, enter your ZIP code and see which nearby stores have it in stock — even pay for it online and just swing by the store to pick it up. These types of stores, however, have seen a decline in recent years, with shifting demographics and more customers buying items online.[20]

Discount Store

A retailer offering a broad variety of merchandise with limited service and low prices.

Off-price Retailers

A seller of brand-name clothing at low prices.

Variety Store

A retailer offering a variety of low-priced merchandise of low to moderate quality.

Hypermarket

A giant shopping facility with a wide selection of food and general merchandise at low prices.

Big Box Retailers

A large retail establishment, usually part of a chain, selling either general merchandise or specialty items (such as electronics) and focusing on large sales volume.

ISSUES IN RETAILING

Retailing changes rapidly. Retailers must address such important factors as diversity, legal and ethical issues, and global retailing.

Diversity and Retailing
Because retailers deal directly with consumers, most of them realize that staffing and marketing programs must reflect the nature of the population they serve. Recognizing diversity and its implications for business practice is a must for top-performing retailers. Sears, Roebuck and Co. is at the forefront in connecting with diverse markets. Some of its stores in Florida have a customer base that is 90 percent Hispanic, and Sears has bilingual signs, sales staff, in-store posters featuring minority models, and four apparel lines designed for multicultural women.[21] With the Spanish-language media market growing at twice the pace of the rest of the market, companies are investing great amounts of money in advertising geared toward the Hispanic population.[22]

> **Recognizing diversity and its implications for business practice is a must for top-performing retailers.**

Ethical Issues in Retailing

Ethical dilemmas often arise over the goods sold by retailers. Consumer action groups may lobby them to stop carrying certain products. More than 10 years ago, Target, under pressure from the growing stigma attached to smoking, eliminated cigarette sales in its stores.[23] Depending on community standards, many stores do not carry certain magazines, or they keep them in locations inaccessible to children. Walmart stopped carrying guns in its stores in 1994. It still sells them through catalogs, though, and it sells many shooting accessories such as gun cases as well. This, predictably, offends many consumer advocates.

Employee relations are another area in which ethical questions arise, such as steps taken to prevent unionization or reduce employee theft. Whatever the issue, if employees are not treated with fairness and respect, then major problems can result. One recent survey found that a two-way performance review is an excellent way to retain good workers. This way, both the management and the employee can comment on the employee's performance, as well as on the management's performance, ensuring the review can be just that, a "review," and not a "criticism." This plan aims to confront problems in the employee-employer relationship before they cause problems for the company.[24]

Global Retailers
For years, a number of U.S. retailers have had successful ventures in global markets. McDonald's, along with KFC and Burger King, have brought fast food retailing to most mature and emerging markets for the past couple of decades. Each of these retailers uses a similar approach with adjustments to local requirements. For example, you will find beer in McDonald's in Germany and Cadbury chocolate sticks in its ice cream cones in the United Kingdom.

Today, retailers from other countries are finding the U.S. to be an excellent market, as well. Recently, European retailer Zara opened its largest flagship store in the United States in Chicago. This three-story clothing and accessory shop boasts 16,000 square feet of retailing space. Situated on Michigan Avenue, Zara engages in competition with other clothing stores like H&M, Banana Republic, and Forever 21.[25] As with most growth-oriented companies, leading-edge retailers emphasize the global nature of business.

Similar to other businesses, retailers are entering emerging markets like China and India. Many companies are seeking to break into the market in India, though the country's laws make it difficult for some; food and grocery retailers, for example, are prohibited, except through cash and carry wholesale trading. In 2011, the government announced it would lift restrictions, but a few weeks later reversed that decision.[26] Walmart is among the companies asking the U.S. government for assistance in entering the Indian market; it spent nearly $1.5 million on lobbying on various issues, including matters "related to FDI in India," in the quarter ending June 30, 2012.[27] Recently, Walmart stood as the world's largest retailer, posting annual sales of $447 billion.[28] The company opened its first store outside the U.S. in 1991 — a Sam's Club in Mexico City; it now has 5,651 stores in 26 countries outside the continental U.S.[29]

Developed markets are also new targets of some U.S. retailers. Drugstore chain Walgreens recently announced its first international expansion when it agreed to buy a 45 percent stake in European chain Alliance Boots.[30]

DIRECT MARKETING

Direct marketing uses various methods to communicate with consumers, generally calling for a direct response on their part. Direct marketing is both a form of communication and a channel of distribution. Direct mail and catalogs have been used for many years. Telemarketing is another prominent method. Advertisements in print media or on television and radio that include toll-free numbers for placing orders have become very popular. The field is being revolutionized by technology — fax machines, email and voice mail, electronic catalogs, infomercials, home television shopping channels, and the Internet.

Many organizations can benefit from direct marketing. A growing number of companies are direct marketers, who conduct business primarily or solely with this method. This kind of direct marketing is most powerful when it communicates product and pricing information, along with guidance for placing orders. The sale is completed by delivery of products via computer (such as software) or through services such as UPS, DHL and FedEx.

> **Direct Marketing**
>
> Uses various methods to communicate with consumers, generally calling for a direct response on their part.

CAREER TIP!

Take a job behind the bulls-eye at one of the most innovative retailers in the United States, where you can expect more and pay less, just as their mantra suggests. Target offers opportunities to work in retail locations or at the corporate headquarters in Minneapolis. Visit the Target career site for more information and to watch videos with interviews from actual employees and their experiences: www.target.com/careers.

According to the Direct Marketing Association, spending for direct marketing totaled $163 billion in 2011 — 52.1 percent of total advertising spent in the U.S. Clearly, direct marketing is very significant in generating sales and is becoming even more important. There are 1.3 million direct marketing employees in the country, and their sales efforts directly support 7.9 million other jobs.[31]

In comparison, total direct marketing expenditures are approximately equal to total expenditures for mass advertising. About 52 percent is spent by B2C businesses, and the remaining 48 percent is directed at the B2B arena. However, the B2B expenditures are growing at a faster rate. Because the B2B arena is larger, direct marketing represents about 4.4 percent of business sales and about 12 percent of consumer sales. Direct marketing is also slightly more productive in generating sales for consumer businesses:

- $1 spent on consumer direct marketing yields $12.66 in sales.

- $1 spent on business direct marketing yields $10.10.[32]

Direct marketing offers consumers a convenient way to shop from the comfort of their home or office. The fast-paced lifestyle of many people leaves little time or energy for shopping trips. Rising gas costs, traffic, parking and retailers' decreased staffing all reduce the convenience of physically traveling to stores. The widespread availability of credit cards, toll-free numbers, Internet connectivity and overnight delivery service has made direct marketing to consumers even more viable. Convenience is also important in business-to-business markets. Direct marketing allows business customers to gain information on products and place orders much more efficiently than having to meet with several salespeople.

Quality and pricing may also be improved with direct marketing. For example, mail-order florist Calyx & Corolla claims that its flowers have superior blooms that last five to 10 days longer by eliminating long truck or retail cooler times. Instead, it partners with growers to send flowers directly using UPS.[33] Another advantage of direct marketing is competitive prices. A company can operate out of an unadorned warehouse in an inexpensive location, keeping overhead low.

Direct marketing is of increasing value to many entrepreneurs as retailers cut back on inventory. For example, many music stores feature only the more mainstream artists and compilations. Music fans can, however, often find exactly what they are looking for through Internet sites such as iTunes.

Direct marketing allows small businesses to access markets without the assistance of retailers, wholesalers or a company sales force. Consequently, the investment required for product launch is relatively low. For example, Ziff-Davis Publishing in New York City puts out a large monthly catalog, *Computer Shopper*, in which companies can advertise. A full-page ad can reach 3.34 million customers per month through the printed magazine. In addition, companies can advertise on the website Computershopper.com. *Computer Shopper* has enabled several small companies to start and successfully maintain their businesses.

Large organizations also benefit from direct marketing. Some use it as their primary means of doing business; others use it in combination with different channels. Swedish furniture retailer IKEA spends 70 percent of its annual marketing budget producing an annual catalog. Last year, 198 million copies of the catalog were printed in 56 editions and 27 languages.[34]

DIRECT MARKETING DATABASES

Figure 16.4 Direct-Marketing Media

All direct-marketing companies maintain a database with customer names, addresses and purchase history. These are often supplemented with lists purchased from market research companies such as Zeller's and Dun's. Some direct marketers have taken the art of database management to a new level. Access Innovations has software called Data Harmony, which helps publishers, corporate libraries and online directory producers design and manipulate databases. The company's Thesaurus Master allows users to tag their own phrases and keywords in a database's thesaurus, and it gives searchers more accurate results by using individualized terms relevant to a specific company, industry, and scientific discipline.[35]

DIRECT MARKETING MEDIA

Direct marketers use many media; some choose only one, but many combine several media in attempts to connect with customers. Figure 16.4 identifies the most popular media which are described in this section. The following sections describe each type of direct marketing media in more detail.

Direct Mail Direct mail is among the most popular method of direct marketing, according to the Direct Marketing Association.[36] Each year, billions of paper-based pieces are sent to prospective customers through the U.S. Postal Service. Direct mail allows organizations to physically place a message in its customers' hands, encouraging a more memorable interaction. Along with the message, many will incorporate elements that actively involve the customer, like samples, coupons, and even DVDs. Mail contact is popular because it hits a select market at a reasonably low cost. Companies can develop selective mailing lists, or tailor mail to target recipients.

Internet Many companies have e-commerce websites, allowing consumers to make purchases directly on the website. However, some people are reluctant to provide credit card numbers online. As technology develops and the Internet is now more accessible to a large percentage of people, e-commerce is able to reach increasingly larger markets. Beyond our borders, however, the web's heavy American influence grates on some in other cultures. Adaptable marketers can use this as an opportunity to provide an inviting environment to people in those cultures.

Companies must decide whether to set up their own web operation or turn to a provider. The trade-off is between greater control and no fees to outside Internet resellers on one hand, and expertise with an existing subscriber base on the other. An annual fee plus some percentage of the company's online sales, typically 2 percent, is paid to the online service. Individuals who do not have their own websites, or who wish to sell their items through larger sites, can use services such as eBay, which allows users to bid on items and then charges the seller a set amount based on the purchase price.

In the consumer market, Amazon.com is an Internet reseller offering books, music, movies, clothing and millions of other goods. Amazon.com owns no inventory; instead it relies on a network of wholesalers to ship orders, normally within 24 hours. Since some companies can not handle large volume shipping, Amazon created one of the most advanced fulfillment networks in the world, offering to pack and ship products for them. The fulfillment centers are so impressive and sophisticated that public tours are offered at several U.S. locations.

Many companies' profits are coming increasingly from Internet sales. By 2017, 60 percent of U.S. retail sales will involve the Internet in some way, either through e-commerce or for research and user reviews.[37] The booming of the Internet in direct marketing has led to a growth of digital printing with personalized targeting possibilities. The Target Marketing's Media Usage Forecast indicates that of the top media channels marketers will use in the year ahead, email is the most favored at 94 percent, then direct mail at 91 percent, and social media at 89 percent.[38]

Catalogs **Mail-order catalogs** publish product and price information in paper form. Annually, more than 19 billion copies paper-based catalogs are sent through the U.S. Postal Service.[39] Some feature general merchandise, such as those by JCPenney. Others focus on a narrow range of products. Omaha Steaks sells beef, seafood, pork, lamb, chicken, pastas and desserts in its catalog. Eddie Bauer catalogs include men and women's apparel, luggage, footwear and accessories.

Some companies, such as airlines and hotels, assemble products from various sources and hire third parties to publish paper-based catalogs. United Airlines provides SkyMall to passengers. It is a collection of upscale, unique merchandise from a number of catalogs, including Brookstone, Disney, Healthrider, Hammacher Schlemmer, and Sharper Image. Customers call an 800 number or visit www.skymall.com to order.

A major disadvantage of catalog marketing is the expense. Paper and postage prices are so high that many entrepreneurs find it impossible to issue their own, and it's very hard to get products included in brand-name catalogs. The Good Catalog Company has filled a need by partnering with producers who can't afford to publish and distribute on their own.

Electronic catalogs are a popular way to store product information, especially in business-to-business markets. iPlanet E-Commerce Solutions, a company formed by the blending of America Online and Sun Microsystems, seeks to meet the needs

Mail-order Catalog

A collection of product and price information that is published in paper form.

of the B2B world by providing services to aid Internet savvy companies. The company collaborated with J. D. Edwards to develop "B2B in a Box," a program and electronic catalog that allows online purchasing and electronic trading.

Telemarketing

Using the telephone to contact leads (potential customers) from a list.

Telemarketing

Telemarketing occurs when salespeople make telephone calls to leads provided by marketing services or from other lists. The timing of calls is very important. Late morning and early afternoon are normally the best times for reaching businesses, while evenings between 7 p.m. and 9 p.m. are best for contacting households — from the marketer's standpoint. You probably have had more than a few interruptions at that time from telemarketers. Telemarketing has a higher cost per contact than direct mail or catalogs. Furthermore, many consumers view unsolicited telephone calls as an annoyance and resent unwanted clutter on voice mail. Salespeople often are poorly trained and may not directly answer consumer questions. In fact, they may be instructed not to deviate from prearranged scripts regardless of what they are asked.

Automated telemarketing uses machines to dial numbers, play recorded messages and take orders either via answering machines or by forwarding calls to live operators. Outbound automated calls meet with strong resistance, and the system is better used for incoming calls — that is, consumers are reached by other means and then place orders through the automated systems.

Precise list selection and development are critical for telemarketing. The sales message must be simple and strong. Salespeople need to receive at least some training on how to make calls and handle customer concerns. Person-to-person telemarketing is best used in the consumer market with current customers who prefer this mode of communication. In business-to-business markets, especially when targeted at employees outside the purchasing area, telemarketing is not very successful. But some professional buyers prefer it to face-to-face dealings because less time is involved. In the business setting, it is especially important that telemarketers be carefully selected, well trained and adequately compensated.

Print and Broadcast Media

Print ads in magazines and newspapers are used a great deal in direct marketing. Along with information on products and prices, toll-free numbers are given. For example, Horizon Instruments of Fullerton, California, sells digital engine tachometers and other instrumentation to owners of private planes through ads in leading aviation magazines.

Direct marketers also rely on television and radio spots, usually ranging from 10 to 60 seconds. Exercise equipment from NordicTrack and Bowflex, publications such as *Sporting News* and *Sports Illustrated*, and music CDs are among the products frequently advertised on television. Oreck Corporation of New Orleans uses radio ads to sell vacuum cleaners.

Infomercials are long advertisements that resemble documentaries. They range from 15 to 60 minutes and often include celebrity endorsers and testimonials from satisfied customers. Such products as smoking cessation, weight-control programs, cosmetics and exercise equipment are promoted this way. Established companies such as Chrysler and Mattel are beginning to use this technique to communicate in depth about product benefits. Some direct marketers use it to obtain distribution in retail stores. For example, pitchman Billy Mays started selling cleaning products like OxiClean for Orange Glo International on the Home Shopping Network in the 1990s. In no time, sales skyrocketed and products were available at retailers across the country. His legendary pitches were so successful, the Discovery Channel show "PitchMen," featured Mays as he attempted to sell various products.

Infomercial

A long advertisement that resembles a documentary.

The legendary pitchman Billy Mays was excellent at selling products like OxiClean, Orange Glo, and Mighty Putty.

Televised Home Shopping

In the past several years, home shopping via cable television has come into prominence. The two largest marketers are Quality Value Channel (QVC) and the Home Shopping Network (HSN), with others including the Home Shopping Mall, Teleshop, and Value Club of America. Themed programs are telecast 24 hours a day, seven days a week, to more than 248 million households worldwide. Program hosts, including such celebrities as Suzanne Somers and Tori Spelling, offer products ranging from books to computers, jewelry to lamps, clothing to power tools. Customers send orders over toll-free lines, enabling companies to adjust inventory minute by minute, not just season by season. Orders are usually shipped within 48 hours. Recently, HSN reported sales of almost $3 billion, and QVC's net sales totaled more than $7.3 billion. QVC and HSN also have websites that allow customers to shop online, track purchases and chat with other users.[40]

DIRECT MARKETING DECISIONS

Direct marketers make several decisions when developing a marketing strategy. The most important relate to target markets, database management, merchandise assortment, pricing, choice of media and other channels, message design, and payment methods and delivery. The steps are depicted in Figure 16.5.

Target Markets Every excellent marketing strategy begins with an understanding of the intended audience, whether baseball hobbyists, newlyweds, cooking buffs or outdoor enthusiasts. Therefore, the first decision is which customers to target.[41] Many direct marketers are small companies content to serve a narrow group of customers in their home territory. Others expand nationally or globally once a strong business foundation is established. Dell Computer Corporation began in 1983 by serving small and medium-sized businesses in Austin, Texas, that needed upgrades on IBM-compatible computers. Dell branched out to serve large businesses and government agencies throughout the United States in the mid-1980s. Today, Dell has regional business units all over the world.[42]

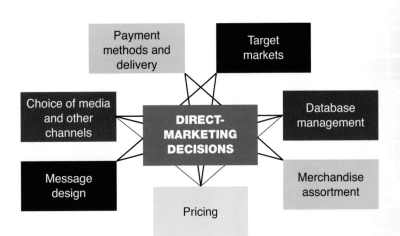

Figure 16.5 Direct-Marketing Decisions

Database Management Maintaining a strong customer database is essential. The database needs current addresses and preference, accurate listings, and notifications of customers with poor credit histories or who no longer desire contact.

Another critical function of a database is tracking. For example a retailer of sports-oriented hats developed a database that tracks individual stores' performances and shows which are falling short of company goals. Because of the stores' limited product line, the company could not afford to overlook missed opportunities for improvement.

Merchandise Assortment The choice of target markets goes hand-in-hand with decisions on merchandise assortment. Baseball enthusiasts will be attracted to fantasy baseball camps and memorabilia. Cooking buffs are interested in exotic ingredients and hard-to-get equipment. Companies need to review and adjust the assortment in light of economic trends, competition and changes in preferences of the target market. Omaha Steaks initially sold beef but responded to the trend toward lower-fat foods by offering seafood, lamb, and chicken. Dell, which focused on desktop computers for years, had to add laptops and local area network (LAN) servers when it expanded to many user segments and began selling numerous handheld devices. It has also started to produce storage, appliance servers and network switches.[43]

Pricing Direct-marketing companies often follow a low-price strategy, facilitated by their low overhead. In contrast, some companies emphasize merchandise quality and follow a premium price strategy. Brigandi Coin Company in New York City has a strong direct-marketing business in baseball cards, team-signed baseballs and autographs. It has developed a reputation for selling only the finest-quality, authentic memorabilia. This is particularly important, since fraud is a major problem in the industry. Many collectors will pay Brigandi's high prices because of their confidence in the company.

Media and Channels Direct-marketing companies normally start with one promotion medium, and many branch out to multiple media over time. Initially, QVC used a home television shopping channel. It now maintains a website and sends out catalogs as well.

Omaha Steaks was one of the first meat companies to sell its products online.

Some direct marketers continue to use traditional channels though they also operate large Internet sites. Omaha Steaks has established more than 80 company-owned retail stores in the United States in addition to its Internet-based business.[44]

Message Design Whatever medium is used, message design and presentation are most important. For paper-based mail, attention must be paid to the envelope, the cover letter and the product brochure. Envelopes of standard size and appearance are often discarded unopened, especially when mailing labels are used. An illustration or an important reason for opening the envelope often helps. The cover letter should be short and clear, using bold type to identify key product or service benefits. Brochures must be of high quality in appearance and content.[45]

Catalogs vary in quality of production depending on the company, its merchandise and its targeted customers. For example, Victoria's Secret sells high-quality lingerie and women's apparel, targeted to an upscale market, and it reflects that through high-quality paper, design and photographs. Hello Direct sells telephone productivity tools, such as cordless headsets and speakerphones, to businesses. It emphasizes low prices, and its catalog is produced at low cost.

On the web, the home page must be eye-catching and provide different categories of information the user can access. Sites must be easy to navigate, and returning to the home page should always be simple. One rule of thumb is that content should never be more than three clicks away. The site must provide a clear overview of the company and why its products are a good buy. Testimonials from satisfied customers are a good idea. Finally, sites must be updated regularly so that users will keep coming back to see what's new.[46] A recent study indicates that the use of lifelike characters, or avatars, can have a significant impact on customers during their online shopping experience. Lifelike characters can engage users and enhance perceptions of social interaction often missed in online shopping, which leads to positive feelings and higher perceptions of value.[47]

Finally, the diversity of a company's customers must be considered when designing direct-marketing messages. A study by Skunkworks of New York said that companies can average a 20 percent increase in sales simply by advertising on Spanish-language network television instead of on English-language broadcast networks. By directly targeting Hispanic communities in ways that appeal to them, companies can increase both sales and increase customer loyalty.[48]

Payment Methods and Delivery Direct-marketing companies serving the consumer market often offer several different payment methods—check, money order, or credit card. Installments also may be possible, especially when the product is relatively expensive, although the final cost to the consumer is greater under that option. Tempur-Pedic company allows a free trial period of 90 days for its mattresses.[49]

In B2B markets, customers often have an account with the direct marketer and pay on a monthly basis. Typically, if the invoice is paid within 10 days, a two percent credit will be applied to the next bill. Payment is normally due within 30 days unless special terms are negotiated.

Customers usually have several delivery options as well. The standard mode at Sharper Image is Federal Express second-day air; the delivery charge is based on the dollar value of the order. For an extra fee, customers can select next-day air or Saturday delivery. Dick's Sporting Goods offers standard delivery (three to six days), two day, and one day shipping at progressively higher charges.[50]

ETHICS IN DIRECT MARKETING

There are a number of ethical problems that confront direct marketers and consumers, including important issues involving fraud, the right to privacy and confidentiality of personal information. Misrepresentation happens often. For example, contests and sweepstakes are sometimes worded so people believe they have won a prize only to find out that their call to a 900 number has rung up a big bill with no prize in sight. In other cases, sales are made and shipments don't occur. Every time you enter a sweepstakes, buy a magazine subscription or register your name online, chances are your name goes into a database that could be accessed by many organizations. It's not unheard of for these databases to be stolen and accessed by people interested in identity theft. All of these ethical issues make it difficult for legitimate direct marketers and consumers. Consequently, the Direct Marketing Association has developed a rigorous set of 53 guidelines for ethical business practice. If you read the complete guidelines, you will probable recognize many situations in which your rights have been violated with direct mail. Figure 16.6 shows some of the guidelines.

Additional ethical guidelines fall into the following categories:

- Advance Consent Marketing: Guidance for credit card usage, advance payments, reminders, refunds, etc.

- Marketing to Children: Suitable communications, parental involvement, information from and about children, marketing by age (i.e., under 13).

- Special Offers and Claims: The meaning of free, price comparisons, and guarantees.

- Use of Test or Survey Data: Valid, reliable, including source and methods.

- Sweepstakes: Prizes awarded by chance (no skill required) without participants rendering anything (including no purchase required), can't represent that the participant has already won, clear representation of prizes vs. premiums,

CREATING & CAPTURING VALUE THROUGH *Relationships*

Costco: The Whole Deal

Where can you can buy groceries, get an eye exam, pick up a designer handbag and enjoy a quick lunch at the cafeteria? The answer is at the successful wholesaler Costco. Its low prices and quality products have made Costco Wholesale Corporation the top wholesaler in the United States, and it's giving the well-known Sam's Club a run for its money. Since the company's beginning in 1983, Costco has grown to have nearly 75 million members, which makes it the fourth-largest retailer in the United States. Costco also has operations internationally, currently present in six countries with plans to expand. Costco's membership-only policy with emphasis on customer satisfaction has led to strong customer loyalty. The wholesaler experiences a remarkable 87 percent member-renewal rate, indicative of the high level of customer satisfaction it provides.

Costco is able to execute its effective wholesaling strategy in part due to its ability to buy merchandise directly from manufacturers. The company buys bulk shipments and routes them directly to the proper storage facilities. This has given the wholesaler the capability to maximize freight volume and handling efficiencies, which leads to the elimination of costs associated with multi-step distribution channels, in turn lowering costs for customers. Costco's policy of offering a very wide variety of categories, each with a limited range of products, has also proven effective. Each warehouse only carries an average of 4,000 products compared to 40,000 found in the average retailer. The merchandise assortment is designed to produce high sales volumes and rapid inventory turnover.

Recently, corporations like Costco have come under scrutiny for their employee standards. One complaint is that "big box" companies will often keep their workers just under full-time status so that they don't have to provide health-care benefits. However, statistics on Costco show that nearly 95 percent of eligible Costco workers have health-care benefits, which is nearly double that of Walmart. At Costco, the starting pay is never less that $10, and the average among all employees is $17, which is nearly double its rival Sam's Club's average pay. Finally, 14,000 of Costco's current employees belong to labor unions, which have been banned by Walmart.

Ethical standards regarding the environment are another way that Costco enhances its company. Costco CEO Jim Sinegal says the company is making a concerted effort to minimize its carbon footprint. Many Costco warehouses are getting facelifts, with new skylights and solar panels. The company is also making small changes that have big impacts. Simply converting from round to rectangular tubs of cashews saved the company 400 truckloads annually because they can be stacked more efficiently. Costco also plans on expanding some of its organic products in the produce department. The success of its fresh produce department has motivated Costco to increase its own Kirkland brand from 330 products to 500. A Costco promise for now and the future is that a member will never pay more than a 14 percent markup on products. Costco continues to aspire to the highest ethical standards in the industry, and customers are responding with loyalty.

"Martha Stewart Living Omnimedia Introduces 'Kirkland Signature Martha Stewart' Prepared Food Program," PR Newswire, New York: Dec 7, 2007; Costco Wholesale Corporation 2009 Annual Report, www.costco.com, site visited January 28, 2012.

THE TERMS OF THE OFFER

HONESTY AND CLARITY OF OFFER: All offers should be clear, honest, and complete. Before publication of an offer, marketers should be prepared to substantiate any claims or offers made. Claims that are untrue, misleading, deceptive, or fraudulent should not be used.

ACCURACY, CONSISTENCY AND CLARITY: Simple and consistent statements or representations of all the essential points of the offer should appear in the promotinal material. Representations which, by their size, placement, duration, or other characteristics are unlikely to be noticed or are difficult to understand should not be used.

ACTUAL CONDITIONS: All descriptions, promises, and claims of limitation should be in accordance with actual conditions, situations, and circumstances existing at the time of the promotion.

DISPARAGEMENT: Disparagement of any person or group on grounds addressed by federal or state laws that prohibit discrimination is unacceptable.

DECENCY: Solicitations should not be sent to consumers who have indicated to the marketer that they consider those solicitations to be vulgar, immoral, profane, pornographic, or offensive in any way and who do not want to receive them.

PHOTOGRAPHS AND ART WORK: Photographs, illustrations, artwork, and the situations they describe should be accurate portrayals and current reproductions of the products, services, or other subjects they represent.

DISCLOSURE OF SPONSOR AND INTENT: All marketing contacts should disclose the name of the sponsor and each purpose of the contract. No one should make offers or solicitations in the guise of one purpose when the intent is a different purpose.

ACCESSIBILITY: Every offer should clearly identify the marketer's name and street address or telephone number, or both, at which the individual may obtain service. If an offer is made online, the marketer should provide its name, an Internet-based contact mechanism, and a street address. For e-mail solicitations, marketers should comply with Article #38 (Commercial Solicitations Online).

SOLICITATION IN THE GUISE OF AN INVOICE OR GOVERNMENTAL NOTIFICATION: Offers that are likely to be mistaken for bills, invoices, or notices from public utilities or governmental agencies should not be used.

POSTAGE, SHIPPING, OR HANDLING CHARGES: Postage, shipping, or handling charges, if any, should bear a reasonable relationship to actual costs incurred.

Figure 16.6 Summary of Direct Marketing Association Guidelines for Ethical Conduct
Source: "Terms of the Offer," Direct Marketing Association

and disclosure of all of the rules.

• Fulfillment: No shipments without permission, product availability, and free test periods.

• Collection, Use, and Maintenance of Marketing Data: Consumer must be told if their information will be rented, sold, or exchanged, provided with source of data upon request, confidential maintenance of data, health-related data use guidelines, promotion and sale of lists, who in the firm sees and uses data, and information security.

• Online Marketing: Notice of online listeners, honoring time of contact, online access for problems, online data security, age restrictions, accountability procedures, commercial email solicitation restrictions and information required, email authentication, use and installation of software on others' computers, getting online leads from people, appending emails to consumer records.

• Telephone Marketing: Calling during reasonable hours, taping only with notice (and a beeping device), not calling unlisted numbers, interfacing with caller ID, limited ring time on automated dialing equipment, diary of call success, appropriate use or prerecorded voice messaging so consumers can gain feedback, use of facsimile machines, promotion with toll-free and pay-per-call numbers, disclosures, fundraising, and compliance with all laws.[51]

WHOLESALING

Wholesaling affects our lives every day, but we rarely notice. We may buy aspirin at Good Neighbor retail pharmacies, not knowing it was purchased from Bergen Brunswig Corporation, a large pharmaceutical wholesaler. We order a pepperoni pizza at a small neighborhood restaurant, not knowing most of the ingredients were acquired from SYSCO, a large wholesaler of food products. ToyDirectory.com Inc. provides a web service that helps retail stores access toys from 2,200 toy importers (wholesalers) and manufacturers. One reason parents and kids can find a broad range of toys at many price points, including the latest dolls or Spider-Man action figures, is because organizations like ToyDirectory.com or WholesaleCentral.com, business-to-business services, provide information for retailers about the vast number of toy wholesalers.[52] Most of us never see these intermediaries, but they are very important to us. **Wholesaling** is selling goods for resale or use to retailers and other businesses. Producers have a number of options in making sales to retailers and other businesses, including company-owned sales branches, brokers and wholesalers.

Many wholesalers are relatively small, filling a certain niche. Others are multibillion-dollar companies serving global markets. Wholesalers help thousands of companies connect with millions of customers. Whatever their size or scope, they all face competition. Their ability to make decisions about target markets, service level, pricing, business locations, merchandise assortment, credit management, use of technology, and image will influence their survival.

A wholesaler is an intermediary that takes title to the products it carries and makes a majority of sales to retailers or other businesses. Many wholesalers make no direct sales to consumers. For others, direct sales may be a significant part of revenue. For example, Smart and Final Inc., sells food products and related merchandise to small businesses and to some consumers. Since more than half of its sales come from small businesses, it is classified as a wholesaler. A pure wholesaler organization does not manufacture any goods. Only firms that sell goods they purchase from manufacturers or other intermediaries are considered part of wholesale trade. As a marketing ploy, many retailers that sell mostly to the general public present themselves as wholesalers. For example, "wholesale" price clubs, factory outlets and other organizations are retail establishments, even though they sell their goods to the public at wholesale prices.

For wholesalers of consumer goods, the primary customers are retailers and service businesses, such as restaurants, hospitals and nursing homes. In business-to-business markets, the primary customers are manufacturing organizations and service firms, such as accountants or contractors.

THE IMPORTANCE OF WHOLESALERS

Wholesalers play an important role in the economy. The roughly 375,000 such organizations in the United States employ approximately 6 million people, with annual sales reaching about $2 trillion.[53] Wholesalers are prominent in a wide variety of product categories, including beverages, climate control equipment, computer hardware and software, electrical products, electronic components, fabrics, flowers and florist supplies, food, giftware, medical supplies, movies, pharmaceuticals, telecom-

Wholesaling

Selling of goods for resale or use to retailers and other businesses.

munications, tools, and toys. They provide value to customers and suppliers, as depicted in Figure 16.7. We will also see that they provide value for one another.

Figure 16.7 Wholesalers Add Value for Suppliers and Customers by Performing Important Channel Functions
Source: Adapted from Bert Rosenbloom, Marketing Functions and the Wholesaler-Distributor (Washington, DC: Distribution Research and Educational Foundation, 1987) p. 26.

Wholesalers are important for product assortment and allocation. They fulfill their **assortment** function by purchasing merchandise from a variety of suppliers for resale. This makes a range of products available in one place for the convenience of customers. They fulfill their **allocation** function by purchasing large quantities to resell in smaller amounts. This means savings for customers in both purchase price and storage costs. In essence, wholesalers make a wide variety of goods available in amounts that can be afforded and handled effectively. Wholesalers also perform other functions, depending on customer needs. They may provide credit, education on product benefits, training in product use, and technical assistance.

Some believe that wholesalers only add to the price of goods. Actually, their price is lower than what individual manufacturers would have to charge on most orders if they were made directly. Wholesalers get a discount for buying in quantity, and part of that is passed on to consumers. Furthermore, overhead is normally lower for wholesalers than for manufacturers. Therefore, wholesalers can serve small or medium-sized companies and still make a profit, whereas most manufacturers cannot.

Wholesalers will do business with one another, often as a matter of courtesy. A wholesaler may need a Black & Decker power drill for an important customer and can get it most quickly by calling a nearby wholesaler. In other cases, the transactions are systematic. Small wholesalers may find it easier to do business with large wholesalers than with manufacturers. As a result, in a number of industries other wholesalers are a primary target market.

Master distributors are wholesaling companies given the right by manufacturers to develop certain geographical areas and recruit other distributors. These, in turn, are called sub-distributors. All sales to sub-distributors go through the master distributor. The system is often used by manufacturers entering a global market, especially if they lack the resources to serve it directly.

TYPES OF WHOLESALERS

Full-service wholesalers perform a wide range of tasks for their customers. **Limited-service wholesalers** provide only some of the traditional channel functions, either eliminating others entirely or passing them on to someone else to perform. Within each category, several types of wholesalers can be identified. Figure 16.8 summarizes the functions performed by different types of wholesalers.

Full-Service Wholesalers *General Line Wholesalers* General line wholesalers carry a wide variety of products and provide a full range of services. Bosler Supply of Chicago and W. W. Grainger are good examples. They stock thousands of different industrial products, provide technical advice on product applications, and expedite shipments when necessary. Another example is SYSCO, which sells a broad array of frozen, dry and refrigerated products to the food industry. It can provide special packaging and delivery schedules. Its cruise ship customers, for

Assortment

A wholesaler function that entails selling a range of merchandise from a variety of sources.

Allocation

A wholesaler function that entails purchasing products in large quantities and reselling them in smaller quantities.

Full-service Wholesaler

An intermediary who performs a wide range of functions or tasks for its customers.

Limited-service Wholesaler

An intermediary who performs only some of the traditional channel functions, either eliminating others or passing them on to someone else.

example, can receive plastic-wrapped pallets of food at any time of day or night.

Specialty Wholesalers Specialty wholesalers focus on a narrow range of products, carry them in great depth and provide extensive services. Ryerson is the largest metals wholesaler in the world, with 50 distribution centers across the United States. It performs a variety of specialized services for customers, such as cutting metals to specification. Ingram-Micro and Tech Data focus on computer hardware and software products, while providing many customer services.

Rack Jobbers Rack jobbers, who sell single product lines to retail stores on consignment, set up product displays and keep them stocked with goods. Retailers pay for the goods only after they are sold to consumers. Krispy Kreme doughnuts are distributed this way. Rack jobbers are common in the music industry, having stepped in to take back new albums with offensive language. For example, Walmart learned of a singer's lyrics suggesting that it sold guns to children and pulled the album from the shelves. These days, in Walmart and Sam's Club, HDTV is one of the most common products using rack jobbers.[54]

Limited-Service Wholesalers *Cash-and-Carry Wholesalers* Cash-and-carry wholesalers are located near customers. They do not extend credit and do not use an outside sales force. Customers perform certain functions for themselves, such as bagging their own goods and delivery. Costs are tightly controlled in order to offer excellent prices.

Drop Shippers Drop shippers arrange for shipments directly from the manufacturer to the customer. They do not physically handle the goods but take title to them, assuming all associated risks (such as damage and theft) while in transit. In addition, they offer credit terms to customers. Drop shippers are prominent in the lumber, chemical and petroleum industries, where goods are bulky and sold in large quantity.

Truck Jobbers Truck jobbers specialize in the speedy delivery of perishables or semi-perishables, such as candy, bakery goods, fresh fruits, potato chips and tobacco products. They use their own vehicles and offer virtually all services except credit. They focus on smaller customers that full-service wholesalers tend to ignore.

Mail-Order Wholesalers Mail-order wholesalers sell through catalogs distributed to retailers and other businesses. They are most popular among small businesses in outlying areas that are not regularly contacted by salespeople. These wholesalers are prominent in the clothing, cosmetics, hardware, office supply, jewelry, sporting goods and specialty food industries.

CHAPTER SUMMARY

Objective 1: Appreciate the important role retailers play in our economy and society.
Retailing is the final stage in the distribution channel for a majority of products sold to consumers. Time, place, possession and form utilities are provided to consumers by retailers. In addition, retailers may promote the general welfare of society through efforts to recruit a diverse workforce. A number of U.S. retailers have been very successful in global markets by understanding important variations in consumer tastes across cultures.

Objective 2: Understand strategy issues confronted by retailers when making marketing decisions.
Retailing strategy must cover a variety of issues. Each retailer must decide on the target market(s) and positioning, then adopt a distinct service level and pricing approach, and decide what type of merchandise assortment it will offer. The geographical location of stores is a very important decision. Some retailers locate stores in low-rent areas off highways and at a distance from other retailers, whereas others place stores close to competitors. Well-run shopping centers have immense

pulling power and are good locations for many retailers. New technologies, such as sophisticated computer systems that allow merchandise to be tailored in individual stores, help improve retailer performance. Furthermore, effectively managing relationships with suppliers — whether manufacturers, wholesalers, or agents — is critical.

Objective 3:   Recognize the diverse array of retailers that compete with one another.

Limited-line retailers include specialty stores, superstores and automated vending operations. General merchandise retailers include department stores, convenience stores, supermarkets, warehouse clubs, discount stores, variety stores and hypermarkets. An understanding of each type is useful in tracking and predicting competitive trends. A number of successful retailers have stores of different types.

Objective 4:   Learn what direct marketing entails, its value, and how it differs from mass communication.

Direct marketing is a powerful selling approach, especially when media are used to communicate information on products and prices and how to place orders. Growth in sales through direct-marketing channels is outpacing growth in U.S. retail sales by about two to one. Direct marketing offers consumers and businesses a convenient way to shop. It enables many small companies to access markets they could not reach through traditional retail and wholesale organizations. It is popular in many parts of the world. In fact, the largest direct-marketing companies are based in foreign countries. International direct-marketers must adjust their strategies to the unique characteristics of each country they serve.

Objective 5:   Be familiar with the different types of direct-response media.

A large number of direct-response media are available. Paper-based mail, fax, email, and voice mail are options. Mail-order catalogs are used by many companies, and electronic versions are gaining popularity. Telemarketing is a major force, especially in business-to-business markets. Advertisements in print and broadcast media are important in direct-marketing activities. Infomercials can be used effectively to sell products and gain distribution through retailers. Television shopping channels have done well, as has the Internet. Each medium has its strengths and weaknesses that must be considered by companies choosing which one or which mix to use.

Objective 6:   Understand the marketing decisions made by direct-marketing companies.

Direct marketers make a number of decisions when developing a marketing strategy. They must carefully select the target market(s). Strong customer databases must be developed and maintained. In particular, direct marketers can put database marketing to great use. Decisions on target markets go hand in hand with merchandise assortment and pricing. Multiple direct-response media should be used with great attention paid to the content of messages in each medium. Each medium has unique challenges with regard to message content. Finally, payment methods and delivery options must be selected.

Objective 7:   Know the different types of wholesalers and the distinct roles they play.

A wide range of functions is performed for customers by full-service wholesalers, a category that includes general line wholesalers, specialty wholesalers and rack jobbers. In contrast, limited-service wholesalers perform only some of the traditional channel functions. In this category are cash-and-carry wholesalers, drop shippers, truck jobbers and mail-order wholesalers.

REVIEW YOUR UNDERSTANDING

1. What is retailing? What is a retailer? List two reasons retailers are important.
2. What are the steps in developing a retail strategy?
3. What is a markup? Markdown?
4. What are the four types of limited-line retailers? What are the seven types of general merchandise retailers?
5. List three ethical issues in retailing.
6. What is direct marketing?
7. List several ways direct marketing provides value to customers.
8. List several media used in direct marketing.
9. List the seven decisions direct marketers make when developing a marketing strategy.
10. What are two ethical problems in the direct-marketing industry? Briefly explain each.
11. What is a full-service wholesaler? What is a limited-service wholesaler? List three types of each.

DISCUSSION OF CONCEPTS

1. Explain the Pathways to Independence program of Marriott International Inc. What are its main benefits?
2. Is following a hybrid strategy on service and price more difficult for a retailer than either a discount-oriented or service-oriented strategy? Explain.
3. What are the pros and cons of following a destination location strategy? Under what conditions would locating stores close to the competition be preferable?
4. Among the various types of limited-line and general merchandise retailers, which have the strongest competitive positions? Why?
5. Some experts view Internet shopping as a major threat to retailers. Do you agree or disagree?
6. What are the major reasons for the growing importance of direct marketing in the United States?
7. What are the pros and cons of using fax, email, and voice mail? Would you recommend their use to a direct-marketing company? Why or why not?
8. What are infomercials? Can they be misused? How?
9. Explain how effective database management can improve the performance of a direct marketing company.
10. Are the efforts of the Direct Marketing Association to promote ethics among its members worthwhile? What else can be done to encourage ethical behavior in the industry?
11. Compare the businesses of limited-service and full-service wholesalers. Can limited-service wholesalers be just as successful financially as full-service wholesalers?

KEY TERMS & DEFINITIONS

1. **Allocation:** A wholesaler function that entails purchasing products in large quantities and reselling them in smaller quantities.
2. **Assortment:** A wholesaler function that entails selling a range of merchandise from a variety of sources.
3. **Automated vending:** The use of machinery operated by coins or credit cards to dispense goods.
4. **Big Box Retailers:** A large retail establishment, usually part of a chain, selling either general merchandise or specialty items (such as electronics) and focusing on large sales volume.
5. **Chain store:** One of a group of centrally owned and managed retail stores that handle the same product lines.
6. **Convenience store:** A small retailer with moderately low breadth and depth of merchandise.
7. **Department store:** A retailer with merchandise of broad variety and moderate depth and with a relatively high level of customer service.
8. **Direct marketing:** The use of various communication media to interact directly with customers and generally calling for them to make a direct response.
9. **Discount store:** A retailer offering a broad variety of merchandise with limited service and low prices.
10. **Full-service wholesaler:** An intermediary who performs a wide range of functions or tasks for its customers.
11. **Hypermarket:** A giant shopping facility with a wide selection of food and general merchandise at low prices.
12. **Infomercial:** A programmatic advertisement of considerable length that resembles a documentary.
13. **Limited-service wholesaler:** An intermediary who performs only some of the traditional channel functions, either eliminating others or passing them on to someone else.
14. **Mail-order catalog:** A collection of product and price information that is published in paper form.
15. **Markdown:** A reduction from the original retail selling price of a product.
16. **Markup:** The amount added to the cost of acquiring a product that determines its retail selling price.
17. **Off-price retailer:** A seller of brand-name clothing at low prices.
18. **Private Label Merchandise:** Products with brand names owned by the retailer.
19. **Retailing:** The activities involved in selling of products to end users for use and consumption by the purchaser.
20. **Scrambled merchandising:** A retail strategy that entails carrying an array of product lines that seem to be unrelated.
21. **Specialty store:** A retailer offering merchandise in one primary product category in considerable depth.
22. **Supermarket:** A large, departmentalized, food-oriented retail establishment that sells beverages, canned goods, dairy products, frozen foods, meat, produce and such nonfood items as health and beauty aids, kitchen utensils, magazines, pharmaceuticals and toys.
23. **Superstore:** A retailer that focuses on a single product category but offers a huge selection and low prices; also called a category killer.
24. **Telemarketing:** Using the telephone to contact leads (potential customers) from a list.
25. **Variety store:** A retailer offering a variety of low-priced merchandise of low to moderate quality.
26. **Warehouse club:** A large, no-frills store that carries a revolving array of merchandise at low prices.
27. **Wheel of retailing:** A descriptive theory about how retailers emerge, evolve and sometimes fade away.
28. **Wholesaling:** Selling of goods for resale or use to retailers and other businesses.

REFERENCES

1. "Facts and Figures," IKEA, www.ikea.com, website visited July 14, 2014; "IKEA Completes Expansion of Round Rock, TX Store," IKEA, www.ikea.com, website visited July 14, 2014; "Swedish giant IKEA close to getting approval for entry into India: report," China Post, www.chinapost.com, website visited July 14, 2014; www.hoovers.com, website visited July 14, 2014; Brad Tuttle, "Marriott & IKEA Launch a Hotel Brand for Millennials: What Does That Even Mean?," Time, March 8, 2013.

2. Lauren Indvik, "U.S. Online Retail Sales to Reach $327 Billion by 2016," Mashable Business, www.mashable.com, website visited February 27, 2012.

3. Venkatesan, Rajkumar; Kumar, V.; Ravishanker, Nalini, "Multichannel Shopping: Causes and Consequences," Journal of Marketing Vol. 70, No. 2, April 2006.

4. Barbara Farfan, "2014 US Retail Industry Overview - Info, Facts, Research, Data, Trivia," http://retailindustry.about.com, website visited July 14, 2014.

5. Wet Seal Inc., www.wetsealinc.com, website visited July 14, 2014.

6. CNW Group, "For the First Time Walmart Canada Stores Add Authentic Merchandise to Help Asian Customers Ring in the New Year," www.newswire.ca, website visited July 14, 2014.

7. Barnes & Noble, www.barnesandnoble.com, website visited July 14, 2014.

8. "Higher Unit Prices, Not Volume, Behind Rapid Growth of U.S. Private Label Sales," Nielsen, www.us.nielsen.com, June 04, 2008

9. Phillips, David, "Not Your Father's Store Brand," Dairy Foods Vol. 107, Issue 6, June 2006, pg. 8.

10. Bolotsky; Fassler, Hard Goods Specialty Retailing, p. 2-4.

11. Levy; Weitz, Retailing Management, pg. 258.

12. www.mallofamerica.com, website visited July 15, 2014.

13. "More challenges from Walmart," Advertising Age 77(17), April 24, 2006, pg. 18.

14. www.japan-guide.com, website visited July 15, 2014.

15. Frank, Robert J.; Mihas, Elizabeth A.; Narasimhan, Laxman; Rauch, Stacey, "Competing in a Value-Driven World," McKinsey & Company Report, February 2003.

16. www.wegmans.com visited July 15, 2014.

17. "Warehouse Clubs and Superstores: Industry Profile," Research and Markets, www.researchandmarkets.com, website visited July 15, 2014.

18. Stern; El-Ansary; Coughlan, Marketing Channels, pg. 43.

19. Levy, Walter, "Are Department Stores Doomed?" Direct Marketing, May 1991, pp. 56-60.

20. "The Era Of Big Box Retail Dominance Is Coming To An End," Bloomberg, www.bloomberg.com, March 30, 2012; www.bestbuy.com, website visited July 15, 2014.

21. Smith, Joyce, "Chain stores change focus," Knight Ridder Tribune Business News, Washington, pg. 1, April 8, 2006.

22. Wentz, Laurel, "Expect More Growth in '07," Advertising Age Vol. 78, Issue 17, April 2007, pg. S1.

23. White, George; Levin, Myron, "Target Stores to Stop Selling Cigarettes," Los Angeles Times, August 29, 1996, pp. A1, A28.

24. Steinberg, Jules, "Worker Performance Reviews Can Be a Two-Way Street," Twice, September 4, 2000, pg. 28.

25. Zara Opens Largest Store in the United States in Chicago, October 30, 2009.

26. 28 "Retailing in India," Sacramento Bee, www.sacbee.com, August 13, 2012.

27. "Walmart, others seek US govt help on India plans," MyDigitalFC.com, http://wrd.mydigitalfc.com, July 29, 2012.

28. "Walmart Stores," CNN Money, http://money.cnn.com, website visited July 15, 2014.

29. "Saving people money so they can live better — worldwide," Walmart, www.walmartstores.com, website visited July 15, 2014.

30. "Walgreen buys stake in European drug store chain for $6.7B," Chicago Tribune, www.chicagotribune.com, June 19, 2012.

31. "DMA Releases New 'Power of Direct' Report; DM-Driven Sales Growth Outpace Overall Economic Growth," Direct Marketing Association, www.the-dma.org, October 2, 2011.

32. Ibid.

33. www.calyxandcorolla.com, website visited July 15, 2014.

34. "Facts and Figures," IKEA, www.ikea.com, website visited July 15, 2014.

35. "Access Innovations Enhances Thesaurus Master," Information Today 22(7), July/August 2005, pg. 38.

36. Fielding, Michael, "Direct mail still has its place: Marketers find it works best as part of integrated campaigns," American Marketing Association, Direct Marketing, November 1, 2006, pg. 31.

37. Amy Dusto, "60% of U.S. retail sales will involve the web by 2017," Internet Retailer, October 30, 2013.

38. "Media Usage Forecast 2013," www.targetmarketingmag.com, website visited July 15, 2014.

39. "Reduce Unwanted Catalogs Mailed to You," National Wildlife Federation, www.nwf.org, website visited July 15, 2014.

40. www.qvc.com, website visited July 15, 2014.; www.hsn.com, website visited July 15, 2014.

41. Stone, Robert, Successful Direct Marketing Methods (Lincolnwood, Illinois, NTC Business Books) 1994.

42. www.dell.com, website visited July 15, 2014.

43. Ibid.

44. www.omahasteaks.com, website visited July 15, 2014.

45. Stone, Successful Direct Marketing Methods.

46. Judson, NetMarketing.

47. Wang, Liz C.; Baker, Julie; Wagner, Judy; Wakefield, Kirk, "Can a Retail Website Be Social?" Journal of Marketing Vol. 71, No. 3, July 2007.

48. Cunningham, Dwight, "One Size Does Not Fit All," Media Week, November 15, 1999, pg. 54.

49. www.tempurpedic.com, visited July 15, 2014.

50. Shipping Methods and Costs, Dick's Sporting Goods, www.dickssportinggoods.com, visited July 15, 2014.

51. "Direct Marketing Association's Guidelines for Ethical Business Practice," Direct Marketing Association, September 2006.

52. www.toydirectory.com; www.wholesalecentral.com, websites visited March 19, 2012.

53. "Wholesale Trade," Bureau of Labor Statistics, http://www.bls.gov, website visited July 15, 2014.

54. Felgner, Brent, "Walmart testing various new CE initiatives," June 19, 2007, pg. 4.

PRICING OBJECTIVES
& INFLUENCES

ALDI Foods, a German-based supermarket chain, entered the U.S. market in 1976 with a goal of offering customers an alternative to the expansive and mega-sized strategies used by its competitors. ALDI has mastered the art of selling its select assortment of groceries at prices that are, on average, 40% less than competitors' prices. Carrying a mere 1,400 grocery items, ALDI is miniature in scale compared to the 30,000 of a typical super center – but the small stores pack a big punch with rock bottom prices on the fastest-moving grocery items. Through the company's commitment to quality, ALDI's low-price strategy has proved very successful in the U.S. over the last 38 years.

The niche grocer is a stickler when it comes to top quality products. ALDI only carries its own national brand products and each product is typically packaged in an average size container. By eliminating the need for a consumer to choose brand or size, ALDI is able to offer a quick shopping experience for today's busy consumer. Limiting its stock to primarily its own brand also allows for some serious buying power with its suppliers. By creating and maintaining great relationships with those suppliers, the company gets the absolute best prices and transfers those savings to its customers. The company believes so highly in the quality of its products that it offers a Double Guarantee on quality, taste, and satisfaction. If for any reason a customer is not 100% satisfied with any product, ALDI will replace the product AND refund the purchase price. ALDI select brands are regularly tested to insure they equal or exceed top, national brands in quality, performance and taste.

In order to maintain its commitment to quality yet offer the lowest prices possible, ALDI has a unique business model that varies from the common grocery shopper's experience. For example, ALDI customers pay for each bag and bag their own groceries. Without having to staff a bagger, the company is able to reduce labor costs. The grocer also has a unique cart system. Customers insert a quarter to release a shopping cart from the cart corral before they begin shopping. When they finish, they return the cart and receive their quarter back. This eliminates the need to hire an employee to gather carts, again reducing company costs. These are two examples of how ALDI reduces operating expenses and passes the savings onto its customers through exceptionally low prices.

While the German company has taken a 'no-frills' approach in many areas of its business model, hiring top quality talent employees and maintaining consistent customer service are two areas in which the company will not cut corners. in order to ensure they have the best of the best, the company is at the top of its industry in pay and benefits. With quality employees and high job satisfaction, an ALDI store runs much more efficiently than many other retailers. Store aisles are stocked with pallets of ready-to-sell products, so restocking is a snap -- a cost saving technique also often deployed by retail giant Wal-Mart. With only four to five aisles per store, ALDI stores are designed to resemble a small town grocery store with familiar faces and excellent service.

ALDI has expanded steadily since first opening its doors in the United States, and has plans to open 80-100 new stores per year in the near future. There are now over 1,100 stores in the U.S. and ALDI is ranked 26th in U.S. grocery chains in terms of gross sales. According to a Market Force study recently released, ALDI was named the nation's low price leader, ahead of competitors such as WalMart, Costco, Kroger, Meijer, and Safeway. Globally, ALDI has become one of the world's largest grocery chains, operating over 9,500 individual stores worldwide. In Germany, ALDI is the leading discount supermarket chain and its sales account for about two-thirds of global company sales.

If you are looking for great food, a streamlined shopping experience and low prices, consider the ALDI experience: honest to goodness savings.[1]

<< ALDI Foods Products & Pricing

Courtesy of ALDI

Learning Objectives

1. Describe how pricing works with the other parts of the marketing mix.
2. Learn how economic factors such as demand and supply influence prices.
3. Understand the legal and ethical constraints on pricing decisions.
4. Use industry structure concepts to understand how competitors determine price in different types of industries.
5. Use competitive factors surrounding industry structure concepts to understand how pricing works in different types of industries.
6. Recognize the conditions that make international pricing complex.

THE CONCEPT OF PRICING

You can purchase a tote bag for as little as $2, but you can also purchase a trendy Louis Vuitton bag for about $5,000. A scarf can cost as little as $10, but a luxury Hermes may cost over $1,000.

A remarkably broad range of prices is charged for items that have similar functions. Ginseng roots grown for tea in Korea and other Pacific Rim nations sell for a few dollars, but a couple of ounces found in the wild will cost nearly $50,000. New cars range from around $13,000 for a 2014 Chevrolet Spark LS to the $4.5 million 2014 Lamborghini Veneno Roadster.[2] Even four years of college tuition can cost anywhere from several thousand dollars to well over $200,000 at a select private school or a prestigious foreign university.

Pricing plays a critical role in the allocation of resources in free market economies. Since prices fluctuate according to competitive forces, their rise and fall directly influence the amount of goods and services consumers are willing to purchase. Pricing is also critical for the firm. The amount consumers purchase multiplied by its price determines the total revenue a company receives. Long before a sale is made, marketers forecast consumer demand at varying prices. This influences the allocation of resources used to create, promote and distribute products. Prices have a dramatic effect in determining the overall profitability of the firm. Consequently, pricing is one of the most important and complex areas of marketing.

Price is also a concept described by many names. These euphemisms "soften" the unpleasant feeling people may have when paying a price for something. How many can you think of? Tuition is what you pay to go to school. Rent is what you pay for your apartment. An honorarium is paid for a speech. A retainer is paid to a lawyer. A fee is paid to a doctor. A premium is charged for insurance. Highways charge a toll. Dues are charged for membership. Assessments are used to calculate property taxes, the ongoing price for real estate ownership. A wage or salary is the price paid for work, and interest is the price paid for using money. Fares are charged for public transportation. Salespeople receive a commission for achieving a certain level of sales, and a bonus is the price paid for extraordinary performance. Whatever the name, price still signals that an amount is exchanged for something.

We have mentioned before that value comes from both the marketing organization and the buyer. In each case, value is given up and received. **Price** is the exchange value of a good or service in the marketplace. We tend to think of price as a set amount of money that can be exchanged for a particular product, but a good or service can also be bartered or traded for other products. Bartering simply bypasses the monetary system.

Price

The exchange value of a good or service in the marketplace.

PRICE AS A PART OF THE MARKETING MIX

We have discussed many of the decisions concerning the elements of the marketing mix. Products, logistics, and promotion create value for buyers. Price captures value from buyers for the firm, in order to cover its costs for other parts of the mix and produce a profit. All parts interact to establish the firm's positioning. In fact, good pricing decisions require analyzing what target customers expect to pay even before products are developed, distributed and promoted. Marketers need to understand ahead of time what customers perceive to be good value. If products cost too much, customers perceive that they are losing value, and they will spend their money on other products or purchase the minimum amount necessary. If products cost too little and the firm loses money as a result, it will eventually become uncompetitive and go out of business.

OBJECTIVES OF PRICE SETTING

Prices are set with profit, volume, competitive and customer objectives in mind. Businesses need to charge enough to make a profit, which satisfies owners (shareholders) and creates the financial resources needed to grow. Even nonprofits must have excess revenues over costs in order to keep pace with inflation and expand operations. Prices are also tailored to the amount of product sold. Like profit, volume maintains or increases the size of the business. In addition to pleasing owners, financial health creates opportunities for employees to progress and prosper. Third, price is often a deciding factor when consumers have to choose among competing brands. Finally, proper pricing helps build customer relationships.

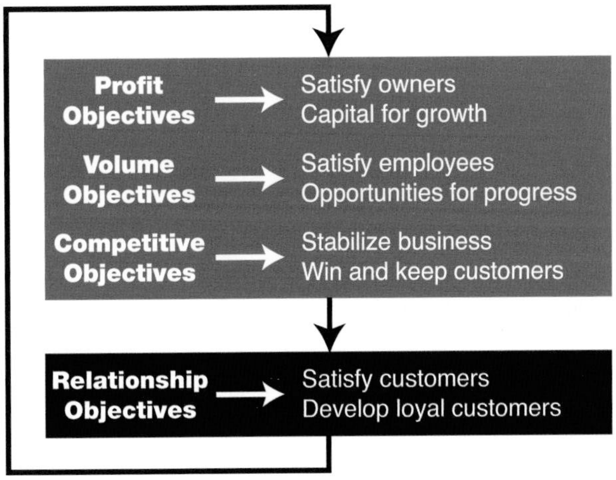

As with the chicken and the egg, it is difficult to determine what comes first; profit, volume, competitive and customer objectives are all linked. Figure 17.1 shows that the satisfaction of all parties to the business is in some way

Figure 17.1   Prices Serve Several Objectives

affected by price. Most important, when an organization meets relationship objectives, it gains satisfied, loyal customers who consistently produce revenues and profit. Yet it takes satisfied shareholders, contented employees and a strong competitive position to make customers happy. Let's look at each set of objectives.

PROFIT OBJECTIVES

Profit is critical for every business. Without it, investors will take their money elsewhere, and the business will cease to exist. In other words, you always need to price in order to make money. In the simplest terms, revenue minus cost equals profit. Price has a direct impact on revenue: multiplying price by volume yields revenue. Later, we will see how price affects volume, which in turn affects cost. The point is that price plays a role in all the major factors that influence profit. To change profit, you simply increase or reduce price, volume or cost. Since these three elements are so closely connected, the situation is very intriguing. Exactly how they interact is a big issue for marketers. Let's say a business makes a 10 percent profit on sales. If nothing else changes, then a three percent price increase means that profits also increase by three percent. A price decrease will have the opposite effect.

Profits are required to cover the risks attached to marketing a product. Price may be designed to create maximum profits, but more often satisfactory profits are the objective. Essentially, satisfactory means that the expectations of investors are met or exceeded. Satisfactory profits are based roughly on how much the company has historically made, how much similar companies make, and the risks involved in the business. Profits are usually stated in terms of return on sales, return on investment, or profit margin. A minimum return on investment is the amount you make when you put your money in a financial institution and earn interest. Companies with significant profit margins will typically be successful. Satisfactory profit goals are designed to reflect what shareholders, management, employees and customers believe are fair for all parties involved.

Profit maximization is often stated as the goal of pricing, but since price is intertwined with volume and cost, it is difficult to project the ideal price for maximized profits. Furthermore, there are limits to what people will pay, and analysis needs to take into account the long-term picture. Customer demand fluctuates with changes in economic conditions and shifts in the marketing mix. Competitive pressures also make it difficult to know exactly what price will maximize profit in dynamic markets.

VOLUME (SALES) OBJECTIVES

The price charged often affects the number of units purchased. Firms must price in such a way that production is maintained at a stable or growing level. Too high a price may result in layoffs, and too low a price may cause difficulty in meeting demand, which means lost sales and damage to the company's reputation. In either situation, employees will be unhappy. As you have learned, too low a price can even reduce the units demanded. Because it influences the overall amount to be consumed, price must be carefully set.

COMPETITIVE OBJECTIVES

Volume translates into market share, which creates market power. Many firms have specific market share objectives and price accordingly. Of course, many factors other than price contribute to high share. Although lowering price to increase share may reduce profits in the short run, it may cause competitors to restrict activities or withdraw from markets. Prices can sometimes be raised later in the absence of competition. But certain predatory pricing is illegal, as discussed later in this chapter.

Aside from gaining share, pricing also can help the organization maintain its market position. Leaders try to establish the market price, while followers have to react to the leaders' change. If either party wants to prevent pricing from being used to adjust demand, then it may choose one of two strategies. **Status quo pricing** maintains the same relative position: Every time a competitor makes a price change,

Status Quo Pricing

When a competitor makes a price change, rivals follow suit.

rivals follow suit. This happens frequently in the airline industry. **Nonprice competition** leaves price at a given level and adjusts other parts of the marketing mix, adding or subtracting value when appropriate. For example, advertising may be increased or decreased, extra products may be piggybacked on packages, or container size may be reduced. Of course, in the short term it is always easier to adjust price than alter other marketing mix variables.

Nonprice Competition

Price is unchanged but adjustments are made to other parts of the marketing mix in response to competitor's price change.

RELATIONSHIP (CUSTOMER) OBJECTIVES

One of the most direct ways to engage in relationship marketing is to establish prices with customer loyalty in mind. The objective is to create sufficient value over time to develop repeat business. In this case, pricing signals the relationship the company desires with customers. This is called value-based pricing and is a major topic in the next chapter. Fundamentally, prices are set to provide value for the customer in both the short term and the long run. Your most loyal customers should benefit to some degree from the extra profit generated through the relationship. You can accomplish this by lowering the price for loyal buyers or by adding value to the product they receive. Most importantly, you must understand your customers thoroughly in order to learn what they value.

MAJOR FACTORS INFLUENCING PRICE

Pricing according to value concepts requires a grasp of several elements, as outlined in Figure 17.2. First, economic factors explain how the demand for and supply of products relate to price. Second, legal and ethical constraints affect pricing decisions. Since price plays a major role in determining how economic resources are distributed, the government and courts have taken a particular interest in pricing. Third, the competitive environment influences price. Marketers must understand how competitors differentiate their products and the effect that substitutes have on price. Fourth, understanding how the company's cost structure is influenced by price decisions is very important. Finally, numerous global factors affect pricing in domestic and international markets. Each of these areas is addressed in the following sections.

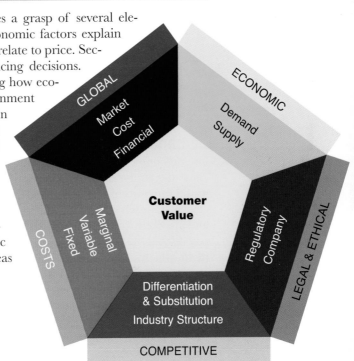

Figure 17.2   Factors Influencing Price

ECONOMIC FACTORS: DEMAND AND SUPPLY

Economists have developed elaborate theories about the effect of consumer demand and product supply. Both have a significant influence on pricing.

The Demand Curve
Demand is determined by the amount of product customers need, plus their willingness and ability to buy. Demand has a major influence on price. It is usually depicted by a **demand curve**, which is a graph showing quantity

Demand Curve

A depiction of the price elasticity demand for a given product.

Price Elasticity

The extent to which changes in price affect the number of units demanded or supplied.

along the horizontal axis and different prices along the vertical axis. Marketers use the curve to estimate changes in total demand for a product based on differing prices. The demand curve describes the price elasticity of a given product. **Price elasticity** is the extent to which changes in what is charged affect the number of units sold. Price elasticity is used to forecast responses to price changes and to define market segments. Knowing the price elasticity for company and competitor products is important in determining a pricing strategy.[3]

When price has a major effect on demand, the product is price elastic. When price has little effect on demand, the product is price inelastic. Figure 17.3 shows two demand curves, one for a price-elastic product (everyday blue jeans) and the other for a price-inelastic product (heart surgery). Blue jeans are useful but not a necessity. If their average price is high, then consumers will demand very few and search for alternatives like khaki pants; if the price goes down, then demand will increase dramatically. In contrast, most consumers who need heart surgery do not care about the price, especially if government or private insurance will cover the cost. Price changes in heart surgery are not likely to influence the total demand to any large degree.

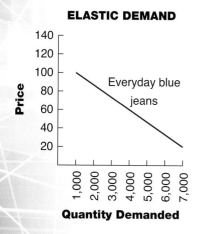

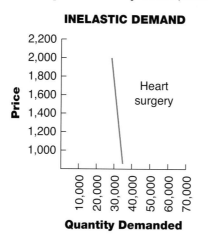

Figure 17.3   Demand Curves

When demand is elastic, prices tend to decrease over time to maintain or increase revenue. As Figure 17.3 shows, when the price of everyday blue jeans drops from $100 down to $20, sales increase from 1,000 units to more than 7,000 units, reflecting elastic demand. For heart surgery, as the price drops from $2,000 to $1,000, demand stays roughly the same. In the elastic case, total revenue rises from $100,000 to $140,000 as increased volume more than compensates for the lower price. In the inelastic case, revenue declines from about $60 million to $35 million.

Demand Sensitivity by Market Segment
In addition to the type of product, differences in market segments explain some of the variation in demand. Because the airline industry believes that the overall demand for business travel is less sensitive to price than the demand for leisure travel, pricing policies are designed specifically for each segment. Business travelers often purchase tickets at the last minute and are likely to pay full fare, while those on vacation can plan well in advance and pay discounted rates. Fares are also lower for trips that include at least one weekend night, which seldom applies to business travelers. Their demand is inelastic because a certain amount of travel is required for the functioning of their firms. Leisure travelers not only have more elastic demand but also are more sensitive to price differences among airlines. Just before spring break, student newspapers are full of ads offering trip packages at greatly reduced prices. StudentBreaks.com, for example, is a website dedicated to offering a great variety of destinations for students for as low as $300 per person.[4] Several travel websites now allow users to view airline prices from hundreds of other sites all in one place. Kayak.com even has a function to track flight prices and notify you when a plane ticket in your price range becomes available.[5]

Cross-price Elasticity of Demand

The extent to which the quantity demanded of one product changes in response to changes in the price of another product

Cross-Price Elasticity of Demand
We find **cross-price elasticity of demand** when the quantity demanded of one product changes in response to price changes in another product. For example, an increase in the cost of lumber in the building industry increases the demand for substitute products made of plastic and steel. At the brand level, an increase in the price of Dasani increases the demand for

Ice Mountain. Marketers use demand curves to describe price elasticity for a product class (all brands) or for a single brand. Price elasticity may differ for the total industry (that is, for all brands) versus an individual brand. Because gasoline is a necessity, variations in the average price charged by all producers may not affect demand dramatically. But British Petroleum-Amoco may find that its demand is elastic if it charges a lot more than the industry average. In other words, cross-elasticity refers to the amount of demand for one company's product based on its difference from the average price. Therefore, the concept of elasticity applies to the total industry, whereas cross-elasticity applies to preferences for individual brands or substitutes. Several marketing factors are likely to have a significant effect on cross-elasticity. For example, customers who are brand loyal to a particular gasoline company, especially those who buy the premium grade, are less likely to buy gasoline elsewhere because of a two- or three-cent difference in price; those with little or no loyalty, and who buy the lowest grade, are more likely to shop around for the lowest price.

Many marketing plans are designed to produce inelastic cross-elasticity for the brand. That means price is less important to buyers than brand attributes, which prevents price competitors from luring them away. Consider Seven for All Mankind jeans, which typically retail for around $200 per pair, whereas Levi's often sell for less than $40. Many consumers are willing to pay more for the Seven brand to satisfy their need for esteem and prestige or because they like its features.

To reduce the cross-price elasticity of their products, marketers may use any of the following approaches:[6]

- *Position the product relative to costly substitutes.* General Motors attempted this when it priced its Aurora to be competitive with BMW, Audi, Lexus and Infiniti in the $40,000 price range.

- *Focus attention on unique features.* Boston Whaler commands a premium for its line of recreational craft due to the company's reputation for safety. The boats can't sink, which is a major reason the U.S. Coast Guard selects the brand.

- *Make it costly or difficult to switch.* ABB Robotics trains users of its systems in programming and maintenance. Retraining on another system is expensive and time consuming.

- *Make cross-brand comparisons difficult.* Prudential says "get a piece of the rock," implying that its size and stability is an asset in financial planning.

- *Use price to signal status, image or quality.* The name Rolex is synonymous with high price. One jeweler says: "If customers have to ask the price, they can't afford it."

- *Put price in the context of high value.* Volvo emphasizes family protection. Assuring the safety of loved ones is a benefit that customers are likely to value more highly than the money they could save by purchasing a cheaper brand.

The Supply Curve

Price, which influences profit, also has an important influence on the willingness to produce. When price is higher, producers are willing to supply more. When profit margins are low, companies are likely to produce less. The supply curves shown in Figure 17.4 depict these relationships. In the elastic curve, an increase in unit price from $20 to $140 causes a dramatic increase in everyday blue jean production, from 1,000 units to 7,000 units. In the inelastic curve, price hikes cause only a moderate increase in supply; there are relatively few trained heart surgeons, and they can squeeze only so many procedures into each day's schedule.

The **supply curve** reveals the amount that producers are willing to provide at each price. Theoretically, it operates very much like a demand curve, but different factors are at work. For example, companies with high fixed investment find it extremely difficult to exit the industry, so supply is inelastic. Another example is lawyers, who are generally reluctant to switch careers because they have invested heavily in education. When the price of legal services drops dramatically because of competition, lawyers are still willing to produce the same amount, reflecting the highly inelastic supply curve. When industry entry and exit are easy, supply tends to be more elastic. As prices rise, firms are willing to produce more; as prices decline, firms produce less or switch to other products.

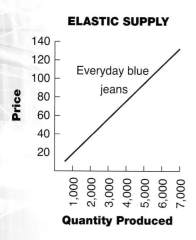
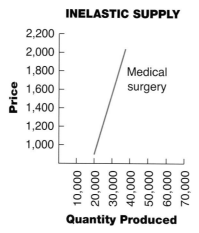

Figure 17.4   Supply Curves

Supply Curve

A depiction of the price elasticity of supply for a product.

Equilibrium Price

In theory, price plays a role in balancing supply and demand. In Figure 17.5, the equilibrium price for everyday blue jeans--the point at which the supply and demand curves cross--is $60. At prices below that point, producers are increasingly reluctant to supply everyday blue jeans; at prices above it, consumers are increasingly reluctant to buy. Market forces work to help balance supply and demand so that products do not go unused and customers do not pay more than is required. Economic theory suggests that, over time, most product prices are somewhat elastic. When prices are high, supply is likely to outstrip demand. Suppliers then lower prices until supply and demand come into equilibrium. When prices are too low, less is produced. Consumers are willing to pay more for scarce products, so supply increases until it is in balance with demand. In other words, supply and demand are related because changes in price affect how both suppliers and consumers respond. The demand for cranberries rose sharply after 1994 after a Harvard University study showed that cranberry juice soothed urinary tract infections, and cranberry growers increased their acreage by 176 percent over the next few years to match the new demand. In 1999, how-

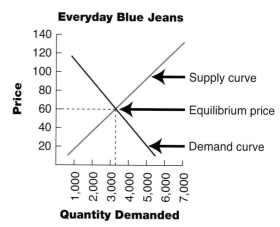

Figure 17.5   Equilibrium Price

Pricing Objectives & Influences **469**

Chapter 17

ever, the new acreage yielded a record harvest and the supply of cranberries surpassed the demand, resulting in the low price of $11 a barrel. Some cranberry farmers went out of business because the price of their product did not cover the costs of growing it, much less produce a profit. With cranberry production scaled back as a result, in 2003 its price rebounded up to $38, and by 2012 it had increased to around $69.90. In 2013, prices plummeted once again to $15.50 because of a near-record 210 million pound supply.[7]

It is important to remember that supply and demand curves work perfectly only in economic theory, which assumes that most variables are held constant. In reality, the marketplace changes rapidly. Indeed, a main purpose of marketing strategy is to alter the supply and demand characteristics of an industry in the company's favor. Unfortunately, this does not always work positively for all competitors. For example, Toyota, Honda and Ford have increased their hybrid car production; environmental concerns among consumers and increasing gas prices have yielded higher demand for these products. As a result, vehicles with poor gas mileage have slowed in sales.[8] In many industries, the tremendous diversity in market segments and individual firms introduces more variables than can reasonably be taken into account. Furthermore, it is very difficult to forecast demand and to predict what competitors will do. For all these reasons, attempts to influence elasticity through marketing strategies may not always work as well in practice.

LEGAL AND ETHICAL INFLUENCES ON PRICING

Both federal and state laws affect pricing decisions. In fact, pricing is one of the most legally constrained areas of marketing. Most regulations are designed to allow prices to fluctuate freely so that market forces can work. Some, however, protect consumers from unfair prices — those that are higher than the value created due to the manipulation of market forces. Pricing practices that are legislatively restrained or regulated include price-fixing, price discrimination, minimum prices (unfair sales), price advertising, dumping and unit pricing, each of which is described later. Figure 17.6 summarizes federal legislation on pricing.

Although marketers certainly must take care to avoid outlawed pricing practices, many companies are equally concerned to

Act	Key Aspects
Sherman Antitrust Act 1890	Restricts predatory pricing (to drive competitors from the market) and makes it illegal to price fix.
Federal Trade Commission Act 1914	Set up the Federal Trade Commission, which is responsible for limiting unfair and anticompetitive practices in business.
Clayton Act 1914	Restricts price discrimination and purchase agreements between buyers and sellers.
Robinson-Patman Act 1936	Restricts discriminatory pricing that diminishes competition, particularly among resellers.
Wheeler-Lea Act 1938	Allows the Federal Trade Commission to investigate deceptive pricing practices and to regulate advertising of prices to help ensure that it does not deceive consumers.
Consumer Goods Pricing Act 1975	Eliminates price controls vertically and horizontally in the market so that channel members cannot set prices and so that retailers do not have to sell according to manufacturer or other channel member price schedules.

Figure 17.6   Major Federal Price Legislation

avoid unethical pricing that could tarnish their reputation and erode consumer trust. "Pricing Ethics," the last topic in this section, describes a number of questionable practices.

Price-Fixing

Price-fixing occurs when one party attempts to control what another party will charge in the market. There are laws against vertical and horizontal price-fixing. **Vertical price-fixing** is an attempt by a manufacturer or distributor to control the final selling price at the retail level. The Consumer Goods Pricing Act of 1975 made all interstate use of unfair trade or resale price maintenance illegal. Retailers cannot be required to use the list price (suggested retail price) set by manufacturers or resellers. Freedom for retailers to adjust prices enhances competition, thereby reducing the overall average price to consumers. The passage of this law was controversial because manufacturers and wholesalers often want to control retail prices in order to maintain consistent positioning. Several practices for controlling retail prices are legal. The manufacturer or distributor may do any of the following:

- Own the retail outlet and establish its pricing policy.
- Suggest and advertise a retail price.
- Preprint prices on products.
- Sell on consignment (own items until they are sold).
- Screen channel members, choosing only those with a history of price maintenance in their retail outlet.

Horizontal price-fixing is an agreement among manufacturers and other channel members to set prices at the retail level. The Sherman Act and the Federal Trade Commission Act outlaw these practices even if the prices are "reasonable." Violations of either statute can be severely punished with steep fines and prison sentences. For example, the Department of Justice investigated several corporations for price-fixing through business-to-business exchanges. Apple has recently been put under federal investigation for possible price-fixing in the e-book industry. The D.O.J., along with the European Commission, launched a price-fixing probe of Apple and five major publishers. Apple is alleged to have placed deals with publishers to raise prices of e-books sold through its iBooks app for the iPad, iPod Touch and iPhone. Traditionally, the book publishing business sells books to retailers at wholesale prices and retailers set the prices to consumers. In this case, Apple and publishers have allegedly conspired to force Amazon to raise its prices and also help publishers regain some power in the electronic publishing business.[9]

Signs of price-fixing include cooperation among competitors on discounting, credit terms or conditions of sale; any discussions about pricing at association meetings; plans to issue price lists on the same date or on given dates; plans to withhold or rotate bids on contracts; agreements to limit production in order to increase prices; and any exchange of information among competitors on pricing. The intent is to prohibit communication among competitors about pricing or any aspects of the business that may influence pricing levels.

On the international level, there are few antitrust sanctions to ensure fair competition. For example, in most countries impartial bidding processes are required, but in others the winners are secretly predetermined. In Japan, this practice is called *dango* and is a common occurrence. In the United States and many other nations, it is known as *bid rigging,* and is responsible for substantial business loss. For example, U.S. builders have been prevented from competing for their share of the $500 billion Japanese construction market. The United States hired a Japanese law firm to file for $35 million in damages against 140 Japanese companies accused of rigging bids. This action resulted in a $32.6 million settlement.

Price Discrimination

Price discrimination occurs when a manufacturer or other channel member charges different prices to retailers competing in the same marketplace. The Robinson-Patman Act of 1936 was designed to enhance competi-

---

Price-fixing

An attempt by one party to control what another party will charge in the market.

Vertical Price-fixing

An attempt by a manufacturer or distributor to control the final selling price at the retail level.

Horizontal Price-fixing

Agreement among manufacturers and channel members to set prices at the retail level.

Price Discrimination

A legally restricted practice in which a manufacturer or other channel member charges different prices to different retailers in the same marketplace.

tion by protecting small retailers against discounters or larger retailers that might obtain favorable treatment from suppliers. Today, this law is a major restriction on how manufacturers price. Essentially, the act permits manufacturer discounts only if the seller can demonstrate that they are available to all competing channel buyers on the same fair basis. Price fluctuations must be developed in such a way that both small and large buyers can qualify for discounts, or the discounts must be cost justified. The law specifies that it is illegal not only for sellers to engage in unfair practices but also for retailers to purchase products when they know that discrimination toward other retailers is occurring.

CAREER TIP!

At British Petroleum, pricing specialists use a combination of data to develop market-based pricing strategies and tactics for gasoline as well as metrics to measure performance for strategies and execution. They are responsible for learning about market structure, product costs, competitive retail tactics, consumer behavior patterns and price elasticities. They are also responsible for profit, volume and margin results as well as for achieving other strategic and tactical goals. If you are interested in this kind of job or another career at BP, then view the current openings at www.bp.com.

The Robinson-Patman Act involves a relatively complex issue. Differential pricing is allowed in many circumstances in which manufacturers are competing to gain or hold business. The law was designed to enhance competition by preventing restraint of trade. Essentially, violation occurs when manufacturers or other channel members charge differential prices that inhibit the ability of one retailer to compete with another. Acceptable price discrimination occurs when the differences are based on time, place, customer characteristics or product distinctions. In other words, any time the marketing mix has been altered, price may reflect those changes.

Consider the annual fees associated with different credit cards. The issuer may charge affluent customers $100 a year for premium gold cards but suspend all fees for students. American Express charges annual fees for many of its cards. The Platinum has a $450 annual fee but comes with extra benefits such as access to airline lounges and a concierge to assist with dinner reservations or concert tickets.[10] The top-tier customers, who charge more than $250,000 annually, may hold the black American Express Centurion Card.

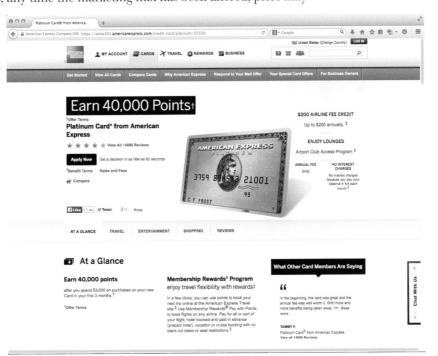

This card has a $7,500 initiation fee plus an annual fee of $2,500. There is no interest rate for this card because cardholders must pay off the balance at the end of each month.[11] Discounts for senior citizens, such as a percentage off on a particular day of the week, are another acceptable form of price discrimination. These practices demonstrate how price deviates among consumer segments.

Minimum Prices

Laws against so-called minimum prices, often called unfair sales acts, have been enacted in a number of states. These prevent retailers from selling merchandise for less than the cost of the product plus a reasonable profit. Many states have such laws in order to protect smaller retailers and agricultural industries from larger competitors. **Predatory pricing** occurs when large firms cut prices on products in order to eliminate small local competitors. Walmart was recently accused of violating predatory pricing laws when it began offering $4 generic prescription drugs. However, other competitors such as Costco and Kroger were able to match Walmart's low price.[12] At the national level, the Sherman and Clayton acts prevent this. Other laws apply to intrastate commerce.

Loss leaders are items priced below cost to attract customers. In some states this practice is restricted. In others it is legal, particularly when it is not designed to injure specific local competitors. Most loss leaders are heavily advertised brands with strong appeal, ensuring volume that compensates for the low price. For example, supermarkets may feature a special on brand-name laundry detergents that have wide appeal. Once in the store, customers are likely to purchase additional goods at normal or even elevated prices. McDonald's and other fast-food chains can lower prices on burgers to increase traffic because its margins on soft drinks and fries make up the difference. Victoria's Secret uses the five pair for $25 deal on its Pink underwear to attract a younger market into its stores to buy its more expensive underwear.[13]

Even investment companies use loss leaders; many waive fees on money funds to attract business, hoping that customers will later invest in other areas.

Black Friday, the day following Thanksgiving in the United States, is traditionally known as the beginning of the Christmas shopping season. Many large retailers offer steep discounted loss leaders to lure consumers into their stores. While thousands line up at the door early in the morning to get the best deals, others are finding similar door-buster deals online. For some, Black Friday shopping has become an important annual tradition to be carefully planned and orchestrated. Websites like blackfriday.com allow shoppers to pinpoint the best advertised deals year-round.[14]

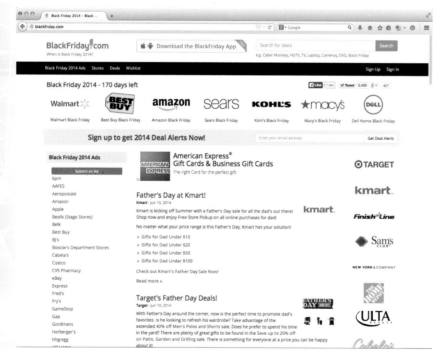

Predatory Pricing

Price-cutting by large firms to eliminate small local competitors.

Loss Leaders

Items priced below cost to attract customers.

Price Advertising

The Federal Trade Commission has set up permissible standards for price advertising. Essentially, these guidelines prohibit marketers from communicating price deceptively. Firms may not claim that a price is reduced unless the original price has been offered to the public regularly and recently. A company can only make price comparisons with the competition if it verifies its claims. Furthermore, pre-marked prices cannot be artificially increased as a point of comparison unless products are actually sold at that price in substantial quantities. In addition, a retailer cannot continuously advertise the same product as being on sale when that price has become standard at that outlet.

Bait-and-switch promotions are specifically outlawed by the Federal Trade Commission Act and various state statutes. **Bait and switch** occurs when the seller

Bait and Switch

An unethical practice in which sellers advertise items at extremely low prices and then inform the customer that the items are out of stock, offer different items, or attempt to sell the customer more expensive substitutes.

advertises items at extremely low prices and then informs the customer these are out of stock, offers different items or attempts to sell the customer more expensive substitutes. In other words, when there is no intent to sell the advertised item, retailers are being dishonest.

Dumping

In the international market, one of the most common regulations relates to dumping, which is a form of price discrimination. **Dumping** occurs when a product is sold in a foreign country at a price lower than in the producing country and lower than its actual cost of production. Because global organizations cover many of their costs in domestic markets, they do this to maximize volume and profit abroad. Dumping is illegal because it puts manufacturers in the local foreign market at a disadvantage. The U.S. Department of Commerce recently placed an anti-dumping tariff on certain steel products imported from China and the United Arab Emirates. The importers were penalized as much as 118 percent of the product value. Often, emerging economies are the source of dumping in the United States because of lower labor costs.[15]

Predatory dumping is pricing designed to drive local firms out of the market. The organization gains strong market share and pushes competitors out of business with low prices, then raises them after establishing this power.[16]

> **Dumping**
>
> Selling a product in a foreign country at a price lower than in the producing country and lower than its cost of production.

> **Predatory Dumping**
>
> Pricing below cost to drive local firms out of business.

Unit Pricing

Container sizes for the same item can vary considerably. In some cases the package may have similar wording, such as "giant" or "large economy" size. This makes it difficult for consumers to compare the price of products based on the size and type of packaging. The unit pricing legislation enacted two decades ago requires that certain types of retail outlets, especially food stores, display price per unit of measure as well as total price. For example, a four-ounce can of tuna selling for $1 is also priced at 25 cents per ounce. In this way, consumers can clearly see whether a larger size makes a price difference. The law is designed to help cost-conscious consumers make wise decisions at the retail level. In fact, according to a survey of customers, the most important attribute in stores is unit pricing signs on the shelves.[17]

Pricing Ethics

Ethical issues in pricing abound. For price-sensitive (elastic) products, they revolve around the creation of demand and delivery of value based on price. For price-inelastic products, particularly because of the captive audience, gouging is an issue.

Although laws protect customers against unscrupulous pricing, companies still find questionable ways of using price to increase demand. For example, an ad for dramatically reduced airfares states (in tiny print) that some restrictions may apply. When you call, you learn that so many restrictions apply that your choices are limited to a few seats and times. Italy's airline Alitalia was fined EUR30,000 for misleading consumers with an ad on round-trip flight fares showing only the one-way ticket cost.[18]

Another way to increase demand is to make the product seem less expensive than it really is, sometimes by not clearly disclosing all costs. For example, a car salesperson may quote a price for the car you're considering. Yet, when you decide to purchase it, you find additional charges, such as administrative expenses and delivery fees, on the invoice. The salesperson tells you that these are standard costs and are stated in small print on the contract.

Perhaps you have noticed that your favorite brand of paper towel or pudding seems to disappear faster than it once did. Check the package. There is a good chance that the price remained the same but the size was reduced. Rather than pass on increased costs to customers, some manufacturers reduce the amount of product contained in a package. To obscure the issue, words like "new convenience package" are printed in small type. You're getting less value but may not be aware of it, because basic package design and price stay the same.

The captive customer creates a tempting target for some marketers. Because demand is already there, the question is how much to charge. Consider the cost of automobile parts. After an accident, you find that replacing one door will cost 20 percent of what you paid for the car. Are you likely to scrap it? It is true that the fee for handling and stocking inventory has to be included in prices, but many companies make a much greater percentage on replacement items than on the original product.

Another way to reduce the amount delivered is to price on an all-you-want basis and then limit the supply. For example, a golf course or tennis club has a monthly fee for unlimited usage, but there are so many customers that you must wait an exorbitant amount of time for space. Some e-retailers experienced a similar circumstance during Christmas, when many online stores did not have enough products, or an efficient system of delivery, to deliver items already bought and paid for by consumers. A number of orders arrived late or did not arrive at all, and hence the Federal Trade Commission fined stores that failed to make good on their delivery promises. As a result, during the next Christmas season, many online retailers improved ordering and shipping practices to meet the consumer demand for their products and services.

COMPETITIVE FACTORS THAT INFLUENCE PRICE

When making pricing decisions, marketers must take the competitive environment into consideration. More specifically, it's important to look at industry structure and the potential for differentiating products through pricing strategies.

Industry Structure The basic definition of industry is a group of firms offering similar products. However, this definition can be applied broadly or narrowly. For example, Pizza Hut executives may view their industry as only establishments that sell pizza, or as all restaurants in a particular price range. As with most other tools, marketers must make sure that the industry concept they use is relevant to the situation at hand.

To understand how competition affects price, we must look at industry structure as well as the behavior of individual firms. Industry analysis examines such aspects as the number of firms, whether products are differentiated, and the freedom of firms to enter and exit. Economists have identified four basic industry structures — perfect competition, monopoly, oligopoly and monopolistic competition. Figure 17.7 shows how each type is likely to affect pricing and other forms of competition.

Perfect Competition In an industry with perfect competition, each firm has little if any control over prices. None is large enough relative to others to control factors of production or market demand. Usually, many small firms produce pre-

Perfect Competition

The industry structure in which no single firm has control over prices.

Type of Structure	Number of Firms	Product Differentiated or Homogeneous	Firms Have Price-Setting Power	Free Entry	Distinguishing Characteristics	Examples
Perfect Competition	Many	Homogeneous	No	Yes	Price competition only	Wheat farmer Textile firm
Monopoly	One	A single unique product	Yes	No	Constrained by market demand	Public utility Brewery in Taiwan
Oligopoly	Few	Either	Yes	Limited	Strategic behavior	Cereal maker Primary copper producer
Monopolistic Competition	Many	Differentiated	Limited	Yes	Price and quality competition	Restaurants Music industry

Figure 17.7   Industry Structure and Competition

cisely the same product. Because they cannot dictate prices, their primary decisions revolve around how much to produce and how to produce it. Since firm size is small, it is generally easy to enter and exit the market. Profits tend to be generated not through price but economies of scale and cost reductions.

Monopoly At the opposite end of the spectrum from pure competition is monopoly, an industry structure in which one organization makes a product with no close substitutes. As the only firm in the market, the monopolist has a great deal of freedom in establishing price. Most monopolies exist because there are barriers to entry for competing firms. For example, governments in many countries establish sole providers for certain services, such as communications or public transportation. Generally, these are heavily regulated to prevent abuses, and prices are set by governing boards rather than company executives. Public utilities that are established as monopolies usually must have their rates approved by a commission whose job is to protect the public interest.

Monopoly

The industry structure in which one organization makes a product with no close substitutes.

From time to time, private enterprises can achieve monopoly status through control of a patent or scarce raw material. Sometimes entry barriers, such as the sheer size of initial investment, may keep competitors out. Intel has been called a monopoly because of its dominance as a technology supplier. Legal experts often refer to companies such as Microsoft and Intel as essential facilities because customers have to buy their products. However, in 2000, federal court judges decided that Microsoft constituted a monopoly because the company illegally tied its Internet browser to the Windows operating system, making it difficult for consumers to buy separate operating and Internet systems.

Wanting lower concert prices for fans, Pearl Jam contended that Ticketmaster inflated the cost with an unwarranted charge, which added as much as 30 percent to the face value. The company argued that the service charge was used to secure venue arrangements, to guarantee performances, and sometimes for marketing purposes. It claimed that its activities may be misconstrued as anti-competitive because small-scale ticket services are unable to duplicate them. Increased competition, however, has not led to an elimination of the service charge. A number of websites sell concert and event tickets, such as TicketWeb.com, Ticketmaster.com, and Tickets.com, and they charge a service fee. But the fee has fallen from the almost 30 percent Ticketmaster was charging in the early 1990s to a price as low as $2. Most ticket sellers now charge a variable fee based on the event, the face value, the demand for the tickets, and the delivery method chosen.[19]

Oligopoly An oligopoly exists when an industry has a small number of companies competing for the same customers. Firms may behave in unusual ways to gain business, such as introducing a new technology, or they may combine a number of factors that can affect their use of price as a strategic tool. They tend to be large, and old rivals engage in strategies and counterstrategies over long periods. The global auto industry, for instance, consists of seven major companies around the world that produce nearly all motor vehicles, and each firm is large enough to commit considerable resources to differentiate itself. Each gains competitive advantage over the others from time to time. A few small firms in a local market also can be considered an oligopolistic situation.

Oligopoly

The industry structure in which a small number of firms compete for the same customers.

Because oligopolies are usually well established and have strong market position, it is difficult for new firms to enter. The incumbents also get to know one another well. Through intelligence gathering, they learn about their competitors' cost

> **Because oligopolies are usually well established and have strong market position, it is difficult for new firms to enter.**

structure and gain insight on their potential for profit. Because members of oligopolies engage in moves and countermoves, planning is essential. This has become evident over the last several years with Boeing and Airbus, as they jockey to win business

Monopolistic Competition

The industry structure in which many firms compete for the same customers by differentiating their products and by creating unique offerings.

Differentiation

A strategy in which product attributes that provide value are stressed.

Price Competition

A strategy that employs price adjustments to gain more customers or to establish a dominant position in the market.

from airline companies. Together, these two companies control the majority of the commercial airline manufacturing industry.[20]

Monopolistic Competition The industry structure known as monopolistic competition occurs when many firms compete for the same customers by differentiating their products. It falls between monopoly and pure competition but is much closer to the latter. Companies create brand loyalty to gain some of the benefits of monopoly. They control price by creating unique market offerings, such as non-fast-food restaurants in urban areas. Both price and quality are important in attracting customers and differentiating the product. Often there are numerous firms that are small or similar in size. Entry and exit are relatively easy, and the success of incumbents invites additional competitors. That's why several similar restaurants are likely to spring up when one starts doing well.

Strong marketing plans help organizations gain monopolistic advantages in highly competitive markets. They do this by creating subtle product differentiation. Rock groups are in this category. Stylistic differences enable you to differentiate between Radiohead, Neon Trees, Coldplay and Maroon 5. Each group also commands a price differential for concerts. Monopolistic competition can be found in the athletic footwear industry as well. Nike, Reebok, New Balance, Adidas and a few others make up the bulk of the competition, with subtle product differences among them.

Differentiation and Price Competition

Nonprice competition usually involves a differentiation strategy. **Differentiation** occurs when product attributes are stressed. Marketers try to demonstrate value and avoid any price reductions. In its purest form, a differentiation strategy relies on little or no mention of price. BMW is positioned as the "ultimate driving experience" to differentiate from competitors, reducing the need to rely on price to influence demand.

Price competition adjusts prices to gain more customers or to establish a dominant position in the market. Recall that nonprice competition occurs when other marketing mix variables, such as product quality and promotion, are adjusted in response to competitors' pricing practices. Marketers need to understand the general approaches to price taken by their key competitors. This helps them anticipate overall market prices and what rivals are likely to do in response to price competition.

Marketing strategists study competitors in order to predict what they are likely to do under various conditions. Most companies respond in fairly consistent ways to price situations. Those that can produce at lower costs are more inclined to engage in price competition. Southwest Airlines cut costs by removing services such as assigned seating, and therefore it can charge less per ticket than other airlines. Furthermore, it sells most of its tickets on the Internet, which eliminates travel agency fees. Because of these differences, Southwest Airlines can offer lower prices and still sustain a profit, whereas companies with higher costs are likely to lose money as prices drop. In countries where wage rates are below average, such as South Korea and Taiwan, production costs are low for many types of goods.

COST FACTORS THAT INFLUENCE PRICE

Although cost alone should not determine price, it is a critical part of determining the profitability of pricing decisions. By understanding costs, marketers can judge profitability in advance. They can move resources to the highest-profit opportunities, avoid losing money, and gain better control of internal processes. By comparing costs with those of competitors, it is possible to assess production efficiency and estimate the relative profits each competitor can expect at various prices. This, in turn, helps to anticipate the pricing choices available to competitors.

Types of Costs

Costs are categorized in several ways. Most simply, accountants look at fixed and variable costs. Marketers also should consider marginal and incremental costs.

Fixed and Variable Costs

Fixed costs are expenditures for items such as production facilities, equipment, and salaries. Regardless of a product's sales performance, fixed costs will not change very much, especially in the short term. Often these are called sunk costs because, once committed, nothing can be done to lower them. In service industries, salaries account for a large portion of fixed costs. For example, hospitals pay nurses regardless of how many patients they serve. In the airline industry, expenses for aircraft, hangar space and salaries are fixed costs. The best a company can do is manage these fixed costs more effectively. McDonald's did this when it introduced its breakfast menu, as well as its McCafe menu, so its facilities could produce more revenue during the same business hours.

Variable costs change depending on how much is produced or sold. They are usually calculated for each unit of production. These costs include raw materials, warranty costs and the aspects of payroll (such as commissions) that rise or fall depending on the units sold. In the airline industry, for example, variable costs include the commissions paid to travel agents and food served on planes.

Total costs (TC) for a given period are calculated by multiplying the variable cost (VC) per unit times the quantity (Q) of units and adding the fixed costs (FC):

$$TC = VC \times Q + FC$$

Total revenues (TR) for a period are calculated by multiplying the price (P) per unit times the quantity (Q) of units sold:

$$TR = P \times Q$$

Profits (PR) are the difference between total revenues (TR) and total costs (TC):

$$PR = TR - TC$$

The average cost (AC) of each unit is the total cost (TC) divided by the quantity (Q) of units:

$$AC = TC/Q$$

The average cost of each unit doesn't provide very much useful information for pricing decisions, however, because average costs are sensitive to volume. The more units sold, the lower the average cost.

Marginal Costs

Unlike many accountants, economists look at marginal costs and marginal revenues. Marginal costs (MC) are expenditures incurred in producing one additional unit of output. These costs often go down with each unit sold and stabilize at a volume of production near full capacity. **Marginal cost** then increases because additional fixed costs must be added, such as more production machinery. Imagine an airline with a plane that normally flies half full. It would not cost much to add one passenger — the cost of another meal and the commission paid to the travel agent who sells the ticket, so that single passenger's price would likely generate profit. The price of the new ticket sold would be the **marginal revenue** (MR), the income from one more unit of the product sold, usually the product price. But let's say the plane is full. Would you add another aircraft to take one more passenger? Obviously not, unless that passenger is willing to pay a huge price.

Fixed Cost

A cost that does not vary with changes in volume produced.

Variable Cost

A cost that changes depending on volume.

Marginal Cost

The expenditures incurred in producing one additional unit of output.

Marginal Revenue

The income from selling one additional unit of output.

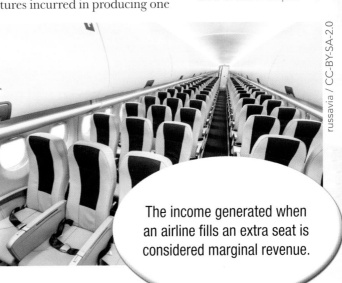

russavia / CC-BY-SA-2.0

The income generated when an airline fills an extra seat is considered marginal revenue.

Economic theory shows that profits are maximized when *MR* equals *MC*. In the airline example, we can continue to lower the price until all seats are gone, or *MC* (the price of food and commissions) equals the price of a ticket. Airlines do this to a degree by offering a few discount seats. But selling a ticket for the cost of food and the agent commission (about $35) is impractical. In reality, you won't often find many marketing executives sitting in their offices looking at graphs of marginal revenues and costs. Yet, like most good theories, this concept provides useful insights.

It was noted that fixed costs do not change with prices and sales volume. Many people assume that these are the costs of being in business. Also called overhead, these fixed costs may be higher or lower for different competitors. For example, the pharmaceutical industry has high fixed costs because of the research and development necessary to yield one profitable drug; of the 5,000 compounds tested in the laboratory, only five make it to the clinical trials, which are expensive and time-consuming to conduct. Of those five drugs, only one is approved by the FDA for patient use. Fixed costs are extremely important in determining the profitability of a firm.

In practice, companies with high overhead may justify high prices if these

CREATING & CAPTURING VALUE THROUGH *Relationships*

Tiffany & Co. - Jewelry at Its Finest

The now-iconic jewelry maker Tiffany & Co. was founded in 1837 by Charles Lewis Tiffany, a man with a vision to change the jewelry industry forever. He coined the company's name after he purchased a 128-carat yellow diamond and named it the Tiffany Diamond. It was famously featured on the neck of famed Hollywood actress Audrey Hepburn in the 1960s film "Breakfast at Tiffany's" and is on display in the company's flagship New York store today. Since its beginning, Tiffany has driven the U.S. jewelry industry to embody the perfect balance of tradition and contemporary style.

While many casual conversationalists probably don't think about it, the Tiffany Company is responsible for many of the standards we refer to when discussing jewelry. Tiffany instituted the standards of purity for both silver and platinum. Sterling silver must meet a minimum millesimal fineness of 925, and platinum must meet 95 percent purity. Always at the forefront of the jewelry market, Charles and his team set out to find precious stones and rare diamonds around the world. Their endeavors led to the discovery of tanzanite (named after the country in which it was discovered) and the rare blush-colored morganite gem. Charles was not only a leader in diamond discovery, but in design. Tiffany prides itself on the design of the quintessential engagement ring, which it introduced in the 1880s and is still a revered fixture of society. The rich history that Tiffany & Co. represents has revolutionized the jewelry industry forever and has led to lasting customer loyalty.

The connection that customers have with their Tiffany purchases are unrivaled by any other jeweler in the world. Tiffany has been able to brand itself as the company with the Tiffany blue box. Because Tiffany isn't allowed to give away or even sell these boxes, it is yet another reason that people covet what's inside. Tiffany offers a vast line of jewels ranging from simple $100 silver chains to $40,000 flower broaches. While Tiffany is really known for its high-end products, the lower-end ones allow everyday consumers to establish a connection with the company. Some of Tiffany's famous designs include gemmed Civil War swords, Congressional Medals of Honor and NFL trophies. With tradition and luxury as its standard for business, Tiffany & Co. continues to be the benchmark for exceptional jewelry.

www.tiffany.com, website visted May 10, 2012.

reflect added value. Often they do not, yet decision makers push prices higher in an effort to obtain maximum revenue. The result may be even lower volume or reduced profit. If fixed costs do not add value for customers, they probably should not be a factor in pricing decisions. This is very difficult for many executives to accept because pricing to cover all costs (cost-based pricing) is initially most lucrative for the company.

Incremental Costs Relevant costs for pricing decisions are **incremental costs**: costs that increase or decrease based on volume. Like variable costs, incremental costs are related to pricing because the price can affect the volume sold. Variable costs are always incremental, whereas only some fixed costs are incremental. For example, if a low price will increase demand to the extent that a new factory will have to be added to satisfy it, then the factory is an incremental cost and becomes a factor in the decision of whether to lower the price. Once the factory is built, the cost becomes fixed or sunk. It has to be paid for regardless of how much is produced.

Cost-Oriented Pricing Both cost-plus and rate-of-return pricing are based on the company's costs. Cost-oriented pricing adds an amount to the product cost, called a markup, which is designed to yield a profit. A percentage markup can be added directly, or additional calculations can be made to determine what percentage rate of return the seller will receive. Either approach has serious problems because each tends to ignore the customer and, to varying degrees, the competition as well.

Cost-Plus Pricing Because of its simplicity, the cost-plus approach is popular. But, as the following example shows, it doesn't necessarily assure a profit. A local furniture store pays $750 to a wholesaler for a sofa and sells it to the consumer for $1,500, a markup of 100 percent. On the surface, it appears that the store has gained $750. But it has many costs to meet, such as salaries and overhead. When these are taken into account, and depending on overall sales volume, the retailer might actually lose money on this sofa and other items. Clearly, to determine whether the sale is profitable and precisely how much is made on the sofa, a portion of the retailer's costs has to be allocated to each of the products sold.

Modern productions of the Kubus sofa, designed by Josef Hoffmann in 1910, retail for about $1500.

Markups are popular because they are perceived to be fair or equitable for both the buyer and the seller. Standard markups have evolved in many industries to help indicate what amount is "fair." Manufacturers or wholesalers often suggest prices to retailers, or retailers form their own conventions. For example, an auto parts dealer may mark up brake assemblies by 40 percent and consumables such as oil by 25 percent. Since all similar retailers use the same basic markup structure, all have approximately the same retail price. Notice that the calculation is based on the wholesale price, which itself is a markup on the manufacturer's price.

Government contracts and some industrial contracts often specify that the seller must use cost-plus pricing. This is full-cost pricing because the markup is based on all costs, including allocations of overhead and other fixed costs. Sellers are expected to provide an accounting upon request. The difficulty lies in determining which costs to assign to which products. Again, even full-cost pricing largely ignores the value of the product to the customer.

Rate-of-Return Pricing A variation on cost-plus pricing, rate-of-return pricing is based on the break-even point. Essentially, the method determines how many units must be sold at a particular price in order to cover fixed costs plus a profit on the investment made. The break-even point is the amount sold at a given price on which the business neither makes nor loses money. Any volume beyond that point makes money.

The break-even point is calculated by dividing the total fixed cost (FC) by the difference between the selling price (P) of one unit and the variable cost (VC) of one unit:

$$\text{Break-even point} = FC/(P - VC)$$

The difference between the price and the variable cost of a unit (P - VC) is called the contribution margin. It tells how much the sale of one unit contributes to covering fixed costs. Once these costs are covered, any remaining contribution is profit. Figure 17.8 shows the break-even concept graphically.

As an example of rate-of-return pricing, assume that you decide to start a small business that will offer house-painting services to homeowners during summer vacation. You calculate that you will have to invest

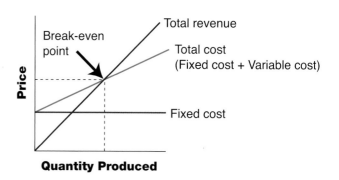

Figure 17.8   Break-Even Analysis

$10,000 in fixed (sunk) costs, including advertising and promotion, insurance, equipment, truck rental, and a salary for yourself. You feel that you should earn a 20 percent return ($10,000 x 20% = $2,000) for having the idea, taking the initiative, and assuming the risk of losing your invested capital. Furthermore, you estimate that labor, paint, and other variable costs for each house will average $2,100, and with four workers your company can paint eight houses in four months. What is the average price you should charge for each house?

To answer this question, you first add your desired return to your fixed costs ($2,000 + $10,000 = $12,000) to determine the total revenue contribution required. Then you divide that sum by the number of houses (units) to find the amount that each unit must contribute ($12,000 / 8 = $1,500). Since the variable cost to paint a house is $2,100, you determine that you must charge $2,100 + $1,500 = $3,600 per house.

Notice in this example that profit is treated much like a fixed cost. This is because if you break even in a strict sense — that is, neither make nor lose money — then your project will not accomplish its profit objective.

Also notice that rate-of-return pricing ignores the customer and the competition. If homeowners consider $3,600 to be too expensive, then they may hire someone who charges less or choose to do the work themselves. If they believe the price is very low, then they may be willing to pay even more. The pricing of competitors is important. Whether competitors are willing to paint a house for $3,000 or $9,000 will influence how consumers perceive your price.

Rate-of-return pricing also tends to ignore the scale of operations you could have. For example, if eight painters rather than four were employed, the fixed costs could be spread across 16 houses rather than eight. That would lower the price, but you would have to supervise more workers while not making more profit. A major problem with the rate-of-return approach is that price will increase when demand declines. For example, if only six houses are painted, the price for each rises by $500, to $4,100. Now, each unit must contribute $2,000 ($12,000/6 = $2,000). Since variable cost to paint a house is $2,100, you determine you must charge $4,100 per house ($2,100 + $2,000 = $4,100). As another example, in the 1990s U.S. auto companies lost share dramatically to foreign rivals. As demand for U.S. cars declined due to competitive pressure, Detroit increased prices to try to compensate for lost unit sales, which simply reduced demand further.

INTERNATIONAL PRICING

Pricing in global environments is affected by several factors not experienced in domestic markets. With markets functioning differently in different countries, international pricing is a complex process. Marketing executives must be knowledgeable about many issues and remain flexible in adjusting to unforeseeable circumstances. The major influencers on global pricing are market, cost and financial factors, as outlined in Figure 17.9.

Market Factors	**Cost Factors**	**Financial Factors**
Local demand	Distance and transportation	Exchange rates
Competitive conditions	Tariffs and homologation	Inflation
Availability of substitutes	Export duties, subsidies, and controls	Government price controls
Gray marketing	Transfer pricing	

Figure 17.9   Influences on Global Pricing

GLOBAL MARKET FACTORS

Market factors such as local demand, tastes and preferences, competitor activities, and gray marketing are important. All of these elements must be considered in international pricing.

Local demand can vary dramatically due to demographic, geographic and political conditions. For example, China is the world's most populous country and is experiencing economic growth at a staggering rate. Yet few Chinese have enough income or even the space for most of the durable goods so common in the West. Consequently, many products for the Chinese market must be designed to be priced very low.

Subtle competitive differences can influence demand, even in fairly similar economic environments. With the advent of the euro, for example, price gaps have narrowed between the countries that adopted it in the past years. Differences in price between countries still exist, however. In Amsterdam, a bottle of whiskey costs almost 80 percent more than in Rome; in Brussels, Pampers cost 56 percent more than in Frankfurt, and a movie ticket costs 170 percent more than in Madrid, but Brussels is the place for Levi jeans — 43 percent cheaper than in Paris.[21]

Globally, tastes and preferences also vary dramatically. A nationalistic bias for domestic products can make them less cross-price elastic in relation to imports. Generally, people in countries where domestic brands are preferred have high incomes and tend to be much less price sensitive across the board, which allows more latitude for premium pricing. For example, companies selling consumer food products in Europe have found themselves in a difficult position recently. The economic unification of the European Union means that many global food retailers want to reduce the number of brands to streamline production processes and lower prices. The customers, however, tend to want to continue to buy specific brands and products, regardless of price, as when British consumers protested Heinz's when it threatened to stop manufacturing salad cream, a type of salad dressing popular among older Britons.

The availability of substitute products also varies widely. The most obvious case is the substitution of automation for labor. Japan — with its high education level, high labor rates, and low unemployment — is highly automated, while Chinese producers use readily available low-cost human labor whenever possible. The market for high-priced robotics is mature in Japan, where many competitors are constantly seeking an edge, but demand is weak in China.

Heinz desktop screensaver, Courtesy of Heinz.

Saved after a campaign by fans, Heinz Salad Creme sales have revived as shoppers identified it as a cheap and low-fat alternative to mayonnaise.

GRAY MARKETING

Gray Marketing

Importing products made in a foreign country back to the company's home market without approval.

A notable feature of many foreign economies is the gray market, which has a significant effect on pricing. Many global companies manufacture in local markets so they can sell at lower prices there, but this also may lead to gray marketing.[22] **Gray marketing** occurs when pirated products made in a foreign country are imported back to the company's home market without approval. They are then sold at reduced prices, usually by unauthorized channel members. The importation of gray market goods is prohibited in the United States by a law that forbids bringing products into the country without permission of the trademark owner. Elsewhere in the world, restrictions vary, may not exist, or may not be well enforced. Many times the foreign-made product is of a different quality but bears the company label, so consumers are confused or deceived. In other cases, prices differ because of manufacturing costs, exchange rates or other reasons.

Companies that want to ensure selective or exclusive distribution must take steps to eliminate gray market problems. If they do not, then the strength and motivation of the authorized channel will be seriously impaired. The company must clearly communicate to all members of the authorized channel the importance of following policy and upholding contracts. They should also monitor activity, especially when dealing with known gray market areas, and be prepared to terminate contracts with those who violate agreements.

GLOBAL COST FACTORS

In calculating the costs of doing business internationally, it is not just distance that matters but the expense of moving goods from one country to another. Transportation and insurance costs escalate when borders are crossed, as do tariffs and red tape. Risks also increase, so prices must cover potential adverse circumstances.

Tariffs — taxes levied against incoming goods — contribute to costs and are sometimes added to price. They affect imports in nearly every country. In Turkey, for instance, vehicle prices are elevated nearly threefold by tariffs. In the United States, importers pay an average of less than 10 percent on all items, much more for some. Recently the World Trade Organization — the entity that regulates importing and exporting — ruled against the European Union's import tariffs for bananas from African and Latin American countries.[23]

Bureaucratic red tape often makes it difficult and expensive to enter a market. The Japanese use it as a barrier to foreign competitors. For example, they lock out international construction companies by claiming that Japan's dirt is unique, or they require considerable testing at border entry points for all sorts of products. Vietnam operated in a similar way. There was so much red tape involved with doing business in Vietnam that many multinational companies decided the hassle wasn't worth the benefit, and they withdrew. In the end though, Vietnamese officials decided that the country needed the investments more than it needed to protect its own industries. The country rescinded hundreds of bureaucratic procedures and tariffs that had prevented foreign firms from doing business in Vietnam. Finally, some European pharmaceutical companies claim that FDA regulations impede their access to the U.S. market. The U.S. federal health agency has streamlined its system, cutting the time needed to help speed the approval process to bring certain new drugs to market from years down to months.[24]

The opposite of a tariff is an **export subsidy** paid by a government to encourage businesses to export. When you compete against these companies, essentially you're competing against their governments as well. When they target a certain market, their prices can be more competitive because the subsidy covers much or all of their export costs, which can put nonsubsidized exports and domestic products at a pricing disadvantage. In other cases, governments may restrict exports by adding costly duties, which raises prices in importing countries. Many countries in the world subsidize big national industries; Canada, Brazil, France and Great Britain all subsidize their aircraft manufacturers, for example.

Risk is also a factor in international business. When risk is high, a company must raise its prices. For example, selling in Russia is risky because of an unstable economy and the possibility of political takeovers. Anywhere in the world, a change in government can affect economic regulations and market access. Furthermore, a weak or indifferent government may permit greater corruption or lawlessness, which can mean that warehousing and distribution channels are insecure.

Tariffs

A tax levied against a good being imported into a country.

Export Subsidy

Funding by a government to encourage businesses to export goods.

www.ball.com

Ball Corporation supplies innovative, sustainable packaging solutions for beverage, food and household products customers, as well as aerospace and other technologies and services primarily for the U.S. government.

Transfer Prices

The amount a company charges its foreign affiliate for a product.

Transfer prices are the amounts that companies charge their foreign affiliates for products. This causes some interesting price variations across countries. By altering the transfer price, both local prices and profits can be dramatically affected. In this way, companies can manipulate their price in markets globally, affecting competition and their sources of revenues. For example, Japanese auto supply companies can charge higher transfer prices for components going to assembly plants in the United States, which increases Japan's profit and lessens the United States'. In turn taxes are paid in Japan, where the rate may be lower than in the United States. Ultimately, the tax savings mean that a lower price can be charged for the product in the United States.

GLOBAL FINANCIAL FACTORS

The primary financial factors influencing international prices are exchange rates, inflation and government price controls. Exchange rates and inflation alter the value of currencies, whereas government price controls prohibit companies from moving prices upward at will. Controls are particularly troublesome when a rapid shift in exchange rates or inflation devalues the price put on a product.

Exchange Rate

The worth of one currency relative to another

Even money has a price, which is reflected in the exchange rate. The **exchange rate** is how much one currency is worth relative to another. If the Chinese yuan has risen about five percent against the U.S. dollar over the past 18 months, Chinese goods will be more expensive in America. Currency exchange rates can fluctuate considerably over time, affecting prices for imported and exported products. Recently, economic conditions in Europe have caused the Euro to decline in value relative to the dollar, making it cheaper for people in the U.S. to purchase European products or travel in that part of the world. At the same time, U.S. products tend to be more expensive in Europe. To avoid these fluctuations, many marketers set pricing in local currencies.

Inflation

The tendency of a currency to be worth less over time.

Inflation is the tendency of a currency to be worth less over time. When inflation occurs, product prices along the supply chain increase. These are passed on in higher prices, so consumers have to spend more money to buy the same item. Most advanced nations now have low inflation rates, often around three percent or even less per year. In some countries inflation is extremely high and escalates monthly or even weekly. In extreme cases, companies may need to raise prices twice a month, by 20 or 30 percent, just to keep up with inflation.

Price Controls

Government restrictions on the price that can be charged for a product.

Governments often use **price controls** in an attempt to keep inflation in check. Essentially, the maximum price increase allowable is set by law. Sometimes the controls are applied to all goods, sometimes they are selective, and sometimes they apply only to imports. In any case, they can make it difficult to earn a profit, so companies may not want to sell in that market. It is not uncommon for people to buy key raw materials, such as coal, cheaply on the local price-controlled market and sell them on the world market for a huge profit, instead of selling the products locally at a price controlled by the state.

Companies consider many factors when making pricing decisions locally or globally. All of these factors are likely to influence price. However, as we will see in the next chapter, the actual pricing strategy must be well grounded in an understanding of how pricing captures value from the market. This requires knowing how customers define value.

CHAPTER SUMMARY

Objective 1: Describe how pricing works with the other parts of the marketing mix.

Pricing is an important element of the marketing mix. Price decisions are made along with product, promotion and logistics decisions. Pricing is influenced by profit, volume, competitive and customer relationship objectives. Consequently, pricing is important for nearly all aspects of the business.

Objective 2: Learn how economic factors such as demand and supply influence prices.

The demand curve helps us understand how price influences the amount of a product customers buy. The availability of substitutes, necessity, the portion of income spent on the product and the timing of price changes affect the price sensitivity of demand. The supply curve tells how much product firms will provide at various prices. Usually, more is produced when prices are expected to rise. By analyzing the supply and demand curves, it is possible to get some idea of future prices in an industry.

Objective 3: Understand the legal and ethical constraints on pricing decisions.

Both legal and ethical factors affect price. Laws prohibit both vertical and horizontal price-fixing by U.S. firms. It is also illegal for manufacturers to sell to different parties at different prices, although some forms of price discrimination are acceptable. To control unfair price competition, many states regulate pricing minimums and the use of loss leaders. The Federal Trade Commission sets permissible standards for price advertising. For example, you cannot advertise a sale price unless it is really a sale and the items are available. International firms must sell at a high enough price to avoid violating antidumping laws. Finally, unit pricing regulations help consumers make comparisons. To be ethical, prices should reflect a fair exchange of value, and marketers must be careful not to misrepresent the terms of an exchange. This requires clear communication of both price and value.

Objective 4: Use industry structure concepts to understand how competitors determine price in different types of industries.

The four basic industry structures are perfect competition, monopoly, oligopoly and monopolistic competition. In perfect competition, many firms vie to provide goods at the going price. A firm with a monopoly can set prices as high as the market will bear, although pricing by public utility monopolies is generally regulated in the public interest. In an oligopoly, a small number of competitors make pricing decisions based on their knowledge of one another's cost structures. Monopolistic competition tends to be based on product differentiation rather than price.

Objective 5: Use competitive factors surrounding industry structure concepts to understand how pricing works in different types of industries.

Pricing decisions must consider variable and fixed costs, marginal costs and incremental costs. Incremental costs, which are the most important, include variable costs and, often, some fixed costs, such as the cost of building a new factory to meet increased demand. Cost-oriented methods, such as cost-plus pricing and rate-of-return pricing, have serious drawbacks because they tend to ignore the consumer and competitors.

Objective 6: Recognize the conditions that make international pricing complex.

Market, cost and financial factors unique to global business must be considered in pricing. Market factors include local demand, competitive conditions, tastes and preferences, the availability of substitutes and gray marketing. Important cost factors are transportation distance, tariffs, red tape and export subsidies. Major financial considerations are inflation, exchange rates, and price controls. Risk is another influence on international pricing.

REVIEW YOUR UNDERSTANDING

1. List 10 names for price.
2. Which constituents of a firm can be pleased with profit objectives, volume objectives, competitive objectives and relationship objectives?
3. What are the major factors that influence price?
4. What is elastic demand? Inelastic demand?
5. What factors influence price elasticity?
6. What is supply and demand equilibrium?
7. What are the laws that affect pricing practices? Describe the restrictions.
8. Describe dumping.
9. What are two ethical issues regarding pricing? Explain.
10. What is industry structure? What are four structures that have price implications?
11. What are fixed and variable costs?
12. What are incremental costs?
13. What is cost-plus pricing?
14. What factors influence pricing in global settings?

DISCUSSION OF CONCEPTS

1. Prices are set with several objectives in mind. What are they, and how are they important to a company?

2. A company's pricing strategy is influenced by many factors: legal and ethical issues, economic conditions, the company's costs, the global environment and competitors. What major effect does each category have on pricing decisions?

3. Product demand is influenced by price elasticity. What does this mean, and what effect does it have on a marketer's pricing policy?

4. Federal and state laws in the United States prohibit unfair pricing. What is meant by "unfair"? Give specific examples of laws and briefly describe their objectives. Do all countries prohibit unfair pricing? Explain.

5. How does the type of competition within an industry affect a company's ability to set prices? Briefly describe the major competitor-based pricing approaches.

6. What types of costs are relevant for pricing decisions? Which are irrelevant? Why? What are some of the main problems with cost-oriented pricing?

7. Despite its drawbacks, cost-oriented pricing is still used by many companies. Briefly describe the two types of cost-oriented pricing.

KEY TERMS & DEFINITIONS

1. **Bait and switch:** An unethical practice in which sellers advertise items at extremely low prices and then inform the customer that the items are out of stock, offer different items, or attempt to sell the customer more expensive substitutes.

2. **Cross-price elasticity of demand:** The extent to which the quantity demanded of one product changes in response to changes in the price of another product.

3. **Differentiation:** A strategy stressing product attributes that provide value.

4. **Demand curve:** A depiction of the price elasticity demand for a product.

5. **Dumping:** Selling a product in a foreign country at a price lower than in the producing country and lower than its cost of production.

6. **Exchange rate:** The worth of one currency relative to another.

7. **Export subsidy:** Money paid by a government to encourage businesses to export goods.

8. **Fixed cost:** A cost that does not vary with changes in volume produced.

9. **Gray marketing:** Importing products made in a foreign country back to the company's home market without its approval.

10. **Horizontal price-fixing:** Agreement among manufacturers and channel members to set prices at the retail level.

11. **Incremental costs:** Costs that increase or decrease based on volume, including variable costs and certain fixed costs.

12. **Inflation:** The tendency of a currency to be worth less over time.

13. **Marginal costs:** The expenditures incurred in producing one additional unit of output.

14. **Marginal revenue:** The income from selling one additional unit of output.

15. **Monopolistic competition:** The industry structure in which many firms compete for the same customers by differentiating their products and by creating unique offerings.

16. **Monopoly:** The industry structure in which one organization makes a product with no close substitutes.

17. **Nonprice competition:** Price is unchanged but adjustments are made to other parts of the marketing mix in response to competitor's price changes.

18. **Oligopoly:** The industry structure in which a small number of firms compete for the same customers.

19. **Perfect competition:** The industry structure in which no single firm has control over prices.

20. **Predatory dumping:** Pricing below cost to drive local firms out of business.

21. **Predatory pricing:** Price-cutting by large firms to eliminate small local competitors.

22. **Price:** The exchange value of a good or service in the marketplace.

23. **Price competition:** A strategy that employs price adjustments to gain more customers or to establish a dominant position in the market.

24. **Price controls:** Government restrictions on the price that can be charged for a product.

25. **Price elasticity:** The extent to which changes in price affect the number of units demanded or supplied.

26. **Price-fixing:** An attempt by one party to control what another party will charge in the market.

27. **Status quo pricing:** When a competitor makes a change, rivals follow suit.

28. **Supply curve:** A depiction of the price elasticity of supply for a product.

29. **Tariff:** A tax levied on a good being imported into a country.

30. **Transfer price:** The amount a company charges its foreign affiliate for a product.

31. **Variable cost:** A cost that changes depending on volume.

32. **Vertical price-fixing:** An attempt by a manufacturer or distributor to control the retail selling price.

REFERENCES

1. ALDI, http://aldi.us/us/html/company, website visited June 4, 2014; Supermarket News, "SN's Top 75 Retailers for 2014", http://www.supermarketnews.com; www.aldi.us, website visited June 4, 2014.

2. Smart, www.smart.com, website visited June 3, 2014; "The Most Expensive Cars of 2014," Forbes, www.forbes.com, website visited June 3, 2014.

3. Stotter, James, "Applying Economics to Competitive Intelligence," Competitive Intelligence Review, Winter 1996, pp. 26-36.

4. Student Breaks, www.studentbreaks.com, website visited May 18, 2014.

5. www.kayak.com, visited May 23, 2014.

6. Nagle, Thomas T.; Hogan, John; Zale, Joseph, The Strategy and Tactics of Pricing 5/E (Upper Saddle River, New Jersey, Prentice Hall), 2011.

7. "U.S.: Banner year predicted for cranberries," Fresh Plaza, www.freshplaza.com, website visited May 20, 2010; Winter, Greg, "Growers Sue Ocean Spray, Seeking Possibility of Sale," New York Times, November 29, 2000, Section C, pg. 6; Lord, Robin, "Massachusetts Cranberries," New England Agricultural Statistics, March 15, 2012; Waterhouse, Gail, "More cranberries mean lower prices for growers," The Boston Globe, October 11, 2013.

8. Ferriss, Paul, Marketing, Toronto, February 11, 2008.

9. Gregg Keizer, "Feds jump on Apple-ebook price-fixing probe bandwagon," Computer World, www.computerworld.com, December 8, 2011.

10. www.americanexpress.com, website visited June 4, 2014.

11. Ibid.

12. Shlachter, Barry, "$4 Generic Drugs Often Loss Leaders for Big Retailers," McClatchy-Tribune Business News, Washington, March 1, 2008.

13. Victoria's Secret, www.victoriassecret.com, website visited May 31, 2014.

14. www.blackfriday.com, website visited May 31, 2014.

15. Addison, Bill, "Nail Dumping Tariffs Approved," New York, February 11, 2008.

16. Associated Press, "Japanese Company Defends Sale of Supercomputers," USA Today, May 12, 1997.

17. "Consumers Are Skeptical Again," Progressive Grocer, April 1996, pp. 40-46.

18. "Alitalia Fined for Misleading Advertising," Airline Industry, December 14, 2005, pg. 1.

19. www.ticketmaster.com, website visited June 2, 2014.

20. Newhouse, John, Boeing versus Airbus, Vintage Books, New York, 2007.

21. "Finance and Economics: The Flaw of One Price; Price Differences in Europe," The Economist Vol. 369, Issue 8346, October 18, 2003, pg. 97.

22. Lansing, Paul; Gabriella, Joseph, "Clarifying Gray Market Gray Areas," American Business Law Journal, September 1993, pp. 313-337.

23. "WTO Rules Against EU on Bananas," Wall Street Journal, February 9, 2008.

24. Gertzen, Jason, "Official Promises at Biotech Convention to Help Speed Up Drug Approval Process," Knight Ridder Tribune Business News, June 8, 2004, pg. 1.

Chapter 18

PRICING STRATEGIES

Southwest Airlines emerged nearly 40 years ago when two Texans got together to start a different kind of company. Rollin King and Herb Keller had one simple idea to entice people to fly their airline: Get passengers to their destinations on time, provide the lowest possible fares, and make sure they have a good time. Southwest's successful recipe allows it to fly more than 100 million passengers to 66 destinations across the United States each year.

As a Fortune 500 company with revenues of more than $17.5 billion in 2013, Southwest has become a leader in the airline industry. Fortune magazine has repeatedly named Southwest one of its Most Admired Companies; in 2014, it was ninth.

A key driver of this success is Southwest's mission, which is a dedication to the highest level of customer service delivered with a sense of warmth, friendliness, individual price and company spirit. A major component of its company spirit is having fun, something all Southwest employees strive to ensure customers.

For example, when Southwest became the official airline of SeaWorld in Texas, "Shamu One," a Boeing 737 painted like Shamu the killer whale, joined Southwest's fleet of 500 aircrafts. On flights into Las Vegas, it is not uncommon to have the flight attendants teach passengers to play craps or find an employee dressed up as Elvis.

Recently, Southwest flight attendant David Holmes became a YouTube sensation when a passenger uploaded a video where Holmes delivered the standard emergency announcements in rap form while passengers clapped the beat. Were executives at Southwest upset when they saw the video? Of course not! Employees are given the authority to take necessary steps to make the flight more enjoyable — as long as they stay within safety regulations — and passengers clearly enjoyed the performance.

One of the keys to Southwest's success is its pricing strategies. It prides itself on keeping ticket prices as low as possible. Recently, SmarterTravel awarded Southwest a Readers' Choice award for "Best Airfare Prices." With its industry-leading website that lets customers easily find the best fares, and email alerts for exclusive offers, the average price for a Southwest flight is $113.97.

Another unique pricing strategy for Southwest is the "Freedom From Fees" promotion. When oil prices began to rise, airlines began imposing additional fees — from checking bags to in-flight snacks — but not Southwest. While other airlines charge passengers $20 to $30 for each bag, Southwest allows each passenger to check two bags completely free. In a New York Times article, David Ridley, senior vice president for marketing and revenue management, said, "We decided to make a strategic business decision that customers would rather deal with transparent pricing." The charges at other airlines are "just a brand violation for us." It is a decision that has made a positive impact on the bottom line and created one more way for Southwest to deliver outstanding service to its customers.[1]

<< **Southwest Airlines Boeing 737-700**

Learning Objectives

1. Understand why an appropriate customer value proposition is a useful guide to pricing strategy.
2. Know what factors to consider when using customer- and competitor-oriented pricing methods.
3. Learn how pricing strategy is implemented by setting prices and communicating them to the market.

THE CONCEPT OF PRICE STRATEGY

Customers should receive an excellent value for the price they pay, and marketers should earn a satisfactory return. The objective of marketing is not simply to sell a product but to create value for the customer and the seller. Consequently, marketers should price products to reflect the value produced as well as received. Innovative marketers create value by offering, for example: a better product, stronger branding, faster delivery, better service, easier ordering and more convenient locations. The greater the value perceived by customers, the more often they demand a company's products, and the higher the price they are willing to pay.

> **Customers should receive an excellent value for the price they pay, and marketers should earn a satisfactory return.**

The firm will likely, but not always, incur higher costs when producing increased value. For example, it often costs more to make innovative products, create better distribution systems or develop service facilities. Gillette can command higher prices because it invests in regular new product development of razor blades. In some cases, companies produce value by reducing their costs relative to those of competitors so that they can pass savings on to the customer in lower prices. That's how Walmart became a leading retailer. It developed very focused marketing strategies that allowed dramatic cost reductions compared with rivals. By passing most of the savings on to customers, Walmart gained considerable competitive advantage.

Whether a company improves its position through innovative products, distribution, communication or cost cutting, the trick is to find a balance between what customers are willing to pay and the costs associated with the strategy. Essentially, the price charged is what marketers think their product is worth, and the price paid is what the customer thinks the product is worth. If both parties have a similar price in mind, there is a strong likelihood that each party will believe it is worthwhile to trade.

It is not easy to establish precisely what price both buyers and sellers agree is appropriate. We need to look at how customer value is derived, recognizing that people place different values on the products they buy as well as the relationships they have with companies. Several pricing strategies may work. It all depends on how price is perceived, how competitors act, and how a strategy is designed and implemented. This chapter is devoted to these issues. First we explore the use of value as the basis for pricing, which is critical for relationship marketing. Next, we discuss the methods used for customer, competitor and global pricing. Finally, we discuss how marketers implement the pricing strategy.

VALUE AS THE BASIS FOR PRICING

Value-based Pricing

A strategy that reflects customer value, not simply costs.

To arrive at the proper balance between the needs of the market and the needs of the firm, it is important to understand a marketing decision approach called value-based pricing. **Value-based pricing**, depicted in Figure 18.1, recognizes that price reflects customer value, not simply costs. Traditionally, firms assessed the costs of doing business, added a profit and arrived at the price. Once it was set, the marketer's job was to convince customers that the product was worth the price. If the marketer was not successful, then the price was lowered. If demand turned out to be higher than anticipated, the price was raised. An important point is that the customer was the last person to be considered in this chain of events.

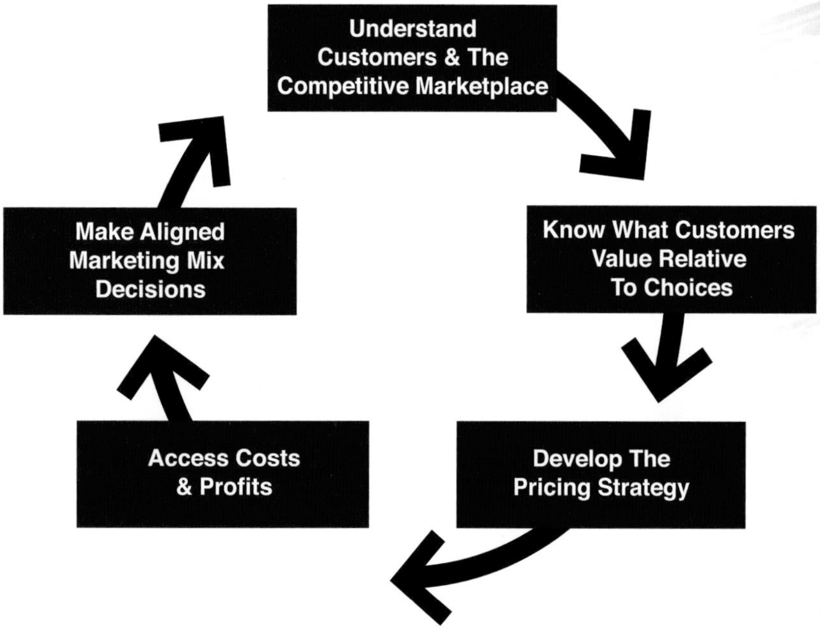

Value-based pricing begins by understanding customers and the competitive marketplace. The first step is to look at the value customers perceive in owning the product and to examine their options for acquiring similar products and brands. In other words, how much satisfaction do they gain from owning the product, compared with what similar items or substitutes cost? Next, the marketer estimates the costs of production and necessary profit. To the extent possible, a similar analysis is usually done for each major competitor. Finally, product, distribution and promotion decisions can be made. Notice that price is defined before developing the rest of the marketing mix. That way the marketer has a better chance of supplying products at a volume competitive with rivals and of earning profits that satisfy the firm's financial objectives.

Although cost-based pricing is easier, it ignores the customer and the competition. Marketers know that it is impossible to predict demand or competitors' actions simply by looking at their own costs. Consequently, cost-based pricing is becoming less popular.

Figure 18.1 Value-Based Pricing

SOURCES OF VALUE

What is value? Generally there are two sources: value in use and value in exchange. **Value in use** is the customer's subjective estimate of the benefits of a particular product. **Value in exchange** is the product's objective worth in the competitive marketplace. Figure 18.2 describes these two concepts. Value in use is what economists call utility. The use value of a product is based on the buyer's needs and his or her understanding of the marketplace at a given time. For example, under normal circumstances a Snickers candy bar may sell for 99 cents. But after working several hours in a location where food is unavailable, a person may be willing to pay $2 or $3 for it. In this case, the use value is high because of the buyer's circumstances. The exchange value is still 99 cents, the price established by competitive forces in the market.

Although general prices are based on value in exchange, companies also need to manage buyer perceptions of the value

Value in Use

The consumer's subjective estimate of the benefits of a particular product.

Value in Exchange

The objective worth of a product in the competitive marketplace.

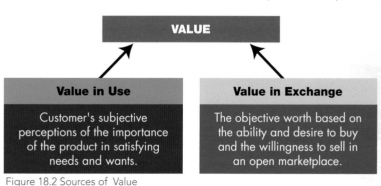

Figure 18.2 Sources of Value

of their products in use. When a product is perceived in a use situation, its perceived value increases. Volvo has captured buyers at relatively high prices for years because of a reputation for durability and safety. The Volvo Saved My Life Club is not an advertising gimmick. On their own initiative, Volvo owners who had survived wrecks wrote to the company about their real-life stories. Volvo then developed a campaign of testimonial print and television ads to promote the safety and reliability of the car and enhance value-in-use perceptions of consumers.[2] Volvo continues to take vehicle safety very seriously. It has recently announced its ambition to prevent anyone from being killed or injured in one of its cars by 2020. By developing seemingly futuristic car technologies and sophisticated sensory devices, Volvo plans on building vehicles that simply will not crash.[3]

CUSTOMER VALUE IN PRICING

Because prices send powerful messages, it is extremely important that they reflect the customer value the company delivers. Customer value is derived from the product itself, the services surrounding it, the company-customer interaction and the image the customer associates with the product. First, we will examine the connection between price and customer value. Second, we will find out how market leaders create customer value.

Price and Customer Value Strategies
The relationship between price and customer value is illustrated in Figure 18.3. FedEx, with its reputation for delivery 100 percent of the time by 10 a.m. the next day, is perceived by many consumers as having a high price and high customer value. The U.S. Postal Service (USPS) scores low on both dimensions. When FedEx introduced overnight delivery, it charged 25 times more than the USPS. Rather than undercut price, it redefined expectations of high customer value.

Two hypothetical price strategies are indicated in Figure 18.3. Most consumers would be unwilling to take to strategy A and pay a high price for something they don't see as worthwhile. How about strategy B -- low price and high value? Buyers would leap at the opportunity, but the company would be pricing at less than buyers are willing to pay. A strategy of this sort is called **buying market share** — that is, setting prices low in order to pull buyers away from competing brands. Trader Joe's wine brand Charles Shaw, better known as "Two Buck Chuck," recently received three gold medals for various wines at a prestigious wine-tasting competition in California. Charles Shaw outshone more than 2,500 Californian wines, nearly all of which were more expensive. "With this month's Consumer Reports Magazine making our Chardonnay a Best Buy and ranking it third of 10 wines rated costing up to ten times as much, it's been a great month for Charles Shaw," said Fred Franzia, CEO of Bronco Wine Company, producer of Charles Shaw. "We thank the American people for recognizing our quality and value and also thank our retail partner, Trader Joe's."[4] The $2.49 price tag is so low that it is taking market share from other labels. The company gives up potential profit it could gain from a higher price in order to gain market share. The payoff —the company sells about 5 million cases of wine per year.[5]

Buying Market Share

A strategy in which prices are set low for the short run to pull buyers away from competing brands.

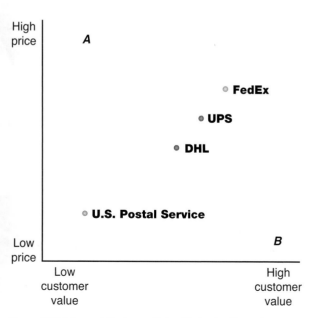

Figure 18.3 Price and Customer Value Strategies Example

A company will select the strategy that best compliments its target market and the number of buyers who want to purchase at each value/price position. Any price strategy has the potential to produce profit or loss depending on the volumes it obtains and the marketing costs associated with it.

Customer Value Propositions

Product leadership, operational excellence, and customer intimacy are the three strategies that deliver customer value. Because different customers buy different kinds of value, it is not necessary to be the best in all these areas. However, an organization should be excellent in one area and good enough in the other two to deliver what buyers want. Essentially, the customer value proposition for each of the three areas is (1) customers want the best products (product leadership); (2) customers want the best price (operational excellence); and (3) customers want the best solution (customer intimacy).[6] Figure 18.4 describes how companies gain leadership in customer value by matching their strategy with what buyers want.

Figure 18.4 Leadership in Customer Value

Product Leadership

The **product leadership** strategy builds customer value by differentiating the product. Nike and Intel, for instance, both provide products whose design and functionality have high perceived value. Both invest heavily in R&D and lead the pack in innovation. Customers have grown to rely on their leadership and are willing to pay extra, knowing they will benefit from the product's supremacy. At the same time, these leaders can cut prices on old models, keeping even price competitors in check. For example, Intel's release of new products like the Core series i3, i5 and i7 processors will result in lower prices for older ones like the Quad-Core Xeon processor series.[7] Each company has very good operations that keep costs in line, but neither is striving to be the absolute lowest cost producer. Both also have good customer relationships, but some might question whether or not they pursue customer intimacy strategies.

Operational Excellence

An **operational excellence** strategy is designed to produce lower costs than competitors while achieving consistent quality. Why can Casio sell a calculator for less than Kellogg can sell a box of cornflakes? For one thing, Casio's operational competencies translate into some of the lowest costs imaginable for manufacturing small objects. This means that no one can offer a lower price and sustain the same margins as Casio. Casio leads with price, its product design is adequate, and its customer service is equitable.

Many companies have trained employees on Six Sigma, a program designed to help companies achieve operational excellence. The rigorous standards of Six Sigma, which was pioneered by Motorola, begins with setting goals such as less than two late deliveries per month, one customer complaint per year, and manufacturing all parts within design tolerances. Six Sigma has been embraced by many leading companies. For instance, Starwood Hotels uses Six Sigma to drive and foster innovation and then rapidly disperse new ideas across the company. Utilizing this strategy enables Starwood to build a sound foundation to continually serve and delight its customers while still improving the bottom line.[8]

Product Leadership

The value strategy that builds value by differentiating the product.

Operational Excellence

The value strategy designed to produce lower costs than competitors while achieving high quality.

Customer Intimacy

The value strategy designed to create close relationships with customers.

Customer Intimacy The **customer intimacy** strategy is about creating very close relationships. DHL has grown faster than rivals FedEx and UPS. It acquired Xerox Corporation as a client with a customer intimacy strategy. By carefully targeting a few accounts and working closely with them to identify and serve their specific needs, DHL has eliminated services the customers do not really want, while customizing services they desire. The company shares the rewards of intimacy by passing some of the savings on to customers, so both parties win.

CUSTOMER, COMPETITOR, AND GLOBAL PRICING

Customer-oriented, competitor-oriented or global pricing describe the three ways to set prices.

CUSTOMER-ORIENTED PRICING

Marketers should keep in mind the effect of prices. Customers can't purchase everything they want, so they have to determine what will give them the "best value" — or, at least satisfactory value — for the money. But value is relative, not absolute, which is why exact prices are not nearly as important as price differences. Among the most important influences on customers are reference prices, price awareness, the association between price and quality, the perception of odd-even prices, and limited offers. Also discussed at the end of this section is target pricing.

Reference Price

The amount that consumers expect to pay for a product.

Acceptable Price Range

All prices around the reference price that consumers believe reflect good value.

Reference Prices Consumers try to obtain satisfactory value, not necessarily the best value. They try to determine how much satisfaction will be gained by comparing the benefits and price of one product relative to another. In most situations it is simply not worth the time to make all the calculations necessary to identify the absolute best value. Instead, buyers use reference prices and a price range. The **reference price** is what consumers expect to pay, and the **acceptable price range** is all prices around the reference point that consumers believe reflect good value.

In many airports, the price of food often so far exceeds consumers' reference points and acceptable range that they are dissatisfied with purchases. The Greater Pittsburgh Airport Authority requires concessionaires to use prices consistent with those in "typical" retail settings. The result is a unit volume of sales and a percentage of satisfied customers much higher there than in many other airports. An important point is that consumers respond more to price differences than to absolute prices. A reference price provides a standard to judge different prices against. For example, if a brand price is greater than a reference price, then the consumer perceives a loss in purchasing that product. If the brand price is less than the reference price, then the consumer perceives a gain.[9]

Researchers have found that consumers are likely to accept a price range for products and adjust their reference price accordingly. The brands lying outside the range will be rejected, and their prices won't be used in creating the reference price.[10] For example, you are looking for a mountain bike to go trail riding and expect to pay about $500 to $600. You find several bikes similar to what you want with price tags from $375 to $450. Your range shifts to about $400 to $500, and your reference price drops to around $425. You also see bikes at $100 and $900 (a midpoint of $500), but those extremes do not figure in your calculations.

The reference price gives consumers an idea about the value they can expect. A reference price is generally based on one or more of the following:

- the last price paid
- the going price (amount paid most frequently)
- the believed fair price
- the average price
- the price limit (what most buyers will pay)
- the expected future price (price based on trends).[11]

Marketers also look at the differentiation value of their product's attributes to determine whether their brand is seen favorably or unfavorably. The buyer looks at the relative price and relative quality. If consumers tend to evaluate a product as better than others, then it has a positive differentiation value. This means that it may have higher demand or command a price on the upper end of the range. The opposite is true if a brand has a negative differentiation value.

Marketers often help consumers establish reference prices. How many times have you seen ads with the original price (manufacturer's suggested retail or list price) and a sale price? In this way, marketers attempt to create favorable differential price impressions. Other methods are "cents off," "everyday low prices," "new low prices" or promotions such as "2014 models at 2013 prices." Marketers must be careful, however, about price changes. If the frequency, length and level of price promotions are not carefully managed, consumers can grow accustomed to the lowered prices and lower their reference price.

Price Awareness Business-to-business customers must be very price conscious. Each item they buy contributes to their costs and, thus, impacts their profits and competitiveness. Many businesses keep extensive records using formalized purchasing systems designed to obtain the best value for the price. Consumers tend to be less aware of actual prices. Studies of grocery shoppers have found that people are inaccurate about the exact price they paid for an item 90 percent of the time, and the range of error is approximately 20 percent.[12]

Price/Quality Association and Product Categorizations When buyers have little information about a product, they often assume a relationship between its price and its quality. In other words, price is a surrogate for quality. A traveler who doesn't know the local hotels may select a medium-priced property, expecting an average room, or the highest-priced hotel, expecting luxury accommodations. Ordinarily, the product delivered should be consistent in quality with its price relative to the competition.

Sometimes putting a very low price on a high-quality item may reduce demand by signaling low quality. Nike found that higher prices on many of its signature lines increased sales because consumers perceived that the price tag matched the company's image. Would it make sense to price Michael Jordan's signature Air Jordan shoes lower than any others? Price indicates not only what we expect to pay but also the value that we expect to gain. If these two are highly inconsistent, we distrust the seller, our own judgment or both. Nike decided not to do business with Sears Holdings, the combination of Sears and Kmart, because the retailers are discounters, which could undermine the premium image that Nike holds. Nike did sell to Walmart, but only its swoosh-free Starter brand, which is now owned by Iconix Brand Group.[13]

The Nike Air Jordan 1, released in 1985, retailed at $65. At the time, it was the most expensive basketball shoe on the market.

Price Ceiling

The top end of a price range.

Marketers often refer to the top end of a price range as the **price ceiling**. Many companies establish ceiling prices from which prices can be reduced.[14] In a product line with several levels of quality, there may be several ceiling prices. When consumers make few or no comparisons among brands, companies can charge prices at or near the ceiling. Companies with strong brands also justify high-end prices, which is why a Samsung cell phone priced just under a $200 ceiling works. It would be less profitable for Verizon to charge $182.99 rather than $199.99. In theory, the $17 difference could increase revenue through more sales, but it doesn't change the consumer's perception of value.

We know from experiments that price comparisons are made on a ratio rather than an absolute basis. If a Honda Insight has a sticker price of $20,000 and is sold for $1,000 less, then that is seen as roughly a five percent discount. The same discount on an Insight with a sticker price of $15,000 is seen as slightly larger, approaching seven percent. Although consumers may not actually compute the percentages, their perception works as if rough calculations were made.[15] Pricing policy must take this into account.

Consider the error made by a discount copying service that didn't understand how prices are perceived. Major copy centers had established copy prices of approximately four cents per page. The discount firm offered the same service for three cents a page. This attracted a lot of customers and produced a substantial amount of sales. The difference of "approximately 25 percent" was enough to entice many students. When the major centers increased price to five cents and then six cents, however, the discounter followed with two one-cent increases. Offering a discount of five cents instead of six was not nearly as enticing, as the differential was only about 17 percent. The discounter's sales volume declined with each price increase, although the one-cent absolute differential in price was maintained.

Performance Pricing Performance pricing provides a warranty that the product will perform as expected. It is generally used with new and uncertain products. Johnson & Johnson has negotiated with Britain's National Health Service using performance pricing, offering money back if its cancer drug Velcade doesn't work. If a patient on the $48,000 per year drug doesn't obtain expected results, Johnson & Johnson will refund the cost. Like in the U.S., British health-care providers are looking for new ways to justify spending great amounts on products that promise outstanding value in use. Likewise, providers such as Johnson & Johnson are looking for ways to charge higher prices for extremely innovative, high value products.[16]

Odd-Even Price Perceptions Prices that end in odd numbers tend to be perceived differently from even-numbered prices. Consumers have learned that discounters tend to use prices ending in a nine, seven or five. Before sophisticated computer systems and inventory control systems were available, retailers used these endings as a code: nine identified a markdown, seven a second markdown, and five a third markdown. Early discounters adopted the odd numbers for all their products to suggest sales prices. Today, odd numbers connote lower quality and price, while even numbers connote higher quality and price.[17]

Limited Offers Limited offers are often used by marketers to encourage consumers to buy types or quantities of products they had not planned to purchase. The special prices are meant to persuade consumers to stock up. Consider for example, the psychology behind a limit on sales. A special promotion for sugar may read "limit four." Why? A study has found that people are more likely to buy an item that has a limit. This is similar to children who want candy because they are told they cannot have any. Furthermore, one study showed that shoppers are more likely to buy an item with a limit of four rather than two.[18]

Target Pricing Customer-oriented pricing focuses on buyers' psychological information processing and their perceptions of value in use and value in exchange. **Target pricing**, which uses price to reach a particular market segment, is a very important strategy. It is a way of matching price with the value perceived by each segment. Burton manufactures and sells snowboards that are marketed towards various types of snowboarders. Distinct lines are priced in relation to an individual's level of interest, ability and income. The Ripcord is a value board priced at $299.95 for beginners and price-sensitive customers, while freestyle riders can choose from more than a dozen boards, including the modestly priced Custom and Restricted models, which sell for about $500.[19] For the ultimate enthusiasts, Burton offers the Mystery Flying V Snowboard for $1,499.95. Burton also markets boards designed especially for women, such as the Feelgood at $549.95, and boards for kids priced at $249.95 or less.[20]

Target Pricing

The use of price to reach a particular market segment.

Sören from Germany - turboed / CC-BY-SA-2.0

Burton uses target pricing to appeal to all skill levels and riding styles.

COMPETITOR-ORIENTED PRICING

Competitor-oriented pricing focuses primarily on prices set by rivals. Leader-follower, going rate, discount or premium, and competitive bids are all price schemes of this type. Carried to its extreme, competitor-oriented pricing can lead to mutually destructive price wars.

Leader-Follower Pricing   When manufacturers of major household appliances, also known as white goods, were faced with rising commodity costs from oil and steel shortages, Whirlpool decided to raise prices by up to 10 percent. Competitors like Electrolux followed by increasing prices. Although material and energy costs were squeezing profits, all were able to produce additional profits through retail prices, which more than compensated for cost increases.[21]

    Competitor-oriented pricing often involves such scenarios. The leader-follower situation tends to occur in oligopolistic industries whose products have relatively inelastic derived demand. The leader usually has considerable strength — high market share, a loyal customer base, an efficient cost structure, moderate inventory, and a technological edge. Leaders generally can exercise power, but often that is not necessary. The reason is that they create competitive environments, which benefit followers by providing fair profits for all. Good followers can also help create a positive industry pricing climate. In banking, most small and medium-sized institutions copy the products and pricing policies of larger competitors.

Price leaders must show a willingness to defend their position when price becomes an issue. Yet, across-the-board cuts may hurt larger companies more, so it's important to be selective. After the Spanish government began taking anti-smoking measures, Spanish-French tobacco company Altadis raised prices in order to pass tax increases on to consumers. However, Phillip Morris' response to the government measures was a price drop on Marlboro cigarettes. Altadis was then forced to lower its prices by 20 percent, taking a huge hit to its profits, and declared that it was the manufacturers' responsibility to price higher in order to maintain a virtuous cycle. Competition drove cigarette prices in Spain down to about a quarter of those in the UK. Later, the Spanish government began enforcing a smoking ban in public places and Phillip Morris again responded by slashing prices, causing other brands to once again follow.[22]

Discount or Premium Pricing Discount or premium pricing positions the company relative to competitors based solely on price. In most markets, there are buyers who seek the cheapest products and those who seek the most expensive. Consider the sale of store-brand hair coloring at very low prices and L'Oréal at higher prices. L'Oréal says its hair coloring is more expensive "because I'm worth it." The Meijer food chain establishes the lowest price possible and asks: "Why pay more?"

Going Rate Pricing The **going rate** price evolves over time when no competitor has power over others so all price at a similar level. This is often the case in monopolistic competition when product differentiation is very minor and firms attempt to gain loyalty while pricing at the going rate. For example, lawyers often charge the going rate per hour, which will vary considerably from one community to another. The going rate tends to avoid price wars. Because all providers charge approximately the same, and these prices are broadly communicated, they usually meet buyers' expectations.

Competitive Bids We tend to think of bids as related to the purchasing function, but they also are a prevalent form of competitive pricing. Sealed bids are opened at a certain time, and the low price usually is the winner. An alternative is for buyers to look at bids as they are received and perhaps give feedback to sellers indicating they are too high. This is called open bidding, and it is intended to get suppliers to lower prices.

By understanding competitors, a company can greatly enhance its ability to win contracts at the highest possible price while still being the low bidder. Competitors often scale prices up or down to meet their own volume or cost objectives. By knowing competitors' capacity and cost structure, marketers can adjust their own bids. At priceline.com, a commonly used web auction site, customers can "name their own price" for airline tickets, hotel rooms, rental cars, cruises and vacation packages. The customer's price is either accepted or rejected. Upon rejection, the customer is able to submit another bid at a higher price.[23]

Price Wars **Price wars** occur when price cuts by one company spur similar reductions by competitors. These price-slashing battles can substantially lower

Going Rate

The price that evolves over time when no competitor has power over others and all price at a similar level.

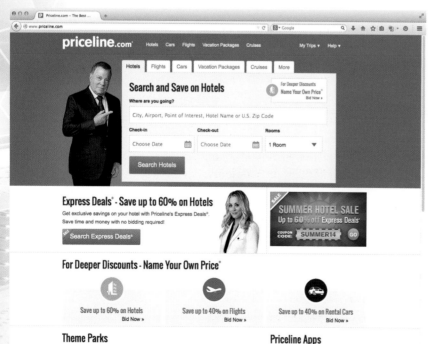

profit margins. The consumer benefits, since products can be purchased below their value. The company most successful at cutting costs is usually the victor — if it can survive despite the meager profit margins. Large organizations with ample reserves have an obvious advantage.

Price wars have been especially common in the airline industry, with the success of low-cost carriers like Southwest and JetBlue. A classic price skirmish ensued one day after Jet-Blue announced a flight from Boston to New York for $69 round trip, American and Delta followed suit by cutting prices by as much as 80 percent. This heavy discounting technique was pioneered by Southwest and has been very successful. If these price wars continued to different routes, profits for American and Delta would undoubtedly take a large tumble. JetBlue, on the other hand, experienced positive moves in market share with better than expected results.[24]

CAREER TIP!

When DuPont says it is "going where the growth is," the company has two destinations in mind — geographic markets and product market spaces with unmet needs that present unique opportunities for DuPont offerings and innovations. The company actively recruits for co-op/internships and regular full-time employment. DuPont offers endless possibilities to utilize your professional and interpersonal skills with internship and co-op assignments that aim to develop students into future leaders. Go online to find out about DuPont's major recruiting events and which campuses are regularly visited at www.dupont.com/careers.

GLOBAL PRICING

Global pricing is complicated by many factors. One of the most important is when a government mandates that imported products cannot be paid for with cash; **countertrade** requires companies from the exporting nation to purchase products of equivalent value from the importing nation. Countertrade affects up to 30 percent of all world trade. When a nation's banking system is poor, countertrade may be the best form of pricing. It also provides governments with a mechanism for stimulating exports. It is common for developing countries to require foreign companies to purchase goods from domestic companies as part of any major trade agreement. In other words, countertrade is a simple barter, the exchange of one good for another.

Countertrade

Government mandates that imported products can't be paid for with cash; the exporting country must purchase goods of equivalent value from the importing nation.

Although technically the term refers to government-regulated exchanges, countertrade also may be initiated by trading partners. There are many arrangements similar to barter that can benefit both parties. Agreements to purchase like values but without exchanging money can increase demand, and avoiding the use of cash can be advantageous when considering taxes. A countertrade deal that covers an extended period can provide a lot of flexibility in scheduling, manufacturing and shipping. Japanese and Dutch trading companies may have hundreds of these arrangements going at one time. The Japanese keiretsu system relies on cross-ownership, cross-ties in banking, and discrimination against outside buyers and sellers to form huge trading organizations.[25] By locking suppliers into the organization, enormous cost savings result. The major keiretsu are Mitsui, Mitsubishi, Sumitomo, Fuyo, Sanwa and Daiichi. However, these arrangements between closely knit Japanese manufacturers, suppliers and distributors are eroding.[26]

International pricing is also complicated by the need to transfer funds. Payment is seldom direct, and generally a bank must be involved. This often requires a letter of credit that specifies the bank will pay a seller under various conditions. Because a good deal of time may pass between the settlement of an international deal and the transfer of products and funds, financing is critical. If it is poorly executed, then a lot of money can be lost.

Exchange fluctuations also influence global pricing. Companies that use value-based pricing tend to treat these fluctuations differently from those that use cost-plus pricing. As exchange rates go up and down, profit margins tend to vary. The cost-plus method simply increases or decreases price to keep the same margins, which changes what buyers pay. The value-based method tends to leave prices the same, varying instead the level of profit. Japanese companies exporting to the United States tend to maintain stable prices, reflecting their tendency to keep them in line with the market as well as profit objectives.[27] This works unless exchange rates fluctuate widely. For example, if the Japanese yen depreciated in relation to the dollar, Japanese companies such as Honda, Sony and Nissan could lower prices on their U.S. products. Many companies benefit when the dollar is strong because foreign-made products and components are cheaper. However, this can also create challenges for domestic companies attempting to keep up with the lower prices offered by foreign competitors.

IMPLEMENTING THE PRICING STRATEGY

Once the overall pricing strategy has been chosen, it must be implemented. Since prices are easier to adjust than any other part of the marketing mix, they tend to fluctuate. Even companies with consistent pricing based on customer value make changes. Whether initiating a new strategy or adjusting an existing one, the first step in implementation is to set prices. The second step is to communicate them to the market. At both stages, ethical issues are involved.

SETTING PRICES

Fundamental Strategies for Price Setting
Price strategies are often categorized according to the following six approaches: skimming, penetration, sliding down the demand curve, the price umbrella, everyday low prices and promotional pricing. Companies can price high, low or in between. Whatever the decision, it is sure to affect buyers and competitors. Figure 18.5 describes the fundamental strategies for price setting.

Skimming and Penetration Pricing
These two approaches are discussed together because they are opposites. **Price skimming** is designed to obtain a very high price from relatively few consumers with the desire to buy regardless of price. The name is taken from the practice of dairy farmers, who once skimmed the valuable cream off the top of non-homogenized milk and discarded the remainder or fed it to farm animals. Today, skimming is used by companies with certain innovations or fads. Marketers charge a very high price, thereby attracting only a small part of the total market. Because use value is high in a product's introductory period, a premium can be obtained. When more producers enter the market, prices tend to move downward as exchange value declines.

If companies perceive they can obtain a monopoly position for a short time, then they might skim to generate profits that provide investment capital for further innovations. To sustain skimming, companies must offer unusual products of the highest quality or artistic value. Many times this strategy does not produce loyal customers, since subsequent entrants eventually will offer a better value at lower prices. In contrast to skimming, **penetration pricing** seeks the maximum number of buyers by charging a low price. This approach is used for products that are very price elastic. If costs are sensitive to volume, then these will drop dramatically as share increases relative to competitors. This is a way to keep rivals from entering the market, since many companies avoid situations in which overall prices are extremely low.

The problem with penetration pricing is that losses are likely, especially in the

Price Skimming

A strategy designed to obtain a high price from relatively few consumers with the resources to buy regardless of price.

Penetration Pricing

A strategy seeking the maximum number of buyers by charging low prices.

Strategy	Objective	When Typically Used
Skimming	High short-term profit without concern for the long run	No competitive products Innovation or fad Block competitor entry due to patent control, high R&D costs, high fixed costs, control of technology, government regulation, or high promotion costs Uncertain demand and/or cost Short life cycle Price-insensitive buyers
Penetration Pricing	Stimulate market growth and capture market share; become entrenched to produce long-term profits	Large markets Products of broad appeal Long product life cycle Very price-elastic demand
Sliding Down the Demand Curve	Gain short-term profits before competitors become entrenched without sacrificing long-term market share	Launch of high-technology innovations Slight barriers to competitive entry Medium life cycle
Price Umbrella Leadership	Encourage competitors to promote the product category to stimulate purchase of all brands and encourage competitors to follow the price leader	Several comparable competitors Growing market Stable competitors One or a few dominant competitors
Everyday Low Prices or Value Pricing	Appeal to buyers willing to shop for the "greatest" benefits for the money	Component parts in industrial markets Repurchased consumer products Mass merchandisers Established products
Promotional Pricing	Stimulate demand to introduce or reintroduce a product, neutralize a competitor, or move excess inventory	Demand fluctuates seasonally or for a certain period Marketing "wars" or head-to-head competition Mass merchandisers Fashion items

Figure 18.5 Fundamental Strategies for Price Setting

short term. Because profit margins tend to be very small, demand must meet expectations in order to generate enough earnings. Furthermore, when customers buy only because of price, loyalty tends to be low. They are likely to switch to competitors offering an even lower price or innovations of higher value at a higher price.

Sliding Down the Demand Curve
To **slide down the demand curve** means to descend from higher to lower prices when competitors enter. When launching its industrial control products, Texas Instruments has been known to use this strategy. First, management establishes a high price for an innovative product to skim the market. Second, when a major competitor follows with its version, Texas Instruments drops its price — sometimes only slightly, often considerably. This aggressive strategy discourages or delays market entrants, and Texas Instruments obtains high short-term profit margins without sacrificing its long-term objective of penetrating the market.

Slide Down the Demand Curve

A strategy that involves setting a high price when a product is introduced and lowering it significantly as competitors enter the market.

Price Umbrella

The leader maintains the price at a high enough level that competitors can earn a profit at the same price or lower levels.

The Price Umbrella

DuPont is known for its leadership in innovations. It produces innumerable plastics, fibers and chemicals used to create thousands of products, and is doing so in more and more sustainable ways. Because of its strength, the company is in a perfect position to use the **price umbrella**; that is, the leader selects the highest price. Competitors can make fair profits at that level or even lower, especially if their costs are relatively low. Price leadership occurs when one or two companies price in such a way that others follow them. In DuPont's case, marketers launch innovations after careful study of the product's likely contributions to customers and society. By assessing the use value relative to substitutes and other brands, DuPont establishes a price commensurate with the high value it typically offers. Along with the product, buyers receive DuPont's uncompromising customer support, which is based on an advanced distribution system, consultative and relationship selling, and service.

Generally, DuPont's price is high enough to encourage other healthy companies to participate in the market. At the same time, because several competitors are promoting a similar product, demand is stimulated for the product category. DuPont even licenses its products to rivals in exchange for a percentage of sales revenue. Since these competitors do not have to engage in basic R&D, DuPont's leadership in product innovation is protected.

Everyday Low Prices

Prices, on average, are consistently lower than those of competitors.

Everyday Low Prices

Walmart is famous for its **everyday low prices**, which on average are consistently lower than those of competitors. Sometimes this strategy is called value pricing (not to be confused with value-based pricing). In order for it to work, retailers need to develop extremely efficient (low-cost) operations. Walmart has the most advanced computerized restocking system imaginable. Rapid turnover (products don't sit on the shelves for long) and aggressive purchasing power provide the basis for keeping prices low. Walmart has approximately $475 billion in annual sales and is the largest retailer in the world.[28] Target and Toys "R" Us also use this strategy — and pledge to meet or beat any competitor's price on any item. In this way, they maximize volume and keep customers from shopping around. Riesbeck's Food Market, an independent supermarket chain in Ohio, Toronto and West Virginia, moved to an everyday low price strategy after noticing the rise in popularity of supercenters and dollar stores. The company was quite successful with this strategy until Walmart stores nearly doubled in surrounding areas and a head-to-head battle ensued. Riesbeck, finding it difficult to square-off with the giant, shifted back to injecting savings into value programs, including multi-day specials promoted in weekly ads.[29]

Everyday low pricing can be highly competitive on an international scale as well. For example, Zellers, Canada's low-price leader, used the slogan "lowest price is the law." Its profit margins shrank when Walmart entered the Canadian market, and the two now compete intensely with their value-pricing strategies. Zellers proclaims, "There's more than low prices," while Walmart continues to implement cuts in order

Courtesy of Walmart

to offer the lowest regular prices to consumers. In an effort to keep its own customers and lure customers from its rival, Zellers became the first retailer in the world to seek and gain from the International Organization for Standardization in Geneva its certification that it meets world-class standards of efficiency and quality. Walmart has run into problems with price controls, strict labor laws, tough zoning regulations and fierce competition. Historically, mature rivals such as Aldi and Lidl have been more than ready to compete on low prices and are familiar with thin profit margins.[30]

Promotional Pricing
Competitive companies such as Coca-Cola and PepsiCo, Burger King and McDonald's, and Toyota and Nissan are nearly always engaged in some form of **promotional pricing**. These battles serve three purposes. First, the price discount is a way to make consumers notice the product. Second, imme-diate purchase is encouraged because promotional pricing gives consumers the impression that the price is likely to rise in the near future. Third, consumers are kept aware of the entire product category. The "wars" between Coke and Pepsi keep buyers loyal to cola at the expense of other soft drinks. Marketers in these two companies expect continuous challenges from one another as price interacts with other parts of the marketing mix to stimulate demand and produce minor market share shifts.

Promotional Pricing

A strategy in which price discounts are used to gain attention and encourage immediate purchase.

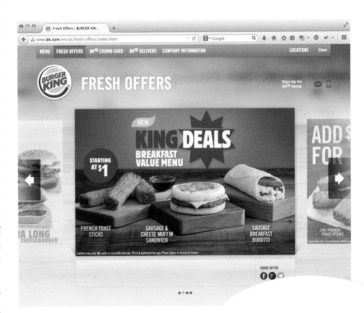

Burger King's "King Deals" are promotional priced breakfast items starting at one dollar.

One kind of promotional pricing is loss leaders, used by retailers to lure consumers into their store. As you'll remember from the previous chapter, these products are priced at or below the retailer's cost. For example, the Midwest grocery chain Meijer often prices milk very low compared to competitors. Because this item is purchased regularly by most consumers, most tend to remember its price. For that reason, milk and similar repeat purchase items provide shoppers with a ready source of comparison among rivals. The theory behind loss leaders is that once customers are in the store to buy the lower priced product, they'll do additional shopping at regular prices. Retailers make up for loss leaders by increased volume or additional purchases made by the customer.

There are many other forms of price promotion. Although we usually assume that price reduction is most likely to stimulate demand, sometimes any message drawing attention to the product, including a price differential, will lead to purchase. Marketing research by a major pharmaceutical company revealed some surprising news. For many years, price promotions had been used to boost sales of selected prescription drugs. Each time the product was promoted at a reduced price by sales representatives, physicians prescribed it more. The assumption was that these products were price elastic for doctors, but the research found that most of them didn't know the price of these drugs and did not especially care. Then why the increase in prescriptions? The study found that the price reduction gave salespeople a reason to discuss the product with physicians; drawing their attention to the product was what increased prescriptions. Subsequent research revealed that nearly any relevant sales message led to a rise in sales because, for established and commonly used drugs, many doctors prescribe the brand that first comes to mind — often the one most recently discussed with a sales rep. The point is that price decreases often stimulate sales, but the attention drawn to a product by price promotions also may be a factor.

PRODUCT LINE PRICING STRATEGIES

Consumers tend to use all products in a company's line as a way of making comparisons. Consequently, marketers use several strategies: product array, bundling, optional product and captive product pricing.

Product Array Pricing Most companies sell several products. These may be offered within the same brand, such as different GMC trucks, or in several lines, such as Buick, Chevy and Cadillac. Prices need to be established across the entire product array. Apple prices its lines of devices so prices go up arithmetically while storage increases exponentially. For example, the new 16GB iPad Air costs $499, the 32GB costs $599, the 64GB costs $699, and the 128GB costs $799.

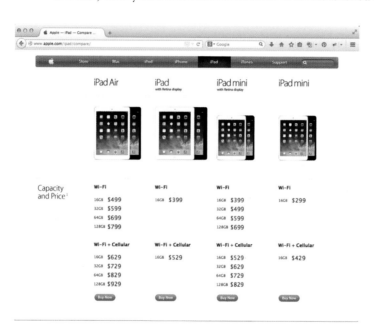

Toyota takes the competition one step further by challenging the entire auto industry on its website. Customers can go to the company's website and click on a tab for cars, trucks, SUVs and vans, and hybrids, then use a side-by-side feature to compare specific Toyota automobiles to three competitive companies. It lists key rivals of each of its car models, ranging from Ford to Lexus. Once you click to compare, it assesses important factors like fuel economy, features, measurements, performance, safety, warranty and price. The website then highlights the advantages that Toyota has over its opposition. Toyota's competitive strategy leads the market by expecting continuous challenges as price interacts with other parts of the marketing mix to stimulate demand and produce minor market share shifts.[31]

Bundled Pricing Products can be bundled or unbundled for pricing purposes. The bundled approach, which gives a single price for the entire package, is used for standardized products, whereas unbundling is often used for customized products. For example, home builders use each method depending on the offering. House prices in a subdivision are usually bundled to include carpeting, fixtures and landscaping, while various items will be listed separately for custom homes. Even property and land preparation cost will be specified. The unbundling helps custom buyers assess the value of each item and make choices according to tastes and budgets. Comcast offers packages that bundle digital cable, high-speed Internet and Comcast Digital Voice®. Other telecom companies also offer discounts to customers that buy more than one service.[32]

Optional Product Pricing

Many products are sold as base units with optional add-ons. Cars are an obvious example. The 2014 Scion IQ has a base price of $16,420 — but by selecting cool options like illuminated door sills, alloy wheels, fog lamps, and a navigation system — the car can cost you $23,000 or more.[33] Add-ons for automobiles include satellite radios, sunroofs, security features and alloy wheels. Companies often price the base product low as a platform for selling other items.

Captive Product Pricing

It is pretty obvious why Gillette prices its razors low. Once you own one, you will buy blades — perhaps for years. In a sense, you're a captive customer, but since razors and blades are not very expensive, the cost to escape is minor. But consider the cost of moving from Xbox to PlayStation video games. You need to purchase a new system (at a price of $350 or more), and your current games will not work with the new system. The average consumer might decide that switching console systems is far too costly and continue to purchase Xbox products. The captive product strategy is used by many marketers. Internet-access cellular phone companies price with a variation on the captive theme. They have an installment fee, then a fixed rate plus a variable usage charge. Often the fixed rate is set very low in order to obtain the more profitable usage fees.

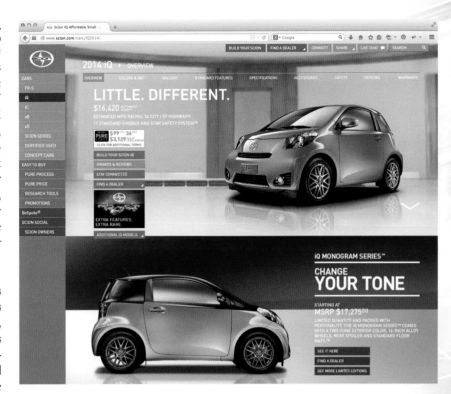

COMMUNICATING PRICE

An important step in price implementation is to communicate with the market. This involves more than just advertising a figure. The price may have several components that are quoted in differing ways, and various kinds of price reductions can be offered.

Price Components Let's say that Joan Martin purchased Rossignol skis, poles and boots at the California Ski Company outlet. The package cost $800, and the total including tax was $848. Her roommate purchased the same package at a Winter Sports Equipment store for $800, but the total including tax was $893. She was charged $30 extra for binding installation and $15 for tuning the skis. Whether the buyer or seller pays for "extras" can make a substantial difference in price.

In consumer markets, there is wide variation in what is included in the price. Playmakers, a sports retailer in Okemos, Michigan, has won national awards for its customer service. Playmakers will return your money if a shoe does not meet your expectations. If the support breaks down before you think it should, then you can take the shoes back for a refund or a new pair, no questions asked. Although the Playmakers' price may be similar to that of other retailers, few provide the same level of customer service. Playmakers' return policy is added value. The most common additions to price are these:

- Finance charges
- Installation fees
- Warranty charges
- 800-number assistance
- Replacement parts inventory
- Shipping and handling
- Training.

It is important to communicate clearly the components that are included within a price quotation. If buyers are hit with unexpected charges for items they thought were included within the original price, they are likely to be dissatisfied. This is because many consumers believe this is unethical behavior on the part of the seller.

Price Quoting
Price quoting is how prices are communicated to buyers. Some companies offer a price quoting service. For example, Progressive Auto Insurance uses online comparative shopping by showing quotes from its competitors as well as its own. This establishes rapport with consumers and makes them feel confident they are getting a fair and reliable price.[34] Sometimes prices are stated clearly and directly, but often an indirect method is used. The **list price** (or suggested retail price) set by the manufacturer usually provides the reference point by which consumers judge the fairness of the market price. The **market price** is the actual amount buyers must pay for the product, and is often much lower than the list price. For example, when Sony introduces a product, the list price may be more than double the market price. The market price is likely to result from several types of reductions, including discounts and rebates.

Price Reductions
Discounts are often given for cash payment, for purchasing large quantities, or for loyalty. Cash discounts are offered to consumers, business-to-business customers, and nearly all channel members. Many buyers look at the undiscounted price as a penalty for delayed payment. Discounts are incentives to speed cash flow from buyer to seller, and they are standard in many industries. It is common for cash discounts to be quoted in terms of a percentage reduction and a specific time for payment, most often 2/10, net 30. This says the buyer has a two percent discount if paid in 10 days, and full payment without a discount is due in 30 days. Many buyers pay within the first 10 days because a two percent discount figured over the remaining 20 days is equivalent to an interest rate of about 36 percent on an annual basis. Sellers use the discounts to speed payment and reduce losses due to bad debts. Many industries have increased their prices by nearly two percent to offset these cash discounts.

Quantity discounts, which are reductions for large purchases, are justified because the seller has lower unit costs when handling larger orders. That is, selling, order processing, billing, shipping and inventory carrying costs are averaged over a greater volume. It is common for a supplier to use quantity discounts to entice buyers to purchase more and to achieve economies of scale for transportation and processing costs.[35] These can be offered at one time or on a cumulative basis. Victoria's Secret PINK sells its name brand underwear for $9.50 per piece. However, a customer can save a substantial amount of money by taking advantage of the ongoing "5 for $25" deal.[36] Another example is pricing of financial mutual funds, which often charge differing commissions, or "loads," depending on the amount purchased. One popular fund charges 4.25 percent for orders less than $50,000, 3.5 percent for $50,000 to $100,000, and 2.5 percent for more than $100,000. The buyer has up to one year to meet the commitment.

Patronage discounts are very similar to cumulative quantity discounts, and

> **Quantity discounts, which are reductions for large purchases, are justified because the seller has lower unit costs when handling larger orders.**

List Price

The price set by the manufacturer and used by consumers as a reference point. Also called suggested retail price.

Market Price

The actual price buyers must pay for a product.

they reward buyer loyalty. An example is a café that stamps a card for each cup of coffee bought and then gives a free cup when the card is full. Another variation is Sam's Club, a no-frills retail buying center developed by Walmart, which offers discounts only to fee-paying members. Discounts should not be used, however, as the sole means for achieving customer loyalty. Customers who buy your product solely because of price are likely to switch to a competitor for the same reason.

Rebates reduce prices through direct payments, usually from the manufacturer to the consumer. In today's competitive car market, rebates are a popular way to move cars off the lot. Rebates may have a greater psychological effect on customers than discounts. A discount is a small percentage of the total price; a rebate is a large amount of money. Remember that price differentials make the largest impression on buyers. With rebates, manufacturers also are more assured that the savings will not be partially absorbed by dealers. Sometimes, when discounts are given to dealers with the idea that they be passed along to consumers, part of the difference is kept by the dealer.

UNETHICAL PRICING PRACTICES

When marketers develop a pricing strategy, it should reflect the value perceived and received. This does not always happen. Abuses can occur through manipulation of the consumer's reference price, quoting overcharged or misleading prices, or using discriminatory pricing practices. Unethical pricing can have legal repercussions, not to mention the risk of losing valuable customers.

As mentioned earlier, the reference price serves as a guideline to consumers. What happens when marketers manipulate that price in order to change the consumer's perception of what is "fair"? Three studies have addressed this issue.[37] When a reference price is set at an implausibly high level, it can influence perceptions about a fair price as well as the highest price. Another study indicates that plausible reference prices can strongly influence customers' estimates of the highest and lowest prices for a given item, but implausible reference prices have little impact on their estimates.[38] Therefore, it is important for marketers to establish reference prices with care.

Another unethical practice is to raise prices to profit from tragedy or natural disaster. Many states have laws to prevent price gouging in the event of a disaster or state emergency. In general, price gouging is the act of raising rates of more than 10 to 25 percent, depending on the state. A Long Island hotel that raised its rates 185 percent after the 9/11 disaster was required to pay $9,500 in restitution, fines and legal costs. Other natural disasters such as tornadoes and hurricanes have spawned unethical pricing practices for items such as food, water and construction supplies.[39]

Discriminatory pricing practices are often very controversial. Is it fair to charge a woman more than a man for dry-cleaning a shirt or for a haircut? This depends on a number of circumstances. Are the shirts similar, or is the service more difficult to perform for one gender versus another? Since most women have longer hair than men, perhaps it is more difficult or time-consuming to cut. Nevertheless, studies have found that women do pay more than men for products ranging from haircuts to cars.[40] In 1995, with the Gender Tax Repeal Act, California became the first state to prohibit gender discrimination in pricing for similar services. Even so, a number of California businesses continue to use different prices. Three years after the passage of the act, the California Public Interest Research Group reported that many dry cleaners and hairdressers continued to charge higher prices for services to women than to men. Because of the small amounts involved in these price differences, however, very few women have chosen to take costly legal action against businesses that violate the law.[41]

CREATING & CAPTURING VALUE THROUGH *Technology*

Banks Coddle Some Customers and Make Others Pay Their Way

The retail banking industry has taken a sharp turn in some markets from focusing on serving its customers to focusing on its bottom line. Feeling the effects of this trend perhaps closest to home are clients of the New England banks that are being taken over by the New Jersey–based FleetBoston Financial Corp.

The general feeling of smaller account customers about these recently acquired banks is that they now need to pay for the services they may have previously enjoyed for free, while the big fish are treated like royalty. John S. Reed, the retired chairman of Citigroup, expressed his concerns by stating that financial institutions "are poorly serving their customers."

The evidence? In the past, banks made their profit on the difference between interest paid to account holders and interest charged to borrowers. However, over the last few years, as interest rates fell and competition for loan customers increased, banks started to rely more on another stream of income: ATM and overdraft charges. While many banks offer free cash withdrawals from their own ATMs, customers are often double charged for using another bank's ATM. After fees from their own bank, customers pay an average of $2.10 for a single withdrawal, and some fees reach as high as $5.00. Many customers are unhappy with the growing expense of accessing their own money.

Since most of a large commercial bank's profits come from big-ticket clients, the attention of the tellers and staff is focused on keeping those people happy, while perhaps neglecting or charging the little guy. Because of this, banks such as Fleet may possibly lose customers to smaller banks that can provide the services that people want.

Not all banks, however, are concerned only with the big-ticket clients. Commerce Bank, the winner of a recent Consumers Report customer satisfaction survey, has emphasized convenience and customer service. "Smart bank executives realized their customers were comparing the way they were treated at their bank with their experiences at places like Nordstrom and Starbucks," says Jim Eckenrode, Managing Director of Banking and Payments for TowerGroup, an industry research firm. So Commerce Bank responded by investing in branches that stay open until 7 p.m., seven days a week. Commerce has also added door greeters and placed its tellers at concierge desks, instead of the traditional booths. With smaller customers in mind, Commerce offers a credit card with no late fee, no annual fee and no balance-transfer fee. It also recently announced a rebate for fees its customers are charged by other banks for using those banks' ATMs

Banks, like all businesses, need to evaluate their pricing policies to insure that profitability and customer satisfaction are both increasing simultaneously. One cannot survive without the other for very long.

Geoffrey Smith, "Bigger Isn't Better for Fleet's Customers," Business Week, July 10, 2000, p. 64; "Customer service is getting new attention, but watch out for those sneaky fees," Consumer Reports, September 2006; Blake Ellis, "ATM fees on the rise," CNN Money, April 17, 2013.

CHAPTER SUMMARY

Objective 1:   Understand why an appropriate customer value proposition is a useful guide to pricing strategy.
Pricing strategies are complex and must balance the needs of both the customer and the firm. Value-based pricing, which includes the concepts of value in use and value in exchange, is increasingly popular. Since customers seek differing types of value and competitors have a broad range of choices in how to price, other strategies are viable as well. In devising a pricing strategy, it is important to identify a customer value proposition that matches the capabilities of the organization. The three types of capabilities are product leadership, operational competence, and customer intimacy.

Objective 2:   Know what factors to consider when using customer- and competitor-oriented pricing methods.
Pricing strategies may focus on customers, competitors or global factors. Customer-oriented pricing requires an understanding of reference prices, price awareness, price/quality association, odd-even perceptions, limited offers and target pricing. Competitor-oriented pricing considers leader-follower scenarios, going rates, discounting and competitive bids. Some companies engage in price wars that can seriously affect industry and company profits. On a global scale, pricing may include countertrading or barter. Funds transfer and exchange rates also affect international pricing.

Objective 3:   Learn how pricing strategy is implemented by setting prices and communicating them to the market.
Implementing a price strategy requires setting and communicating prices. One of six fundamental approaches can be used to set prices: skimming, penetration pricing, sliding down the demand curve, price umbrella, everyday low prices and promotional pricing. Product line pricing complicates matters. Options are product array, bundled, optional product and captive product pricing. When prices are communicated, various components may be specified or only the overall price, and various reductions may be offered. Price communication must be done carefully to avoid unethical practices, such as false impressions about price or unfair discrimination.

REVIEW YOUR UNDERSTANDING

1. What is value-based pricing? How does it differ from cost-based pricing?
2. What is value in use? Value in exchange?
3. What three leader strategies match what buyers want?
4. What are reference prices? Give several categories.
5. What is a ceiling price, and how is it used in setting prices?
6. How are odd and even prices perceived?
7. When is going rate pricing used?
8. How is pricing used to attract senior citizens?
9. What are price skimming and penetration pricing?
10. What is umbrella pricing?
11. List three aspects of product line pricing.
12. How are prices quoted?
13. What is discriminatory pricing?

DISCUSSION OF CONCEPTS

1. How are price and value related? What are the advantages of value-based pricing over the traditional cost-based approach?
2. What is the difference between value in use and value in exchange? How could a marketer use these concepts to improve profitability?
3. What is required if a company wants to use product leadership, operational competence or customer intimacy as the basis for establishing a customer value proposition? Give examples of each.
4. How does competition affect a company's prices? Briefly describe the major competitor-based pricing approaches.
5. We know that several factors influence consumer responses to prices. What psychological factors should marketers keep in mind when using consumer-oriented pricing? Describe each.
6. How is a company's market position related to price leadership? What does this have to do with price wars?
7. Describe the six fundamental ways to set price. In what situations is each strategy typically used?
8. How does the communication of price present ethical dilemmas? Give examples of several questionable practices.

KEY TERMS & DEFINITIONS

1. **Bait and Acceptable price range:** All prices around the reference price that consumers believe reflect good value.
2. **Buying market share:** A strategy in which prices are set low for the short run to pull buyers away from competing brands.
3. **Countertrade:** Government mandates that imported products cannot be paid for with cash; instead, companies from the exporting nation are required to purchase products of equivalent value from the importing nation.
4. **Customer intimacy:** The value strategy designed to create close relationships with customers.
5. **Everyday low prices:** Prices that, on average, are consistently lower than those of competitors.
6. **Going rate:** The price that evolves over time when no competitor has power over others and all price at a similar level.
7. **List price:** The price set by the manufacturer and used by consumers as a reference point. Also called suggested retail price.
8. **Market price:** The actual price buyers must pay for a product.
9. **Operational excellence:** The value strategy designed to produce lower costs that competitors while achieving high quality.
10. **Penetration pricing:** A strategy that seeks the maximum number of buyers by charging low prices.
11. **Price ceiling:** The top end of a price range.
12. **Price skimming:** A strategy to obtain a very high price from relatively few consumers, who have the resources and desire to buy irrespective of price.
13. **Price umbrella:** The leader maintains the price at a high enough level that competitors can earn a profit at that or lower levels.
14. **Price war:** A cut by one company spurs similar reductions by competitors, resulting in price slashing that can lower profit margins.
15. **Product leadership:** The value strategy that builds value by differentiating the product.
16. **Promotional pricing:** A strategy in which price discounts are used to get attention and encourage immediate purchase.
17. **Reference price:** The amount consumers expect to pay for a product.
18. **Slide down the demand curve:** Set a high price when a product is introduced and then lower it significantly as competitors enter the market.
19. **Target pricing:** The use of price to reach a particular market segment.
20. **Value-based pricing:** A strategy that reflects value, not just cost.
21. **Value in exchange:** The objective worth of a product in the competitive marketplace.
22. **Value in use:** The consumer's subjective estimate of the benefits of a particular product.

REFERENCES

1. "Fact Sheet, Southwest Airlines, www.southwest.com, website visited April 30, 2014; Southwest Airlines, www.southwest.com, website visited April 30, 2014; "Record revenue performance led to our 39th consecutive year of profitability — a feat unmatched in U.S. aviation history," Southwest, www.southwestonereport.com, website visited website visited April 30, 2014; "World's Most Admired Companies," Fortune, www.fortune.com, website visited April 30, 2014; Maynard, Micheline, "At Least the Airsickness Bags Are Free," New York Times, www.nytimes.com, August 16, 2008; Maciborski, Walt, "(Full) David Holmes - Southwest Airlines - Rapping Flight Attenttendant," YouTube.com, website visited April 30, 2014.

2. www.volvocars.com, website visited March 19, 2014.

3. "Volvo Crash Test Lab photos: Crashing cars, saving lives," Cnet, May 7, 2010.

4. "Charles Shaw Wins Triple Gold in Orange County ," http://www.winebusiness.com, June 27, 2013.

5. Erica Ho, "Trader Joe's Two-Buck Chuck Gets a Price Hike," Time, January 25, 2013.

6. Treacy, Michael; Wiersema, Fred, The Discipline of Market Leaders (Reading, Massachusetts, Addison-Wesley), 1995.

7. Intel Microprocessor Quick Reference Guide, www.intel.com, website visited May 12, 2014.

8. Starwood Hotels, www.starwoodhotels.com, website visited January 24, 2014.

9. Kopalle, Praveen; Rao, Ambar G.; Assoncao, L. J., "Asymmetric Reference Price Effects and Dynamic Pricing Policies," Marketing Science 15, no. 1, 1996, pp. 60-85.

10. Urbany, Joel E.; Bearden, William O.; Weilbaker, Dan C., "The Effects of Plausibile and Exaggerated Reference Prices on Consumer Perceptions and Price Search," Journal of Consumer Research 15, June 1988, pp. 95-110.

11. Morris, Michael H.; Morris, Gene, Market Oriented Pricing (Lincolnwood, Illinois, NTC Business Books) 1990, pp. 5-8.

12. Urbany, Joel E.; Dickson, Peter R., Consumer Knowledge of Normal Prices: An Exploratory Study & Framework (Cambridge, Massachusetts: Marketing Science Institute, 1990), pp. 7-8.

13. "Nike, with little explanation, has decided not to do business with Sears. Whose image suffers?", New York Times, May 5, 2005.

14. Chen, Yongmin; Rosenthal, Robert W., "On the Use of Ceiling Price Commitments by Monopolies," Rand Journal of Economics 27, Summer 1996, pp. 207-220.

15. Harrell, Gilbert D., Consumer Behavior (New York: Harcourt Brace Jovanovich), 1986, pg. 68.

16. Pollack, Andrew, "Performance Pricing: Drug Company Offering a Money-Back Guarantee," New York Times, July 14, 2007, pg. B1.

17. Harrell, Gilbert D., Consumer Behavior (New York: Harcourt Brace Jovanovich), 1986, pg. 68.

18. Staten, Vince, "Can You Trust a Tomato in January?", Library Journal, July 1993, pg. 179.

19. Burton, www.burton.com, website visited July 16, 2014.

20. Ibid.

21. "Whirlpool lifts prices to offset commodity costs," Financial Times, February 4, 2005.

22. Woolls, Daniel, "Spain fumes over Marlboros / Lower prices anger government trying to curb youth smoking," Associated Press, January 28, 2006; Jacobs, Rose, "Imperial suffers as price wars hit Spain," www.ft.com, June 13, 2011.

23. www.priceline.com, website visited March 24, 2014.

24. "American, Delta cut JFK air fares to match JetBlue," Knight Ridder Tribune Business News, October 2005.

25. Hesna, Genay, "Japan's Corporate Groups," Economic Perspectives 15, January/February 1991, pp. 20-30.

26. "Japan: Just the facts," Journal of Commerce, June 2005.

27. Onkvisit and Shaw, International Marketing, pg. 614.

28. http://investors.walmartstores.com, website visited February 3, 2014.

29. "Why Follow the Leader Isn't Best Pricing Game," www.supermarket-news.com/blog, website visited February 12, 2014.

30. "How big can it grow," The Economist, March 2004.

31. Toyota, www.toyota.com, website visited May 3, 2014.

32. Comcast, www.comcast.com, website visited March 24, 2014.

33. "Build Your Scion," Scion, www.scion.com, website visited April 5, 2014.

34. Progressive, www.progressive.com, website visited March 24, 2014.

35. Benton, W.C.; Park, Seungwook, "A Classification of Literature on Determining the Lot Size Under Quantity Discounts," European Journal of Operational Research, July 19, 1996, pp. 219-238.

36. Victoria's Secret, www.victoriassecret.com, website visited May 5, 2014.

37. Suter, Tracy A.; Burton, Scot, "Believability and Consumer Perceptions of Implausible Reference Prices in Retail Advertisements," Psychology and Marketing 13, January 1996, pp.37-54.

38. Alfor, Bruce L.; Engelland, Brian T., "Advertised Reference Price Effects on Consumer Price Estimates, Value Perception, and Search Intention," Journal of Business Research Vol. 28, No. 2, May 2000, pg. 96.

39. White, Martha, "Travelers Charged $1,000 by Hotel in Irene's Wake, http://moneyland.time.com, August 3, 2011.

40. Myers, Gerr, "Why Women Pay More," American Demographics 18, April 1996, pp. 40-41.

41. Bazar, Emily, "Women Pay More for Services, Study Finds," The Nando Times, October 29, 1998.

Credits

Photo credits are listed throughout the text adjacent to the appropriate image. Images not credited in the text are property of the author, GNU Free Documentation License, Non-Attributed Creative Commons (CC) license or deemed public domain.

Index